MAGILL'S
LITERARY ANNUAL

1986

MAGILL'S
LITERARY ANNUAL
1986

*Essay-Reviews of 200 Outstanding Books
Published in the United States during 1985*

With an Annotated Categories Index

Volume Two
Lam-Z

Edited by
FRANK N. MAGILL

SALEM PRESS
Englewood Cliffs

LIBRARY OF CONGRESS CATALOG CARD NO. 77-99209
ISBN 0-89356-286-6

FIRST PRINTING

PRINTED IN THE UNITED STATES OF AMERICA

MAGILL'S
LITERARY ANNUAL

1986

THE LAMPLIT ANSWER

Author: Gjertrud Schnackenberg (1953-   )
Publisher: Farrar, Straus and Giroux (New York). 83 pp. $12.95
Type of work: Poetry

An exposition of the art of human purpose

The four sections of Gjertrud Schnackenberg's *The Lamplit Answer* view from various angles how humans imagine the shapes of their condition and destiny. The first section focuses on childlike perceptions and their sinister outcome, the second on dreams and the machinery of death, the third on personal love, and the fourth on altruistic love.

The major poem of the first section of the book is "Kremlin of Smoke," which is about Frédéric Chopin's life as a child in Warsaw and as a grownup in Paris. In both cities he is lionized and pampered, and in Paris he remains childlike, prone to tantrums and vaporous moods, eager to act out charming stories for his audiences. An ominous note in this long poem is sounded by the political reality lurking behind Chopin's genius and popularity. As a child he asks his mother where snow comes from; eventually the answer comes—left over, as it were, from her elegant idleness and all but insubstantial passion: She tells him that it comes from Russia, alluding to the fact that Poland at the time was a political victim of Russia. Later, part of his Parisian audience is composed of the very rich; the sinister smoke rises from their pipes and cigars to the pleasantly adorned ceiling of the salon where Chopin is playing. This image helps to identify them with those who plot the destinies of countries, with the smoke that rises from the pillage and ruin of a city such as Chopin's native Warsaw.

Chopin is protected from such machinations and horrors, but part of his genius is that he senses what is really going on beyond the hothouse of his fame. His sudden fits of temper, especially as a child, puzzle his piano teacher and, later on, his maid. The poem suggests, though, that his fits result from his knowledge that he is trapped in romantic ephemera. His sense of the brutality of life foreshadows the destruction of his piano in Warsaw by Russian soldiers. On the other hand, he comes to know that his art, fragile as it may be, attracts the better side of those who hear it. Not only the cultivated appreciate his music but also the uncultivated, those shoveling snow outside the window of the salon in the Faubourg Saint-Germain where he is performing. The paradox of power and fragility inhabit his art, but it is the latter that imposes itself most on him. The former virtuoso who was his teacher in 1822 gives Chopin several rules by which to guide himself. Most of them are warnings against certain kinds of music, including that of Ludwig van Beethoven. One, however, cautions him to ignore the real world—to play for anyone who will listen without thinking about them or about where he is playing. This "art for art's sake" prescription is rounded off when Chopin's teacher tells him, in effect, that art has no motive beyond itself. As a result, when Chopin, at the height of his powers, tries to discover a more profound source of music than himself, he feels guilty about it, while at the same time he sees himself and his art falling apart like a short-lived flower.

If Chopin is trapped in a solipsistic world typical of children, the naïve or childlike painter in "The Self-Portrait of Ivan Generalić" must watch his Christian assumptions stripped away one by one. The light that he once painted by, so to speak, has already gone out of his world, as he gradually realizes. Disasters yet to come are the subject of "Signs"; the childish perfection people want to see in the world is eventually overwhelmed by sinister omens. The poem infers that maturity is measured by one's perception of such omens.

Ending the first section of Schnackenberg's book is "Two Tales of Clumsy." The hero, Clumsy, behaves like a child throughout. In the first part of the poem, his appetite for food and love are simple—that is, he does not reflect upon them. No-No (or Death) enters the picture and kills Clumsy's mother, who also seems to be his wife (another sign that he has not advanced beyond the stage of a child's perceptions). Even at the end, Clumsy's grief is selfish, and he fails to understand what has happened. In the second part of the poem, the fact of death is replaced by its meaning, as No-No becomes Clumsy's teacher. Clumsy is illiterate, though poetic in his ignorance. Under the pressure of No-No's complex and cruel intelligence— in short, his maturity—Clumsy accepts (though without seeming to know what he is doing) the essential meaning of death: its finality. No-No is a sort of Satan who stands for entropy and promises knowledge in exchange for Clumsy's servitude.

"Imaginary Prisons" and "Darwin in 1881" constitute the second section of Schnackenberg's book. The first poem features the human longing for perfection, for the ideal. This ideal is impossible, for time and nature defeat it. Man's condition, however, is to be cursed by the sole timeless aspect of time that allows him to entertain one longing: the present. Interpreting the fairy tale *Sleeping Beauty* in detail, Schnackenberg presents the frozen dreams of various characters in the story. The future carries out the orders of the past, meaning that mortality consigns man to failure and death. The princes whose dream it is to possess the princess die of hunger in a wilderness of rose thorns, while those in the castle and on the castle grounds are stuck in the timeless spell of their dreams. The kitchen maid dreams of her betrothed, but he is a woodcutter from another area, and he, like the princes, is dead, as she will discover when she awakes. The truth, that is, is death and the reversal of man's dreams, though the curse of having them is a blessing insofar as they last. The court astronomer, paralyzed like the others in the present, has a theory of the universe that is false but nevertheless comforts him. Ironically, the insomniac dreams of falling asleep, while the princess' uncle, already enamored of his crazy theory of the world's construction, dreams that the flaw he has seen in it will prove to be the reason for its perfection.

There are also those in the poem who undergo a double imprisonment: Not only are they locked in their own dreams, but also they have been locked up by the king for challenging in one way or another his own insistence on perfect order. The court poet has become too obscure in his writing to suit the king, and he continues to indulge his surreal imagination. The bird keeper, jailed for importing unfamiliar and therefore dangerous birds, imagines the details of his confinement as birds. The traitor cannot help but dream of an escape that fails because of his own image of himself, and the court seer, whose misfortune was to dream the fate of Sleeping Beauty (to dream, as it were, the collapse of the king's dream of his daughter), now dreams about the past—his wife finding out that he has been arrested. The king himself is the maddest dreamer of all, for he tried to banish time from his kingdom to save the princess. Caught in the act of doing so—of disemboweling the clocks—he comes to see that the source of the misery of time is the past.

The dreamer in "Darwin in 1881" is Charles Darwin's wife. She dreams that life is a flight that somehow evades death, whereas Darwin has discovered the machinery of death in the shapes that evolve to die, leaving the imprint of oblivion on their successors. Death defines not the abstract theories imposed on the whole of life but life's individual embodiments, such as the scientist himself.

In the third section of the book, Schnackenberg focuses on the love she feels for an absent lover. First she wonders about the mystery of real love for someone who is unreal in not being there. "Love Letter" concludes that personal love is a condition that does not require any particular quality of the beloved to exist. It has no reason, and as such it is not bound by time. "Sonata" develops this idea of the ineffable. Without her lover close by, her physical surroundings seem unreal, which leads her to speculate that the physical world, without the overlay of mental abstractions like Plato's Ideals, cannot be proven to exist, though the reader is sure that it does in much the same way that the narrator of the poem feels that her beloved, though absent, is extant to her. It is all an elaborate joke making light of her longing and pointing out the dreamlike quality of impassioned perception.

Schnackenberg continues the theme of separation in "Paper Cities." Here the narrator likens her situation to that of Gustave Flaubert's lover, who is left alone to amuse herself while he is writing far away. Unlike Emma Bovary, she and the narrator are condemned to fidelity, but like her they are crazed with loneliness among their dreams and the books they read. Indeed, frustration makes them paranoid and prone to gruesome imaginings, from which the narrator, a writer herself, constructs her poem. The failure implicit in this situation informs "Snow Melting," where the narrator suffers separation from the one she loves but who does not love her; the loneliness engendered in her because of this seems both to dwarf the universe and to make her feel remote from it.

Altruistic love is the focus of the last section of the book. Simone Weil's death is the subject of "The Heavenly Feast." In her refusal to eat after she escaped to England from France during World War II, she demonstrates a tragic generosity, wishing her food to go to those whom she left behind and who have nothing to eat. Nature itself seems in sympathy with this wondrous love as the birds communicate Weil's plea and sacrifice to the grim landscape. In "Advent Calendar," Schnackenberg longs to be part of the Christian vision of love expressed by a German Christmas tableau, while in "Supernatural Love," she finds Christian equivalents for pain and love in various definitions in her father's dictionary.

Love in one form or another defines human purpose and anguish in *The Lamplit Answer*. Chopin loves his art and his country, Darwin loves the truth, the poet loves men from whom she is separated and the ideal of compassion. Schnackenberg treats the variations of this theme in an intensely literary way, moreover. Her prosody is deliberately formal or "literary," featuring meter and rhyme. Also, her subjects and starting points often belong to the world of art. Chopin is a composer and performer, "Imaginary Prisons" is a gloss on a fairy tale, the poet's lover and Simone Weil are writers, and the calendar in "Advent Calendar" is a construction of painted cardboard. Finally, perhaps because of the power of love, human perception tends to favor the mental aspect of reality in Schnackenberg's poems, giving them a somewhat elitist veneer and limiting them—despite their genuine passion and inclusive concerns—to a highly cultivated audience.

Mark McCloskey

Sources for Further Study

Booklist. LXXXI, July, 1985, p. 1506.
Boston Review. X, November, 1985, p. 28.
The Georgia Review. XXXIX, Summer, 1985, p. 414.
Library Journal. CX, May 1, 1985, p. 64.
Los Angeles Times Book Review. July 28, 1985, p. 3.
The Nation. CCXLI, December 7, 1985, p. 621.
The New York Times Book Review. XC, May 26, 1985, p. 16.
Publishers Weekly. CCXXVII, March 1, 1985, p. 77.
Washington Post Book World. XV, August 25, 1985, p. 4.
Yale Review. LXXIV, Summer, 1985, p. R11.

LATER THE SAME DAY

Author: Grace Paley (1922-   )
Publisher: Farrar, Straus and Giroux (New York). 211 pp. $13.95
Type of work: Short stories
Time: The 1970's and 1980's
Locale: New York City

Seventeen stories selected from the past ten years' work show the humane voice and impeccable craft that make Grace Paley one of the most distinguished contemporary writers of short fiction

Grace Paley's output is small—three books of short stories in twenty-five years—but even at a time when markets for short fiction are limited and the literary stars are novelists and poets, her reputation has grown steadily. Paley's work is particularly savored by writers and teachers of writing. This new collection, like *The Little Disturbances of Man* (1959) and *Enormous Changes at the Last Minute* (1974), displays the apparently effortless simplicity and clarity of her work.

As in any craft, the appearance of natural ease in storytelling requires not only great skill but also respect for both the medium and the material. Fiction's material is human life. Paley's characters command attention as distinct individuals from the moment of their first appearance, a feat that she manages even in the absence of introductory comments or descriptions of their work, background, or physical appearance. In similar fashion, Paley can provide a sense of resolution and meaning without shaping tidy plots or constructing scenes that put opposing values in conflict. Her distinctive viewpoint includes the wider world as an important element in the context of daily life and thus makes her work impressively humane, responsible, and—ultimately—hopeful about the human condition.

One secret of Paley's craft is her seeming absence of craft. She ignores both Edgar Allan Poe's prescriptive definition and the structural rules promoted when short fiction was a commercial staple; she neither strives for a single emotional effect nor builds plots that reveal characters at carefully limited moments of significant conflict, change, or revelation. It would be difficult to chart one of Paley's stories so as to discover the exposition, point of attack, rising action, and climax. Paley shows people in the process of living and convinces readers that she has accurately rendered their experience; and at the same time, she successfully manages to avoid the ambiguous, unfinished, and often unsettling quality of the fiction once referred to as "slice of life."

The absence of crisis and conflict throws the emphasis on character; the reader's impatience with open endings is dissipated because the characters satisfy. They behave understandably—and like most people, are unlikely to be dramatically altered by one single event, though their interests, and also their feelings and responses, are likely to change over the years as circumstances change. Though Paley does not quite write linked stories that can be put together into something approaching a novel, many characters from her earlier collections reappear. The young women who were rearing preschoolers alone in the 1960's are now coping with their parents' old age, a friend's death from cancer, the end of childbearing years, and the loosening bonds of motherhood.

Most of the stories are set in a world as distinctive as any local colorist's Kentucky or Maine or Mississippi. It seems less limited primarily because residents of college towns across the country are citizens—either in spirit or in exile—of Paley's small square of New York. There, rehabilitated tenements and surprising patches of green create a walking neighborhood with its own school and greengrocer and butcher and deli and well-known faces; where the church is important primarily as a building whose basement holds a meeting room and a mimeograph machine that can be used to promote peace, ecology, and neighborhood causes.

Though there is a certain amount of parochialism in its specifics, the world of Paley's stories is impressive because its people are engaged by a range of concerns. Love and affection and friendship are important in their daily lives, but so are China, the educational bureaucracy that refuses to let parent volunteers tutor Spanish-speaking children, the Strategic Arms Limitation Talks (SALT), the PTA, Union Carbide, and a grandmother's recollections of Russia in 1905. Her characters are adults, with a long perspective not only in their own maturity but also in memories across the cycle of years; their energies may shift focus and their friendships be interrupted by political differences, but they are part of an enmeshed continuity.

Although most of the stories in the volume are told by or about Faith—the character that many readers assume is a fictionalized version of Grace Paley herself—some reach into other lives. "Lavinia: An Old Story" convincingly creates the mingled hope, joy, and anger of a black woman who sees her daughter's life repeat her own. "A Man Told Me the Story of His Life" is an extraordinarily economical monologue that explicates a whole history of ambition frustrated by class and schooling in the space of two pages. The choice of four or five words in the very last sentence enriches the story's emotional tone so as to save readers from despair without diminishing their anger or weakening the message.

Paley refuses to settle for easy pessimism, on the one hand, or privatization, on the other. She writes primarily about women: Love and family are women's topics, and so are race, violence, ecology, class, and disarmament. These public issues are not simply platform causes but part of life's daily texture; how can a woman who gives birth be oblivious to nuclear weaponry or environmental damage or the effect of mothering on the adults that children will become? In "The Expensive Moment," a visitor from China speaks to Faith:

May I ask you, do you worry that your older boy is in a political group that isn't liked? What will be his trade? Will he go to university? My eldest is without skills to this day. Her school years happened in the time of great confusion and running about. My youngest studies well. Ah, she said, rising. Hello. Good afternoon.

Ruth stood in the doorway. Faith's friend, the listener and the answerer, listening.

We were speaking, the Chinese woman said. About the children, how to raise them.... Shall we teach them to be straightforward, honorable, kind, brave, maybe shrewd, self-serving a little?... You don't want them to be cruel, but you want them to take care of themselves wisely. Now my own children are nearly grown. Perhaps it's too late. Was I foolish? I didn't know in those years how to do it.

Yes, yes, said Faith. I know what you mean. Ruthy?

Ruth remained quiet.

Faith waited a couple of seconds. Then she turned to the Chinese woman. Oh, Xie Feng, she said. Neither did I.

Faith, the most prominent character in *Later the Same Day*, is seen from various narrative viewpoints: sometimes in the first person, sometimes as viewpoint character in a third-person story, once (in "Zagrowsky Tells") as an outsider. The choice of angle from which to tell a story is one of several techniques that Paley employs to give the illusion that she is presenting life rather than constructing plot. Three stories are drawn from the same day's events. In "The Story Hearer," Faith (as an unnamed first-person narrator) tells Jack about some of the things she did and thought; she uses them to make an interesting but undemanding narrative of the kind that will please someone who says, "Tell me about your day." Because Jack is interested in ecology and the economics of food, she particularly emphasizes her discussion with the greengrocer and the thoughts that spring from his situation.

Yet no narrative ever tells about a whole day—and this one, though serious and interesting, is also shaped by Faith's affectionate interaction with Jack. Because the conversation and the story's shape lead in a particular direction, she does not mention another brief incident from the same day, which appears in "Anxiety." In that story, Faith—again speaking as "I"—is absolutely central. She watches young fathers picking up their children from school, thinks about change and authority and the sources of war, and leans out the window to give a brief lecture. Most of the action in "Anxiety" is a kind of internal speechmaking, the commentary on an incident that one shapes mentally into words to put feelings into context. As a story it works exceedingly well, just as a single transcendental image can generate a very large point—and yet the very concentration and focus would make it unnatural if, in "The Story Hearer," Faith tried to fit it into her dinner-table chat.

Finally, on the same day, Faith has the encounter with the pharmacist who is the narrator and viewpoint character of "Zagrowsky Tells." Zagrowsky's words and thoughts subtly reveal the mixture of pride and discomfort he feels over his black grandchild, Emanuel—a child conceived in the mental hospital where his daughter Cissy had been a patient. Cissy's breakdown first took shape after Faith and three other women picketed Zagrowsky's store over an incident of racism.

The story is one of the most powerful in the collection, yet its effect is not to cast judgment on Faith nor arouse pity for the pharmacist, but to extend empathy. As Thomas Hardy pointed out, the hero of one story is the walk-on in another's life. Well-crafted fiction, in the old sense of the word, does violence to the world by ignoring the intersections to focus on one person's tale, just as many people want to see life as if it were a story in which they play the only interesting role.

The sense of story is also necessarily selective. The writer chooses—out of all the materials available in even one day's experience and thought—a limited few that deserve attention. On the book's last page, Faith's friend Cassie asks why she has been left out. Where, she asks,

> is my woman and woman, woman-loving life in all this? And it's not even sensible, because we *are* friends, we work together, you even care about me at least as much as you do Ruthy and Louise and Ann. You let them in all the time; it's really strange, why have you left me out of everybody's life?

Grace Paley avoids traditional plots because they are both unreal and inhumane; they provide a false sense of ending. The tendency to see life in terms of fiction—to see one's feelings as dramatically important, one's self-fulfillment interesting to other people, to see life made up of actions with direct causes, consequences, and resolutions—is both simplistic and quite possibly (in the largest sense) immoral. Thus, though her stories are often unconcluded, they do not leave tensions unresolved or make readers close the book wondering what will happen next. There can be no doubt that Paley's characters will go on doing what needs to be done (even if things look bad for the moment) and will go on changing in the way that all interesting people change. When, on the last page of a book, a character who has not been noticed before demands attention—and demands it in a way that engages the author's humane and ethical standards—it is also clear what Grace Paley's readers must do next: patiently wait for more.

Sally Mitchell

Sources for Further Study

Book World. XV, April 28, 1985, p. 3.
Booklist. LXXXI, February 15, 1985, p. 802.
Christian Science Monitor. May 7, 1985, p. 25.
Commonweal. CXII, June 21, 1985, p. 376.

Kirkus Reviews. LIII, February 1, 1985, p. 107.
Library Journal. CX, April 1, 1985, p. 159.
Los Angeles Times Book Review. May 19, 1985, p. 2.
Ms. XIII, April, 1985, p. 13.
The Nation. CCXL, June 15, 1985, p. 739.
New Directions for Women. XIV, May, 1985, p. 5.
The New Republic. CXCII, April 29, 1985, p. 38.
The New York Review of Books. XXXII, August 15, 1985, p. 26.
The New York Times. April 10, 1985, p. 22.
The New York Times Book Review. XC, April 14, 1985, p. 7.
Newsweek. CV, April 15, 1985, p. 91.
Publishers Weekly. CCXXVII, February 8, 1985, p. 68.
The Village Voice Literary Supplement. June, 1985, p. 9.

LETTERS
Summer, 1926

Authors: Boris Pasternak (1890-1960), Marina Tsvetayeva (1892-1941), and Rainer
Maria Rilke (1875-1926)
Translated from the Russian by Margaret Wettlin and Walter Arndt
Edited, with an introduction, by Yevgeny Pasternak, Yelena Pasternak, and
Konstantin Azadovsky
Publisher: Harcourt Brace Jovanovich (San Diego, California). Illustrated. 251 pp.
$24.95
Type of work: Letters
Time: 1926

An exchange of letters between two young Russian poets and one established German poet, reflecting their common belief in the restorative power of poetry

>*Principal personages:*
>BORIS PASTERNAK, the author of *Doctor Zhivago*, and an important Russian poet
>MARINA TSVETAEVA, a gifted Russian poet not acknowledged until after her suicide
>RAINER MARIA RILKE, a renowned German neoromantic poet
>LEONID PASTERNAK, Boris Pasternak's father
>EVGENIYA PASTERNAK, Boris Pasternak's first wife
>SERGEY EFRON, Marina Tsvetaeva's husband

The lofty musings of gifted solitary poets do not find better expression than in this correspondence between three highly individualistic lyricists who shared, or imagined that they shared, a spiritual and creative affinity. Though the letters cover but a brief interval in the authors' lives—five months—all three regarded the unexpected contact as miraculous, as preordained, and invested the relationship with a corresponding degree of awe. The glimpses revealed here reach far into their thought processes and biographies, and without the running commentary provided by the editors of the collection, the material would have been inaccessible to anyone but the Slavicist. As it is, letters and notes together form a comprehensible whole.

Rainer Maria Rilke was a renowned and established but already seriously ill poet in the summer of 1926. It is possible that he entered into the exchange for sentimental reasons, for his two visits to Russia in 1899 and 1900 had affected him to such an extent that he termed them the decisive events of his creative existence. In Russia, in its traditional Orthodox festivals and its undeveloped expanses, he discerned a life unspoiled by the vicissitudes of Western ways, and he invested the land with his own vision of a superior, nontechnological future. He spent much time and effort mastering the language; for a time, he planned to settle there altogether but then converted his Russian impressions into verse in *Das Stundenbuch* (1905; *The Book of Hours*, 1968). When Boris Pasternak's father, in exile in Berlin, modestly reminded Rilke in 1925 of their acquaintance during those fabled journeys a quarter of a century earlier, hinting in passing at his son's admiration for Rilke, the latter responded with words of warm remembrance and encouragement for the budding poet. For young Pasternak, then struggling to make a literary name for himself in postrevolutionary Moscow, the possibility of entering into discourse with Rilke was electrifying. At age ten, he had seen Rilke during a fleeting train station encounter, and, intrigued by Rilke's enthusiasm for Russia, the boy soon found himself drawn to the poet's neoromantic worldview. While still in school, Pasternak endeavored to make Rilke known in Russia, translated several of his poems, and throughout his life acknowledged the impact of Rilke's creative force on his own development.

Among the few Russian contemporaries whom Pasternak considered worthy to be called poets, Marina Tsvetaeva, in exile in France during the 1920's and 1930's, occupied first place. (The editors of this collection give her name as Tsvetayeva, but this is not the form preferred by Slavic scholars, nor is it consistent with the transliteration system employed throughout the book.) They had barely met but soon recognized each other as kindred spirits. Both came from artistically gifted upper-class families, shared liberal childhood travel and schooling in Germany, a fluent command of German, a veneration of Rilke, and a refusal to become involved in the political turmoils of the time. Their correspondence, commencing in 1922, continued sporadically until 1935, during which time they never saw each other. Many of their exchanges will not be published until after the year 2000, in accordance with Tsvetaeva's wishes, so that the selections contained in this book are highly prized for the light they shed on the lengthy and often-mercurial relationship. Pasternak received the news of his family's contact with Rilke while reading a new arrival of Tsvetaeva's verse, and this coincidence moved him to include Tsvetaeva in an envisioned poetic union. He even commended Tsvetaeva to Rilke as the more worthy soul mate. His first and only letter to Rilke, as it turned out, written in German, on April 12, 1926, is striking for its somewhat naïve outpouring of sentiment. Pasternak considers himself reborn from death and despair by the happy (he calls it magical) concurrence of hearing from Rilke and Tsvetaeva on the same day. Curiously intersecting the many avowals of love is a wordy hint that he has sheaves of poems lying about, available for Rilke's perusal, and the repeated request to Rilke to honor Tsvetaeva with an inscribed copy of the *Duineser Elegien* (1923; *Duino Elegies*, 1930). The circuitous route by which this missive found its way to Rilke attests the significance which Pasternak attached to the step. He first sent the letter to his father in Berlin, from whence it went to other family members and friends spread throughout Germany, each offering criticism and corrections until Pasternak's father finally directed the letter to Rilke with a long cover message of his own.

Overlapping these efforts is a frantic epistolary exchange between Pasternak and Tsvetaeva, which provides considerable insight into their beliefs and explains not only why they regarded one another so highly but also obliquely reiterates certain aspects of Rilke's worldview particularly attractive to the young Russians. All three poets shared a disdain for a reality they saw obsessed with bourgeois material values, bereft of all spirituality. All three believed that contact with truly important human events, such as birth and death, had become impossible in their world and that only the creative poetic spirit was able to bring an understanding of these notions to humankind. Hence, in their view, the craft of poetry represents the highest calling mortals can achieve. Their poetry, consequently, was often abstract, difficult to comprehend, reaching into spheres that were otherworldly, mystical, separate from traditional religious ideas yet utilizing religious symbolism for its own purposes. All three regarded themselves as correspondingly exalted and chosen. Keeping other close human contact at arm's length, they tended to go overboard at the occasional prospect of what they considered a genuine union of poetic souls, a circumstance which explains the eagerness with which they embarked on the correspondence under discussion. Tsvetaeva more so than the other two worshiped the realm of the disembodied soul. In nine letters to Rilke between May 9 and August 22, 1926—their correspondence was in German—Tsvetaeva defines for him her absolute delineation between the commonplace, detestable world of the body and the sublimely radiant, metaphysical domain of the soul, an ideal made imperfectly manifest by the rare poetic genius of a Rilke, a Pasternak, and herself. Tsvetaeva's words frequently hint at aversion to all physical contact. She writes to Rilke, on August 22, 1926, "The farther from me—the further *into* me. . . . He who kisses me misses *me*." This dualism between body and soul pervades her every letter. She considered it necessary for the execution of her art to free herself from desire and human touch. She craved to be kissed by words and visited in dreams. In fact, she often exchanged dream content with her correspondents, speculating on its possible significance for their craft and calling. The exquisite precision of some of these dream sequences suggests a certain literary polishing, but the poets took them seriously and placed their communicative value far above that of ordinary discourse.

Another aspect of Tsvetaeva's letters to Rilke is the boundless admiration of a disciple for her master. Showering him with such accolades as poetry incarnate, elusive phenomenon of nature, spirit from a timeless region, raw poetic force, topography of the soul, addressing him with the *Du* reserved for deities, she displays an unabashed romanticism. Though her style has a certain originality and whimsicality, the overall impression is one of restlessness and urgency. Her thoughts are not easily followed. Parentheses, dashes, exclamation marks, and dangling phrases abound, chopping sentences into disparate segments, thereby accentuating incongruously joined themes. The dialogic nature of the discourse, the ever-present rhetorical questions, the intonational markers, the frequent poetic fragments, and, above all, the heavily emotional tenor of her language—all this compels the reader to delve into her prose as into a poem. Tsvetaeva herself regarded the letters as artistically valuable, copying most of them in her notebook for preservation. In fact, part of this correspondence would not be available at all were it not for copies in her notes.

The intent to create a spiritual community with this interchange of thoughts was not realized as planned, primarily because of certain traits in Tsvetaeva's personality. Despite the posited primacy of ideal over real, she exhibited a jarring possessiveness where personal relationships were concerned. Rather than permit a real communion to develop among the trio, she reserved for herself the role of intermediary between Rilke and Pasternak and in effect hindered contact between them. Pasternak, unable to correspond directly with the Switzerland-bound Rilke because of the absence of Soviet-Swiss diplomatic relations, trustingly relied on Tsvetaeva in France to act as his postal intermediary. In his first letter to Tsvetaeva, Rilke dutifully enclosed a warm note to Pasternak which she did not forward right away. To Pasternak's subsequent and repeated pleas to keep him informed of whatever passed between her and Rilke, she responded laconically and in cryptic phrases, teasingly dangling excerpts from Rilke's letters in front of Pasternak. Only rarely did she copy out an entire Rilke letter addressed to her. So completely and innocently did Pasternak rely on her judgment that he did not dare to write a second letter to Rilke, believing himself unworthy in the shadow of their genius. Rilke likewise received word of Pasternak only through Tsvetaeva's tidbits. When at last he expressed concern at Pasternak's silence, she freely and dramatically blamed herself, but buried in her usual convoluted syntax is an assertion of her right to sole access to Rilke, an insistence that she alone should represent Russia to him. As a result, the exchange between Rilke and Pasternak is limited to one introductory letter from each. The rest of the correspondence is between Rilke and Tsvetaeva, and Pasternak and Tsvetaeva.

Pasternak had initially hoped to join Rilke and Tsvetaeva in France for an extended poetic gathering. In a letter to her of April 20, 1926, he carefully lays the groundwork by emphasizing his reverence for her, assuring her that they are made for each other, that her inspiration guides his every thought and word and that she is his only aim in life. (Both Pasternak and Tsvetaeva had spouses and children, none of whom was allowed to interfere in these high poetic passions.) He was eager to join her immediately, but Tsvetaeva, feeling no need for his physical presence, quickly dampened his hopes. Yet, quite ironically, by August of that year she found herself in the same impatient position in regard to Rilke. By then, Rilke had so completely engulfed her attention that she exaggerated her role in his life and pressed for a meeting. Her usual total self-absorption prevented her from acknowledging

Rilke's repeated allusions to his failing health and from noting his reserve in the face of her impetuousness. Rather crassly, in a letter of August 22, 1926, she asks for a precise meeting time and place and, apparently envisioning a long stay, begs him to accept her as a guest because of her own strapped pecuniary circumstances. Rilke, in the advanced stages of leukemia, did not answer the brash inquiry, though he kept up other correspondence, continued to compose and to receive selected visitors right up to his death on December 29, 1926. Tsvetaeva never accepted the diminution. She preferred to believe that Rilke had stopped writing after creating an elegy as a secret farewell message to her. She also confided to Pasternak that Rilke's death was the best thing for her, since it deported him to that ideal domain where he could belong to her without earthly interference.

Tsvetaeva can perhaps be excused for expecting too much from the Rilke interlude, since the latter himself initially joined in the enthusiasm of their epistolary acquaintance. In seven letters, from May 3 to August 19, he regaled her with a poem, "Elegie für Marina," with inscribed copies of his works, occasionally accompanied by cover verses just for her, with snapshots of himself and his surroundings, and in general reinforced Tsvetaeva in many of her beliefs. He did, however, confess that her verse was difficult for him to grasp in spite of her explanatory footnotes in German. Possibly, he indulged Tsvetaeva because he was moved by memories of another Russian charmer in his life, his longtime friend Lou Andreas-Salomé, who had accompanied him on his trips to Russia. He very likely was forced to break off contact because his deteriorating health could not accommodate the presence of such a powerhouse as Tsvetaeva promised to be.

Tsvetaeva's correspondence with Pasternak had come to a halt at the end of July 1926, after she had once more firmly refused his visit and after rather uncavalierly downgrading his poem "1905: Lyutenant Schmidt." After Rilke's death, she quickly commanded Pasternak to resume their relationship. Although they kept in touch for many more years, and Pasternak's admiration for her craft at no time wavered, their actual meetings between 1939, when she returned to the Soviet Union, and her death by suicide in 1941 were devoid of the earlier emotional overtones. By that time Pasternak had a new wife, a certain renown, and full confidence in his talent; he no longer needed the by then quite spent Tsvetaeva as a crutch. Toward Rilke, however, his feelings never changed. His autobiographical *Okhrannaya gramota* (1931; *Safe Conduct*, 1949) is dedicated to Rilke, who also appears in the opening pages as a traveler in Russia.

The publication of these letters, made possible when Tsvetaeva's fifty-year ban expired, will supplement future Rilke biographies as well as illuminate Tsvetaeva's complex relationship with Pasternak. It comes as a surprise that the authors do not really discuss one another's work from a technical or creative point of view, except for an occasional comment by Pasternak on

Tsvetaeva's new verse. Neither do the poets offer many comments about their contemporaries. The book, then, reports private, subjective, philosophical views, artistic visions valuable for the insight they afford into revered personages. The translators have done an excellent job of transforming Tsvetaeva's difficult syntax into credible English equivalents. Readers will be struck by two things: first, the unrestrained and often sentimental outpourings of correspondents famous for their terseness, control, and high craftsmanship in verse, and second, the irony of three great artists disavowing the importance of bodily existence, while it was that very existence, through personality and illness, which dictated the course of their interaction.

Margot K. Frank

Sources for Further Study

Booklist. LXXXI, June 15, 1985, p. 1431.
The New Republic. CXCIII, September 2, 1985, p. 38.
The New York Review of Books. XXXII, December 5, 1985, p. 3.
The New York Times Book Review. XC, July 21, 1985, p. 8.

THE LETTERS OF D. H. LAWRENCE
Volume III, October 1916-June 1921

Author: D. H. Lawrence (1885-1930)
Edited, with an introduction, by James T. Boulton and Andrew Robertson
Publisher: Cambridge University Press (New York). Illustrated. 762 pp. $49.95
Type of work: Letters
Time: October, 1916-June, 1921
Locale: England and Italy

The third of seven volumes of the collected and newly edited letters of D. H. Lawrence, covering the period of his isolation and disillusionment in provincial England during the last half of World War I through the completion of Aaron's Rod, *chiefly written in Taormina, Sicily*

When complete, the Cambridge edition of D. H. Lawrence's letters will run to seven volumes (with an eighth volume devoted to addenda, corrections, and a comprehensive index), containing some 5,600 pieces of correspondence written between 1901 and 1930. Considering the relatively short span of Lawrence's career—he died of tuberculosis in his forty-fifth year—as well as his chronically poor health and his frequent travels to far-flung spots around the globe, this is an astonishing amount of correspondence. Although the Cambridge edition includes every available scrap, from postcards and telegrams to the most ephemeral of notes, the overall quality of the correspondence is such that Lawrence's reputation as one of the greatest English letter writers will be even more secure than previously.

The fact that so many of Lawrence's correspondents held on to his letters, even when he was persona non grata in literary circles, testifies in itself to the remarkable impact of his letters. His reputation as a formidable correspondent became more widespread, however, with the publication of a large volume of letters edited by his friend Aldous Huxley in 1932, only two years after Lawrence's death. Huxley's edition, which contained 790 letters, eventually played an important role in the rescuing of Lawrence's reputation as a major writer, after a series of sensationalistic memoirs written by so-called friends and admirers during the 1930's and 1940's had seriously damaged it. Pioneering scholars and critics such as F. R. Leavis, Harry T. Moore, and Graham Hough frequently quoted from Huxley's edition in an attempt to shed light on the character and ideas of the man and his work. Unfortunately, Huxley had found it necessary to delete many proper names and "feeling-hurting passages" without systematically indicating where the omissions occurred; furthermore, his chronological arrangement of the letters (Lawrence frequently dated them only with the day of the week) was often inaccurate. Partly to rectify these limitations, Harry T. Moore, Lawrence's biographer, edited *The Collected Letters of D. H. Lawrence* (1962). In two volumes, Moore published 1,257 letters, of which 520 had already appeared in Huxley's edition, 296 had been published in various other sources, and 441 appeared in print for the first time. Although this clearly represented an advance, Moore's edition was hardly definitive. Nearly one hundred of the letters in Moore's edition had incomplete or inaccurate texts. His edition, like Huxley's, was highly selective and, intended as it was for a general audience, carried a minimum of scholarly apparatus. Finally, some eight hundred additional Lawrence letters were published in such volumes as *The Quest for Rananim: D. H. Lawrence's Letters to S. S. Koteliansky, 1914-1930* (1970); *Letters from D. H. Lawrence to Martin Secker, 1911-1930* (1970); and *Letters to Thomas and Adele Seltzer* (1976). Even with these new additions to the epistolary canon, however, nearly half of Lawrence's extant letters had still not been published until the Cambridge edition, the first volume of which, spanning the years 1901 to mid-1913, appeared in 1979. (The second volume, spanning June 1913 to October 1916, was published in 1981.)

The four-and-a-half years covered in volume 3 of the letters amounted to a crucial turning point in Lawrence's life and career as novelist, a period that he would later recount in an episode aptly called "The Nightmare" in his novel *Kangaroo* (1923). The wounds caused by official suppression of *The Rainbow* in the fall of 1915 were still fresh. Lawrence has not only been charged publicly with "immorality" on both sexual and political grounds and reviled by the patriotic press, but also had been effectively deserted by the book's publisher and, still more painfully, by many of his supposed friends and literary associates. Though not directly connected with the scandal surrounding *The Rainbow*, important friendships and collaborations with Bertrand Russell and John Middleton Murry also collapsed at this time. The prolongation of the war, sporadic illness, and increasing poverty all further contributed to his growing depression. Lawrence determined to leave England for America, where he hoped to found a sort of Utopian community called Rananim, but he was denied permission to leave the country. His notoriety as a perpetrator of "dirty" books, his pacifist activities, and the fact that his wife, Frieda, was German by birth (and, in the bargain, a cousin of the famous flying ace Baron Manfred von Richthofen)—these factors worked together to arouse official suspicion that the Lawrences were, at best, German sympathizers and, at worst, enemy spies. As a result, the couple was hounded and persecuted by the authorities. Lawrence was subjected to a series of humiliating medical examinations, even though he was clearly unfit for military service. His living quarters were searched, his mail monitored, his manuscripts tampered with. In October 1917, the Lawrences were summarily ordered to leave Cornwall, where they had lived in seclusion for twenty months, yet still they were not allowed to leave England. Meanwhile, Lawrence had great difficulty finding an English publisher who would accept his work, and so he was forced to rely in part on the generosity of friends to make ends meet. *Women in Love*, considered by many his masterpiece, was completed by 1917, but he could not find a publisher for it until 1920—and then it was published not in England but in the United States, in a limited edition.

This barrage of painful experiences turned Lawrence against his homeland. Finally after the war, in November 1919, he and Frieda departed for Italy and entered on a phase that has aptly been called the "savage pilgrimage." Never again would they live in England. Settling for the next sixteen months in Italy, mostly in Sicily, Lawrence worked sporadically on such novels as *The Lost Girl* (1920, but begun in 1912), *Aaron's Rod* (1922, but begun in 1917), and *Mr Noon* (written in 1920-1921, but never completed and published in 1984). Such fitfulness was quite atypical of Lawrence and seems, along with the uneven quality of all these works, indicative of the spiritual anomie from which he suffered after his bitter severance from England.

Because the period covered in this volume was one of transition between the more sharply defined phases that preceded and followed it, these letters reflect the uncertainties, the false starts, the frustrations, and the vulnerability of a man fundamentally uprooted from the environment—and the readership—that had nurtured his sensibility and, to a considerable extent, shaped his art. Confined to provincial England during the war, cut off from his literary friends, unable to get his completed work published, and dispirited by the apparent endlessness of the conflagration in Europe, Lawrence longed for escape. In letter after letter he described plans to embark—for Palestine, for Russia, for Zululand, for the South Seas, for Colombia, but mostly for America. America attracted him in part because he felt confident of finding there a market for his writing. It also fit into his apocalyptic scheme: "America, being so much *worse*, falser, further gone than England, is nearer to freedom. England has a long and awful process of corruption and death to go through. America has dry-rotted to a point where the final *seed* of the new is almost left ready to sprout." Yet when at last he was free to go to America, arrangements having been made for him to lease a farm in Connecticut, he decided instead to go to Italy (he would not arrive in America until the fall of 1922, settling in Taos, New Mexico).

If Lawrence's life was fraught with indecision and uncertainty in these years, certain of his ideas seem to have been strengthened by adversity. His wartime isolation, for example, forced him to find a religious dimension in solitude that he urged on others. To Catherine Carswell he wrote:

> Shelter yourself above all from the world, save yourself, screen and hide yourself, go subtly in a secret retreat, where no-one knows you...living busily the other, creative life, like a bird building a nest. Be sure to keep this bush that burns with the presence of God...hidden from mankind: or they will drag your nest and desecrate all.

To Lady Cynthia Asquith he confided that "the whole crux of life now lies in the relation between man and woman, between Adam and Eve. In this relation we live or die." As for humanity at large, he had come to hate it. In a letter to E. M. Forster, he proclaimed that "there ought to be a flood to drown mankind, for there is no health in it, and certainly no *proud* courage . . . of life, no independent soul anywhere." At such moments, and they are frequent in the wartime letters especially, Lawrence assumed the tones of a latter-day prophet. In this way, he transformed the war itself symbolically into his own war, a war against "the whole body of mankind," and his self-appointed role was that of the preserver of the purified nucleus which would somehow survive the apocalypse, "when the existing [societal] frame smashes, as it must smash directly." Meanwhile he placed his faith, as he passionately urged his most intimate friends to do, in "the creative unknown." These are among the ideas that would be explored repeatedly in Lawrence's postwar fiction, in which the "creative unknown," the nucleus of "new life," would increasingly be embodied in the dark-skinned natives of the "primitive" lands to which he journeyed: southern Italy, Australia, and Mexico.

Not all the letters, certainly, are doctrinal and hortatory. There are numerous letters to his British and American publishers, Martin Secker and Thomas Seltzer, and his agents, J. B. Pinker, Robert Mountsier, and Curtis Brown. Lawrence's always precarious finances required him to become deeply involved in the often complicated negotiations over advances and royalties, while his perennial battle with the censors resulted in numerous disputes over passages deemed too "raw" for contemporary readers. Though occasionally such conflicts touched a nerve and provoked vivid Laurentian tirades, in the main these business letters have limited interest for the general reader. Other letters, particularly those to his sisters back home in the Midlands, offer welcome glimpses of a humbler, less self-centered Lawrence, concerned about the education and the various illnesses of his nieces. (It is interesting to note, however, that there are no letters in this volume to Lawrence's now-elderly, former coal miner father, Arthur Lawrence, and only a few very brief references to him in letters to others.) There are surprisingly few letters to other notable contemporary writers: one to Forster, one to Norman Douglas, fourteen to Compton Mackenzie, twenty-two to Amy Lowell (a generous benefactor), ten to Katherine Mansfield, and only six to his one-time friend John Middleton Murry. These letters are among the most interesting in the volume, for in them Lawrence gives free reign to his volatile feelings about literature, politics, mutual friends, and, above all, the various locales in which he found himself. Lawrence was at his best in his spontaneous descriptions of places, as in this lyrical account to Katherine Mansfield of a walk in the snow near his cottage in Derbyshire.

> I climbed with my niece to the bare top of the hills. Wonderful [it] is to see the
> footmarks on the snow—beautiful ropes of rabbit prints, trailing away over the brows;
> heavy hare marks; a fox so sharp and dainty, going over the wall; birds with two feet

that hop; very splendid straight advance of a pheasant; wood-pigeons that are clumsy and move in flocks; splendid little leaping marks of weasels, coming along like a necklace chain of berries; odd little filigree of the field-mice; the trail of a mole   it is astounding what a world of wild creatures one feels round one, on the hills in the snow.

Like the other two volumes in the Cambridge edition of Lawrence's letters, volume 3 is the product of impeccable scholarship and bookmaking. The 940 letters are numbered consecutively, beginning where volume 2 left off. The names of recipients and the dates of composition are printed in boldface above the letters; the source for each text is given next in reduced type. The annotations, appearing as footnotes, usefully explain the identities of the correspondents, unfamiliar allusions, and foreign phrases. Occasionally the letters to which Lawrence is responding are provided in full in the footnotes. The book is further graced with a very ample and easy-to-use index, two maps, and a detailed chronology. There are also twenty-three black and white photographs of some of the more important correspondents. The editors' introduction is comparatively short but informative, calling attention to those such as Robert Mountsier and Douglas Goldring, whose correspondence with Lawrence has not been previously or fully published. Altogether this is an exemplary edition of Lawrence's letters, which, while intended chiefly for scholars, should be of interest to a general readership as well.

Ronald G. Walker

Sources for Further Study

The Economist. CCXCIV, January 5, 1985, p. 71.
Listener. CXIII, January 31, 1985, p. 22.
The London Review of Books. VII, February 7, 1985, p. 6.
Los Angeles Times Book Review. May 12, 1985, p. 11.
Modern Fiction Studies. XXXI, Summer, 1985, p. 357.
New Statesman. CIX, January 4, 1985, p. 22.
The New York Review of Books. XXXII, January 16, 1986, p. 33.
The Observer. December 2, 1984, p. 24.
Times Literary Supplement. February 1, 1985, p. 108.
World Literature Today. LIX, Summer, 1985, p. 434.

LINDEN HILLS

Author: Gloria Naylor (1950-   )
Publisher: Ticknor & Fields (New York). 304 pp. $16.95
Type of work: Novel
Time: The 1980's
Locale: An unnamed Midwestern city

Two young men wind their way through Linden Hills, an affluent black neighborhood, doing odd jobs to earn Christmas money, but money becomes secondary as they begin to gain insight into the horrors and hypocrisy that lie behind the picture-perfect façade of the neighborhood

Principal characters:
　　LESTER TILSON, a would-be poet and a cynical Linden Hills resident
　　WILLIE MASON, Lester's best friend and a fellow poet, a resident of Putney Wayne, a poor neighborhood
　　LUTHER NEDEED, the head of the Tupelo Realty Corporation and the controlling force in Linden Hills

Linden Hills, Gloria Naylor's second novel, is, in some ways, a sequel to her first, *The Women of Brewster Place*, for which she won the American Book Award for First Fiction in 1982. (In paperback, both novels have appeared in Penguin's prizewinning Contemporary American Fiction Series.) The neighborhood of Linden Hills plays a significant role in the earlier novel; it is the place to which many residents of the Brewster Place project aspire, the reward awaiting those who work hard and fast enough to reap it here on Earth. Even in the first novel, Naylor suggests, however, that Linden Hills is not exactly the place her less privileged characters imagine it to be.

In *The Women of Brewster Place*, a young woman, Kiswana Browne, leaves her parents' secure Linden Hills home, moves into Brewster Place, and begins working as a black activist. While such a downward move mystifies her parents and many of her Brewster Place neighbors, Kiswana is Naylor's foreshadowing of the secrets to be unraveled in the second novel. In *Linden Hills*, Kiswana comes to the home of the would-be poet Lester, seeking clothing donations for the Liberation Front in Zimbabwe. When Lester's upwardly mobile, Wellesley-educated sister, Roxanne, tells Kiswana that Zimbabwens are not ready for independence and therefore Linden Hills blacks should not support the liberation cause, Kiswana's stunned reaction is one spur to Lester's own feelings that Linden Hills is a hell instead of the heaven most of its residents and, more important, most of those who aspire to be residents believe it to be.

A major difference between Naylor's two novels is that *Linden Hills* focuses on male characters. In the first novel, as its title suggests, Naylor was primarily concerned with female characters, and although the plight of black women is not ignored in the second book, the plot revolves around the struggle of Lester and his best friend, Willie, to make sense of the world of Linden Hills. Because that world is controlled by another man, Luther Nedeed, and because he is almost obsessively protective of the mystique that his empire has acquired over the 150 years since his great-great-grand-father, the first Luther Nedeed, came to the area, settled with a light-skinned bride, and began the Nedeed rise to economic and political power, *Linden Hills* becomes a classic story of good and innocence versus evil and experience.

The classical overtones of the novel are reinforced by Naylor's having structured her story, quite self-consciously, along the lines of Dante's *Inferno*. Because Linden Hills is built on the side of a very steep plateau, its streets wind and spiral from the top of the neighborhood, where Lester lives with his mother and his sister, down through increasingly luxurious accommodations, culminating, at the bottom, in the ultimate status of Tupelo Drive, home of Luther Nedeed himself. Thus, as Lester and Willie spend the week before Christmas doing odd jobs for customers whose wealth increases the lower they move down the incline, their "journey" approximates the descent into Hell, with Nedeed's home, surrounded by a lake, protected by a drawbridge, and backed up against a cemetery, representing Hell itself. (Despite the obvious parallels and the mythic weight Naylor's story gains from the connection to Dante, it should be noted, the reader of *Linden Hills* need not be an expert on the *Inferno* to appreciate the hellish quality of Nedeed's empire or to recognize Nedeed as a devil incarnate.)

One of Naylor's "travelers," Lester, the native, has grown up with his poet's soul tormented by the hypocrisy and materialism that rule his community, but as Willie rightly points out to him, he has also quite willingly accepted the security and comfort of that world. Lester is skeptical about the values of *Linden Hills*, but not skeptical enough to leave and risk life in the harsher outside world. By teaming Lester with Willie, the other "traveler," Naylor not only makes the reader dubious about the depth of Lester's negative feelings but also contrasts him with a character who has experienced the longing to make it to Linden Hills. Willie, a dropout after ninth grade and a drifter sprung from a home crowded and explosive with tension and violence that come from a man's not being able to provide for his family and not being able to stop squandering what little he does have on drink to ease the guilt of his failure, has taken the risk Lester has not. He lives on his own in a cold, spare room where the idea of Linden Hills seems much less repugnant than it does to his friend in the warm comfort of his home, with its stereo system and its always-loaded dinner table. Together, they make reliable seekers.

They had met in the seventh grade, when Willie had helped Lester in a fight with an older boy. That was the genesis of the relationship, but its lasting value springs from their shared love of poetry, a passion they revealed to each other, with much embarrassment and trepidation, as junior high students. Naylor explains their bond this way: "Bloody noses had made them friends, but giving sound to the bruised places in their hearts made them brothers." Thus, even after Willie dropped out of school, the two have stayed in touch and exchanged verses—Lester's written, and Willie's alive only in his head and recited to his friend from memory.

Because poetry is an unmarketable commodity in the world in which these men live, they find themselves doing odd jobs, scrounging for whatever dollars they can earn without selling out. To them, retaining the soul of the poet is more important than possessing material wealth. Still, Willie at least suspects that there will be some ultimate dissatisfaction in being a gray-haired grocery boy who happens to be able to recite a thousand verses. Consciously or unconsciously, both Lester and Willie are hovering on the brink of manhood, looking for the experience that will remove them forever from their somewhat boyish and romantic view of themselves and their world.

The novel's structure is episodic in that the people Lester and Willie meet appear only in the chapter of the novel where a job is being performed for them by the two friends. The only other character who appears throughout is Luther Nedeed, whose presence is increasingly felt by the two young men as they move closer and closer to Tupelo Drive and his home.

The first episode in their journey takes place on December 19th, when the two long-time friends meet on the street during the coldest weather of the year. While they stand talking on the wintry street, they meet Norman and Ruth Anderson, who invite them to their apartment for warmth and coffee. Norman is a good, hardworking man who finds himself possessed every third spring by mental demons that he calls "the pinks." When they attack, Norman loses his job, and he and Ruth must live off the money they have managed to save during his safe time, only to begin the struggle to save again when Norman is well enough to get another job. Ruth, a defector from Linden Hills after six months of unhappy marriage to one of its residents, is the one who suggests to Lester and Willie that they might be able to pick up some money for Christmas by doing odd jobs in the neighborhood. She even volunteers to make contacts for them.

The Andersons represent, from the very beginning of the novel, an alternative to the corruption and sterility Willie and Lester will find in Linden Hills. Ruth, an informed source, suggests that turning one's back on that world is the only way to have a chance at happiness. The fact that her happiness comes at such an enormous cost, what with the personal demons that torment Norman, indicates that life outside Linden Hills cannot be idealized as simple and undemanding. The Anderson apartment is as devoid of material objects as a home can be. Because the pinks cause Norman to be self-destructive, any object that he might use to hurt himself has been eliminated from their lives. The coffee must be served in Styrofoam cups that Ruth washes and reuses in order to boost their savings in preparation for the inevitable fall from peace. In addition, after years of experience, Ruth has stopped replacing furniture and other items most people would consider essential.

Thus, the Andersons provide for Willie and Lester a model of true love, content in and of itself, not connected to ambition or wealth. Ruth stays with Norman despite the strain of the bad times, because once, when she was prepared to leave him, unable to bear the pressure any longer, he brought to her an aspirin and a glass of water to comfort her—even though at that very moment the onset of the pinks was causing him almost unbearable pain. Their mutual sacrifice, typified by the aspirin incident, serves as Naylor's counter to the horrible acquisitiveness in Linden Hills.

When Ruth arranges for them to work early the next day, Willie agrees to spend the night in Lester's home, a plot device that allows him to see Linden Hills from the inside before he begins to explore it from the outside. Lester has nothing but contempt for the values of his mother and his sister. When Willie chats with Mrs. Tilson and later watches the entire Tilson family at the dinner table, he comes to realize that Lester is somewhat unfair in his view. He sees in the Tilsons, who live barely on the edge of Linden Hills, the innocent desire to make their lives better. The impetus for Nedeed's original plan for this community had been the assumption that men and women possessed just such a desire.

After dinner, Lester shares with Willie an image passed on to him by his grandmother, one of the few people in Linden Hills never intimidated by the awesome power of the Nedeeds. Grandma Tilson had once told the young Lester that the way to survive in Linden Hills was to retain possession of what she called the mirror in the soul. To her, that mirror was the one thing that allowed people to retain a sense of their own identity, separate and distinct from the identity constantly being imposed from without. If Willie and Lester are to survive the journey they will embark upon the next morning, Naylor implies, they must emerge on Christmas Day with those mirrors in their souls intact.

Their first job is helping out in the kitchen—out of sight, for the waiters must all be white—at the wedding of Winston Alcott, a young Linden Hills lawyer. Winston is a homosexual, deeply in love with his best man, David. They have been lovers for several years, and their relationship is apparently one of deep commitment and trust. Yet, Winston succumbs to the pressure of his father and sells out the love he shares with David for all the things that life in Linden Hills means. Willie and Lester watch from the kitchen as Luther Nedeed, one of Winston's groomsmen, toasts the bride and the obviously straining bridegroom, and they see what the reward for selling out is: Nedeed presents the newlyweds with a Tupelo Drive mortgage.

The next day, December 21, Willie and Lester clean out the garage at the home of Xavier Donnell and his mother. They had seen Xavier and his date, a white woman, at the wedding reception, something that infuriated Lester, since Xavier has been dating Roxanne, his sister, for some time. Xavier is angry about the presence of these lower-class blacks at his home, because he has invited Maxwell Smyth, his friend from work, over for a drink and a chat. Maxwell and Xavier are the two highest-ranking blacks at the General Motors plant where they work, and since Maxwell is ahead of him in the climb up the corporate ladder, Xavier wants his advice on the dilemma that he faces. Much against his will, Xavier finds himself falling in love with Roxanne Tilson, who is, he suspects, not the sort of wife who would help him get where he wants to go. In putting the problem in Maxwell's hands, Xavier is essentially writing Roxanne off, for Maxwell is a man bent on eradicating his own blackness.

As expected, he advises Xavier against such a match, and when Lester and Willie knock at the door, the four young black men meet in the kitchen and discuss the role of blacks in the contemporary world. Maxwell tries to prove to the two garage cleaners that blacks have enormous opportunity in that world. His evidence is a *Penthouse* magazine centerfold, which features a black woman subduing a wimpy, bespectacled white man. His attitude and Xavier's obviously compromised life only serve to reinforce the hollowness of the Linden Hills value system.

Later that same day, Lester and Willie go to the home of Lycentia Parker, who has just died and whose wake is to be held that very night in the home. Her widower has summoned them to begin painting her bedroom, as, he tells them, she would have wanted. Lester and Willie, however, are not fooled—they know that Parker is readying himself for an instant remarriage. Being at the scene of the wake allows Willie access to a community debate about a proposed low-income housing project to be built near the boundary of Linden Hills. The project is intended to improve the lives of Putney Wayne residents, such as Willie's family. Most Linden Hills residents, certainly those attending the wake, oppose the project. The moral issue at stake is whether the community should join forces with the Wayne County Citizens Alliance, an openly racist organization, to stop the project. Standing on the stairs, Willie overhears Nedeed speak to the issue; he acknowledges the overt racism of the alliance, yet at the same time he admits that he will work with the alliance for the pragmatic reason that he does not want Linden Hills property values to decline. Willie admires and respects Nedeed for his honesty.

On December 22, the workers help Reverend Hollis of Mount Sinai Baptist Church prepare for the annual Christmas party for poor children, an event that Willie loved as a child. Hollis proves to be another Linden Hills sellout. He is enormously hostile to Nedeed but unwilling to give up the economic power and prestige that come from being Nedeed's minister. An alcoholic and a womanizer, Hollis lives alone, his wife having abandoned him because of his weaknesses. Willie, reminded of his own father, sees through Hollis' slick ministerial appearance, and Willie talks so honestly, if indirectly, with the minister that he temporarily breaks free of the false self he has become to preach Lycentia Parker's funeral sermon with an openness and emotional fervor long absent from Linden Hills. Still, the congregation finds comfort and ease only when Nedeed assumes the pulpit to deliver the eulogy in the formal, repressed way the people have come to expect of their church.

After the service, Willie, who had been very ill the night before, after eating some of the cake Nedeed had brought to the wake, observes Nedeed, the community's undertaker, working over the body. What he sees so frightens him that he wants to refuse Nedeed's offer, made to Lester, of work on Christmas Eve. Lester, however, wants the money and the chance to get inside the mysterious Nedeed home. As the two friends argue about whether to accept the undefined job, they are almost arrested walking along Tupelo Drive. Fortunately, Norman Anderson appears in a taxi and rescues them by arranging work the next day shoveling the walks at the Dumont home on Tupelo.

As the young men shovel the walks during a storm the next morning, Nedeed appears as if from nowhere, ready to evict Laurel Dumont from Linden Hills. Her husband, a district attorney, has left her, and the mortgage, held by his corporation, can only be granted to a direct descendant of the original Dumonts. He tempts the young men with an offer to match whatever they have earned thus far if they will come to his home to decorate his tree the next evening, an offer neither can refuse. He also discusses with them his theory of life, that some, the strong, choose to live, and that some, the weak, to die, a conversation that foreshadows Laurel Dumont's suicide.

In a flashback, Naylor recounts Laurel's experiences growing up with a stepmother and living in the summers with her grandmother Roberta, who encouraged her love of swimming and music, who finally cashed in her life-insurance policy to send Laurel to Berkeley, where she could train as a swimmer while getting an education. That education turns Laurel into a woman her grandmother cannot recognize, a high-powered computer executive married to a high-powered attorney, from whom she daily grows more distant. When Laurel faces the emptiness of her life on Tupelo Drive, she withdraws from everything—marriage, job, all connection with the outside world. When Roberta comes at Christmas, the grandmother's strength is almost enough to pull the beloved granddaughter out of that life. Laurel begins to emerge from the depression that has paralyzed her, only to have Nedeed appear with his eviction notice. A short time later, Laurel commits suicide by diving into the wintry pool, destroying her face as it crashes into the cement hole. It is Lester and Willie who find the body.

At the Dumont house after the tragedy, Lester and Willie meet Daniel Braithwaite, Nedeed's handpicked historian of Linden Hills, who provides the final widening of their perspective necessary to make them the fully prepared emissaries to the Nedeed home. Willie finds himself troubled by the nameless, faceless quality of Nedeed's wife, who was not seen at the wedding or the funeral, who is said to be out of town, but who is never named. On the night before he and Lester are to go to Nedeed's house, Willie struggles for the first line of the poem he knows he must create to order the experiences of the past week. When he finds the lines that will start his poem, "There is a man in a house at the bottom of the hill. And his wife has no name," he is able to sleep soundly for the first time since he began the journey through Linden Hills, and he awakes the next morning ready for whatever awaits him at the Nedeed house.

Woven through the adventures of Willie and Lester is the story of the nameless, faceless wife of Luther Nedeed, Willa Prescott Nedeed, who is being held prisoner in her own home, the captive of her husband, who has paranoid fantasies that their child, the next Luther Nedeed, is, in fact, the child of some other man. He has locked the two of them in the basement, where the child has eventually died. At first, the wife, who literally cannot remember her own name for most of her captivity, keeps herself alive by reading the journals and cookbooks of her predecessors, the other wives of the Nedeed patriarchs. From those documents she finds that the terror she is experiencing is part of a multi-generational pattern whereby the wives of the Nedeeds have been stripped of all identity and discarded as if for dead once they have produced the single male heir that is expected of them. Through tremendous will and courage, she remembers her name and asserts her identity by coming upstairs and through a magically unlocked door, into the very room where Nedeed, Lester, and Willie have just finished decorating the tree and lighting the candles that are a tradition with the Nedeeds. She carries the corpse of her child, long since rigid, frozen in a position of desperate clinging to his mother's body.

As Lester and Willie hasten away from the hellish vision of the Nedeed family gathered around the beautiful, old-fashioned tree, the house begins to burn, and the last of the Nedeeds and their legacy of terror and abuse die, burned away in the unwinding of the patriarch's obsessions. Because they escape with profound knowledge, Willie and Lester are saved when they could as easily have been victims, like Willa Prescott Nedeed and her child, like all those whose mirrors in the soul had been sold to buy a place in Linden Hills.

Back of the episodes in Naylor's plot has the unity and focus of a short story, but Naylor never loses sight of the fact that this is a novel and that her conflict must always come from the struggle between innocence, represented by Lester and Willie, and experience, as embodied in Nedeed. Her characterizations are accomplished on two levels: The outer character traits are conveyed in broad strokes, verging almost on stereotype, or perhaps archetype, but the inner characters are precisely detailed and realistic.

Perhaps the most interesting narrative strategy of the novel is to be found in that which Naylor allows her two seekers access to and that from which she protects them. Willie and Lester certainly see enough to be knowledgeable and experienced by novel's end, but they are protected from some of those painfully detailed inner lives, so that they emerge without suffering the sort of irreparable damage with which some of the characters have lived and from which they have sometimes died. Willie and Lester have, almost miraculously, retained those mirrors in the soul, which Lester armed them with by recounting his grandmother's story on the night before their adventures began.

Naylor weaves myth and realism in such a way that her theme is inescapable. When people, black or white, make possession their god, they lose everything that can give life meaning. They lose life itself. Yet she also provides an alternative to such a death-in-life existence. That alternative lies in the sparse apartment of the Andersons, who are committed to each other, not to places or things, and in the friendship of the two young men, who enter Linden Hills aspiring poets and who leave possessed of the wisdom from which true poetry comes.

Jane Bowers Hill

Sources for Further Study

Booklist. LXXXI, January 15, 1985, p. 688.
Commonweal. CXII, May 3, 1985, p. 283.
Essence. XV, March, 1985, p. 52.
Library Journal. CX, April 15, 1985, p. 86.
The London Review of Books. VII, August 1, 1985, p. 26.
Los Angeles Times Book Review. February 24, 1985, p. 3.
Ms. XIII, June, 1985, p. 70.
The New York Times Book Review. XC, March 3, 1985, p. 11.
Publishers Weekly. CCXXVI, December 14, 1984, p. 39.
Times Literary Supplement. May 24, 1985, p. 572.

LONESOME DOVE

Author: Larry McMurtry (1936-   )
Publisher: Simon and Schuster (New York). 843 pp. $18.95
Type of work: Historical Western novel
Time: The late 1870's
Locale: From Lonesome Dove, Texas, to northern Montana

Lonesome Dove *chronicles the fortunes of a colorful variety of characters involved with or intersecting with a cattle drive from the Rio Grande to Montana*

Principal characters:
> AUGUSTUS "GUS" McCRAE, a former Texas Ranger who is half owner of the Hat Creek Cattle Company
> WOODROW F. CALL, a former Texas Ranger who owns the other half of the Hat Creek Cattle Company and who organizes a trail drive to Montana
> LORENA WOOD, a prostitute at the Dry Bean Saloon
> JAKE SPOON, a former Texas Ranger, on the run from an Arkansas sheriff
> NEWT, a seventeen-year-old boy who may be Call's illegitimate son
> BLUE DUCK, a murderous Comanchero
> DISH BOGGETT, a top hand among Call's cowboys
> JULY JOHNSON, a sheriff from Fort Smith, Arkansas, looking for Jake Spoon

Since the publication of his first novel, *Horseman, Pass By* (better known by its film title, *Hud*) in 1961, Larry McMurtry has written about the modern West in such works as *The Last Picture Show* (1966) and *Leaving Cheyenne* (1971). In *Lonesome Dove*, he has finally turned to the frontier heritage of the West and written an epic historical novel. Set probably in the late 1870's (no date is given, but General George Armstrong Custer's death at the Battle of Little Bighorn is a recent event), *Lonesome Dove* is a panoramic narrative centering on a cattle drive from the Rio Grande to northern Montana, spanning more than two thousand miles of frontier. Western enthusiasts will find that the novel has a bit of everything: rustling raids into Mexico, stampedes, lightning and hail storms, river crossings, drought, deadly outlaws, gunfights, lynchings, murderous Indians, and Indian fights.

Full as it is of action, however, *Lonesome Dove* is essentially a novel of character. Leading the large and varied cast are Augustus McCrae (Gus) and Woodrow F. Call, owners of the Hat Creek Cattle Company in the town of Lonesome Dove on the Rio Grande. Both are veteran Texas Rangers who spent dangerous years fighting Indians and outlaws. The gregarious Gus is a compulsive talker and a humorist who, while impressively effective in action, usually prefers to relax, enjoy himself, and let Call do most of the work. Even though Call complains, he is temperamentally suited to the arrangement, for he is a workaholic, a laconic loner who drives everyone else as hard as himself. The genial and expansive Gus embraces life; he enjoys his whiskey, good books, an occasional woman, and an amused observation of human nature. The indrawn Call's accumulated frustrations have built up a store of suppressed violence. The two of them are perfect foils to each other.

The inspiration for the cattle drive comes from Jake Spoon, a former Ranger crony of Gus and Call, who turns up with tales of tall grass and wonderful country in Montana, available for the first settlers to stake out a claim. Though Call and Gus are rich enough and have no need to make a fortune, Call determines to assemble a herd and be the first cattleman to enter Montana, mainly because it will provide an outlet for his pent-up energies and because it has not been done before. Gus thinks that the enterprise is foolish but agrees to go along for the show.

To collect a herd, Call undertakes a series of nightly raids into Mexico, from which he steals about three thousand head. To handle them, he hires on additional cowboys, most notably Dish Boggett (so named because he was once so thirsty he drank a pail of dishwater rather than wait his turn at the pump).

Call also permits Newt to go on the drive. Newt is a seventeen-year-old boy whom Call and Gus reared when the boy's mother, a prostitute, died. It is rumored that Jake may be Newt's father, but it is more likely that his father is Call, who, though usually indifferent to women, had a brief but intense relationship with Newt's mother. Newt has no last name, for no one has acknowledged him. For him, the long trek will be an initiation into danger, responsibility, and manhood.

Meanwhile, Newt has a platonic crush on Lorena Wood, the prostitute at the local Dry Bean saloon. Dish Boggett and most of the other men are less platonically in love with her, but since her past relationships with men have been a series of disasters that drove her into her present position, she does not care for any of them. Lorena is most at ease with Gus, whose conversation is amusing and who treats her with consideration. Jake Spoon, however, has an irresistible way with women, and when he appears, Lorena goes out of business and devotes herself entirely to him. To his dismay, she insists on accompanying him on the cattle drive in the hope that he will carry out his promise to take her to San Francisco, the utopia of her dreams. The irresponsible Jake has no intention of keeping his word, but he is too easygoing to resist Lorena.

The rest of the outfit are a colorful crew: Deets, a black cowboy, who is the best tracker and pointer on the frontier; Pea Eye, simpleminded but a persistent worker; Bolivar, the Mexican cook who is a retired *bandito*; Po Campo, who replaces him and creates unusual dishes from food he has foraged off the land; the O'Brien brothers, Irish immigrants who sing at night to the cattle; Lippy, former piano player at the Dry Bean, who leaks from an unhealed bullet wound in his stomach; Jasper Fant, obsessed with a fear of drowning; Needle Nelson and Soupy Jones; and Gus's two pigs, who walk all the way to Montana, thus making history after a fashion.

Crossing the path of the cattle drive are numerous other characters. July Johnson, a naïve husband newly wed to a domineering wife who he does not realize used to be a prostitute, is an inexperienced sheriff from Fort Smith, Arkansas. He reluctantly goes after Jake Spoon, who accidentally killed his brother, but gets sidetracked into a search for his wife when she runs off on a whiskey boat to find a former lover. July's hopelessly incompetent deputy, who goes after July with the news of his wife's departure, falls into a series of hapless misadventures from which a runaway teenage girl and July must rescue him. The Comanchero Blue Duck, a cold-blooded and vicious killer who hates Gus and Call from their Texas Ranger days, abducts Lorena, who undergoes a ghastly ordeal before Gus rescues her. Without Lorena to look after, Jake falls in with the Suggs brothers, who go on a rampage of casually demented murder that Jake is unable to prevent and for which he must share the penalty.

After Gus rescues her, Lorena thinks that she is in love with him, though she is more terrified of losing his protection. Gus becomes increasingly devoted to her, but he thinks that he is still in love with Clara, whom he courted sixteen years earlier. Though no one else could make her feel as fully alive as Gus, Clara rejected him to marry a horse dealer, who was dull but provided the sort of security she needed. She realized that Gus loved his freedom even more than her and that she was the type of person who needed to put down roots, not blow around like a tumbleweed. While the cowboys are wanderers, happiest when on horseback savoring the excitement of new land, Clara is anchored to her chosen plot of earth. Now her husband is slowly dying from a horse kick to the head, and Clara is doing her best to take care of the farm in Nebraska and to raise her two daughters. If Gus is the most colorful character in the novel, Clara is the strongest—an uncomplaining, self-reliant frontier woman who commands the men around her without being domineering. She and Gus have an affectionate reunion, but they cannot reverse their choices.

Among other things, the novel is an elegy for an era that was ending. Gus observes that when the Texas Rangers killed off Indians and outlaws, they removed some of the most interesting people in the territory, and he admits that he himself would rather be an outlaw than a doctor, lawyer, or member of some tame and respectable profession. He is also aware that the land will not stay untamed for long; all too soon, settlers, merchants, townspeople will fill up the empty spaces and take away the wild freedom that he has enjoyed.

For most of the characters the action is tragic. Many of them die violently, either murdered or the victims of accidents on the trail. Death comes casually, in episodes of startling and unexpected violence. The survivors are initiated into painful reality as they experience loss or disillusionment. After spending much of the trek in tears or terror, Newt develops into a capable young man. Call gives him increasing responsibility, makes him his second-in-command, but cannot quite bring himself to acknowledge his son, and the bond that was almost established between them dissolves in frustration and inhibition on Call's part and bitterness on Newt's. Other characters suffer bereavement.

Yet the overall impression is of the vitality of life. As Gus observes, "It's a fine world, though rich in hardships at times." The novel is full of energy. Its language, both in narrative and dialogue, is a lively vernacular, full of unexpected metaphors and turns of phrase, and there is a considerable amount of mellow, deadpan, and offbeat humor. Written on a large scale, *Lonesome Dove* chronicles both an epic journey and the picaresque adventures of other wanderers. The narrative shifts from group to group, connecting them in surprising but logical ways. Both McMurtry's storytelling verve and the vitality of his characters will catch readers and keep them deeply involved. McMurtry re-creates the details of Western Americana, geography, history, weather, and trail driving with such vividness and authenticity that the reader vicariously experiences the life of the 1800's. *Lonesome Dove*, winner of the 1986 Pulitzer Prize in the category of fiction, is not a formula Western but a major novel with a breadth, variety, and liveliness that recall Charles Dickens. As Gus puts it, "I wouldn't have missed coming up here. I can't think of nothing better than riding a fine horse into a new country."

Robert E. Morsberger

Sources for Further Study

Booklist. LXXXI, May 15, 1985, p. 1274.
Kirkus Reviews. LIII, April 15, 1985, p. 341.
Library Journal. CX, July, 1985, p. 94.
Los Angeles Times Book Review. June 9, 1985, p. 2.
The New Republic. CXCIII, September 2, 1985, p. 26.
The New York Times Book Review. XC, June 9, 1985, p. 7.
Newsweek. CV, June 3, 1985, p. 74.
Publishers Weekly. CCXXVII, April 19, 1985, p. 71.
Time. CXXV, June 10, 1985, p. 79.
The Wall Street Journal. CCVI, August 15, 1985, p. 25.

THE LONG MARCH
The Untold Story

Author: Harrison E. Salisbury (1908-   )
Publisher: Harper & Row, Publishers (New York). Illustrated. 419 pp. $22.95
Type of work: Current history
Time: 1934-1935
Locale: China

The epic march of the Chinese Red Army in search of a secure territorial base

Principal personages:
MAO ZEDONG, the leader of the Long March and the chairman of the Chinese Communist Party
ZHOU ENLAI, a top commander of the Long March and later the premier of the People's Republic of China (PRC)
LIN BIAO, a top commander of the Long March and later the defense minister of the PRC
ZHU DE, a top commander of the Long March
DENG XIAOPING, a ranking party functionary and later the senior vice premier of the PRC
CHIANG KAI-SHEK, the leader of the Kuomintang

Harrison Salisbury retells the story of the Long March in fresh and illuminating detail and with many new insights. It is the fascinating story of one of the most astounding feats of all time, an epic on the grandest scale. The Red Army marched some six thousand miles across some of the most inhospitable and difficult terrain imaginable, while constantly being harassed by sizable enemy forces. In 1984, the fiftieth anniversary of the Long March, Salisbury was able to travel along most of the original routes. It was an enterprise that represented an impressive personal achievement for the author, a man well into his seventies. He had the opportunity to interview numerous men and women who were veterans of that march. Among these were the paramount leaders of China, as well as ordinary citizens. Salisbury was also afforded access to archives and documentary materials heretofore not open to any Westerner.

Surprisingly little was known of the conditions of the Long March outside China. They resulted from the conflict between the Chinese Communist Party (CCP) and the Kuomintang (KMT), the Nationalist movement founded by Sun Yat-sen. The CCP was formally established in 1921, ten years after the overthrow of the Manchu dynasty by the KMT. Still, conditions in China remained rather chaotic in the newly proclaimed republic. The central government was unable to assert control over vast areas ruled by rapacious warlords. As dedicated Nationalists, the Chinese Communists collaborated with the KMT and contributed to the latter's gradual consolidation of power. By 1927, Sun's successor, General Chiang Kai-shek, was able to unify most of China under the banner of the KMT. At this juncture, Chiang decided to eradicate the Communists, whom he perceived as a

threat to his rule. Vicious death squads were unleashed on Communist func-
tionaries in Shanghai, touching off the struggle between the CCP and the
KMT, the elemental struggle over which version of the Chinese Nationalist
Revolution would prevail.

The CCP was able to establish enclaves under its rule, notably in the
southern area of Jiangxi province. Here the Communists captured the city
of Nanchang on August 1, 1927. The date was designated as that of the
founding of the Red Army. It was an event of great importance to the Chinese revolution, for it brought together the group of men who would assume the leading roles. One of the central figures—then and throughout—
was Zhou Enlai, offspring of a "bankrupt Mandarin family." Other key figures present were Lin Biao and Zhu De—and, of course, there was Mao
Zedong. Mao was familiar with Jiangxi, a particularly backward and poor
area of China, and he organized the so-called Autumn Harvest Uprising in
September, 1927. Winning over the bandits of the region and setting up a
fortress in the remote mountains, Mao was instrumental in carrying on the
struggle. The initial base was expanded and transformed into a Soviet
republic in 1932. Nevertheless, Chiang had huge numbers of troops at his
disposal. He surrounded the Communist area and relentlessly intensified the
pressure. In 1934, Chiang's stranglehold over the CCP in Jiangxi was strong
enough to threaten imminent collapse. These developments set the stage for
the Long March. The Communists determined that in order to survive, they
had to break through the encirclement and move westward to set up a new
base.

The Red Army marched out of Jiangxi with more than eighty thousand
men. Probably no one anticipated the enormity of the enterprise that lay
ahead. Still, it must have been a most difficult step to take. For most of the
men, Jiangxi was home. They must have been greatly troubled by the
thought that they might never return. The decision was taken reluctantly.
Within the CCP leadership, considerable disagreement over policy and strategy existed. There was also, at the time, strong opposition to Mao. Yet, the
prospect of eventual annihilation at the hands of an enemy hundreds of
thousands strong left few options.

The Red Army moved to the southwest corner of the Communist zone
and from there slipped quietly into "white" territory. They were able to get
out of the vicinity without military clashes through an arrangement with the
Guangdong warlord. The Communists were further aided by their ability to
intercept and read KMT wireless exchanges, with the KMT apparently
unaware of this. By the time Chiang Kai-shek had fully realized what was
afoot, the Red Army had extricated itself from the entrapment. Interestingly, both sides had a German as key military adviser: Chiang had the
famed General Hans von Seeckt, who was credited with developing the
stratagems that pressured the Communists ever more intensely, while the

CCP had a German revolutionary named Otto Braun, who was at first virtually in overall command of the Communist forces. Later, many of Braun's decisions proved damaging to the Red Army, and he was forced to the sidelines once Mao was able to assert his leadership.

The early military battles were clearly won by the Red Army. Surprise, mobility, and superior discipline would carry the day. Nevertheless, as Salisbury so vividly conveys, the Long March was not only military combat. It required the simultaneous waging of three separate battles—the battle against the KMT forces, the battle against nature and the elements, and the internal leadership and policy battles. Still, the men and women of the Red Army were highly motivated, firm in the cause for which they were fighting. The discipline of the troops was excellent; they did not maltreat the civilian population, and they paid for their supplies. In general, the Red Army constituted a potent force. High morale and impressive mobility would give it the edge over a numerically far-superior enemy. One of the most perilous episodes for the Red Army was the crossing of the great Xiang River. Chiang's forces attacked at the time when some groups had already crossed, while slower moving columns had only just reached it. The battle of the Xiang lasted from November 25 to December 3, 1934, and was fought desperately. The crossing was achieved at a disastrously high price. By Salisbury's account, more than half of the troops were lost.

Once they were across the Xiang and had moved into the rugged mountainous terrain, they were relieved of military pressure. Yet now they faced the enormous physical obstacles posed by the dangerous mountain paths, perilous rivers, exhaustion, and hunger. The peasantry of this part of Guizhou province was appallingly poor and miserable. The landlords from whom supplies could be expropriated were few in number. Moreover, the Miao, a minority people populating the area, were not merely distrustful, but outrightly hostile. It was an extremely trying time for the Red Army, whose numbers had shrunk to about thirty thousand. At the fateful meeting of party leaders in Liping, highest authority fell formally to Mao. It spelled the end of Braun's influence over the Communist forces. Braun had advocated direct military confrontation and sought decisive battles. Mao, by that time having developed his theories on guerrilla warfare, set a different course designed to avoid an all-out clash with the powerful forces Chiang could position against him.

The Wu River was successfully crossed, and the city of Zunyi captured. Nevertheless, plans to establish a new base here had to be discarded. The Zunyi region was economically quite backward and not suitable to support a sizable army. The chief crop—as in so many other regions of China at the time—was opium. Moreover, Chiang would be able to array against them some four hundred thousand men. So they continued the march, but they were only a remnant of the original force that had moved out of Jiangxi. To gain access to the north of China became the chief objective. This, however, required the crossing of the mighty Yangtze River. The Red Army endeavored to gain a direct northerly route to the Yangtze. That effort was foiled by the KMT, as Chiang's best troops engaged the Communists in a critical battle along this approach to the Yangtze. The fighting raged for ten days, reports Salisbury, and the Red Army's fate hung in the balance. Mao and his close associates Zhou Enlai and Zhu De took personal command, making every effort to preserve the Red Army as a fighting force. The direct route to the north had to be abandoned. Instead, it was decided to move south—backtracking over Zunyi—and then west into Yunnan province for refuge. Doggedly they fought on, knowing that defeat or surrender would mean certain death. A vital victory that ensured escape once again was won at Louchan Pass.

Through Yunnan, the march went northward again up to the Yangtze, known in this region as the Golden Sands River. This time, the troops were able to cross and move into Sichuan province. After seven months in the field and extremely heavy losses, they had finally gained some freedom of operation. The next big obstacle was the Dadu River. Crack troops under Lin Biao raced to beat Chiang's forces to a suitable river crossing. The Luding Bridge was captured in a daring attack. In the annals of the Long March, this feat would be singled out as particularly important; it ensured the Red Army's escape through Sichuan.

Nevertheless, still more severe trials were in store for the battered and worn army before a safe haven could be reached. In their eighth month on the move, they crossed the Snowy Mountains. The accounts of the veterans that Salisbury relates suggest that the Snowies were the worst yet that most of the men had experienced. The high altitude and extremely cold temperatures caused many casualties among the insufficiently clothed and fed men. Beyond the mountains, Mao's forces met up at Dawai with a separate Communist force, the Fourth Front Army under the leadership of Zhang Quotao, which had established itself in the area. Mao and Zhang celebrated their reunion, even agreed to a joint command. Yet, apparently the two leaders were unable to put their earlier quarrels behind them. Suspicion and outright hostility welled up, causing leading functionaries to fear an open conflict between the two Red Army contingents. Mao was determined to continue to push northward. Zhang, persuaded that the southwesterly Tibetan region offered a safer base, moved in that direction with his troops.

Mao's army had to overcome still one more incredibly severe trial: the crossing of an area consisting of vast and treacherous marshes known as the Grasslands. Many hardened veterans succumbed to the extreme hardships they had to endure: No landmarks, no trees, no dry place to rest, and no food. Yet after this ordeal, the worst was over. More battles would have to be fought, but there would be no more starvation, no more retreats.

Indeed, Mao was able to turn the Long March into a great victory upon reaching northern Shaanxi province, his new base. The Long March ended officially at Wuqui. It had been a trek more than six thousand miles long. There had been more than eighty thousand men at the start; there were barely four thousand at the finish. There are no statistics to show how many were dropouts and how many were casualties; certainly there were plenty of both. As Salisbury so skillfully relates, the march was an epic in blood and courage. Those who survived it were steeled for the Chinese revolution and the sweeping social changes to be effected. Even in 1985, more than fifty years later, veterans of the Long March are among China's highest leaders. One of the most outstanding among them is the indomitable Deng Xiaoping, who is pushing China along new paths of modernization and development.

Salisbury's work, although not the first on the subject, as claimed by the publisher, makes for highly interesting reading and provides a lot of new information on a great historical event. The reader is apt to see it with Salisbury as a human undertaking without parallel. Having covered much of the ground himself, and talked to so many who remembered, he enlivens the story with personal anecdotes and graphic visual accounts. Photographs, maps, and extensive notes further enhance the book's value as an admirable contribution to modern Chinese history.

Manfred Grote

Sources for Further Study

Booklist. LXXXII, September 15, 1985, p. 104.
Kirkus Reviews. LIII, July 15, 1985, p. 710.
Library Journal. CX, September 15, 1985, p. 80.
The New Republic. CXCIII, December 16, 1985, p. 41.
The New York Times Book Review. XC, September 29, 1985, p. 7.
Newsweek. CVI, October 14, 1985, p. 87.
The Observer. November 24, 1985, p. 29.
The Wall Street Journal. CCVI, October 10, 1985, p. 30.
Washington Journalism Review. VII, October, 1985, p. 51.

LOUISE BOGAN
A Portrait

Author: Elizabeth Frank (1945-   )
Publisher: Alfred A. Knopf (New York). Illustrated. 460 pp. $24.95
Type of work: Literary biography
Time: 1897-1970
Locale: The United States and Europe

A rich and well-researched study of the life and work of one of America's finest and most neglected poets

> *Principal personages:*
> LOUISE BOGAN, a poet and critic
> MARY HELEN SHIELDS BOGAN, her mother
> DANIEL BOGAN, her father
> RAYMOND HOLDEN, her second husband
> MAIDIE ALEXANDER SCANNELL, her daughter

When she died in 1970, Louise Bogan had received most of the accolades the United States bestows on its best writers: membership in the Academy of American Poets, the American Academy of Arts and Letters, and the National Institute of Arts and Letters; a Guggenheim Fellowship; the Harriet Monroe Award for Poetry; the Bollingen Prize. She had lectured and taught at several colleges and universities, sat on panels with many distinguished colleagues, and served as poetry consultant to the Library of Congress. In addition to being recognized as one of the best lyric poets of the century, she had become an important critical voice, helping to determine the nation's literary tastes as the poetry critic for *The New Yorker* for more than three decades. Yet, as her biographer Elizabeth Frank shows in her sympathetic study, these successes came late in Bogan's life and were wrought out of great emotional pain. They brought her neither widespread fame nor personal happiness, and her last years were marred by paralyzing depression.

At the heart of Frank's book is her understanding of the paradoxical connection between Bogan's artistic achievement and her psychological struggles. Though her poems are almost never autobiographical in the strictest sense, they are nevertheless profoundly tied to the events of her life. In her spare, crystalline lyrics she was able to express her alternating moods of despair and serene acceptance—the spiritual "chiaroscuro," the blend of light and dark, which Frank uses as a dominant metaphor throughout her work.

Using as her sources Bogan's brief memoirs and autobiographical stories, her letters to friends and family, and personal interviews with many of those who knew her, including her daughter, Maidie Alexander Scannell, Frank has been able to reconstruct her life in remarkable detail. The biographer has given special attention to those events and relationships that provide clues to Bogan's art. She puts special emphasis on the poet's early childhood and the character of her mother—influences which Frank, as did Bogan herself, identifies as central to much of her later distress.

Bogan was born in 1897 in Livermore Falls, Maine, where her father, Daniel Bogan, was superintendent at a paper mill. Her mother, Mary Helen Shields Bogan, was a volatile, unhappy woman who quarreled constantly and bitterly with her husband and was often unfaithful to him. On at least one occasion she involved her young daughter in one of her affairs in some profoundly traumatic way. As Frank notes, Bogan never revealed—if she even remembered clearly—the nature of the experience, but she did record the fact that she once went blind for two days in her early childhood, apparently reacting against some sight she desperately needed to block out. By the time the family moved to Boston in 1909, the situation had stabilized enough for Bogan to have a satisfactory, productive career as student and apprentice writer at the Girls' Latin School and as a freshman at Boston University. Yet her marriage at nineteen to Curt Alexander, a German-born soldier, seems a classic case of a young woman seeking escape from her parents.

As Frank observes, one critical result of Bogan's family heritage was a lasting difficulty in establishing permanent relationships. She found it hard to trust anyone and at times seemed to expect betrayal from both lovers and friends. Within a few months of her first marriage, she recognized that it had been a terrible mistake. She and Alexander had little in common, and she was miserable during the months they were stationed in Panama as she awaited the birth of their daughter. She soon took the baby home to her parents in Boston. Although she and Alexander were briefly reunited when he was sent back to the United States, they separated again and would almost certainly have divorced had he not died of pneumonia in 1920. By then Louise had moved to Greenwich Village and had at least one short and painful love affair.

Second only to her conflict with her mother in its damaging effects was her relationship with Raymond Holden, whom she married in 1925 after living with him for a year. Their ten years together brought her the greatest happiness she was to know, but they also moved her inexorably toward a complete breakdown. Socially and temperamentally they differed greatly. He came from a well-established, wealthy New York family; she still smarted from the insults she had suffered as an Irish working-class girl in Boston. He disliked scenes; she, like her mother, was given to violent rages. In addition, she was almost pathologically jealous.

Frank's description of the last years of the marriage suggests that Bogan forcibly broke it apart. The cost of her anger and suspicion was depression, which became so severe that she hospitalized herself for treatment in 1931. Two years later, perhaps sensing restlessness in Holden and certainly feeling unhappy about the marriage herself, she applied for and won a Guggenheim Fellowship for travel to Europe. Her husband was unhappy about her departure, and Frank quotes extensively from letters that reveal Louise's jealousy and Raymond's exasperation. By the time Bogan ended her six-month trip, Holden had, in fact, taken a mistress. Frank asks whether Bogan's obsessive suspicions produced the very outcome she feared most. The two did make several abortive attempts at reconciliation, but within two months of her return, Bogan was once again hospitalized for mental illness. In the spring of 1934 she left her husband permanently, recognizing that she would not be able to sustain her newly won stability if they remained together.

Although the end of her marriage brought an end to the kind of consuming passion she and Holden had shared, their break did not immediately end Bogan's emotional attachments. She and poet Theodore Roethke were briefly lovers in 1935, when he was twenty-six and she thirty-eight. Two years later, in the throes of an attack of paranoia during a trip to England and Ireland, she was befriended by an electrician from New York. Their affair continued for eight years, very privately. Her friends knew nothing of him, and she was evidently able to keep their relationship in balance in a way that she could not do earlier.

In the last third of her life, Bogan avoided passionate commitments, recognizing that to continue functioning she could not risk the psychic toll of intense involvements, and she relied increasingly on the emotional support of her circle of friends, mostly writers. Some, like Edmund Wilson, Rolfe Humphries, and Morton Dauwen Zabel, were part of her life from the 1920's and 1930's. Others, including May Sarton, William Maxwell, W. H. Auden, and her literary executor, Ruth Limmer, entered her orbit in her middle years. Through them she remained at the center of American literary activity, nurturing their work with her incisive critical comments and welcoming their companionship for listening to the classical music she loved, discussing literary theory, or eating and drinking well.

The postwar years might appear to an outsider the most satisfactory ones for Bogan, bringing economic security and a measure of fame in literary circles. Pictures of her at this period show a handsome, imposing woman, apparently in full control of her life and talent. Yet the structure of Frank's book, as well as its content, suggests a different conclusion. Nearly two hundred pages are devoted to the eleven years from 1930 to 1941, while a little more than one hundred cover the period from 1942 to Bogan's death in 1970. Clearly, it was during the most stressful times that Bogan did her best work. In the poetry, Frank notes, she tried always "to seek alliance with life, through art, rather than escape, and to set the wintry, betrayed, stunned, and sleeping heart to beating."

While the most immediately appealing sections of Frank's book are the biographical ones that bring Bogan vividly before the reader, it is perhaps the extensive, thoughtful analyses of her writings that will prove of more lasting value to scholars and students of poetry and criticism. These critical discussions are carefully interwoven with the biographical materials to show the ties between the experience and the art derived from it. Frank provides detailed commentary on the major themes and images of each volume of Bogan's work, quoting copiously to allow the reader unfamiliar with the poetry to derive a full appreciation of the poet's achievement.

Bogan's first volume, *Body of This Death* (1923), Frank writes, shows a "sequence of moods" reflecting the female experience. Out of her childhood, her failed marriage, her unfulfilling affairs came a succession of images of women "wounded and spiritually ravaged," at times transfixed, frozen in time. The image of Medusa, turning to stone those who look upon her, is a recurrent one. The second volume of poems, *Dark Summer* (1929), is somewhat more positive. A product of the happier years of Bogan's marriage to Holden, it moves away, Frank notes, from the earlier volume's "almost exclusive preoccupation with the psychology of sexual" conflict toward greater pleasure in the natural world.

With *The Sleeping Fury* (1937), which contained the poems written during the tormented years of Bogan's breakdown and divorce, she reached the height of her powers. In this work, says Frank, can be seen "the story of her spirit's trial, death, and rebirth, the 'dark night of the soul' which she had traversed like any seeker for salvation." In the title poem, Bogan moves "from high tension to calm insight," and the whole volume shows the magnitude of her technical and artistic skill.

Bogan seemed at this point in her career to be on the verge of a breakthrough to new levels of accomplishment. Yet with the publication of *The Sleeping Fury*, Frank observes, "Her most productive days as a poet were over." Bogan was to publish three more volumes of poetry: *Poems and New Poems* (1941), *Collected Poems, 1923-1953* (1954), and *The Blue Estuaries: Poems, 1923-1968* (1968). Yet, as their titles indicate, each of these volumes relied heavily on the earlier works. Bogan was never a writer who could sit down to write a poem at will. Though she could dash off amusing rhymes in letters to her friends, her real poems "arrived," and as she grew older and more detached from her deepest feelings, they came less and less often. From 1941 to 1948, according to her biographer, she produced no poems at all. There were, certainly, successful works in her later years, among them "After the Persian," one of her relatively rare ventures into free verse, and "Song for the Last Act," which Frank calls "the great poem of Bogan's poetic decline." The latter is a lyric full of her favorite symbols: "the garden with statues; flowers; the late summer about to become autumn; the text which must be painfully spelled out; the quest or voyage." The poem recapitulates the themes of renunciation and acceptance that were so prominent in Bogan's later work and life.

As her powers as a poet diminished, Bogan turned her energies toward criticism, and Frank provides her readers with a balanced and accurate assessment of Bogan's gifts in this genre. Bogan's greatest talent as a critic, she concludes, was "her ability to place herself at the center of another's work." She produced essays on Henry James, William Butler Yeats, Rainer Maria Rilke, and W. H. Auden that are still considered among the finest commentaries on their writings.

Bogan held to strong critical principles for the four decades of her career as a reviewer, insisting always on the essential connection between emotion and art. She detested the political themes that many of her colleagues adopted in the 1930's, when Marxism became fashionable in intellectual circles, and she did not hesitate to make her scorn known. She later reacted equally strongly against the New Critics, whom she viewed, in Frank's words, as "an encroaching phalanx of abstract, overingenious, and deliberately obscure mandarins, out to safeguard their academic and social prestige by demonstrating the need for a priestly class of explicators and interpreters."

In her portrait of the complex woman and artist who was Louise Bogan, Elizabeth Frank has provided her readers with a model of what every literary biography should be. Her book is both scholarly and readable, and she has achieved a superb balance between objectivity and sympathy. This book has won high praise for its author, including the 1986 Pulitzer Prize in the category of biography, but, perhaps more important, it should win new attention for its subject, who clearly deserves greater recognition for her contributions to American letters.

Elizabeth Johnston Lipscomb

Sources for Further Study

The Atlantic. CCLV, February, 1985, p. 100.
Boston Review. IX, December, 1984, p. 33.
Library Journal. CIX, November 15, 1984, p. 2145.
Los Angeles Times Book Review. March 31, 1985, p. 1.
Ms. XIII, December, 1984, p. 39.
The Nation. CCXL, February, 23, 1985, p. 215.
The New York Times Book Review. XC, March 3, 1985, p. 1.
The New Yorker. LXI, July 29, 1985, p. 73.
Publishers Weekly. CCXXVI, July 12, 1984, p. 61.
Washington Post Book World. XV, February 24, 1985, p. 5.

THE LOVER

Author: Marguerite Duras (1914-   )
Translated from the French by Barbara Bray
Publisher: Pantheon Books (New York). 117 pp. $11.95
Type of work: Novel
Time: The late 1930's to the mid-1940's
Locale: Saigon

A French Caucasian woman recollects an affair with a Chinese lover, her school, and her family life in Indochina

> *Principal characters:*
> A GIRL, unnamed, who is fifteen and a half years old
> HER MOTHER, headmistress of a girls' school in Sadec
> HER OLDER BROTHER
> HER YOUNGER BROTHER
> A CHINESE MAN, the son of a rich local landlord

Marguerite Duras spent her early years in prewar French Indochina. After a series of relatively conventional novels, she came to express dissatisfaction with writing as a medium that continued to serve the contemporary world. No one, she said, read anymore, including herself, although she said that writing was a personal necessity, a compulsion that threw her into a highly charged relationship with words. Yet perhaps the result was obsolete. Instead, Duras proposed the "multiple work of art," material that might find expression equally in the form of an opera, a film, a play, a dance, a novel. *India Song* (1976) served as an example, appearing simultaneously in film and play form and soon after published by Gallimard as a novel.

In company with such other modernist writers as Alain Robbe-Grillet and Jacques Sternberg, Marguerite Duras had earlier turned to cinema as a new medium to explore. Significantly, each collaborated with the French director Alain Resnais; the Resnais-Duras venture was the memorable *Hiroshima mon amour* (1959).

In their film, one may identify elements common to subsequent motion pictures and novels by Duras. Characters are unidentified by name. A woman transgresses social boundaries to experience erotic love with an Asian man. Memory, one's avenue to the past, figures centrally in both dialogue and images.

Repressed or intruding involuntarily, memory patterns Duras' shifting narrative fabric. Who is remembering? Who agrees so that the reader-viewer may measure contradictory information? A moment of the past—a photograph, a town once frequented—tantalizes by promising to unlock a secret of personal history and frustrates by its distance, its refusal to yield.

In films she has directed (*Destroy She Said*, 1969; *Woman of the Ganges*, 1972; and *India Song* are examples), Duras structures her work by playing picture against sound. A segment of dialogue runs counter to what the audience sees; two people will be shown talking while the audience hears voices of another couple. It is often unclear whether what is seen and what is heard are taking place in a common time frame. Voices may be past, the picture present. Or the image may frequently reoccur, sometimes identical, sometimes subtly changed so that the audience repositions its place in time. Such static, minimalist images find Duras' prose equivalent in carefully described moments from the past.

Calling up such recollected moments (it was the French philosopher Henri Bergson who had likened memory to successive still frames of motion-picture film), Duras carefully details the backgrounds of her composition while leaving other areas vague. Then she will qualify, shift, and reposition her view or her understanding of what there is to be witnessed. The audience's stability is undermined with doubt, by new information, by a different thought. Such strategies are evocative more of modern painting, sculpture, and serial music than of traditional narrative. Called upon constantly to share the task, the reader undertakes a joint venture in the creation of an ever-tentative reality. Language misleads as it clarifies.

Working with so demanding and so elusive an aesthetic, it is a wonder Marguerite Duras has continued to operate with sufficient commercial appeal. *The Lover* (published in France in 1984 as *L'Amant*) met unexpected public response in the summer of 1984: Nearly seven hundred thousand copies were sold in France by the year's end, and Duras won the prestigious Goncourt Prize. In addition, *The Lover* received the Ritz Paris Hemingway Award, the world's largest prize for a novel. The explanation may be found in another shift in her aesthetic tactics. With *The Lover*, Duras mutes modernist strategies without betraying their spirit. What had sometimes in her fiction been frustrating puzzles appear here as poetic evocation. For a general reader attuned to her style, *The Lover* is rewardingly accessible.

The novel's major characters are unnamed. The narrator is a French woman, now in her sixties, recounting her life in Indochina before the outbreak of World War II. At fifteen and a half, she has an affair with an older Chinese man, the son of a wealthy builder and landlord. The man falls in love; the girl experiences deep, erotic passion while preserving a kind of startling self-awareness and objectivity. Their liaison lasts a year and a half, known to her family but unacknowledged. The girl's mother is a schoolteacher, prone to periods of morose despair and possessively attached to an older son, who is a thief, a gambler, and a bully. A younger brother and the girl have a close, if unexpressed, alliance against the others. The girl attends a boarding school, sneaking away regularly to meet her lover.

All this information is disclosed in bits and pieces. There is no direct dialogue; everything is filtered through the narrator's memories, tied to old photographs and remembered images, such as the girl's ragbag costume as she rides a ferry across the Mekong River to her school, or a photograph of her mother, or washing the family house by running water across the floors through back door to front while neighbors visit to watch the spectacle. Some settings are permeated with smells, such as the lovers' quarters where street odors drift through the flimsy wall into the room.

The girl's emotions are not so much confused as they are complicated, extreme, and intense. She loves and hates the mother who alternately understands her altogether and slips away into melancholic reverie or obsessive attachment to her firstborn. The older brother is a tragic, despised burden. The younger one dies in 1942 during the Japanese occupation. By then the girl has been sent to Paris, and there are moments of that city in wartime. Sometimes the narrator recollects more current events: the older brother's sordid career, the mother's last return to Indochina, a call from the lover years later.

Sensually described, the intensity of the love affair is complicated by money (the girl's family is desperately poor) and by race. The wealthy father cannot condone such a relationship; the girl's family accepts her lover's generosities without admitting his existence. While experiencing the deepest pleasures, the girl is remarkably clear-sighted, in contrast to the man's sometimes-desperate emotionality, and yet her sexual relation to him is one of traditional pornography—that is, the passive love object brought to heights of ecstasy by the ever-potent male.

All of this is set in the last days of French colonial Indochina. The native population figures as a constant presence without intruding into memory's foreground. Along with the smells of jasmine, herbs, and incense there are beggars' cries, housekeepers, houseboys, and Indian moneylenders who wait, smiling, in the family parlor for their payments. The triumph of Duras' prose, wonderfully translated by Barbara Bray, who won the PEN Translation Prize in the category of prose for her translation of the novel, rests finally in the form she has engendered to evoke so broad a range of attitudes and feelings, many so sexually charged. The prose is beautifully clear, precise, candid, and economical, for *The Lover* is more novella than novel. Indeed, ties between reader and writer seem finally almost to turn invisible, like those between history and invention. The novel ends with a signature: "Neauphle-le-Château—Paris; February-May 1984," as if Marguerite Duras herself were the girl in her story. In a way, she is, but so is the reader.

John L. Fell

Sources for Further Study

Booklist. LXXXI, June 1, 1985, p 1370.
Boston Review. X, July, 1985, p. 26.
Harper's Magazine. CCLXX, June, 1985, p. 28.
Library Journal. CX, June 1, 1985, p. 142.
Los Angeles Times Book Review. July 14, 1985, p. 3.
The New Republic. CXCIII, September 9, 1985, p. 26.
The New York Times Book Review. XC, June 23, 1985, p. 1.
The New Yorker. LXI, July 22, 1985, p. 90.
Newsweek. CVI, July 8, 1985, p. 67.
Publishers Weekly. CCXXVII, May 3, 1985, p. 64.
Saturday Review. XI, May-June, 1985, p. 12.
The Wall Street Journal. CCVI, July 10, 1985, p. 26.
World Press Review. XXXII, September, 1985, p. 56.

LOW TIDE

Author: Fernanda Eberstadt (1960-   )
Publisher: Alfred A. Knopf (New York). 173 pp. $13.95
Type of work: Novel
Time: The late 1970's and 1980
Locale: New York, London, Oxford, and Mexico, near Veracruz

An adolescent tells the story of her infatuation with two brothers and of the violent outcome of their relationship when she follows one of them to Mexico in search of the estancia he inherited from his mother

> *Principal characters:*
> JEZEBEL WESTERN, a precocious adolescent who lives in a gloomy brownstone in New York City and follows the fortunes of the Chasm brothers
> NICOLAS JANUARIUS "JEM" CHASM, a youth in perpetual mourning for his mother who lives in Oxford on a trust fund
> CASIMIR CHASM, Jem's younger brother and an adventurer of great imagination
> EUSTACIUS, the ancient cook at the Western home who fusses over Jezebel and who is prescient despite being illiterate

Low Tide presents little plot but develops a series of relationships in expressive, poetic language. The title originates in a conceit explained at the beginning of the novel. After giving a brief account of her father's return to England when she was twelve, Jezebel notes that "when the tide goes way out, sometimes odd sea things are stranded in the sand." Thus, she and many of the other characters are, in Jezebel's own words, just "such creatures—landed, salt-dried, and petrified in our monstrousness."

These exotic figures cluster around two families—the Westerns and the Chasms. Jezebel Western's mother, Pomelia, secludes herself in her brownstone crypt, feeding off her cache of memories and delusions of the Great House at Terrebonne: a "tottering Third Empire delirium of glory-be" hunched down in front of a Louisiana mangrove swamp. She married her Englishman husband when he was foraging among the debutante parties deep in bayou country, and their New York City life soon became a series of extravagant soirees. Eventually the appeal of the extended party dies out, and after twelve years Jezebel's father decamps in disgust at a wife who lies in a darkened room all day "in a rat's nest of black cashmere." It is then that Jezebel realizes "how carefully life had been arranged" and understands "that forced gaiety after all couldn't save the day."

With Mr. Western back in England, responsibility for life in the decayed brownstone bastion devolves on Eustacius, a "righteous Baptist" black man, a lucky gambler, a bayou-born seer to whom strange angels grant secret visions. He cooks his own exotic recipes, "voodoo each time," as Jezebel says. He runs a well-ordered but idiosyncratic domestic economy, admonishing Jezebel when she wears a dress that is too "heady." He hints to Jezebel

of "the great divide," the boundary between the sane and the mentally dis-
possessed, and restricts her to the rational side. Jezebel complains that "it
was an edict confining me to the sane and self-ruled." Jezebel laments one
fault in both Eustacius and her father: their fondness for "mad girls," whom
they promptly drive even madder before leaving them for partners who are
still more abandoned. Unfortunately for Jezebel, she picks up this same
trait as she falls under the spell of the driven youth Jem Chasm.

Jem is the older son of Professor Charles Chasm, her father's oldest
friend and a frequent reveler at the Westerns' parties, one whose fond
attentions to the child Jezebel made him her great favorite. Chasm's first
wife, mother of Jem and Casimir, is from an estate in Mexico almost on the
Guatemalan border. Professor Chasm had visited there before taking up a
teaching post at Duke University, and he had met the flamboyant Boca-
negra family with its three daughters—Ifigenia, Ofelia, and Consuelo—
living practically in purdah. Chasm's engaging style—especially his ability to
absorb copious amounts of alcohol—wins the father's favor and Ofelia's
hand in marriage. Ofelia rides horseback like a daredevil, smokes her father's cigars, and slugs down flasks of pulque expropriated from her father's
tenants. For Chasm, the Oxford don, she is just the wife to take to an academic assignment in the New World.

Alas, bridge clubs and committee work in Durham do not suffice for
Ofelia. After three years in North Carolina, the Chasms depart for George-
town, where the two boys grow into young teenagers. When Jem is fourteen, Ofelia's father dies, leaving a fortune in trust to them. By this time,
the Chasms' marriage is a dead thing, and Ofelia takes to a life of restless
travel, tugging Jem along with her while Casimir is left in junior high school.
When Ofelia is afflicted with stomach cancer, the pace of travel becomes
even more feverish. When she dies, the boys get a generous amount of
money which they spend in Spain and Italy while living "free as pirates."
Jem soon wins a scholarship to Oxford, confirming for the fifteen-year-old
Jezebel her conviction of the "prosperity of sinners."

Two years later, Jezebel is in England visiting her divorced father and dining one evening with the Chasms. (The professor is now remarried to Stephanie, a "pulpy" faced Englishwoman with "leftist leanings.") At this time
Jezebel is discovered by Casimir, already clearly won to a life of dissipation
and adventure, and he introduces her to the heedless life that he and Jem
lead. It is now that Jezebel learns that she cannot resist the lure of obsessive, mad mates any more than can Eustacius and her father, for she is
immediately caught up by a "trembling crazy exaltation" in the presence of
Jem: "It seemed to me mad and sinful, this love of Jem that was more like
fear and scorn."

Jem soon involves himself in a variety of pursuits after Jezebel returns to
America. A sudden whim prompts Jem to leave Oxford and remove himself

to Salamanca, where he studies for a while with Jesuits before packing up ("under rather a cloud," Casimir reports). Back at Oxford, he occupies himself temporarily with studying Russian, but all other pursuits soon succumb to the intensity of his outlandish affair with a Mrs. Shaw of London. The determined Mrs. Shaw tracks him to Oxford one time and, wrapped in a sable coat, spends the night on the street in front of his house. They sit up nights drinking vodka, while Jem talks of the Church Fathers. Eventually, Mrs. Shaw takes Jem to a new flat: "a rajah's suite, all orchids and elephant tusks, a carved, entwined fourposter bedstead swathed in flaming brocades and taffy-colored fur blankets."

While Jem is in Salamanca, Jezebel is back home in New York, where her only friend is a dogmatic and bad-tempered Spanish teacher, "one of those ardent Communists who have their shoes made in Italy." The Spaniard's eccentricities infuriate Jezebel's father, and the relationship is aborted by its own built-in impossibilities, leaving Jezebel with only her Puerto Rican boyfriend admirers from the New York City streets.

Two summers after she first falls in love with Jem, Jezebel goes back to England to stay with her father, and she immediately—to her father's dismay—begins spending all of her time at Oxford with Jem and Casimir. Jezebel is now deep in her own detachment from the world; Jem even calls her "autistic" and accuses her of callousness, lecturing her on morals: "Perhaps you're frightened of seeming judgmental, along with everyone else these days. Well, it's a piece of dangerous lunacy, this new prohibition against morality."

Jezebel wonders what gives this "spoiled idler" his moral authority, as he boasts of his silk shirts and his life of leisure. Jezebel observes Jem closely, seeing in him "a figure whose every sunken hollow and jutting bone expressed a self-scrutiny stirred to suffering, a passion such as one saw, sometimes, in seventeenth-century Spanish crucifixions. So much for covering the scars in raspberry silk, so much for the debutante rounds. Let him dance."

While in London with her father, Jezebel meets his old friend Mrs. Palafox, "a preserved white monkey of a lady." After an adventurous life as the wife of a big-game hunter, Mrs. Palafox has settled down in Long Island to last out her widowhood. A true cosmopolitan, Mrs. Palafox gathers around her a circle of admirers and hangers-on. Jezebel is annoyed because Mrs. Palafox pinches her, and Jem scorns her. Nevertheless, Jezebel is fair and realizes that Mrs. Palafox "missed sleeping under the stars with a rifle and a man."

Jem's behavior becomes even more frenetic during Jezebel's stay in London. He professes his love for Jezebel and moves in with her and her father. With Casimir, Jem and Jezebel follow idle courses, shoplifting for the mere pleasure of the kill, and picnicking on Gorgonzola and chocolate. Desmond Western cannot tolerate Jem in his house, especially with his daughter, and a big blowup ensues, culminating in Jezebel's return to New York.

The pointlessness of her life with Eustacius and her mother drives Jezebel to accept Mrs. Palafox's invitation to stay with her on Long Island. ("I felt like a released patient in my street clothes.") The two women get along fine: Mrs. Palafox does not like girls and Jezebel does not like women, so they stay out of each other's way. Jezebel learns to live on black coffee and yogurt, on jellied soups and steamed vegetables. Whenever "trying" guests come for the weekend, Mrs. Palafox sends them off with picnic baskets or has Jezebel take them to the beach club.

With Jem's arrival, the tone of the weekend changes. Jezebel is dismayed to find him on Long Island. ("The chatter of those powdered sepulchers had soured the thought of him.") Jem immediately cuts a vapid secretary who presents herself seductively, tells Jezebel that Mrs. Palafox will sell her to the highest homosexual bidder, and brutally scolds a trivial male admirer of Jezebel for his pawing at her. He has turned up in New York after six weeks in a research center in Southern California, where his studies of terrorism led to a report recommending that terrorists be shot on the spot by an international paramilitary squad—and with no media coverage.

The result of his visit is that he convinces Jezebel to leave with him immediately for Vera Cruz on a freighter from New York. His purpose is to take her away from her "chimpanzee's tea party of a life" and establish her as his woman in the house where his mother had been reared. Jezebel agrees: "I was held in God's palm," she tells her mother in a farewell note.

Their experience in Mexico is surrealistic for Jezebel. First, the boat trip sickens her, and then Jem conducts her on a hallucinatory tour by bus and train that seems to have no fixed destination. They visit a church where Jezebel is repulsed by the spectacle of dolls dressed up at the expense of the villagers' earnings, and they attend a Communion dinner at a small café in San Saturnino. Jem's confusion and aimlessness depress Jezebel, and she hops off the bus finally and walks to San Sepulcro, where she finds him waiting for her. Finally, they come to rest in a small hotel, but the end of their "driven pilgrimage" occurs suddenly. Jem sends Jezebel out in the morning to get a bottle of water, and when she returns, she finds him lying on the bed with his Luger in his hand and a bullet through his brain. Jezebel reacts with anger: All she can do is "curse that parched body" for this "lowest trick yet." Then there is nothing left to do but scavenge his belongings for what items she wants and throw a thousand pesos on the bedside table to cover the trouble they have caused.

The posturings of the precocious youths in *Low Tide* dramatize their spiritual and moral confusions. One of the guests at Mrs. Palafox's says of Jem and Jezebel, "My God, coming from those two families, the kids must be crazy as coots. I wouldn't be surprised if it doesn't end in murder." Certainly if they, intelligent and blessed with advantages, are doomed by the decadence of their parents' lives, then Fate must exert a stranglehold on human life that is inescapable.

If the ending of *Low Tide* is abrupt and perhaps not completely convincing, and if the whole story of doomed youth is a reprise of sentimental Romantic fictions, the novel still impresses by Fernanda Eberstadt's virtuoso control of language and her ability to create bright characters with economy.

Frank Day

Sources for Further Study

Booklist. LXXXI, April 1, 1985, p. 1098.
Kirkus Reviews. LIII, February 1, 1985, p. 98.
Library Journal. CX, March 15, 1985, p. 72.
Los Angeles Times Book Review. June 2, 1985, p. 9.
The New York Times Book Review. XC, May 26, 1985, p. 13.
Publishers Weekly. CCXXVII, February 1, 1985, p. 350.
Times Literary Supplement. June 28, 1985, p. 733.
Vogue. CLXXV, April, 1985, p. 242.
Washington Post Book World. XV, May 12, 1985, p. 9.

LUISA DOMIC

Author: George Dennison (1925-   )
Publisher: Harper & Row, Publishers (New York). 192 pp. $14.95
Type of work: Novel
Time: October, 1973
Locale: Rural Maine

A victim of the Chilean revolution comes to visit a happy family in rural Maine, forcing the family to face the evils of the world outside their Eden

> *Principal characters:*
> THE NARRATOR
> PATRICIA, his wife
> IDA, their twelve-year-old daughter
> LIZA, their nine-year-old daughter
> JACOB, their six-year-old son
> HAROLD ASHBY, their friend, a musician
> RICHARD RASMUSSEN, Harold's lover
> MARSHALL BERRINGER, a friend of the narrator and a Marxist poet
> LUISA DOMIC, the widow of Chilean Alejandro Domic

George Dennison is best known as the author of *The Lives of Children* (1969), a narrative account of twenty-three students at Manhattan's First Street School, where he was a teacher. He is also an accomplished writer of fiction; his previous works include *Oilers and Sweepers* (1979), a collection of stories, and *Shawno* (1984), a short novel.

"It was this call . . . that set in motion the events of that weekend," says the unnamed narrator of *Luisa Domic*. The telephone call to which he refers is from Harold Ashby, a longtime friend of the narrator, who has appeared unexpectedly to spend the weekend with the narrator, his wife, Patricia, and their three children, Ida, Liza, and Jacob. The family is already expecting another friend, Marshall Berringer, a Marxist poet, and Luisa Domic, a refugee from the Chilean military coup that has toppled Salvador Allende.

The world into which these guests come has been established in the first pages of the book as a Maine paradise, complete with turning leaves, ripening apples, and ponies free to race their own course. The narrator has found happiness with Patricia, his second wife, marred only slightly by her ventures into the outside world as a nuclear protestor and by what he sometimes thinks is her too-cavalier attitude toward his writing. Such disagreements, though, are as insignificant as the squabbles of the children, in the context of a life in harmony with nature and most of the time in harmony with each other. That life is symbolized by the spider mentioned on the second page of the book, which clings to its filament as it moves, for every member of the Maine family can move as he wills, knowing that he is still attached to nature and to those he loves.

The first person to bring an alien world into this atmosphere is Harold

Ashby. The narrator had known Harold many years before, when Harold was a famous composer. More recently, Harold has abandoned that career and now works with disturbed children, using his music to make contact with them. In the narrator's accounts of the work of Harold and his lover, Richard Rasmussen, he dramatizes the plight of children who feel intense pain but cannot express it except in cries or screams. Somehow the music imitates those cries and thus joins each child in his tortured isolation. The narrator comments, "What I had just witnessed in the basement of the church, that calling out of souls from perdition, or of the unformed from their chaos of mere sensation, was not like anything I had ever seen before." Out of pain, Harold and Richard bring joy. Even though Richard's world has been darkened by the death of his mother, it was a natural death, he still has Harold, and it is clear that the grief can be followed by a cessation of grief and by a renewal of joy. It is significant that this section of the book is concluded by Harold's story, told for the children, about one of Harry Houdini's successful escapes. The narrator's earlier unhappiness, the pain of disturbed children, Richard's grief, Houdini's entrapment—all can be or have been cured by human efforts.

When the activist Marshall Berringer appears with the Chilean refugee Luisa Domic, it is with the hope that the idyllic natural environment, the uninhibited children, dogs, and ponies, and the tactful concern of other people will begin to make her pain bearable. Berringer does not know what has happened to Luisa's husband and children; he knows that she is silent and sedated. At first, there is hope. Luisa seems to feel a bond with Patricia, probably because she is also a mother, and she enjoys the children. When Ida falls down the stairs, however, frightening the family and skinning her arm, Luisa begins to scream uncontrollably. Only Harold's music, joining her, can bridge the abyss between her consuming pain and the world of ordinary life. She is calmed, and after a long sleep, she returns to the group, discovers that the pianist is a musician whom she has long admired, and talks happily about her teen-age musical children. When she leaves, she speaks of her happiness in knowing Harold and of her joy in her new friendship with Patricia. Again, it seems that human efforts have succeeded in effecting a cure, that her isolation is ended, that the filament has been spun that will connect her to life. Just before supper, however, Marshall telephones to say that Luisa Domic has killed herself. In the last pages of the book, the narrator relates the torture of her children, ended by brutal death, which Luisa had been forced to witness and which had left a hurt too deep for cure.

Thus the novel falls structurally and thematically into three sections. In the first, a nearly perfect world is established. In the second, pain is introduced, but the hurts can be healed. In the third, Dennison suggests that some human memories are unbearable, no matter what human concern attempts. Significantly, the nearly perfect world is a world dominated by nature, and the world which inflicts unbearable pain is the world of men, operating through their governments.

In that Maine paradise, though the lion does not lie down with the lamb, harmony is always a goal. Thus the narrator, annoyed with his wife because of her attitude toward his writing, realizes that the quarrel which has been developing will not happen, simply because nature on that day has made "a momentarily undemanding world, and because one did not have to struggle with it, one was free to look at is gratefully." Although Harold and Marshall have never been friends in the city, the aesthetically oriented homosexual and the activist heterosexual come to appreciate each other during the weekend. When Marshall is leaving, he comments that the two live in different worlds and that he would like to see Harold sometimes. Harold agrees, and yet the narrator doubts that they will ever continue the friendship when they are in the fragmented outside world. At one point during the weekend, the narrator quarrels with the aggressive, argumentative Marshall; yet when he remembers Marshall's courage in good causes, he can no longer be annoyed. Thus, though there are human jarrings in Eden, they are resolved by the essentially good people there, who are made better by their Wordsworthian contact with nature. Once Dennison has established this gentle world, the descriptions of terror and torture, of cruelty as a policy of state, are more shocking.

Certainly there is death in Eden, but it is merely natural. The old man who knew which orchard every apple came from has passed away, and the ninety-nine-year-old milkman is in his last golden days. From time to time the farmers must hire the local bear hunter to save their cows. Yet the death of Luisa Domic has been first a death of the heart. Like the disturbed children with whom Harold works, Luisa has been imprisoned in a world so horrifying that consciousness itself is an unbearable torment. Unlike those children, she cannot continue to live, even with the temporary help from contact with nature, the kindness of friends, and the solace of Harold's music.

This careful patterning of incident and symbol in *Luisa Domic* is perhaps Dennison's greatest achievement. He should also be praised for the lyric evocation of nature at its most beautiful—New England in the fall. His details—the quiet air and water, the persistent sunlight, the sweet smell of apples, the feel of a pony's head, the dance of the falling locust leaves—all are presented precisely and economically.

Dennison, drawing on his long experience as a teacher, also has a talent for observing the details of the children's lives, in what some reviewers have described as a sentimental manner. Thematically, his approach seems justified. If his intent is to dramatize the horror of events in a country ruled by a military junta, he can achieve this purpose first, as has been noted, by contrasting life in Chile with life in an idyllic natural setting, and second, by contrasting the happy lives of the narrator's sheltered children with the terrible deaths of Luisa's children. What Luisa cannot forget is being forced to watch the torture and death of her children; it is interesting that the same instinct to protect the innocence of children operates after the narrator and his wife have heard about Luisa's death. Hearing the children, Patricia dries her tears, and she and the narrator agree that "it would be pointless to tell them."

Unfortunately, Dennison does not let his story speak for itself. He finds it necessary to speak through the narrator, in answer to supposedly artless questions from fourteen-year-old Ida, about capitalism, nuclear waste, and the environment. Elsewhere, he lets Harold tell the Houdini story in that kind of patronizing tone which some adults adopt toward children, and which children generally resent, though the narrator's children are charmed. In both cases, it is as if the audience is not the children, but the readers, who are supposed to subscribe to Dennison's opinions as congregations are supposed to agree with comments addressed to God.

Elsewhere, too, Dennison's dialogue is sometimes artificial, too little like speech, too much like sermonizing. Probably it is his passionate convictions that are the cause of another flaw: the unnecessarily graphic detail of the bloodbath in Chile. One remembers Anton Chekhov's philosophy: A few images are enough; the reader can supply the rest.

Despite the flaws which result from more passion than art, *Luisa Domic* is an effective and moving novel. Its characters are well drawn and clearly motivated. Its structure is masterful, its symbolism subtly handled. There are scenes in the book that are unforgettable—the ponies joyfully racing; the whole family sleeping together on an improvised "raft," secure in a harsh world; Luisa Domic collapsed and screaming; the old milkman recalling the world as it once was. In the closing sentences of the book, the narrator suggests that it is a memorial, dedicated to victims such as the Domics. Although Dennison emphasizes the fact that his novel is fiction, the Domic family fictitious creations, *Luisa Domic* may be regarded as a memorial to all those children in the world, mentally troubled or physically tortured, who are bereft of innocence.

Rosemary M. Canfield-Reisman

Sources for Further Study

Booklist. LXXXII, October 1, 1985, p. 191.
Kirkus Reviews. LIII, August 1, 1985, p. 726.
Library Journal. CX, November 1, 1985, p. 109.

The New Republic. CXCIV, January 27, 1986, p. 37.
The New York Review of Books. XXXII, December 19, 1985, p. 54.
The New York Times Book Review. XC, September 22, 1985, p. 22.
Publishers Weekly. CCXXVIII, August 30, 1985, p. 413.
Washington Post Book World. XV, November 10, 1985, p. 8.

THE MAKING OF MARK TWAIN
A Biography

Author: John Lauber (1925-   )
Publisher: Houghton Mifflin Company (Boston). Illustrated. 298 pp. $17.95
Type of work: Biography
Time: 1835-1870
Locale: The United States, Europe, and the Middle East

An account of the experiences and influences that transformed Samuel L. Clemens into Mark Twain

> *Principal personages:*
> SAMUEL LANGHORNE CLEMENS, an American author and lecturer
> ORION CLEMENS, his older brother
> JANE LAMPTON CLEMENS, his mother
> JOHN MARSHALL CLEMENS, his father
> OLIVIA "LIVY" LANGDON CLEMENS, his wife
> HORACE BIXBY, the riverboat pilot under whom he trained

Perhaps no other American writer represents so much a mixture of fact and legend as Mark Twain. His popularity, his flamboyant style, and his own storytelling combined to form the myth that most people accept as the genuine person involved in actual events. As a professional humorist, particularly in the lecture hall, Twain himself delighted in making poor stories good and good stories better, thus creating and perpetuating the myths he so enjoyed. John Lauber suggests that, having repeated tales over decades, even Twain forgot the actual incidents. Other than the author himself, the greatest single source of the myth-fact blend which formed the legend of Mark Twain is probably Albert Bigelow Paine, Twain's companion-secretary during the final traumatic and cynical years, when one of Twain's primary escapes was nostalgia. He dictated his autobiography to Paine, an almost worshipful admirer who would not have believed anything negative and who would have cheerfully altered whatever he thought the public might construe to be negative. Those who are familiar with Twain's canon may recall that it was Paine along with Frederick Duneka, an editor from *Harper's Magazine*, who emendated *The Mysterious Stranger* (1916), creating a new character out of whole cloth and generally cleaning up, something on the order of what Alfred, Lord Tennyson did with Sir Thomas Malory's work to make it more palatable to British Victorian sensibilities. Lauber's two main thrusts in *The Making of Mark Twain* are to delineate the very human individual who was Sam Clemens and to separate him from the myths that abound regarding him.

The Making of Mark Twain is a lively, well-researched, clearly documented biography of Samuel Clemens from his birth in Florida, Missouri, to his marriage to Olivia Langdon at age thirty-four. Lauber arranges his book into fifteen chapters ranging from five to thirty-five pages, with a brief epilogue. The chapter titles designate the time period, such as "Little Sam,"

"Pilot," "Correspondent," and "Pilgrim." The length of the chapters is determined not so much by the actual time elapsed but rather by the significance of the events occurring. Thus, Twain's very brief and even less important military career, "Rebel," comprises only five pages; while "Lover," his courtship of and marriage to Olivia Langdon—a union much debated and central to Van Wyck Brooks's thesis in *The Ordeal of Mark Twain* (1920)— receives thirty-five pages.

In most Americans' minds, Mark Twain was a sophisticated and wealthy world traveler who smoked cigars, entertained audiences, and gazed with happy amusement at his fellow beings. The Samuel Clemens who became Mark Twain did smoke cigars, but he learned to delight audiences in an attempt to find the security and acceptance denied him in childhood. His father, John Marshall Clemens, was a hapless man with little business sense and even less luck, whose schemes and ineptitude took the family steadily downward. As a result, Sam Clemens knew both poverty and neglect as a child. There were several moves to less and less desirable homes, culminating in 1846, "when even the furniture was lost and the Clemenses were reduced to sharing quarters with another family for whom Mrs. Clemens cooked." Lauber maintains that these circumstances left Sam with "a lifelong horror of debt [and a desire for] absolute security," associations that later led him into ruinous speculation.

The Clemens family had moved from Jamestown, Tennessee, to Florida, Missouri, during Jane Clemens' pregnancy. Samuel was born two months premature on November 30, 1835. Before his fourth birthday, the family moved again—to Hannibal, Missouri, where he encountered the Mississippi River, a meeting of natural phenomenon and vivid imagination that would result, some forty-five years later, in the publication of *The Adventures of Huckleberry Finn* (1884).

Having shown the family settled in Hannibal, Lauber carefully deals with "Tom Sawyer Days," those mythically idyllic but often painful times varying between joy and fear wherein the boy first began to comprehend the relationships among individuals and, particularly, between races and classes. Here Lauber establishes those major threads which would weave into the fabric of Mark Twain's later life and works—boyhood escapades, constraints of school, the death of John Clemens, avid reading, religious fundamentalism, and the institution of slavery.

Lauber's remaining chapters proceed in much the same fashion, as he continues to separate fact from legend and to anticipate Twain's future, pointing out how particular elements in Sam Clemens' formative years affected the later choices and writings. Lauber establishes Twain's knowledge of printing and his seemingly natural style by showing how Sam Clemens learned to set type and to acquire a sense of the distinction between good and poor prose. Sam's not-always pleasant adventures in becoming and being a riverboat pilot are intermingled with comments about *Life on the Mississippi* (1883) and learning judgment of both men and situations. The obvious reason Sam left this occupation was the intervention of the Civil War and subsequent halting of river traffic; Lauber surmises, though, that Sam had realized that he could be only a competent pilot—and his ego was such that that was insufficient.

The next significant period involves Sam Clemens' move west, first as secretary to his brother Orion, who had supported Abraham Lincoln in the 1860 election and been rewarded with the secretaryship of the Territory of Nevada. Brash, brawling Virginia City welcomed Sam's kindred spirit, and the novice writer absorbed yet another culture—the one that would first provide the material to make his name famous across the nation with "The Celebrated Jumping Frog of Calaveras County." Sam left Orion's employ and became first a miner, then a reporter. Lauber shows that Clemens saw himself as a miner only as a means of growing rich; journalism, however, beckoned as a genuine career, and Clemens devoted time and effort to his trade. Lauber establishes that journalistic standards in the 1800's in wide-open mining towns were somewhat flexible, with reporters who embellished and even invented news as well as engaging in running printed verbal battles with one another. This milieu reinforced Clemens' assumption that a good story was superior to a merely factual one.

Sam Clemens moved to San Francisco, a city sophisticated in comparison with the mining towns but raw in comparison with the Eastern Seaboard, where he would have to adjust to yet another culture. San Francisco eliminated some rough edges, extended Clemens' reputation, and provided the opportunity for his first real adventure in traveling—a trip to the Sandwich Islands, as Hawaii was then known. Clemens' only obligation to his newspaper was to write letters about what he did and saw. Lauber shows that Clemens succeeded in the assignment and also benefited from an unusual stroke of luck. When the survivors of the shipwrecked *Hornet* arrived in Honolulu, Clemens interviewed them, wrote desperately through the night, and sent his report off the next morning in a packet boat for the mainland. His paper got an important news scoop, and Sam Clemens got his name spread across the nation.

Never content to stay anywhere long, he returned to San Francisco and left almost immediately to sail to Central America and on to New York. It was on this trip, as Lauber demonstrates, that Clemens met Captain Ned Wakeman, whose influence was brief but pervasive. Wakeman was, Lauber believes, the prototype of Twain's main character in *Captain Stormfield's Visit to Heaven* (1907).

The New York days were long and tiring as Clemens did hack-work reporting. Long hours and little pay made him yearn for his favorite solution to any unpleasantness or dilemma—travel. His reputation having grown somewhat, though more by virtue of the lecture platform than his writing, he secured a place on the *Quaker City*, a cruise ship bound for the Holy Land. Financed once again by a newspaper, he began offhandedly and lightheartedly the trip which perhaps included the single most significant incident of his life. One of his companions, seventeen-year-old Charlie Langdon, casually showed Clemens a miniature of his sister. From that day, Sam was determined to meet her, though not as intensely as his later recounting would indicate. The cruise took almost five months and involved land trips in eight nations. Clemens wrote frequent letters about the trip, his fellow passengers, the events he observed, and the tourist sites. Instead of reporting from the standard American uncritical stance, Clemens used fresh eyes, describing, for example, *The Last Supper* as poorly done, with faded colors and dim outline. His American audience responded appreciatively and thus reinforced the humorously satirical vein that came naturally. His skepticism of guides and their claims reached its height in the Holy Land.

Having detailed the *Quaker City* trip thoroughly, Lauber narrates Clemens' return to New York and then his almost-immediate trip west to earn money by lecturing on his European and Mideastern experiences. He contracted with Elisha Bliss for a book—which turned out to be called *The Innocents Abroad* (1869)—also based on the trip. These activities provided Clemens with the confidence and funds to approach the conservative, proper, and wealthy Jervis Langdon household with its female treasure, Olivia. The courtship was not always smooth, but it was successful. Sam Clemens and Olivia Langdon were married February 2, 1870. The "wedding day began auspiciously with the postman bringing him a royalty check of $4,000, representing three-months' sales of *The Innocents Abroad* [which] served to remind everyone, including himself, that at thirty-four he was as successful in his own trade as his father-in-law to be, Jervis Langdon, had been in the coal business." Lauber's text forms Sam Clemens' childhood, adolescence, and young adulthood into a coherent image of Mark Twain.

Lauber's style reflects the same blending as the content. He frequently uses quotations from contemporary Clemens materials interspersed with observations of the future Twain. There are also numerous quotations from persons in Twain's immediate environment as well as those, again, from the future. For example, in the very early chapter "Tom Sawyer Days," in which Lauber discusses young Sam's introduction to racial differences, Lauber quotes Twain's friend William Dean Howells, not to be met for four decades, to clarify a point. In some hands, these frequent quotations could be interruptive and disconcerting; Lauber, however, skillfully blends and merges them with his own prose so that their presence is unobtrusive. The smoothness of the insertions belies the benefit of the added dimensions. Lauber's own style is eminently readable. He takes a direct approach to his subject and appears to deal almost casually with it—the same seeming ease Twain himself displayed on the lecture platform where he appeared to be speaking spontaneously, when in fact the entire presentation had been meticulously planned and completely memorized.

In addition to his main text, Lauber provides a brief epilogue which points to the future, standard acknowledgments, and three other very helpful items. The first, "For Further Reading," is far more than its title suggests. Instead of a cursory list of books and periodicals, Lauber provides the reader with more than seven pages of discussion of both primary and secondary materials. It is here that Lauber shows the need for his own volume when he remarks "Justin Kaplan's *Mr. Clemens and Mark Twain* . . . is thoroughly researched and modern in its approach. But it omits the first thirty years of its subject's life." *The Making of Mark Twain* fills that gap. Next is "Author's Notes," arranged by chapters and headed by those sources particularly useful for that period. There are relatively few notes per chapter, but these are ordinarily lengthy and explanatory—not simply sources and page numbers. Finally, Lauber includes a detailed and convenient index.

John Lauber's *The Making of Mark Twain* is an enjoyable book which makes a substantial contribution to the already abundant scholarship devoted to one of America's finest writers. Correcting popular misconceptions as he brings the young Samual Clemens to life, Lauber makes his subject not only more human but also—amazingly—as likable as in the legends.

Stanley Archer

Sources for Further Study

Booklist. LXXXII, November 15, 1985, p. 461.
Choice. XXIII, February, 1986, p. 870.
Christian Science Monitor. LXXVIII, November 29, 1985, p. 38.
Kirkus Reviews. LIII, September 15, 1985, p. 1016.
The New York Times Book Review. XC, November 24, 1985, p. 30.
Publishers Weekly. CCXXVIII, September 27, 1985, p. 90.

THE MAMMOTH HUNTERS

Author: Jean M. Auel (1936-   )
Publisher: Crown Publishers (New York). 645 pp. $19.95
Type of work: Novel
Time: The late Pleistocene Epoch (35,000-25,000 B.C.)
Locale: Eurasia

A young Cro-Magnon woman, reared by a clan of Neanderthals, finds acceptance and self-worth in an advanced society of mammoth hunters

> *Principal characters:*
> AYLA, a beautiful young woman of unknown origin, whose search for identity leads her to join a band of Mamutoi (mammoth hunters)
> JONDALAR, Ayla's lover, of the Zelandonii people, who encourages Ayla to leave her Neanderthal past and learn the ways of the Mamutoi
> RANEC, master carver of the Lion Camp of the Mamutoi, who falls in love with Ayla
> MAMUT, the old spiritual leader and holy man of the Lion Camp of the Mamutoi, who adopts Ayla to his hearth

The Mammoth Hunters is the third novel in Jean Auel's Earth's Children series, the unfolding story of a young woman's life and search for family, identity, and community during a unique period in the evolutionary development of Man. While continuing the series' emphasis on romance and adventure, *The Mammoth Hunters* explores various themes of universal nature: Man's conscious acknowledgment of his evolutionary possibilities; his relationship with his environment; the conflict in reconciling the demands of the individual with the demands of society; and the struggle for personal growth.

It is the author's intention that each novel in the series stand as a complete and individual story. Nevertheless, the tragedies and successes of Ayla, the heroine of *The Mammoth Hunters*, can be best appreciated in the light of the two preceding volumes, which also feature Ayla in a central role.

In *The Clan of the Cave Bear* (1980), the five-year-old Ayla is taken and reared by a clan of Neanderthals after a devastating earthquake kills her people and destroys her home. Ayla struggles for acceptance despite the striking physical and mental differences between the Clan and herself—differences which prevent her from conforming with Clan laws and customs. She secretly develops the ability to hunt with a slingshot, obtains the knowledge of a medicine woman, and gives birth to a son of mixed blood. Rejected by the Clan at fourteen, Ayla is separated from her son and forced to leave in search of her own people, the Others.

In *The Valley of Horses* (1982), Ayla finds refuge from the oncoming winter in a valley, where, for the next four years, she establishes her home. To survive, she perfects her hunting skills and draws upon her innate creativity, repressed while living with the Clan, to make important discoveries (fire from flint stone, riding horseback, medicinal techniques). To conquer her loneliness, Ayla domesticates a wild horse and befriends a lion cub. To communicate, she develops a language with these animals and becomes, herself, a part of the natural environment, efficiently making use of the valley's natural resources. When she rescues Jondalar (an Other, like herself) from a lion's attack. Ayla nurses him back to health, learns his language, and falls in love. After years of self-sufficiency, Ayla makes the transition from solitude to companionship. As the novel closes, she and Jondalar journey from the valley to find their own people.

The events of the series' first and second novels shape Ayla's character in profound ways. As a female member of the Clan, Ayla is forbidden to learn about and participate in hunting forays. She must seek permission to speak about important matters from male Clan members, and she is obligated to acquiesce to any male's desire for sexual activity. In addition, Ayla is regarded as a misfit because of physiological and mental distinctions that lead her to feel ugly and misunderstood by the Clan. Despite these obstacles, Ayla proves herself to be a fast learner and innovator, and from her achievements she derives a measure of inner strength.

During the years of solitude that follow these experiences, Ayla articulates and strengthens her innate talents and comes into her own as an individual. Still, the adversities she endured in her early years with the Clan combined with those years without human contact leave Ayla lacking comprehension of a fundamental concept: how a society of her own people might work and what her role in that society might be.

Here develops a major theme in the series that finds embellishment in *The Mammoth Hunters*: the significance of society to the individual and the ability to maintain individuality while seeking conformity and fulfilling the community's collective needs.

When Ayla meets Jondalar in *The Valley of Horses*, the experience of finding and living with a member of her own kind is almost a shocking one. Ayla must learn basic skills necessary for life in the progressive society of the Others: employing verbal language (the Clan used sign language to communicate); sharing thoughts freely; equal dialogue in communal matters; participation in community hunts; and personal sexual fulfillment. These are monumental tasks for Ayla that require the reversal of years of Clan conditioning.

As *The Mammoth Hunters* begins, then, the promise of a new life brings conflict to Ayla. Leaving an existence of independence, she doubts her ability to be accepted by the Mamutoi, the mammoth hunters, or to achieve personal fulfillment, yet she instinctively knows that neither she nor Jondalar can exist outside a structured society.

Ayla's unique talents are unfolded to the Mamutoi—her healing abilities;

her command of the animals; her hunting prowess; the ease with which she is able to learn their language; her beauty and grace—revealing a woman of strength, mystery, and passion. The enigma of Ayla's past enhances her mystique, yet it also discourages understanding and acceptance.

With the presentation of this paradox, the author examines the tensions between Clan (Neanderthal) and Other (Cro-Magnon) cultures in Ice Age Europe through the story of Ayla, who experiences both. Through anthropological study, the author reveals the timeless struggle of coexistence among peoples of different cultures.

Paleontologists have determined that, in fact, the Homo neandertalis and Cro-Magnon species were contemporaneous. In the Earth's Children series, Auel suggests that, while the two Homo species coexisted, there arose a confrontation between the soon-to-be-extinct Neanderthals and the more adaptable Cro-Magnons—a confrontation that is at the heart of *The Mammoth Hunters*.

When Ayla recounts her experiences to the Mamutoi band that welcomes her—the Lion Camp—she is met with varying reactions of shock and amazement. The Mamutoi, and in fact all Others, consider the Clan animals, not humans. (Called "flatheads," because of the Neanderthal flattened forehead, Clan people are short and muscular, with heavy brow ridges and a chinless jaw that juts forward.) Ayla does not suspect so severe a response, since living within the Lion Camp is Rydag, a small boy, half Clan, half Other, who reminds Ayla of her own son. Nevertheless, the Others consider such a child an "abomination," one who is half animal, half human.

Ayla, who is sensitive to the very human qualities of the Clan, threatens to dispel these notions, first by teaching Rydag how to communicate with hand signals. She succeeds in appealing to his "racial memory," that ability of the Clan to recall information concerning their survival with instinct rather than learning. When Ayla shows that the flatheads communicate with a rich language of their own and suggests that by rescuing and rearing her they have demonstrated their capacity for human feelings, she places the Lion Camp in a state of turmoil, threatening, as it were, "the whole structure of comfortable beliefs."

Ayla, then, represents a new way of thinking to the Mamutoi. When Rydag, who suffers from a congenital disease, dies at the Summer Meeting of the Mamutoi, Ayla and the Lion Camp conduct a Clan funeral for him, reflecting the growing awareness of the real nature of the Clan:

> He had been called an abomination, an animal, but animals were not buried; their meat was stored. Only people were buried, and they did not like to leave the dead unburied for long. Though the Mamutoi weren't quite willing to grant Rydag human status, they knew he wasn't really an animal, either. . . . He was an abomination precisely because they saw his humanity, but degraded it and would not recognize it.

When Ayla performs an ancient Clan ritual for the Lion Camp, she demonstrates a culture rich in ceremony and detail. "It was not simply a different style of tunic, or choice of predominant color tones, or spear-type preference, or even a different language. It was a different way of thinking, but they did recognize that it was a human way of thinking."

Ayla ultimately validates her contention that there is an evolutionary bond between Clan and Others, but she fails, for a time, to transcend the emotional barriers that inhibit acceptance in Jondalar. Jondalar's experiences with the Mamutoi provide the vehicle through which he unwittingly eliminates these barriers in order to allow his relationship with Ayla to proceed as the novel closes.

Ayla and Jondalar are passionate lovers, who share the same spirit guide, or "totem," and have similar perceptions and talents. Jondalar, however, must overcome his embarrassment at having chosen one who has lived with flatheads and who has conceived an "abomination." He fears bringing Ayla to his people, the Zelandonii, only to be rejected and cast out.

The situation is complicated by the attentions of Ranec, a dark-skinned carver of ivory, an artist, who loves and pursues Ayla toward matrimony. Ranec offers Ayla unconditional love and acceptance—something Jondalar must learn to do in view of Ayla's past. Ranec has lived with Rydag and, because of his own skin pigmentation, empathizes with being different and unusual. Ayla's past is of little consequence to Ranec; his artist's appreciation of Ayla's skills, talents, and beauty only heightens his love and desire for her.

It is difficult for Ayla to disregard the temptation of Ranec's complete acceptance. She is emotionally, physically, and spiritually attached to Jondalar, yet his hesitation allows the complications of a love triangle to dominate their relationship. It is only when Jondalar realizes his priorities—those of love over conformity—that he and Ayla are able to renew their love for each other. Having almost married Ranec and lost Jondalar, Ayla herself learns to fight for the attentions of the man she truly loves.

Amid a complicated romance, Ayla grows both as an individual and as a member of a community. With her awesome ability to ride horses, Ayla adds a new dimension to the Mamutoi's hunts. Her ability to command animals brings to her the added status accorded to one who has great spiritual and mystical connections. Her prowess with the sling earns for her respect and admiration, as do her treatments for various ailments. When the Lion Camp proposes to adopt Ayla into their society as a valuable and appreciated companion, Ayla is able to counter one member's opposition with her demonstration of the more advanced and valuable method of using flint to make fire, which she developed in the valley. At her Adoption Ceremony, a major obstacle to Ayla's self-worth is removed as Ayla of No People becomes Ayla of the Mamutoi.

Having achieved a sense of belonging, Ayla is now free to expand her individuality. While learning how to make clothing, she conceives the idea for a sewing needle, which the Camp creates communally. Returning from a hunt, she brings home an orphaned wolf pup, who is raised at the Camp as a pet—a pet whose descendants are modern-day canines.

Concurrently, Ayla becomes a worthy Mamutoi, whose value is expressed in economic terms as the Bride Price. In Mamutoi society, brides are a standard of currency and can bring husbands riches in the form of great status, by their talents, hunting prowess, skills, or charm. Ayla, who possesses all these traits, increases the status and worth of the Lion Camp, allowing her to command a costly Bride Price.

In addition, Ayla's contributions to the Mamutoi are noteworthy in that they add new dimensions to the ways in which environment can serve society. Ayla's horses can scout during mammoth hunts and alleviate the burden of transporting home large amounts of mammoth meat. The creation of the sewing needle facilitates a tedious labor, and the knowledge of medicinal herbs and plants can often mean the difference between life and death. In a more profound way, Ayla partakes in a fundamental change in man's relationship to his environment, as the Mamutoi move from activities primarily directed toward survival to those more of leisure and recreation. Only a society well organized and successful in providing the necessities of life can afford to enjoy life and increase its quality.

As the prehistoric societies of Earth's Children attempt to control their environment, they simultaneously acknowledge the supremacy of a cosmic force that directs their activities. While the Clan and Others pay homage to different gods, Ayla perceives the underlying metaphysics that creates such a human need. A woman of great inspiration, Ayla is regarded by the Mamutoi as a Healer; a Caller and Searcher of animals; and, ultimately, as a chosen one of Mut, the Great Earth Mother.

Ayla is encouraged along this route by Mamut, the Mamutoi's spiritual figurehead, who adopts Ayla to the Mammoth Hearth, the spiritual essence of the Mamutoi, with hopes that he may train her to serve the deity. Mamut sees in Ayla the innate abilities of a spiritual leader, a potential he hopes Ayla will one day realize. Mamut's role as a spiritual father to the Mamutoi, and specifically to Ayla, is one of guidance, interpretation, protection, and revelation. Apart from his calling, Mamut carries with him his own mystique: living longer than many ever dream to—long enough to witness five generations of Mamutoi—Mamut suspects that the Mother has destined him to realize fully his own potential within the context of his relationship with Ayla.

Mamut offers Ayla additional insight when he reveals that he lived with and was nursed by the Clan a few generations earlier during a time of illness. His compassion for Ayla and his respect for her mystical talent results, in large part, from her ability to master the complex spirit worlds of both cultures.

At the close of *The Mammoth Hunters*, Ayla has changed the nature of the Mamutoi way of life and matures in matters concerning her own happiness: her past, her self-esteem, and love. Having lived in a hostile society in *The Clan of the Cave Bear*; both in solitude and with Jondalar in *The Valley of Horses*; and estranged from Jondalar in the Lion Camp of the Mamutoi in *The Mammoth Hunters*, Ayla embarks on a journey to the Zelandonii people where, she hopes, she will find with Jondalar both a love that fulfills her and a community that accepts her. While it is easy to regard Ayla as a caricature of a feminist superhero, the author's message is clear: It is possible for the potential in each person to be realized if there exists the willingness to struggle with the internal and external obstacles that hinder success.

Shelly Usen

Sources for Further Study

Booklist. LXXXII, November 1, 1985, p. 353.
Cosmopolitan. CXCIX, December, 1985, p. 34.
Kirkus Reviews. LIII, November 1, 1985, p. 1144.
The New York Times Book Review. XC, November 24, 1985, p. 24.
Newsweek. CVI, November 18, 1985, p. 100.
Publishers Weekly. CCVIII, November 1, 1985, p. 54.
Time. CXXVI, December 9, 1985, p. 107.
Vogue. CLXXV, December, 1985, p. 195.
The Wall Street Journal. CCVI, November 26, 1985, p. 28.

MARXISM
Philosophy and Economics

Author: Thomas Sowell (1930-   )
Publisher: William Morrow and Company (New York). 281 pp. $15.95
Type of work: History of economic thought
Time: 1840 to the 1980's
Locale: France, Great Britain, and Germany

A summary and explication of Marxian theory, intended for the general reader rather than the specialist

> *Principal personages:*
> KARL MARX, a German social theorist and revolutionary agitator
> FRIEDRICH ENGELS, a German social theorist and revolutionary agitator
> GEORG WILHELM FRIEDRICH HEGEL, a German philosopher
> DAVID RICARDO, an English economist
> ADAM SMITH, a Scottish political economist and philosopher
> ROBERT OWEN, a British social reformer
> PAUL HENRI DIETRICH, BARON D'HOLBACH, a French materialist philosopher
> LUDWIG FEUERBACH, a German materialist philosopher
> FRANÇOIS-MARIE-CHARLES FOURIER, a French social reformer
> JEAN-CHARLES-LÉONARD DE SISMONDI, a Swiss economist and precursor of Marx
> JEAN BAPTISTE SAY, a French economist
> THOMAS ROBERT MALTHUS, an English economist and demographer
> PIERRE JOSEPH PROUDHON, a French advocate of social reform

Thomas Sowell, an American economist and a leading black neoconservative, is best known for his work on American race and ethnic relations. Yet his first academic contributions, more than a quarter of a century ago, dealt with the ideas of the German socialist philosopher Karl Marx. In *Marxism: Philosophy and Economics*, Sowell offers, for the general reader, a guide to one of the most significant intellectual products of the nineteenth century.

Marxism is the official social and economic dogma of the Union of Soviet Socialist Republics, whose political elite uses that ideology to justify its possession of absolute power. Yet the average American does not know what Marxism means or how this doctrine originated. Sowell's work, although not particularly original or path-breaking, does perform a valuable service: It gives Americans a thoughtful, although occasionally a bit overly polemical, exposition of Marxist theory, based on a close reading of the writings and correspondence of Karl Marx and his collaborator, Friedrich Engels.

Sowell's book is especially useful to such beginning students of intellectual history as college undergraduates. In each one of chapters 2 through 8, the author examines in depth a different aspect of Marx's thought; the inclusion of a summary at the end of each of these chapters makes it easier to remember the author's main points. Sowell devotes three chapters apiece to the economic theory of Marxism and to the philosophical underpinnings of that economic theory; chapter 8 deals with Marx's theory of politics. The last two chapters are an account of Marx's life and a sharply critical assessment of Marx's legacy.

Marx's works, Sowell makes clear, have often confused later generations of readers because the German philosopher's writing is so epigrammatic, relying on catchy phrases at the expense of clarity. As the author repeatedly reminds his readers, Marx, both during his early life in Germany and throughout his long years of exile in France, Belgium, and Britain, was a polemicist as well as a scholar. He was engaged not merely in economic research but also in a continual debate with both the defenders of the existing social order and his rivals within the European radical movement. In most of Marx's writings, Sowell explains, the German philosopher's position was defined by contrast with that of his rivals; only in *Das Kapital* (1867; *Capital*, 1886) did Marx give his own ideas systematic exposition.

To understand Marx's economic theories, Sowell contends, one must first comprehend the dialectic, a philosophical tool taken from the kit of the German philosopher Georg Wilhelm Friedrich Hegel. When one uses the dialectic, one sees the world as a series of processes rather than a set of isolated facts; one looks for the inner tensions that propel the transformation of something from one state to another, rather than simply accepting the surface appearance of things as the ultimate reality. Thus, Marx speaks of the everyday idea of price as a surface phenomenon, beneath which lies the truer notion of value. Marx looks beneath the surface of capitalist society and sees those forces which are working to transform it into a totally different type of society.

To illustrate Marx's distinction between the essence of something and its outward appearance, Sowell uses the example of the metamorphosis of the caterpillar into the butterfly; throughout the discussion of Marx's thought, Sowell adeptly employs such simple but powerful illustrative examples in order to make murky concepts clearer and easier to grasp. Having made the dialectic more comprehensible, Sowell goes on to explain, clearly and carefully, the equally difficult concepts of alienation, philosophical materialism, and the labor theory of value.

Sowell is willing to aid the untutored reader by pointing out possible misunderstandings that might arise from changing meanings of certain words. Thus, Sowell informs his readers that the materialism inherited by Marx from such ancient philosophers as Epicurus and Lucretius, and from such later European philosophers as Baron Paul Henri Dietrich d'Holbach and Ludwig Feuerbach, had nothing to do with the greed and gluttony associated with that word in popular usage; it simply meant a belief in matter as the ultimate reality. Similarly, the author warns, the fact that Engels and Marx called the future society a communist one and wrote *Manifest der kommunistischen Partei* (1848; *Communist Manifesto*, 1888) does not, in and of itself, prove that they wished to see a society like the Communist regime currently existing in the U.S.S.R. The word "communism" must be understood in its proper historical context.

Americans have an unfortunate tendency to think of Karl Marx and Marxism in a historical vacuum, as if socialism began only yesterday, and only in the U.S.S.R. Sowell is careful to place Marx firmly in the context of his time. Marx was, Sowell demonstrates, by no means the first Western European thinker to argue in favor of socialism; other thinkers, earlier in the nineteenth century, had also expressed their hopes of seeing a new social order replace the old system of private property. It was in his emphasis on the historical relativity of moral judgments, derived from the dialectic of Hegel, and in his faith in the historical inevitability of the transition to the new society, Sowell shows, that Marx differed most strikingly from such earlier socialist thinkers as the British reformer Robert Owen and the French theorist François-Marie-Charles Fourier, and from such contemporaries as the French radical thinker Pierre Joseph Proudhon. For Marx, capitalism was not simply evil, as it had been for earlier socialists; it was historically necessary, but also inevitably fated to be replaced by socialism.

Giving the reader the full benefit of his long years of research on the classical economists, Sowell also fruitfully compares and contrasts Marx's economic theories with those of the British economic thinkers David Ricardo and Adam Smith, the Swiss economist Jean-Charles-Léonard de Sismondi, and the French economist Jean Baptiste Say. It was from Ricardo, and ultimately from Smith, Sowell points out, that Marx took the labor theory of value, although the notion of surplus value as a measure of the exploitation of labor was Marx's own idea. Although Sowell is critical of Marxism, he is fair-minded enough to recognize at least one instance where Marx's powers of economic analysis were equal or even superior to those of some of the classical economists: the question of the causes of economic crises. Unlike Sismondi, Marx believed that economic crises were caused by sectoral disproportionality of production rather than by general underconsumption; unlike Jean Baptiste Say, who believed that supply created its own demand, Marx showed how such sectoral disproportionality could cause monetary reactions that would temporarily push aggregate demand below aggregate supply.

While Sowell does generally succeed in placing Marx within the context of his time, his treatment of Marx's idea of progress is misleading precisely because it fails to offer such comparative perspective. Sowell criticizes Marx, in the final chapter on Marx's intellectual legacy, for failing to take into account the possibility of retrogression as well as progress, for failing to recognize that capitalism could as easily be replaced by something worse as by something better. Yet naïve faith in the inevitability of progress was by no means a failing peculiar to Marx; it can be found in many nineteenth century thinkers, including such Social Darwinists as the English sociologist Herbert Spencer. The crucial difference is simply that Marxist naïveté had more serious political consequences.

Besides placing Marx's teachings in their proper historical perspective, Sowell also takes account of change in Marx's ideas through time; by doing so, the author helps resolve some of the apparent inconsistencies in Marx's thought. Over Marx's forty-year career as theorist and agitator, his opinions on certain issues were modified in significant ways. Thus, during his young manhood, in the period of Europe-wide economic distress known as the Hungry Forties, Marx predicted that the workers' lot was bound to grow ever worse in absolute terms. Later, when the European economy had improved somewhat, Marx redefined the immiserization of the masses to mean a continual fall in the relative share of economic growth obtained by the proletariat; such immiserization could occur even if the workers were somewhat better off in absolute terms than they had been before. Similarly, Marx's idea of revolution, clearly foreseen as a violent uprising in the Europe of voteless workingmen that existed in the 1840's, had been transformed by the early 1880's, with the growing enfranchisement of the working classes throughout Europe, into something that could as easily be achieved by peaceful as by violent means.

Marxism has, as Sowell recognizes, been thoroughly tainted for the average Western man (including the average workingman) by its use as an ideological fig leaf for some of the most brutally tyrannical regimes in human history. Yet Sowell can only wrestle somewhat inconclusively with the ambiguous legacy of the German philosopher's teachings concerning the State. Sowell argues, in his chapter on Marx's political philosophy, that Marx's concept of the dictatorship of the proletariat meant not the narrow elitism propounded by the Russian revolutionary leader Vladimir Ilich Lenin but a democratic, republican form of government by the workers themselves. Somewhat inconsistently, however, Sowell, in the final chapter, blames the allegedly totalitarian heritage of Marx's thought for the sins of the regimes that later bore Marx's name in the U.S.S.R. and elsewhere; the tyranny of Joseph Stalin is pointed to as one particularly horrible example. In the chapter on Marx's life, the author even argues that Marx's dictatorial personal style exerted an especially malign influence on future Marxist revolutionaries. Sowell ignores the possibility, raised by the historian Robert V. Daniels in *Russia: The Roots of Confrontation* (1985), that the crimes of Stalin may owe as much to the autocratic tradition of pre-Communist Russia as they do to the ideology of Karl Marx.

Sowell's case for the baleful legacy of Marx's economic thought is a bit more persuasive. The author concedes that Marx did sometimes recognize, in his off-the-cuff remarks, the importance of skills and risk-taking in a capitalist economy. Yet Sowell firmly insists that such occasional bursts of insight into economic reality were vitiated by Marx's failure to incorporate the factors of skill and risk-taking into either his labor theory of value or his general theory of capitalism as expounded in the seminal work *Capital*. Marx made an even more serious mistake, Sowell argues, by naïvely assuming that a future socialist economy could easily dispense with the pain of capitalism's economic crises without endangering the gain of efficient allocation of resources, or eliminate the supposedly unjust profits of the capitalist at the expense of the worker without also stifling badly needed incentives for innovation in the interests of the consumer.

Sowell is right in pointing out the naïveté of Marx's vision of a future socialist economy in which all human and material constraints could be easily overcome. Yet the author fails to see that criticism of such a vision can as easily be made by a theologian as by an economist. Marx postulated the coming of a future in which neither the apparatus of police coercion nor the mechanism of economic incentives would be necessary to ensure the smooth functioning of society. The traditional Christian doctrine of the innate sinfulness of man, reasserted in recent times by thinkers such as the American theologian Reinhold Niebuhr, is a warning against Marx's belief that a mere change in social institutions can radically transform human nature.

In giving reasons for the success of Marxism, Sowell mentions the appeal of Marxism as an intellectually coherent system, its popularity among the highly educated scions of the elite, and its convenience as an excuse for ambitious politicians' hunger for absolute power. The author ignores, however, yet another important reason for the popularity of Marxism: its role as a substitute religion for those who have abandoned the certitudes of orthodox Christianity or the time-honored ways of life of traditional Judaism. Sowell correctly notes that Marx's steadfast refusal to provide any detailed blueprint for the future socialist state and economy made it possible for governments calling themselves Marxist to carry out many unwise and tyrannical policies in the master's name. Sowell fails to recognize that this very vagueness about the future society, by enabling men to see this future society as the embodiment of all of mankind's most strongly felt millennial longings, probably did much toward permitting the Marxist version of socialist thought to displace other competing versions of socialism in nineteenth century Europe. For a fuller discussion of the religious appeals of Marxism, one can consult *The Opium of the Intellectuals* (1957), by the French anti-Communist intellectual Raymond Aron.

Sowell has also failed to touch on other interesting subjects. Thus, Karl Marx's teachings on the family and sex roles in capitalist society and in the future socialist state deserve a bit more attention from the author. The only mention of the subject in Sowell's work is a citation, in the chapter on Marx's life, of a plank in the *Communist Manifesto* as evidence of Marx's totalitarian intention of destroying the existing family structure; this citation is not an adequate treatment of an issue of considerable importance. A better treatment of this issue can be found in Lise Vogel's *Marxism and the Oppression of Women: Toward a Unitary Theory* (1983), although it does have a strong pro-Marx bias.

Sowell could have provided greater insight into Marx's ideas by providing a fuller comparison of them with those of the English population theorist Thomas Malthus. Sowell gives Malthus' views on economic crises but does not say anything about Malthus' population theory as such. Malthus, like Marx, did have a model of immiserization, one in which the steady impoverishment of the masses was caused not by the inner workings of the capitalist system but by the mechanism of unchecked population growth. For Malthus, a pessimistic conservative rather than a revolutionary socialist, such immiserization led, not to a radical leap into a higher social order, but to a reestablishment of the old equilibrium between population and resources. Some historians have offered a Malthusian explanation of the very economic misery, prevalent in the England of the 1840's, that Marx's longtime collaborator, Friedrich Engels, saw as evidence of the instability and unfairness of capitalism. The reader of the 1980's living in a world troubled by the problems of rising population might be more interested than Sowell seems to be in finding out how Marx dealt with the implicit challenge to his theories posed by Malthus' theory of population growth.

Thomas Sowell's *Marxism: Philosophy and Economics* is by no means the first work in English to attempt to provide a summary of the thought of Karl Marx for the general reader. Marx can be profitably studied from the vantage point of more than one author and more than one scholarly discipline. In *Marxism: For and Against* (1980), Robert Heilbroner, an American who has written many popular works on economics, presents a view of Marx which, while not uncritical, is considerably more sympathetic to the German philosopher than is Sowell's. Heilbroner's rather brief book, however, lacks the sophisticated understanding of economic thought found in Sowell's work. The Australian professor of philosophy Peter Singer, in *Marx* (1980), one of the Past Masters series, provides a better insight than does Sowell into some aspects of Marx's thought, even though his coverage of Marx's economic concepts is as sketchy as Heilbroner's. Singer's discussion of Marx's concept of freedom, for example, demonstrates an awareness of the collective irrationality that free individual choice can sometimes bring. Such a treatment of this issue seems more enlightening than Sowell's broadbrush condemnation of Marx's attitude toward freedom as a form of totalitarian elitism. All these various approaches to Marx add something to an understanding of the man and his theories; of them all, Sowell's is, on balance, the one that best combines, for the general reader, scholarship, readability, and comprehensiveness.

Paul D. Mageli

Sources for Further Study

Barron's. LXV, July 8, 1985, p. 50.
Choice. XXII, June, 1985, p. 1545.
Human Events. XLV, January 12, 1985, p. 17.
Kirkus Reviews. LIII, January 15, 1985, p. 89.
Library Journal. CX, March 1, 1985, p. 91.
National Review. XXXVII, May 3, 1985, p. 54.
The New York Times Book Review. XC, March 31, 1985, p. 18.
Publishers Weekly. CCXXVI, January 18, 1985, p. 67.
The Wall Street Journal. CCV, March 29, 1985, p. 26.
Washington Post Book World. XV, March 24, 1985, p. 11.

MASTERS OF ATLANTIS

Author: Charles Portis (1933-   )
Publisher: Alfred A. Knopf (New York). 248 pp. $15.95
Type of work: Novel
Time: From World War I to the 1980's
Locale: The United States

Told with tongue in cheek, this comic novel is a warm and sometimes moving account of misfits and con men, tracing the history of the secret Gnomon Society in America following World War I

> *Principal characters:*
> LAMAR JIMMERSON, Master of the Gnomon Society in North America
> SYDNEY HEN, Master of a rival branch of the Gnomons
> FANNY HEN, Sydney's sister and Lamar's wife
> AUSTIN POPPER, a con man and the chief spokesman for the Society
> PHARRIS WHITE, an FBI agent determined to expose Gnomons and arrest Austin Popper
> CEZAR GOLESCU, a Romanian scientist with interest in alchemy and the lost continent of Mu
> BATES,
> MAPES,
> HUGGINS, and
> EPPS, members of the Gnomons
> MAURICE BABCOCK, a Chicago court stenographer and late initiate of the Gnomons
> MOREHEAD MOALER, a Texas millionaire and Gnomon
> ED, a World War II veteran of uncertain sanity
> THE STRANGER, one who has numerous identities but who admits to the name of Robert and who gives Lamar the *Codex Pappus*

Charles Portis, a native of Arkansas, is one of America's very best comic writers. He is perhaps best known for his wonderful Western, *True Grit* (1968), which was made into a fine film starring John Wayne as Rooster Cogburn (the role which won for Wayne his only Academy Award for Best Actor). Portis' other novels—*Norwood* (1966) and *The Dog of the South* (1979)—were not as popular, although *Norwood* was also made into a film, and *The Dog of the South* enjoys a cult reputation as one of the best least-known novels of the 1970's.

It is easy to see why Portis has become such an appreciated writer, compared to Mark Twain *and* Woody Allen by way of Buster Keaton. His protagonists are often befuddled or lost innocents adrift in a vastly complex world. They ask little more than to discover some kind of order, some degree of reason, although their quests may seem foolish or impossible or insignificant. They are surrounded by a rich variety of characters: heroes and villains, madmen and con artists, obsessives and fools. Few of Portis' characters are actually evil, and, indeed, he presents them with a warmth that is sweet and contagious.

Masters of Atlantis is a lovely addition to Portis' work. In a sense, it is a one-joke novel. In 1917, near the end of World War I, Corporal Lamar Jimmerson, an American soldier, meets a mysterious stranger who introduces him to the secret society of the Gnomons. The stranger, who has numerous identities but finally admits to the name of Robert, gives Lamar a book written in Greek, the *Codex Pappus*, which "contained the secret wisdom of Atlantis." The original manuscript, the stranger explains, came from the Lost Continent. It was sealed in an ivory casket and survived the sinking of the island. After floating for nine hundred years, it was discovered by a Hermes Trismegistus, who then became "the first modern Master of the Gnomon Society." The present Master, Lamar is told, is one Pletho Pappus, who lives on the island of Malta. Pletho has now ordered that the Society be expanded, and Lamar has been chosen to take the Order to America. Leaving the book in Lamar's hands and fleecing him of two hundred dollars for a never-delivered ceremonial robe, Robert disappears. The credulous Lamar reflects: "There was no question of [Robert] having run off with the robe money," for Lamar has the precious book, not to mention Robert's Poma, a conical goatskin cap "signifying high office."

As this opening scene suggests, the jest of the book comes from the difference between Lamar's steadfast faith in this new creed and the reader's more skeptical perception of the events that are related. The narrative voice is never judgmental; the facts of Lamar's life are recounted in a masterful deadpan delivery. Portis never encourages the reader's sense of superiority to Lamar; indeed, there is always the slightest possibility that Lamar—or Mr. Jimmerson, as he is respectfully addressed once he becomes Master of the Gnomons—is wiser in his apparent silliness than those who otherwise fail in the test of faith.

Shortly after being introduced to the mysteries of Gnomonism, Lamar meets an Englishman named Sydney Hen, who shows an immediate interest in Lamar's discoveries. Although Sydney seems suspect in some ways, Lamar decides to bring him into the Order. "This is marvelous stuff!" Sydney enthuses. "I can't make head or tail of it!" Soon thereafter, Sydney comes to the conclusion that both he and Lamar are further along in their studies than Lamar had realized. "Can't you see it, man? You're already a Master! We're both Masters! You still don't see it? Robert was Pletho himself! Your Poma is the Cone of Fate! You and I are beginning the New Cycle of Gnomonism!" Sydney convinces Lamar that he should return to America immediately, while he himself takes charge of Europe and Asia.

This account of the rise and fall of the Gnomon Society in the world covers a period of approximately sixty years. During this time, Mr. Jimmerson devotes himself more and more to meditation on the mysteries of the lost lore of Atlantis. He works specifically on the theory he calls the Jimmerson

Spiral, a foggy explanation for the vagaries of history. He establishes the first Pillar of the Society in Gary, Indiana, shortly after his return from Europe. Pillar No. 2 is set up in Chicago by Mr. Bates, a traveling salesman, and Pillar No. 3 in Valparaiso, Indiana, by Mr. Mapes, a football coach who "hoped that Gnomonic thought might show him the way to put some life into his timorous and lethargic team." The Society, however, does not really begin to grow until 1929, after the stock market crash and the beginning of the Great Depression when people are looking for a sense of order and purpose, or some form of escape. Mr. Jimmerson has by this time married Fanny Hen, Sydney's sister, who acts as his secretary and types his first books: *101 Gnomon Facts*, *Why I Am a Gnomon*, and *Tracking the Telluric Currents*. In 1936, the Gnomon Temple is dedicated in Gary, and Mr. Jimmerson retreats to the Red Room, there to continue his life of contemplation.

The man who is most responsible, however, for the success of the Gnomon Society is not Lamar Jimmerson but Austin Popper, one of Portis' finest creations. Popper insists that the precepts, requirements, and secrets of the Society be revised and simplified for the common man. Mr. Bates at first has his doubts:

> [Popper] was willful, erratic. He was vain in his personal appearance. He was sometimes facetious in a most unbecoming way. In his writing he had a vulgar inclination to make everything clear. He had not yet learned to appreciate the beauties of allusion and Gnomonic obfuscation—that fog was there for a purpose. He couldn't see that to grasp a delicate thing outright was often to crush it.

Popper is a go-getter, a fast talker, and a man easily caught up in his own schemes. As Mr. Jimmerson draws back into his inner sanctum, Popper takes center stage. Early in his association with the Society, he incurs the enmity of a potential initiate, Pharris White, who then dedicates himself to the destruction of Popper and the Society. Popper disappears for long periods of time, only to return when least expected. Whenever Popper shows up, however, White follows soon thereafter, as obsessed with his revenge as the Gnomons are with their knowledge.

Austin Popper is a fascinating character. He is, in his own way, devoted to Mr. Jimmerson and to the Gnomon Society, although he clearly has no real understanding of either. His ideas are often fantastic. For example, he takes Mr. Jimmerson to Washington at the beginning of World War II to discuss with the War Department "a carefully prepared plan for winning the war through the use of compressed air and the military application of Gnomonic science." The trip leads to humiliation for Mr. Jimmerson, but Popper is never defeated, nor does Jimmerson lose his trust in his assistant.

Popper's greatest disappointment occurs soon after when he joins forces with Professor Cezar Golescu, who is convinced that he can extract gold from the leaves of bagweed plants rooted in soil containing microscopic traces of the metal, which would be absorbed into the vine. Popper and Golescu travel to the town of Hogandale, Colorado, site of numerous abandoned mines, there to put the "Banco Plan" into effect. Popper takes on the aliases of Commander DeWitt Farnsworth, one of many disguises he assumes to avoid local suspicion and to beat the draft. The plan is a failure; Popper and Golescu quarrel over a girl, and Austin turns to drink. He returns years later to the Society after a life as a drunken bum:

> He had been on the road living a life of stupor, filth, irregular meals and no certainty of shelter from one night to the next. Pedestrians in many cities had been obliged to step over him as he lay curled up on the sidewalk wearing four shirts, three sweaters and multiple layers of verminous trousers, the cuffs bound tightly at the ankles with rubber bands, so that he was sometimes taken for a downed cyclist.

When Austin, now reformed, returns, Mr. Jimmerson and the Society have reached their own personal nadir. Sydney Hen has started his own rival Society. Fanny has long since left her husband and become a wealthy woman in her own business. The Gnomons have dwindled down to two Pillars: the Temple outside Gary and the Texas Order near Brownsville, ruled by Mr. Morehead Moaler. Mr. Jimmerson has evolved a new theory, the Jimmerson Lag, to explain the situation, but it is up to Popper to revitalize the Order. Taking Jimmerson in hand, he moves the entire Society to Texas, where they establish themselves in Morehead Moaler's three trailers, one set aside especially as the Great Hall to take the place of the abandoned Temple in Gary.

If there is a weakness in the book, it is found in the ending of the story. *Masters of Atlantis* is, finally, a shaggy-dog story of the highest order, but it does lose energy as it winds to a conclusion. There is no clear resolution to the tale. Portis retrenches his characters and allows the entropy to continue. It is, in some ways, a sad and wistful ending, and one might wish for a more definite solution. On the other hand, Portis shows a wisdom and sympathy in leaving his characters as he does. They are now old, still deluded, but happy in their brotherhood. Friendships have been renewed, and new bonds have been made. The book ends on Christmas Day. The Telluric Currents again begin to flow. A "New Cycle" may be about to begin. "What a wonderful Christmas!" one character exclaims. "This is the best party I've ever been to!" another answers. There should be few readers who would dare disagree.

Edwin T. Arnold

Sources for Further Study

Booklist. LXXXII, October 1, 1985, p. 192.
Kirkus Reviews. LIII, August 15, 1985, p. 815.
Library Journal. CX, October 15, 1985, p. 103.
The Nation. CCXLI, November 30, 1985, p. 593.
The New York Times Book Review. XC, October 27, 1985, p. 32.
The New Yorker. LXI, November 25, 1985, p. 163.
Newsweek. CVI, September 30, 1985, p. 73.
Publishers Weekly. CCXXVIII, August 23, 1985, p. 60.
Texas Monthly. XIII, December, 1985, p. 194.
Washington Post Book World. XV, October 27, 1985, p. 7.

MEMORY OF FIRE
I. Genesis

Author: Eduardo H. Galeano (1940-   )
Translated from the Spanish by Cedric Belfrage
Publisher: Pantheon Books (New York). 293 pp. $17.95
Type of work: Latin American history
Time: Pre-Columbian period to 1700
Locale: Primarily Central and South America; also North America and Europe

Selecting bits and pieces from everything that has been written about the colonization of South America, Galeano has fused them into daring testimony that the past is still alive

The Library of Congress has placed this book of Latin American history in a category of "light" works, works of anecdote, witticism, and satire. Yet it is a minor miracle that the book reads so smoothly and so pleasurably. For the fire that the title remembers is the auto-da-fé in which Christian Europe incinerated the Indian civilizations of South and Central America while filling its coffers and founding its colonies. The subject of this entertaining volume is genocide.

The modulating of this material into prose that human eyes can read without flinching is accomplished by an extraordinary feat of technical virtuosity. *Memory of Fire: I. Genesis* (the second volume of the projected trilogy has already been published in Spanish) is made up of more than three hundred brief passages, averaging less than a page. With the exception of the passages in the opening section, "First Voices," which presents myths and folktales of pre-Columbian America, each entry is headed by a date and a place-name. Arranged in chronological order, these passages string together some luminous moments in the history of America's colonization. Like the "magic realism" that is so distinctive of recent Latin American fiction, Galeano's writing manages to personalize history; as he says at one point, one learns to smell history in the wind. Each snapshot reminds the reader of how much ordinary life, how much ordinary suffering, is glossed over by any continuous, totalizing, synoptic history of conquest or nation-building. Refusing to rise to the Olympian heights that such subjects seem to call for, Galeano pushes one's nose in the present-tense particularity, the experiential intensity of the lives that were battered and lost. Yet his format also attenuates this misery: Some of the passages combine to form sequences (the life of the pirate Henry Morgan or the poet Sor Juana Ines de la Cruz, for example), but most do not; as a result, the reader is not bludgeoned into acquiescence by a repetition of horror after horror but, rather, involved in an active, ceaseless weaving and interweaving of pieces, a fitting together of fragments. What is left out is as important as what is said. No scene of horror lasts too long; in a moment one is elsewhere, distracted by new issues, seeking connections. As in a well-conducted slide show, much of the pleasure comes from the brevity of each slide and the spaces for thought that come between them.

Another effect of the slide-show form is to eliminate or at least play down the overarching, omniscient presence of a narrator who would tie everything together in the bitter indignation of a single voice or a single vision. Thus the book is curiously impersonal; the images come out of nowhere. One is left wondering who has undertaken this work of historical reconstruction, to what sort of present life all of this is the background. Perhaps the succeeding volumes of the trilogy will answer these questions.

The Library of Congress classification, perhaps inspired by Galeano's early work as a political cartoonist, correctly notes that this form is hardly that of academic history, yet it has its own rigor. Galeano has done his homework; the list of source materials at the back of the book, to which the numbers following each passage refer, permits the reader to check up on any episodes that catch his fancy. There is, to be sure, a considerable amount of humor in the book, some of it satiric and some more unsettling than satire. For example, reading the Indian creation myths and folktales that Galeano reproduces in "First Voices," one's laughter is mixed with awe. What a sense of human existence this was, which could found itself on a comic view of the creation. By contrast, our own myths of creation—of which the "discovery of America" is one—seem dour.

A vast mosaic of folklore and history, poetry and political analysis, *Genesis* has more than its share of surprises. It contrasts the creativity of Indian mythology, the fresh discovery of life that leaps from the pages of these native versions of genesis, with the relentless, repetitive greed and dogma of the European invaders, but it also brings their myths closer to ours: One reads Indian variants of Noah's Flood and of Orpheus' trip to the underworld. More important, perhaps, it refuses to idealize the victims. Aztec human sacrifice is referred to repeatedly, and when the Aztecs arrive victorious at Tenochtitlan, the prophecies that they hear from the defeated of their eventual fall function as an anticipation of the conquistadores. Told that they will subjugate all the peoples and cities around them from sea to sea, they also receive prophecies of their own subjugation by strangers, people with clothes on, who will draw a spider web around their people and turn men into slaves.

By adhering strictly to chronology, Galeano pulls off another nicely relativizing touch. It is customary to divide the history of Latin America into the period before and after Christopher Columbus' arrival, but the entrance of the Europeans did not automatically make them the central focus of attention. Much of what had been happening before Columbus simply continued. In a number of passages, the reader watches the Aztecs still pushing forward their conquests, sacrificing prisoners to their gods. One sees conquered Indians paying unwilling tribute to Inca tax collectors, and one sees the Inca empire extended further and further, until it is larger than Europe. Thus the god to whom Montezuma's prisoners are sacrificed in 1506 and the god who presides over the Inquisition's burning of European heretics in the same year stand out in clear parallel.

The voyages of Columbus, which have always seemed so natural a beginning for American history, look different from the point of view of those who were there to greet him. After interrogating the natives in Hebrew, Chaldean, and Arabic, Columbus takes captives. None of the women and children survives. It is the beginning of a long succession of atrocities. Almost immediately, the scene shifts forward to Columbus himself dying in disgrace, and then, just as quickly, the hidden history of rebellion and reaction also begins. In 1511, the Indian inhabitants of Puerto Rico realize that the invaders are not immortal and rise against them. The reader watches the Spanish shoot an old Indian woman with a crossbow; one watches a Haitian chief, about to be burned at the stake, choose Hell rather than join the Christians in their Heaven. In 1522, one watches the first rebellion of black slaves. One watches Balboa, only two days away from his discovery of the Pacific Ocean, setting his dogs to tear apart fifty Panamanians accused of the sin of sodomy. The Araucanians rise against the Spaniards in Chile with extraordinary success; the slave Lautaro makes Valdivia eat Chilean soil. In Peru, the death of Tupac Amaru in 1572 ends forty years of Inca resistance. The Indians of the Caribbean fight for the freedom to make love as they wish. In Mexico, the converted Indians who are dying in the mines of Durango rise against the priests and renounce their religion. In Santa Fe, New Mexico, the Spaniards take thirteen years to reconquer the lands the Indians have liberated.

Above all, there is the century-long story of Palmares, a nation-state set up in the Brazilian jungle by escaped slaves. Reading of its fortifications, its two corn harvests a year, its use of Portuguese as lingua franca, its negotiations with delegates of the king, its resistance to all expeditions until cannons were brought to the region in 1694, it becomes clear how much history has been hidden and how that history lives on. Chief Zumbi, the last leader of Palmares, was murdered by a traitor, but all the leaders of later rebellions were called Zumbi.

Though Galeano is primarily interested in Latin America, the English colonies to the north do not serve as any sort of moral contrast to the savagery of the Spanish and Portuguese. Beginning with the death of Pocahontas on the Thames before her twenty-first birthday, Galeano proceeds through the bloody suppression of Chief Opechancanough's rebellion, which leaves nine-tenths of the Indians who had greeted the first settlers at Jamestown dead. One is reminded of the Puritan slave traders and of how the Duke of York's men burn the initials "DY" with hot irons into the chests of the three thousand slaves sent each year to Jamaica and Barbados.

In the Yorktown of 1674, Galeano notes, it is a crime for a laborer to challenge a gentleman to a horse race. As smallpox devastates the Indians of New England, the Puritans turn to the Old Testament to justify their policy of massacring Indian women and children.

In one of the book's more interesting motifs, Galeano pauses frequently to consider how much and how variously European culture has depended on and been fashioned out of what happened in the colonies. This concern extends from dances such as the saraband and chaconne, which were influenced by the slaves, to the link between Thomas More's *Utopia* and the "primitive communism" discovered in the New World. Quevedo and Cervantes come off as valuable early critics of the colonial passion; William Shakespeare's Caliban and John Donne exploring his mistress' body in a poem as one discovering America become evidence that the monuments of culture, as Walter Benjamin said, are simultaneously monuments of barbarism. Following the exploits of the pirate Henry Morgan against the Spanish fleet and Panama City, the reader watches as, in 1674, after his casual murder of a half-witted boy, he is appointed by the king to serve as lieutenant governor of Jamaica—with instructions for government drawn up by John Locke.

This is a story with European heroes as well as European villains. Those who made it their business to see and who bore witness, always at serious cost to themselves, show the reader that atrocities cannot be explained away with the assertion that "everyone thought that way back then." Of these heroic witnesses, the most famous is Father Bartolomé de las Casas, who tried to deprive the conquistadors' sons of Indian slaves. The book also surprises the reader with the number of kindred spirits, such as the Jesuit Father Ragueneau, who defended Huron Indian dream interpretations (in terms of unfulfilled desires). The Mexican poet Sor Juana Ines de la Cruz, who refused to accept the servile status of women, came to "write like a man" and compared her sufferings to those of Christ, represents another sort of exception. Given Galeano's sensitivity to any and all subversive behavior, even the existence of a single (unfairly treated) woman conquistadora is credited to the account of the human race.

All Galeano's fond attention to moments of individual experience does not obscure the large patterns of history. From the beginning, the hold of foreign bankers over the Spanish monarchy is evident, and Galeano notes how the merchants defeat the conquistadores without once drawing a sword. As the decades go by, it is increasingly clear that, thanks to the theological, unproductive bias of its rulers (the gentry have the bedroom as their only battlefield, Galeano says), Spain is losing the wealth of its colonies to Northern Europe. The atrocities of forced labor in Peru's silver mines are traced to Spain's need for booty from abroad to make up for the lack of a modernizing economy at home. Producing fewer and fewer things and more and more coins, Spain watches its neighbors modernize while its own board of theologians turns down a project to channel the Tagus and Manzanares rivers in 1641, on the grounds that if God had wanted those rivers navigable He would have made them navigable. In 1655, England begins to seize the Spanish empire. It is something less than justice, but Galeano's satisfaction as Spain itself collapses, like his careful notation of each horrible death of each conquistador and, finally, of Charles II and the dynasty that conquered America, helps give his narrative an emotional roundness.

The European conquest of the Americas has been narrated before. Information has been available concerning the ruthless extermination of native peoples, the destruction of their cities and cultures, the death ships full of African slaves, and the founding of new colonies on the blood and ash of the conquered. Galeano has not done original research; he has not unearthed previously unknown atrocities. He merely retells stories that have been documented by others. Why has he chosen this duplication of labor? Perhaps the clue lies in his title. The Bible's Genesis celebrates a divine creation out of nothingness. The New World, on the other hand, came into being by massacre; Europeans found a world already there and turned it into nothingness. Yet those who celebrate the "civilization" of the New World have remained loyal to the biblical model. Our myths, the stories we tell our children, the versions of the past that we not only find in our reference libraries but also live by day to day, integrated into the way we think about ourselves, have not changed. Hence the daring literary experiment of inventing a new form in which to tell it all again—so freshly that it will become our creation myth. For many readers, Galeano has certainly succeeded; his pages will take on the personal intensity of memory and the authority of a story to live by.

Bruce Robbins

Sources for Further Study

Booklist. LXXXII, November 15, 1985, p. 464.
Choice. XXIII. January, 1986, p. 746.
Kirkus Reviews. LIII, August 15, 1985, p. 807.
Library Journal. CX, October 1, 1985, p. 101.
The New York Times Book Review. XC, October 27, 1985, p. 22.
Publishers Weekly. CCXXVIII, August 16, 1985, p. 62.

MEN AND ANGELS

Author: Mary Gordon (1949-   )
Publisher: Random House (New York). 239 pp. $16.95
Type of work: Novel
Time: The 1980's
Locale: Selby, Massachusetts, a fictitious college town

This tense, eloquent tale describes the fatal consequences that follow when an art historian, trying to juggle research, housekeeping and child rearing, hires an emotionally disturbed young woman to care for her children

> *Principal characters:*
> ANNE FOSTER, an art historian
> MICHAEL FOSTER, her husband, in France on a sabbatical
> PETER, their son, age nine
> SARAH, their daughter, age six
> LAURA POST, a twenty-year-old woman hired to care for Peter and Sarah
> CAROLINE WATSON, an early twentieth century painter whose life and works Anne is researching
> JANE WATSON, Caroline's daughter-in-law, who is assisting Anne's research
> BEN HARDY, an art historian and Anne's friend
> ED CORCORAN, an electrician rewiring the Foster house
> BARBARA GREENSPAN, Anne's neighbor and close friend

Men and Angels is Mary Gordon's third novel. Like her highly acclaimed *Final Payments* (1978) and *The Company of Women* (1981), *Men and Angels* focuses on an engaging heroine who, in crisis, must rely on her own character in the absence of an authoritative male. Anne Foster, ambitiously attempting to be mother, housekeeper, and researcher while her husband Michael teaches in Europe for a year, unknowingly shapes a tragic fate for the girl hired to care for her children. Like Isabel Moore in *Final Payments* and Felicitas Taylor in *The Company of Women*, Anne struggles with the burden of being thought stable and good even as she learns that life is unpredictable and that love is not innocent.

Men and Angels is a more complex, richer work of fiction than the previous novels. Its scope extends beyond the Irish Catholic world of ethnic solidarity and clerical sway. Its central situation is complicated by mirroring subplots and characters. It offers an additional poignant theme: the human yearning to reestablish the Edenic harmony—real or imagined—of the childhood home before the Fall into adulthood. It employs two alternating points of view to record the fatal interaction of Laura Post and Anne Foster.

Laura is the central consciousness of the first chapter (and subsequent odd-numbered chapters). These chapters take the reader inside Laura's heart and head. Laura's heart shriveled when her mother rejected her for a younger, more attractive daughter, and her father only halfheartedly compensated for his wife's withdrawal. Laura's withered heart creates the conviction that the Spirit of the Lord has chosen her for a revelation. Laura imagines herself the apostle of the Spirit to children, preaching that parental love is transient and unreliable. Purged of illusion, children shall turn to stable, divine love.

Laura's determination to estrange child and parent deepens after she leaves home in a vain search for surrogate parents. For a while she helps the ministry of a faith healer, until he dismisses her for aspiring to become herself a channel of restorative grace. Briefly she lives in a religious commune where she becomes its leader's mistress in the belief that the Spirit wills it. When Laura discovers that her lover appropriates the community's money, he banishes her as the sinner.

Laura comes to work for Anne after dismissal from another family. Realizing that she must now, as the Bible enjoins, be as cunning as a serpent, Laura stealthily plans a revelation for the Foster children. Despite attention to Peter and Sarah, Laura is increasingly attracted to Anne. She soon receives a new injunction from the Spirit: Free Anne from the cares and physical love of family. Laura envisions living with Anne in harmonious hermitage until death takes them home to the Spirit. One winter day, however, the girl carelessly leads Peter and Sarah onto the thin ice of a pond; Anne immediately fires her. Angry yet contrite, Laura takes revenge against Anne: She slashes A-N-N-E on her wrists and bleeds to death.

Reading Laura's chapters is an excursion into pain, desperation, and fanaticism. Laura seeks love, but each denial further twists and distorts her perceptions. Though Laura's plight deserves pity, the reader cannot ignore Laura's descent into madness. Her faith is obviously compensatory, a psychological mechanism for repairing the disintegration of her life. Though biblical quotations come trippingly to Laura's tongue, she acts irreligiously. She is blind to the irony of lying, manipulating, or fornicating to achieve the Spirit's will.

The even-numbered chapters, told from Anne's point of view, are different: Neither narrow nor paranoiac, Anne's chapters open to the world. They are longer because Anne's life is fuller. Divided into sections, each chapter reflects the complexity of Anne's roles as wife, mother, friend, professional.

Anne might have been what Laura became. Like Laura, Anne disappointed her mother by forswearing exclusive attention to housekeeping and motherhood. Worse yet, Anne's mother withdrew her love in proportion to the affection that Anne drew from her father. Yet the withdrawal of love did not wither Anne's heart.

She married Michael. Partially romantic love made them marry, partially the desire to end childhood and enter adulthood, partially the will to "reinvent domestic life." Like Anne, Michael came from a house with "deficient parents" and wanted to create a home nearer the ideal.

Anne found love too in producing Peter and Sarah. She knows them with the surety of body and the intuition of soul. To Anne, motherhood is a relationship, not of logic and sentiment but of passion: With "fear, longing and delight," Anne observes in her children's daily activities the gestation of their characters.

Anne has wrought love out of friendship too. Her neighbor Barbara Greenspan shares domestic tribulations and the career handicap of an advanced degree in an impractical subject. Ben Hardy, an art historian, offers her platonic affection and help in getting assignments. Jane Watson shares her admiration for the character and art of Caroline Watson.

Bathed in love that Laura missed, Anne constructs an existence more solid and purposeful. To outsiders her life appears easy, tranquil, and unchanging. Anne is acutely aware, however, that her life supports are fragile, the guideposts not always illuminated. As the novel progresses, Anne struggles with the added fears of Michael's infidelity and wrestles with her sexual attraction to Ed Corcoran, the affable electrician rewiring the Foster house.

Anne at first refuses to hire Laura; there is something about the girl that Anne distrusts and dislikes. When circumstances force Laura's hiring, Anne determines to make the best of it. She ignores the young woman's constant introversion, her maddening silences, her annoying habit of poking into Anne's possessions. Indeed, Anne instinctively senses a growing responsibility for Laura.

In death, Laura establishes with Anne the bond she failed to effect in life. Her suicide spites Anne, as a chastised child's misbehavior spites a parent. Anne meets Laura's death not with parental anger but with maternal pity. Realizing that Laura died because of a failure to love, Anne offers to Laura's corpse the motherly care Laura's soul craved. Anne clothes Laura's nude body before the police arrive to protect it from "violations of the outside world," just as she would protect her own children. Then Anne carries the news of Laura's death to her parents. Death does not lessen Mrs. Post's antipathy to her daughter, nor does it move Mr. Post enough (although he offers to pay expenses) to see Laura's remains. Anne alone carries out the burial rites: She scatters Laura's ashes in the peaceful woodland near Selby.

Since Laura and Anne connect only after the suicide, their stories are appropriately told in separate sections. In Laura's chapters, Anne is never a real person; she is an obsession born of desperation. Laura is equally without substance in Anne's chapters; Anne never pierces the taciturnity of this reclusive, troubled young woman.

Laura's fate justifies Anne's fears about her own life that outsiders think so solid. Laura confirms Anne's deepest fears: that destiny is obscure, that living is a ceaseless effort to compensate for disappointment, that parents have little to say but much responsibility for their offspring's fate, and that love is not a callus against life's lashes but an open wound through which pain and despair enter.

Enriching the novel's exploration of these themes are mirroring subplots and characters. Ed, for example, works weekends and nights at the Foster house. He often brings his son and frequently lingers for tea with Anne. She considers this intimacy to be friendship at first and later thinks it an incipient romance, but finally she realizes that Ed finds in her home the domestic idyll missing in his own. Since his wife has been stricken by a disease and rendered older, unattractive, and helpless, the Corcoran house has become an ill-kept ward.

Jane Watson is another version of the impulse to re-create what destiny has denied or destroyed. In the Paris of the 1920's, Jane shared Caroline Watson's passion for the arts and yearned to be more than a friend. Yet Jane fit no niche of natural relationship. Therefore she married Stephen Watson to be close to his mother. Like the Fosters, Jane married to invent domestic life.

The richest mirroring subplot is Caroline's story. Caroline fascinates Anne as artist and as mother. Anne recognizes that Caroline's painting is the work of a major twentieth century artist; Anne's catalog of her works will be a major scholarly accomplishment. Like Anne, Caroline is a mother. Anne wonders what is the relationship of career and biological fate?

Anne's insight is that the story of a successful woman is a story of escape from being female. It is an escape seldom successful because the world, Anne realizes, is fascinated by the private life of notable women in a way it is not curious about the personal dimension of famous men. To study an accomplished woman is to wonder whether she lived up to—or failed—the expectations of being a daughter, a lover, a wife, or a mother.

Like Anne, Caroline pursued a career despite her family's opposition. Caroline battled her father's will as Anne fought against her mother's expectations. Like Anne, Caroline worked at the same time she reared her son. Caroline succeeded at the first and failed at the second. She left Stephen to her family in the winter while she painted in Paris; in the summer she tried to be a mother. Even that short time was too long, so Caroline often locked herself away from Stephen to paint. Trying in later years to enter intellectual circles at Paris and failing, Stephen killed himself. Like Anne, he took revenge against the mother who kept distant.

Anne recognizes both Stephen's plight and Caroline's dilemma; she has been in their places. Thus Anne resists the temptation to judge artistic achievement by maternal ability. She concludes that Stephen's death is no argument against Caroline's merit as a painter or against a woman's pursuit of her talent.

Right after Laura's death Anne is unable to judge herself so dispassionately. Reared to accept responsibility and the world's opinion of appearances, Anne believes that Laura's suicide indicts her life. She readily accepts guilt for failing to love the unlovable girl. She convicts herself with the biblical passage that gives the novel its title: "Though I speak with the tongues of men and of angels, and have not charity, I am become as sounding brass, or a tinkling cymbal."

Later Anne realizes that she is no more brass or cymbal than anyone else. The death of Laura is a lesson about one of life's inevitable, unpleasant realities. Maternal love is no more innocent than any other love. It can create or it can murder. It draws everyone into the maelstrom of human interaction. It predictably falls short, not only of perfection but of expectation.

Men and Angels employs the remarkable style found in Gordon's earlier novels. It is simple, direct, provocative. Gordon's forte is the declarative sentence of one or two independent clauses built upon a metaphor or simile. Even as it quickly advances the plot, her style surprises the reader with striking images that amplify the emotion of a passage:

> The house in the morning thrummed with expectation. The morning sunlight, weak and ordinary, took on purpose. For the children, life was shining: they were going to the city. A wave of strangers would engulf them, beautiful, treacherous, and carry them on. They might see a movie being made; they might see a murder. It was nearly Christmas. Stores would be lit up, lights would be strung through the dense air.

Another dimension of Gordon's imagistic style is the resonance of names. Consider, for example, the implications of Anne's married name. Anne becomes a foster mother to Laura; her house is a foster home for the reinvented domesticity of Michael and Ed. "Foster" not only implies surrogate care, but also means to nuture helpless things. Just so, Anne fosters the growth of Peter and Sarah and fosters intimacy with Michael and her friends.

The only flaw in *Men and Angels* is Gordon's tendency to put explicit statements of theme into the mouth (or head) of the protagonist. Since the novel's events usually lead the perceptive reader to the same observation, these thematic assertions sound contrived. It is a minor lapse compared to the virtuosity of the alternating narrative and figurative language.

Men and Angels is an excellent novel. Its plot moves inevitably to catastrophe; its characters' fates engage the reader's sympathy; its themes challenge contemporary assumptions about home and parenting. Most important, its author cares about the best words in the best order.

Robert M. Otten

Sources for Further Study

America. CLIII, July 6, 1985, p. 19.
Christian Science Monitor. LXXVII, April 22, 1985, p. 21.
Commentary. LXXIX, June, 1985, p. 62.
Commonweal. CXII, May 17, 1985, p. 308.
Library Journal. CX, March 15, 1985, p. 72.
Los Angeles Times Book Review. April 14, 1985, p. 3.
The New Republic. CXCII, April 29, 1985, p. 34.
The New York Times Book Review. XC, March 31, 1985, p. 1.
The New Yorker. LXI, April 29, 1985, p. 132.
Newsweek. CV, April 1, 1985, p. 75.
Publishers Weekly. CCXXVII, February 8, 1985, p. 68.
Time. CXXV, April 1, 1985, p. 77.

MICROWORLDS
Writings on Science Fiction and Fantasy

Author: Stanisław Lem (1921-   )
Translated from the German by Bruce R. Gillespie, Werner Koopman, R. D. Mullen, Robert M. Philmus, Franz Rottensteiner, Elsa Schieder, and Darko Suvin; from the Hungarian by Istvan Csicsery-Ronay and Etelka de Laczay; and from the Polish by Robert Abernethy, Thomas E. Hoisington, and Darko Suvin
Edited, with an introduction, by Franz Rottensteiner
Publisher: Harcourt Brace Jovanovich (San Diego, California). 285 pp. $14.95
Type of work: Critical essays; memoir
Time: 1971-1984

A collection of Stanisław Lem's critical essays on science fiction published during the 1970's and 1980's, supplemented by an autobiographical essay

Stanisław Lem's *Microworlds* is a collection of his previously published essays, with an introduction by his longtime friend, translator, and literary agent Franz Rottensteiner. While it is very helpful to have these essays easily available, they represent a fraction of Lem's critical output. Since they were selected to meet different editorial requirements when first published, some subjects are dealt with in depth and some not at all.

Lem has written a full-length study of science fiction, *Fantastyka i futurologica* (1970); two of the chapters, "The Time-Travel Story and Related Matters of Science-Fiction Structuring" and "Metafantasia: The Possibilities of Science Fiction," are included in *Microworlds*. Rottensteiner observes that Lem had problems in locating sources for his history of science fiction, which may further account for his not dealing with certain subjects and authors. Balancing this weakness is Lem's strength as a scientist. Trained as a doctor, he rigorously applied both scientific knowledge and scientific method to his science-fiction essays and fiction. Lem has additionally published numerous scientific articles; he has a special interest in cybernetics. Two other significant untranslated works are *Summa Technologiae* (1964), now undoubtedly dated as to content but nevertheless still of interest to Lem's readers, and *Filozofia przyypadku* (1968), an attempt to construct an empirical theory to account for variant responses to works of literature by different cultures at different times.

Lem, though a writer of science fiction, is sharply critical of the genre, so much so that Science Fiction Writers of America once revoked his honorary membership. The articles related to the controversy, not included in *Microworlds*, were published in several successive issues of *Science-Fiction Studies* (July 1977, ff.). Though Lem is more concerned with intellectual and structural problems than he is with belletristic literature, he edited a series of works published in Poland, which included short stories by M. R. James and Stefan Grabiński and Ursula K. Le Guin's *A Wizard of Earthsea* (1968). Lem contributed an afterword to each volume; the analysis of Arkady and Boris Strugatsky's *Roadside Picnic* (1977), a Soviet work, appears in *Microworlds*. Of this essay, Rottensteiner observes that while Lem criticized American and English writers negatively, he was more cautious with comments on the Soviets since "objective discussion of the better works would be fraught with dangers for the writers discussed."

The essays are not presented in chronological order, the most recent, written in 1984, "Reflections on My Life," appearing first. Its place in the volume, however, is logical: The reader has an overview of Lem's life and the development of his thought and also his present evaluation of his work, including allusions to other essays appearing in *Microworlds*, and therefore has reference points from which to evaluate the subsequent articles. In the essay, Lem speculates on the relationship of chance and order in shaping his career not only as a writer but as a writer who "ceaselessly strives to reconcile contradictory elements of realism and fantasy." The theme recurs in many of the essays, notably in "Todorov's Fantastic Theory of Literature,"

The son of a wealthy doctor, Lem grew up in a safe and affluent household in Lemberg, now Lvov, in the Ukraine. Still, he constantly escaped into fictitious worlds, which he documented in detail, keeping all of his fantastic worlds and equally fantastic inventions and drawings secret. As a boy, he had access to his father's library, including medical books and specimens, sometimes with permission and sometimes without it. The library contained books in German and French as well as Polish; Lem learned to read these languages and also Latin. World War II abruptly changed his family situation, and Lem could easily speculate that the world was a "preestablished disharmony, ending in chaos and madness." In two novels, he deals with his wartime experiences, when he resembled more "a hunted animal than a thinking human being." In the first, *Wysoki zamek* (1966), he tries to recapture his childhood, "to peel away, as it were, the overlying strata of war, of mass murder and extermination, of the nights in the shelters during air raids, of an existence under a false identity, of hide-and-seek, of all the dangers, as if they never had existed." *Szpital przemienienia*, though all the settings and characters are imaginary, explores and attempts to exorcise one of the horrors of occupied Poland: the murder of mentally ill persons and the insane. Written in 1948, Lem's last year as a student, it could not be published until 1957.

In 1946, reduced to destitution by the war, Lem and his family moved to Kraków, living in a single room, while Lem's father, by then seventy-one, worked in the hospital. Lem began writing to help support the family. By 1947, he was employed as a junior research assistant for Konwersatorium Naukoznawcze (the Circle for the Science of Science). Lem read and compiled surveys of scientific periodicals, learning in the process to read English, though he has never learned to speak it or to understand spoken English. Here he had access to recent scientific works from around the world. The reading provided him with background for many of his subsequent works "that I can still acknowledge without shame," such as *Eden* (1959), *Solaris* (1961), and *The Invincible* (1964). His earlier works, he says, "oversimplify the world." Lem here applies to his own works the critical standards he stresses for all others: the necessity for rigorous logic based on scientific fact, the necessity of then stretching scientific concepts to new boundaries, and the necessity of creating works of literature rather than mass-produced variations on worn-out themes. In fact, Lem by precept and example approaches his works as a scientist or philosopher approaches the testing of a hypothesis or the development of a theory.

Despite his many works of science fiction, Lem became increasingly critical of the genre. H. G. Wells and Olaf Stapledon, he contends, were discoverers; most science-fiction writers after them became imitators. Attempting himself to break new ground, Lem experimented with reviews of fictitious scientific works. His own fiction, he admits, is not logically planned from beginning to end; spontaneity and trial and error play a large role in its creation. Lem has also written several comic, satiric science-fiction works. It is surprising that there are so few comic science-fiction writers, in view of the satiric content of much science fiction and the strong relationship between satire and fantasy.

In "On the Structural Analysis of Science Fiction," Lem first defines the "rules of the game" in conventional literature and goes on to point out how science fiction often violates these rules. Unlike mathematics, in which the terms used have no outward semantic meaning, literature uses words that refer to reality. In other words, the usual world of affairs is needed as a given if one is to appreciate the different worlds of myth and fairy tale. Lem distinguishes between "final" fantasy—fairy tales and science fiction—and "passing" fantasy. The latter is exemplified by Franz Kafka's "Metamorphosis" (1915), in which the fantastic outer events refer to inner realities. Science fiction is expected to be empirically realistic; if it is not, it becomes fantasy and is at its worst when its impossible aspects—time travel, for example—are used solely to illustrate impossible situations created by impossible premises. Then it becomes a game that, Lem suggests, is not worth playing. The bounds of the fantastic are limited and defined by knowledge. For example, when space travel was not a reality, one could travel as one pleased in space. Now one cannot. Science fiction could become a first-rate literary genre if it followed the rules, but to do so, Lem contends repeatedly, a new group of readers would have to be recruited from the mainstream. This has taken place since Lem's 1973 essay was written and, to some extent, was indeed the case at the time he wrote it. In the early 1970's, science fiction was beginning to be accepted on a scholarly level.

"Science Fiction: A Hopeless Case—with Exceptions" is introduced by a footnote in which Lem admits that there are errors in the essay, caused by the unavailability of books. His main point, that it is impossible to read everything and therefore it is the critic's job to winnow the mass of material, still holds. Especially in science fiction, he observes, one cannot read everything, and indiscriminate critics are worse than useless. In this essay, Lem addresses some of the reasons that science-fiction criticism is so weak.

Science fiction now belongs to the "Lower Realm" of literary genres and achieves the "Upper Realm," or mainstream, when it does at all, by virtue of excellence. For earlier writers such as Wells and Henry James, the barrier between fantasy and realism was nonexistent. Lem defines "trivial literature" as a mass product consumed by mass readers, whose merit is defined in terms of sales and which is perpetuated by the publishers' treatment of the writer as a commodity rather than as an artist, demanding alterations in works to fit the market. When science-fiction writers do succeed, they often attempt to break away from the Lower Realm and into the Upper. What the Upper Realm has is a critical establishment independent of the publishers, and this establishment does not allow science fiction equal status. One science-fiction writer whom Lem finds deserving of such status is Philip K. Dick. Lem later devoted an entire essay to Dick's work, also reprinted in *Microworlds*: "Philip K. Dick: A Visionary Among the Charlatans."

At his most pessimistic, Lem suggests that the sheer volume of published books may make mainstream literature go the way of science fiction, as the selection process is now often the result of "the random collision between prominent books and prominent critics." Lem does emphasize that any culture contains entertainment and passing trends. They are an essential part of the Zeitgeist, but an ephemeral one. The rules for selecting enduring literature do not deny entertainment value, but they do require something more. Let criticism cease to function, and works will be judged solely on their commercial success, the measure of their entertainment or fashionable value. Lem's pessimism about the power of criticism in mass culture has to some extent been validated as each year money looms larger in all cultural fields, though the number and variety of critics have multiplied. Criticism may not therefore be as influential as Lem contends. Contributing to the decline is the widespread prevalence of kitsch, a debased or sentimentalized version of an original masquerading as the real thing.

In his essay "The Time-Travel Story and Related Matters of Science-Fiction Structuring," Lem elaborates on the possible ramifications of logic in a science-fiction context. Considering the proposition "John is the father of Peter, or John is not the father of Peter," in the context of genetic engineering possibilities, Lem demonstrates how an individual could, given time travel, not only be his own father but also his own mother and how the definition of father can become extremely ambiguous in terms of genetic engineering possibilities. Time travel abounds in such paradoxes, and one can deal with them or ignore them entirely to establish another theme, as Ray Bradbury did in his short story "A Sound of Thunder."

Though Lem maintains that most time-travel themes are a device to write melodrama, romance, or adventure stories, he does note that the best of them are "pure" science fiction, logically built upon current scientific hypotheses, or departing from them only with reason. The difficulty with this approach, as in Lem's own *His Master's Voice* (1968), is that the novel can become a scientific or philosophical treatise rather than a novel showing an idea in action. Lem comes close to this defect in some of his other works as well. In general, science fiction is not a pure exercise in logic but involves at least the perspective of the author and (usually) the development of characters.

One of Lem's major points is that the realistic novelist does not invent the world he depicts; the science-fiction writer to a greater or lesser extent does and is therefore accountable for it. Lem maintains that most science-fiction writers do not create a truly original world but variations on a previous theme, usually with minimum intellectual structure and maximum peripheral plot. Even the better writers, such as Bradbury and J. G. Ballard, have emphasized literary quality at the expense of logic, providing "nonfantastic content, already old-fashioned, in an ethical, axiological, philosophical sense," and perceive science as having a negative impact altogether, leaving their works invariably pessimistic about the modern world and providing escapist and sentimental solutions. Thus, Lem concludes, they have "seriously damaged literature and culture" by abandoning "intellectual imagination."

Though Lem himself admits that the task is not now possible, in "Metafantasia: The Possibilities of Science Fiction," he attempts to construct a metatheory of science fiction. Here again he stresses the appeal of "intellectual adventure" rather than the conventional adventure story, admitting that to depict such adventure would require numerous changes in conventional narrative structure. What he suggests—a "collage" of hypotheses, newspaper articles, speeches, and the like, already used by John Dos Passos in *U.S.A.* (1937-1938)—is closer to docudrama than to the novel. Lem does not deal at all with the dramatization, stage or screen, of science fiction, though in some ways it is easier to get the kind of effect he is seeking in these media. On stage, where the actors make direct contact with the audience, abstract ideas become more accessible; on screen, by being able to show an experiment in action rather than describing it, or to express concepts in visual images, film or television can help the viewer to visualize ideas. Lem, however, is not advocating abandoning traditional narrative methods and structures altogether. Rather, he is suggesting possible new literary directions for which science fiction is uniquely suited.

Lem observes that a metatheory of literature has one major problem that metatheories of science do not: Creative works cannot be "facts" in the sense in which two plus two equals four. One can, however, trace the development of a given literature and attempt to predict its possible directions. Further, while narrative structures may become exhausted, new events do bring with them new content for fiction.

Content, however, is not literature's major problem in the twentieth century. Rather, it is the weakening and collapse of value systems, cultural norms, and the power of myth and religion; as old ones decline, no new ones take their place. Writers are left with neither taboos to resist nor a cohesive culture from which and to which to address their work. In the contemporary novel, the reader usually has to search for the meaning, and there may be multiple interpretations of each novel, or there may be deliberate meaninglessness. If an entire novel is structured on the principle of chance, the reader nevertheless attempts to make it a coherent whole.

Further, Lem continues, in science fiction there is no really agreed-upon theoretical base, including a definition of the genre itself. In a novel with a simple narrative line such as Daniel Keyes's *Flowers for Algernon* (1966), one sees the results for an individual but not for a society of the sudden artificial elevation of intelligence, leaving the story a variation on a theme, as are most others. The detective story, the romance, the adventure novel, the fairy tale, are the usual modes of narrative structure, and Lem finds them inadequate to deal with scientific phenomena: The "slick, closed, and completely ambiguous structures" will not do. Nor does criticism provide any guidelines for development. The greatest deterrent to the development of science fiction as literature is this lack of "independent, rational, and normative criticism that is neither destructive nor apologetic," Lem again concludes.

In a prefatory footnote appended to "Cosmology and Science Fiction," Lem warns that cosmology can quickly become outdated and is, on several counts, a difficult problem for science-fiction writers. Cosmologists, even those associated with such projects as Contact with Extraterrestrial Intelligence (CETI), are accumulating more and more evidence of the lack of other life-forms in the cosmos. What Lem does not note is the role of science fiction in stimulating exploration of the cosmos. Scientists interviewed at the time of the first flights to Mars commented that reading science fiction when they were young was a major factor in developing their interest in space, and even the dissenters muttered that it was necessary to take elaborate precautions on the assumption that one might encounter other life-forms because of the influence of science fiction. Lem observes that most science-fiction writers tend to ignore the major cosmological discoveries of their day, relying instead on fantasies of space and time travel. Lack of intellectual content in depicting alien cultures and outmoded attitudes toward warfare persist. A completely falsified and sentimentalized version of the cosmos results, as opposed to its actual "strange, icy sovereignty." This simplification of the cosmos, a literary device to which Lem himself has resorted, is a gradual mass development in science fiction with no individual writers really responsible. Also, the cruelty of the cosmos is not so readily understood as the cruelty of warfare. In concentrating upon the cosmos' population—human and alien—science fiction moves away from questions that might shed further meaning on human existence, as in Blaise Pascal's meditations on the universe. Instead of avoiding it, Lem's suggested solution is to take cosmic theory to even further logical limits. The concepts Lem describes are as much in the realm of poetry as philosophy, though Lem does not discuss poetry. Some contemporary poets, trained in science, do communicate accurately both the emotional and the intellectual content of contemporary science, but it would be highly improbable for science fiction written as poetry to be published or read, given the present state of literary culture.

In "Todorov's Fantastic Theory of Literature," Lem discusses the failure of logic when confronted with literary phenomena. Discussing Tzvetan Todorov's *Introduction à la littérature fantastique* (1970; *The Fantastic: A Structural Approach to a Literary Genre*, 1973), Lem argues that Todorov's structuralist approach is not valid, since complex literary works, in particular fantastic literature, resist being reduced to one structure. Further, as Lem observes with numerous flashes of his ironic wit, a piece of kitsch and a piece of genuine literature may have the same structure—it is by other means that one distinguishes them. The structuralists' theoretical equality of all works on the one hand, and a very selective examination of works to support the theory on the other, results in large, logical gaps in a system that prides itself on its logic. After this demolition of Todorov's theory of fantasy, Rottensteiner includes Lem's essay on Jorge Luis Borges, written in 1971. Here, Lem shows how successful fantasy is constructed, both greatly admiring Borges' work but also highly critical of it. It is the "logically perfect structure" Lem most admires, but he sees Borges as bound to the past. He constructs marvelous paradoxes and embellishments on the myths of the past, but, living at the end of this past as a creative source, he is an epigone. Lem's summary of Borges might well stand as his summary of other writers as well: "He has explicated to us paradises and hells that remain forever closed to man. For we are building newer, richer, and more terrible paradises and hells; but in his books Borges knows nothing about them."

Arkady and Boris Strugatsky's *Roadside Picnic* is also a science-fiction work that Lem admires. In his 1983 essay, the final one in *Microworlds*, he discusses the skill with which the Strugatskys maintain the mystery of the aliens and the logic with which they account for the objects the aliens have let fall from the sky or left behind them. Lem does find some logical discrepancies, adding that the writer of fantasy or science fiction has a much more difficult task in maintaining both scientific fact and mystery than does the theologian.

Lem's very insistence on logic is both one of his weaknesses and his strengths as a critic. As he repeatedly asserts, order, logic, and objectivity have long been needed in science-fiction criticism. Yet, as noted above, if a short story or novel is a mere exercise in logic, it can rapidly become a treatise instead. The method that works well for Lem is his own style and approach, and not necessarily one that is valid for others. It is a great temptation for writer as critic to attempt to rewrite another's work, and Lem does succumb to this temptation at times. Lem also can be dogmatic, and his language is often extremely abstract. Nor does he give many examples, and some of these are writers not easily accessible to English-speaking readers. Lem does not address the communication problems created for writers and readers by language barriers, though he himself has been limited in his studies by lack of access to the books, not only through lack of translations but also by the barrier of the Iron Curtain. Nevertheless, Lem is a pioneer in the field of serious science fiction and has many valid opinions and insights. Further, Lem's criticism, like that of any other author, is also part of his work and, as such, illuminates his own writings and approach. Despite his quarrels with the genre, despite the fact that he is "probably both dissatisfied with everything that I have written and proud of it," Lem continues to write. *Microworlds* is a useful guide to Lem's work as well as worth reading for itself. Rottensteiner's judicious editing has placed the essays in a logical sequence for the development of Lem's ideas. The bibliography includes essays, letters, interviews, and reviews; it would be even more useful if it included a chronology of Lem's life and works.

Katharine M. Morsberger

Sources for Further Study

Choice. XXII, June, 1985, p. 1488.
Kirkus Reviews. LII, November 1, 1984, p. 1039.
Library Journal. CX, February 1, 1985, p. 99.
Los Angeles Times Book Review. April 14, 1985, p. 10.
The New York Times Book Review. XC, March 24, 1985, p. 28.
The New Yorker. LXI, April 22, 1985, p. 143.
Publishers Weekly. CCXXVI, November 30, 1984, p. 85.

MIDAIR

Author: Frank Conroy (1936-   )
Publisher: E. P. Dutton/Seymour Lawrence (New York). 149 pp. $15.95
Type of work: Short stories
Time: The mid-twentieth century
Locale: The United States

> *The eight short stories in this collection examine various types of relationships such as those between people, between the past and the present, and between the rational and the irrational*

Midair is Frank Conroy's second book. At thirty-one, Conroy published his autobiography, *Stop-Time* (1967), the poignant account of a young boy growing up in the 1940's and early 1950's. The book received praise for its richly detailed picture of adolescence. In the eighteen-year interim between books, Conroy has taught at various universities and published short stories in *The New Yorker, Harper's Magazine*, and *Ararat*, some of which are collected in *Midair*. In 1981, he became the director of the literature program at the National Endowment for the Arts. Although the stories in this collection are not overtly autobiographical, Conroy has drawn on his many experiences to add color to his short stories.

In *Stop-Time*, Conroy focused on the relationship between an adolescent boy and the adult world surrounding him. In *Midair*, Conroy continues to explore the effects of various types of relationships, the most important of these being that between parent and child. He suggests that there is a deep and often unexplainable bond between children and parents that can be the cause of deep scars or the basis for profound love. Three of the eight stories in the collection present variations on this filial theme. The first of these is the title story, "Midair."

In "Midair," the relationship between Sean and his father is examined. As a six-year-old, Sean hardly knows his father, who has been confined in a mental hospital. One day, however, his father materializes and abruptly picks up Sean and his nine-year-old sister from school. They return to their fourth floor apartment, but since no one has a key, the father and the children ascend to the roof, climb down the fire escape, and enter through an open kitchen window. Later when the hospital attendants and the doctor arrive, the father refuses to unlock the door. As the attendants forcefully enter, he snatches Sean and rushes to the open window. Sean, for the moment, is suspended four flights above the street.

Although Sean blocks the incident from his memory, it affects him for the next forty years; he often dreams of people falling out windows, and years later he even duplicates the earlier incident. Determined to enter his absent lover's apartment, he goes to the roof of her apartment building. This time there is no fire escape, and he must lower himself down a steeply angled roof until he is poised above her window. Although he cannot reach the window, he is not disappointed because "he becomes aware that there is a reality that lies behind the appearance of the world, a pure reality he has never sensed before." Still he does not remember his earlier, frightening experience, which will continue to haunt him even when he himself becomes a husband and a father. When he hears of a baby falling out a window, he is alarmed and must sleep in the same room as his two young sons, Philip and John.

As the years pass, Sean is divorced, remarries, and teaches at a university. Finally forty years after the first incident, another one, equally harrowing, causes him to recall it. As Sean rides an elevator to his office on the sixty-fifth floor, it malfunctions, stopping between floors. The only other passenger, a young man who bears a strong resemblance to his son Philip, is terrified. Sean calms him, helping the young man to overcome his fear. Soon the elevator proceeds to the next floor, and the young man hurriedly gets out, astonished that Sean remains in the elevator to continue the ride to the sixty-fifth floor. Sean is no longer afraid. That night he remembers the early incident and finally accepts and understands who he is.

The narrative structure that Conroy employs in "Midair" will appear throughout the volume. In many of the stories, the present is juxtaposed against the past with rapid shifts from one to the other. In this manner Conroy implies that the present is determined by past events; the present can only be understood through reference to the past. Sean's difficulties can only be explained on the basis of an incident that happened when he was six, an incident that he himself had forgotten.

The theme of parent-child relationships that Conroy introduces in "Midair" is continued in several other stories. "Celestial Events" describes the closeness of Lewis, an adult, and his mother who dies from cancer. The death has left Lewis feeling dismantled—"in a dozen pieces" somewhat like his mother, who earlier had lost a breast to cancer. Lewis feels unconnected until, as in "Midair," a second incident occurs, which enables him to accept her death. When his mother was suffering from the intense pain of cancer, Lewis had purchased for her a radio with earphones so that she, concentrating on the music, could block out the pain. After her death, he listens to the same radio. One night he imagines that his mother is speaking to him over the earphones, reassuring him that everything is all right. He cries and finally is able to come to terms with his grief. Thus the pattern established in "Midair" is repeated here. The first incident disrupts the character's life, and the second one pulls the pieces of that life together; the result is a final acceptance of past events and an integration of those events with the present.

In "Midair," a man comes to terms with a father who has failed him, and in "Celestial Events," a man accepts the loss of a parent. In the concluding story, "The Sense of the Meeting," a father recognizes that, as his son matures, his love for his son must change as well. He no longer needs to protect him but must accept him as an adult.

One weekend Kirby travels to Philadelphia to visit his old college roommates of thirty years ago and to watch Alan, his son from his first marriage, play basketball for a college that is also Kirby's alma mater. Visiting his son causes Kirby to reconsider his relationship with him. When Alan was a young boy, Kirby was afraid of failing him and thus losing the boy's love. He also thought that he needed "to shelter the boy against some vague, unnamed threat." Now he wonders how his actions have affected Alan. Did Alan start playing basketball because that is what he thought his father wanted?—while all the time Kirby only showed an interest in the sport because he thought that his son was interested. Kirby concludes that love is complicated.

Kirby's confusion is resolved during the two basketball games that Alan plays. The first game on the weekend of the reunion is a disaster. Alan fumbles the ball and is taken out of the game until the final minutes, when the game is already lost. The rematch on the following weekend is the opposite of the earlier game. Alan smoothly orchestrates the play. He is in top form as he controls the ball and directs his teammates. During the second game, Kirby realizes that he no longer needs to protect his son nor does he need to be afraid of disappointing him; instead, they can meet as equals. A deep, strong, and secure bond has evolved.

"Midair," "Celestial Events," and "The Sense of the Meeting" examine close relationships. In "Car Games" and "Roses," Conroy considers the consequences when people fail to establish bonds with others. In "Roses," a bachelor artist has many brief encounters with lovely women, but since these are only casual contacts, the relationships are meaningless. Thus his life, an endless round of women and parties, is empty and unfulfilling.

In "Car Games," Conroy again uses an early incident to help explain the present events. In 1946, when Jack was twelve, he drove a car, his uncle Charlie's Model A, for the first time, and thus began his obsession with cars. Throughout his adolescence, cars were Jack's passion. He and a friend devised a race course through the campus of a local college, and nightly the two would challenge each other. On one memorable winter night, the two took turns making elaborate patterns in the newly fallen snow on a parking lot. Twenty-three years later and after sixteen years of marriage, Jack has lost interest not only in his wife but also in his Aston Martin.

Feeling uneasy at home, Jack takes his Aston Martin out on the expressway. When a distraught woman driving a Chrysler cuts in front of him, Jack catches up with her, driving as a good ice skater moves, weaving in and out of the traffic. Reminiscent of his high school days, the two are soon in a contest, traveling down the highway at one hundred miles per hour. As they vie for a single lane, the woman's car breaks through a guardrail and sails off over the river. Jack is amused at her plight, but a moment later his own car crashes into a concrete abutment. Having lost interest in his car and having failed to establish a relationship with another person, Jack, perhaps subconsciously, chooses suicide. Fittingly he dies in his car, the one thing that has given him pleasure.

The title story, "Midair," hints at the possibility of another level of reality, which Sean had sensed that night when he was high above the street on the steep roof of his lover's apartment building. In "The Mysterious Case of R" and "Transit," Conroy more explicitly questions the accepted concept of reality, suggesting that there are other levels beyond what can be seen. These stories present events for which there are no rational explanations.

On one level, "The Mysterious Case of R" can be read as a humorous justification of why Conroy himself has written so little since the publication of his autobiography. On another level, the story suggests that there is much that is unknown and not understood. The story, in the form of a letter, concerns a psychiatrist who at the end of his career writes of an incident that occurred when he was establishing his practice years ago. One of his first patients was R, a self-destructive but wealthy novelist. After many daily sessions at one hundred dollars each, R was no longer a danger to himself, and the psychiatrist was no longer struggling with his new practice. Unfortunately, after the analysis, R abandoned his fiction. When the psychiatrist urged him to write, he replied that it was not a writer's block, but that his reluctance was "due to the intercedence of particular Gods whose special interest was the prevention of bad prose on earth." R continued that he was to be believed because he was an angel. R's explanation astounded the psychiatrist, since he had been totally unaware of what seemed to be schizophrenic behavior. R concluded that "the artist who works without inspiration creates a dead child," and then he literally disappeared. Conroy leaves unresolved the question of whether R is truly an angel or if the highly respected doctor is in need of treatment himself.

Like "The Mysterious Case of R," "Transit" concerns the interpretation of reality, and also like the earlier story, it is written in the form of a letter. The epistolary form allows Conroy to establish evidence by which to judge the veracity of the narrator. In the story, E. Worel designs transit systems and has the opportunity to travel on one of his first projects, a system that runs from an airport to the center of the city. Instead of a routine trip, Worel experiences a series of bizarre incidents, which he describes to a colleague. He and several others wait for a train, but although the trains slow down, none stops. A young student reports that the exit from the station is locked. Finally a frustrated man stands in front of a slowly approaching train. The operator of the train is visible, but he takes no notice of the man on the tracks, and the train slowly knocks him down. When the crowd pounds upon the train, it finally stops, the man crawls out from under the train, and the people board. Worel is at a loss to explain the two-hour wait and the behavior of the trains' drivers. He concludes that the incident is "some kind of message, some kind of coded, whispered message that I should be able to figure out, but can't." The reader is also puzzled since there appears to be no rational explanation.

Conroy's stories are interesting statements on relationships. There are the relationships between parent and child, between student and teacher, and between lovers or husbands and wives. He also writes of other relationships. How does the past affect or determine the present? Conroy's frequent juxtaposition of the two suggests that there is a strong link. Several of the stories treat the relationship of the artist to his art. In "Roses," a model has no being outside of what she creates for the camera; in "The Mysterious Case of R," it is suggested that a novelist must be inspired. Finally Conroy asks his readers to consider their understanding of reality. Is reality only what is tangible? Some of the stories seem to indicate there are other unseen levels.

Conroy is an effective storyteller whose stories contain sharply detailed characters and finely drawn settings. He is adept at creating a believable fictional world.

Barbara Wiedemann

Sources for Further Study

Booklist. LXXXII, September 15, 1985, p. 107.
Kirkus Reviews. LIII. August 1, 1985, p. 725.
Library Journal. CX, October 1, 1985, p. 111.
Los Angeles Times. October 28, 1985, V, p. 6.
The New Republic. CXCIII, November 18, 1985, p. 48.
The New York Times. CXXXIV, September 7, 1985, p. 15.
The New York Times Book Review. XC, September 22, 1985, p. 12.
Publishers Weekly. CCXXVIII, August 9, 1985, p. 63.
The Village Voice. XXX, September 24, 1985, p. 51.
Vogue. CLXXV, September, 1985, p. 498.
Washington Post Book World. XV, September 15, 1985, p. 2.

MIKHAIL BAKHTIN

Author· Katerina Clark (1941-   ) and Michael Holquist (1935-   )
Publisher: The Belknap Press of Harvard University Press (Cambridge, Massachusetts). Illustrated. 398 pp. $25.00
Type of work: Biography and literary criticism
Time: 1895-1975
Locale: The Soviet Union

A biography that attempts to describe the life and to explain the complex texts of a thinker who is beginning to have an impact on several different disciplines a decade after his death

The problems of writing a biography of Mikhail Bakhtin are formidable, and this book has only partly solved them. It is difficult to speak in a clear, readily understandable manner about Bakhtin. What field was he in? For many years he had no institutional or academic affiliation at all. Was he what might be called vaguely a "thinker," or, as the authors suggest, was he a "philosophical anthropologist"? Was he primarily a literary critic? Or was he a linguist, religious philosopher, Marxist theoretician, folklorist, psychologist, or social scientist? One of the most fascinating aspects of Bakhtin's writings is that he resists all these pigeonholes. Above all he is synthetic, forging new, original, and convincing unities.

This would seem to point toward a biographical approach that follows Bakhtin's intellectual growth and evolution, charting the strands of these different syntheses during Bakhtin's life. Instead of this format, however, Katerina Clark and Michael Holquist alternate chapters about Bakhtin's life with chapters explaining his works. The authors have done thorough research into Bakhtin's life, and this material is as abundant as that of the interpretive chapters—the proportions are about equal. This is not only biography but also a scholarly investigation of texts. Unfortunately, the abrupt alternations between the two reduce the sense of development and flow that a genuine intellectual biography is capable of giving. Why did the authors decide against a uniform, consistent approach? Perhaps they thought some problems had to be cleared up first.

There is the problem of the "disputed texts." According to Clark and Holquist (and others—the contention is not theirs alone), several of Bakhtin's writings were published under the names of friends: "Vološinov" and "Medvedev." A reader unacquainted with the texts in question might think, perhaps this is true, but in the view of the present writer, even a cursory examination of the disputed texts shows that they differ from Bakhtin's works both in form and in content. For example, Vološinov was a committed Marxist while Bakhtin was a Neo-Kantian. Why do the authors make this rather doubtful claim? It is true that Bakhtin and Vološinov were friends and members of the same discussion group. They were influenced by similar books and lectures; possibly they shared notebooks. Yet they remain far apart. The Vološinov books are fascinating, their intellectual and literary quality is high, but this is not in itself a reason for attributing them to Bakhtin. The thesis of Clark and Holquist has already received some sharp rejoinders in specialized publications; the balance of evidence does not yet favor it, and it remains speculative.

One of the problems with this book is that the chapters devoted to the explanation of texts tend toward paraphrase and are far too uncritical, making few distinctions between what is original in Bakhtin's thought and what is derivative or opportunistic. Much is strikingly original. Bakhtin might well have been one of the more interesting philosophical minds to survive in Russia in the postrevolutionary period. The authors' practice of explaining all of Bakhtin's ideas together, however, of identifying with him too closely and failing to assume critical distance, undercuts the higher claims that might be made for him. A more critical, nuanced interpretation of Bakhtin will have to wait for a future study.

The chapters on Bakhtin's biography are easier to read and clearer than those on the texts, and the investigation of his life is probably the most valuable part of the book. The authors did much original research in the Soviet Union, interviewing friends and acquaintances of Bakhtin. (There is a tantalizing reference to Yuri Andropov, who took an interest in Bakhtin.) The Soviet authorities seem to have been quite forthcoming in aiding Clark and Holquist with their research. Bakhtin's life was an interesting one. He had the misfortune to live in the least auspicious of times—at some points the book almost seems to be about madness, or about the madness of a period. Bakhtin's coming of age coincided with the revolution. He lived most of his life in complete obscurity, and as Clark and Holquist make clear, this was largely his own fault: "Bakhtin's problem in publishing . . . continued to be his phlegmatic nature and his inability to bring any text to completion." He had almost none of the aggression, or narcissism, that writers often have. During World War II the publishing house that was to print his manuscript on Johann Wolfgang von Goethe was destroyed by a German bomb, and his manuscript was lost. He had one carbon copy, but paper was scarce and he used most of this copy for rolling cigarettes. It was difficult to publish without an institutional affiliation, and later, after his arrest and exile to Kazakhstan, he was an "undesirable." It seems that Bakhtin did not have a highly developed sense of individuality or a unique personalized style. This corresponds to his philosophical position, which was highly skeptical of the role of the individual, which he tended to denigrate as "subjective." Some of his essays read like a string of highly generalized assertions with few links between them. Often they lack the apparatus of orderly, gradual development; clearly made, careful distinctions; and a regular appeal to persuasion, analogy, evidence, and professional authority that the Western reader might expect. Further, Bakhtin did not respect the divisions between disciplines—

his interests shifted numerous times during his life, with the result that his writings cannot have an impact on any single "field." He had a unique personality: absorptive and synthetic, accepting, modest, not rebellious—it is claimed that he loved disguises. Bakhtin believed that meaning is always a function of two or more consciousnesses: "Creativity is in essence anonymous."

One of the most interesting aspects of Bakhtin's thought is his belief that there is no such thing as single "fields" or "disciplines," at least as these are currently defined. This absence of demarcations is not a trifling matter and goes to the heart of Bakhtin's philosophy: He wanted to abolish the traditional distinction between the subject and the object as a basis for a theory of knowledge. He believed that the act of communication, whether in life or in literature, is always dual, requiring a speaker and an addressee. Communication is unthinkable without the two being present. Hence all speech and writing is a form of dialogue, and its basic building block is what he calls the "utterance," a social act requiring a social context. In Bakhtin's words: The "individual and subjective are both grounded . . . by the social and objective. What I know, see, want, love, recognize, and so on, cannot be assumed. Only what all of us speakers know, see, love, recognize—only those points on which we are all united can become the assumed part of an utterance."

The "other," or interlocutor, with whom the individual speaks has an enormous importance in Bakhtin's schema. Dialogue can become internalized, resulting in what Bakhtin calls "inner speech"; in literature, the writer internalizes his audience. For Bakhtin, man is above all a social animal, and his individuality has narrowly circumscribed limits. Speech is impossible as an individual act—it requires a social context to come into being. This has important implications for literary theory and for what is often called the "triangle" of literary communication with the writer at one point, reality or experience at a second point, and the reader at the third. Bakhtin's contention that the writer internalizes the audience has a broad array of specific applications. Literary creation, and especially the novel, can be "polyphonic"—to use Bakhtin's term—with a variety of dialogues taking place; these manifold interactions are explained in detail in Bakhtin's books on Fyodor Dostoevski and François Rabelais. Clearly, Bakhtin's literary theory is entirely different from that of the Formalists, with whom he frequently polemicized. As Clark and Holquist put it, "There is no such thing as 'the text itself,' that autotelic object dreamed up by Russian Formalists and American New Critics. There are only texts that are more or less implicated in their environments." Bakhtin's theories are also at the opposite pole from those of Jacques Derrida and the deconstructionists, who tend to deny to literature any reference to reality.

The implications of Bakhtin's philosophy for linguistics are equally radical and far-reaching. He stressed the primacy of dialogue over monologue, the importance of what he termed the utterance, and the inability of descriptive systems based on logical models to comprehend the variety and historicity of meaning. Bakhtin was at odds with Ferdinand de Saussure and Structuralist linguistics; he wanted to include in his description of language all the factors arising from dialogue and social context—all the factors outside words that have a profound bearing on their meaning. The number of these factors is so high it is almost inconceivable, and most linguists have carefully excluded them from their accounts because they undermine the attempt to describe language as a system. For Bakhtin, the conceptual power of these systems is limited; "by concentrating on words outside the contexts in which they are used, linguists have bought their neat paradigms and dictionary definitions at the price of what is most important in language, the capacity of words to mean." According to Clark and Holquist, "Linguists have looked at language from the wrong end of the telescope in their attempts to gain a global view. Bakhtin, by contrast, focuses his attention on the individual speaker rather than on the chimera of 'the words themselves.'" Bakhtin considered an utterance a more comprehensive unit than a sentence; it underlies the completeness of sentences which act as its parts. Bakhtin has some excellent thoughts on the inadequacy of pronouns and on discourse as action. He has harsh words for traditional linguistics, which he describes as a child of philology, growing out of the study of dead languages. The first philologists and the first linguists, he says, were always and everywhere priests, who elevated their study to the level of a mystery, thereby removing it from the domain of everyday communication. For Bakhtin, language was not a "Platonic dream," nor did it partake of Leibnizian timelessness or Cartesian logic: "It is not the abstract system of linguistic norms . . . but the social event of verbal interaction implemented in an utterance." Bakhtin recognized that he was more concerned with communication than most linguists, so perhaps his "philosophy is a 'meta-' or 'trans-' linguistics insofar as it includes in language factors that are shunned by most linguists."

One major weakness in Bakhtin's thought that the authors do not take fully into account is his anti-individualist bias. The stress upon social context is fine and relatively easy to accept; it is one of Bakhtin's major theses and a welcome corrective. What does not come into focus in this study, however, is the real nature of the individual in Bakhtin's thought and its implications. Bakhtin's social environment is all-encompassing. The individual is not a self but a "nonself" who, through the acquisition of different "languages," moves to a "self" that is the sum of his discursive practices. Bakhtin's individual has little ability to present effective resistance to evil in society or to make significant choices. Perhaps this reflects Bakhtin's youthful ideal of collectivity, or *sobornost'*. The concept deprives the individual, however, of an important moral dimension. The difficulty is compounded by the tendency of Clark and Holquist to use the term "moral" or "ethics" in far too loose a manner. There is no discussion whatever of the ability of the single person to criticize his society or follow his conscience. No doubt these topics were taboo in Bakhtin's day, but to what degree is this taboo incorporated into the fabric of Bakhtin's thought? The authors do not make this clear. As a result, their use of words such as ethics or morality comes perilously close to conformism and compulsion.

A final problem in the presentation of the book has to do with Stalinism. One of the authors, Katerina Clark, has discussed Stalinism in an earlier study, *The Soviet Novel: History as Ritual*, which is referred to in the discussion of Bakhtin's response to Stalinism. In Bakhtin's book on Rabelais, he compared the "official language" in the 1530's—in the court of François I— to the "official language" in the 1930's under Joseph Stalin. (Bakhtin's treatment owed much to the dissertation and articles on Rabelais by the Austrian-American scholar Leo Spitzer; it is peculiar that the authors do not mention this fact.) This comparison is tenuous enough, containing obvious Aesopian references; it recalls a study by the Polish critic Jan Kott comparing the politics in William Shakespeare's plays to twentieth century politics and war. The statement by Clark and Holquist that the epistemological principle of Stalinism is "the vertical ordering of all reality," however, and their assertion that this is "a crude form of Neo-Platonism," are serious blemishes on the book. The reader is referred to Clark's *The Soviet Novel*, which describes parallels between what she calls "High Stalinist myth" and Plato's myth of the cave in *The Republic*. The differences between these doctrines far outweigh any similarities. The notion of archetypes, or *paradeigmata*, has no counterpart in the literature—or propaganda—of Stalinism, nor does the key Platonic concept of participation. The comparison with Platonism is not merely fanciful impressionism, it is a mistake and disfigures both books. When Clark and Holquist refer to "the prevailing idealism" of Bakhtin's day, it is unclear what they are writing about. Clearly the Stalinism of Clark and Holquist is not the Stalinism of Alexander Solzhenitsyn, Roy Medvedev, or A. Antonov-Ovseyenko. There was ritual in Stalin's day, but there was much more than that. The authors' treatment of the period is peculiarly abstract, sanitized, and one-sided.

Mikhail Bakhtin emerges from this study as a figure of major importance. The authors have unearthed useful, relevant information, and their presentation of Bakhtin's ideas communicates their overall thrust as well as their originality. Perhaps the stress on Bakhtin's life and the outline of his ideas are what is needed at the present moment. The authors' claim, however, of his authorship of the Vološinov texts is premature, and more skepticism toward their subject would have been in order. A more refined and critical treatment of Bakhtin's ideas will have to wait for a future book.

John Carpenter

Sources for Further Study

Choice. XXII, April, 1985, p. 1148.
Kirkus Reviews. LII, December 1, 1984, p. 1129.
The New Republic. CXCII, April 8, 1985, p. 38.
The New York Times Book Review. XC, February 10, 1985, p. 32.
Publishers Weekly. CCXXVI, December 14, 1984, p. 47.
Science and Society. XLIX, Fall, 1985, p. 373.
Times Literary Supplement. June 14, 1985, p. 675.

MINDS, BRAINS AND SCIENCE

Author: John Searle (1932-   )
Publisher: Harvard University Press (Cambridge, Massachusetts), 107 pp. $10.00
Type of work: Philosophy

An inquiry into the relationship of human beings to the rest of the universe, from the perspective of philosophical analysis and modern physical science

In 1948, the British Broadcasting Corporation (BBC) established the annual Reith Lectures, six half-hour radio talks broadcast over the BBC Home Service, in honor of Sir John C. W. Reith, managing director (1922-1926) of the BBC and director-general (1927-1938) of the successor corporation. The first Reith Lectures, given by the noted philosopher Bertrand Russell, set the tone for those that followed. Since that inaugural series, the talks, on many issues of contemporary intellectual, political, or social importance, have been addressed to a general audience with curiosity and intelligence enough to follow the development of a coherent argument, despite the lack of technical expertise in the field discussed.

Minds, Brains and Science is a slightly revised version of the 1984 Reith Lectures given by John Searle, professor of philosophy at the University of California, Berkeley, and only the second philosopher (after Russell) to have been honored as Reith Lecturer. In his introduction, Searle explains that the general theme of the lectures—"the relationship of human beings to the rest of the universe"—is easily adaptable to the special format of the radio series, six independent but related talks, each of which can stand alone or be taken together with the others in a broader examination of the central theme. In choosing so large a general theme, Searle admits to a missionary interest in making "the results and methods of modern analytic philosophy [with which Searle is particularly associated] . . . available to a much wider audience." By his own account, Searle resisted the temptation to revise and annotate his lecture texts, preferring instead to make the book as informal as possible, in the hope of reaching the same sort of audience that the radio series anticipated.

The book thus carries with it both the advantages and the liabilities of its original form, expanded for clarity in some places but altered only by the greater ease with which a reader may move back and forth in the overall argument. First among the advantages is Searle's characteristic conversational style—fluid, witty, pugnacious—which keeps the essays from bogging down in any of the numerous philosophical quicksands that lie in their way. Searle's capacity for the brief but telling outline of various philosophical positions not only makes sense of the immediate context but also places the issues under discussion in a larger framework of philosophical debate over perennial questions. Finally, the frequent repetition of major points—always necessary in a lecture format—usefully keeps the reader on track in the development of occasionally abstruse or complex ideas.

The liabilities of the form stem partly from the very complexity that Searle is seeking to untangle and illuminate. Searle's central focus on the conflict between the conception of freely willed mental experience and that of a deterministic physical universe creates a difficult problem in itself, since its presuppositions sometimes run counter to commonsense ideas of the natural order—ideas that Searle's lucid exposition of alternative views can only partially replace. Searle's accounts of his philosophical opponents and their views, necessarily abbreviated by the requirements of the format but sometimes too slight to provide a useful sense of the opposition's real depth, occasionally verge upon caricature. Finally, Searle's own vigorous and combative style occasionally features rhetorical feints to ward off possibly mortal assaults that are never completely put to rest.

Even with these formal liabilities, Searle's book is a richly challenging analysis of important questions about the human place in the universe, beginning in the first essay with the relationship between the human mind and the human brain. In the second, Searle considers "artificial intelligence" and the idea of "thinking machines," extending his inquiry, in the third essay, to the accuracy of the "computer" model for the human mind. The fourth essay advances an argument about intentionality, the structure of human action in the world, which seeks to clarify and resolve some of the difficulties already presented. Having given these arguments, Searle uses the last two essays to consider consequences in particular areas of concern: the status of the social sciences in the hierarchy of scientific endeavor (in the fifth essay) and the freedom of human will (in the sixth). Closing with a brief reading list for further study and a name-subject index, the volume thus surveys some of the most provocative and contentious areas in the realm of epistemology, ethics, and philosophy of mind.

Searle's method in dealing with these various problems is grounded in his philosophy, the study of the formal relationships between the ultimate structures of language and reality. In general, he approaches the claims made for each position as definitions reducible by strictly logical, syntactic analysis to lucid statements of relationship between ultimately existent things; definitions which fail this test of lucidity and relationship must therefore be regarded as errors distorting accurate knowledge of reality. Unlike Russell, the originator of the analytical school, Searle does not finally identify an irreducible pluralism—as between mind and matter, for example—in the constitution of the universe; indeed, the earlier chapters of this book support a fundamentally materialist, monistic constitution of reality, whereby appearances of pluralism are explained by the differences in the manifestations of physical reality at the subatomic (Searle's "micro") and sensible ("macro") levels.

An outline of the austere analytical method, however, does not do justice to its manifestation in this book, which, although occasionally difficult, is neither arcane nor academically pretentious. In part because Searle sometimes bases his arguments upon "commonsense" propositions (that is, upon the use of language by naive speakers who accept without question the conventions of their language system), his development of analytical constructs generally proceeds by analogy from the immediate and familiar to the abstract and difficult. Furthermore, the analogies themselves provide Searle with the opportunity to display both the acuity and the whimsy that are characteristic signs of his wit. Overall, then, despite the rigorous approach and the intellectual difficulties, the text itself is highly readable and comprehensible if one is willing to accept the conditions of the various arguments' development.

The first essay, "The Mind-Body Problem," addresses the central topic from which the topics of the later essays may be drawn as corollaries. Searle attempts to answer the long-canvassed problem of mental-physical dualism by pointing out that the mind and the body interact, but not as separate or discrete entities, since the mind is a "macro" manifestation of physical characteristics of the brain. This position allows him to address several related problems—the possibility of consciousness and of intentionality, the accommodation of mental subjectivity in objective physical reality, and the mental causation of physical events—by asserting that, since mental experiences have their basis in physical reality (that is, in the microstructure of the brain), there is no inconsistency in holding both the physicalist and the mentalist views simultaneously: "As far as we know anything about how the world works, they are not only consistent, they are both true."

As its title suggests, the second essay, "Can Computers Think?" considers the matter of artificial intelligence and the claims of computer technology to have created "thinking machines," claims that would necessarily deny the biological nature of human thought. Through a series of "thought experiments," Searle argues that, since computers are machines, physical systems that perform certain kinds of binary manipulations with data, they may be said to possess a syntax (that is, the rules for manipulating the data) but not a semantics (that is, the system by which meaning may be derived from the data). Thus, computers may be able to simulate certain processes without being able to duplicate their meaning. In other words, computers are defined by their formal structure, whereas minds are defined by their mental contents (or semantic systems). As a result, Searle argues, a computer program may provide the syntax (or formal structure) that mimics a mind, but no program could provide the semantic powers necessary to create a mind—a position that reinforces the first essay's claim of the biological nature of mental states.

In the third essay, "Cognitive Science," Searle investigates the validity of attempts to place theories about human behavior on a scientific footing of the same kind as used in physics or the other hard sciences. In attacking cognitivism, Searle admits its attraction: Our present explanatory models for human behavior (often derived from computer technology) incline us mistakenly to assume an identity between the "rules" that machines follow and the "rules" that humans follow, especially when no other explanation of the relationship between mind and brain is available. Using material developed in the previous lectures, Searle argues that cognitivism mistakes the character of the rules that humans follow, since those rules do not strictly depend upon the formal structure of behavior but rather upon the meaning that shapes that formal structure. From the outside, Searle argues, machines and humans appear to follow the same kinds of rules; the differences—overlooked by cognitivism—lie in the mental content with which humans invest such rules and which machines can simulate but not duplicate. In conclusion, Searle argues that there is no need to posit an area of inquiry such as that claimed by cognitivism, since there is no intermediate level of phenomena between the mental states and the physical structures that produced them.

As a group, the first three essays lead directly to the inquiry set out in the fourth essay, "The Structure of Action," which addresses the place of intentionality in human behavior, a topic that Searle examines in much greater detail in *Intentionality: An Essay in the Philosophy of Mind* (1983). Searle identifies three characteristics of human behavior: first, that intentional states have both a form and a content of a certain type; second, that these states include notions of the conditions of their satisfaction; and third, that these states sometimes cause things to happen. In less abstract terms, human intention includes both a mental and a physical component (as, for example, the intention to walk home), the conditions necessary to realize the intention (walking toward, then arriving at home), and sometimes the beginning of that realization (by engaging in the appropriate physical actions of directed walking, and so on). Second, since human beings in intentional states can identify both the intention and the physical action that they think will realize the intention, any explanation of behavior must have the same content as the intention that causes that behavior. Finally (and most significantly in terms of Searle's other work), intentions are shaped by their relationship to a "network" of other intentions that qualify and characterize the conditions of satisfaction represented in the intention itself, and the whole network of satisfactions is itself shaped by human characteristics and qualities that are not themselves mental phenomena.

The fifth essay, "Prospects for the Social Sciences," takes up some of the material already canvassed in the third essay in order to examine the claims of the social sciences to be scientific in the strictest sense. Searle points out that the social and natural sciences are radically unlike in character and quality. This unlikeness is not merely the consequence of the difference between social and (nonhuman) physical phenomena nor that of the unsystematic form that social phenomena present. According to Searle, the fundamental difference between the natural and social sciences, and the reason that the social sciences will never be able to attain to the same level of systematic application, lies in the different sources of action that apply to the different areas of inquiry: The physical sciences address actions that spring from wholly physical sources, whereas the social sciences address actions springing from the mind. Thus, as Searle argues in the earlier essays, since the kinds of actions addressed are constitutively different, the criteria of judgment must also be different, so that the social sciences err insofar as they attempt to pursue the goals appropriate to the natural sciences.

Searle undertakes an examination of perhaps the most basic of the questions that he addresses in the last essay, "The Freedom of the Will." He begins with a review of the three positions that are most commonly offered to the problem of human will: determinism, the idea that all events and actions are determined by physical constraint; free will, that all mental events and intentions are open to the free choice of the human being; and compatibilism, the position that accepts a human free will limited but not constrained by physical necessity—"it is that corner of determined human behaviour where certain kinds of force and compulsion are absent." After reviewing the positions and the various arguments and evidence in support of each, Searle considers whether any of the three is consistent with the view of human mental and physical reality as outlined in the earlier essays, concluding that the model of the mind-brain relationship that he provided in the first essay (and supported by scientific inquiry since the beginning of the modern period) offers no place for truly free will. Rather, Searle argues, human beings live their lives upon the founding assumption that their actions are free and that they remain free in intention despite physical constraints that prohibit the satisfaction of some of those intentions.

As a whole, *Minds, Brains and Science*, although witty and refreshing to read, presents a bleak picture of the human relationship to the physical universe. On the one hand, the early parts of the book appear to reclaim some particularly human characteristics of thought and intention from the grasp of those who champion artificial intelligence; on the other, Searle's basic model of the mind-brain relationship and its implication in the structure of a universe determined at the microlevel make those human characteristics perhaps less valuable. His general argument, that there is no fundamental inconsistency between the commonsense notion of mental life and the nature of the physical universe as described by the sciences, may resolve a long-standing philosophical question, but it does so by abandoning humankind's claims to any conspicuous singularity.

Dale B. Billingsley

Sources for Further Study

Best Sellers. XLV, May, 1985, p. 76.
Choice. XXIII, September, 1985, p. 133.
The New York Times Book Review. XC, May 12, 1985, p. 20.
Times Literary Supplement. December 14, 1984, p. 1442.
Virginia Quarterly Review. LXI, Summer, 1985, p. 99.

MR. PALOMAR

Author: Italo Calvino (1923-1985)
Translated from the Italian by William Weaver
Publisher: Harcourt Brace Jovanovich (San Diego, California). 130 pp. $12.95
Type of work: Novel
Time: The twentieth century
Locale: The modern world

In a series of anecdotal visions and analyses, Mr. Pálomar, a representative of twentieth century man, contemplates

> Principal character:
> PALOMAR, the protagonist, a representative of twentieth century man

Mr. Palomar (published in Italy in 1983 as *Palomar*) joins an ample body of work by the late Italo Calvino, the best-known author of Italian fiction in the twentieth century. Calvino's works, both short stories and novels, seem to run in two streams or extremes. On the one hand, he is known as a masterful storyteller, as is suggested by his popular *Italian Folktales* (1956). On the other, he has attained even more fame as an innovator of and experimenter with fictional form (see, for example *If on a Winter's Night a Traveler*, 1979). While it may seem contradictory to acclaim an author as both a grand storyteller and as one who shuns traditional narrative to focus on form, both extremes work for Calvino, perhaps because of his clear devotion to writing and to language.

The fact that so many of Calvino's works have been translated into English, as well as into many other languages, attests the universal appeal of his writing. *Mr. Palomar* should prove equally successful. As to which stream it follows, readers should be aware that there is no full story here. Instead, Calvino offers glimpses into the thoughts (rather than the life) of one Mr. Palomar, about whom the reader knows very little, at least in terms of conventional characterization. Yet, what Mr. Palomar thinks about his surroundings finally does reveal much about his own character and about twentieth century man in his technical world.

Mr. Palomar consists of a series of anecdotal visions and analyses. One follows the protagonist as he moves from place to place, contemplating aspects of nature and civilization. The basic divisions of the novel are three: "Mr. Palomar's Vacation"; "Mr. Palomar in the City"; and "The Silences of Mr. Palomar." Following Calvino's attachment to numerical symmetries, each of these sections is subdivided into three, and these, in turn, have three sections. Thus in the vacation segment, Mr. Palomar's thoughts are focused on phenomena that he encounters at the beach (a wave, a topless bather, and a sun ray); in the garden (tortoises mating, blackbirds' whistles, and the idea of a lawn); and in contemplation of the sky (the moon, the planets, and the stars).

Mr. Palomar seems obsessed by his personal relationship with the cosmos. In the segment on the sun's ray, for example, he resists leaving the sea, for he perceives a direct link with the sun based on the fact that, as he swims westward, the sun's sword appears to move with him. He has a similar reaction to his viewing of the moon, although he finally gives that up, too: "At this point, assured that the moon no longer needs him, Mr. Palomar goes home."

This personalized relationship is but one way to establish a link with his surroundings. Another, even more prevalent, is to analyze, in minute detail, all that he sees. It is not a coincidence that the protagonist shares his name with a famous observatory (Mount Palomar in California). To make sure that no reader misses the connection, Calvino includes a specific reference to the telescope in the section devoted to the planets. By examining his environment so closely, Mr. Palomar would seem to make it his own. His desire would be to master one element, then move on to another, slowly but surely conquering the universe.

The pattern is announced in the very first section, entitled "Reading a wave." At first glance, the reader might well mistake the "reading" for "riding," as the letters are very close, and riding is an activity one associates with waves. Mr. Palomar, however, is not an active man, as the reader will soon learn. Instead, he is a passive individual who analyzes, in addition to those things mentioned from the first section, such items as going shopping to buy goose fat or cheese, going to the zoo, and thinking about death. For Mr. Palomar, even a trip to the cheese shop can turn into an allegory of life.

One might very well question the type of life Mr. Palomar leads, if he spends so much time analyzing. If he is thinking all the time, it seems that there would be few moments left for feeling or for enjoyment. This is precisely Calvino's message, as shown particularly in the segment concerning the topless bather. Mr. Palomar passes her by several times, always conscious of what his actions might convey as a communication to the young woman or to society in general. Once again, the activity is to read a sign into the scene. Mr. Palomar is so lost in his thoughts, however, that he fails to realize how annoying his frequent passings have become. The woman finally departs in disgust.

The drawing on the dust jacket of the English-language edition suggests the same theme. Against a white background and within a pink frame, there is a copy of Albrecht Dürer's *Draftsman with Reclining Woman*. The black-and-white drawing shows a draftsman gazing from a special optical device through a rectangular-netted screen enclosed in a wood frame. In the past, it was common for artists to use such devices to make drawings of landscapes as accurate as possible. The object of this draftsman's gaze, however, is not a landscape but a woman in a very seductive pose. The frame is appropriately placed in the center of the drawing, with the two figures on either side—appropriate, in that analysis is incompatible with eroticism. Thus, the frame separates the two, establishing a space, or a distance, between them.

This notion of pitting what is natural against what is imposed through science or through other artificial means is consistent with the rest of the book. An important theme soon emerges: that twentieth century man, as a true child of his civilization, tries to relate all that he sees to what is technical. Even phenomena that are the very essence of Nature are in this book compared to man-made or man-conceived things. Examples abound, and they generally appear in the form of similes—thus Calvino, through Mr. Palomar's thoughts, moves from relatively obvious comparisons (birds are like airplanes) to others which are quite unusual, if not startling or even silly. To Mr. Palomar, for example, a giraffe's neck resembles the arm of a mechanical crane; the iguana's skin is like a dress; the white plates on the iguana look like a hearing aid; and Jupiter has something in common with a scarf.

Mr. Palomar observes, describes, questions, and analyzes all that meets his gaze. He considers everything from objects to ways of thinking and states of being. This pattern is established quickly and developed carefully throughout the novel. At this level of meaning, the reader should recognize Calvino's underlying contention that man has become too involved in analyzing life to live it. Yet there is more to be gained from a reading of *Mr. Palomar*. At the end of each segment, contained in a mere couple of sentences or in a short paragraph, a parallel pattern soon emerges. After the meditation, after the abstractions, Mr. Palomar, the thinker, returns to his status as Mr. Palomar, the man. The reader is able to catch him at his most vulnerable moments, as he reacts with unmasked feelings to what is happening. It is this vulnerability which contributes to the reader's appreciation of the character of the protagonist. Mr. Palomar might well protest that he wants to be a detached observer, a thinker who tries to keep sentiment or feelings out of his perceptions, but in his effort to represent modern man, or Homo sapiens, as a thinking creature, he remains a man after all, a man of feelings as well as knowledge.

Beyond this level of appreciation, there is a more serious aspect to the novel. As Mr. Palomar focuses on his environment, there is a progression from the somewhat frivolous to the more serious, from the mating of tortoises to the contemplation of death. One can learn from this book as from a series of essays treating aspects of the condition of man. Thus the reader is invited to contemplate philosophical issues and to evaluate the questionable value of certain of civilization's "contributions."

Finally, one must appreciate *Mr. Palomar* as a delightful work that engages the reader on the level of language. Although there is a certain loss from any translation, the prose of this novel has a wonderful rhythm; it is clear that Calvino takes great care in his selection of words and in their effect when assembled in particular ways. A striking example can be found in the section that begins Mr. Palomar's experiences in the city, "From the terrace." Calvino takes his time in describing, little by little, the assortment of buildings and traces of humanity, of colors and textures. The beauty of the prose suggests a verbal painting. At the same time, the slowness of the description and the sense of movement as the gaze falls on new delights makes one think of a panoramic shot by a gifted filmmaker. This effect is enhanced by the slow progression within the lengthy paragraphs, almost unbroken by periods which would disturb the flow.

Occasionally, one has the feeling that the narration has escaped the author's control, such as when describing the delights to be found in a Parisian special-foods store or the array of meats in the butcher shop. The same thing happens at times in an extended comparison, in which an item is likened to one thing, then to another, then to another, as if each simile inspired yet one more. Frequently these gushes of language are cut off, but gently, by the use of ellipsis points. One senses that the narration could go on and on, so full is it of the joy of the moment. The reader then can share Calvino's pleasure of language, an almost erotic enjoyment of words and their power.

Carol Clark D'Lugo

Sources for Further Study

Library Journal. CX, September 15, 1985, p. 91.
The London Review of Books. VII, October 3, 1985, p. 17.
Los Angeles Times Book Review. October 6, 1985, p. 3.
New Statesman. CX, September 27, 1985, p. 34.
The New York Times Book Review. XC, September 29, 1985, p. 1.
Newsweek. CVI, October 21, 1985, p. 80.
The Observer. December 2, 1984, p. 19.
Publishers Weekly. CCXXVIII, August 9, 1985, p. 63.
Time. CXXVI, September 23, 1985, p. 81.
Washington Post Book World. XV, September 22, 1985, p. 5.

MONEY
A Suicide Note

Author: Martin Amis (1949-   )
Publisher: The Viking Press (New York). 368 pp. $16.95
Type of work: Novel
Time: The 1980's
Locale: New York and London

A successful film director, whose life is based solely on immediate personal grati-
fication, discovers slowly that he is being or has been betrayed by all of his associates
and that not only his work but also his life is a sham

> Principal characters:
> JOHN SELF, the director of *Bad Money*
> SELINA, his sexual partner, eventually pregnant by Ossie Twain
> FIELDING GOODNEY, an actor and swindler pretending to be Self's
> backer
> DORIS ARTHUR, the scriptwriter of *Bad Money*
> MARTIN AMIS, the author, hired as second scriptwriter
> MARTINA TWAIN, Self's "good angel"
> OSSIE TWAIN, Martina's husband
> BARRY SELF, Self's mother's husband, but not his father

Money: A Suicide Note may be seen as a satire on metropolitan life in the
late twentieth century. Its central character, John Self, incorporates all the
worst aspects of an acquisitive society. He is extremely aggressive. Little
homilies on the art of street fighting are delivered by him at various points
in the narrative. Near the end, he is involved in two critical brawls, both of
which he wins (in spite of being fat, unarmed, and allergic to any form of
exercise), solely because of his no-limit ferocity. He is also sexually voracious. Much of the story consists of visits to striptease clubs, topless bars,
and pornographic displays of one kind or another, while his main attachment in the novel, to Selina, is founded solidly on her sexual athleticism,
with almost no hint of sentiment. Self believes furthermore that both sex
and aggression are essentially matters of money. Money can buy sex, and
sex can always be sold for money. Yet the key to gaining money is aggression, and once one has money, aggression can be bought. This is what happens, for example, when a small, cheap "contract" is taken out on Self, with
a specific purpose—one blow in the face with a blunt instrument—and a
specific price, fifty pounds. Self is also bone idle, often passing entire days
in drunken stupor, and compulsively addicted to fast foods. In an earlier
age, he would certainly have been taken as a living example of the Seven
Deadly Sins: Gluttony, Lust, Sloth, Wrath, Envy, Pride, and Avarice.

Self, however, is not living in an earlier age, but in the 1980's, and with
that in mind, it is possible to assemble for him some faint shreds of an excuse. For example, though he does exemplify all the Seven Sins listed above,
he is clearly much more guilty of the first four corporeal sins than of the last

three spiritual ones. He is vain about his clothes and his car but not especially proud. His envies are by no means devouring. Though he is greedy for money, which is one kind of avarice, he is the reverse of miserly once he has got it. In one scene, he wanders through New York (admittedly drunkenly), handing out dollars, and in many scenes, one sees him compulsively spending. There is also a very obvious suggestion that Self's actions are not so much sins as adaptations. He *is* aggressive, but then everyone else around him is as well, and there is an old saying that "attack is the best form of defense." The crazy telephoner whose threats punctuate the book insists all along that Self has injured him, but when the caller's identity is revealed, it looks at the very least as if his revenge is out of all proportion to Self's original offenses. Self is surrounded, in short, by what he calls "sickoes," "devoes," and "crazoids"; he cannot help being affected by them. In a way, he resembles a character glimpsed briefly in one New York street scene, a man lashing wildly round him at cars and passersby with a length of chain, until he is shot by a policeman. The man looks aggressive, but he has been made so. Conceivably, underneath, he might be classified as a victim.

Another way of regarding *Money*, therefore, is to see it as a "psychomachy," or even a "morality play," in which the soul of Everyman, or John Self, is battled for by troops of opposing Vices and Virtues. In this struggle, it has to be said that the forces of Vice are far more prominent. The most ludicrous are those associated with Self's job. By trade a director of television commercials, he is now attempting to make his first full-length feature film, titled alternatively (and significantly) *Good Money* or *Bad Money*. His main backer is Fielding Goodney, by comparison with Self, a paragon of youth, beauty, self-confidence, and wealth. His actors, though, are all in different ways egomaniacs. His older female lead presents an image of Italian maternal love and sentiment; really, she hates children. His younger female lead is sex-mad. His younger male lead is a born-again Christian and, to all outward appearances, totally wholesome; he is, however, a victim of any passing fashion. Finally, his older male lead, Lorne Guyland, is vulnerable to the slightest reflection on his talents, his age, his size, his virility, or his culture, and spends most of the book determinedly trying to rewrite the script of *Bad Money* so that it will correspond to his childish wish-fulfillment fantasies. Self copes in the end by getting a second scriptwriter to insert large chunks of flattery in the script to pacify his actors—though he intends to cut all of it out of the film after it has been shot. Self, in short, is surrounded by people who are completely self-ish. In one way, they make him worse; as with the crazies and muggers of the street scenes, he has to defend himself against them. In another way, though, he has to show responsibility and make some effort at understanding them, an effort they never reciprocate.

Even including Self's unreliable inner promptings to responsibility, though, the side of Virtue in *Money* is significantly underrepresented. It could be said to consist of only one character with a real life of her own—namely, the first scriptwriter of *Bad Money,* one Doris Arthur. She is the only person in the story who tries, for no reason other than altruism, to warn Self of the fact that almost all the other characters are either part of a plot against him or else hired unknowingly by the plotters. Self, however, instantly erases the warning from his mind, so it has no effect. Since he does not even report the warning in his rambling I-narrative, referring to it only in very delayed flashback at the end, the reader shares Self's delusion, participating in his increasing realization that something bad is going on but as unable as he is to find out what. The truth is that Fielding Goodney, apparently a millionaire film backer, is in reality Self's mysterious threatening telephoner, and he has set up the whole confidence trick of making a film in order to make Self personally liable for all the costs, and so ruin him. All this says for Virtue, though, is that even characters who appear to be good influences are not; the only one who might be, Doris Arthur, is distrusted and dismissed.

This, however, leaves out one further strand in the novel, which reinforces the notion of *Money* as a "morality play," or allegory, namely, the presence inside it of the author as a character, Martin Amis, seconded by a further character acting as the author's female double, Martina Twain. These two—"twain" is incidentally a genuine Old English form of two—do their best to haul Self back from various brinks. One has to wonder, though, what the function of such evidently nonrealistic figures is, and the answer is that they exist as culture bearers, figures who resist the twentieth century trend away from literature to film, from the enduring to the instant, from personal to commercial values. At the lowest level, both talk to Self about books. Martina (with whom Self eventually falls in love) even refuses to associate with him until he has read a selection of them, no doubt a significant selection. Her first offering is George Orwell's *Animal Farm* (1945), with its famous last scene in which the exploited have become exploiters, the pigs farmers. Self, obviously, is an exploiter and, in many senses, a pig. This is what he has to be saved from. Martin Amis, meanwhile, inside his own novel, tries to talk his character—his Self—into a better understanding of money, with at least partial success.

Who will gain Self's soul? Why is it diseased? Once questions of this generality have been framed, even quite minor scenes in the novel begin to take on significance. Yet, another way in which the novel's significance can be interpreted is as a Freudian "family drama." Martina makes Self read a book about Sigmund Freud, which is a heavy hint, but most readers could manage without it. Near the end of the story, Self is tempted—of course he falls—to have intercourse with his father's wife, apparently his stepmother. He is disturbed by his father, in a reversal of Freud's famous "primal scene."

It turns out, though, that Barry Self is *not* his father, which explains, among other things, why Barry charged John nineteen thousand pounds for the expense of his upbringing. Escaping from this encounter, Self is confronted by the thug who intends to earn fifty pounds by striking him one blow in the face with a blunt instrument; the thug is his real brother. Meanwhile, Selina has been made pregnant, but Self is not the father. One can only say that this kaleidoscope of relations, pseudorelations, and nonrelations functions almost as a parody of Freudian theories. Self has two "fathers," two "mothers," a brother who is in a way his own double, a "good" and a "bad" partner in Martina and Selina respectively, and two psychic mentors in "Amis" and "Twain." Realism again is eroded. The suggestion of the Freudian parody is, perhaps, that Freud's theories of ids and Oedipuses, repulsive as they seemed at the time, were nevertheless not complex, selfish, or treacherous enough to deal with the normality of the late twentieth century.

Money does indeed function as an explanation, as well as a satire, of the 1980's. It points to genuine difficulties, such as the disappearance of families under the pressures of increased sexual expectation, divorce, and personal anxiety. It is even unexpectedly sympathetic to Selina, Self's corrupt and ruthless sexual partner, as it points out the deep financial insecurity of her life. *Money* stresses also the way in which artificiality has crept up even on its central topic (money), as society has gone from gold to paper to the plastic credit card; it is both a realistic scene and an eerily symbolic one when the waiter in a restaurant brings Self his credit card ceremoniously chopped into four pieces. The scissoring symbolizes how one can go from riches to poverty in an instant. It is also something that might really happen. One might sum up by saying that, overall, Martin Amis, as author and as character, is telling the reader that, in his view, the twentieth century is turning into an illusion, a film set, a giant sting, a plastic credit card, a pornographic magazine. They all look good, but there is nothing behind them. The nothing, though, is what people are not prepared to face. They prefer the illusion of feeling good—of Fielding Goodney?

In the end, Self does face the nothing. He smashes Fielding Goodney (literally), he escapes from New York, he loses both his money and his debts, he is forced into total immobility by Martin Amis in a chess game. One sees him, finally, poor, happy, and befriended by a highly unpornographic fat girl who looks after him and stamps firmly on any recidivism toward aggression or lust. His soul has been saved, but one final question remains: Whose soul was it? It is tempting to conjecture that it was Martin Amis' and that the novel is in a way addressed by the author to himself. Certainly the novel is ambiguous to an extent that can only be hinted at here. It claims to be on the side of virtue, reality, culture, Martin, and Martina. Nevertheless, the delight in vice found in its pages approaches the pornographic, and the author takes many opportunities to express (via Self) opinions that are illiberal, misogynistic, or cruel, but also uncomfortably sharp and plausible. There is much to be said for Vice (declares *Money*). Self may be saved for Virtue, but he is only one case.

A final opinion of *Money*, indeed, may be this: It expresses contempt and loathing for the shallowness and cheap successes of the 1960's, in whose shadow both Self and Martin Amis grew up, but, at the same time, a deep and yearning nostalgia.

T. A. Shippey

Sources for Further Study

Library Journal. CX, April 1, 1985, p. 155.
Los Angeles Times Book Review. March 31, 1985, p. 3.
The New Republic. CXCII, June 10, 1985, p. 40.
The New York Times Book Review. XC, March 24, 1985, p. 36.
The New Yorker. LXI, June 10, 1985, p. 136.
Newsweek. CV, March 25, 1985, p. 80.
Publishers Weekly. CCXXVI, December 21, 1984, p. 84.
Time. CXXV, March 11, 1985, p. 70.
The Wall Street Journal. CCV, April 24, 1985, p. 28.
Washington Post Book World. XV, March 24, 1985, p. 3.

MOUNTBATTEN

Author: Philip Ziegler (1929-   )
Publisher: Alfred A. Knopf (New York). Illustrated. 784 pp. $24.95
Type of work: Historical biography
Time: 1900-1979
Locale: Great Britain and India

A biography of Lord Mountbatten, a prominent member of the British royal family and the last viceroy of India

> *Principal personages:*
> LOUIS MOUNTBATTEN, Supreme Allied Commander for Southeast Asia, 1943-1946, Viceroy of India, 1947, First Sea Lord, 1955-1959, Chief of Defence Staff, 1959-1965
> EDWINA, Countess Mountbatten of Burma, his wife
> JAWAHARLAL NEHRU, first Prime Minister of an independent India, 1950-1966
> CLEMENT ATTLEE, Prime Minister of Great Britain, 1945-1951
> WINSTON CHURCHILL, Prime Minister of Great Britain, 1940-1945 and 1951-1955

Mountbatten is a full-length biography of a man who played a vital role in British public life from World War II until his retirement in 1965. It is the official biography of Mountbatten and, in addition to making extensive use of interviews and other primary sources, Philip Ziegler had unrestricted access to Mountbatten's private papers in preparing his study. It is gracefully written and makes an important contribution to understanding a major public figure.

From the very beginning, Mountbatten's family ties set him apart from his contemporaries. He was the great-grandson of Queen Victoria, nephew of Nicholas II, the last czar of Russia, a cousin of kings Edward VIII and George VI, and an uncle of Queen Elizabeth's husband, Prince Philip. Mountbatten took great pride in his family line; one of his favorite diversions was to trace his ancestry back to the Emperor Charlemagne. Mountbatten's father, Prince Louis of Battenberg, married Queen Victoria's granddaughter, Princess Victoria of Hesse, entered the British navy and rose to the position of First Sea Lord. Anti-German feeling became so strong during World War I, however, that he was forced to resign. Mountbatten, then a young naval cadet, was stunned by his father's treatment and vowed that he would some day succeed him as First Sea Lord. Ziegler suggests that this incident was a source of the driving ambition which was so prominent a feature of his personality.

Ziegler devotes considerable attention to Edwina, Mountbatten's wife, and their troubled marriage. Edwina Ashley was the granddaughter of Sir Ernest Cassel, one of the wealthiest men in Europe at the beginning of the twentieth century, and she inherited the bulk of his fortune. Mountbatten, in contrast, although of royal blood, had an annual income of only six hundred pounds at the time of their marriage in 1922. Nevertheless, the disparity in wealth proved less of a source of conflict within their relationship than other factors. Edwina cherished her independence and resented the bonds of matrimony. Within seven months after the birth of their first daughter, she temporarily deserted Mountbatten. Although she later returned to him, this was only the first of a series of extramarital relationships she established; in 1928, she was named corespondant in a threatened divorce action. Although deeply unhappy with her behavior, Mountbatten continued to try to regain Edwina's affection. Ziegler suggests that his inability to satisfy her left Mountbatten with a sense of failure for which he compensated with an exceptionally fierce determination to be successful in his naval career.

World War II was a decisive turning point in Mountbatten's career. He entered the war as an undistinguished destroyer commander with no reason to anticipate promotion to high office. He emerged from the war as Supreme Commander of Allied Forces in Southeast Asia with an enhanced reputation for his political skills, which made him a logical choice to serve as the next viceroy of India. This meteoric series of promotions owed less to his success in the various positions he held than to his having become a protégé of the prime minister, Winston Churchill.

At the beginning of the war, Mountbatten nearly ruined his reputation as a naval commander through repeated errors of judgment, which led to the ships under his command suffering unnecessary damage. Mountbatten's decision to signal another destroyer at night with a bright light while cruising in the North Sea early in 1940 led to his ship being torpedoed and very nearly sunk. Yet his skill in preventing his ship from sinking while it was being towed back to port attracted considerable publicity and caught Churchill's attention. Churchill was so impressed that he proposed that Mountbatten be granted a medal, but this was vetoed by Mountbatten's fleet commander, who pointed out that there would have been no need for Mountbatten's heroism had it not been for his initial mistake. The episode proved invaluable to Mountbatten, however, for it left Churchill convinced that Mountbatten was a man of great talent whose abilities were being ignored by petty-minded superior officers.

After this inauspicious beginning, Mountbatten continued to compile an unenviable record as a naval officer. He was placed in charge of a flotilla late in 1940, but he proceeded to commit errors in strategy while engaging a German fleet, which led to his ship being hit by torpedoes and put out of action. In the following year, he was commander of a flotilla assigned to assist British troops resisting the German invasion of Crete. On this occasion, his ship was sunk. Even Ziegler admits that Mountbatten's superiors were correct in claiming that he was no better than second-rate as a destroyer or flotilla commander. Happily for Mountbatten, however, Churchill had become convinced that he was an innovator with the drive to find new ways of waging war on Germany, and he appointed him Chief of Combined Operations in October 1941.

Combined Operations was a special group responsible for planning and conducting operations in which forces from more than one service were involved. Although initially limited almost entirely to commando raids on the French coast, it was the organization specifically charged with preparing for a full-scale invasion of the Continent. Mountbatten's appointment to such a responsible position was quite amazing, considering his age and limited experience: Virtually all of his staff were older than he, and most held higher rank than he until his sudden promotion over them. In his new position, Mountbatten became the fourth military member of the Chiefs of Staff, the supreme military council charged with directing the war. Initially he was regarded with skepticism bordering on hostility by the other Chiefs of Staff who suspected that he owed his appointment more to his political connections than his ability, but eventually he gained their acceptance.

Mountbatten's tenure as Chief of Combined Operations is most often remembered because of his role in the disastrous raid on Dieppe in August 1942. Ziegler acknowledges that, with the possible exception of the partition of India, Mountbatten received more criticism for the Dieppe raid than for any other episode in his career. On this issue, as on most others, he insists that Mountbatten has been treated unfairly. The raid was originally planned in part because of pressure from Churchill to initiate an operation that would tie down German divisions on the French coast, thereby relieving some of the pressure on Russia. At one point, the proposed raid was abandoned because of bad weather. Mountbatten's chief responsibility stems from the fact that he was the one who resuscitated the plan and persuaded Churchill and the Chiefs of Staff to go ahead with it after they had put it aside. Ziegler notes, however, that the operation which was conducted deviated in several crucial respects from the plan Mountbatten had proposed: Inexperienced Canadian troops were substituted for British commandos, the advance air attack was canceled, and the artillery support from a battleship was eliminated because of fears that the ship would be sunk by enemy aircraft. Ziegler also suggests that the lessons learned from the Dieppe fiasco enabled the Allies to avoid similar mistakes during the D-day invasion, thus enhancing its chance of success.

Despite Mountbatten's mixed record at Combined Operations, Churchill continued to have confidence in him and in 1943 appointed him Supreme Commander of Allied Forces in Southeast Asia. Mountbatten's performance in his new position was not an unmitigated success. He established his headquarters in Ceylon, two thousand miles away from the fighting front. It soon developed a reputation for elegant and expensive living; even Ziegler comments that "Mountbattens do not come on the cheap." Many visitors came away from his headquarters with the impression that an undue emphasis was placed on public relations and show. Military leaders under his command were often not impressed with his direction of the war effort; a surprising number of them resigned or were dismissed for questioning his military strategy. While quick to draw attention to Mountbatten's accomplishments, Ziegler's account enables the reader to understand why P. J. Grigg, the Secretary of State for War, had opposed Mountbatten's appointment as supreme commander on the ground that he was an "aristocratic playboy."

Happily, Mountbatten's political instincts were often more impressive than his military judgments. At the end of the war, he was responsible for accepting the Japanese surrender in French Indochina, Java, and Borneo, as well as in Burma and Malay. This placed him in a position in which he had to make crucial political decisions that affected the future of Asian nationalist movements. Rather than attempting to reimpose prewar colonial administrations, Mountbatten worked closely with native independence movements, especially when the latter had actively participated in the war against Japan. In part, this stemmed from a practical need for their assistance in maintaining order, but it also reflected Mountbatten's sense that it would be both unwise and unjust to attempt to reestablish the authority of a colonial power over a hostile population. After accepting the surrender of Japanese forces in Indochina, for example, Mountbatten urged the French to negotiate with the Viet Minh and, if necessary, to grant Indochina independence rather than use force in an attempt to restore French control. Ziegler suggests that the prolonged fighting in Indochina since 1945 might have been avoided if the French had followed Mountbatten's advice.

When the 1945 Labour government took office, it was committed to the rapid termination of British authority in India. Mountbatten's selection in 1947 to implement this decision seems surprising at first glance, but there are at least three reasons why it was a shrewd choice. Labour leaders were impressed with Mountbatten's handling of Asian independence movements and recognized that he had built up a large reservoir of goodwill among Asian nationalists. Also, unlike many Britons in this period, he had no racial prejudice. Finally, the fact that he was related to the British royal family enhanced his position when negotiating with Indian princes, and it was hoped that British Conservatives would find it easier to accept Indian independence if it were negotiated by someone with close ties to the British monarchy.

Mountbatten was at the peak of his power and influence during 1947 and 1948 while he served as viceroy, then governor-general of India. It is thus appropriate that Ziegler devotes a full ten chapters to this critical stage in Mountbatten's career. When Mountbatten arrived in India, he inherited a situation in which large-scale fighting had broken out between Hindus and Muslims, and both sides distrusted the British. Although he had to accept the partition of India with Pakistan, Mountbatten succeeded in preventing the remainder of India from breaking up into numerous small states. He gained the friendship of Jawaharlal Nehru, and with his assistance he persuaded the new Indian government to remain in the Commonwealth, contrary to its original intentions. Mountbatten has been criticized for the speed at which independence was granted, but Ziegler observes that the government's authority was degenerating rapidly in 1947, and if Mountbatten had not moved quickly there might have been a complete breakdown of law and order.

After his return to England, Mountbatten declined an offer to become minister of defence under the Labour government, choosing instead to work his way up the naval hierarchy until he became First Sea Lord in 1955. It is surprising that one of his first initiatives in that position involved opposing government policy. When asked to prepare plans for the invasion of Egypt during the 1955 Suez crisis, Mountbatten objected to this step and influenced the Chiefs of Staff to express similar reservations. He felt so strongly about the issue that at one point he wrote out a letter of resignation but allowed himself to be dissuaded from sending it. Some have claimed that Mountbatten should have gone through with his resignation, but Ziegler insists that this would not have prevented the invasion and that it is unrealistic to expect a military officer to resign on political and moral grounds at the onset of a war.

Mountbatten's opposition to Anthony Eden's Suez policy certainly did not harm his career, for in 1959 he became Chief of the Defence Staff, the direct supervisor of the Chiefs of Staff. In this new position, Mountbatten played a key role in the modernization of the British armed forces, but in so doing he antagonized many service ministers. Mountbatten was instrumental in persuading the British government to acquire nuclear submarines and in convincing Admiral Hyman Rickover to assist the British in developing their nuclear submarine fleet. Funding this program during a period of financial constraint inevitably meant less money for the other services, however, and Mountbatten was accused of showing favoritism toward the navy. His opposition to the creation of an independent British nuclear deterrant also made him unpopular in some circles. He insisted that an independent British force would be "neither credible as a deterrant, nor necessary as part of a Western deterrant." Furthermore, for Great Britain alone to use her nuclear weapons in defense of Western Europe would be to commit "national suicide."

After his retirement in 1965, Mountbatten continued to make himself available for public service, but he was not involved in Irish affairs, nor was he a prominent spokesman on matters relating to Northern Ireland. It is thus a mystery why the Irish Republican Army chose to assassinate him in 1979, and Ziegler is unable to shed any light on their motivation.

Ziegler is sufficiently objective to admit that there were striking defects in Mountbatten's character. He was vain, inordinately ambitious, and never considered a profound thinker. In spite of these flaws, Ziegler insists that Mountbatten was a great man whose special talent lay in executing policies set by others. Mountbatten was thought by some contemporaries to be "the greatest fixer of all time." This judgment draws attention both to his tremendous determination to get things done and to the methods that he employed, which caused some colleagues to consider him shifty and untrustworthy. Ziegler's study is of special value in part because he is so frank about Mountbatten's limitations as well as his accomplishments. It supersedes all previous studies and should be considered the standard work on the life of Mountbatten.

Harold L. Smith

Sources for Further Study

History Today. XXXV, July, 1985, p. 64.
Library Journal. CX, May 1, 1985, p. 57.
The London Review of Books. VII, March 21, 1985, p. 5.
The New York Review of Books. XXXII, May 9, 1985, p. 6.
The New York Times Book Review. XC, May 26, 1985, p. 18.
The New Yorker. LXI, September 9, 1985, p. 101.
Newsweek. CV, June 3, 1985, p. 75.
Publishers Weekly. CCXXVII, March 8, 1985, p. 80.
Time. CXXV, May 13, 1985, p. 73.
Times Literary Supplement. April 12, 1985, p. 401.

MOVE YOUR SHADOW
South Africa, Black and White

Author: Joseph Lelyveld (1937-   )
Publisher: Times Books (New York). 390 pp. $18.95
Type of work: Current affairs
Time: 1980-1984
Locale: South Africa

Highly personal observations and reflections on the apartheid system in South Africa

Principal personages:
STEVE BIKO, a South African black nationalist martyred by the white police
THOZAMILE GQWETA, president of the black South African Allied Workers Union
NELSON MANDELA, an imprisoned black South African leader
ROBERT SOBUKWE, leader of the Pan-Africanist Congress
DESMOND TUTU, the Anglican bishop of Johannesburg

Joseph Lelyveld, a veteran of two postings as *The New York Times* South African correspondent, provides a penetrating, discomforting view of apartheid in *Move Your Shadow: South Africa, Black and White*. His informed and comprehensive perspective derives from his having lived in the country during two separate periods of time: Returning to Johannesburg in 1980 after almost fifteen years, he was in a unique position to explore and assess trends as well as discern the realities camouflaged by official double-talk. Lelyveld's credentials as an American reporter provided access to the inner sanctums of the government bureaucracy, the legal and penal systems, and other dimensions of South African society and government normally closed to outsiders. His determination and zeal led him to many black areas infrequently visited by nonblacks. During the early 1980's, he traveled regularly to each of the major cities and to the ten so-called homelands, noting ironically that probably fewer than one hundred South Africans have seen more of their country than he.

Move Your Shadow is an intensely felt, impressive, personal work filled with vivid and haunting portraits of despair and unfeigned courage. The author provides a multidimensional analysis of the South African racial system through the concrete day-to-day experience of blacks and whites. In vivid human terms, he shows what it means to live under the shadow of apartheid.

One of the strongest themes of the book is that South Africa is a land of paradox and contradiction. These complexities are defined and described through a series of poignant anecdotes. In great detail, Lelyveld covers the living conditions in black townships that are analogous to other countries after famine or war; institutionalized violence and torture; the elaborate government-subsidized bus system that transports black workers to their city

jobs; and black-white interactions in a society designed to minimize communication.

The author's greatest strength is in developing character sketches of the
citizens of South Africa. With empathy and insight, he presents people such
as the Afrikaner farmer's wife who expresses her belief that some blacks
"try to think, really they do"; a visiting American black who manages to live
as though he is white; a black diesel mechanic fired for putting a civil rights
slogan on his coffee mug (his jail sentence for this act was longer than the
sentence he received for a previous homicide conviction); a black security
director in Ciskei who directs his power against his own people by playing
the role of an anti-Communist crusader in a "theatre of the absurd"; a black
faith healer, or seer, who makes his living on the government payroll, telling
whites what they want to hear about blacks; and a now-deceased Afrikaner
churchman who was the first white minister to refuse ordination in the
white branch of his church and seek a life of service among the blacks.

The author also points out the bona fide bridgeheads of multiracial interaction uneasily coexisting side by side with the institutions of the apartheid
state. For example, the plays of Athol Fugard, full of passion and pain, are
presented in integrated theaters under the close scrutiny of the security police. Lelyveld chronicles the efforts of clergymen and other mavericks who
dare to bridge the institutionalized racial gap to bring about change.

The central paradox of South African life stems from the Afrikaner struggle to achieve freedom and identity. There is an obvious contradiction that
has never been resolved: The freedom they sought for themselves from
externally imposed laws meant, of necessity, the freedom to impose their
laws on others. Thus, a people who bravely fought Africa's first anticolonial
struggles, who were native to the land and not colonists in any normal
sense, have established one of the world's most retrogressive colonial systems. The Afrikaner establishment has a disposition for control that extends
far beyond political exigencies. It is almost a physical sensation, habitually
expressed in images of grip or stress; for example, extremist conservatives
often use the slogan "Don't Let Go" in presenting themselves as defenders
of "white self-determination" in a country that is 85 percent nonwhite. The
blacks, too, view white power in physical terms, as a force squeezing or
pressing down upon them. The raw, cruel reality of that power is often
veiled from the white beneficiaries, but it is part of the daily existence of
blacks. There is nothing subtle about the plainclothes white security police
who cruise through the black townships with their guns visible. Clearly, they
are there to remind, harass, and intimidate.

Sometimes, the white power structure hides behind a black façade, but
there is no question about who exercises control. There are a handful of
blacks with doctorates in education working for what is known as the Ministry of Education and Training, but they never are assigned to the head-

quarters in Pretoria from which control is exercised over the entire black educational system. The greatest bureaucratic horror, however, is the Byzantine and secretive Ministry of Cooperation and Development. This holy of holies of South African apartheid changes its name every five or six years to sanitize and mask its real role—which is to regulate the movement of blacks and rationalize the pattern of black living patterns to minimize inconvenience to whites. It is a vast warren of racist ideologues, constantly refining the vast corpus of apartheid law, which dictates to millions of blacks whether, where, and when they can live with their families.

Lelyveld also points out how the efforts to resettle blacks in their own supposedly sovereign homelands are really an ill-disguised campaign of removal and subjection. "Repatriation," as this process is called, represents the final stage of a 140-year campaign to alienate blacks from their land. For more than seventy years, it has been illegal for blacks to purchase land in more than 86 percent of South Africa. For thirty-five years, blacks have been forced, cajoled, or squeezed off "black spots," land to which they had earlier secured proper title according to the white man's law. Between 1960 and 1980, some 3.5 million blacks were forcibly removed from their land, more than two million into so-called "closer settlements" in the homelands. Most rural people who had lived as sharecroppers and labor tenants on white farms lost even the hope of subsistence farming, for what made a closer settlement "closer" was the absence of grazing land and the restriction of cultivation to small gardens. It is estimated that 3.7 million South African blacks were living in these squalid encampments by 1980. In 1960, 39.8 percent of the total black population was jammed into the former tribal reserves; by 1980, resettlement and gerrymandering had raised that proportion to 53.1 percent. In absolute terms, the number of blacks living on the same 13 percent of the land more than doubled during the two decades. Furthermore, nearly half had been stripped of their South African citizenship.

For the sake of maintaining white privilege, large portions of the countryside have been systematically turned into catchment areas for surplus black population. The distribution of land is astounding—fifty thousand white farmers have twelve times as much land for cultivation and grazing as fourteen million rural blacks. Thus, apartheid deliberately compounds mass rural poverty in order to preserve white elitism and power. It is ultimately a divide-and-rule strategy—portioning the land into racially designated areas and bogus homelands, and the population into distinct racial castes and subcastes. The whites are free to move into any area except those designated nonwhite; the coloreds and the Indians can move freely in the country but are barred from owning land in more than 95 percent of it; the blacks are subdivided by law into six distinct impermeable or superimpermeable categories.

The most hard-hitting portion of the book deals with one hardship imposed on blacks never noted in the press. By virtue of their isolation in segregated communities far from major urban centers, a host of blacks routinely endure long hours on uncomfortable commuter buses. Lelyveld rode with commuters who reside in a black area outside Pretoria. The black settlers of this new state had to ride about ninety-five miles before transferring to local buses that would take them to factories where they worked. This meant a minimum of 190 miles every working day in buses with hard seats, buses designed for short hauls on city streets. These people were fortunate in a sense—unlike many others, they were employed—but they were spending up to eight hours a day on buses.

Through the use of anecdotes and his remarkable eye for detail, Lelyveld portrays South Africa as a real place rather than an abstract moral or international problem. The people in *Move Your Shadow* are not clichés. One sees the many faces of white South Africa in the words of bogus intellectuals who espouse diaphanous theories of racial superiority and the convoluted reasoning of jurists whose system of laws is founded on shabby tenets. One sees the other side of the nation in the words of black nationalists and Afrikaner clergymen ostracized for their support of black causes. The awful reality of apartheid is also seen in glimpses of squatters near Cape Town sheltering themselves from winter rains in makeshift structures of twigs and polyethylene garbage bags; in the experience of black students jailed and tortured for their beliefs; and in the legal horrors faced by a light-skinned "colored" single mother found living in a white area.

With every vignette, with every story of brutality and courage, with every description of a life preordained for doom, South Africa becomes a vivid landscape over which a shadow grows ominous and larger each day. The title *Move Your Shadow* was derived by Lelyveld from a language manual intended to help whites learn phrases for communicating with black workers. After they are told to carry the clubs, clean the balls, and remain quiet, black caddies are instructed to move their shadows from a certain portion of a golf green. The title's implications extend to the dominance of South African white minority, the apartheid system, South Africa's place in a black continent, and even a strong sense of impending bloodshed and violence. This classic, definitive book, winner of the 1986 Pulitzer Prize in the category of General Nonfiction, makes the current turmoil in South Africa more vivid and eminently comprehensible.

Michael C. Robinson

Sources for Further Study

Business Week. December 30, 1985, p. 16.
Kirkus Reviews. LIII, September 1, 1985, p. 935.
Library Journal. CX, November 15, 1985, p. 85.
The New Republic. CXCIII, December 23, 1985, p. 29.
The New York Review of Books. XXXII, November 7, 1985, p. 5.
The New York Times Book Review. XC, October 13, 1985, p. 1.
Newsweek. CVI, November 4, 1985, p. 70.
Publishers Weekly. CCXXVIII, October 4, 1985, p. 65.
The Wall Street Journal. CCVI, October 24, 1985, p. 30.
Washington Journalism Review. VII, November, 1985, p. 51.

NAOMI

Author: Jun'ichirō Tanizaki (1886-1965)
Translated from the Japanese by Anthony H. Chambers
Publisher: Alfred A. Knopf (New York). 237 pp. $15.95
Type of work: Novel
Time: Approximately 1918 to 1926
Locale: Tokyo, Japan

A chronicle of the ill-fated, humorous, and mordantly rendered love affair between Jōji Kawai, a young Japanese gentleman, and Naomi, a Westernized and exotic young woman whose portrait serves as a piquant satiric metaphor for the newly liberated Japanese women of the period

> Principal characters:
> JŌJI KAWAI, a young Japanese office worker
> NAOMI, his mistress, eventually his wife
> KUMAGAI, her lover, later Jōji's confidant
> HAMADA and
> MA-CHAN, other lovers of Naomi

For many Japanese readers and a growing coterie of Western admirers as well, Jun'ichirō Tanizaki continues to rank as the most sophisticated and imaginative Japanese novelist of the century. Few before him have written with such elegance and wit, and few after him, with the possible exception of Yukio Mishima, have been able to link the powerful literary traditions of classical Japanese literature with the social concerns of the contemporary world. *Naomi*, presented in this elegant and accurate translation, shows at once how Tanizaki has earned and sustained his reputation. This work has long been admired as one of his masterpieces and, along with the six other novels or collections now available in English, helps to reveal the wide span of Tanizaki's concerns, both in terms of style and of philosophy.

Published in 1924, about the time of the disastrous Tokyo earthquake, Tanizaki created in *Naomi* a vehicle for a social satire on a Westernizing Japan. In the aftermath of the earthquake, which destroyed many of the locales described so wittily in the novel, Tanizaki was to move to the middle of the country, the region of Kyoto and Osaka, where he slowly became interested in certain more traditional aspects of his culture. That fascination culminated in the composition of his novel *Sasame-yuki* (1949; *The Makioka Sisters*, 1957), written during World War II. *Naomi*, however, was a product of an earlier phase of Tanizaki's work, composed at a time when so many artists and intellectuals congregated in Tokyo in order to draw as close as possible to the kind of artistic ferment they found there. Much of this excitement involved the importation of Western modes of thinking and living. High culture brought translations of Charles Baudelaire and Immanuel Kant; popular culture imported American silent films, bobbed hair, and dance halls.

Satō Haruo, a distinguished poet and novelist who knew Tanizaki well, insisted that his colleague remained, despite his frequent choice of decadent or sensational subject matter, a real moralist at heart. *Naomi* shows Satō to be right. The original title of Tanizaki's novel, *Chijin no ai*, which might be translated as a fool's love, shows at once Tanizaki's point of view on the relationship he creates in the novel, in which Jōji Kawai, a gentle and fastidious young Japanese gentleman, becomes increasingly ensnared in his complex relationship with the beautiful, narcissistic, and intriguing Naomi. No matter how ridiculous the relationship becomes, Kawai finds himself dragged further and further into an intimate connection in which he finds himself completely dependent on this beautiful woman, who eventually manages to engulf him completely. Their final marriage is in reality a kind of financial and psychological slavery. The young man willingly places himself in a subordinate role in every aspect of the life they share together.

The setting of the novel, Tokyo from the late 1910's until the middle 1920's, is particularly crucial for Tanizaki, who sees the two main characters as very much a product of their times. In that sense, the relationship between the pair does show a wider symbolic significance. Kawai, in his twenties when he first meets Naomi, is very much, on the surface at least, a product of traditional Japanese values; he seems a gentle man, with good manners, who maintains proper filial relationships with his mother and treats his coworkers with dignity and reserve. Naomi, who is about fifteen when he meets her in a café, enchants him precisely because she seems to stand for something ineffable, different from anything he has ever known. Her name is actually a Japanese one that is written in Japanese characters, but to him it sounds Western. Kawai is intent on finding in her boyish charm a certain resemblance to the silent film star Mary Pickford, who was as popular then in Japan as she was in Europe and the United States. Once Kawai takes Naomi on, he finds himself completely manipulated by this modern flapper; she is altogether hedonistic and openly inconsiderate of him, showing no regard for her putative obligations to the man who will, eventually, virtually ruin himself for her. She spends his money, takes lovers, laughs at his clumsiness, and eventually runs away, all without the least pretense of apology. Some critics have described her as a kind of Carmen figure in modern Japanese literature; and in Tanizaki's ironic mode, her Don José, far from killing her, can only grovel at her feet in uncritical admiration. Naomi has her antecedents in some of the raffish women characters in the comic novels of the great Tokugawa satiric novelist Ihara Saikaku, but she is an authentic modern creation.

Much of the mordant humor of the narrative arises from the way in which Tanizaki chooses to tell his story. Kawai serves as his own narrator. The novel is written as a kind of confession, all in the first person. The reader, following the story along, thus becomes an often rueful confidant to Kawai's drubbings, observing him as he knowingly commits mistake after mistake.

The first-person narrative style is one of the oldest devices employed in classical Japanese fiction, going back to the poetic diaries of the Heian period (794-1185), but no traditional author made use of the form for such consistently self-conscious and ironic ends. Kawai's account thus serves both as narrative and running commentary on his own emotional state of mind. Tanizaki's technique can thus sustain for the reader, able to observe both layers at once, a degree of objectivity that makes the tone of the story humorous rather than pathetic.

Literary historians in Japan have sometimes suggested that *Naomi* can be read as a kind of extended metaphor for the Japanese worship of all things Western in the popular culture of the time. Naomi as a woman certainly represents something that Kawai, for all his homegrown virtues, cannot hope to obtain. In trying to take on Western customs, and a Western-style mistress, he can only remain clumsy, and his uncritical worship of the West through these means only makes him denigrate the Japanese virtues that provide him what dignity he has. Certainly there are aspects of this worship of the West running through the story, but Tanizaki, always a master of subtle social commentary, never intended to adopt such a simplistic view. *Naomi* is no tract. Much of the wry tone of the novel, in fact, comes from the fact that Kawai, in several important aspects of his own life, is not a reliable narrator. His desires, particularly in the erotic areas of his psyche, are often at best half articulated, even to himself. There is a droll hypocrisy about many of his responses and attitudes. Thus, many of Naomi's responses must be judged in terms of Kawai's own possessiveness and self-serving sentimentality. In one way, Naomi, as sketched by Tanizaki, seems to represent Kawai's own Freudian slip, a needed, objectified figment of his erotic imagination. She allows him to find out things about himself that he is quite incapable of articulating in any straightforward manner.

Although the novel centers on Kawai and Naomi, there are several minor characters sketched with deftness and humor by Tanizaki, and they contribute considerably to the deftness and humor of the narrative. In particular, two Westerners living in Japan are described with special panache. One is the woman who teaches the couple Western social dancing, Aleksandra Shlemskaya, a white Russian refugee who presumably learned dancing in her former social milieu and is now looking for an income in Tokyo. Limpid, bejeweled, and holding a short whip, she commands her cowering students to learn their steps as though they were military recruits. Another satiric figure is a slim foreigner who wears white makeup, William McConnell, "the Wolf of the West," to whose house Naomi goes when she runs away from Jōji. Naomi's band of lovers, too, most of them college students, provide a winsome chorus of complaint and disappointment to echo Kawai's longer and louder laments.

Tanizaki has created a series of satiric settings that do much to fix the ironic and amusing tone of the narrative. In particular, Kawai's peculiar and ill-planned Western-style house, which he rents for Naomi and himself, seems a virtual symbol for a misunderstanding of the West, and such spots as the El Dorado Dance Hall are redolent with the atmosphere of imported delight that attracts Jōji and Naomi alike.

At the beginning of his career, Tanizaki often identified as his masters such writers as Oscar Wilde and Edgar Allan Poe. By 1924, however, Tanizaki was himself a full-fledged master, and the tone and style of *Naomi* are altogether his own. Indeed, Tanizaki's voice is virtually unique in the literature of Japan and remarkable enough in the modern literature of any country, for its suggestive, sophisticated ironic tone is used in *Naomi* to render to the reader a wise understanding of the necessarily ludicrous aspects of human sexual and sentimental relationships. *Naomi* makes a perfect companion to the more elegiac *The Makioka Sisters* in capturing the limits of what men and women can, in the end, make of each other.

J. Thomas Rimer

Sources for Further Study

Booklist. LXXXII, October 1, 1985, p. 193.
Kirkus Reviews. LIII, September 1, 1985, p. 904.
Library Journal. CX, October 1, 1985, p. 117.
The New Republic. CXCIII, November 11, 1985, p. 36.
The New York Review of Books. XXXII, November 21, 1985, p. 23.
The New York Times Book Review. XC, October 20, 1985, p. 12.
The New Yorker. LXI, November 18, 1985, p. 171.
Publishers Weekly. CCXXVIII, August 9, 1985, p. 63.
Vogue. CLXXV, September, 1985, p. 498.

NATIVES AND STRANGERS

Author: Louisa Dawkins
Publisher: Houghton Mifflin Company (Boston). 404 pp. $18.95
Type of work: Novel
Time: 1956-1973
Locale: East Africa and London

A European girl, tied to England by blood and to Kenya by emotion, struggles to tame the forces and relationships competing in her disordered life

> *Principal characters:*
> MARIETTA HAMILTON, a white girl born and reared in colonial East Africa
> VIRGINIA HAMILTON, her mother, an innkeeper with a taste for the wanderer's life
> NEVILLE BILTON, Virginia's short-term husband and Marietta's long-term stepfather
> JONATHAN SUDBURY, Marietta's husband, a white hunter and gentleman farmer
> JUSTIN, a Ruba man who keeps house for Virginia and Marietta
> VIOLET, his daughter and Marietta's only real friend
> MICHAEL KAGIA, Jonathan's foe and Marietta's lover
> CATHERINE ONGAKI, Marietta's schoolmate

For most American readers of fiction, Africa remains, even in the late twentieth century, a largely unknown territory. Peopled in our imaginations at worst with Tarzan and Cheetah and at best with characters created forty years ago by Ernest Hemingway, Graham Greene, and Isak Dinesen, the countries of this vast continent, so carefully printed in contrasting colors in the atlas, have a distressing tendency to move and blur in our minds, coming into focus only when they temporarily capture headlines or are mentioned in the evening news. Apart from Nadine Gordimer and perhaps Athol Fugard, contemporary African writers are not widely read in North America, and for most of us, the African landscape of our imagination is as unexplored as the sands of the Sahara.

Louisa Dawkins' subtle and moving novel, *Natives and Strangers*, cannot in itself relieve this ignorance, but it does succeed in providing the rudiments of a new fictive geography. In this story of a girl growing to adulthood during the 1950's and 1960's in the Great Rift Valley of East Africa near the shores of Lake Victoria, the author has evoked with great precision the emotional power of a very particular place. The beauty of the vast, rich landscape where Mt. Elgon, the tip of its cone broken off in some long-past volcanic eruption, towers above the dusty towns and fertile farms of the valleys, has entered into the blood of Dawkins' characters; it draws them back when they attempt to leave and makes them fight bitterly against their own logic to remain when time and history are clearly against them. The texture of small-town life in Kenya and Tanganyika as it is felt by a child scuffling barefoot through the heat and dust has the weight of authenticity: One can hear the prostitutes argue with their customers through the board walls of back country hotels and smell the stock growing beneath the rails of colonial verandas.

Like Paul Scott's *The Raj Quartet* (1966, 1968, 1971, and 1975) *Natives and Strangers* is about the colonial experience—more specifically, about the end of the colonial experience. Dawkins' characters, the children and grandchildren of settlers who left England for Kenya when the British empire was already in decline, must come to terms with the legacy bequeathed them by their parents and define their roles in a world that they only gradually learn is in the process of transformation. More direct and less intricate than *The Jewel in the Crown* (1966), this novel shares with the Scott books a breadth of vision that enables the reader to comprehend the moral landscape that lies behind and beneath the action.

Is Marietta Hamilton, Dawkins' heroine, a native or a stranger in East Africa? Certainly, as the daughter and granddaughter of white British colonials, she can hardly be defined as a native in the aboriginal sense, but like most of the men and women who are important in her life, she was born in the Great Rift Valley and feels lost and alien elsewhere. Mari's restless and beautiful mother, Virginia, herself an alien of sorts in rebellion against a narrow colonial family, runs a series of guest houses and hotels for touring British officials in the small towns of Kenya, transforming run-down watering places into modern resorts and moving on to new places when her life threatens to become too settled. Mari is cared for by Justin, Virginia's African houseman, whose daughter Violet is Mari's best friend, and who is involved in some way that Mari does not understand with the mystery of her father, who committed suicide six months before she was born.

When Virginia returns to England for an extended vacation, on one of the trips regularly made by settlers to reinforce their identities after years of exposure to the debilitating African heat, it is only natural that six-year-old Mari, nominally in the care of a neighbor couple, will travel with Justin and Violet to their home on the island of Galana in the Kavironda Gulf. Sleeping on floor mats with Violet, doing chores, and listening to the enthralling stories of the co-wives of Justin's father, Mari feels at home. Justin is, after all, her second father: He provides the only real stability and continuity in her life. When she is teased by the family she expresses no doubt about the fact that, like the grandmothers, she will share a husband with Violet when they both are grown. Certainly England, the fabled paradise of her mother's friends, could be no more pleasant than lake-washed Galana.

Dawkins blends the personal story—Mari's coming of age, physically and, much later, emotionally—with the political situation that shapes her character's consciousness and fate with unusual skill. Because of Virginia Hamilton's stubborn independence and her refusal to be bound by the conventions of colonial life, the Hamiltons have more freedom than the settlers around them. Mari grows up aware of the barriers of race and class but relatively untouched by them. Violet may not be able to eat in the hotel dining room, but except at mealtime the girls are seldom separated. They share the correspondence course sent out from South Africa, handing their lessons to Justin to mail each week, and hide in ditches together to watch the Indian girls in pleated skirts and patent leather shoes walk in lines to the school behind the hotel where neither of them, for opposite reasons, is permitted to go.

Virginia impulsively marries, but the idyll continues. Neville, Mari's new stepfather, whisks the entire household to his bizarre home, a Romanesque castle with turrets and a telescope that he has had built for him on a mountainside near the Kenya-Uganda border. Mari loves Neville immediately. The only fairy tale she knows is "Sleeping Beauty"; can this be her prince? With him she goes camping and explores the mountainside, even turning away from Violet in her passion to learn and to belong to this gentle and cultivated man, who is in turn awakened and enchanted by Mari's curiosity.

The marriage lasts only a few months. Virginia has misjudged her ability to tolerate a man whose life is rooted in a building and a piece of land. Mari reluctantly returns to the old life, close again to Violet and Justin, but conscious now of loss and betrayal. When her mother, in a fit of compunction, enrolls her in a local school, she finds herself comfortable neither with the stolid children of the European farmers nor with the clever daughter of the local black ruler, Chief Matthias, whose rather sharp comments about her mother—the "wanderer"—confuse and anger Mari. Still on the fringes of Virginia's life, Mari writes to Neville and longs for rescue.

Virginia is not evil, only thoughtless and caught up in her own problems. Eventually Mari, lonely and curious, allows herself to be seduced by one of her mother's boyfriends. Virginia, shaken at last, realizes the precariousness of her position and sends Mari first to boarding school, where she finds herself rooming with Catherine Ongaki, her nemesis from the Keriki school, and then to England, where the girl stays with Neville's mother and plans to study art. She watches her former stepfather's plane crash moments before they are to be reunited.

Virginia Hamilton's detachment, unsettling as it may have seemed to the child, assured her survival in a country which was beset by social change throughout most of her lifetime, and Mari eventually learns to follow her example. Passion and involvement can only destroy. In England, Mari meets and, against her better judgment, marries another child of the Great Rift. Jonathan Sudbury makes a living running safaris for rich Americans, but he is obsessed with the farm which his parents have spent their lives establishing and haunted by the "ancestors," lingering specters of the colonial past that overwhelm him with guilt. Mari, pregnant, returns to East Africa to have her child and manage the land. When Jonathan, bitter and pathetic, shoots himself, Mari's African lover, a politician whose rivalry with Jonathan dates back to their childhood, makes it clear that she has been an instrument of his revenge. Thus, she finds herself on her own, just as her mother had been, neither a native nor a stranger. In order to exist with her child, she must finally leave. Violet asks her,

> "What kind of life will you lead?"
> "An ordinary life."
> "And what is that?"
> "It's one without myths or special privileges. Without the burden of what happened once and of how things used to be. It's a life in which you choose what to do, the choice hasn't been made by others before you were born."

Louisa Dawkins is an anthropologist. What distinguishes her novel is the trained eye she brings to the plight of her heroine and the persuasive analysis she makes of the conflicting cultures which have formed her. As she moves from native huts to London town houses and Chicago living rooms, Mari comes to understand that she has spent her life trapped in a world whose artificiality is as blatantly absurd as the architecture of Neville's castle on Mt. Elgon. Yet the new Kenyans, unlike Violet and Justin, who belong to the past, are in some ways as remote from her as the old settlers. Michael Kagia, her lover, and Catherine Ongaki are fierce and cold in their rational demands to control the future and avenge the past. New forms of social organization must evolve for both blacks and whites in Africa, and at the end of the book it is not clear to anyone what these forms will be.

Dawkins' clarity and precision are effective in conveying Mari's plight, but the emotional power of the book has another source. *Natives and Strangers* is at heart neither a novel about the decline of colonial power nor the story of a sensitive adolescent coming of age in a brutal culture. It is an exploration of the relationships between parents and children, of the universal struggle for love and recognition within the family and of the legacies that are passed on from one generation to the next. Violet feels that Mari has displaced her as Justin's daughter. Mari seeks a father in every man to whom she is attracted, hoping to reach through some magic paternity a sense of security and peace. Michael, having ousted Jonathan Sudbury from his parents' affections as a child, can never forget the white boy's jealous arrogance and seeks somehow to appease the spirit of his own father, put to death in the British hysteria that followed the Mau-Mau uprising. Catherine, the child of a prostitute—like Virginia, a "wanderer"—who became her father's favorite wife, seeks to consolidate her power and wield it against a world that scorned her mother.

In a sense, Africa is itself the parent whose embrace they all seek, the body that they simultaneously long to be a part of and to escape. The landscape of Kenya thus becomes an aspect of the theme. Multiple meanings accrue to the Great Rift which gives the valley its name: It is the gap between the colonial past and the African present, between the blacks and the whites, between the natives and the strangers, and finally between the childhood unconsciousness that establishes the image of a home to which we can never return and the adult perception of a bleak, inhospitable society in which no one seems to have a continuing place.

Natives and Strangers is a first novel. There are occasional and jarring lapses in point of view, but these are compensated for by the freshness of the author's tone and her ability to make the reader see a potentially trite situation with new eyes. The clichés and stereotypes that hover about the edges of most popular novels are deftly avoided. One of Jonathan's American customers, seeing Justin playing with Mari's baby, Charles, makes a fatuous remark about *Gone with the Wind*. The inane comparison serves to point up the achievement of Dawkins' novel. The consequences of Kenya's civil tumult in the twenty-odd years are as dramatic as those of America's Civil War. In both cases, the lives of the dominant and subservient classes were intertwined and the dislocation of the former was abrupt. Yet political dislocation is less important in Dawkins' novel than the internal tumult that is at once a result and a symptom of the change. The educated Africans and their often interracial families, who populate Mari's social world at the end of the book, are certainly different from the Europeans who only a decade before refused them admission to her mother's hotels, but it is to the author's credit that the reader cares less about the enormity of the social change than about the fates of the individual characters who have lived through it. The interrelationships of Mari and Justin and Catherine and Michael may embody the revolution, but the links between these people transcend the class and racial differences that place them. One is not conscious of Africans and Europeans in reading the novel, only of people undergoing change and stress.

Because it manages to connect the forces of political upheaval to the patterns of human growth and emotional need, *Natives and Strangers* has unusual power. It presents a vivid picture of one corner of contemporary Africa and places recognizable people in an exotic landscape which they, like the reader, find difficult to control or comprehend.

Jean W. Ashton

Sources for Further Study

Booklist. LXXXII, October 1, 1985, p. 190.
Glamour. LXXXIII, November, 1985, p. 210.

Kirkus Reviews. LIII, August 15, 1985, p. 804.
Library Journal. CX, October 1, 1985, p. 111.
The New York Times Book Review. XC, December 22, 1985, p. 11.
The New Yorker. LXI, February 10, 1986, p. 113.
Publishers Weekly. CCXXVIII, August 23, 1985, p. 60.

NERO
The End of a Dynasty

Author: Miriam Tamara Griffin (1935-   )
Publisher: Yale University Press (New Haven, Connecticut). Illustrated. 320 pp.
   $25.00
Type of work: Historical biography
Time: A.D. 54-69
Locale: Rome

A scholarly examination of how imperial policies to weaken senatorial opposition evolved into such tyranny and financial mismanagement that the Roman nobility had to remove Nero to save itself

> *Principal personages:*
> NERO, Roman emperor, A.D. 54-69
> AGRIPPINA, his mother
> AUGUSTUS, the first Roman emperor, 27 B.C.-A.D. 14
> TIBERIUS, Roman emperor, A.D. 14-37
> CALIGULA, Roman emperor, A.D. 37-41
> CLAUDIUS, Roman emperor, A.D. 41-54
> SENECA, Nero's tutor and adviser
> BURRUS, the commander of the Praetorian Guard

Many readers of the History Book Club's recent main selection will be stretched to finish this volume. Expecting to find sex and violence, they will instead encounter detailed analyses, repetition, and mild humor intended for specialists. One wonders what the lay reader is to make of a sentence that ends: "...when Helvidius thought the time was propitious, he first fought explicitly for senatorial independence and then, when disillusioned, chose a more outspoken and provocative way of fulfilling his senatorial duty than absention." This book is intended for readers who know what Helvidius did without being told, because the author does not tell.

Miriam Griffin is a fellow of Somerville College at Oxford and has previously published a monograph on Seneca. She writes for such a small audience that even the dedication is something of an inside joke: "To JG, JBG, MCG, VTG Nero's latest victims." Nevertheless, for the specialist, Griffin has some very interesting ideas buried in her chapters—each of which stands much as a separate essay.

The thread which binds the whole together is a belief that the Roman nobility held to such strong conservative ideas about the superiority of amateurs over professionals that effective government would have been impossible if emperor after emperor had not fought for efficient bureaucracies staffed by freedmen and slaves, and for financial security through a great imperial household estate, by personal intervention crushing dangerous individuals as they arose to threaten the precarious stability of the regime. This strong conservative nobility would not cooperate effectively with the emperors, as repeated efforts at senatorial reform demonstrated, and it could not be trusted to govern, since it was composed of individuals whose secret hope was to succeed to imperial power themselves. To avoid deadlock in government or civil war, one emperor after another tired of efforts at cooperation and assumed full responsibility for governing.

This meant that each emperor ultimately had to face the temptation to govern tyrannically. Whether he did so or not was a matter of personality. So far, this theory offers nothing new. What Griffin does with it is both remarkable and understated. She removes the moralistic wrapping that has enveloped the Julio-Claudian emperors to such an extent that one cannot see them in a human-sized perspective. In the place of moralism, she proposes a dilemma in situational ethics that explains the choices that each emperor made: Those who came to office as mature, experienced men with a good reputation as politicians and generals were able to deal with the nobility easily—few dared to challenge their policies. Emperors who acceded to office while young and inexperienced had to buy an offsetting support from the mob and the army. This policy could be maintained for a few years (each time a golden age) until they had dissipated the resources brought together by their predecessors. When the moment of reckoning came, they had to replenish their finances through confiscations and heavy taxes. These policies ultimately brought about their overthrow.

The lay reader will not readily see this thread of argument, nor can he be expected to see its importance. The specialist, however, will quickly grasp the essentially revisionary nature of this book and eagerly follow the scholarly debate that can be expected in the future. Anyone looking for lurid episodes of imperial life had better look elsewhere. This is a scholar's book.

Griffin analyzes Nero's policies as conflicts with the social conservatives who dominate the Senate, the army, and many high government posts. Central to her approach is the much-debated role of Seneca and Burrus as the powers behind the throne during the first five years of Nero's reign—the golden age. Griffin discounts their importance, dismissing Dio Cassius' account as self-serving advice to his own ruler, and demonstrating Suetonius' self-contradictions. She holds with Tacitus that Nero was his own man from the beginning, a young man of talent who took advice because he thought it good, not because he was anybody's lackey. She backs this claim with an analysis of governmental decisions so detailed that she probably loses most readers before the book is a third along.

Tacitus has been criticized for failing to explain properly the suddenness of Nero's change from a good to an evil ruler. Surely there was more than personality involved. Tacitus' strong point was as moral history, with his emphasis on the necessity of listening to sage advice, especially from historians. Griffin shows that the change was not sudden; rather, by about A.D. 62, the effects of earlier policies had become noticeable. The crisis was essentially financial, beginning with a storm that destroyed the ships bearing corn from Egypt and culminating with the Great Fire of 64. Nero was unable to correct the situation because, in playing the role of the generous benefactor, he had bankrupted the imperial finances.

Nero worsened his prospects by embarking on a building program in the heart of Rome that emphasized imperial power and vanity and required heavy contributions from all classes. This came at the moment that Nero's personal life and public conduct were causing the upper class to doubt his sanity. Unconventionally, Griffin ignores the well-known excesses described by the ancient historians associated with the nobility and concentrates on outlining policies that ran counter to upper-class mores. Her description of Nero's Golden House emphasizes the public nature of the building, argues against its disrupting life or commerce, and demonstrates that Nero was not likely to have set the fire to clear an area for his project. In fact, the extensive series of buildings that composed the Golden House were constructed in areas spared by the fire. What offended senators was the great cost of the place (which caused Nero to look among their numbers for potential expropriations), the display of arrogant power, and the inconvenience occasioned by Nero's residing temporarily in more private quarters (which made access more difficult). Moreover, Nero soon undertook a trip to Greece; the senatorial class considered Greeks to be something less than real men—businessmen, perverts, and generally soft—and the acclaim that Greeks gave Nero confirmed the senators in their opinion that he was seriously lacking in Roman virtues.

The Roman historians have caused us to sneer at Nero's pretensions as an artist; Griffin encourages us to look again at what he was doing. Nero was not an innovator in the arts. He took what was popular, encouraged it, and subsidized it. Roman nobles were not equipped to make good aesthetic judgments, but his Greek subjects were, and they were wildly enthusiastic about Nero's efforts. It was not merely that Nero supported art by patronage—the emperor encouraged, by personal example, the development of talent through study and training. Unfortunately, Nero's disturbed personal life and his financial incompetence undermined much of the influence this might have had among the nobility.

In short, the spendthrift financial policies that Nero undertook as a patron of the arts were not solely the result of artistic desires: They were part of a cultural policy designed to undermine the old mores. Nero used his plays, his music, and the games to lure away noble youth from the ancient concept of a gentleman as a member of a closed caste who could involve himself honorably with war, high public office, country life, and the arts only as an amateur pastime. The senatorial class, Griffin implies, wanted power and all that came from power without exerting themselves unduly. Shortsighted, arrogant, and self-righteous, they frustrated the imperial bureaucracy in every way they could. Nero needed professional men who could manage the extensive Roman government and understand the needs of the varied Mediterranean cultures, especially the Greeks, who provided the bulk of the taxes. When Nero eventually concluded that senatorial cooperation was not forthcoming, he began to block the ambitions of even the most able opposition senators by promoting ahead of them men such as Otho, who were willing to break with the past (and who then were considered dissolute and unrespectable) or talented individuals from the lower classes, such as Vespasian. In doing this, he frightened the Senate. When the conservatives realized that they were losing their monopoly on high office in the state and the army, they began to think about replacing Nero.

The lack of a law of succession and the longtime imperial policy of intermarrying with the leading Roman noble families meant that hundreds of individuals could consider themselves eligible to succeed Nero, should he die. Since Nero was periodically ill and did not produce a son, he had reason to fear the ambitions of those senators who opposed his policies. He began to strike them down. The more he killed, the more he came to fear the survivors. Nevertheless, the more he killed, the closer he came to coping with his financial troubles, since he could confiscate the estates of his victims. Ultimately, he had murdered so many of his near and distant relatives that the imperial family became extinct, and the old Roman nobility was so reduced in numbers that it never recovered.

After A.D. 65, Nero turned from this horror to art and began to live increasingly in a fantasy world. As his behavior became ever more bizarre, the commanders of the armies believed themselves both unappreciated and threatened. A revolt of some kind was inevitable—to save the human race, as Roman nobles put it. Nevertheless, so strong was the belief that the emperor alone guaranteed political stability that Nero could probably have prevailed had he but exerted himself. Many officers and officeholders were beholden to him for their posts, and he was extremely popular in the East. Many nobles understood that civil war would cost them lives and property—hence their propensity for a quick, clean coup d'état. The failure of several conspiracies, however, had cost them their best leaders and convinced others that silence and acquiescence was the only way to survive until the gods removed Nero from the scene.

Nero came to despise his opponents, first returning sneer for sneer, then executing his detractors without mercy. This had dire consequences. His military commanders knew that their armies protected the empire against very real enemies, and they were not amused by suggestions that their contributions were unimportant; they were understandably concerned by Nero's mockery of military virtues and his devaluation of martial honors. When, in addition, they feared their replacement by men whose qualifications hardly extended beyond imperial favor, they acted to save the Roman state. Even so, they were far from united. Many legions and many commanders put their faith in Nero. At the critical moment, Nero demonstrated once more his basic incompetence. Ignoring pleas to put himself at the head of his army, he abdicated the crown to his enemies. He knew that he was a failure as an emperor and had no faith in his ability to play the part even for a short while. All he could think about in his last moments was his reputation as an artist. Having confused his artistic goals with his political purpose, he fled his responsibilities, sealed his doom, and brought his dynasty to a squalid end.

William L. Urban

Sources for Further Study

The Atlantic. CCLV, May, 1985, p. 105.
Best Sellers. XLV, April, 1985, p. 21.
Choice. XXII, July, 1985, p. 1679.
Library Journal. CX, April 1, 1985, p. 137.
Times Literary Supplement. May 10, 1985, p. 517.
Wilson Library Bulletin. LIX, June, 1985, p. 709.

NICARAGUA
Revolution in the Family

Author: Shirley Christian (1938-   )
Publisher: Random House (New York). 337 pp. $19.95
Type of work: History and current affairs
Time: 1978 to 1984
Locale: Nicaragua and the United States

A fact-packed, lucidly written account of Nicaraguan history from the overthrow of the last Somoza to the outbreak of the Contra rebellion against the Sandinistas

Principal personages:
ANASTASIO SOMOZA DEBAYLE, President of Nicaragua, 1967-1979
DANIEL ORTEGA SAAVEDRA, head of the nine-man Sandinista Directorate after 1979; President of Nicaragua after 1984
JIMMY CARTER, thirty-ninth President of the United States, 1977-1981
MIGUEL OBANDO Y BRAVO, archbishop of Managua and principal leader of the Roman Catholic Church in Nicaragua
PEDRO JOAQUÍN CHAMORRO CARDENAL, editor of *La Prensa* and critic of the Somoza regime
VIOLETA BARRIOS DE CHAMORRO, his widow; one of the leading critics of the Sandinistas
EDÉN PASTORA GÓMEZ, one of the Contra military leaders
ALFONSO ROBELO CALLEJAS, one of the Contra civilian leaders
RONALD WILSON REAGAN, fortieth President of the United States, 1981-

The Sandinista National Liberation Front, founded in 1961, at first posed little threat to the Somoza dynasty, which was solidly entrenched in power since the mid-1930's. After the assassination of opposition journalist and editor of *La Prensa* Pedro Joaquín Chamorro Cardenal, however, violent rebellion against President Anastasio Somoza Debayle spread throughout Nicaragua as the moderate opposition joined forces with the Sandinista guerrillas. A seesaw military struggle culminated in Somoza's flight into exile in July 1979.

Shirley Christian, currently a foreign-affairs reporter for *The New York Times*, was formerly an Associated Press reporter for the *Miami Herald*, and has contributed stories to *The Atlantic Monthly* and *The New Republic*. In 1981, she won the Pulitzer Prize in International Reporting and was the first to win that award solo. She also won the George Polk Award for the best foreign reporting in perilous circumstances. In this work, she stresses the crucial role played by President Jimmy Carter in the Sandinista triumph. Christian tells the reader a fascinating inside story of how an inexperienced American administration, traumatized by memories of the Vietnam War and guilt-ridden over earlier American interventions in Central America, proved unable to do anything to avert a Sandinista takeover. According to Christian, this unwillingness to intervene prevailed despite an explicit warning from Harold Brown, the United States secretary of defense, that the Sandinista front was probably dominated by Marxist-Leninists. Following the overthrow of Somoza, the Carter Administration watched helplessly as moderates were gradually but inexorably squeezed out of the new revolutionary regime.

Some Americans praise the Sandinista government as the first regime in the country's history to pursue policies favoring the poor majority rather than the upper classes; such observers tend to view opposition to the new regime within Nicaragua as reflecting the class interests of the well-to-do. Christian, unlike such American sympathizers with the Sandinistas, does not believe that the political history of Nicaragua can be interpreted as a simple conflict between rich and poor. The peasants of Somoza's Nicaragua, she insists, were long indifferent to the appeals of the Sandinista guerrillas. Somoza's regime, she argues, was overthrown only after it had incurred the opposition of the overwhelming majority of the Nicaraguans, including the wealthy. The split over Sandinista policies, Christian shows, runs not between the educated elite and the masses, but within the elite itself, and sometimes even within elite families: Violeta Barrios de Chamorro, widow of the martyred newspaper editor, is a vocal critic of the Sandinistas, while one of her sons, Carlos Fernando Chamorro Barrios, is a fervent partisan of the new regime.

Although conceding that wealthy businessmen and rich landowners often did come to oppose the new regime's policies, the author shows that other social groups also collided with what she sees as a movement toward totalitarianism. Thus the petty food vendors of the Managua market fought in vain against the Sandinistas' determination to control distribution. Independent trade unionists protested unsuccessfully against official harassment. By trying to promote a separate, pro-government People's Church, the new regime brought upon itself the wrath of the Roman Catholic hierarchy, led by the outspoken archbishop of Managua, Miguel Obando y Bravo. Even the Miskito Indians rebelled against Sandinista encroachments over their traditional autonomy.

Citing mob intimidation and harassment of opposition rallies, Christian questions the democratic legitimacy of the November 1984 elections, boycotted by the opposition and won by Daniel Ortega Saavedra. Although conceding that there is strong support for the regime as well as strong opposition to it among the Nicaraguan people, she concludes that most Nicaraguans simply want to go with the winner.

For Christian, the Sandinista leaders are not well-meaning social reformers, driven toward alignment with Moscow only by the hostility of the administration of President Ronald Reagan, but power-hungry Marxist-Leninist ideologues. She shows that as early as the end of 1979, well before Reagan was first elected president, the new Nicaraguan regime had already begun to arm itself heavily, to import educators and military advisers from Cuba, and to set up block committees to control food rationing and to spy on those suspected of disloyalty. In April 1980, well before Reagan's election, with the resignation of Violeta Barrios de Chamorro and Alfonso Robelo Callejas from the government, the nucleus of determined opposition to the leftward course began to form.

Those Americans who sympathize with the Sandinistas tend to see the armed opposition to the regime, which emerged in 1982, as a purely artificial creation of the United States government. Christian, while conceding the role played by the Central Intelligence Agency (CIA) and American money, regards the rise of the Contras as a natural reaction to the Sandinistas' undemocratic policies. It was these policies that spurred even former foes of Somoza, such as onetime Sandinista military commander Edén Pastora Gómez, to raise the flag of revolt in 1982.

Christian admits that former Somoza military officers, as well as disaffected democrats, take part in the Contra insurgency. Unfortunately, she makes no attempt to assess the significance of these Somocistas in the overall Contra effort, even though the assertion that former henchmen of the fallen dictator dominate the anti-Sandinista resistance is frequently made by American sympathizers of the Sandinista regime. This assertion cannot fairly be ignored; it must be answered in some way. If such an assertion has even a grain of truth in it, it raises the possibility that the overthrow of the Sandinistas might bring with it not democracy but a right-wing military dictatorship such as the one that prevailed in Guatemala for thirty years following the overthrow of a left-wing regime in 1954. For a closer look at the Contra insurgency than that provided by Christian, one more willing to point out their faults as well as their virtues, the reader should consult Christopher Dickey's *With the Contras: A Reporter in the Wilds of Nicaragua* (1985).

Christian builds a persuasive case against the Sandinista regime, but she fails to present any clear prescriptions for American policymakers. She endorses American support for the Contras, but she expresses qualms about the ethics of the American government's manipulation of these men simply to extract foreign-policy concessions from the Sandinistas. Christian never addresses the question of what the United States should do if the Contras fail completely, leaving in power an unrepentant and increasingly pro-Moscow Sandinista regime. She does not say whether, in the event such a scenario should take place, an American invasion of Nicaragua could be justified or whether such an invasion could achieve quick and lasting success.

Christian relies chiefly on the testimony of the Nicaraguan moderates who once supported the Sandinistas but turned to the opposition as the regime moved leftward. The author also makes use of her interviews with high American officials of the Carter era, talks with ordinary Nicaraguans, and personal observations made while in Nicaragua.

Despite some flaws, Christian's book is essential reading for every concerned citizen who wants to become better informed about the Central
American crisis. Although a reporter, the author has a novelist's gift for
description that helps give the reader an intimate acquaintance with the bitter conflicts of Nicaraguan politics.

Paul D. Mageli

Sources for Further Study

Commonweal. CXII, November 1, 1985, p. 611.
Foreign Affairs. LXIV, Fall, 1985, p. 182.
Library Journal. CX, September 15, 1985, p. 71.
The Nation. CCXLI, September 7, 1985, p. 181.
The New Republic. CXCII, September 30, 1985, p. 32.
The New York Times Book Review. XC, July 28, 1985, p. 1.
Publishers Weekly. CCXXVII, June 7, 1985, p. 71.
The Wall Street Journal. CCVI, August 1, 1985, p. 15.
The Washington Monthly. XVII, July, 1985, p. 50.
Washington Post Book World. XV, July 14, 1985, p. 4.

NO MORE VIETNAMS

Author: Richard Nixon (1913-   )
Publisher: Arbor House (New York). 240 pp. $14.95
Type of work: Historical autobiography
Time: 1954-1985
Locale: Washington, D.C., and Vietnam

An often intemperate polemic defending the author's decisions regarding war in Vietnam, with a concluding chapter advancing a program for United States action in the Third World

Even veteran Nixon-watchers have difficulty recalling the number of "new" Nixons who have appeared since the 1950's, and the redoubtable former president is not through yet. Since his resignation under certainty of impeachment in 1974 and a three-year period of anonymity, he has sought to fill another new role, that of elder statesman and chief foreign-policy adviser to the powers-that-be. He has published a new book overy other year since his presidential memoirs, *RN*, appeared in 1978: *The Real War* (1980), *Leaders* (1982), *Real Peace* (1984), and now, *No More Vietnams*.

Of the postpresidential books (*Six Crises*, published in 1962, clearly belongs to earlier image-building efforts), the most useful has been *RN*. It was written close to the events it relates and is a personal record of the Nixon presidency. While far from being a detached and objective report, *RN* represented an attempt at credibility. Subsequent works appear to have more immediate and personal goals: to establish Nixon's authority as a foreign-affairs expert and to prepare reception for his views in the appropriate circles. His real influence has been exercised through carefully orchestrated interviews and private dinners for sympathetic journalists and politicians, appearances before prestigious foreign-policy groups, and contacts with highly placed officials. The fall 1985 issue of the influential journal *Foreign Affairs* featured Nixon's article "Superpower Summitry," and, in April of that year, he gave *Time* magazine editors a private interview on that subject.

In *The Real War*, *Leaders*, and *Real Peace*, Nixon perhaps unconsciously constructed a three-dimensional image: toughness, to conform to the hard-line anti-Communism of the Ronald Reagan presidential campaign and the rising bellicosity of a public opinion frustrated by the humiliation of the Iranian hostage crisis; personal acquaintanceship with many world leaders; and the vision and diplomatic skill to fashion what he still liked to call "a structure of peace." Perhaps he really wanted to be President Reagan's secretary of state.

No More Vietnams differs from his previous books. It is an uncompromising defense of his Vietnam policies, which is not surprising, and a detailed indictment of his critics, which is not only mean but often mistaken. Nixon presided over the war longer than any of his predecessors. When the last American troops departed, he certainly knew that, without half a million

Americans and billions of dollars' worth of munitions and equipment, the regime of South Vietnamese president Nguyen Van Thieu could maintain itself only for a "decent interval." In that context, the Christmas bombing at the end of 1972, the fiercest and most concentrated of the war, could neither have diverted the North Vietnamese from their march toward total victory nor convinced Thieu of continued American support. In retrospect, it seems to have been a pointless and atrocious spasm born of frustration.

That is not the way Nixon explains the situation. Quite the opposite:

> When Secretary of State William Rogers signed the Paris peace agreements, we had won the war in Vietnam. We had attained the one political goal for which we had fought the war: The South Vietnamese people would have the right to determine their own political future.... We won the war in Vietnam, but we lost the peace. All that we had achieved in twelve years of fighting was thrown away in a spasm of congressional irresponsibility.

Nixon does not explain what his course would have been, although one can assume that it would have involved more "Christmas bombings" and, inevitably, the reintroduction of American troops. Nixon was too astute to think that the American people would have stood for that—and in any case he was by then too mired in Watergate (which he mentions here only incidentally) to turn his attention back to Vietnam.

America's involvement in Vietnam, Nixon contends, was punctuated by "fundamental" errors, beginning with President Dwight D. Eisenhower's refusal in 1954 to send B-52s from Guam to bomb the Viet Minh besieging the French at Dien Bien Phu, as Nixon and Admiral Arthur W. Radford, chief of the Joint Chiefs of Staff, wanted to do. That decision, Nixon argues, cost the United States a last chance to stop Communist expansion into Southeast Asia. Eisenhower is blamed for not having sent aid to the Hungarians in 1956. President John F. Kennedy should have invaded North Vietnam in 1961 and at the same time provided air cover for the Cubans at the Bay of Pigs. Although almost no one familiar with the circumstances now believes that the U.S.S. *Turner Joy* and *Maddox* were really attacked by North Vietnamese torpedo boats in the Gulf of Tonkin in August 1964, Nixon holds to his opinion: "While some respected military observers have questioned whether the attack took place, I have concluded that it did and there is no credible evidence that we provoked it."

Harsher than his castigation of the Congress and of the press and television is the author's denunciation of antiwar demonstrators, particularly student activists. They, he says, "shot at firemen and policemen, held college administrators hostage at knifepoint, stormed university buildings with shotguns in hand, burned buildings, smashed windows, trashed offices, and bombed classrooms."

Nixon confidently analyzes the thinking of enemies. Thus, Ho Chi Minh's "guiding maxim" was: "It is better to kill ten innocent people than to let one enemy escape," and, in the aftermath of World War II, Joseph Stalin "began scanning the world for possible Communist conquests like a vulture searching for fresh carcasses." Sweeping assertions have long been a Nixon trademark: "The idea that Ho Chi Minh was primarily a Vietnamese nationalist has no basis in fact," and again, "the issue of religious repression [in South Vietnam] was a complete fabrication."

Nixon's airy dismissal of every opinion which does not suit his self-serving view of history ultimately undermines his credibility. His first chapter, "The Myths of Vietnam," begins with a list of some twenty statements, some generally accepted as true, a few patently false, and some merely tendentious. For example, Nixon insists that the domino theory has been proved true. Aside from the fact that such a "theory" is hardly susceptible to proof, there remain, after the Communist victory in Indochina (Cambodia and Laos are parts of the region the North Vietnamese claimed as successors to the French), Thailand, Burma, Indonesia, Malasia, Singapore, and others. Sturdy dominoes, Nixon to the contrary notwithstanding, they disprove the domino theory.

Opponents of the war in Vietnam and of all American efforts to prevent Communist expansion in the Third World, according to Nixon, base their positions on what he calls "four articles of faith": The Vietnam War was immoral, it was unwinnable, the United States was on the wrong side of history in Vietnam, and diplomacy alone is the best answer to wars of national liberation.

The last point is untrue; few of the Vietnam dissidents were pacifists, as Nixon surely knows. Nevertheless, they did believe that the war was both immoral and unwinnable, and for both those reasons the United States was on the wrong side of history. On a superficial level, the war was immoral because no vital American interests were at stake, and therefore the United States had no business intervening. On the other hand, as many opponents of the war conceded, the United States acted morally in going to the aid of a government and people threatened by conquest by their neighbor. The difficulty here is that rational analysis of the problem had to show that intervention in the end would leave the supposed beneficiaries worse off than before, and it might also inflict unpredictable damage on the United States itself. Hindsight makes such a conclusion easy, but there were many men in authority from 1961 to 1973 who made just that argument.

President Lyndon B. Johnson's under secretary of state, George Ball, was a kind of official naysayer within the administration. Richard Holbrooke, a foreign-service officer who resigned in protest, spoke for many others after the South Vietnamese collapse in 1975. He wrote that he had concluded early in the conflict that the North Vietnamese would continue to fight indefinitely despite all the United States could do and regardless of the cost to themselves. The problem thus became one of means and ends.

Would the United States conduct permanent war in Vietnam, scorching the land both north and south and inflicting millions more casualties, bombing the North Vietnamese "back to the Stone Age," as one air force general suggested? What of the cost at home? In Vietnam, would the United States continue to destroy villages in order to "save" them? After four, six, or eight years, could Americans continue to believe that their mission in Vietnam was humane? As Hendrik Hertzberg pointed out in *The New Republic* after the North's victory, American intervention in Vietnam was immoral because the ends sought were from the beginning unattainable, especially with the means that could be employed.

Thus, three of Nixon's supposed "articles of faith" turn out to be interconnected. The war on the American side was immoral because it was unwinnable, and since it was unwinnable, the United States was on the wrong side of history. Nixon asks whether the South Vietnamese would be better off if the Communists had not won, and the answer is yes. Yet that is not a serious question. If put realistically, the question would be: Would they be better off after another ten years of suffering and dying than under Hanoi's rule? Perhaps there is no answer to that, but it is certain that the American people would not and could not have put up with another ten years of the war.

In a final chapter, Nixon abruptly abandons his querulous review of the Vietnam War and offers advice on how to fight the Third World War, which he dates from 1945. His counsels, however, are contradictory. On the one hand, he would have the United States and its allies oppose the Soviet Union wherever it seeks to expand—a call to arms reminiscent of the Truman Doctrine and Kennedy's inaugural address. Aggression is most likely to occur in the Third World and be carried out by Soviet proxies; therefore "it is no longer enough to look for the smoking gun; now we must look for the hidden hand."

Nixon wants to repeal the War Powers Act and other congressional measures that inhibit the president's war-making capability, and he supports President Reagan's bellicose policies regarding Nicaragua, Angola, Afghanistan, and elsewhere. Such policies tend to contribute to the institutionalization of the military-industrial complex, which the unprecedented Reagan military buildup is promoting. At the same time, Nixon complains that the government spends 7 percent of the gross national product on defense and only two-tenths of 1 percent on economic aid. "This means," he argues, "that we are spending thirty-five times as much in preparing for a war that will probably never be fought as we are for programs that can help us win a war we are losing."

Which is the real Nixon? Probably the one represented in the chapter's final sentence: " 'No more Vietnams' can mean that we will not *try* again. It *should* mean that we will not *fail* again."

Meanwhile, Nixon continues to cultivate his image and enhance his private interests. A long piece he contributed to *The New York Times* op-ed page in January 1986 resurrected his first political triumph in the case of Alger Hiss. His lawsuit to recover some forty-two million pages of his presidential papers held in the National Archives, with a value reportedly in the millions of dollars, seems at last to be moving forward. There are more "new" Nixons in the American future.

Albert Hall Bowman

Sources for Further Study

Christian Century. CII, August 28, 1985, p. 775.
Foreign Affairs. LXIII, April, 1985, p. 919.
Library Journal. CX, April 1, 1985, p. 145.
Los Angeles Times Book Review. April 28, 1985, p. 2.
The New York Review of Books. XXXII, May 30, 1985, p. 11.
The New York Times Book Review. XC, April 7, 1985, p. 5.
Policy Review. Summer, 1985, p. 87.
Publishers Weekly. CCXXVII, March 15, 1985, p. 104.
The Wall Street Journal. CCV, April 11, 1985, p. 28.
Washington Post Book World. XV, March 31, 1985, p. 1.

NORTH GLADIOLA

Author: James Wilcox (1949-   )
Publisher: Harper & Row, Publishers (New York). 264 pp. $15.95
Type of work: Novel
Time: The 1980's
Locale: Tula Springs, Louisiana

A farcical look at small-town life

> *Principal characters:*
> ETHYL MAE COCO (MRS. COCO), a fifty-seven-year-old mother of six, who is a cellist and the manager of Pro Arts, a string quartet
> GEORGE HENRY, her thirty-seven-year-old son; first violinist in Pro Arts
> DUK-SOO YOON, a forty-nine-year-old violinist in Pro Arts, who secretly loves Mrs. Coco
> RAY JR., a seventeen-year-old schizophrenic who becomes a ward of Duk-Soo
> MR. COCO, the husband of Ethyl Mae
> HEIDI, George Henry's fiancée and the local hot-tub saleswoman
> TEE TEE, the murdered Chihuahua

Now that her six children are grown, but hardly what she would call settled, Ethyl Mae Coco's main concern is promoting Pro Arts, a chamber music group which she manages and in which she plays cello. As the book opens, the group is scheduled to perform at the black-tie opening of the town's first BurgerMat. Such are the goings on in Tula Springs, Louisiana, where no event is too small to cause a stir.

The musicians of Pro Arts are memorable, offbeat characters such as George Henry, the third of Mrs. Coco's six children, who plays first violin and anticipates his second marriage to Heidi, the local hot-tub saleswoman. Two six-packs of beer a day and only a bit of gray frizz on the top of his head make him appear older than his thirty-seven years. Mrs. Coco (as she is always referred to) cannot quite believe that someone so large and so old could have been her baby. Duk-Soo Yoon, a Korean completing a doctoral dissertation on tourism, plays second violin and struggles with his undeclared love for Mrs. Coco.

The title of the book comes from the street North Gladiola, where the Cocos reside. About midway through the book, Duk-Soo ponders the name:

Take North Gladiola, for instance. It was in the southern half of Tula Springs, and furthermore, there existed no South Gladiola, no Gladiola even. What did *North* in this case signify? And why *Gladiola*? The street was not a flower, not even a metaphorical flower, being as it was in the heart of the business district. Was it named after another North Gladiola by a homesick settler from Virginia or Illinois, thus making North Gladiola not a "here," after all, but a "there"?

Nothing more is made of North Gladiola, and it is left to the reader to ponder its significance, if any, as the book's title.

At an engagement in a mental institution, Mrs. Coco meets Ray Jr., a seventeen-year-old schizophrenic who inexplicably appeals to her. With this meeting, her life becomes considerably more complicated. This mixed-up, uncontrollable young man takes on a central role when Duk-Soo agrees to live with and care for him. At the Cocos one night, while briefly unsupervised, Ray Jr. murders a Chihuahua, believing it to be a killer rat. Duk-Soo plans an elaborate cover-up, mistakenly believing the tiny dog to be Mrs. Coco's beloved pet. Actually Tee Tee, the Chihuahua, belonged to the Tiger Unisex Hair Styling Salon, next door to the Cocos on North Gladiola Street. The dog had been a point of dispute between Mrs. Coco and the Tiger Unisex for some time. Thus the salon views Tee Tee's disappearance suspiciously, casting Mrs. Coco in the role of murderer.

Because of all the difficulty, Ray Jr. is returned to the institution. Duk-Soo attempts to make his love known to Mrs. Coco, but she, shocked at the very idea of it, cuts him off. After all, she is fifty-seven years old, has been married to Mr. Coco for forty years, and is the mother of six grown children. She knows that she should fire Duk-Soo, because he is even a terrible musician, but there is too much going on in Tula Springs just now. For example, it is time for the annual beauty pageant, and, according to the town gossip, Pro Arts is not being asked to perform at the event because of its suspected involvement in murder; Heidi, a heroin addict, is in a drug rehabilitation program, having been apprehended as a first-time user; and Mrs. Coco is distraught because the townspeople suspect a liaison between her and Duk-Soo.

Mrs. Coco is the focal point of the book. She is the kind of woman who refers to people as Sug, Heart, or Hon, the familiar, middle-aged woman from fiction who wonders about the man she married and about the young woman she was. She frets about her grown children, wondering how their lives went awry, how and when they became complaining, tiresome adults. While effectively communicating Mrs. Coco's existential dilemma, James Wilcox still manages to present a refreshingly comic image of this character. Mrs. Coco, for example, pops Sominex (no Librium for her), which she keeps handy for those times when her nerves get the best of her. Once, preoccupied with too many problems, she made Kool-Aid for the group during a practice. It seemed natural, somehow, to mix up in a pitcher raspberry Jell-O and Sweet'n Low instead of the more ordinary Kool-Aid. "Mrs. Coco had noticed her mistake in the kitchen but, not wanting to waste good food, served it anyway, without, of course, mentioning the mixup."

Mrs. Coco has the ability, along with most of the residents of Tula Springs, to give equal weight to the important and the mundane. In the middle of a conference with an attorney discussing Pro Arts' grievance with the beauty pageant for not being allowed to perform, Mrs. Coco looks out of the attorney's window where she can see her own backyard. Ray Jr., now her ward, is busily hanging up the laundry. "It was good that he was keeping himself occupied, but she was worried that he might be mixing the coloreds with the whites." This would be a trivial matter for some, but not for Mrs. Coco.

Then there is the matter of her children, who all descend on her for the wedding of George Henry and Heidi. None of the six has met her expectations. For their part, they have relocated as far from the family home as is geographically possible. One teaches horseback riding in Australia, one is a weaver in Canada, one studies nutrition in New York, and one writes obscure poetry in New Orleans. She is quick to point out their shortcomings. Wilcox, however, presents this classic struggle between a mother and her grown children with a light touch and a comic view.

Helen Ann, of all Mrs. Coco's offspring, presents special worries. As a teenager, she had an affair with Mayor Binwanger, resulting in a pregnancy terminated by abortion. It was then that she moved to Australia. Mrs. Coco never forgave herself, her daughter, and especially the hated Binwanger for this sordid affair. Helen Ann, graying and plump, has never put her life together and seems unable to succeed at anything.

Another main thread running through the novel is Mrs. Coco's struggle with Catholicism, to which she converted upon her marriage to Mr. Coco. She has been a devoted Catholic for forty years, but recently she is having doubts. For one thing, there is Helen Ann's abortion, which she not only sanctioned but also arranged and then conveniently swept under the carpet of her mind. Now, seventeen years later, she is confronted with the memory and the morality of it. She also sanctioned her oldest son's second marriage by attending the wedding, paying for the rehearsal dinner, furnishing him with a car, and paying for the honeymoon. With George Henry, however, she plans to put her foot down. He can marry Heidi, his second wife-to-be, but Mrs. Coco will not give her approval by attending the wedding.

In the end, the dead Chihuahua, Duk-Soo's unrequited love, Ray Jr.'s situation, Helen Ann's abortion, the future of Pro Arts, the place of Catholicism, and George Henry's marital state are all resolved. As is the case in many stories of small-town life, unlikely relationships between characters from the past and the present are revealed. While issues of family life and relationships are frequently treated in contemporary fiction, Wilcox's lighthearted approach is both welcome and highly distinctive.

In his first novel, *Modern Baptists* (1983), Wilcox introduced the town of Tula Springs, Louisiana, and its inhabitants, some of whom make a cameo appearance in *North Gladiola*. It is hoped that he will delve further into the life of this town with future offerings. Although the author treats relatively unsophisticated characters, his style is hardly minimalist; he writes long, involved sentences which, attesting his talent, read clearly and precisely. With remarkable attention to details of speech, gestures, and eccentricities, Wilcox creates small-town America comically skewed.

Terrill Brooks

Sources for Further Study

Kirkus Reviews. LIII, March 15, 1985, p. 249.
Library Journal. CX, April 1, 1985, p. 161.
National Review. XXXVII, August 23, 1985, p. 47.
New Statesman. CX, August 30, 1985, p. 26.
The New York Times Book Review. XC, June 30, 1985, p. 12.
Newsweek. CV, June 10, 1985, p. 79.
The Observer. September 1, 1985, p. 18.
Publishers Weekly. CCXXVII, April 12, 1985, p. 87.
Vogue. CLXXV, May, 1985, p. 210.
Washington Post Book World. XV, May 8, 1985, p. 2.

NOTHING HAPPENS IN CARMINCROSS

Author: Benedict Kiely (1919-   )
Publisher: David R. Godine, Publisher (Boston). 279 pp. $16.95
Type of work: Novel
Time: The early 1970's
Locale: Northern Ireland, Eire, and New York City

A meditative lament for the suffering incurred by political violence in Northern Ireland

Principal characters:
> MERVYN "MERLIN" KAVANAGH, a teacher who is a native of and visitor to Carmincross
> MR. BURNS, a hotelier and boyhood friend of Mervyn
> CECIL MORROW, a member of the Royal Ulster Constabulary and a boyhood friend of Mervyn
> DEBORAH, Mervyn's holiday girlfriend, an employee of Mr. Burns
> JEREMIAH GILSENAN, a cynic, civil servant, and new acquaintance of Mervyn

Since the onset of political violence in Northern Ireland (popularly but inaccurately known as Ulster) in 1969, a large number of novels have appeared, varying widely in quality and genre, purporting to depict the character of the opposing sides, the impact of the violence on noncombatants, and occasionally, going so far as to sketch in a certain amount of historical and sociological background. Some of these works have reached best-seller lists, and some of them are not entirely devoid of literary merit. None, however, begins to approach the range of allusion, intimacy of detail, and bitterness of exposition present in *Nothing Happens in Carmincross*.

That so comprehensive and devastating a statement has been made by Ulster's senior novelist should not be thought surprising. Yet, there is a note here, similar to but more audible than that in the concluding quartet of stories in Kiely's acclaimed collection, *The State of Ireland* (1980). This note, which is of lamentation—piercing yet subdued, furious but stoical—goes beyond fictive glibness and artistic puppetry to express the despair of Benedict Kiely, citizen and son of provincial Ulster. Perhaps this note has swollen in volume as the author has come to realize that the impatience with the sociopolitical reality of his native province in his early work has been harnessed for exclusively destructive ends by some of his fellow citizens. Where Kiely may have sought to reveal injustice and initiate discourse, the aim of the militarists (of all persuasions), as *Nothing Happens in Carmincross* implies, is to reduce the world they live in to silence.

The journey made by the protagonist, Mervyn Kavanagh, from his comfortable academic position in the southern United States to his native village of Carmincross is made in the name of harmony and renewal: the wedding of a favorite niece. Yet, with the destruction of the village by bombers, it becomes clear that Mervyn has been traveling toward the unspeakable.

Despite his being nicknamed Merlin, no charm, spell, or formulaic utterance can protect him, try as he might to use the glories of English poetry as talismans and traditional Irish ballads as amulets. One of the novel's least-harsh ironies is that Mervyn the academic has a mind like a haunted house.

Nevertheless, despite having nightmares of increasing severity, Mervyn does have a wonderful holiday prior to his arrival in Carmincross. The delights of normality are his to enjoy, largely in the person of an old girlfriend, Deborah, who accompanies him northward. (Carmincross is situated, as are the settings of most of Kiely's novels and stories, in western county Tyrone, a placid, river-rich country—in Kiely's imagination, an Eden.) To keep the sense of vitality alive, and to show the mind to be as playful as the body, Mervyn pretends that he and Deborah are the mythical Irish lovers, Diarmuid and Gráinne. It seems natural for him to do so; his mind is compulsively allusive. Moreover, to provide a romantic precedent for present pleasures reveals an understandable yet not entirely explicit need on the part of both Deborah and Mervyn to defend themselves against the depredations of the day—namely, the incessant reports of Northern atrocities. If their route to Carmincross parallels, as is suggested, the route of a celebrated retreat by a sixteenth century Irish chieftain, Deborah and Mervyn are anything but on the defensive. If the elopement of Diarmuid and Gráinne ended tragically, no such possibility is contemplated by their modern counterparts. The couple's unusual yet simple happiness is ironically glossed by the novel's structure, which places the section entitled "The Honeymoon" before the one called "The Wedding." Since Mervyn is Merlin, Deborah's name too must be allowed the resonance of its biblical origin. She is a prophet, Mervyn jokes. Tragically, her witnessing of the murder of a British soldier does foreshadow more traumatic killings—not only that of Stephanie Curran, Mervyn's niece and the bride-to-be, and not only that of Cecil Morrow, an amiable policeman and one of Mervyn's boyhood friends, but also the murder of a place, Carmincross.

Much of this novel's rich, dense texture is provided by detailed references to notorious episodes from "the troubles," as Ulster's ongoing political violence is euphemistically known. In fact, the central event, the murder of Carmincross, is clearly based on the destruction, also with numerous innocent victims, of the village of Claudy, county Derry, some twenty-five miles north of Omagh, county Tyrone, capital of Kiely country. (This event occurred on July 31, 1972, and has already entered Ulster literature and song by being the subject of a ballad by the poet James Simmons.) As Mervyn discovers, the violence is as inescapable as it is incomprehensible. Stories about it break in unexpectedly on Mervyn's consciousness. Violence is presented as an atmosphere, an additional dimension of the environment. Because of the informal, guerrillalike nature of paramilitary violence, there is no such condition as ordinariness in Ulster. The most inoffensive object might contain explosives; the most commonplace item may be employed in murder. The world cannot be trusted. The most likely victim could also be the most innocent citizen. The shooting to death of a deaf mute is cited. (Kiely spares none of those engaged in the violence—the deaf mute was shot by a British soldier.)

In saturating Mervyn's consciousness with this material, Kiely is rearranging the historical record, mainly by means of compression. As a note at the end of the novel declares: "The earnest student of atrocities will detect anachronisms. Some specimens have been moved about in time. And in place. Does it matter?" Compression creates the effect that by virtue of its omnipresence, violence makes the actual world as potentially nightmarish as anything the disturbed psyche can conceive. Internal unreason finds its counterpart in militaristic escapade, though the latter is executed in the name of cherished principles and traditions. Rationales, while they may provide the perpetrator of violence with a framework of self-justification, discipline the mind in a manner that is explicitly antithetical to Mervyn's associative, commemorative way of thinking. Furthermore, it is clear that Kiely's concern here is not so much with style as with value. Mervyn's appetite for experience, and his perhaps naïve but engaging gratitude for what each day brings, are clearly directly at odds with those who would reduce all experience to one purpose. It is difficult not to recall William Butler Yeats's "Easter 1916":

> Hearts with one purpose alone
> Through summer and winter seem
> Enchanted to a stone
> To trouble the living stream.

Kiely's main target in his excoriation of violence is the Provisional IRA (Irish Republican Army). When he quotes the opening phrase of the Proclamation of an Irish Republic, signed by the leaders of the Easter 1916 rebellion ("Irishmen and Irish women, in the name of God and the dead generations..."), his bitterness is palpable. While proclaiming itself to be the heir of the Irish Republican tradition, one of whose climactic occasions was Easter 1916, the Provisional IRA, by virtue of its anticivilian brand of violence, defaces that bequest. Kiely seems most concerned that this critique be established as early in the novel as possible. Mervyn's leisurely but clearly schematic reestablishment of his native credentials includes a visit to an old die-hard Republican, whose repetitious and cliché-ridden endorsement of events in the North is the mindless manifestations of an inanimate heritage. Yet Mervyn is unable to reject cynically the Republican heritage, as one of his companions on the visit does. The cynicism of this companion, Jeremiah Gilsenan, is in effect as mindless as the Republican veteran's slogans. There may be a strong desire, and an even stronger need, for a more humane embodiment of the Republican tradition (as is indicated by the set piece, toward the end of the novel, by the statue of Thomas Davis, proponent of Irish cultural nationalism and egalitarianism). Yet neither desire nor need receives public recognition. For this state of affairs, the South, or Republic of Ireland, is in some part to blame, it seems. References to it as "maimed" and "crippled" implicate it in one of the novel's most powerful imagistic motifs, that of amputation.

This motif, together with numerous references to the Crucifixion, reinforce the relentless disgust with and bewailing of violence that is the core of *Nothing Happens in Carmincross*. Though the text does contain fine outbreaks of candor, its somber effects are achieved more often by juxtaposition and association than by flat declarations, protests, or rebukes. On the whole, the novel keeps Kiely's reputation as a wordsmith intact. The familiar occasions of his verbal felicity are here again much in evidence. Love of lore, of the peculiarity and idiosyncrasy of the world of mortal men, is as prominent in this novel as in earlier works. Love of nature and of physical grace shines through, as does a relish for spontaneous singing and dancing, together with a delight in the enthusiasms of athletes, ridiculous in their excessiveness, magic in their momentariness (what Mervyn remembers best of all when he meets Cecil Morrow is playing football). In addition to, and amplifying, the novel's numerous endearing coinages is Kiely's most celebrated artistic trait—the storyteller's tone. Following the bombing of Carmincross, Mervyn becomes noticeably less garrulous and is most articulate when addressing remonstrances to death ("You ..."). Yet the flexibility and fluency of Kiely's tone sustains itself. The reminiscent, buttonholing, anecdotal voice speaks on in defiance of would-be silencers, celebrating even as it enacts its sense of life as an endlessly digressing yarn. Against what seems almost a denial of such a possibility, the author emerges in his most persuasive guise, as the loving (if profoundly embittered) chronicler of his native place. Not for nothing is Mervyn reminded that "perhaps the only real thing in the world is fidelity."

Resilience of tone, however, does not overcome some of the novel's structural problems. Some of these derive from the integrity with which the author maintains the view that the ultimate enemy of violence is love. Both honeymoon and marriage are desecrated by bullet and bomb. There is a sense that, given the ineffaceable reality of such events, acts of the mind seem impotent and irrelevant. The last third of the novel deteriorates as a narrative, and Mervyn's sojourn eventually terminates instead of reaching a satisfying conclusion. Prior to this final Dublin sequence, there is a productive interaction between an expository journalistic mode and a meditative poetic one. This partnership collapses in Dublin. While it may be argued that the result is a convincing depiction of Mervyn in a state of shock, Dublin offers little to make that state dramatically compelling for the reader.

Mervyn's failure to mobilize the resources and consolations of literature to allay the nightmare of violence finds an unsettling parallel in Kiely's apparent disinclination to bring a greater degree of formal and thematic integration to *Nothing Happens in Carmincross*. Yet, it is this aesthetic disappointment which reveals the author to be impotent in the face of his material, so much so that he declines to exercise his authorial privileges, refuses to tidy the Irish scenario. The novel ends with Mervyn—drunk, tentative, yet vigorous—on the point of rejoining his estranged wife. Yet that is in another country; by this time he has already returned to the United States.

Despite its structural looseness, this novel gives substantial and rewarding evidence of the brand of sanctity that graces Kiely's preoccupations. Piety toward place, reverence toward persons, respect for the past, hope in community remain fundamental tenets of his sentimental, humanistic, and lyrical talent. This novel silently inquires if such principles are tenable in today's Ulster. Bitterly, but honestly, the author answers in the negative. When Cecil Morrow remarks that nothing happens in Carmincross, he characterizes a peaceful backwater. When Benedict Kiely says the same thing, he means that nothing can happen there: The name of the village is synonymous with bomb craters, severed limbs, murderous strangers in explosives-laden cars. Nevertheless, by its unblinking gaze on the tenuousness of the ordinary under the shadow of murder, *Nothing Happens in Carmincross* becomes an indispensable act of witness, and thereby a creative alternative, to the destructiveness of political violence in Northern Ireland.

George O'Brien

Sources for Further Study

Booklist. LXXXII, November 1, 1985, p. 376.
Boston Review. X, November, 1985, p. 21.
Kirkus Reviews. LIII, September 1, 1985, p. 894.
Library Journal. CX, November 1, 1985, p. 110.
Los Angeles Times Book Review. October 20, 1985, p. 3.
The New York Times Book Review. XC, October 27, 1985, p. 7.
The New Yorker. LXI, October 21, 1985, p. 146.
Publishers Weekly. CCXXVIII, September 13, 1985, p. 125.
Times Literary Supplement. November 1, 1985, p. 1229.

THE OLD FOREST AND OTHER STORIES

Author: Peter Taylor (1919-   )
Publisher: The Dial Press/Doubleday & Company (Garden City, New York). 358 pp.
   $16.95
Type of work: Short fiction
Time: Primarily the 1930's and 1940's
Locale: Primarily the middle South

Fourteen stories, including one in dramatic form, representing more than forty years of fiction by an American master of the short story

The work of the Southern writer Peter Taylor has often been compared to that of Henry James, Jane Austen, and Anton Chekhov. Like theirs, his stories and plays are leisurely paced and focused on the manners and assumptions of the middle class. Influenced by John Crowe Ransom, Allen Tate, and Cleanth Brooks, the formalists with whom he studied as a college student, Taylor writes primarily traditional, realistic stories concerned with the disintegration of family life and the vanishing values of bygone eras. His settings are usually the cities of the middle South he knew growing up, particularly Nashville and Memphis and, occasionally, Saint Louis. *The Old Forest and Other Stories*, Taylor's eighth collection of short fiction, winner of the PEN/Faulkner Award for Fiction, includes fourteen stories, more than half culled from previous collections. Linked by the theme of time's effects on the values and relationships of upper middle-class Southerners and their servants, the stories in this new grouping offer stunning examples of Taylor's craftsmanship. Each is an intricate, ironic portrait that moves subtly yet inexorably toward a quiet moment of insight and truth.

The most common type of story in this collection is the memoir, a progressive retrospective usually narrated by an elderly man. Seven, fully half of the stories collected here, have first-person male narrators. Five of these stories are retrospectives. Of the remaining seven stories, one, "The Death of a Kinsman," is written as a short play; four are narrated in limited third-person point of view, evenly divided among male and female centers of consciousness; and one, "Bad Dreams," is told from the omniscient point of view. "A Walled Garden," the remaining story, is the only first-person retrospective narrated by a female; it represents a form of dramatic monologue spoken by an elderly Memphis matron to a young man waiting to escort her daughter out for the evening. Like many of the stories focusing on male protagonists, "A Walled Garden" concerns the relationship of parent and child. Here the mother relates a past incident from her daughter Franny's childhood. Unconsciously paralleling her cultivated garden with Franny, the mother reveals her struggle to civilize and control her daughter as well as the walled garden.

More common, however, are stories depicting the ironic, often strained relations between father and son. Three pieces offer examples: "The Gift of the Prodigal," "Promise of Rain," and "Porte Cochere." Of these, the first two are first-person retrospectives; the last is a third-person study in the paranoia of an aged father.

In "The Gift of the Prodigal," an elderly man watches from an upstairs window of his home the approach of his son Rick, the black sheep of the family who returns repeatedly needing help from his aging father. Told primarily through flashbacks, "The Gift of the Prodigal" paints a portrait of two intertwined lives: the son's sordid adventures and the father's gradually diminishing life. A widower crippled by the diseases of old age, the father frets about the gravel in his driveway, the few remaining duties he has at his business since he has partly retired, and the meaningless morning mail. Still an influential figure in his community, the father is in a position to rescue his son and thus, indirectly, hold the reins on his son's life. Yet, ironically, the father needs his son as much as the son relies on his father. Not only does the father delight in recounting Rick's troubles to other family members, but through his son's adventures, the father also escapes vicariously the narrowness of his own life. This is the "gift of the prodigal" that no one else can offer: exciting stories of passionate women, scandalous love affairs and spoiled marriages, tales of gambling and violent encounters with mobsters and corrupt policemen. "I find myself listening not merely with fixed attention," the father says at the end of the story, "but with my whole being. . . . I hear him beginning. I am listening. I am listening gratefully to all he will tell me about himself, about any life that is not my own." Appropriately, "The Gift of the Prodigal," which subtly depicts the interrelationship and mutual need of father and son, of listener and storyteller, is the first story in this new collection by Peter Taylor. The concluding words of the grateful, listening father offer an invitation to the reader to listen carefully to the voices and the stories that follow.

While "The Gift of the Prodigal" captures a father's perverse delight in the circumstances of his son's life, "Promise of Rain" records a father's disappointment in his youngest son and his struggle toward acceptance of the boy. The voice is that of the father. Will Perkins, a small financier, finds himself at fifty nearly idled by the Depression of the early 1930's. With his idle time, Mr. Perkins becomes a keen observer of his youngest son, Hugh Robert, who displays a self-absorption and vanity repugnant to the older man. A young man of Mr. Perkins' day was not so fascinated with himself. He studied serious subjects in school, history and Latin, not the speech courses that interest Hugh. His education completed, he took a position under his father in the family business, as the older Perkins sons do, and filled the roles prescribed by family and community. Hugh Robert is the first to seek an identity of his own, and his father fears he will leave home without warning, with only a note to say he is gone. The boy's fascination with himself clearly reflects the narcissism of a new generation; his interest in speech and theater—he later becomes a director of a small theater in another town—presages the occupational direction and mobility of a later era. To his father, however, these are troubling, even embarrassing signs, and the tone of his narrative reflects this concern. Yet Taylor skillfully allows his narrator's tone to modulate, so as to capture not only the father's disappointment but also his fondness and love for his son, even his nostalgia for the Depression era. The father, in fact, struggles to see his son sympathetically, and he is rewarded for his efforts with a rare insight one afternoon when his son waits anxiously to hear his own recorded voice on the radio. "I had a strange experience that afternoon," the father comments at the conclusion of the story.

> I was fifty, but suddenly I felt very young again. As I wandered through the house I kept thinking of how everything must look to Hugh, of what his life was going to be like, and of just what he would be like when he got to be my age. It all seemed very clear to me, and I understood how right it was for him. And because it seemed so clear I realized the time had come when I could forgive my son the difference there had always been between our two natures. I was fifty, but I had just discovered what it means to see the world through another man's eyes.

In contrast to the leisurely paced "Promise of Rain," with its depiction of empathy between father and son, "Porte Cochere" is a tightly structured tale about the growing paranoia of an elderly man with regard to his children. The events take place within a short time on one afternoon. Old Ben, the central character, has been celebrating his seventy-sixth birthday with his grown children, several of whom have traveled distances to be with their father. Nearly blind, old Ben faces encroaching darkness and death, but, more immediately, the loneliness and desolation of old age. He longs for love and respect from his children to lessen his pain, yet he is incapable of evoking or asking for the attention he craves. Instead, he attempts to manipulate his children to get his wishes, especially his favorite son, Clifford, whom, ironically, the old man admires and respects for his knowledge of history and his athletic prowess. Haunted by memoires of the harsh punishment he suffered from his own father, old Ben has granted his children a freedom he never had, yet he maintained tabs on them by building his study over the porte cochere, or drive-through, attached to his house. In an angry confrontation between Clifford and old Ben, both the old man's desperate need for his children and their justifiable anger and struggle for power and freedom vividly emerge.

Perhaps because it captures this unending struggle, "Porte Cochere" is one of the most disturbing stories in this collection. Its central symbol, the porte cochere itself, suggests the departure of old Ben's children from his life and, thus, the fate that awaits him. Though the children's struggle for freedom is both justifiable and essential for their growth, Clifford is nevertheless harsh and heartless with his father, whose main need, after all, is thoughtfulness and affection from his children. Moreover, although the story is set in Nashville, it offers none of the familiar Tennessee vistas Taylor adroitly paints elsewhere. The external landscape is old Ben's study, shadowy and secluded; the internal landscape is his mind, his memories and thoughts, and, above all, his growing confusion and fear. When, at the conclusion of the story, old Ben recognizes how his children have suffered at his hands, he is too frightened and confused to realize that they will not harm him. In a disturbing act of isolation and paranoia, he locks himself in his study and, too late, strikes at his children with his father's cane, the same cane which his father had used on him when he was a boy. Pitiably, it is only the chairs in his study that he strikes while calling "the names of children under his breath."

"The Old Forest" and "A Long Fourth," two other stories in this collection which focus in part on the relationship of parents and children, are less violent and, typical of Taylor's work, more slowly paced. Both, however, develop the familiar theme of time's effects on an older generation's values. Indeed, the "old forest," a section of Memphis near Overton Park, is a fitting symbol for the entire collection, for it suggests the social values and class and racial assumptions of the South's "old order"—values and assumptions that are central to most of the stories.

Another first-person retrospective narrated by an elderly man, "The Old Forest," the longest story in the collection, looks back forty years to draw contrasts between the working-class girls of the 1930's, the "demimondaines" as they were playfully called, and the independent young women whom the narrator, a college professor, encounters in the 1970's. The story's plot centers on a search for one of these "city girls" of the 1930's. Lee Ann Deehart is involved in an automobile accident with the narrator, Nat Ramsey, a week before his wedding. Immediately after the accident, she disappears mysteriously into Overton Park. Because the accident and disappearance occur in 1937, it is unthinkable to Nat's family or his fiancée's family that the wedding should go on as planned unless the girl is found. Thus the search involves not only Nat but also his father and his attorney, Nat's fiancée's father and his attorney, a local newspaper editor, and the mayor of Memphis. "They were a generation of American men," Nat reflects, "who were perhaps the last to grow up in a world where women were absolutely subjected and under the absolute protection of men." They believed that girls such as Lee Ann, whom they admired, were their special responsibility. "The Old Forest" looks nostalgically at the values of these men and their sense of "communal fatherhood." Like the early periods of Memphis history associated with Overton Park and the old forest, their generation's assumptions about women, the narrator's early assumptions as well, have given way to the manners and mores of a new age. Strongly feminist in its sympathies, "The Old Forest" also focuses on the relationship of Nat with his fiancée, Caroline Braxley, who is as much an injured party in the accident and Lee Ann's disappearance as Nat himself. "The only power I had to save myself," Caroline comments near the end of the story, "was to save you. . . . I know now what the only kind of power I can ever have must be." Unfortunately for Caroline, a debutante of 1937, that power could only be obtained through assistance to the man she had chosen to marry. As for Nat, the very fact that he could date another woman, one about whom he was not serious, so close to his wedding, suggests the double standard prevalent in the South of the 1930's.

Several notable stories in this volume capture the relationship of middle-class Southern whites and their black servants—among them "Bad Dreams" and "A Friend and Protector." Set in Saint Louis, "Bad Dreams" focuses on the lives of two black servants, Bert and Emmaline, employed by the Tollivers of Thorton, Tennessee. (Both the servants and the Tollivers also appear in "Two Ladies in Retirement," another story in this collection, set at a later time.) Written in third-person, omniscient point of view, "Bad Dreams" centers on the disruption of Bert and Emmaline's lives and dreams when Mr. James Tolliver brings home an ignorant and filthy "Old Negro" man to share their living quarters. Through this gesture, Mr. Tolliver illustrates his callous disregard for the privacy of his servants. For him, as for Harriet Wilson, blacks are not to be judged as white people. Thus, he can casually disregard their need for dignity and privacy. This action shocks Emmaline into the recognition that the quarters she had envisioned as home for her, Bert, and their four-month-old baby are really nothing more than a converted barn. The stifling limitations, the loneliness and despair of the lives of Southern blacks rise before the reader. Nowhere in this collection, in fact, does Taylor so vividly evoke these stunted and hollow lives, dependent as they are on the munificence of white people, than in his description of the Old Negro, a symbol of the poverty Bert and Emmaline thought they had left behind them in west Tennessee. "Though the evening was one in early autumn," Taylor writes,

> and warm for the season, the old fellow wore a heavy overcoat that reached almost to his ankles. One of the coat's patch pockets was gone; the other was torn but was held in place with safety pins and was crammed full of something—probably his spare socks, and maybe his razor wrapped in a newspaper, or a piece of a filthy old towel.

This "shiftless and lousy-looking creature," whose hair is "uncut and unkempt . . . precisely like a filthy dust mop that ought to be thrown out," is nevertheless a fellow human being, one who will, as Emmaline helplessly realizes, come to share the remainder of her and Bert's lives in the Tolliver household.

"A Friend and Protector," a first-person retrospective narrated by the nephew of a wealthy Memphis cotton merchant and his wife, depicts the gradual ruin of a black servant of the family, Jesse Munroe, brought by his employers from a small Tennessee town to the city. Both the narrator's Aunt Margaret and his Uncle Andrew contribute to Jesse's dissipation: Uncle Andrew, by his continuing good humor and willingness to rescue him, and Aunt Margaret, by her "censorious words and looks" that encourage his complete ruin. Both, the narrator sees, are victims of their own assumptions and prejudices. They are unable "to reverse a view" of Jesse "based upon impressions received before any of them ever knew Jesse, impressions inherited from their own uncles and aunts and parents and grandparents." In a passage echoing the depiction of mutual need in "The Gift of the Prodigal," the narrator comments on his recognition that his story is "not merely the story of that purplish-black, kinky-headed Jesse's ruined life. It is the story of my aunt's pathetically unruined life, and my uncle's too, and even my own." They all

> most certainly forced Jesse's destruction upon him. . . . But they did it because they had to, because they were so dissatisfied with the pale *un*ruin of their own lives. They did it because something would not let them ruin their own lives as they wanted and felt a need to do—as I have often felt a need to do, myself.

Perhaps the most poignant, lyric story in this collection is "Rain in the Heart." Set in the Tennessee mountains, the story illustrates the best features of Taylor's writing: his sensitivity to nuances of feeling and mood in his characters and his haunting use of imagery and pictorial detail. The focal character in "Rain in the Heart" is an army sergeant who has only recently married. On the occasion of his first leave since his wedding he faces a disturbing contrast between the loud, vulgar joking of the soldiers he commands, his life in the barracks, and the gentle beauty, sensitivity, and compassion of his bride. Faced with this "terrible unrelated diversity in things," the sergeant is unable to forget the bitter and insensitive women he encountered on the transit ride to his bride's apartment. The sounds of the soldiers' voices haunt him even while he is with his wife. Just as the evening rain that falls while he is with his bride shuts out the sounds of the street below, so also the sounds and images from his experiences throughout the day create a "rain" in his heart, temporarily shutting him off from his wife. The first rain, symbolic of a purification, fails to wash away all the day's impressions. Yet the sergeant's perception of life's fragmentation is one his wife shares. "These hours we have together are so isolated and few," she tells him, "that they must sometimes not seem quite real to you when you are away." The depth of this understanding draws the sergeant to his wife, overwhelming him with a desire to "tell her everything he had in his mind." Ironically the moment passes; another rain must fall before he is able to embrace her. The quiet tone and pace of "Rain in the Heart" are matched with striking details of setting and imagery: the "magnificent view of the mountains" the sergeant sees from his window, "rising up on the other side of the city," "the last few seconds of a sunset—brilliant orange and brick red—beyond the blue mountains."

Like the other stories in Peter Taylor's latest collection, "Rain in the Heart" concerns a conflict of values, of two ways of viewing life. It suggests, as do other stories here, a quiet truth about the transience of human values and feelings. To learn these truths of the human heart, the reader needs to listen attentively. Like the father in "The Gift of the Prodigal," he must listen with his "whole being." If he does, he will be rewarded by insights only a master storyteller, such as Peter Taylor, can give.

Stella Nesanovich

Sources for Further Study

American Libraries. XVI, March, 1985, p. 157.
Booklist. LXXXI, March 15, 1985, p. 1032.
Book World. XV, January 27, 1985, p. 3.
Christian Science Monitor. LXXVII, March 26, 1985, p. 25.
Kirkus Reviews. LIII, January 15, 1985, p. 64.
Library Journal. CX, March 15, 1985, p. 74.
The London Review of Books. VII, September 5, 1985, p. 15.
Los Angeles Times Book Review. February 13, 1985, p. 1.
The New York Times Book Review. XC, February 17, 1985, p. 1.
Newsweek. CV, March 11, 1985, p. 74.
Publishers Weekly. CCXXVI, December 21, 1984, p. 81.
Saturday Review. XI, May, 1985, p. 73.
Time. CXXV, February 4, 1985, p. 74.
USA Today. III, January 25, 1985, p. 3D.

THE OLD GRINGO

Author: Carlos Fuentes (1928   )
Translated from the Spanish by Margaret Sayers Peden and the author
Publisher: Farrar, Straus and Giroux (New York). 199 pp. $14.95
Type of work: Novel
Time: 1914
Locale: The desert in northern Mexico

The fate of an aging and embittered American newspaper writer, an American woman hired as the teacher for a prosperous Mexican landowner's children, and a peasant leader who is part of Pancho Villa's marauding rebel army forms the narrative triangle in which personal as well as national destinies are put under scrutiny

> *Principal characters:*
> AMBROSE BIERCE, the "old gringo" of the title who at seventy-one has come to Mexico to die
> HARRIET WINSLOW, an American schoolteacher hired to teach the children of Miranda, a prosperous Mexican landowner
> TOMÁS ARROYO, a rebel leader, who accepts Bierce into his army for his valor
> LA LUNA, Arroyo's female companion who follows him across northern Mexico

Originally published in Spanish in 1985 as *El gringo viejo*, Carlos Fuentes' novel *The Old Gringo* is a fascinating historical fiction which takes as its theme the deforming effect of borders, describing the mental and physical boundaries that both separate and join Mexican and North American cultures. As such, the novel addresses readers of both countries and asks them to ponder the question of personal and national identity that artificial borders have constructed for them. Fuentes has long been recognized as one of his country's leading artists and thinkers. The success of his novels outside Mexico attests his ability to universalize the Mexican historical and cultural experience and thereby to challenge some of the basic assumptions about the exotic picturesqueness of Mexico and its people. In fact, the ironic tension between the stereotypes that foreigners, mostly North Americans, have of Mexico and the intimate rapport by which geography has bound the two countries is the thematic centerpiece of *The Old Gringo*.

Set in the northern Mexican desert in 1913, the novel is inspired by the rich folklore surrounding the disappearance of the American writer Ambrose Bierce, the "old gringo" of the title. At the age of seventy-one, Bierce, a reporter for the Hearst newspapers and a short-story writer known for his misanthropic views, sets out to join the rebel army of the legendary Pancho Villa. In real life, Bierce disappeared, never to be heard from again. Fuentes, inventing the details of Bierce's travels, constructs his story through the flashback memories of an American schoolteacher, Harriet Winslow, whom Bierce meets when he joins one of the Villista armies headed by the peasant leader, Tomás Arroyo. The circumstances of Bierce's death and Harriet's reasons for pretending that he was her father (she had him buried with military honors in Arlington National Cemetery) make up the intricate weave of this many-layered historical fiction.

The novel's twenty-three chapters blend violence and fast-paced action with a series of dramatic meditations by the three protagonists on national and personal destiny. The whole story, in turn, is expressed as Harriet's memories of her encounters with Bierce and Arroyo. The first and last lines of the novel are the same: "Now she sits alone and remembers." The sentence is also repeated at least a half dozen times within the intervening narration to remind the reader that all actions are essentially retrospective. Characteristic of Fuentes' master design for the work, and not unlike his earlier novels, personal memory parallels and, in important ways, illuminates national history. For that reason, particular attention is paid to a series of historical details which suggest that the fortuitous pairing of Bierce with Harriet and the later triangular relationship that emerges between the two Americans and Arroyo are part of a larger historical allegory of national rather than simply individual fortunes and identities.

That chain of historical details includes the Spanish-American War of 1898, in which Harriet's father presumably died; the Mexican-American War of 1847, in which Bierce's own father was a participant; and finally, the American Civil War, in which Bierce fought for the Union army. Through the accumulation of such background detail, Harriet and Bierce are gradually viewed as symbolic characters, expressing through the crises which have brought them to Mexico the deeper crisis which Fuentes suggests lurks in the American collective psyche.

Similarly, Arroyo is depicted as an amalgam of features that arises from Mexican and pre-Hispanic cultural myths. At points he is described as embodying and being trapped within the violent, destructive destiny of the Mexican revolution. At other points, the reader is brought to perceive a more arcane symbolism, as when his silent female companion, a woman named La Luna (the moon), is introduced into the story. The allusion here is to the son of the Nahuatl mother-goddess, Coatlicue, whose warrior son appears to be one of the mythic inspirations for Arroyo. Such touches clearly serve to free the novel's action from a too-literal historical reading and move it into a more symbolic key.

Though the framing device of the flashback foregrounds Harriet's position, the heart of the novel, as its title indicates, is the enigmatic figure of Bierce. In part, the logic of this detailed portrayal of Bierce is Fuentes' fascination with the eccentric and embittered character of the real Ambrose Bierce; in part, it is to set in motion the intricate series of events which will transform Bierce's final days from a mere footnote in history into a renewed vision of national cultural identity on both sides of the border.

The old gringo has come from San Francisco, a place which, perched on the coast, serves as a constant reminder to his countrymen that they have run out of frontiers and thus have reached the end of their manifest destiny. In coming to Mexico, Bierce is not looking for a new frontier but, rather, acting out his understanding of the meaning of the end of frontiers: the long-delayed confrontation with his own mortality. Bierce's appointment with destiny transcends the personal, however, through the intricate weave of events that finally brings the old man to his death and an eventual burial at Arlington cemetery. The intrigue begins when he is quickly taken into Arroyo's confidence after he demonstrates his skill with a gun. He accompanies the rebel band to the vast Miranda hacienda in the Chihuahua Desert, where Arroyo shares with him his dream of regaining for his people their rights to the lands usurped by the Mirandas. In a fateful move, which the old gringo will later use to his own advantage, Arroyo shows Bierce the ancient land grant, signed, he claims, by the king of Spain, proving the peasants' rights to the land.

While Bierce's efforts to construct his own death provide a springboard for many of the novel's philosophical reflections, they also trigger a series of episodes that dramatically reinforce the broader national themes. After his failure to get himself killed by volunteering for the most dangerous actions in battle, Bierce finally provokes Arroyo to murder him by burning the coveted land grants. Yet through his death, Harriet Winslow's life suddenly seems ironically redeemed, for she claims, quite falsely, that Bierce's body is that of her father, long missing in the Cuban War. Furthermore, she tries to have it disinterred and brought for proper military burial at Arlington National Cemetery. The notoriety surrounding her claim reaches all the way to Washington, D.C., and contributes to the growing criticism in the American press of the barbarous massacre of innocent foreigners by the rebel forces. To retain support for his cause in the United States, Pancho Villa has Bierce's body disinterred, brought to his headquarters in Camargo, then shot "formally" by a military firing squad, and finally turned over to Harriet Winslow for proper burial in the United States. To close the book on these events, Villa then personally executes his faithful supporter Arroyo for killing Bierce without proper orders: "When it comes to killing gringos," one character observes, "only he, Pancho Villa, would say when and why."

As the plot clearly demonstrates, the destiny of a single man is necessarily tied up with the larger issues of collective historical destiny. To give prominence to that meditation, Fuentes centers an important phase of the novel's action in the symbolic setting of the abandoned ballroom of the Miranda hacienda, curiously spared from destruction by Arroyo's order. The ballroom first appears simply as the setting of Bierce's first conversation with Harriet, as these two displaced North Americans briefly describe their background to each other. Later, when Harriet is in the same ballroom with Arroyo, she speaks to him of the self-consciousness that the reflecting mirrors provide.

He explains to her that what the gringo and the Miranda family took for granted, each individual's self-image, his ability to see himself represented as a human being, was something denied to the peasants by the entire social and political system represented by the Mirandas.

Arroyo's particular attachment to the mansion and to the room, it turns out, derives from the fact that he is the old landowner's natural son and that, as a child, he could only view the glitter of life within the Miranda house from a distanced peephole. With time, the idea had grown in Arroyo's mind that the ballroom signified the achievement of identity, something politics denied his people. For Harriet, the mirrored room became the embodiment of the dreams of splendor and of escape which have filled her life since her father's departure for the war in Cuba thwarted her possibilities of a socially prominent marriage.

These same reflecting mirrors emblemize the condition that Bierce calls "fragmented consciousness," an ability to see the world, and also to step outside oneself as in a dream and view oneself as from a distance. The very way in which the entire novel is constructed, as distanced reflections of fragmented moments and recollections within recollections, seems to embody the order of that fragmented consciousness. Fuentes' novels and short stories have often used similar narrative devices to present the multiple historical and cultural identities of characters. In *The Old Gringo*, however, the choice of this technique seems especially appropriate, in that it takes its inspiration from the best-known story of the real Ambrose Bierce, "An Occurrence at Owl Creek Bridge," a tale set in the midst of the Civil War and dealing with a soldier's efforts to escape the death to which he seems predestined. Fuentes even has Bierce allude to the story, as the old gringo sets about to precipitate his own death:

> The old man is plodding along in a straight line, muttering to himself stories he had once written, cruel stories of the American Civil War in which men succumb and survive because they have been granted a fragmented consciousness: because a man can be at once dying—hanging from a bridge with a rope around his neck—and watching his death from the far side of the creek: because a man can dream of a horseman and kill his own father, all in the same instant.

Insistently, this condition of splintered or errant consciousness, as Fuentes has his characters call it, pervades the entire fiction and underscores the novel's thematic core: destiny, identity, and the need to transcend the borders that confine individuals and communities. It is a theme that has particular import in terms of the Mexican national history and is pointedly dramatized in the life of Tomás Arroyo. Though seemingly less important than the two North American protagonists, Arroyo helps forge the destiny of the two gringos: Harriet finds in Bierce the father who has abandoned her; Bierce sees in Harriet the daughter who has scorned him. Yet, in the process of bringing about this reciprocal encounter between the two, Arroyo is martyred. Finally that martyrdom moves the reader's focus to a more expansive arena, as Arroyo's death brings to the surface of the novel the intricate reciprocity among individuals and nations that has been ignored in the lives of the characters up to this point. Indeed, one purpose for the elaborate flashback mechanism of the novel is to suggest that the value of the twin deaths of Bierce and Arroyo is to trigger in Harriet a belated recognition of that reciprocity.

In a novel of a narrower, less ambitious scope, Arroyo might well have appeared to be merely a picturesque figure, allowed to fulfill the heroic image of the peasant revolutionary who martyrs himself for a just cause. Yet, in Fuentes' effort to transcend the fragmented consciousness of Mexicans and North Americans, Tomás Arroyo becomes the symbol of that subtle and often-ignored reciprocity that has shaped the destines of individuals on both sides of the border.

The Old Gringo is a novel of subtle and complex ideas and characters which seeks to shatter the simplistic stereotypes of both nations. Yet, despite such complexity, the force of its characters, the craftsmanship of its plot, and the skill of Fuentes' storytelling make it a pleasurable and rewarding reading experience.

Marvin D'Lugo

Sources for Further Study

The Atlantic. CCLVI, December, 1985, p. 118.
Booklist. LXXXII, November 1, 1985, p. 374.
Library Journal. CX, November 1, 1985, p. 109.
Los Angeles Times Book Review. October 27, 1985, p. 1.
The New York Review of Books. XXXII, December 19, 1985, p. 54.
The New York Times Book Review. XC, October 2, 1985, p. 1.
Newsweek. CVI, December 23, 1985, p. 76B.
Publishers Weekly. CCXXVIII, September 27, 1985, p. 87.

ON DISTANT GROUND

Author: Robert Olen Butler (1945-   )
Publisher: Alfred A. Knopf (New York). 245 pp. $14.95
Type of work: Novel
Time: 1975
Locale: Baltimore, Maryland; and Saigon, Vietnam

A novel about a captain in the United States Army Military Intelligence who attempts to come to grips with the meaning of his actions during the Vietnam War

> *Principal characters:*
> DAVID BATES FLEMING, a young career officer
> JENNIFER FLEMING, his American wife
> CARL LOMAS, his army lawyer
> NGUYEN THI TUYET SUONG, his Vietnamese lover
> PHAM VAN TUYEN, a North Vietnamese officer

Robert Olen Butler is becoming recognized as one of the best writers on the Vietnam War. Butler, who was with the United States Army Military Intelligence in Vietnam, speaks Vietnamese, and his portrayal of the army and its involvement in the Vietnam War carries the authority of his experience—the facts are right. Furthermore, his clean style and his tight focus on event make for easy reader access. Yet he is more than a reporter: He has the novelist's strong sense of story and character, which enables him to explore the moral ambiguities of that experience for the kind of meaning that only an artist can wrest from his materials.

On Distant Ground completes a loosely joined trilogy focusing on three men who made up a small intelligence unit that operated just north of Saigon. Each novel has a different protagonist, who appears as a secondary character or who is at lest mentioned in the other novels. Although each novel touches on events that involved direct fighting, Butler is not primarily concerned with the experiences of combat but, rather, with the "clash of specific cultures, back where the gunfire was out on the horizon, that had the larger, unique effect." This concern is most dramatized in *Alleys of Eden* (1981), Butler's first published novel and the first novel of the trilogy, whose protagonist is Clifford Wilkes, an army deserter who falls in love with a Vietnamese prostitute and, when Saigon falls, who escapes with her to the United States. Although *Alleys of Eden* opens a bit awkwardly, which is typical of many first novels, the characters in their situations become powerfully compelling to a degree Butler has never quite matched in his subsequent, more carefully constructed novels. In *Sun Dogs* (1982), the middle novel of the trilogy, the protagonist, Wilson Hand, is an investigator in the oil fields on the North Slope of Alaska, whose life is haunted by flashbacks to an incident when he was taken prisoner by the Vietcong before being rescued by Captain David Fleming, the protagonist of *On Distant Ground*.

Butler has written a fourth, unrelated novel, *Countrymen of Bones*

(1983), about an archaeologist who is excavating an important burial site near Los Alamos, New Mexico, concurrent with the testing of the first atomic bomb. Butler's concerns in *Countrymen of Bones* are similar to those in his trilogy. He writes of the relationships between an individual's sense of his own identity and the cultural surroundings in which he lives—in particular when those surroundings involve the violence of war (World War II is part of the fabric of *Countrymen of Bones*). Also rooted in the subject of self-definition is his concern with relationships between men and women, with the accompanying exploration of the sexual impulses toward life or death involved in such relationships. Although Butler portrays his women characters with sensitivity, he has always presented his materials through the consciousness of men. The point of view in *Countrymen of Bones* switches between the consciousness of the two leading male characters, and each novel of the trilogy remains tightly focused on the mind of the protagonist.

Butler has been termed a novelist of ideas. In his exploration of moral ambiguities, as in the fiction of Saul Bellow or Norman Mailer, the ideas arise from the actions of fully developed characters involved in significant situations. The central situation in *On Distant Ground* is the court-martial of David Fleming in the spring of 1975 at Fort Holabird, Maryland, for an action that he himself does not understand: During the war, he went to inordinate lengths to free an important North Vietnamese officer—Pham Van Tuyen—held by the South Vietnamese in the infamous Con Son Island tiger cages; after whisking Tuyen away at gunpoint in a dramatic helicopter escape, David returned him to his base of operations where Tuyen could continue to wage war against the United States military and the South Vietnamese army. The key factor in the trial is David's motivation for freeing the officer.

Butler took a master's degree in playwriting before going to Vietnam, and his training as a playwright is evident in the novel's sharp dramatic focus, whereby he uses the apparatus of the trial to force David to explore his motives for his past actions in Vietnam. (The playwriting experience is also a contributing factor in Butler's ability to write crisp, character-revealing dialogue, which—given Butler's focus on the mind of the protagonist—is essential in portraying secondary characters.) Initially, as David sorts through his war experiences in a series of flashbacks, no clear answers emerge. Yet, as the trial develops, his reflections intensify into a journey to self-knowledge that provides the key structuring device of the novel.

This journey will lead Butler to explore what Duncan C. Spencer has termed "the highest themes of literature, the exploration of the human heart, the terrible loyalties of blood, the instinctive springs of honor." David has a great sense of integrity; he is an honorable man. His trial lawyer, Carl Lomas, suggests the possibility of a defense based on his Central Intelligence Agency (CIA) related activities: Because David was a model career officer who was very effective in achieving military objectives in conjunction with CIA operations in Vietnam, the lawyer would like to suggest that the freeing of the officer was part of a CIA operation whose scope cannot be investigated at the trial because of its secret nature. Yet David knows that he cannot fabricate such a lie; that defense might indeed by successful, but it would rely on his convincing the officers of the jury. His sense of integrity in juxtaposition with his past actions has created a present indecisiveness, which he senses would betray him on the stand.

Since returning from Vietnam, David has married a young woman, Jennifer, who is very devoted to him and who gives birth to their first child during the course of the trial. Jennifer Fleming is Butler's best American woman character, a stable middle-class woman who reflects David's essentially middle-class views of the world. All of Butler's protagonists are basically middle-class people, college educated, with typical middle-class biases and prejudices, and the majority of his secondary characters—even his Vietnamese characters—are middle class, with the notable exception of Lanh, the prostitute in *Alleys of Eden*. This is one of Butler's limitations and one of the reasons that his trilogy seems more narrow than such earlier war-related novels as Norman Mailer's *The Naked and the Dead* (1948) or James Jones's *From Here to Eternity* (1951), which treat the concerns and lives of essentially working-class characters with as much weight as those of middle-class characters. In fact, the initial reason for David's interest in the North Vietnamese officer is that David finds scrawled on the wall of a cell where prisoners are held the words *ve-sink la khoe*—in English, "hygiene is healthful"—an attitude most tightly embraced by the American middle class, at times to the point of obsession. David is captivated by these ironic words—the cell is dirty, dingy, bleak, without light, without any sign or symbol of humane consideration (in its way, it is a symbol of the larger war itself)—and David feels an immediate kinship with the man who could write such words in such circumstances, while waiting for his captors to torture him. It is this sense of kinship, this empathetic feeling for another human being who is in some essential way the same as he is—the theme of the double—that eventually leads David to find and free Tuyen.

Although Butler's characters are middle class, Butler is not really a novelist of manners, no more than, say, Joseph Conrad is. A comparison to Conrad is illuminating on further points, for Conrad also was concerned with the clash between Western cultural values and non-Western values, in particular in such a novel as *Lord Jim* (1900); also, Conrad's novella "The Secret Sharer" is a classic work on the theme of the double. The sense of mystery about motives, the need to protect the double from members of his own community who would "lawfully" bring him to death, the great urgency involved in such action—an urgency that becomes an obsession—are common to Conrad's protagonist and to Butler's David Fleming. One reviewer has found David's actions "incomprehensible" and has faulted Butler for not being even more action-oriented, but Butler's concerns are rightly in exploring the *meaning* of certain actions—the moral ambiguities involved in those actions—as Conrad's were before him, and not in presenting the simple experience of action itself. In fact, Butler becomes thin as a novelist and is least satisfying when he relies on the details of unreflected action and plot to carry his story, as he occasionally does in *On Distant Ground*. (The same weakness is more apparent in *Sun Dogs*, where the "detective" elements become the least memorable aspect of the book.) Finally, the comparison to Conrad must be qualified: Butler's work is good, but it does not finally achieve the compelling, rich complexity of a masterpiece such as *Lord Jim* or "The Secret Sharer."

During the course of the trial, David comes to realize that his freeing of Tuyen is in some way related to a love affair he had had with a middle-class Vietnamese, Nguyen Thi Tuyet Suong. Although the affair lasted only a few months, until Suong terminated it, the intensity of it in some subtle way changed David—as love affairs change all of Butler's protagonists.

The idea of exploring cultural differences through interracial affairs is not new: From Giacomo Puccini's *Madame Butterfly* (1904) to Pearl Buck's *The Hidden Flower* (1952) and James Michener's *Sayonara* (1954), the tensions between cultures find a natural focus in the subject. The reason that Butler handles the situation so successfully in both *Alleys of Eden* and *On Distant Ground* is that he goes beyond the surface passions and interracial tensions to explore that larger significance of the relationship between man and woman. David now senses that the positive, life-giving nature of his relationship with Suong enabled him to become more fully human and thus have the experience of the double with Tuyen, the North Vietnamese officer. In turn, David also realizes that it was paradoxically his experience with Tuyen that enabled him to love Jennifer and thus be placed in a situation whereby he can be convicted of a crime, which will deny him the presence of Jennifer and of his newborn son. The portrayal of this link of passion to compassion—achieved through the love relationship between a man and a woman—is at the center of each of Butler's four novels, and it is this element that creates much of the underlying tension, and beauty, in his work.

Because of his present experience with Jennifer in her pregnancy, David becomes convinced that Suong broke off their affair because she had become pregnant with his child and did not want him to know. He feels a great urgency to find his Vietnamese child—an urgency equal in intensity to that involved with his actions in freeing Tuyen. David is indeed convicted of the charges of aiding the enemy but is expelled from the military instead of receiving a prison sentence. Through the media attention invited by Carl Lomas, David's case becomes widely publicized, against his own wishes, and the justification for the verdict is that the military refuses to make a martyr.

As soon as he is freed, David arranges to return to Saigon, during what proves to be the final week before its fall to the North Vietnamese in April, 1975, to search for his child. The arrangement develops from his contact with a CIA agent, whom David knew when both men were in Vietnam and who highly respected David's professionalism. The agent agrees to provide David with a cover—as a Canadian radical—in exchange for potential information on Saigon after its imminent fall.

The setting for the second half of the novel thus shifts from Baltimore to Saigon, where Butler once again presents the actions of those final few days before its fall—he used the same setting for the first part of *Alleys of Eden*. The great confusion and hysteria of the events serve as a backdrop to David's frantic search for the child, a symbol of the identity that David "left" in Vietnam when he returned to the United States. His desperate need to find his own offspring becomes an obsession. The outer search mirrors an inner search for his own motives, and when David finally finds the child— Suong, a political prisoner, had died in prison the year before—he realizes that a selfish sense of "self" has driven him in his actions, has created his obsession. This Vietnamese boy does not physically resemble him, as his American son does, and David has trouble viewing him as a son. He realizes that the search for this son springs from the same motive as his freeing of Tuyen: It was his own identity that he saw in Tuyen which prompted him to action, and it is his own identity that he was seeking in this Vietnamese child. Nevertheless, the freeing of Tuyen was at the same time a compassionate act: The ambiguities involved in any man's actions are complex, and to assign any one motive for any one action is impossible. Butler suggests through the events of the novel that, on a larger scale, this final ambiguity parallels the involvement of the United States in the Vietnam War: No one motive can explain the actions of a nation. Self-interest, an obsessive selfishness, compassion—no one slogan or one way of viewing the action is the final word, the ultimate measure.

The events of the conclusion of the novel, however, do suggest an absolute, which is the final value of a compassionate act. When David is frantically searching for his child, he must place himself in the hands of the new government in Saigon, and once again David becomes involved with Tuyen, who has become the director of security in Saigon for the North Vietnamese. David, while at Tuyen's mercy, is given his life and the help he so desperately needs to find the child. This act of compassion sets the stage for David's final awareness of his great obsession with self—which is a Western concern—and it frees him to view the child in a different light. The child is a human being, with needs that can be supplied by David, and in one last action-filled escape, David flees to freedom with the child so that he can rear him back in the United States. David's journey back to Vietnam is thus completed physically, as is his journey to self-knowledge.

On Distant Ground has received mixed responses, from those who view the novel as one of the best in recent years, to those who see it as "labored" with "serious problems of credibility." If Butler's characters are not always compelling, if the reader senses that occasionally he has his eye too strongly on the kind of action that attracts the best-seller mass audience, his basic impulses are those of a fine novelist, and he follows those impulses in much of *On Distant Ground*. Ultimately, his value as a novelist will reside not in presenting exciting action but in exploring the moral ambiguities of that action.

Ronald L. Johnson

Sources for Further Study

Booklist. LXXXI, February 15, 1985, p. 820.
Kirkus Reviews. LII, December 1, 1984, p. 1104.
Library Journal. CX, February 15, 1985, p. 178.
Los Angeles Times. February 12, 1985, V, p. 8.
The New York Times Book Review. XC, April 21, 1985, p. 26.
Publishers Weekly. CCXXVI, December 21, 1984, p. 82.
Washington Post Book World. XV, April 21, 1985, p. 11.

ON THE ROAD WITH CHARLES KURALT

Author: Charles Kuralt (1934-   )
Publisher: G. P. Putnam's Sons (New York). Illustrated. 316 pp. $16.95
Type of work: Social science
Time: 1966-1985
Locale: The continental United States

Charles Kuralt has been on the road for more than eighteen years chronicling the characters, the curious, and the commonplace of back-roads America

> *Principal personage:*
> CHARLES KURALT, a traveler and chronicler

Charles Kuralt is a professional wanderer. He has been all over the place and seen just about everything, and he wants to keep on doing it. If you ask him what he is, he will tell you what he is not. He is not a real reporter, neither the kind his boss at CBS wanted him to be nor the kind that informs on moonshiners in Tennessee. He likes old folks. He will tell you that—and when he goes on the road, he is drawn to them. They tell him about the way things used to be, what they did when they were young, and what their grandparents taught them. Best of all, he tells us.

On the Road with Charles Kuralt is the second collection of vignettes of Americana adapted from Kuralt's regular segments on the *CBS Evening News* and *Sunday Morning*. The vignettes seem to be transcripts largely taken directly off the air. Most readers will be able to "hear" Kuralt as he interviews his subjects, and those who have watched some of the "On the Road" segments will be able to "see" them too. For fans of Kuralt, the book is nothing less than a series of meetings with old friends. At the same time, the absence of the video portion of the interviews is a significant handicap for those new to Kuralt's work, because their original visual freshness and sparkle simply cannot be transferred to the printed page.

Kuralt says, "I was a real reporter once, but I was not suited for it by physique or temperament." In 1966, when he first suggested to Fred Friendly, president of CBS News, that he would like to roam the country looking for stories rather than covering "hard" news in places such as Vietnam, Friendly sent him to the North Pole. By the time he got back, things had warmed up at CBS, and the new boss, Richard S. Salant, let him go on the road with only a few words of wisdom: "Keep the budget low." Since then, Kuralt has sent back stories from anywhere his motor home can take him, relying "on dumb luck and letters from viewers" to find them. The popularity of both the television and book versions of *On the Road* attests the success of this approach.

Kuralt has come across a variety of "Unlikely Heroes" in his travels. The doctor who accepts apple strudel or a jar of buttermilk as payment for his work and the man who repairs dozens of bicycles so that even the poorest kids in his neighborhood can ride one are heartwarming stories, but only mildly surprising. That the liberator of Bulgaria is named MacGahan and came from New Lexington, Ohio, comes as more of a shock.

Kuralt has also come across many characters who march to the beat of "Different Drummers," perhaps because he does so himself. Along with the "Dreamers" Kuralt has met on his travels, he lets them demonstrate the independence of thought and diversity of attitude of the American people. As Kuralt puts it, "You can't get your thumb on America's mood. I never try." Yet without trying, he has come as close as anyone has since the famous wanderers he admires, Alexis de Tocqueville and Mark Twain. "Each of them caught a little bit of the truth about America and wrote it down." So has Kuralt. The mood is upbeat; the attitude is step to the beat you hear; and who is in Washington at the moment does not much matter.

> Hardly a week goes by that I don't come across a poet at some country crossroads. I don't mean a writer of verse. I mean somebody who has inside of him such a love of something—farming, flying, furniture-making—and talks about it so lyrically and intensely, that in telling you about it, he makes you love it, too.

That is a good enough definition of a poet for most people. The poets that Kuralt encounters, the lover of steam engines, the builders of the Golden Gate Bridge, the fishing judge, the hex-sign painter, make one long to be in their shoes. By his own definition, Kuralt must be a poet, too. In watching his show or reading his book, it is easy to catch oneself wishing to go on the road with him. Only later does the thought of spending most of one's waking and sleeping hours in a motor home make one glad that he and his companions, Isadore Bleckman, the cameraman, and Larry Gianneschi, Jr., the soundman, are doing the hard part and sharing the best part. They say, "We feel we have the best jobs in journalism," and readers and viewers are lucky that they do.

"Drive across the country and you find that hardly anybody makes anything." That is what Kuralt tells the reader, but he manages to find the builders anyway. The men who braved wind and storm and earthquake to put up the Golden Gate Bridge say simply, "I worked on that. I remember being there." That feeling is familiar. The men who build moonshine stills in Tennessee are proud of their work too, and they do not appreciate the ones who tip off the law. "The mountain folk have an awful name for these informers. They call them reporters." So Kuralt is not a reporter, not a "real one" anyhow.

He is, however, a storyteller. He goes wherever the stories are and brings them back alive. He revels in the places he visits ("I hate getting to know small towns and then having to leave") and has even found places to which, in an absurd game of international tit-for-tat, Russians are not allowed entry for no other reason than "the Russians do it to us, so we do it to them." He has visited a man who has recorded the names of everyone he has ever met and one who has made the biggest ball of twine in the world. He has come across the only parking meter in Lookingglass, Oregon; a coffee shop in Illinois where each regular patron has a personalized cup; and a town in California that has invented its own vocabulary to confuse tourists.

These anecdotes do not add up to merely another collection of trivia, though. They show the variety that abounds in the country and reveal what one can see when willing "to go slow, stick to the back roads, take time to meet people, listen to yarns, notice the countryside go by, and feel the seasons change." The humor that emerges is generally homely, and the stories are filled with clichés, but it is evident that Kuralt's affable manner has put his subjects at ease and that what one reads is heartfelt and honest (except perhaps for the jackalopes in Wyoming and the trees that follow the dogs around in a particularly arid part of Arizona).

The heartwarming nature of several of the stories does not get in the way of the message that Kuralt claims he tries to avoid. "I have attempted to keep 'relevance' and 'significance' entirely out of all the stories I send back. If I come upon a real news story out there On the Road, I call some real reporter to come cover it." The story of the Chandlers of Prairie, Mississippi, a pair of sharecroppers who reared nine children and managed to send them all to college, is a moving example of the value of hard work. So many of Kuralt's subjects value hard work that it becomes clear that "dumb luck" is not the only thing he relies on to get his stories. As Lula Watson, age 103, puts it, "hard work and strong coffee" probably help.

Just as *On the Road* is not "real reporting," it is not news either. There is no dateline on any of the vignettes (the reader is left to figure out when each was chronicled, by calculating from ages, durations, and beginnings). There are only a few updates to the stories. (The man who was building his own road has died, and the state plans to make it into a bike path. The library of the "scholar of the piney woods" burned down, but so many people sent him replacements that he will not need more books for quite a while.) One is left to assume that Americans are still grunting for worms in Sopchoppy, Florida, searching for mushrooms in Illinois, speaking Boontling in California, catching jackalopes in Wyoming, playing croquet in Kentucky, making bricks in North Carolina, and misspelling and telling tall tales all over the country. Presumably the Monarch butterflies still return to Pacific Grove, and there are still oysters in Chesapeake Bay. With luck, the Franciscan Sisters of Perpetual Adoration are still praying for peace—as they have been "*without interruption* for a hundred years!" These stories may not be news, but in these cases, no news is good news.

That leaves one with what *On the Road* is. It is storytelling at its best, at once surprising, amusing, enlightening, moving, and educational. It is a book worth reading, even if it is not literature.

James A. Woodhead

Sources for Further Study

Booklist. LXXXI, July, 1985, p. 1476.
Kirkus Reviews. LIII, July 15, 1985, p. 700.
Library Journal. CX, September 15, 1985, p. 71.
Publishers Weekly. CCXXVIII, July 12, 1985, p. 43.
TV Guide. XXXIII, August 3, 1985, p. 40.
Variety. CCCXX, September 18, 1985, p. 92.
The Wall Street Journal. CCVI, October 1, 1985, p. 30.
Washington Post Book World. XV, October 13, 1985, p. 10.

ON WRITING AND POLITICS
1967-1983

Author: Günter Grass (1927-   )
Translated from the German by Ralph Manheim
Introduction by Salman Rushdie
Publisher: Harcourt Brace Jovanovich (San Diego, California). 157 pp. $13.95
Type of work: Literary and political essays

A collection of essays and political addresses focusing on Grass's view of the writer's political role and describing the relationship between literature and politics in his own work

Günter Grass is the best known and easily the most successful of the small group of contemporary German writers to find an audience in the United States. In particular, his early international best-seller, *Die Blechtrommel* (1959; *The Tin Drum*, 1961), together with the other two books of his Danzig trilogy, *Katz und Maus* (1961; *Cat and Mouse*, 1963) and *Hundejahre* (1963; *Dog Years*, 1965), and later the novel *Örtlich betäubt* (1969; *Local Anesthetic*, 1969), served to establish Grass's reputation in the United States as Germany's leading postwar writer. Grass's success outside Germany is no doubt in large part achieved through the power of his fanciful and at times bizarre imagination, an imagination that has produced some of the most memorable figures and scenes in all modern fiction. In fact, the opulence of Grass's fantasy and his often grotesque vision of twentieth century reality leave such a strong impression on the reader that it is, at first, all too easy to overlook the political intention at the center of his work. Grass remains a committed and distinctly political writer, a writer whose work is clearly informed by a coherent moral and political purpose.

Grass's writing is never far from politics and the political realities of his country's past and present. In his work, he insistently challenges his reader to confront the past with its uncomfortable lessons in order to be able to contend with the problems that Germany and the world must face in the present and in an increasingly uncertain future. A writer is, as he recalls having told his children once, "someone who writes against the passage of time." Like other writers who began their careers in the new Germany of the 1950's, Grass has sought in his work to keep the reality of Germany's recent history before his audience, to counteract the all-too-ready forgetfulness of an increasingly affluent postwar generation, and to remind everyone, German and non-German alike, of the lasting consequences and only partly learned lessons of what he refers to as the "German crime."

The essays and miscellaneous political addresses included in the collection *On Writing and Politics, 1967-1983*—the second book of Grass's essays to appear in English—provide an informative parallel to Grass's development and activity as a political writer. In the material gathered here from various sources and occasions spanning the period from 1967 to 1983, Grass holds forth on his experiences as a writer and a reader and on the role that literature plays in shaping one's view of the world. At the same time, the pieces included here suggest a political role for the contemporary writer that, if one is to take Grass's own example to heart, extends beyond the writer's desk and into the day-to-day political life of his country and the world. Thus, the five longer essays drawn together under the heading "On Writing" focus on Grass's view of literature and its role in making both the past and the future part of one's present reality, a visionary role that he sees realized, for example, in the work of his "teacher," the German futurist Alfred Döblin, and in the novels of Franz Kafka. The eight political addresses presented in the book's second and concluding part, under the title "On Politics," offer concrete testimony to the political activism that has characterized Grass's career since the early 1960's.

The frequent autobiographical references in this volume provide considerable insight into the relationship between Günter Grass as a literary figure and as a private citizen. In several essays, Grass reflects on the role that German Fascism and the Third Reich had upon the shaping of his political consciousness. He was, he notes, only seventeen as the war ended, "too young to participate in the crimes of National Socialism, but old enough to have been shaped by their consequences." His first tentative acquaintance with democracy came, as for his entire generation, in those first postwar years, when he was nearly a grown man. Like many of his colleagues who took a similar path toward political involvement, Grass acted upon the lessons that the failure of the Weimar Republic had for him as a writer and citizen. For the failure of German democracy in the 1930's is, in Grass's view, to be blamed in part on Germany's writers, who for the most part "made no attempt to defend the Republic, while not a few of them deliberately held it up to ridicule." A second lesson was clear as well: Those writers who did warn against the rise of Fascism went largely unheard, as— Grass adds parenthetically—they still continue to be.

Grass's view of literature and the writer's political role and responsibility reflect his distinctly German experience. His political activism and involvement with partisan politics as a supporter of West Germany's Social Democratic Party arose from his conviction that writing by itself is insufficient to the political task that the writer, as well as each responsible citizen, must set for himself. In Grass's view, even "engaged" literature can only have long-term effects. The writer who wants to have an effect with respect to the political issues of the day must leave his desk and become an active participant in the democratic process.

In repudiation of the long-standing German tradition which sees intellect and political power as incompatible, Grass became actively involved in the "dirty" work of politics in the early 1960's. He chose to support an "evolutionary democratic socialism" and the path of slow reform via the par-

liamentary process of electoral politics; for it was and is here that he sees
the possibility for positive social change in the spirit of the European
Enlightenment. Grass declares his "evolutionary" colors in the piece "Literature and Revolution, or The Rhapsodist's Snorting Hobbyhorse," an
address that he gave at the Belgrade Writers' Conference in 1969, which
begins rather shockingly—considering the date and setting: "I'll come right
out with it: I'm against revolution." Grass's rejection of revolution, be it
motivated by rightist or leftist aims, derives from his conclusion that the
mechanisms of revolution are fatally flawed, that revolutions tend inevitably
to reestablish and institutionalize traditional structures of political power,
often at an unacceptably high human price. Thus, he rejects the "revolutionary rhapsodists" among his colleagues in the West, for whom revolution had
become the latest fashion in the late 1960's. Similarly, he attacks those on
the radical Left for their "revolutionary sandbox games" and for the endless
ideological bickering in which they engage, when they could instead be
involved in the arduous, long-range work for democracy and social justice.
Grass freely admits to his audience: "I am a revisionist and worse—I am a
social democrat."

Grass's avowal of revisionism and the path of gradual social and political
reform is one of several unifying motifs in the essays. In the speech "Erfurt
1970 and 1891," given even as the newly elected West German government
under social democratic chancellor Willy Brandt was making the first conciliatory gestures at Erfurt toward a rapprochement with its Eastern European
neighbors, Grass relates the events of the day to the reformist tradition
within the Social Democratic Party, a tradition born in the party's Erfurt
Program of 1891. In placing Brandt's "Ostpolitik" against the background of
the Erfurt Program and the subsequent split of the party into revolutionary
and reformist factions, Grass celebrates the victory of practical striving for
reform over inflexible ideological posturing and honors the work of early
party reformers such as Eduard Bernstein, who laid the foundation for the
"modern, undogmatic socialism" in which he invests his hope.

The relationship of Grass's political activism to his work as a writer is
addressed most directly in the essay "What Shall We Tell Our Children?"
Here, Grass recounts in some detail the genesis of his 1972 novel *Aus dem
Tagebuch einer Schnecke* (*From the Diary of a Snail*, 1973), a book in which
his fictionalized account of the expulsion and persecution of the Jews in his
home city of Danzig alternates with diarylike accounts from the present that
deal both with his private family life and with the Bundestag election campaign of 1969, in which he took an active part. As he explains, he sought in
his story of the Danzig Jews to illustrate the "onset and slow development
of the German crime." For what happened in all of Germany in the late
1930's happened in Danzig as well: "The same limitless hatred was proclaimed in posters and in shouted slogans. The same cowardly silence on the

part of the Christian churches. There too the citizenry adapted to the new situation. There too the people deliberately disenfranchised themselves."

Grass's account of the "German crime" is tied here, as elsewhere in his work, to his responsibility as a writer to keep the past alive, or, as he states this purpose in another context, "to throw it [the past] in the path of the present to make the present stumble." At the same time, the parallel narration of the novel provides him the means by which he can suspend chronology. He forces the reader to relate the past to the political realities of the present, in this case, to the specific political reality of the 1969 election campaign which, in Grass's view, pitted Germany's past, in the person of the former Nazi Kurt Georg Kiesinger, against Germany's hope, in the person of the social democratic candidate Willy Brandt. The close juxtaposition of past and present underscores Grass's view that human progress toward the ideals of social justice and tolerance is a slow and gradual process which is constantly threatened by ideological intolerance and individual complacency. Progress is, as Grass declares, a snail. As difficult to accept as the snail's slow pace may be, Grass sees its barely noticeable but quietly sure course as the only real path from the present into the future. The choice of the snail as a symbol for his social democratic coat of arms underscores further Grass's rejection of the ideologically tainted view, prevalent on both the Right and the Left, which holds history to be an inexorable process leading toward an inevitable goal. Instead, as Grass suggests at numerous times in these pages, he views the snail's progress to be ever in danger and ever needful of the individual's active commitment to the spirit and ideals of the Enlightenment.

The individual's right and responsibility to "resist" provides another unifying focus in these essays. In Grass's view, such "resistance" is characterized by a spirit of skeptical opposition to one's time and to the traditional structures of political and economic power. In an address delivered in 1983 on the fiftieth anniversary of the National Socialist seizure of power, he asks his audience the still relevant questions: "When is resistance imperative? What sort of resistance does democracy not just admit of but demand for its protection?" Although he sees no new Adolf Hitler in Germany's future, he worries about his state's "well-nigh-hysterical security-mindedness" and about the tendency of a passive and complacent citizenry to accept "security" and "order" as justification for measures that can only undermine democracy. When he pleads the case for resistance, he does so in the name of democracy. It is his intention, as he summarizes in the speech entitled "The Artist's Freedom of Opinion in Our Society,"

to plead for diversity, to protect the desperately blasphemous outburst, to tolerate the kitsch that blooms everlastingly, to grant admittance at all times to subversive doubt, even where faith has established an entrenched society, to live with the contradictions characteristic of man and human society.

Thus, while Grass himself enjoys the freedoms of the writer in the West and readily recognizes the existence of artistic repression in the Soviet bloc, and while he daily exercises his political freedom as a citizen of West Berlin with the knowledge that the same freedoms do not exist on the other side of the wall that divides his city, he is nevertheless insistent upon voicing his opposition to the abuses and to the potential abuses of power in his own country.

For Grass, resistance means above all a vehement rejection of ideology and the excesses that derive from ideological intolerance. This message is implicit in the tone of skeptical wariness that underlies his discussion of the Cold War and the ideological confrontation between East and West. In the essay "Racing with the Utopias," he uses Alfred Döblin's and George Orwell's futurist visions to suggest an inevitable convergence of ideologies. Indeed, he finds it difficult even now to discern essential differences between the structures employed in both the East and the West to ensure a political and economic status quo. Likewise, in the essay "Kafka and His Executors," Grass uses the occasion of the tenth anniversary in 1978 of the occupation of Czechoslovakia by the troops of the Warsaw Pact to comment on the all-too-similar "bureaucracies of Eastern as well as Western obedience." In the omnipresent, impenetrable bureaucracy in Kafka's novel *Das Schloss* (1926; *The Castle*, 1930), Grass discovers a vision of totalitarian administration that, quite apart from military, economic, and political considerations, demands the individual's acquiescence in Bonn and Washington, as it does in Prague and Moscow. In East and West, the structures of power seem in Grass's view to resemble one another more and more, as the real world of the present races to outdo Kafka's vision of the future.

Grass's apparently undifferentiated repudiation of both sides in the Cold War presents the greatest difficulties for American readers of these essays and has drawn considerable critical fire in the United States. To reject Grass's warnings, however, because of their critical assessment of Western democracies, is to misunderstand the origin and nature of his opposition. If he seems all too simply to declare East and West equally guilty of "executing" Kafka's vision, it is because his experience as a German suggests that underlying structures of power and oppression can and do outlive ideology. For Grass, his role as a writer necessarily precludes his close identification with either the state or a particular ideology. His role is and must remain one of questioning skepticism and determined resistance. Only in this manner can the snail's progress be assured.

James R. Reece

Sources for Further Study

Best Sellers. XLV, September, 1985, p. 231.
Booklist. LXXXII, September 1, 1985, p. 19.
Books and Bookmen. October, 1985, p. 29.
Kirkus Reviews. LIII, May 1, 1985, p. 412.
Library Journal. CX, July, 1985, p. 73.
Los Angeles Times Book Review. July 21, 1985, p. 2.
The New Republic. CXCIII, August 12, 1985, p. 31.
New Statesman. CX, September 20, 1985, p. 27.
The New York Times Book Review. XC, June 23, 1985, p. 17.
The New Yorker. LXI, August 26, 1985, p. 88.
Publishers Weekly. CCXXVII, May 3, 1985, p. 59.
Washington Post Book World. XV, August 11, 1985, p. 9.

ONE EARTH, FOUR OR FIVE WORLDS
Reflections on Contemporary History

Author: Octavio Paz (1914-   )
Translated from the Spanish by Helen R. Lane
Publisher: Harcourt Brace Jovanovich (San Diego, California). 213 pp. $14.95
Type of work: Essays

A medley of essays about political developments in the world since 1970, with special reference to Mexico and Latin America

One Earth, Four or Five Worlds: Reflections on Contemporary History is unique in the overall output of Octavio Paz—it is about contemporary politics. He is primarily a poet. In addition, he has written many prose works about literary topics; his well-known study of Mexico, *El labertino de la soledad: Vida y pensamiento de México* (1950, revised and enlarged edition, 1954; *The Labyrinth of Solitude: Life and Thought in Mexico*, 1961), touched on politics, but it stressed the cultural and historical background; *Los hijos del limo: Del romanticismo a la vanguardia* (1974; *Children of the Mire: Modern Poetry from Romanticism to the Avant-Garde*, 1974), *El arco y la lira* (1956; *The Bow and the Lyre*, 1973), *Corriente alterna* (1967; *Alternating Current*, 1973), and *Conjunciones y disyunciones* (1969; *Conjunctions and Disjunctions*, 1974) were studies of literature and poetry. The book *One Earth, Four or Five Worlds* (originally published in Spain in 1984 as *Tiempo nublado* with three additional essays) addresses head-on the major international political issues of the times. It has a broad range of reference, however, which makes it more interesting than most political studies that ignore the connection between politics and broader cultural, historical trends. The closest parallel is with the prose works of the Nobel Prize-winning poet Czesław Miłosz, for example his *Zniewolony umysl* (1953; *Captive Mind*, 1953)—both poets have succeeded in writing about politics with greater incisiveness and depth than the majority of specialized political historians and journalistic commentators.

The book has great strengths and also some weaknesses. Its strengths are originality and broad range of reference, both horizontal—Paz is informed about many regions: the United States, Europe, and the Soviet Union; also the Third World, Mexico, Latin America, India, and the Muslim countries—and vertical, ranging far back in time and history. He has great erudition, and his knowledge of underdeveloped countries provides a special perspective to his commentary on the United States and the Soviet Union. For the reader in the United States, one of the most important and insistent points raised by Paz is the destructive influence of that country on the development of democracy in Latin America. He writes, "The United States has fostered divisions between countries, parties, and leaders; it has threatened to use force, and has not hesitated to use force every time it has seen its interests endangered; when this was to its advantage, it has backed rebellions or strengthened tyrannies."

This is not entirely new, but Paz presents an image of the United States that will surprise many American readers. He shows how Alexis de Tocqueville predicted long ago, in 1845, that the foreign policy of the United States would not necessarily reflect the democratic nature of the society itself—or, as de Tocqueville wrote, "Almost all the defects inherent in democratic institutions are brought to light in the conduct of foreign affairs; their advantages are less perceptible." Paz presents an image of the United States that many Americans will not recognize or want to recognize. Is it a true image? This reviewer believes that it is and does not think that Paz overstates his case. The journalistic origins of *One Earth, Four or Five Worlds* do not permit Paz a methodical and detailed historical analysis. He presents a critique that America should have the courage to make itself— American journalists, investigative reporters, and historians—yet it seems that America prefers to remain blind.

According to Octavio Paz, the United States is a country that has very little ability to understand the outside world. A genuine democracy itself, founded upon and still practicing the ideals of the Enlightenment, it drops those ideals once it acts beyond its borders and turns into an empire, an imperium. Paz is puzzled by this strange duality or double standard of Americans, and he traces its origin to the intense concern of the early Puritans for the state of their own consciences. One of their favorite activities was soul-searching—a type of humility, perhaps, but also a form of self-absorbed egotism that put the fate of the individual's own soul before outside concerns. Not intent upon the conversion of others, this self-righteousness permitted the individual to ignore the outer world with complacency. The point is made briefly; Paz's knowledge of Protestantism and of the pre-Revolutionary history of the United States is skimpy, but his theory is extremely suggestive.

Americans instinctively seem to draw a curtain over what happens south of the border without being aware that they are doing so. There are additional reasons for this that Paz does not mention. American foreign policy is almost never debated in elections, and there is great confusion about the concept of foreign aid. Investigative reporting by the American press rarely extends beyond the borders of the United States or to the actions of its embassies abroad; ambassadors rarely come from the foreign service but usually are businessmen who have made large campaign contributions to the party currently in office—one example among many is Joseph P. Kennedy, the father of John Kennedy and a real-estate investor who was given an ambassadorship to Great Britain. A pork-barrel approach has characterized much of American foreign policy, above all in Latin America. It is both primitive and against the true national interests of the United States. Paz generally praises the objectivity of the United States press; clearly it lacks a mandate, however, or constituency for reporting beyond America's borders. It was not in *The New York Times* but the *Journal de Genève* that, years ago, one could read how Nicaragua was ruled by an "iron triangle" in downtown Managua: One angle was located at Anastasio Samoza's palace, another at the American Embassy, and the third at the main prison. Many reforms have been made in the United States in the intervening decades, but the pork-barrel practice of treating ambassadorships as spoils has not changed. George Kennan, Malcolm Toon, John Paton Davies, and others regularly lament this practice, but without any effect. As Paz points out, it was largely American actions that provoked the downfall of both Samoza and Fulgencio Batista, two dictators friendly to the United States. Hence it is not a paradox to say that the United States itself "produced" both Daniel Ortega and Fidel Castro.

One of Octavio Paz's major points is that Americans do this to their own peril; they inflict a wound on themselves and on the whole continent. For Paz, Castro is not a harmless, colorful "gadfly." Communism in Latin America is not to be taken lightly. On the contrary, it might have an enormous, incalculable future there. Paz believes that Marxism and Communism, according to the Soviet model, are largely dead in Europe—the ideology has become a hollow shell, with fewer and fewer believers. It has an enormous potential in Latin America largely because of the region's unique history. The Enlightenment had only a superficial influence on Latin America; the Counter-Reformation triumphed in both Spain and Portugal and, consequently, in Latin America. The revolutions there overthrew Spain and Portugal, but not their heritage: the Counter-Reform continued as a living influence long after independence and still continues. This continuation of the Counter-Reform, and of what Paz calls the "Islamic" component of Spanish culture—its penchant to fuse the religious and political in the form of a crusade—persists in Latin America and provides fertile ground for Marxism. In Russia, as in Latin America, the Enlightenment had been negligible, without widespread acceptance: Their histories have traits in common. According to Paz, neo-Thomism and the Jesuit education that shaped Latin American thought produced attitudes that include "little respect for the opinions of others" and prefer "ideas to reality, and intellectual systems to the critique of systems." He adds that the Mexican middle and upper classes are far less attracted to Western or "modern" ways than the Americans who meet them might believe—they are friends of the United States, he writes, "for reasons of interest, but their real moral and intellectual affinities lie with authoritarian regimes. Hence their sympathy for Germany during the two world wars of this century." Although Paz can be bitingly critical of the United States, he does not spare his own country, Mexico, either, and this gives his argument extra force.

North Americans would do well to be as self-critical as Paz and to heed his warning. Marxism is dying in Western and Eastern Europe; as Hans Magnus Enzensburger has mockingly said, real socialism is the highest stage of underdevelopment. Yet there is the paradox of dying Marxism in Europe and resurgent Marxism in Latin America. Czesław Miłosz has explained this by saying that different places on the globe do not necessarily exist within the same time frame—one should not assume that they are synchronous. Paz adds that both Latin America and the Soviet Union live outside the influence of the Reform and the Enlightenment—for them, "modernity" has meant bypassing these major historical movements, or leapfrogging them. For fifty years, Paz writes, Latin American dictators felt bound to do lip service to democratic constitutions and to promise to obey them. Certainly they broke the promises, yet they thought their legitimacy derived from them. Now with Castro, this weak link to the Enlightenment has for the first time been deliberately thrown to the winds. In the political and cultural context of Latin America, Paz regards this gesture as very significant. It has excited many intellectuals and people of the "Left"—a term that Paz says has no meaning in Latin America, as those who apply it to themselves are invariably products of the Counter-Reform and hostile to the Enlightenment.

Paz considers the future of Latin America with very qualified hope. Since 1975, several countries have evolved from dictatorships to democracies. The United States no longer applies the Monroe Doctrine. Yet with the Sovietization of Cuba and Nicaragua, the Soviet Union has become a very active presence on the continent, which he deplores. Paz expects little constructive action from the United States, the country that might seem, superficially, the most interested in ending that presence. The book contains many provocative insights, some only hastily sketched. His views on the Soviet Union are consistently interesting, although that country is not the center of his concern. He sees the Soviet Union as having become a rigid, petrified "stratocracy," entirely dependent on the army and the Party. Paz's Catholic and Latin American background permits him numerous insights denied, perhaps, to specialists on the Soviet Union who are products of the Reform or take it for granted; he has observed a broad variety of dictatorships in action and compared them. He does not believe the myth of the Soviet Union's "paranoia"—he claims that *all* dictatorships shift the locus of conflict from inside to the world outside. This shift, he thinks, and inner repression are the two pillars upon which the Soviet Union is founded.

Also of great interest are his observations about the "Third World," a term he does not like, as there are so many great differences among the countries to which it gives an artificial unity. Yet they do have a connecting thread—the experience of colonialism and a dislike of the West. His observations on the Third World range widely, with a fascinating discussion of the relations between colonial influence and modernization. All the countries influenced by China, he concludes—Singapore, Korea, Japan—have modernized faster than those influenced by Islam or, often, Catholicism.

This is a scintillating, provocative book; it is packed with insights and suggestions that are rarely developed at length but prod one to further thought. The book's greatest weakness is that it is a collection of essays pieced together to make a whole. These essays were often written for different newspapers and different audiences with quite different expectations. Consequently, their arguments do not build upon one another the way they might, and often they are presented in an impressionistic style. Many of the most valuable, original ideas are touched upon, put on record, then the author moves on to cover new ground. There are, finally, some lacunae in his considerable erudition. His knowledge of Protestantism is somewhat superficial, as is his knowledge of the history of the United States during the eighteenth and nineteenth centuries. Sometimes his terminology is uncritical—Paz uses terms such as "capitalism," "bourgeoisie," "hegemony," and "modernity" too loosely, often as gestures. The critical reader genuinely interested in the argument longs for more distinctions and qualifications. The requirements of good newspaper copy are different from those of excellent literature, even when the author is one of the most perceptive contemporary writers. Despite its origins, however, the book is a striking success; it is consistently lively, thought-provoking, and succeeds in relating politics to an admirably broad cultural background.

John Carpenter

Sources for Further Study

Booklist. LXXXI, August, 1985, p. 1628.
Commentary. LXXX, September, 1985, p. 70.
Kirkus Reviews. LIII, May 15, 1985, p. 472.
Library Journal. CX, August, 1985, p. 100.
Los Angeles Times Book Review. June 16, 1985, p. 3.
The New York Times Book Review. XC, August 11, 1985, p. 18.
The New Yorker. LXI, October 7, 1985, p. 134.
Publishers Weekly. CCXXVII, May 24, 1985, p. 56.

ORIENTAL TALES

Author: Marguerite Yourcenar (1903-)
Translated from the French by Alberto Manguel in collaboration with the author
Publisher: Farrar, Straus and Giroux (New York). 147 pp. $12.95
Type of work: Short stories

A series of evocative renderings of ten stories and fables set in a variety of locales and periods from both the Near and the Far East, recast in contemporary language, style, and psychology

Ever since the publication in English in 1954 of Marguerite Yourcenar's 1951 novel *Memoirs of Hadrian*, this French novelist has maintained a high reputation among American and British readers, but until the growth of her more general popularity in the 1980's, many of her other representative works were not available in translation. Thanks to her continuing popularity, however, many of her earlier works, such as *Alexis* (1929) and *Coup de Grâce* (1939), have been made available in English. Of all these earlier books, however, none has found a more enthusiastic welcome than her *Oriental Tales* (published in France in 1938 as *Nouvelles orientales*). The charm, wit, and learning of these stories, as well as the particular combination of literary techniques involved in composing them, give them a special place not only in her own work but also in the history of modern French letters.

The ten stories collected here were not originally written to be read or linked together. A helpful postscript by the author indicates both general sources and a list of the various magazines and journals where they first appeared in 1928 over a period of more than a decade. The word "oriental" as used in the title reflects an older European usage of the word and one that may not be familiar to American readers, who may well anticipate a collection of stories from Korea, China, and Japan. Here the term is taken to refer to any area that lies east of Europe. "How Wang-fo Was Saved" is set in China and "The Last Love of Prince Genji" in Japan, for example, but "Marko's Smile" takes place in Montenegro in Yugoslavia, "Kali Beheaded" in a mythic India, and "Aphrodissa the Widow" in modern Greece. What links the stories together is rather the similarity in literary method by which the stories are retold. The reader can take considerable pleasure in observing the same congruence of perception and imagination applied to an extraordinarily wide variety of subject matter.

To some extent, most of the stories involve adaptation of older literary materials. Although the author does not indicate her precise sources, the reader's sense that the tales represent an art consciously and lovingly constructed from art is always strong, giving the prose something of the effect of a musical theme and variations. There is a tonality in the texture of virtually all the stories that suggests that, while these fables and legends could well have been reconstructed using quite a different set of elements that doubtless defined the contours of the original, Yourcenar has chosen to emphasize one particular set of possibilities to bring into relief some special element that drew her to the tale in the first place, perhaps an erotic or ironic possibility. This multilayered effect gives a density, an almost archetypal quality, to the best of these stories, suggesting as it does a richness that confirms the poetic truth of the narrative.

"How Wang-fo Was Saved" recounts the last hours in the life of a Han dynasty painter so skillful in evoking a realistic reproduction of nature in his works that the emperor of China, learning of the world through a selection of the artist's paintings, becomes disillusioned to find actual life less exciting than the art he once loved. To gain his revenge, the emperor decides to blind the artist but first demands that he finish an impromptu work begun many years before. Wang-fo does so, then saves himself by disappearing into the world of his own painting. The language of the story is arch, creating the effect of a piece of chinoiserie, but the narrative line, filled with ironic twists, is suitably stylish.

"Marko's Smile," which retells a Serbian legend, begins in a realistic vein but soon slips into a heroic and romantic mode as the narrator, a Greek archaeologist, recounts the story of a famous fighter against the Turks and of his escape from the enemy, to whom he has been betrayed by his jealous mistress. The tale provides a compelling mixture of bravado and fancy in a highly sensual atmosphere. Marko makes an escape fully worthy of a legendary hero, a feat greater, the archaeologist comments, than any in the *Illiad*.

"The Milk of Death" is set in the same area and begins in a similar realistic fashion with a modern narrator, this time an engineer, who recounts the story of three brothers who wall up the wife of the youngest in a tower. Again, the mixture of the contemporary and the mythic serves well as a vehicle to manifest Yourcenar's touching theme.

"The Last Love of Prince Genji" is an attempt to create an incident never included in Lady Murasaki's great twelfth century Japanese novel, *The Tale of Genji*, a description of the death of the Shining Prince himself, an event that occurs about two-thirds of the way through the lengthy narrative. Murasaki wrote of Genji's decline and then of the shock to the ensuing generation of his death, but the final period of his life was never chronicled in the original novel. Yourcenar's fanciful attempt to do so turns him more into a French aristocrat in retirement, always ready to play the Casanova, than into the ailing and world-weary figure in the original, but there is no denying the ironic charm of his last liaison as she has imagined it.

"The Man Who Loved the Nereids" puts the reader in Greece, where fabled creatures can strike even a modern man dumb, while "Our-Lady-of-the-Swallows" celebrates a Christian rather than a pagan myth in the same culture. "Aphrodissia, the Widow" is also set in Greece. The author's laconic recounting of this tale of lust and death is filled with a powerful eroticism altogether at odds with, say, the delicacies of "How Wang-fo Was Saved," yet the two stories share a similar narrative technique in which small details, beautifully observed—the trail of an ant along the cracks in a wall in the former, dogs sleeping in a thin ribbon of shade in the latter—objectify and help render credible the more fabulous elements in the narrative.

Two briefer stories, "Kali Beheaded" and "The End of Marko Kraljević," deal respectively with Hindu myth and contrasting ideals of Slavic heroism. "The Sadness of Cornelius Berg," the slim fragment that concludes the book, provides a brief sketch of an artist, an unknown contemporary of Rembrandt, who, having roamed Asia, has now returned to contemplate ruefully his past life while living in obscurity in Amsterdam. The sketch is perhaps too short to make a strong effect, but it does serve to pull the reader back into Europe and strikes a nice balance, as the author notes in her postscript, to her story about the painter Wang-fo, whose story opens the collection.

Sophisticated, elliptical, and often ironic, these tales are highly poetic and subtly moving. In virtually all these narratives, Yourcenar manages to establish and sustain a sense of the fabulous, and the reader is thus beguiled into finding again in himself that rarest of modern responses, a genuine sense of wonder. In terms of the author's intentions, then, *Oriental Tales* is an unqualified success.

J. Thomas Rimer

Sources for Further Study

Booklist. LXXXII, September 15, 1985, p. 109.
Kirkus Reviews. LIII, July 1, 1985, p. 613.
Library Journal. CX, September 15, 1985, p. 96.
The New York Review of Books. XXXII, December 5, 1985, p. 19.
The New York Times Book Review. XC, September 22, 1985, p. 42.
The New Yorker. LXI, October 21, 1985, p. 149.
Publishers Weekly. CCXXVIII, July 12, 1985, p. 44.
Times Literary Supplement. November 8, 1985, p. 1266.
The Wall Street Journal. CCVI, August 27, 1985, p. 28.
Washington Post Book World. XV, September 22, 1985, p. 4.

ORSON WELLES
A Biography

Author: Barbara Leaming
Publisher: The Viking Press (New York). Illustrated. 562 pp. $19.95
Type of work: Biography
Time: 1915-1985
Locale: The United States, Europe, and the Middle East

The colorful life of a theatrical genius

> *Principal personages:*
> GEORGE ORSON WELLES, an actor, director, playwright, screen-writer, and novelist
> BEATRICE WELLES, his mother
> RICHARD HEAD WELLES, his father
> MAURICE "DADDA" BERNSTEIN, his guardian
> ROGER E. "SKIPPER" HILL, a teacher and later headmaster of the Todd School; Welles's lifelong friend and occasional collaborator
> MICHAEL MACLIAMMOIR, an Irish actor who worked on numerous projects with Welles
> JOHN HOUSEMAN, the producer of Welles's plays at the Federal Theatre Project and Mercury Theatre
> DOLORES DEL RIO, a film actress with whom Welles had an affair
> VIRGINIA NICOLSON WELLES, Welles's first wife
> JOSEPH COTTON, a member of Welles's Mercury Theatre company and an actor in his films
> RITA HAYWORTH, a film actress, Welles's second wife
> SHIFRA HARAN, Welles's private secretary
> PAOLA MORI, Countess di Girfalco, Welles's third wife

Most show-business biographies, even of major stars, tend to be superficial and to consist largely of gush and gossip. Yet some figures have made such a formidable contribution to theater and film that they warrant a scholarly study. Such a one was Orson Welles, who was a giant in every aspect of theater. Welles was protean, a modern Renaissance man—stage, screen, radio, and television actor and director, magician, matador, playwright, novelist, screenwriter, politician, and bon vivant. Barbara Leaming's *Orson Welles*, which appeared just before the subject's death at the age of seventy, is at once a scholarly and an immensely readable biography whose subject is more fabulous than the hero of many a novel.

Welles was always interested as much in how a story is told as in the story itself; several of his films, beginning with *Citizen Kane* (1941), and his stage version of *Moby Dick*, deliberately let the framework show. Thus when Leaming obtained his cooperation to work with her on his life story, Welles insisted that she put herself into the book, like a James Boswell, or like a reporter trying to get at the truth about Charles Foster Kane. Accordingly, Leaming often takes the reader behind the scenes, becoming a character in the narrative and at the same time giving intimate glimpses of Welles that might not have been available in a different format. Leaming, a professor of theater and film at Hunter College and the author of previous books on Grigori Kozintsev and Roman Polanski, has produced a work which is far more scholarly than the usual Hollywood biographies, most of which lack documentation, let alone critical rigor. Her extensive research was supplemented by months spent taping Welles's reminiscences. Perhaps Welles is not always reliable on himself, but he makes extremely lively copy.

It is hard to realize that by the time Leaming's book appeared, the "boy wonder" had become a man of seventy, for despite his increasing years and girth, Welles never lost his energy and enthusiasms. By ordinary standards, he was a man of great accomplishment, yet his reach exceeded his grasp, and his career exemplified the fate of the person of genius hobbled by team players afraid of individuality and thinking chiefly of commercial considerations.

Welles's talent was recognized early. While he was still an infant, he was proclaimed a prodigy by Dr. Maurice Bernstein, an orthopedist, who claimed that young Orson examined him from his crib and observed, "The desire to take medicine is one of the greatest features which distinguishes men from animals." Fascinated, Bernstein became a sort of foster father to young Welles, providing him with a violin, a conductor's baton, a magic kit, art supplies, a stage makeup kit, and a puppet theater. A great womanizer who was infatuated with the celebrated beauty of Beatrice Welles, Bernstein insinuated himself into the family and became "Dadda" to Orson. Yet Orson's childhood was not painless; his mother died when he was nine, and his father, an occasional inventor, became an alcoholic. A restless globetrotter, Richard Welles took his son Orson with him on some of his journeys and thus started him on a lifetime of wandering.

Meanwhile, Orson, not yet nine, became a hit as "Trouble" in *Madame Butterfly* in the Chicago Opera. At home, he had an informal education, reading William Shakespeare, making himself up and performing *King Lear*, putting on puppet shows, sketching and painting, and studying music. His only formal education was five years at the Todd School in Woodstock, Illinois, where he became the protégé of the headmaster's son, Roger "Skipper" Hill. Just entering his teens, Welles adapted, designed, directed, and performed in numerous plays, in which he portrayed both Dr. Jekyll and Mr. Hyde, Androcles and the Lion, Richard III, Cassius, and Mark Antony. When he played the latter two in a school competition at Chicago's Goodman Theatre, he was accused of being an adult professional actor.

At the age of fifteen, Welles adapted and staged several of Shakespeare's historical plays as one drama, the prototype of the Mercury Theatre production *Five Kings* and of Welles's film *Falstaff* (1966). About this time, his father died, and Welles selected Dadda Bernstein to be his guardian.

Graduated at the age of sixteen, Welles sailed for Ireland and launched himself as a professional actor, with remarkable results. At first, fortune favored Welles in everything he touched. At sixteen, he became a leading actor in six plays at Dublin's Gate Theatre. At eighteen, he was playing Mercutio opposite Katherine Cornell as Juliet. At nineteen, he married socialite Virginia Nicolson. At the same time, his deep, resonant voice made him the world's best-paid and most-in-demand radio actor.

By twenty, Welles had his own theater in New York with the Federal Theatre Project, where he teamed up with producer John Houseman and directed an all-black voodoo *Macbeth* that became a sensational success. When the leading actor, a chronic alcoholic, had a breakdown, Welles replaced him, playing the title role in blackface. At twenty-one, he directed several other smash hits for the Federal Theatre Project—a farcical extravaganza, *Horse Eats Hat* and Christopher Marlowe's *Doctor Faustus* (in which he also played the lead), while also staging Marc Blitzstein's "labor opera," *The Cradle Will Rock*, for the Actors' Repertory Company. The government tried to ban the latter, so Welles left the Federal Theatre Project and founded, with Houseman, the Mercury Theatre, for which he directed a succession of brilliant hits—a modern-dress *Julius Caesar* that indicted Italian Fascism, Thomas Dekker's bawdy Elizabethan comedy *The Shoemaker's Holiday*, and George Bernard Shaw's *Heartbreak House*, in which he played the aged Captain Shotover. A second season was less successful, but in 1938, Welles stunned the nation with a radio adaptation of *The War of the Worlds* on Halloween, a broadcast that created widespread panic with its verisimilitude. Simultaneously, he starred on the radio as The Shadow. In 1940, he directed a dynamic stage adaptation of Richard Wright's *Native Son*.

By the age of twenty-three, Welles was on the cover of *Time* magazine and was profiled in *The New Yorker*. The following year, RKO gave him an unprecedented contract to write, produce, direct, and star in whatever film he wanted to make, with complete control and final cut. Coming to motion pictures with no previous experience in the medium, Welles in a few months of intense study so mastered the art of the cinema that his first film, *Citizen Kane*, became a dazzling example of the resources of camera and sound track, a classic film that many critics hail as the greatest American picture ever made, one that has influenced all subsequent filmmakers. Only twenty-five when he produced, directed, starred in, and cowrote *Citizen Kane*, Welles seemed to have reached the pinnacle of his profession.

Ironically, it was indeed the pinnacle for him, for everything after it was anticlimactic, and from being fortune's favorite, Welles became something of fortune's fool. Enraged at the faintly disguised portrait of himself as Kane, William Randolph Hearst became Welles's implacable enemy, and Hearst's hired gossip columnists lost no opportunity to undermine Welles's career. Getting the reputation of being an unreliable maverick whose work was uncommercial, Welles lost control of most of his later pictures and after 1958 never directed another film for a Hollywood studio. Practically all of his films after *Citizen Kane* were taken away from him and cut and mangled by others. His second picture, *The Magnificent Ambersons* (1942), may have been his masterpiece, but it was butchered by the studio while Welles was in South America on a government assignment, and forty-five minutes of it were thrown into the Pacific, leaving a brilliant but botched work, like a defaced statue or temple. The irony is, according to Leaming, that Welles was an extraordinarily resourceful and efficient filmmaker, who brought in pictures on time and under budget and whose work probably would have had greater commercial success if it had been left intact.

Meanwhile, Welles seriously considered shifting his career to politics. The Franklin D. Roosevelt Administration sent him as a goodwill ambassador to South America. This led to his radio show, *Hello Americans*, in which he informed North Americans about conditions in South America, and to another political show, *Ceiling Unlimited*, about aviation's role in the war. In 1943, he wrote the foreword to a pamphlet about the injustice of the Sleepy Lagoon murder case in Los Angeles. From 1943 to 1946, Welles gave numerous political speeches for the Roosevelt Administration and for the Free World Association. He campaigned actively for Roosevelt's reelection, participated in War Loan Drive shows, wrote editorials for *Free World*, and contributed a syndicated political column to the *New York Post*. He considered running for the Senate and was even spoken of as presidential material. Welles worked for the establishment of the United Nations and was proposed as its first secretary general. During the war, Welles produced and starred in several long-running political radio shows. His most successful was a series he did in 1946, defending a black veteran who had been blinded by an unprovoked beating by police. Week after week, Welles investigated the case on the air and finally got the Justice Department to bring charges against the guilty officer.

In films, Welles directed and starred in the anti-Nazi suspense drama *The Stranger* (1946). This was his most conventionally commercial film, and the studio left it more or less alone. Yet his brilliant *Lady from Shanghai* (1948), costarring his second wife, Rita Hayworth, was taken away from him and tampered with, and Republic Studio butchered his low-budget *Macbeth* (1948). Many of Welles's projected productions were vetoed for lack of funding: *War and Peace*, with Welles as Pierre and Laurence Olivier and Vivien Leigh as André and Natasha, *The Little Prince*, *Cyrano de Bergerac*, and the life of Christ. After *Macbeth*, Welles became a wanderer, living for extended periods in Europe and financing most of his later films himself or with what funds he could scrape up from unlikely sources, such as the Iranian government. Though he had a reputation for being unable to finish his films, he persevered for years to get the money to complete

Othello (1952) and *Falstaff*. Made on a shoestring budget, his Shakespearean films nevertheless have a visual richness and even a sense of opulence that attest Welles's resources as a filmmaker. When he could not get money for sets for *The Trial* (1962), he filmed it ingeniously in an abandoned Paris train station.

Leaming finds it ironic that in 1976 the American Film Institute gave its Life Achievement Award to Welles, who had virtually been blackballed as a Hollywood director and who used the occasion to plead for funds to complete *The Other Side of the Wind*, a potential masterpiece left unfinished because of lack of funds. In the last year of his life, he wrote a script that promised to rival the quality of *Citizen Kane*, but he could get no one to star in it. It is a tragedy and a waste that Welles, one of the most brilliant film directors, was allowed to direct only six pictures in Hollywood and only twelve in all.

Fortunately for the multitalented Welles, he could always fall back on acting to recoup his finances. A formidable performer, he did some of his best work in the films of others, as Edward Rochester in *Jane Eyre* (1944), Harry Lime in *The Third Man* (1949), Cesare Borgia in *Prince of Foxes* (1949), Father Mapple in *Moby Dick* (1956), and Clarence Darrow in *Compulsion* (1959). Welles also appeared in several potboilers, but he always bounced back, following such a failure as *The Tartars* (1961) with a brilliant performance as Cardinal Wolsey in *A Man for All Seasons* (1966). He played the first King Lear ever televised, and he staged and played Ahab in a highly successful *Moby Dick—Rehearsed* (1955). He also appeared in many cameos and did numerous radio and television commercials.

The final two decades of Welles's life had more professional frustrations than triumphs, and Leaming devotes only forty-eight of 514 pages to them. Yet perhaps it was Leaming rather than Welles who was running out of steam, for she gives only a cursory treatment to his films of these years, omitting *A Man for All Seasons* altogether, whereas she goes into meticulous detail in the early years.

Nevertheless, Leaming's is a superior biography, far above most Hollywood lives. She provides complete documentation on sources but curiously fails to include a filmography and chronology of Welles's activities on stage, television, and radio, and of his publications and awards, though they are included in a publicity brochure. Perhaps, therefore, the omission was the decision of the publisher rather than the author.

Besides chronicling the public Welles, Leaming does well with his private life as well, in which he was Gargantuan in his appetites for food, women, and high living. At seventeen, he had the run of a Moroccan pasha's harem. He was the lover of Dolores Del Rio, the husband of Rita Hayworth when she was every soldier's favorite pinup girl, and a spectacular womanizer.

Nicknamed "Crazy Welles," he nevertheless comes across as a sensitive, even shy, individual whose flamboyance was something of a defensive mask. In any event, it is well worth making his acquaintance in Leaming's fascinating portrait of a remarkable individualist.

Robert E. Morsberger

Sources for Further Study

American Film. XI, December, 1985, p. 75.
Library Journal. CX, August, 1985, p. 113.
Los Angeles Times Book Review. September 22, 1985, p. 8.
The New York Times Book Review. XC, September 15, 1985, p. 9.
The New Yorker. LXI, November 11, 1985, p. 157.
Publishers Weekly. CCXXVIII, July 26, 1985, p. 158.
Time. CXXVI, October 7, 1985, p. 70.
Variety. CCCXX, October 16, 1985, p. 165.
Vogue. CLXXV, September, 1985, p. 502.
Washington Post Book World. XV, September 15, 1985, p. 1.

ORWELL
The Lost Writings

Author: George Orwell (1903-1950)
Edited, with an introduction, by W. J. West
Publisher: Arbor House (New York). Illustrated. 304 pp. $20.00
Type of work: Radio journalism and letters
Time: 1940-1943
Locale: Great Britain

A record of some of the talks Orwell produced while employed at the BBC during World War II, along with pertinent correspondence relating to this work, the book includes a historical and biographical introduction by the editor, which links these recently discovered writings with Orwell's mature fictional works, Animal Farm *and* Nineteen Eighty-Four

It has long been known that George Orwell drew upon his wartime experiences when he came to write *Nineteen Eighty-Four* (1949) in the immediate aftermath of World War II. The drab, forbidding landscape of Winston Smith's Oceania (subject of two films, the most recent of which captures this aspect of the novel rather better than the 1950's version) reflects Orwell's almost phobic aversion to the England that emerged during and after the war, revealing not only the bombed-out buildings and the war-enforced deprivations but also the generalized regimentation and imposed conformity in domestic and public building, which became part of the postwar Labour government's effort to rebuild and reshape a shattered nation. INGSOC, the political and social dogma of Oceania, while it was in part motivated by a generous dose of anti-Communist ideology (deriving from Orwell's long-standing contempt for the Soviet Union and its local incarnation, the Communist Party of Great Britain), was more directly a representation of the Clement Attlee government's attempt to direct social spending toward the masses of underprivileged British workers and the unemployed, to give them for the first time in history a solid and secure material basis upon which to build a decent life. To the extent that any such program of general social improvement would require centralized bureaucracy and state control, it can be said that Orwell's horrific fantasy of the future (he himself always insisted that this is what the world of *Nineteen Eighty-Four* was) had no particular government or social system as its model. Nevertheless, given what is known about Orwell's political beliefs and prejudices, it is not so wrong to say that the novel gives warrant for the Cold War appropriation of it that ensued immediately upon its publication, and that has shaped its reception down to the mid-1980's. That Big Brother was intended to suggest Joseph Stalin (once more, Orwell made no bones about this) is but another indication of the book's basic polemical thrust. England is there all right, but behind the picture of war-ravaged London lay Orwell's nightmares about a Socialist future, which he thought he detected emerging in Labour-led Great Britain and which had as its ultimate avatar what Orwell thought he knew about Stalin's Soviet Union.

The value and interest of *Orwell: The Lost Writings* lies in the light it sheds on that period in Orwell's life when he worked for the India Section of the Far Eastern Service of the British Broadcasting Company (BBC), writing and broadcasting radio scripts and arranging for speakers and programs. This period was undoubtedly influential upon Orwell's ultimate picture of those aspects of Oceania which he saw already incarnated in His Majesty's government's wartime organization and administration. It is by now a commonplace in the scholarship on Orwell that much of what Winston Smith experiences in his work for the Ministry of Truth reflects Orwell's own experiences at the BBC, then under tight rein by the Ministry of Information. Even the physical description of the Ministry of Truth building resembles quite closely the actual University of London Senate House on Malet Street (pictured in a recent photograph in the present book), where the Ministry of Information was headquartered during the war. To a degree, then, Orwell's novel was less a projection than a recollection, a kind of report of what things were like for at least some of those employed by "our side" in the "struggle against Fascism." One might profitably read *Nineteen Eighty-Four* with Thomas Pynchon's *Gravity's Rainbow* (1973), rather than, as has most often been the case, in the company of Eugene Zamyatin's *We* (1959) and Aldous Huxley's *Brave New World* (1932). Orwell's supposed fantasy might well be taken less as a dystopian fantasy than as a grim, but scarcely exaggerated, historical novel.

The point, however, should not be overdramatized. One can see fairly clearly from the present book that on a daily basis Orwell's life was not all that distressing. The correspondence reprinted in the second section of the book suggests that the difficulties he faced were scarcely more menacing than the ones met every day by anyone who works in a relatively impersonal organization of any size, whether it be a university or a government agency of ministry. The sense of having someone always looking over one's shoulder, which W. J. West emphasizes in his introduction and in his commentary on the general governing wartime censorship at the BBC, was perhaps exacerbated during the war. Yet the bureaucratization of the mind (the phrase originated, after all, not in reflections on totalitarian states of the twentieth century but in Max Weber's analyses of the German imperial bureaucracy whose servant he was), the tendency to adapt oneself to what Orwell would label "doublethink," is probably part and parcel of the contradictory loyalties anyone is bound to experience when trying to balance personal moral beliefs (for example, simply honesty) with the demands of living in a social environment. The only place where outright lies and plain truth can be directly and without ambiguity opposed is precisely in the realm of fiction.

That said, one can discern in the writings collected here the kind of genuine moral bind in which Orwell most probably felt he had been trapped by agreeing to produce propaganda in support of the British government's war effort. The difficulties were most acute over questions of political and social commentary on India and the overseas colonies. Orwell complained loudly over the wish of his superiors to have him broadcast under his pen name. He protested that since the reputation of "George Orwell" was, in South Asia at any rate, primarily as an anti-imperialist, to appear suddenly as an agent of the British Crown and perforce an opponent of Indian nationalism (some of those who were pursuing this struggle had gone to Berlin and Tokyo, where they were understandably given cordial treatment) would not only damage his own image (about which he rather disingenuously professed not to care) but also would undermine the credibility of his views. Better, Orwell reasoned, to come over the air waves under the unknown moniker of Eric Blair.

West suggests that Orwell's consciousness of the extent of real censorship at the BBC was really only awakened after he left the service and tried to find a publisher for *Animal Farm* (1945). If, however, as West himself argues repeatedly, the experiences and feelings of Winston Smith are indeed derived from Orwell's own at this period, it is difficult to believe that he was not acutely aware of at least the general run of practices that characterized the Ministry of Information's scrutiny of every word that was to be broadcast. Possibly the most revealing incident of all concerns the rejection of a script by Barbara Ward on "British Colonial Policy." West prints the text of the memorandum ordering cancellation of the talk as well as the censor's detailed criticisms—a masterpiece of the rewriting of history books Orwell was to pillory in *Nineteen Eighty-Four*. Here are some excerpts:

> The less said about India at the present time the better. In any case, the Indian problem is not related to Colonial problems.

> Whereas there is much to explain about our Colonial Empire, on balance there is surprisingly little of which we need to be ashamed.

> It has been no part of British Colonial Policy to consider any members of the British Colonial Empire as "racially inferior."

> As for the "colour bar" this has been fought wherever it has reared its ugly head.

> When has Great Britain taken "riches out of the Colonies"?

To this last bit of brilliant doublethink, one can only reply: "When did Great Britain, or any other imperial power, not?" The author of this incredible (although under the circumstances of wartime censorship, completely effective) tissue of distortions was one H. V. Usill. Since the techniques of secrecy and repression in Great Britain have not reached quite the degree of efficiency predicted by Orwell himself, Usill, if he or she is still alive, will have the opportunity to rue the bad faith exhibited here. Whatever may be said of Orwell's subsequent political betrayals, one cannot imagine the author of *Burmese Days* (1934) stooping this low. Small wonder that he ultimately grew disenchanted with the role he was compelled to play in Great Britain's war effort, resigning his post to become the literary editor of the *Tribune*, and to work on his allegorical novel *Animal Farm*.

Interesting as some portions of *Orwell: The Lost Writings* are, and valuable as West's introduction undoubtedly is in filling in the blanks that have remained in one's knowledge about this brief but important period in Orwell's career, one's sense of Orwell as a writer and as a person will not be substantially altered by this book. West's claim that "the key to Orwell's evolution from the slightly pedantic and unpolished author of pre-war days lies in the two years he spent" at the BBC, is, frankly, rather dubious. Leaving aside the caricature of Orwell's writings prior to the war (*Homage to Catalonia*, 1938, unpolished or pedantic?), nothing in the materials collected here points toward the two works of fiction that would establish his subsequent reputation. What one sees from this book is a competent performer of mundane bureaucratic tasks and a no-more-than-ordinarily literate Englishman called upon to disseminate some bromides about culture at a time when such an activity was a very low priority of the British government. Orwell aficionados will be pleased and delighted by the publication of these writings; the general reader will benefit more from West's competent and informative introduction. Yet to claim that these documents constitute a great find strains credulity. While one does not wish to endorse the activities of paper shredders and incinerators the world over, there is one principle that can reasonably be applied in deciding what to preserve and what to leave to what Karl Marx once called the "gnawing criticism of the mice": Not all words and documents are worth preserving, not even all the words of important writers.

Michael Sprinker

Sources for Further Study

Booklist. LXXXI, August, 1985, p. 1598.
Kirkus Reviews. LIII, July 15, 1985, p. 706.
Library Journal. CX, October 15, 1985, p. 88.
National Review. XXXVII, November 29, 1985, p. 56.
New Leader. LXVIII, September 9, 1985, p. 19.
The New York Times Book Review. XC, November 17, 1985, p. 18.
The New Yorker. LXI, October 21, 1985, p. 151.
Newsweek. CVI, October 28, 1985, p. 89.
Publishers Weekly. CCXXVIII, August 2, 1985, p. 56.
Washington Post Book World. XV, September 8, 1985, p. 11.

OUR THREE SELVES
The Life of Radclyffe Hall

Author: Michael Baker (1948-   )
Publisher: William Morrow & Company (New York). Illustrated. 386 pp. $17.95
Type of work: Literary biography
Time: 1880-1943
Locale: England, France, and Italy

A carefully researched biography that illuminates both the life and the literature of Marguerite Radclyffe Hall, better known to her contemporaries as "John"

> *Principal personages:*
> MARGUERITE "JOHN" RADCLYFFE HALL, a British novelist
> RADCLYFFE "RAT" RADCLYFFE-HALL, her father
> MARIE DIEHL VISETTI, her mother
> MABEL "LADYE" BATTEN, her first, long-term lover
> MRS. OSBORNE LEONARD, a celebrated medium
> UNA VINCENZO TROUBRIDGE, the companion, lover, and amanuensis of John
> ADMIRAL SIR ERNEST TROUBRIDGE, K.C.M.G., Una's husband
> ANDREA TROUBRIDGE, their daughter
> EVGENIA SOULINE, the great passion of John's twilight years

Michael Baker's *Our Three Selves: The Life of Radclyffe Hall* is the third and the most satisfying full-length biography of Marguerite Radclyffe Hall. In order to appreciate fully what Baker has accomplished in *Our Three Selves*, it is necessary to understand the limitations of its predecessors. The first, *The Life and Death of Radclyffe Hall* (1961), was written in only four weeks in 1945 by Una Vincenzo Troubridge and was withheld from publication until 1961, when it was presumed that most of the principal persons were deceased. It is the distinctive work of an adoring lover and life companion: It is eulogistic and quaintly Victorian in its discretion. It displays, unfortunately, almost none of the wit, vivacity, and trenchant observation of Troubridge's carefully kept daybooks. It has, however, despite its anachronistic reticence, a charm and an eye for ostensibly trivial detail, which Baker has been careful to notice and to cultivate in his use of this source for *Our Three Selves*.

The second biography, by Lovat Dickson, is entitled *Radclyffe Hall at the Well of Loneliness: A Sapphic Chronicle* (1975). Dickson was in the enviable position of having been left the copyrights to Radclyffe Hall's books, with Troubridge's stipulation that they would only be published in the most dignified fashion, this referring especially to *The Well of Loneliness* (1928), Radclyffe Hall's book concerning "sexual inversion," which had faced so many court proceedings because of its then-unusual subject matter. As literary executor, Dickson felt compelled to write a more complete and more carefully documented life of the much-misunderstood novelist. One of several areas in which Dickson's book significantly increased public knowledge about Radclyffe Hall's life was in its account of her late, and very painful, affair with Evgenia Souline. This affair received a scant three pages in Troubridge's earlier biography, even though the episode lasted, off and on, for a full eight years before Radclyffe Hall's death. Despite the additional information made available in *Radclyffe Hall at the Well of Loneliness*, Dickson's book suffers from a disturbing penchant for impressionism and a rather florid style when dealing with matters of the heart and loins. The following description of Troubridge at a luncheon that she and Dickson shared in the 1950's is typical: "I could see that she had been very beautiful. It was not difficult to imagine her suffused with that hot content that burns away the flesh; and to imagine this flame lit by someone other than a man." This is clearly the style of the romance-novel genre. Throughout Dickson's biography of Radclyffe Hall, one senses the storyteller, the stylist, and perhaps the unwary sensationalist getting the upper hand over the objective recorder of fact.

To be fair, Radclyffe Hall's story is so dramatic and unusual that the temptation to romanticism must be nearly irresistible. Nevertheless, it is to Michael Baker's credit that in *Our Three Selves* he manages, in the main, to steer a more scholarly, but no less interesting, course.

The sources from which a biography of Radclyffe Hall must be fashioned make objectivity a very difficult goal. To begin with, Radclyffe Hall never kept a diary, nor was she a prolific letter writer, with the exception of a relatively short period at the end of her life. To use Baker's words, "Her story is thus predominantly one told by others." The major sources for *Our Three Selves* are the diaries and letters of Mabel "Ladye" Batten, which chronicle Radclyffe Hall's first significant love affair; the records of the proceedings of the Society for Psychical Research, which engaged the energies of both Radclyffe Hall and Troubridge immediately following Batten's death; the Radclyffe Hall Collection at the Humanities Research Centre at the University of Texas, which houses Radclyffe Hall's letters to Evgenia Souline; and the extensive daybooks of Troubridge, without whose careful attention to the author's life, more than twenty-eight years of intimacy, any attempt at a biography would have been speculative indeed.

One cannot overlook the prose fictions of Radclyffe Hall herself: *The Unlit Lamp* (1924), *The Forge* (1924), *A Saturday Life* (1925), *Adam's Breed* (1926), *The Well of Loneliness* (1928), *The Master of the House* (1932), and *Miss Ogilvy Finds Herself* (1934). One of the excellences of Baker's method is in his use of these fictional sources. Rather than play the amateur literary critic, attempting to explicate the novels in terms of Radclyffe Hall's life, he takes the more interesting approach of showing how each of the novels illuminates a facet of the personality being examined in the biography. He is less interested, for example, in how much the character Stephen in *The Well of Loneliness* resembles Radclyffe Hall in superficial details as in how the writing of a ground-breaking book on "inversion" affected Radclyffe Hall, the woman, in her views of herself as a "congenital invert" and as a champion of a weak and oppressed minority. He focuses on the research that went into writing the book—which, interestingly enough, put Radclyffe Hall in touch with Havelock Ellis, the foremost authority on inversion in her day. Baker chronicles her frustration with the book's reviewers, who so clearly failed to accept *The Well of Loneliness* on its own terms. Baker shows both her determination to fight the banning of the book in England and her elation at its vindication in the United States. He makes the reader experience her disappointment when her fellow writers prove chary of taking a strong stand in defense of the book. The reader comes to see the prosecution of *The Well of Loneliness* not simply as a cause célèbre but as a touchingly sincere effort by one dauntless woman to garner empathy for a group that she believed was tremendously misunderstood.

Always in Baker's *Our Three Selves*, the focus is rightfully on the author rather than on her works. The conservative politics, the preoccupation with the welfare of animals, the care for the weak and the disenfranchised, the Catholicism infused with spiritualism, the strong sense of duty, and the passion for ethical convictions are all characteristics of the novels, which are skillfully used to shed light on the actions of an intense and complex woman, who left little other direct record of the inner workings of her mind.

In Radclyffe Hall's first major successful novel, *Adam's Breed*, she initiated a dedication that would appear in all of her future works: "To Our Three Selves." The three selves referred to are Mabel Ladye Batten, Una Vincenzo Troubridge, and Radclyffe John Hall herself. They formed a special trinity, which Baker recognizes in the title and in the structure of his book. The prologue to the book, in fact, begins in the dark rooms of Mrs. Osborne Leonard, a celebrated medium, who is possessed by the spirit of the recently deceased "Ladye." "John" and "Una" are taking notes and asking careful questions. Like so many of the bereaved of World War I, they looked to spiritualism for comfort, and their intellects, more rigorous than most, soon convinced them to take part in the serious psychic research of their day. No less a scholar than Sir Oliver Lodge championed their membership in the Society for Psychical Research, an honor which they felt greatly and which appears to have awakened a diligence in Radclyffe Hall that would later be transferred to the writing of her novels.

Some of the early feminist reviewers of *Our Three Selves* have doubted the ability of a male author, despite his prestigious degrees in modern history and British literature from Oxford University, to tackle the biography of a turn-of-the-century lesbian author. They could easily cite lines such as the following from *Our Three Selves* to argue their case: "John was certainly a stickler for what one might call 'husband's rights' in the home, chief of these being her own study and dressing room." This sounds, out of context, like a remark that could only be made by a biographer who had never even heard of Virginia Woolf's famous feminist manifesto *A Room of One's Own* (1929). Yet Radclyffe Hall was, in fact, a woman who from an early age emulated the desultory, squirely habits of her father, Radclyffe "Rat" Radclyffe-Hall. She wore publicly, and attractively, as one can see from the illustrations in the biography, handsomely tailored but decidedly masculine clothing; she spent the early years of her life more engaged with hunting and hounds than with poetry and prose; she shouldered the major financial and decision-making responsibilities in her affairs with women; and she was known by her contemporaries not as Marguerite but simply as "John." This was a woman who, for all her sartorial eccentricities, had extremely conservative political views, including her conviction that her lesbianism was an unfortunate, albeit unavoidable, congenital plight. Such a view, odd as it may appear to modern readers, seems tame compared to her championing of Benito Mussolini and the Axis Powers in World War II. The notions that seem anachronistic in *Our Three Selves* are especially important, because they are the sure signs of the precision with which Baker has attempted to relate the story of Radclyffe Hall in a way that avoids the subjectivity of his predecessors. As he explains in the preface: "I have avoided the worst excesses of modern psychiatric jargon and placed my speculations in the context of her [Radclyffe Hall's] own times rather than what passes for fashionable thinking today."

Most readers will be glad that Baker has not only set such a worthwhile goal for himself but, what is more, has achieved it.

Cynthia Lee Katona

Sources for Further Study

Booklist. LXXXI, August, 1985, p. 1621.
Kirkus Reviews. LIII, June 1, 1985, p. 512.
Library Journal. CX, October 15, 1985, p. 81.
The New Republic. CXCIII, November 25, 1985, p. 34.
The New York Times Book Review. XC, September 8, 1985, p. 3.
The Observer. June 23, 1985, p. 22.
Publishers Weekly. CCXXVII, May 24, 1985, p. 59.
Washington Post Book World. XV, August 18, 1985, p. 4.
Wilson Library Bulletin. LX, October, 1985, p. 70.

OUT IN THE WORLD
Selected Letters of Jane Bowles, 1935-1970

Author: Jane Bowles (1917-1973)
Edited, with an introduction and notes, by Millicent Dillon
Publisher: Black Sparrow Press (Santa Barbara, California). Illustrated. 319 pp.
$20.00; paperback $12.50
Type of work: Letters
Time: 1935-1970
Locale: Primarily Tangier, Morocco

A selection of letters by a talented writer thwarted by psychological and physical problems

> *Principal personages*:
> JANE BOWLES, an American woman of considerable writing ability
> PAUL BOWLES, her husband, a composer and writer
> LIBBY HOLMAN, her friend
> HELVETIA PERKINS, her lover
> CHERIFA, a Moroccan woman pursued by Jane Bowles

During her lifetime, Jane Bowles produced a novel, *Two Serious Ladies* (1943), a play, *In the Summer House* (1954), which ran briefly on Broadway, seven short stories, and some fragments of works that were never completed. She was of interest to such writer friends as Truman Capote and Tennessee Williams and to a small group who admired her experimental style. Her reputation has grown as society has changed. It is now somewhat difficult to disentangle the interest in her works from the interest in her life—a life tortured by anxiety, tormented by writer's block, committed to open marriage that permitted her lesbian affairs, hampered and shortened by ill health. To some degree, feminism is responsible for the increasing interest in Bowles, a woman who sought independence at a time when few women had that goal. Recent publications have at last made it possible to study Jane Bowles fully. *My Sister's Hand in Mine: An Expanded Edition of the Collected Works of Jane Bowles* (1978) includes fragments along with the previously published works. It was followed in 1981 by Millicent Dillon's biography of Bowles, *A Little Original Sin: The Life and Work of Jane Bowles*. The 133 letters in *Out in the World*, assembled from various collections by Millicent Dillon, who has also dated them and provided necessary editorial comments, further illuminate both the life of this unusual writer and her works.

In her letters, Jane Bowles writes frequently about the difficulty she has in writing. Sometimes she finds excuses: The weather is humid, or she has guests, or she is ill. Certainly after she had her stroke in 1957, ill health was a valid reason. Though in her early years, she bemoans her slowness without finding either cause or remedy. For example, in 1947, she was in Connecticut working on a second novel. She writes to her husband, Paul, that her lover, Helvetia Perkins, on whom a character is based, intrudes in the novel, so that Jane finds herself dwelling on Helvetia, who always makes her feel "uncertain," rather than working at the writing itself. Jane forces herself to remain in her room, but she cannot force her thoughts to remain with her work. As a result, she averages only a page a day. Often she comes close to despair, but then her imagination saves her, and she turns out a few more sentences.

Jane's depression was exacerbated by her knowledge that Paul wrote rapidly and efficiently. To her, his facility seemed a rebuke, and the fact that he and some of her friends regularly sent her money on which to live put even more pressure on her. For Jane Bowles, writing justified her existence. In 1950, she wrote to Paul about her current block. What if she cannot write, she muses, continuing that she sees her options as suicide or as life as a nonperson, a writer's wife. "I don't think you'd like that, and could I do it well? I think I'd nag and be mean, and then I would be ashamed. Oh, what a black future it could be!" Clearly, her very identity depended on her writing; only her career marked her individuality.

There was, however, another area in which Jane Bowles exercised her creative powers. In 1948, she expresses her dream of what marriage should be: "If *only* you had been here. . . . I wish . . . you liked Tangier. I cannot imagine a better time really than being in a place we both liked and each of us being free and having adventures." Throughout the letters, it is clear that Jane viewed life as an artistic creation, which she and her husband would produce together. In her letters, she dreams that other affairs will not hinder their relationship; like friends, she and Paul will discuss their lovers, encourage each other in romantic difficulties, and even suggest possible partners. Thus Paul suggests the Moroccan woman Cherifa as an interesting lover for Jane. These sexual "adventures" will keep life interesting and presumably stimulate their marriage as well as their work.

For Jane, however, the dream of an open marriage did not work; it only increased the anxieties of a person who was already extremely nervous. In her desire to be independent, was Jane forcing herself into a life more adventuresome than she could handle? Not only does she write frequently about her frustrations in her relationships with Cory, Helvetia, Cherifa, and others, but she seems also to be jealous of Paul's relationships with others. Frequently he is absent for long periods of time. Is it, as she suggests, simply that he dislikes Tangier? Is it the pressures of his work, as when he must write for a travel magazine? Or does he prefer friends such as Tennessee Williams and Gore Vidal to her? She loves him, she writes; she needs a word of comfort or encouragement, and she is embarrassed that she constantly needs money from him. Is the relationship totally free, she asks, or are they husband and wife, whatever that means? There are many long and confused passages in the letters to Paul, as in a letter written in July 1948:

> I feel both things at once. That you are completely free and someone who will help me when he can, out of affection, and yet also that you are a husband. . . . I am not sure either that being confined a bit by the social structure is altogether bad for either one of us. We will see.

Paul was loyal to her, supporting her financially, as far as he could, and emotionally, caring for her in the later years that brought ill health and mental disorder. His devotion carried over in those years to checking her spelling after that capacity was lost. Yet much as she apologized to him, she seemed to need more.

Certainly the writing block and the attempt at an unusual marital relationship contributed to the nervousness evident in all the letters, as did the financial pressures and Jane's indulgence in alcohol. She frequently calls herself an "agonizer"; everything worries her. She cannot make plans and keep to them. She analyzes every possibility until at last she cancels a trip, then writes letter after letter alternately justifying her decision and insisting that she made a mistake in not making the trip after all. Long passages are devoted to her need for money, interspersed with apologies for asking for it and excuses for her expenditures, whether for new clothes or for a sheep to take to a Moroccan feast. Other long passages speculate as to why she has not heard from Paul: Where is he? Is he annoyed with her? When will he come to see her? Should she be living somewhere else? Then later in the same letter, or in one following, she apologizes for her dependence on him.

The fact that her works were coolly received, except by a few enthusiasts, continued to depress her. In September, 1947, she wrote to Paul, "I seem to be completely ignored by the whole literary world just as much as by the commercial one." Although she was encouraged by the production of *In the Summer House* and by some good reviews, she recognized that its tenure on Broadway was very brief and that many people would never see it. Again, a kind of independence was required of her—to continue writing despite public apathy—which was more than she could manage.

Nor could Jane Bowles walk away from her emotional relationships, not even from those which were intended to be merely "adventures." After an intense relationship with Cory (the editor's pseudonym for a lover of Jane), she found herself wishing that Cory would leave and resolved not to get involved with "the innocent" again. The Moroccan woman Cherifa, who fascinated Jane for many years, limited her liberties and constantly drew on Jane, herself living on a skimpy allowance, for as much money as possible. From sheep to doctor bills, Jane seemed to be the Moroccan family's source of funds. Sometimes Jane realistically wonders whether Cherifa really cares for her, even physically, or simply submits to Jane's attentions because there are financial rewards. To Jane, relationships with women seemed to involve fewer demands than those with men. Paul, she thinks, would not want to see her if she were not producing literary work, but Cherifa does not understand about the work and thus can be seen as a more perfect lover. Undoubtedly Jane misinterpreted Paul's encouragement as demands, just as she tried to persuade herself that Cherifa was truly disinterested. Despite her ambivalence about Paul, he seems to have been the most stable influence in her shaky world, and she needed stability. The adventures which provided escape for a time finally produced hangovers—doubts and agonies. As her women lovers disappeared, Paul remained.

Despite the wit which is evident—particularly in the early letters— despite the occasional descriptions of the outside world, with its eccentric people and charming animals, despite the interesting comments on writer friends and acquaintances, ranging from Alice B. Toklas to Tennessee Williams, the recipients of Jane's letters must have had mixed feelings about the long, repetitive, desperate documents. If some annoying qualities, however, are evident in the letters, so are her honesty and courage. Even after the stroke, even after hospitalization for breakdowns, she never resorted to self-pity but continued her self-examination and her brave attempts to be independent. She apologizes because her letters are dull or words are misspelled; she hopes that she has not complained; she asks about other friends and about children; she expresses gratitude for emotional and financial help but insists that friends must not send her money when it becomes a burden for them. Bravely, she says that she is unsure to what extent her ailments are physical and to what extent mental, and she considers arrangements to be made after her death. Thus when she is most dependent, financially and physically, she is still maintaining her own separateness, reporting on her own agony but blaming no one else for it. Her character Emmy Moore, in the unfinished novel *Out in the World*, worried because, she said, "I have not justified myself." Jane Bowles hoped to justify herself by creating literary works or by creating an adventure-filled, independent life. Her letters prove that she accomplished something else: From all of her agony, she produced a life of honesty and courage and thus was more of a success than most of the similarly uncertain characters in her works.

Millicent Dillon's selection of Jane Bowles's letters fulfills its purpose—to reveal the various aspects of a complex personality and to trace the gradual breakdown of a talented writer. The volume will be invaluable to the scholars, feminist and otherwise, who are at last discovering Jane Bowles.

Rosemary M. Canfield-Reisman

Sources for Further Study

The New York Times Book Review. XC, July 28, 1985, p. 10.
Quill & Quire. LI, October, 1985, p. 54

THE PAST

Author: Galway Kinnell (1927-   )
Publisher: Houghton Mifflin Company (Boston). 57 pp. $13.95; paperback $5.95
Type of work: Poetry

In this splendid collection—his first since Selected Poems *won the Pulitzer Prize in 1982—Galway Kinnell continues to explore the tensions between literary sophistication and primal utterance*

The evolution of Galway Kinnell's poetry has a few things in common with that of some of his contemporaries. James Wright, W. S. Merwin, and Adrienne Rich, for example, began their careers, as Kinnell did, in an era when the "well-made poem" was metrical, precise, and responsive to the inquiries of the New Criticism. All four poets, as well as others, found in the 1960's various reasons for casting aside the strictures of meters; several of them published defiant statements of their purposes in doing so, and Kinnell, for one, went so far as to indicate that he was stating principles that ought to apply to all poetry of our time, not only to his. Having begun with poems displaying ease and confidence with formal devices, these poets (some of whom, such as Wright, never completely forsook them) found ways of establishing the integrity of their lines and of maintaining the uniqueness of their voices; Kinnell is among the most versatile handlers of open forms now writing in English. Though he has striven for a quality of speech which might have the immediacy and urgency of the first words spoken by humans, he is also quite at ease with the language of cultural sophistication. If many of his poems are set in the woods, or in rural areas, among animals, and take up ancient themes of love, parenthood, and mortality, he has no problem mentioning in passing such cultural totems as George Frideric Handel's concerto for harp and lute, *Australopithecus robustus*, Wolfgang Amadeus Mozart, or "the angle the bow makes/ when the violinist effleurages out of the chanterelle/ the C three octaves above middle C ("The Seekonk Woods").

Including such details in poems that strive for primal intensity has never been easy, and Kinnell's mastery of his broad vision has been gradual; even in such a masterpiece as "The Bear," first collected in *Body Rags* (1968), the powerful simplicity of the vision is shattered by the phrase "parabola of bear-transcendence," as if the poet had momentarily forgotten that he was not William Butler Yeats.

The ease with which Kinnell now achieves difficult things might partly be attributable to a certain relaxation that characterizes his recent work. (Relaxation is not slovenliness, as any sprinter knows who has learned to increase his speed by relaxing as he runs.) Kinnell is now prepared to accept images and narratives which must not be rendered with fierce intensity; humor, rare in Kinnell's work before *Mortal Acts, Mortal Words* (1980), now greatly enlarges the humanity of his vision and gives individual poems an emotional scope much richer than pure solemnity could achieve.

The Past opens with just such an inclusive poem; "The Road Between Here and There" picks out, on a familiar route between, say, work and home, private landmarks that evoke responses:

> Here a barn burned down to the snow. "Friction" one of the ex-
> loggers said. "Friction?" "Yup, the mortgage, rubbing against
> the insurance policy."
> . . . .
> Here I hurt with mortal thoughts and almost recovered.
> Here I sat on a boulder by the winter-steaming river and put my
> head in my hands and considered time—which is next to
> nothing, merely what vanishes, and yet can make one's elbows
> nearly pierce one's thighs.

These almost-prose lines, all beginning with "Here" and ending with periods, sinuous and energetic, make a fine invitation into the book, which is divided with unusual symmetry into three sections of eleven poems each. Part 1 touches on many of the themes and preoccupations taken up in the other two sections—a deepening sense of mortality, handled with a remarkable honest wistfulness; moments when the awareness of love—of a woman, a child, a friend—is almost too much to bear; and brief anecdotes of rural existence, pointing toward something that endures. The second section consists of shorter poems, most of them moments of piercing awareness, as some natural event takes place. "Prayer," the first poem in the section, though it is only three lines, seems to speak for most of the rest: "Whatever happens. Whatever/ *what is* is is what/ I want. Only that. But that."

It is easy to make too much of a poem as short as this, but it is noteworthy that its clarity and urgency emerge from what might have been a game or a challenge: In fourteen words, three of them appear twice each, one pair to a line; "is," in defiance of expectation, appears three times in a row. Despite this careful exercise of artifice, the poem at first seems to speak conversationally, though with memorable conviction.

The final section of The Past contains the title poem and several others whose meditations on the passing of time and of friends are as moving as any poems recently published. Yet even here, where things are at their most serious, the occasional joke appears. The tact with which Kinnell has found the place for humor is among the most interesting developments in his poetry; there is a calm assurance about that difficult matter which would have been hard to predict from a reading of even his best earlier work.

In part 3, for example, there is a stunning series of three poems in memory of several fellow poets. The first, "December Day in Honolulu," is the shortest of these, though its tone is perhaps the most complex of the three. It begins with a conversational comparison of the days' lengths in Honolulu and in Sheffield, Vermont; the longer day in Honolulu allows time for three separate postal deliveries. This day, each mail delivery brings something connected with the deaths of James Wright, Muriel Rukeyser, and Robert Hayden. The last is touchingly eccentric:

> Last, around the time of stars in Sheffield, a package holding four
> glass doorknobs packed in a *New York Times* of a year ago,
> which Muriel Rukeyser had sea-mailed to me, to fulfill if not
> explain those mysterious words she used to whisper whenever
> we met: "Galway, I have your doorknobs."

The poem ends with the wail of a cat in heat and the speaker's speculations on the noise's meaning. The balance here between literalism and oracular affirmation that, paradoxically, *"this one or that one dies but never the singer"* is a beautiful embodiment of the necessity to accept "whatever happens."

"On the Oregon Coast" and "Last Holy Fragrance" are dedicated to the memory of Richard Hugo and of James Wright, respectively; the one is written in the same one-sentence line form as "December Day in Honolulu" and "The Road Between Here and There," while the other is composed of some 120 lines which range from seven to perhaps sixteen syllables, set without stanza breaks. This progression seems arbitrary in the context of these three poems, but since they are a series only in that they appear together, it is more important that the forms surge forward toward the remaining six poems in the collection. "On the Oregon Coast" evokes an amusing yet serious memory of a conversation between the speaker and Richard Hugo on the problem of personification in poetry in a post-Darwinian age. There is some indication in the recollection that, in retrospect, the speaker finds parts of the conversation pretentious, but his sense is balanced with the conviction that they were on to something that day and that poets with any ambition had better think about these things.

The James Wright memory, however, complicates this issue a little further, in its portrayal of a man struggling to say the unsayable:

> But poetry sings past even the sadness
> that begins it: the drone of poetry readings
> or the mutterings coming from poets' workrooms—
> as oblivious to emotion as the printed page—
> are only seeking that chant of the beginning,
> older than any poem, that the song men
> of Arnhem Land, who jolt their clapsticks
> with a rebuking force like a spank, think
> they summon, or the shaman in Point Barrow,
> Alaska, having trance-learned it, translates,
> or gopher frogs put to us in *parellelismus membrorum*,
> or, now and then, a pure poem glories in.
> As do those last, saddest poems of his,
> which overtake the chant, synchronize

with its happiness, and, as when first light blooms
clouds of night, give us *mourning's* morning.
"How am I ever going to be able to say this?
The truth is there is something terrible,
almost unspeakably terrible in our lives,
and it demands respect, and, for some reason
that seems to me quite insane, it doesn't hate us.
There, you see? Every time I try
to write it down it comes out gibberish."

It is conventional in workshops to advance the dictum that, since all poetry is ultimately about itself, one should not write overtly about poetry.
Though this is usually sound advice, it is well to remember that direct treatment of poetry as subject is conventional in certain kinds of elegies; it might
be added that when such direct treatment is as splendid as the foregoing, it
should be welcome almost anywhere. It is hard to recall, in the work of contemporary poets, a more moving evocation of what poets strive to do.

From these three poems dwelling on the deaths of contemporaries,
Kinnell passes to poems that touch on his own approaching death and on
recollections of intense living-in-the-present. The title poem and "The
Seekonk Woods," with which the volume concludes, are masterful meditations that shift with graceful fluidity from *now* to *then*; "The Waking" and
"That Silent Evening" re-create moments between lovers and speak strongly
for *now*. In the midst of this progression, terror intrudes in "The Fundamental Project of Technology." This poem begins in a museum of the
aftereffects of Hiroshima and Nagasaki; its epigraph, from Tatsuichiro
Akizuki's *Concentric Circles of Death*, is "A flash! A white flash sparkled!"
Variations upon this oddly ambivalent phrasing appear in the last lines of
each of the poem's seven stanzas, gathering force as the context moves from
mere objects to old people to children. The "project" of the title is not,
however, expressed directly as the extinction of the human race; it is
described more ominously as the removal from human mentality of our
connection with other animals, to disconnect us from natural processes,
especially of death. Yet to eliminate death, "it is necessary to eliminate/
those who die; a task attempted, when a white flash sparkled."

This brave poem is in many ways not up to the standard met by most of
this collection. Several passages in it seem products more of the will than of
the deeper imagination that informs most of Kinnell's poems; the final
stanza, however, comes close to those in its sad near resignation, imagining
the day when there will be no one to look back and say what happened.
Nevertheless, the effect of this poem's presence, among personal meditations on what is lost and what persists, is extremely powerful, for it raises
questions—indirect ones, as words may be inadequate to the task of raising
them directly—about what meaning life can have when contemplation of
the future results in fear and grief. In "December Day in Honolulu," it is

suggested that the cat's wail may be saying *"one singer falls but the next steps into the empty place and sings."* The inclusion of "The Fundamental Project of Technology" requires that one consider the absence of all singers, and of all listeners.

Such a prospect can be put in words, but truly to imagine it is nearly impossible. It is one of this wonderful collection's many triumphs that it sings toward the emptiest of places.

Henry Taylor

Sources for Further Study

Booklist. LXXXII, November 15, 1985, p. 462.
Library Journal. CX, November 15, 1985, p. 100.
The New York Times. CXXXV, November 2, 1985, II, p. 13.
Publishers Weekly. CCXXVIII, October 4, 1985, p. 65.
Vogue. CLXXV, November, 1985, p. 280.

PEARL HARBOR
The Verdict of History

Author: Gordon W. Prange (1910-1980), with Donald M. Goldstein and Katherine
V. Dillon
Publisher: McGraw Hill Book Company (New York). Illustrated. 699 pp. $19.95
Type of work: Military history
Time: 1941
Locale: Pearl Harbor and Washington, D.C.

A sequel to At Dawn We Slept *and a fitting tribute to the life and work of Gordon
W. Prange*

> *Principal personages:*
> FRANKLIN DELANO ROOSEVELT, thirty-second President of the
>   United States, 1933-1945
> HUSBAND E. KIMMEL, commander, United States Pacific Fleet at
>   Pearl Harbor
> WALTER C. SHORT, commander, United States Army, Hawaiian
>   department
> GEORGE C. MARSHALL, Chief of Staff, United States Army
> HAROLD STARK, Chief of Naval Operations, United States Navy
> ISOROKU YAMAMOTO, Commander in Chief of the Combined Fleet

In the little more than four decades since the Japanese surprise attack on
Pearl Harbor, historians, journalists, and participants have produced a tremendous volume of literature on the subject. For thirty-seven of those
years, Gordon W. Prange researched the Pacific war and the events leading
to its outbreak on December 7, 1941. Unfortunately, he did not live to see
the results of his labors brought to fruition. Nevertheless, his massive work
on Pearl Harbor, *At Dawn We Slept: The Untold Story of Pearl Harbor*, was
completed and published in 1981 by two of his former students, Donald M.
Goldstein and Katherine V. Dillon. Drawing on Prange's vast research
collections, these two authors also collaborated to produce *Miracle at Midway* (1982) and *Target Tokyo: The Story of the Sorge Spy Ring* (1984). Now
Goldstein and Dillon have completed the prodigious sequel to *At Dawn We
Slept*, entitled *Pearl Harbor: The Verdict of History*.

During World War II, Prange served on the United States Army Historical Staff and afterward was chief of the Historical Staff in Japan under General Douglas MacArthur. In 1949, he joined the faculty of the University of
Maryland and taught there until his death. A prolific researcher, Prange was
steeped in the details of the Pacific war. He believed that there were no villains in the Pearl Harbor story. Many individuals made mistakes both of
commission and omission, but they did not do so with the sinister motive of
thrusting the United States into a world war. In *Pearl Harbor*, Prange thus
rejects the premise of many revisionist historians who maintain that conspiracy alone suffices to explain the ineptitude of American defense and intelligence systems prior to Pearl Harbor. The lack of preparedness in Hawaii

on the fateful morning of December 7 sprang not from the seed of conspiracy but from the seed of lethargy—a seed widely sown in the United States during the 1930's.

As that troubled decade progressed and ominous clouds of war began to gather on the horizon, there seemed to be two distinct groups in the United States who had a clearly defined foreign-policy agenda—isolationists and interventionists—and both were minorities. The vast majority of Americans languished between these two positions, neither demanding nor desiring decisive leadership at a time when circumstances called for precisely that. It is not surprising that these divisions in society were projected into the Congress. Appropriations for the army and navy were consistently reduced. In fact, the latter service did not reach its 1934 authorized strength level until 1944. Even more astounding is the fact that in 1941 the House of Representatives approved extension of the military draft by only one vote.

Prange does not place all the blame at the door of Congress. Between 1937 and 1941, President Franklin D. Roosevelt's Bureau of the Budget regularly made reductions in defense spending before giving Congress a chance to act. Prange also believes that Roosevelt and most of his advisers were too preoccupied with events in Europe to comprehend fully what was happening in Asia. Fearing that hostilities in the Pacific would divert American resources away from the more important European theater, Roosevelt adopted what Prange describes as an "overly placating attitude" toward Japan.

Indecision on the part of Congress and the administration was unfortunate. For the military, it was disastrous. Prange believes that there was a definite connection between the two. He quotes approvingly from an editorial in the *Chicago Sun* that "the mentality that prevailed at Pearl Harbor . . . was the mentality that prevailed at home." Although Prange does not excuse the military for its mistakes, he does suggest that a fair evaluation of the military's performance in the months immediately prior to Pearl Harbor must take into account the paralyzing ambivalence that was so pervasive at the time.

Prange recounts in great detail the numerous paradoxical and ironic events that occurred in the months and weeks prior to the Japanese attack. He cites several instances where high-level officials in Washington, D.C., withheld vital information from officials in Hawaii because they did not think it important enough to forward. Then, too, there were examples of critically important intelligence being forwarded to Hawaii, only to be misinterpreted altogether. Certainly, the failure to assess and disseminate adequately the intelligence that was available prior to December 7 contributed to the success the Japanese enjoyed on that day. Prange emphasizes that Washington's failure to "evaluate this information at its real worth is inexcusable."

Though critical of Washington for its poor handling of intelligence, Prange maintains that the information that was made available to Pearl Harbor should have produced a greater state of readiness than it did. In retrospect, it is clear that Admiral Husband E. Kimmel and General Walter C. Short had certain preconceived ideas about how a war might start in the Pacific, and neither considered a surprise air attack on Pearl Harbor a very likely prospect. Kimmel feared a submarine attack; Short feared sabotage. Moreover, both men believed that if the Japanese were to attack Hawaii, they would do so when the fleet was away. According to Prange, both Kimmel and Short had come to lean psychologically on the fleet. They saw it as something that afforded protection, not as something requiring protection. Neither man realized that to the Japanese the fleet was not a shield but a lightning rod.

The mistakes and errors of judgment made by the commanders at Oahu and by the civilian and military hierarchy in Washington were symptomatic of a more fundamental cause for the disaster of Pearl Harbor. Prange writes: "One cannot emphasize too strongly that all of the American failures and shortcomings contributing to the Japanese victory at Pearl Harbor stemmed from the root disbelief that the Japanese would undertake such a risky venture." Prange maintains that "this lack of genuine, gutlevel belief . . . was the fundamental cause of the United States being caught flat-footed on December 7, 1941," and that "all other sins of omission and commission were its sons and daughters." Most American military experts assumed from the standpoint of logic that Japan would not initiate hostilities with the United States and start a war she could not hope to win. They also assumed that the Japanese would be just as logical. As Prange points out, however, the Japanese government was dominated by a military caste whose code demanded death before dishonor—a code applicable to the nation as well as to the individual. Logic therefore was not the key to the Japanese mind and undue reliance on it precluded American strategists from elevating the possible to the realm of the probable. For their part, the Japanese blundered when they nurtured the illusion that a succession of quick victories in the Pacific would confront the United States with a fait accompli and thus lead to a negotiated settlement. This strategy was predicated on the belief that while the United States had the potential industrial and military might to crush Japan, she lacked the will to use it. The Japanese grossly underestimated the resolve of the American people and suffered terrible retribution as a result.

Prange comes to the conclusion, therefore, that the more obvious political and military errors frequently cited as causes for Pearl Harbor might well be viewed as symptoms of less apparent psychological errors committed by both sides. As a result of these errors, the Japanese committed what must be viewed as a strategic blunder of the first order, despite the fact that they did so with an initial tactical success.

Prange's book is not a whitewash of the major personalities involved in the Pearl Harbor tragedy. He does not shrink from assigning blame where it belongs, but not culpability as the revisionists are wont to do. In fact, much of this work represents a point-by-point refutation of the revisionists, whom Prange excoriates for their rather cavalier treatment of historical evidence. It is doubtful, however, that this tome, impressive though it is, will serve as the headstone for revisionism; one need only recall that *At Dawn We Slept* was followed one year later by John Toland's *Infamy: Pearl Harbor and Its Aftermath*. As a sequel to *At Dawn We Slept*, *Pearl Harbor* seems far too lengthy a work. Impact has been sacrificed for volume. Consequently, some of Prange's most salient findings are made not with the point of the rapier but with the redundant pounding of the pile driver. Equally regrettable is the failure of Prange's associates to take into account several pertinent works published since 1981 by Jonathan Utley, Jeffrey Dorwart, and Ronald Lewin which touch on various aspects of the Pearl Harbor story.

There are also some areas where Prange's arguments seem to need refinement. On page 80, for example, he discusses Roosevelt's pledge of "armed support" to Winston Churchill given on December 3, 1941. Prange notes that the "armed support" did not imply belligerency—citing as an example the support of the United States for Great Britain against Adolf Hitler. It may well have been that Roosevelt had exactly that parallel in mind when he spoke to Churchill, but here Prange assumes and does not prove the president's intent. Another apparent disparity occurs in a discussion of the alternatives open to Roosevelt prior to December 7. Prange asserts that the president's "overly placating" attitude toward Japan "may well be judged a major error." Then, seven pages later, he appears to find validity in Secretary of War Henry Stimson's suggestion that the main strength of the fleet should have been transferred to the Atlantic in the spring and summer of 1941. How one is to reconcile the criticism with the implied alternative is not at all clear.

Drawing on a vast treasure of sources, both official and unofficial, from Japan and the United States, Gordon Prange clearly demonstrates that a story often told need not necessarily lose its interest and fascination. Undoubtedly, the Pearl Harbor story will continue to be told and retold, but no serious account will fail to acknowledge the substantial contribution of Prange and his associates, Donald Goldstein and Katherine Dillon. Their conclusions rest on solid research and are, for the most part, sustained by convincing argument. Nevertheless, there will be many who will continue to believe that when Churchill described Soviet foreign policy as "a riddle wrapped in a mystery inside an enigma," he might just as easily have been speaking of Pearl Harbor.

Kirk Ford, Jr.

Sources for Further Study

Booklist. LXXXII, October 15, 1985, p. 291.
Business Week. February 3, 1986, p. 12.
Kirkus Reviews. LIII, October 15, 1985, p. 1128.
Library Journal. CX, November 15, 1985, p. 94.
The New York Times Book Review. XCI, January 5, 1986, p. 9.
Publishers Weekly. CCXXVIII, November 1, 1985, p. 60.

PLAUSIBLE PREJUDICES
Essays on American Writing

Author: Joseph Epstein (1937-   )
Publisher: W. W. Norton and Company (New York). 411 pp. $15.95
Type of work: Literary essays

A collection of witty and pugnacious essays on various topics in twentieth century American prose

Joseph Epstein is a virtuoso of the essay, and *The Middle of My Tether: Familiar Essays* (1983) assembled some of the pieces that, under the nom de plume Aristides, he contributes to each issue of the quarterly *American Scholar*, of which he is also the editor. *Plausible Prejudices: Essays on American Writing*, Epstein's fifth book, reprints articles that first appeared in *Commentary*, *The New Criterion*, the *Times Literary Supplement*, and *Book World*. Commissioned by other editors on particular literary subjects, the pieces in this book do not have quite the character of familiar essay shared by those in the earlier volume. Nevertheless, they are brilliant performances displaying again Epstein's wit, insight, and passion.

Plausible Prejudices derives its title and its epigraph from a statement by H. L. Mencken: "Criticism is prejudice made plausible." Mencken is, along with Edmund Wilson and Lionel Trilling, one of three tutelary spirits of the book. With Mencken's provocative declaration, Epstein serves notice that he has no intention of disavowing the subjectivity of the literary experience. Instead, he savors it, relishing the opportunity for a bravura demonstration of his own sensibility colliding with contemporary literature. If he cannot win his reader over by the force of logic, he will do so through the power of style. He rejects the academic paradigm of literary science and celebrates the irreducible vitality of the individual reading experience.

The essays in the book are organized into four sections. The first, "The Scene," provides Epstein's general observations on the current situation in literature and literary studies. Section 2, the emotional focus of his energies, is entitled "Portraits of Novelists" and consists of Epstein's animadversions on many of the most acclaimed contemporary authors: Robert Stone, John Irving, Bernard Malamud, John Updike, Ann Beattie, Gabriel García Márquez, Norman Mailer, Philip Roth, Cynthia Ozick, Renata Adler, and Joan Didion. The third section, "The Older Crowd," is a reassessment of earlier figures, most of whom Epstein respects more than is currently fashionable: Van Wyck Brooks, Edmund Wilson, Maxwell Perkins, A. J. Liebling, Willa Cather, John Dos Passos, and James Gould Cozzens. The final section of *Plausible Prejudices*, called "Amusements and Disasters (Essays on Language)," is a miscellany on the current state of reading, writing, and the American language. Its culminating entry, "Piece Work: Writing the Essay," functions both as a coda to the volume and, through appreciations of Joseph Addison, William Hazlitt, Max Beerbohm, George Orwell, Edmund

Wilson, and H. L. Mencken, as a testament to Epstein's own enterprise.

As a reviewer and a critic, Epstein presents himself in the role of literary sheriff, "ready to apprehend delinquent writers." As "part of a posse to head writers off at the pass," he claims that he has more than enough work to keep him busy; the current scene is beset with vastly inflated reputations and with critics intent on puffing new books rather than skeptically appraising them. Epstein resists becoming either a publishing-industry press agent or an ivory-tower obscurantist. He strives to be faithful to Van Wyck Brooks's ideal of being "kind to the dead and hard on the living."

Living writers do not enjoy Epstein's high esteem. He maintains that contemporary literary culture is second-rate, its mediocrity exacerbated by a pervasive failure to acknowledge that fact. Epstein, who is a professor of English at Northwestern University, ascribes much of the blame for this dire situation to the fact that universities have become the center of literary life in America. He attributes the thinness and claustral self-consciousness of current American fiction to the fact that it is being written from within the narrow confines of academe and that it is being written primarily in order to be taught. Epstein also indicts the university for the compartmentalization of experience, for an infatuation with abstractions, and for the politicization of literature. Writing for the conservative journals *Commentary* and *The New Criterion*, he deplores what he describes as the fondness of authors for leftist clichés.

Not only is there a dearth of great writers now, according to Epstein, but literature has also ceased to be central to the culture in the way that it was in earlier eras. He exempts only Saul Bellow, V. S. Naipaul, Isaac Bashevis Singer, Andrei Sinyavsky, Alexander Solzhenitsyn, Vladimir Voinovich, and Marguerite Yourcenar from his invective. Each of these, Epstein contends, possesses gravity—"the quality that confers greatness in literature, even on comic literature; gravity has to do with spirituality, with high and undeflected seriousness, with recognition that literature provides the best record of the common humanity of all." Yet, it is noteworthy that Epstein merely mentions the names of those authors he admires, whereas he provides extensive, detailed analyses of those authors who repel him. He is indeed more comfortable in the role of sheriff than in that of encomiast. He is energized by indignation.

Much of *Plausible Prejudices* thus is animated by its author's resentment over the lack of a worthy subject. Epstein deplores "the vast overproduction of criticism devoted to contemporary writers," particularly since those writers do not merit such sustained attention. Yet, surely he must also be aware that this volume, concentrating on contemporary writers, would likewise be a contribution to that plethora and hence superfluous. One wonders what Epstein would have to say about earlier writers from other cultures to whom he might be expected to be sympathetic. What, for example, might he write about Dante, Erasmus, Michel de Montaigne, Johann Wolfgang von Goethe, or Charles Dickens? It is also not clear to what extent his summary dismissal of the current literary scene is implausibly prejudiced by an exclusive concentration on prose works. Nowhere does Epstein discuss the achievements of a contemporary poet or playwright.

In attempting to salvage Brooks from unmerited oblivion, Epstein finds in the older critic, whom he portrays as another eloquent voice crying in the wilderness of an age of zinc, concerns akin to those of his own maverick enterprise. Brooks was out of temper with the dominant ideology of modernism, and Epstein, who faults the residual effects of modernism for the current malaise, is as well. He even goes so far, during the course of an invective against Mailer, as to proclaim: "The methods of modernism, with very few exceptions, have not been successful in the novel." The remark is made merely en passant, and one waits in vain for Epstein to elaborate on whether and why he judges James Joyce, William Faulkner, and Marcel Proust to be among those "very few exceptions."

In characterizing Brooks as a lonely figure out of sync with cultural fashion, Epstein lauds his determination to confront questions that he deems still crucial to criticism in 1985:

> Is literary criticism strangling on the umbilical cord of its own increasingly arcane analysis—an analysis of a kind that places it at further and further removes from life? And is it not merely that modernism is overrated as a body of literature but, more important, that it represents a dead stop to literature's once central place in the strivings of men?

Even when exercised on trivial texts, literary criticism is, according to Epstein, a high calling, and some of his sharpest barbs are reserved for those who demean the profession. John Leonard is assailed for being frivolous, and Harold Bloom for being unintelligible. "Love of life," a quality as vague as it is inspiring, is the criterion by which Epstein judges his colleagues and by which, presumably, he would himself be judged.

Epstein's review of the *Harvard Guide to Contemporary American Writing* (1979), "one of the most impressive omnium gatherums of literary cliché ever assembled," typifies much of his displeasure with the current state of literary studies and literature. He sees the collective volume as an oblique attempt at literary history—a discipline that has fallen out of fashion—and as a victim of factitious categorization. He deplores the inflation of reputation that the book helps to perpetuate and the generally fuzzy writing of most of the contributions. Most fundamentally, he faults the *Harvard Guide to Contemporary American Writing* for accepting without question what he considers the dominant left-wing sociology and metaphysics.

Politics have, according to *Plausible Prejudices*, disfigured the work of Robert Stone and, even more dramatically, Gabriel García Márquez, writers whose enormous talents have been put at the service of simplistic and banal ideologies. Most of Mailer's most ambitious productions are dismissed as inane, pretentious, and dull. As "chief purveyor of her own generation's leading clichés," Ann Beattie is attacked for preaching a trendy gospel of gloom.

Epstein presents an earlier generation of writers as likewise victims of politics—the erroneous perceptions of current critics and readers. He seeks to recover Dos Passos from the disfavor into which he has fallen simply because he turned from the Left to the Right. He attempts to repair the injustice of a widespread contempt for Cozzens as the laureate of privilege and the status quo. He is intent on rescuing Cather, whom he adores precisely because she did not write for academics, from the crude attempts by feminists to adapt her to their canon by portraying her as a lesbian.

Despite, and perhaps because of, his strain of anti-intellectualism, A. J. Liebling inspires the closest thing to rhapsodic tribute in *Plausible Prejudices*. Epstein is inspired by Liebling's masterful command of language, his immersion in his subjects, and his zest for life. Epstein feels a special kinship to this essayist whose prose, he declares, he has missed "more than that of any other writer who has died in my lifetime."

Given his respect for those intent on mastering the craft of writing, it is no surprise that Epstein bemoans the current state of the English language. Even, and especially, the college-educated have, according to Epstein, become verbal slobs. By precept and example, he insists that it is our duty to use language with respect and precision.

Some repetitions in *Plausible Prejudices* betray the volume's origins as an accumulation of occasional assignments. Yet they also reinforce its author's abiding concerns. Epstein does not reject the label reactionary, as he is intent both on articulating his own reactions to selected writers and on retarding the collective rush to consume ideas. Like that of the essayists he most reveres, his playful prose engages the reader with wit and verve. Epstein complains that "Updike simply cannot pass up any opportunity to tap dance in prose," and that might be an accurate self-assessment as well. The trenchant, epigrammatic sentences he fashions out of a language so abused elsewhere command attention if not assent. The sheer power of its style makes this book's observations plausible, if not compelling.

Steven G. Kellman

Sources for Further Study

Christian Science Monitor. LXXVII, April 17, 1985, p. 22.
Encounter. LXV, July, 1985, p. 59.
National Review. XXXVII, September 6, 1985, p. 60.

The New York Times Book Review. XC, February 24, 1985, p. 8.
Times Literary Supplement. August 2, 1985, p. 857.
The Wall Street Journal. CCV, April 2, 1985. p. 26.

POETRY INTO DRAMA
Early Tragedy and the Greek Poetic Tradition

Author: John (C. J.) Herington (1924-   )
Publisher: University of California Press (Berkeley). Illustrated. 292 pp. $29.50
Type of work: Literary criticism

Fifth century Athenian tragedy is seen as a continuation of the performative poetry of the song culture of Greece in the sixth century B.C.

Poetry into Drama: Early Tragedy and the Greek Poetic Tradition is the forty-ninth volume of the Sather Lectures, a major series of classical studies based upon public lectures given by the Sather Professor of Classical Literature at the University of California at Berkeley. John Herington is a distinguished classical scholar whose most important previous book, *The Author of Prometheus Bound* (1970), supports the strongly disputed Aeschylean authorship of this play.

Turning his critical attention in *Poetry into Drama* to the contributions of early Greek poetry in the development of Athenian tragedy, Herington has changed significantly the ways in which Greek poetry and tragedy are understood and has painted an excellent picture of what he calls the "song culture" of Greece. *Poetry into Drama* is as much about pre-tragic Greek poetry as Greek tragedy and treats the epics of Homer, the lyrics of Sappho, and the tragedies of Aeschylus as part of one poetic evolution. Herington revives literary bonds which united these genres in the ancient Greek world, when tragedy was considered a subform of poetry rather than a separate genre and when the word "poet" was applied equally to composers of epic, lyric, and tragedy. Pre-tragic Greek poetry included several forms, such as lyric (or monody), elegy, and iambic, classified according to the meters used and the contexts of performance. By discussing all these diverse ancient poetical categories as part of a single song culture in pre-fifth century B.C. Greece, Herington makes a significant contribution to the criticism of Greek poetry and drama.

Both the original lectures and the published book are directed to the general reader as well as the classical specialist, and each audience will find much of value in the book. For the sake of the general reader, most of the documentation has been placed in a series of ten appendixes containing information about ancient Greek poetry not otherwise available in a single source. Making up about 20 percent of the text, these appendixes include evidence for musical performances at religious festivals, for performances of various types of Greek poetry, and for texts and reperformances of such poetry. These appendixes would have been easier to use if page headings had distinguished each one by title or by number. Fortunately, Herington's theory that tragedy was created out of the oral song cult in Greece can be followed without giving overdue attention to the documentation in the appendixes.

Poetry into Drama is divided into three parts. In the first, Herington describes the pre-tragic poetry of Greece and discusses several important ways in which the oral and performative features of this poetry are similar to those of dramatic performances. In the second part of the book, Herington describes the confluence of pre-tragic Greek poetry in sixth century Athens, which led, within a few decades, to the invention of drama. In the last part, Herington studies features of Greek tragedy that show a deliberate blending of several types of pre-tragic poetry. This poetic integration can especially be noted in the innovative assimilation in tragedy of several diverse metrical forms found in earlier forms of Greek poetry.

Unlike most modern poetry, pre-tragic Greek poetry was directed toward live audiences rather than to readers. Oral, traditional, performed publicly, often in a competitive context, poetry of this type in Greece can be traced back to the preliterate world of Homer, when poetry based on traditional tales and vocabulary was composed in performance by illiterate singers. In *Poetry into Drama*, Herington is interested less in that stage of Greek poetry when the Homeric epics were a living form than in the sixth century B.C., when the Homeric texts had become more fixed and were being performed by reciters called rhapsodes, not by creative poets. While the combined poet-performer of epic was no longer active during this period, other kinds of poets continued to perform their own compositions. The works of Sappho, Alcman, and Pindar provide Herington with important evidence for the role of performance in Greek poetry. Herington might have added that early Greek tragedians, such as Aeschylus, continued this poetic practice by acting in their own productions.

Herington considers pre-tragic Greek poetry a performing art. In the first chapter of *Poetry into Drama*, he provides a detailed comparison of four kinds of pre-tragic poetic performances: the rhapsodic recitations of Homer; solo performances of songs sung to the accompaniment of a lyre or kithara; performance of choral lyrics, such as those of Alcman and Pindar; and the performance of solo lyrics, such as those of Sappho and Anacreon. Discussing both literary and artistic evidence for such performances, Herington notes the need for declarative and histrionic skills not unlike those needed for drama. Performers of such poetry were not much different from actors.

These poetic performances also shared with later dramatic performances an element of competition. Herington provides a catalog of the many religious festivals at which poetic contests were held. Viewed from this perspective, the famous dramatic competitions during the Festival of the Greater Dionysia in Athens were not then unique but a regular feature of the Greek poetic tradition.

The dramatic aspects of Greek poetry in performance are especially visible in an epilogue to *Poetry into Drama*, in which Herington reconstructs the first performance of the *Persians*, a kitharodic poem of Timotheus of

Miletus in the late fifth century B.C. While not widely known in the modern world, this poem was contemporary with the later tragedies of Euripides and shares a context of public performance with its tragic cousins

In a chapter entitled "Text and Re-performance," Herrington discusses the relationship between oral performance, written text, and poetic transmission in pre-tragic Greek poetry. He has collected here impressive evidence that reperformances of these poetic texts continued in Greece for many years following their initial performances. The closeness of these poetic performances to drama is particularly emphasized by reperformance, which was a kind of dramatic re-creation often demanding impersonation by the performers. Herington notes several fragments of Sappho that speak in two voices and offer dramatic dialogues more than a century before the first tragedies were performed in Athens.

If reperformance were an assumption of these poems, how could such reperformances occur without some tangible preservation of the original? In attempting to answer this question, Herington notes that written texts, devoid of choreography and musical scores, existed for these poems as early as the Hellenistic period (the second century B.C.). Since some evidence, collected in an appendix, suggests that poetic texts existed in various forms before the fifth century, Herington argues that the sixth century poets themselves, while composing their poems orally, were producing written texts to serve as documentation for reperformance.

The existence of such working texts is questionable. Albert Lord's definitive work on oral transmission (*The Singer of Tales*, 1960) has shown the ability of oral poetry to be created and transmitted orally in performance without a written text. There is no evidence, for example, of a written text of Homer before the Peisistratid recension of the late sixth century, yet the text itself had reached some form of stabilization before this date. It is most unlikely that written texts were needed in an oral song culture to preserve the poems. It is also significant that most of the written texts collected in Herington's appendix were not texts used for recollection or preservation, but for religious dedications, family histories, and pedagogical tools. Further, what use would a written text serve for a performance without accompanying choreography and musical score? If the dance and song were preserved orally, could the words not be also?

In a chapter entitled "The Forest of Myths," which is intended for the general reader and which specialists are expressly invited to ignore, Herington turns from performance and text to context and discusses the close relationship between myths and poetry in Greece. Even specialists can benefit from the picture that Herington paints of the traditional world in which Greek poetry functioned, for such mythic themes created a poetry that is quite foreign to the modern experience.

Herington suggests that, as part of a mythic and poetic tradition, Greek poetry assumed a multifaceted context difficult for anyone outside that tradition to appreciate fully. Unlike a modern poem, which is usually presented as the poet's own personal insight and as the product of a private, usually emotional experience, a Greek poem, because of its traditional nature, absorbed a concentric series of experience, including not only those of the immediate poet, his audience, and his society, but also those of other poets, both living and dead, their audiences, and their societies.

The universal context of Greek poetry was reinforced by several features of the myths. The Greek poet's traditional prayer to the muse for inspiration, for example, resulted both in a deliberate distancing of the poet from his poetry and in a divine authority that sanctioned the relevance of this poetry for all men and insured for the poem a *kleos*, or "fame," through reperformance in other communities and later generations. The poem, like its divine source, is not ephemeral but immortal; within its Greek context, it is for all men in all times. Such poetry never became "dated" but remained part of a poetic tradition and dialogue in which poets conversed with poets across distances of both space and time. The myths represented in this poetic tradition thus reflect the accumulated experience and knowledge of previous generations and were used by contemporary poets to educate their audiences and to interpret human life. In its use of these traditional myths, Athenian tragedy is indebted to the Greek poetry that preceded it.

A long-standing debate about the origin of tragedy, a question which has vexed classical scholars and students of the theater for more than two millennia, hovers constantly in the background of *Poetry into Drama*. The general reader should at least have the following bare outline of the debate before beginning the book.

The history of Western drama clearly begins in ancient Athens, where the surviving plays of Aeschylus, Sophocles, and Euripides were produced in the fifty century B.C. Tragedy is said to have been invented in Athens in the late sixth century by a mysterious figure named Thespis, about whom almost nothing further is known. Two centuries later, in a scintillating piece of ancient literary criticism called the *Poetics*, the great philosopher Aristotle traced the development of tragedy past Thespis to traditional songs called dithyrambs and dedicated to the god Dionysus.

Aristotle's association of tragedy with cult captured the imagination of modern scholars who have sought the origins of tragedy in sundry religious contexts. In *The Birth of Tragedy* (1872), Friedrich Nietzsche contrasted the irrational Dionysiac spirit with the subdued Apollonian soul and found the source of drama in the power of Dionysus. Early twentieth century scholars such as Jane Harrison and Gilbert Murray (*Themis*, 1927) sought the origin of tragedy in more hypothetical religious rites celebrating the suffering and victory of a year-spirit. Others, such as Martin Nilsson (*Greek Festivals of Religious Meaning*, 1906), found the antecedents of tragedy in Greek ancestor worship or rites of the dead. More recently, the religious origin of tragedy has been deemphasized by Gerald Else (*The Origin and Early Form of Greek Tragedy*, 1965), who has suggested a more secular and more individual development for tragedy beginning not with vague year-spirits or ancestor cults but with individuals such as Thespis and Aeschylus.

Herington, a student of Else, follows in his teacher's footsteps and argues that the poetic antecedents of Greek tragedy are more important than its cultic heritage. Like Else, Herington believes that tragedy's association with the Festival of Dionysus may have been based upon political rather than religious motives. While the Peisistratids, a family of unconstitutional rulers called tyrants, controlled Athens in the late sixty century B.C., a conscious effort was undertaken to make Athens the Panhellenic center of culture and poetry to attract poets to the city and to provide favorable contexts for poetic performances. Such a convergence of poets from all over Greece created in Athens an environment conducive to the integration of the diverse meters, diction, and mythic themes of the Greek poetic tradition into a new genre. This integration took the form of tragedy in the Theater of Dionysus. The derivation of Greek tragedy from the earlier Greek poetic tradition rather than from a religious cult is thus Herington's central hypothesis.

In the last chapter of *Poetry into Drama*, Herington considers how the first authors of Athenian tragedy could have invented tragedy from the poetry that existed before. Comparing tragedy to a crucible of earlier poetic forms, Herington notes how tragedy assimilated the meters, diction, and myths of earlier poems and applied dramatic techniques learned from earlier poets, such as Homer, to other contexts. Greek tragedy, then, was essentially poetry, not cult, to which dramatists such as Aeschylus added powerful visual elements, such as the carpet scene in *Agamemnon* (456 B.C.) and the appearance of Darius' ghost in *The Persians* (c. 410 B.C.).

In *Poetry into Drama*, Herington thus offers a unique and exciting view of Greek tragedy as an integration of Greek performative poetry with innovative stage effects.

Thomas J. Sienkewicz

Source for Further Study

Choice. XXIII, October, 1985, p. 287.

POUND/LEWIS
The Letters of Ezra Pound and Wyndham Lewis

Author: Ezra Pound (1885-1972) and Wyndham Lewis (1882-1957)
Edited, with an introduction, by Timothy Materer
Publisher: New Directions (New York). 346 pp. $37.50
Type of work: Letters
Time: 1914-1957

The lifelong correspondence of Ezra Pound, a central figure in twentieth century literature, and Wyndham Lewis, an important English writer and painter

This volume of letters between two makers of modernism records the dialogue of two obstreperous craftsmen over a lifetime of controversy and creativity. The letters are short on many of the things for which typically one pries into famous people's private correspondence. There is little that is directly personal here. Both men rejected their time's preoccupation with the probing of the unconscious, and their letters reveal little about any private selves that might lie behind their public images.

Neither does one find here those unguarded reflections on the human dilemma or on their own hopes and fears that often make writers' letters worth reading. Wyndham Lewis gives a clue to the nature of the correspondence when he suggests that Ezra Pound's letters "can be of no interest to anyone but a writer. It is a craftsman speaking throughout about his craft, and the single-minded concentration is magnificent." Lewis is right to say that Pound is first and last concerned with the arts and artists but wrong to suggest that only fellow writers could be interested in such things.

Lewis' observation notwithstanding, what one has in these letters is not so much technical talk about the craft of writing or about specific works as the record of Pound's tireless efforts to promote and Lewis' ambivalent feelings about being promoted. In the process, one also discovers interesting tidbits from the early days of modernist manifestos and movements and, almost accidentally, insights into Pound's decline from the heights of those heady early days.

Editor Timothy Materer groups the correspondence into four parts, the first beginning just before the start of World War I when Pound and Lewis were busy inventing Vorticism and trying to give it the look of a major movement. Their letters reveal the nuts and bolts of their efforts—dealings with printers, publishers, patrons, and fellow artists—but little of their vision. Materer provides background introductions and explanatory notes for this period and for the others to aid the uninitiated reader. His introduction to Pound and all the supporting material in the book are finely done, enlightening without obtruding.

The brief months when they worked together on Vorticism and *Blast* (1914), Vorticism's great, pink, public manifesto, were also the last in which they had close personal contact. *Blast*, however, continues to echo throughout their correspondence over the years. Pound, especially, liked to refer back to those early days when they were young and full of fire and determined to create a new renaissance. A decade after the first issue of *Blast*, Pound writes from Italy to Lewis,

> I have just, ten years an a bit after its appearance, and in this far distant locus, taken out a copy of the great MAGENTA cover'd opusculus. We were hefty guys in them days; an of what has come after us, we seem to have survived without a great mass of successors.

Although there is very little self-pity in Pound's letters, even when his circumstances are at their worst, one detects here and in later years the wistfulness of a campaigner in a revolution that never quite succeeded.

Vorticism died aborning when Lewis went off to war. The letters exchanged with Pound while Lewis first trained in England and then went off to fight in France are perhaps the most interesting of the entire collection. Lewis, never one to suffer fools quietly, chaffs under the feeling that he is surrounded by idiots, who, not incidentally, are often his military superiors and hold his life in their hands. At times, the situation elicited from him his famous gift for invective, as in describing a fellow officer whose dangerous job Lewis had volunteered to take over:

> The young man in question,—a sharp-featured, horse-toothed, narrow-browed, vain, crotchety young board-school master accepted my offer at once as though he were conferring a great favour upon me. Why treat these animals like human beings? I shall not in future offer my skin in place of the cheap pink trash that covers the absence of brain, heart and stomach of pedagogic or other colleague.

Other humorous incidents (both bilious and sanguine) are recounted, including Lewis' futile attempt to explain Pound's Imagism movement (1912-1914) to a befuddled commanding officer. At other times, however, Lewis attempts to convey the great devastation, spiritual and physical, of this war which altered Europe's way of seeing itself. His 1917 description of no-man's-land shows his painter's eye and novelist's gift:

> The moment you get in this stretch of land you feel the change from the positions you have come from. A watchfulness, fatigue and silence penetrates everything in it. You meet a small party of infantry slowly going up or coming back. Their faces are all dull, their eyes turned inwards in sallow thought or savage resignation; you would say revulsed, if it were not too definite a word.

Pound's response to Lewis' war letters was typically practical. Lewis was valuable as an artist; the arts were the key to any society, so Lewis could best serve his country and civilization by staying alive to produce more art. Pound's characteristic brusque straightforwardness, perhaps masking a genuine concern for Lewis, typifies the tone of many letters: "I can not see that the future of the arts deamns [*sic*] that you should be covered with military distinctions. It is equally obvious that you should not be allowed to spill your gore in heathen and furrin places."

If one sometimes thinks that Pound only valued even his friends in terms of the contribution he thought they could make to arts and letters, one nevertheless sees throughout this correspondence that Pound would work tirelessly and selflessly for anyone whose work he valued. Pound not only placed Lewis' writing and sold his paintings, but he also lent him money when he had none to lend, worked to get him a commission in the army, softened up publishers and patrons, stored and shipped his artwork, and agreed to be his executor (and even to take partial responsibility for his illegitimate children) if Lewis were killed in the war.

Usually Lewis was grateful for all this. At times, however, Pound's activities on his behalf struck him as those of a well-intentioned but suffocating mother. In the mid-1920's, Lewis dropped out of sight to work on a mammoth prose manuscript that was later cut up into many different books. He obviously wanted to be left alone. His reply in 1925 to another of Pound's endless promptings about possible projects demonstrates his exasperation at Pound's tireless art entrepreneuring and more than a little of Lewis' famous testy paranoia:

> Please note the following: Because in the glorious days of Marinetti . . . we were associated to some extent in publicity campaigns, that does not give you a mandate to interfere when you think fit, with or without my consent, with my career. If you launch at me and try and force on me a scheme which I regard as malapropos and which is liable to embarrass me, you will not find me so docile at [as?] Eliot.

That Pound could be seemingly unfazed by such a response to his unselfish efforts is a testimony to his lifelong practice of putting art before his personal well-being. His reply to Lewis, however, reveals that while he was almost incapable of being insulted, Pound was no less willing than Lewis to say exactly what he thought. After assuring Lewis that he will do nothing on his behalf without permission, he closes as follows: "There are some matters in which you really do behave like, and *some* ‹some not all› lines in this letter of yours in which you really do write like, a God damn fool."

Unfortunately both Pound and Lewis were capable of more dangerous foolishness. Lewis' dabbling with Fascism was damaging but relatively brief. Pound was more seriously infected. All the good aesthetic judgment of his youth was no protection against the illusions of Italian Fascism that he embraced so uncritically. Pound became as tireless (and tiresome) in trying to convert Lewis to his vision and to get him involved in propaganda schemes as he was earlier in regard to art and literature. The ever-present anti-Semitism of the letters becomes even uglier, especially in the light of historical events that provide their context. To his credit, Lewis rebuffed Pound's efforts and tried to disabuse him of some of his more persistent illusions.

Pound's tragic decline culminated, following World War II, in his long confinement among the insane at Saint Elizabeths Hospital in Washington, D.C.—the alternative to a trial for treason. At this point, the two former Vorticists had not seen each other for many years, and both had fallen on difficult times. Lewis initially attempts to make light of Pound's situation, not knowing it would take thirteen years for Pound to gain his freedom: "I am told that you believe yourself to be Napoleon—or is it Mussolini? What a pity you did not choose Buddha while you were about it, instead of a politician!"

As the years dragged on, their lifelong roles changed somewhat. Whereas Pound had always been the promoter and encourager, now Lewis tries to encourage Pound, not least by reminding him of his important contributions to the arts. Lewis is still feisty and straightforward, however, in a letter that once again rejects Pound's hobbyhorse efforts. He declares, once and for all, "Do understand that I am politically a complete agnostic. No theory of the State interests me in the slightest," adding, "You are in a chaos. Why not face the fact and sing the chaos, songbird that you are?"

From the 1930's on, Pound's letters became increasingly cryptic and typographically outrageous. By the Saint Elizabeths years, they are at times almost incomprehensible. There is something deeply sad about Lewis' brutally honest question in a letter a year before his death: "Your last letter undeciperable [*sic*], just cannot imagine what lies beneath the words. Have you anything really to say?" It is a question some still ask about the *Cantos* (1925-1968), the work to which Pound devoted fifty years of his life.

There are many things of interest to be found in a correspondence between two creative geniuses that stretched over forty years. Among them are their views of other writers, such as D. H. Lawrence, Ford Madox Ford, James Joyce, and, more often than any other, T. S. Eliot. Lewis was obviously more than a little irritated that the young American, whom he and Pound had published in *Blast* so many years before, was, at the end of all their lives, not only lionized and comfortable but pious and proper to boot. Having called each other Ez-*roar* and WynDAMN over the years, they took delight in referring to Eliot by names such as "Rev. Possum" and "His somnolences."

These letters will be of more interest to students of modern literature than anyone else. In that somewhat narrow vein, however, they are significant and worthwhile reading.

Daniel Taylor

Sources for Further Study

Kirkus Reviews. LIII, January 15, 1985, p. 80.
Library Journal. CX, April 15, 1985, p. 68.
National Review. XXXVII, June 14, 1985, p. 45.
New Leader. LXVIII, April 22, 1985, p. 16.
The New York Times Book Review. XC, June 30, 1985, p. 21.
Publishers Weekly. CCXXVII, January 11, 1985, p. 64.

THE PRICK OF NOON

Author: Peter De Vries (1910   )
Publisher: Little, Brown and Company (Boston). 233 pp. $14.95
Type of work: Novel
Time: The 1980's
Locale: Merrymount, Connecticut

An engaging comedy which satirizes the manners and morals, the pleasures and pretensions of both the country-club set and those who eagerly seek to become a part of it

> *Principal characters:*
> EDDIE TEETERS, the narrator, a man who longs to become accepted as a member of the upper middle class
> CYNTHIA PICKLES, an attractive bluestocking who is the object of his desires
> TOBY SNAPPER, a waitress who, despite her lowly origins, is irresistible to Eddie
> JERRY CHIROUBLE, a good-natured dilettante

The Prick of Noon is Peter De Vries's twenty-second novel. Longtime fans will recognize the stylistic mannerisms of this work as typical of De Vries's love of language and deft verbal twists. In its bawdy humor, social criticism, and irreverent (and seemingly irrepressible) puns, malaprops, and double entendres, it is vintage De Vries. The story of Eddie Teeters' rise and fall is not profound, but it is thought-provoking. Although it lacks the strong religious or moralistic undercurrent of De Vries's best work, such as *The Blood of the Lamb* (1962), the author's wit and irony create a humorous and eminently readable tale.

De Vries employs the time-honored technique of relating his story through the language of an uneducated narrator-protagonist, one who is blind to his own best qualities. As in so many American novels, the protagonist longs to rise from his humble origins to become a respected member of the Eastern Establishment. Eddie Teeters is from Backbone, Arkansas, and has "vowed never to come from there again"; he longs to adopt the casual ways and affected vernacular of the country-club set of Merrymount, Connecticut. A self-described "knight in shiny armor," he intends to win the heart, or at least the hand, of Cynthia Pickles and thereby move up into the upper middle class. Cynthia epitomizes the "smart set" of "Rolling Acres," where, as Eddie notes, "men in bleeding madras shorts bounced golf balls off pre-Revolutionary gravestones." He first encounters her at poolside, racket in hand, and is smitten immediately, both by "the princess" and her "habitat group," who urbanely discuss little restaurants in Trieste and similar pressing subjects. Eddie wants in, and the novel is his account of his increasingly ludicrous attempts to ingratiate himself with Pickles and Company.

Eddie's role model and his means of introduction to this smug little group is Jerry Chirouble, a wealthy man who plays at being a publisher. Most of his time, however, is spent over leisurely lunches at the club or giving expensive parties for the moneyed set of Merrymount. Eddie envies Chirouble's cool nonchalance and smooth one-liners. "Being precocious," Chirouble comments, "I naturally age very fast as well. In fact, at only twenty-five I was already young at heart." To Eddie's uneducated ears and upwardly mobile sensibility, this remark, like Chirouble and Cynthia Pickles, is "sheer class." Eddie would trade in his birth certificate to be reborn into this rarified society where one can "opine" casually, "everything couched in an epigram and whatnot.... Lightly bandying what-do-you-call-it, persiflage and never hurting anybody."

Through Chirouble, Eddie meets Cynthia Pickles and begins a hilarious courtship. In his eagerness to adopt the mannerisms of Merrymount, however, he inadvertently reveals his down-home upbringing; persiflage is not his strong suit. Still, one cannot help but admire the effort and energy—itself a middle-class trait—with which Eddie tries to climb out of his social station. His air of nonchalance requires much rehearsal; he finds that it takes a lot of sweat to look cool.

In contrast, being cool is a natural state for Cynthia Pickles. "The ice princess," as a rival for Eddie's affections terms her, is the essence of what Eddie sees as sophistication. When not discussing favorite restaurants over planter's punches in her tennis whites, she is busy recruiting investors for her pet project, *Overview*, a "journal of opinion for all sides." She has an easy laugh and a facility for inane banalities equaled only by F. Scott Fitzgerald's Daisy Buchanan. She tells Eddie that his "expression of resented alienation" is "most appealing.... Don't boggle at the 'alienation' either. Alienation is big these days. Without it you have no sense of belonging." The paradox does not bother Eddie Teeters. He sees only a vision—a beauty whose figure has "the trim concision of a Congregational church," and Eddie appears ready to believe in God in order to become a member of the congregation.

He soon discovers that sexual conquest is much easier than social acceptance. Marriage is definitely out of the question for the princess, although she casually sleeps with Eddie and wants to continue to see him. He even ingratiates himself with Cynthia's prissy old stepmother, Mrs. Pickles (who "didn't think that people who subscribed to the *National Geographic* ever had affairs"), all to no avail. The ice princess sparkles, but she will not melt. Eddie's initial impression of her as "unbridled chastity" proves, in the end, strangely appropriate. Cynthia enjoys Eddie's company but stays within her class and eventually marries Chirouble.

Eddie finds solace in the arms of a local waitress, Toby Snapper, who is both his comfort and his conscience. He enjoys taking her to bed but is disconcerted that she keeps popping up, in uniform, at every party and poolside encounter. She teases him, in a mock Cockney servant-girl accent, for his pretensions and ambition to be "wif the quality 'e's bent on gettin' in wif." At night, Toby, the delectable "peach tart," seems to be all he has ever dreamed of. In the daylight, as she waits upon the "tight little, right little group" at poolside, she drops sarcastic remarks which scratch the thin veneer of Eddie's patrician pose.

Toby's behavior annoys Eddie as he reflects on the importance of class distinctions in a democratic society. In fact, the novel opens on this note: "The trouble with treating people as equals is that the first thing you know they may be doing the same to you. Such reprisals seriously disrupt the pecking order, especially in a democracy where the class distinctions are so much more finely balanced than in other systems." Eddie energetically endeavors to upset this balance in his own case. At the same time, he is irked by Toby's refusal to accept her station and resents the little barbs she drops in public. She is "about as obsequious," Eddie remarks, "as your next door neighbor's mastiff sinking his teeth into your shins." Toby gives democracy a bad name. As Eddie notes, "This is what Chirouble's permissiveness led to. Equality was fine, liberalism was admirable, but you had to draw the line or all was chaos. Here was a chick who had slept with me acting like she was one of us."

Actually Toby and Eddie have much in common. Once Eddie has had his fill of upper crust he is ready for a wholesome peach tart. Eventually the "smart set" becomes, for Eddie, the "smart-assed set," and he realizes that he would much rather be home with a six-pack of Heineken, watching television, and eating fast food. The rightness of the match is evident to the reader long before it is to Eddie. The reader's first indication of this comes early in the novel when Toby is the only one privy to Eddie's secret identity.

Eddie has his deceptions as well as his desires. He is careful not to reveal that his way to wealth was as producer and stuntman for "Sexucation" films, a screen equivalent to *The Joy of Sex*. Eddie, known in the skin trade as Monty Carlo, more than once finds himself in a tight spot because of his work. Through Eddie's discomfiture, De Vries humorously points out the double standard of the upper class. They enjoy the films yet would not enjoy being seen with their producer. Eddie attempts to confess his history to his princess but cannot. Appropriately enough, he gets a piece of chicken caught in his throat and is rushed to the hospital. (He tells the doctor, whom he suspects of being a swell, that it is pheasant.) On his way to respectability, Eddie must conceal his means. As he himself remarks, he is "the Gatsby du nos jours."

Indeed, there are numerous references to *The Great Gatsby* throughout: *The Prick of Noon* might be seen as a raw, bawdy rewrite of Fitzgerald's masterpiece. Jay Gatsby's romantic shading has been replaced in this 1980's version by Eddie Teeters' lusts and humorous vulgarity. Gatsby's ornate white Rolls Royce, for example, becomes Eddie's twenty-eight-foot, lilac-colored stretch limousine, "The Land Yacht."

The approach is uniquely De Vries, but the conflict is as old as American culture. The battle between new and old values, money and expression has been ongoing since the separatists landed at Plymouth Rock in 1620. Merrymount was the name given to Thomas Morton's liberal, carefree community established in 1624, only thirty miles from Plymouth. The Pilgrim histories record their disapproval of Morton's "laciviousness," promiscuity, drinking, and trading with the Indians. Eventually, Miles Standish led a company which invaded Merrymount and put an end to Morton's freewheeling life-style. De Vries's modern-day equivalent is to have Eddie appear before a Moral Majority judge who effectively puts an end to Eddie's source of income—and his hopes of trading in one life-style for another.

The story may be an old one, but De Vries keeps the reader laughing and wincing from a barrage of puns, malaprops, and parodies. No pun is too ridiculous ("It Midas well be spring," sings Eddie's dad as he installs a muffler) nor any one-liner too offbeat for De Vries ("To have read nothing by Bulwer-Lytton," quips Chirouble, "can give a man a solid sense of accomplishment"). Literary references and parodies abound. William Shakespeare, Herman Melville, Walt Whitman, Oscar Wilde, Edith Wharton, William Burroughs, Marcel Proust, F. Scott Fitzgerald, Ernest Hemingway, William Faulkner, Thomas Mann, and Agatha Christie all make cameo appearances. The film industry is also subject to De Vries's light, sardonic touch. Dozens of actors and film titles are woven into Monty Carlo's narrative: "I liked Mrs. Pickles, although I wished she didn't look so much like William Powell."

The title itself, from *Romeo and Juliet*, exemplifies De Vries's tone and technique. Mercutio tells Juliet's nurse that "the bawdy hand of the dial is now upon the prick of noon." The several puns in the statement are both witty and erotic. Like Shakespeare, De Vries enjoys seeing how close literary license can come to licentiousness. Love and lust are not always clearly distinguished; the protagonist is appropriately named since he indeed teeters between the two throughout the novel.

In the end, Eddie accepts that "in the long run you can't climb out of your social class. The jockey can't ever hope to marry into the horsey set." Yet he does run an energetic race. Despite his faults, he wins the reader's sympathy through his earnest naïveté. Through him, one sees that self-conscious does not mean self-aware. He remains full of middle-class contradictions to the very end. On the one hand, he is able to see that the rich are "plastic" and "rigid with frigid," and yet he still longs to lead the leisurely life. Eddie concludes his narrative puzzling over how he might make a million on a motion picture, the theme of which would be that money has nothing to do with happiness.

Danny Robinson

Sources for Further Study

America. CLIII, August 31, 1985, p. 96.
Booklist. LXXXI, March 15, 1985, p. 1010.
Christian Century. CII, May 15, 1985, p. 492.
Kirkus Reviews. LIII, March 1, 1985, p. 187.
Library Journal. CX, May 15, 1985, p. 78.
The New York Times Book Review. XC, May 19, 1985, p. 16.
The New Yorker. LXI, June 10, 1985, p. 139.
Publishers Weekly. CCXXVII, March 15, 1985, p. 100.
Time. CXXV, April 22, 1985, p. 69.
West Coast Review of Books. XI, July, 1985, p. 29.

RANDALL JARRELL'S LETTERS
An Autobiographical and Literary Selection

Author: Randall Jarrell (1914-1965)
Edited by Mary Jarrell, assisted by Stuart Wright
Publisher: Houghton Mifflin Company (Boston). Illustrated. 540 pp. $29.95
Type of work: Letters
Time: 1935-1965

A collection of nearly four hundred of Randall Jarrell's letters, ranging from 1935, when he was a student at Vanderbilt University, to his death in 1965

This collection, although selective, presents the many faces of Randall Jarrell, showing him as meticulous poet, penetrating literary critic, enthusiastic teacher, member of the United States Air Force, husband, friend, and poetry consultant to the Library of Congress. The letters, edited by Jarrell's second wife, Mary von Schrader Jarrell, number just under four hundred, selected from about twenty-five hundred extant Jarrell letters that were available to her. Unfortunately, not all the existing letters were available for this edition. Among some important letters missing from it are those to Peter Taylor, Jarrell's friend of long standing, who would not allow any of Jarrell's letters to him to be included in this volume.

In spite of this omission and a few smaller ones, the book is valuable because it shows Jarrell's growth from his student days at Vanderbilt University, when he became deeply involved in the New Critical Movement that was developing there, to his final days when, having attempted suicide by slashing his wrists, he went to Chapel Hill, North Carolina, to be treated at the Hand House. Jarrell died instantly of a fractured skull after having been struck by a car in Chapel Hill on October 14, 1965.

The collection will be valuable to Jarrell scholars and enthusiasts. It gives new insights into the poet's literary relationships, which were far-ranging, and into his critical acuity, which was legendary and considered by some to be brutal. Jarrell deplored weak poetry, and some of his early reviews severely castigated such poets as Ezra Pound, Frederic Prokosch, and Conrad Aiken, who called him a "self-appointed judge and executioner." The Aiken-Jarrell exchange is fascinating.

Jarrell's detailed letters to Robert Lowell reveal his admiration for Lowell's work. In a letter dated November, 1945, he tells Lowell, "I think you write more in the great tradition, the grand style, the real *middle* of English poetry, than anybody since Yeats," certainly high praise from a poet and critic who never compromised his critical integrity because of friendship. In the same letter, Jarrell deals specifically and at length with some of Lowell's unpublished poems, providing the poet with sharply focused and enormously detailed suggestions about them.

The collection includes more than thirty of Jarrell's letters to Mackie, his first wife, as well as many he wrote to Mary von Schrader. Jarrell always appeared in his romantic relationships to be a sort of teacher: He shared his literary enthusiasms with the women he loved, and he sent them detailed reading suggestions. The breadth of his own reading, as it is revealed in most of the letters in this book, was gargantuan. His reading routine broke down only during the academic year of 1951-1952 when he taught at Princeton University and found his living expenses so great that he had to do considerable free-lance writing to survive financially.

The letters which Jarrell wrote during World War II, when he served from 1942 until 1946 in the air force, are revealing in that they show how well attuned to modern poetry he remained during his military service. He entered the air force shortly after the Japanese bombing of Pearl Harbor on December 7, 1941, and was trained first as a ferry pilot in Austin, Texas, where he had been teaching at the University of Texas. He washed out of this training program and was dropped in rank from sergeant to private, yet his letters reveal no bitterness about this failure. He continued training at Sheppard's Field in Wichita Falls, Texas, and was transferred from there to Chanute Field in Rantoul, Illinois. Finally he was moved to Davis-Monthan Field in Tucson, Arizona, where he taught celestial navigation to crewmen of B-29 bombers until the end of the war.

Jarrell kept up a lively correspondence with his wife, Mackie, from the time he went to Sheppard's Field until she joined him in Tucson, where they stayed until 1946. This correspondence amounted to more than one hundred letters. While only about one-third of it is reproduced in this book, the editor has provided excellent commentary on this group of letters and has provided general paraphrases of a great many of the letters that are not reproduced. This correspondence is important because it provides details about what Jarrell was reading and writing during this period and also because it contains some quite unrestrained critical judgments. For example, he writes to Mackie in a letter dated April 25, 1943, "[Delmore] Schwartz's *Genesis* is just *awful*: I wouldn't dare write a line about it anywhere, I'd be too embarrassed."

During the same period, Jarrell corresponded quite regularly with both Allen Tate and Edmund Wilson. Toward the end of the period, he wrote frequent long, detailed letters to Lowell, who was incarcerated as a conscientious objector during the war years. Jarrell also had established a close tie with the *Nation* and with its literary editor, Margaret Marshall, whom he was to replace, at her suggestion, as acting poetry editor in 1946-1947, when she was away on leave.

During the war years, Jarrell, who had had twenty poems published in James Laughlin's *Five Young American Poets* (1940), published two volumes of poetry. *Blood for a Stranger* (1942) was completed before but published after he began his military service, and *Little Friend, Little Friend* (1945) was published as he was nearing the end of his military service. It contained many poems Jarrell wrote during his enlistment. Some of the poems in *Losses* (1948) also are from the years when Jarrell was in the air force.

The letters written shortly after the end of the war reveal Jarrell's anxiety about whether he would receive a Guggenheim Fellowship in 1946, when he was mustered out of the air force. Then, after a period of uncertainty, a veritable cornucopia of good fortune burst upon Jarrell. He received the Guggenheim Post-Service Award, the first of two he was to receive; he was offered the opportunity to replace Margaret Marshall on *The Nation* during her leave; and he was appointed a part-time instructor at Sarah Lawrence College. In the autumn of 1946, Taylor, his friend from Kenyon College, was hired by the Women's College of the University of North Carolina in Greensboro, and he was to be instrumental in bringing Jarrell to the same institution the following year, when Jarrell was appointed assistant professor and Mackie instructor.

The letters of the New York period reveal a Jarrell who loved teaching at Sarah Lawrence, who was challenged by and extremely competent at his editorial work for *The Nation*, but who hated living in New York City. Although his earlier letters give clear indications that Jarrell was not the enthusiast for agrarian reform that his mentors and close friends at Vanderbilt had been, the New York letters show with equal clarity that Jarrell was not a city person. He left New York gladly in 1947 for Women's College, where Mackie was also afforded an opportunity to teach.

The early Greensboro years were happy ones for the Jarrells. They thoroughly enjoyed the company of the Taylors, beside whom they lived in a duplex that they had bought jointly. Jarrell was stimulated by his teaching. In the summer of 1948, Jarrell took his first trip to Europe to teach American Civilization at the Salzburg Seminar. An impressive group of poems grew out of this trip: "A Game at Salzburg," "A Soul," "Hohensalzburg: Fantastic Variations on a Theme of Romantic Character," "The Orient Express," "An English Garden in Austria," "Seele im Raum," and "Quilt Pattern." This was the same year in which *Losses* was published.

In Salzburg, Jarrell met and fell in love with a twenty-eight-year-old artist, Elisabeth Eisler. Of his seventy extant love letters to her, ten are reproduced, all of which are of literary and autobiographical interest. This romance presaged marital problems that would lead to Jarrell's separation and eventual divorce from Mackie, but these events were still three or four years in the future.

In the summer of 1951, while he was attending a Summer Writers' Conference in Boulder, Colorado, Jarrell met Mary von Schrader, who was to become his second wife and who has edited this collection of letters. Jarrell spent the year between his separation from Mackie and his divorce from her as a visiting professor of literary criticism at Princeton. The letters to Mary during this period are curiously reminiscent of his letters to Mackie during his military service. Jarrell was not unqualifiedly happy at Princeton. He was overwhelmed by the cost of living there and he felt direly his physical separation from Mary. His letters to her reflect a great longing and a sense of isolation, despite the fact that he was immensely involved in Princeton's social circuit.

Oddly enough, the letters from the 1951-1952 academic year project a Jarrell who was reading less and producing less poetry than he had during his service in the air force. Mary lived in California during this period, and Jarrell spent as much time as he could with her there. The two were married in 1952, about a week after his divorce from Mackie had become final.

The later letters quite often reflect Jarrell's struggles against depression. He tried to be upbeat in these later letters, as he had in the letters he wrote during his service in the air force, but he could not always manage to be. In a despairing letter to Michael di Capua, his editor, written five months before his death, he says, "I want you to disregard almost everything I said in my last letter—I was not only depressed but very much under the influence of Thorazine, a drug which makes thought and action so difficult for you that you can't be your real self." During this period, he and Mary separated but were soon reconciled.

Although one cannot call Mary Jarrell a disinterested editor of her husband's letters, one must certainly admire her magnanimity in dealing with his love letters to Mackie and to Elisabeth Eisler, and must be impressed by the balanced portrayal that her selection of about one-sixth of the letters available to her project of her husband, who has rightly been called a poet of talent and a critic of genius. Her explanatory notes, with which the text is interlarded, are invaluable.

R. Baird Shuman

Sources for Further Study

Book World. XV, April 28, 1985, p. 1.
Kirkus Reviews. LIII, February 15, 1985, p. 172.
The New Republic. CXCII, June 3, 1985, p. 32.
The New York Review of Books. XXXII, May 9, 1985, p. 29.
The New York Times. CXXXIV, May 6, 1985, p. 19.
The New York Times Book Review. XC, May 19, 1985, p. 11.
Parnassus. XII, Fall, 1984, p. 281.
Saturday Review. XI, May, 1985, p. 66.
Time. CXXV, April 29, 1985, p. 80.

REDESIGNING THE WORLD
William Morris, the 1880s, and the Arts and Crafts

Author: Peter Stansky (1932-   )
Publisher: Princeton University Press (Princeton, New Jersey). Illustrated. 293 pp.
$27.50
Type of work: Cultural history
Time: 1876-1896
Locale: England

The Arts and Crafts Movement, through the organizations that arose under William Morris' influence, left a legacy of functional simplicity in architecture and design

> *Principal personage*:
> WILLIAM MORRIS, a designer, author, and Socialist

William Morris (1834-1896) was one of the great Victorian polymaths. As an author, his earliest work appeared in the *Oxford and Cambridge Magazine*, which he founded as an undergraduate in 1856. He wrote poetic romances, including *The Defence of Guenevere* (1858) and *The Earthly Paradise* (1868-1870); translated Icelandic sagas as well as the *Aeneid* and the *Odyssey*; penned an enormously popular Utopian novel, *News from Nowhere* (1891); declined appointment as Professor of Poetry at Oxford University in 1877, and was mentioned as a possible Poet Laureate in 1892. He painted frescoes in the Oxford Union, was apprenticed to an architect, and revitalized both calligraphy and typography. He designed wallpaper, stained glass, cloth, tapestries, and carpets—though not the furniture which his firm also produced, and which made his name a generic term for a popular style of chair. He was one of the founders of the Socialist League and editor of its monthly journal, *Commonweal*. In the 1890's, he began both the Kelmscott Press and the Hammersmith Socialist Society. He was also a creature of contradictions—an atheist who designed stained-glass windows for churches, a lover of things medieval who opposed the movement to restore Gothic churches by reproducing their original decoration, a proselytizing Socialist (arrested more than once at open-air meetings) with a comfortable inherited income whose own capitalist business firm was both successful and profitable.

Morris embodied a particular constellation of attitudes that can still be recognized. In rejecting much of his own society, he was artistically avant-garde (responsible, in Peter Stansky's opinion, for setting the course toward modernism in architecture and design), politically radical, and, at the same time, reactionary in many of his ideas about life and work. His vision originated in a romantic attachment to the past—a trait common enough in periods of rapid change and shared by many of Morris' contemporaries who were distressed by the ugliness and social upheaval that followed industrialization. Going up to Oxford, in 1853, for a gentleman's education, he was first drawn toward the pseudomedievalism of the High Church movement, then fell into company with poets, then decided on a apprenticeship with Gothic Revival architect G. E. Street, and soon became friends with Dante Gabriel Rossetti and the poets and painters of the Pre-Raphaelite Brotherhood.

In each case, it appears, Morris felt an urge to create, yearned for something in the past that seemed missing in the present, and wanted fellowship with like-minded people working together for similar aims. Eagerly reading the works of John Ruskin, he perceived the intimate relationship of art to the society in which art is created, and thus he arrived at a diagnosis: Ugliness results when industrial capitalism subdivides tasks and separates work, beauty, friendship, and pleasure.

The practical direction of Morris' life took shape when, on his marriage in 1859, he commissioned an architect to build a house to his design. Designing a house and then planning its furnishings, decorations, and details, he became potently aware of the relationship of "material, working process, purpose, and aesthetic form." He also saw that a process which should be a single creative act had been subdivided. Architecture was an art, and an architect primarily a gentleman—but how could an architect create a functional dwelling unless he understood lighting and heating and plumbing? Furthermore, the artificial division between art and craft—and the specialization of individual crafts—made it almost impossible to harmonize the dwelling with its furniture and decoration. Frustrated by trying to put together the unsatisfactory and unrelated bits and pieces available in the marketplace, Morris eventually built or designed almost every object in the house for himself.

The immediate result was the formation, in 1861, of the design firm of Morris, Marshall, Faulkner and Company, a collection of artists and craft workers working together—both individually and in collaboration—to produce mural decoration, stained glass, metalwork, furniture, wallpapers, textiles, embroidery, carpets, and painted tiles. Morris himself set out to become a master of as many of the crafts as possible.

In theory, Morris had found his key in the relationship between history, the working process, and aesthetics. He believed that the debased nature of industrial products was not necessarily the fault of machines themselves but arose from the division of labor between design and manufacture. He believed that work and production could be made harmonious—and satisfactory—only if workers had control over the whole of the objects they produced. He did not quite manage to put all of his principles in practice: Running the firm as a successful business required divisions of labor (and women workers were often responsible for the most tedious and mechanical parts of the process).

His concept, however, was important. Other artists dissatisfied with industrialism and the ugliness of manufactured goods were taking a different direction, into the movement known as "art for art's sake," which divorced art from function and increased the distance between artists and commerce or working life, making art a special province for the cultivated few. Morris, however, reversed the traditional aesthetician's definition of art—art, in his view, existed only as an aspect of function, and "pure art" was therefore an impossibility.

Morris' greatest productivity as a designer came in the early 1880's—and it was also in these years that his political activity became most intense. As he saw the connections between work and aesthetics, he realized that aesthetics could not be isolated from economics, politics, and the conditions of labor. His concept of design, then, led to a belief that society itself must be redesigned and, in 1883, to his announcement that he had been converted to socialism—though, significantly, not to the state socialism that was becoming marginally respectable but to a vision of a society truly organized from below and based on the nature of work.

This period is the focus of Peter Stansky's *Redesigning the World: William Morris, the 1880s, and the Arts and Crafts*. Specifically, Stansky discusses the organizations that grew under Morris' influence in the 1880's and 1890's. Separate chapters are devoted to the Century Guild (formed in 1882), the Art Workers' Guild (1884), and the Arts and Crafts Exhibition Society (1887). All arose from concerns articulated by Morris—and all, in addition, shared his ideal of brotherhood created through mutually supportive work by artists and craft workers in a variety of fields. By the time they were formed, however, Morris personally was more involved in politics than in art. In an essay printed in *The New Review*, in 1891, he wrote:

> Art was once the common possession of the whole people; it was the rule in the Middle Ages that the produce of handicraft was beautiful. . . . At present art is only enjoyed, or indeed thought of, by comparatively a few persons, broadly speaking, by the rich and the parasites that minister to them directly. . . . 'The Socialist claims art as a necessity of human life. . . . When people once more take pleasure in their work, when the pleasure rises to a certain point, the expression of it will become irresistible, and that expression of pleasure is art, whatever form it may take. . . . Our business is now and for long will be, not so much attempting to produce definite art, as rather clearing the ground to give art its opportunity. . . . To condemn a vast population to live in South Lancashire while art and education are being furthered in decent places, is like feasting within earshot of a patient on the rack.'

Yet, while the social revolution Morris sought did not come about, Stansky argues that much of his proposed revolution in design did. The book's thesis is that "how we view the world, and how it should look, changed in the 1880s under Morris's influence." Stansky traces the connections between the renaissance in British design and the ideas which Morris espoused in speeches, by writing, and through the multiple personal relationships he established in architects' offices, artistic brotherhoods, and organizations magnetized by his enthusiasm.

The Century Guild, a collective of designers and an agent for associated individuals (including Agnes Garrett, the first woman in Great Britain to be officially designated an interior designer), worked in both handicraft and manufactured goods. While the handcrafted objects produced by Morris' firm remained (by and large) quite expensive, Century Guild designers worked with manufacturers to create attractive machine-made products for domestic use and thus made new and simpler tastes available to the middle class. The associations developed within the guild were also important in promoting the concept of total design; although the guild itself was rather short-lived, Stansky argues that its ideas led toward modernism and the Bauhaus style.

The Art Workers' Guild was originally a loose combination of architects interested in retaining their status as artists (and thus opposed to the movement toward professionalization and certification through examinations) who joined forces with a society of designers to facilitate working together. The organization was perhaps as much social as functional, and deliberately low-profile—what it provided, Stansky argues, was a sense of identity to the young architects of the generation after Morris. Thus, some of them chose to forsake designing stately homes and monumental public buildings in favor of creating functional domestic architecture and searched for a plain English style arising from the materials, the site, and the work process.

The Arts and Crafts Exhibition Society grew out of the chronic discontent with the Royal Academy's elitism and its insider selection methods. (The Academy's Annual Exhibition not only defined the respectable in art but also was the primary source of sales once art patronage moved from the hands of aristocrats to newly rich manufacturers looking for something certifiably valuable to put on their walls.) Various proposals were made throughout the 1880's for a truly national exhibition that would include painting, sculpture, architecture, engraving, and the arts of design. What emerged, in 1888, was an exhibition primarily for decorative and applied arts, largely (it would seem) produced by gentlemen-craftsmen of the middle class, whose work was for sale but not in shops. It included metalwork, lighting schemes, furniture, bookbinding—and, from William Morris himself, tapestry, silks, chintzes, carpets, and calligraphic manuscripts. The Society's exhibits and associated lectures aroused interest in handicraft techniques (and ultimately in local craft shows). Furthermore, some of the designers (particularly of furniture) began to work with machine technology and discover how the machine also could become a part of a production process suited to the design and the method of work to create functional mass-produced wares with a beauty of their own.

The strength of Stansky's book is his emphasis on connections, most particularly his tracing of the ways that artistic styles are tied, on the one hand, to history, economics, and politics and, on the other, to the personal relationships and quirks and lives of practicing artists. He convincingly sees the shifting concerns and crosscurrents in the art world of the 1880's as part of the general breakup of high Victorian prosperity and complacency. Strikes, the broadened franchise, and a stirring social conscience all worked to redefine the world, while the industrial revolution (essentially complete by 1880) had utterly changed both technology and the worker's relationship to production and consumption.

This strength, however, also makes the book rather difficult to read, because explaining connections requires providing a considerable amount of information from various fields, so that Morris' ideas, the biographies of other figures of the Arts and Crafts Movement, the politics of church restoration or Irish Home Rule, and the internal organizational disputes of, say, the Arts and Crafts Exhibition Society must all be grasped at virtually the same moment. Despite all the specific detail, there is an odd lack of concreteness about the book. The passages on the Arts and Crafts Exhibition Society, for example, are crammed with details about organizing the exhibitions yet give no real sense of precisely what objects were shown and what they looked like. Yet, although it is necessary to have some acquaintance with the Arts and Crafts Movement to appreciate the book fully, its union of art, politics, and social history is instructive. Furthermore, some of Morris' ideas about the nature of work and the organization of the workplace are still quite surprisingly relevant.

Sally Mitchell

Sources for Further Study

The New York Review of Books. XXXII, April 25, 1985, p. 22.
The New York Times. February 20, 1985, p. 19.
The New York Times Book Review. XC, March 10, 1985, p. 18.
Publishers Weekly. CCVII, June 15, 1985, p. 65.

REINHOLD NIEBUHR
A Biography

Author: Richard Wightman Fox (1945-   )
Publisher: Pantheon Books (New York). Illustrated. 340 pp. $19.95
Type of work: Biography
Time: 1892-1971
Locale: Missouri; Logan County, Illinois; Detroit, Michigan; New York City; and Stockbridge, Massachusetts

A thorough, well-researched biography of Reinhold Niebuhr, an influential theologian and social activist who made a significant impact on American religious thought

> *Principal personages:*
> REINHOLD NIEBUHR, a major Protestant theologian and longtime professor at Union Theological Seminary
> H. RICHARD NIEBUHR, his younger brother
> URSULA KEPPEL-COMPTON NIEBUHR, Reinhold's wife
> CHRISTOPHER ROBERT NIEBUHR, their son
> BARBARA ELIZABETH NIEBUHR, their daughter
> HENRY SLOANE COFFIN, president of Union Theological Seminary
> WILL SCARLETT, Episcopal bishop of Missouri

Reinhold Niebuhr rose from humble beginnings to become one of the most spellbinding preachers and influential theologians of his time. During the 1920's, Niebuhr in many ways was to intellectuals what Billy Sunday was to the masses. Throughout his life, Niebuhr was a much sought-after preacher and was looked upon by many as the thinking man's theologian.

Born in rural Wright City, Missouri, to a clergyman in the German Evangelical Synod and his wife, Niebuhr grew up speaking German more than English. The family moved to Logan County in Illinois when Niebuhr was a small child, and he grew up around simple farm folk. He learned a considerable amount about the evangelical style of preaching from hearing his father's sermons.

Niebuhr attended Elmhurst College in Illinois and Eden Theological Seminary in St. Louis, Missouri, before matriculating in the Yale Divinity School, from which he received a bachelor of divinity degree in 1914 and a master of arts degree in 1915. Niebuhr quickly became a rousing preacher with an ever-expanding following, first in Detroit, where he had a church in a middle-class neighborhood, and later, as his fame spread, across the entire nation. Niebuhr traveled from his base at Union Theological Seminary to churches throughout the country to bring his special brand of Christian socialism to the people.

Richard Fox, a professor of history at Reed College, has drawn from a broad range of primary sources in preparing this well-balanced, meticulously researched biography. Not only has he read and provided critical commentary on all of Niebuhr's books, but he has tracked down as well a huge mass of Niebuhr's voluminous correspondence, sermons, letters to the editor, and articles and essays, many of which appeared in journals not readily available to the public. Working from this staggering quantity of material, Fox has written an engaging and lively biography that combines scholarly rigor with popular appeal.

Fox is a discriminating critic. He greatly admires his subject, but not to the point of losing his objectivity about him. Niebuhr was a prolific writer, and his books are uneven in depth and quality. Fox recognizes this unevenness and assesses Niebuhr's output with objectivity and intellectual integrity. The Niebuhr who emerges from his study is a many-sided, fascinating man.

Indeed, Niebuhr's life was filled with contradictions and ironies. He had essentially a populist view of society during his years as pastor of the Bethel Evangelical Church in Detroit, from 1915, the year in which he received his master's degree from Yale, to 1928, when he left to assume his post at Union Theological Seminary. Niebuhr liked to think of the congregation of the Bethel Evangelical Church as working class. The church had served a middle-class neighborhood, but under Niebuhr's pastorate, the congregation grew to six times its original size, attracting many factory workers from Detroit, who were moved by Niebuhr's attacks on such industrialists as Henry Ford. Niebuhr, a Socialist, favored the collective ownership of industry by the workers.

Niebuhr came to Bethel at a difficult time. Germany was at war with England and France, and the United States was in danger of being drawn into that war. Niebuhr, preaching to, largely, German-Americans, called for them to support the Allied cause in this conflict, although to do so meant repudiating their allegiance to their closest ties. Despite his pacifism, Niebuhr supported his country's engagement against Germany in both World War I and World War II.

It was during his period at Bethel that Niebuhr began to emerge as a social critic—a role for which he was known during his long and distinguished tenure at Union Theological Seminary. Niebuhr was sometimes simultaneously the darling of the political Right and the political Left. His basic posture was that of a liberal, but he was quite aware of some of the limitations of liberalism. He was fervently anti-Communist, believing that Communism destroyed the very roots of a free society, and he went so far as to suggest that right-wing extremism, when directed against Communism, was less dangerous to an open society than Communism was. Such sentiments gained for him a substantial following among conservatives and neoconservatives.

Niebuhr's growing national reputation as an outspoken social critic prompted Henry Sloane Coffin to seek Niebuhr out for a position at Union Theological Seminary, despite the fact that he did not hold a doctorate and despite opposition from a substantial number of the seminary's faculty, many of whom never came to respect Niebuhr. Coffin believed, probably correctly, that Niebuhr's dynamism and national visibility would attract students to the seminary.

When Niebuhr came to New York City in 1928 to assume his associate professorship in the Philosophy of Religion department, he had many rough edges and was in many ways still a country bumpkin. He arrived at white-tie functions dressed in a rumpled business suit. His table manners were atrocious. Some of his colleagues contended that he wrote before he thought, and fifteen years after he began his post at Union, he was still being castigated by theological scholars for his failure to explore data relevant to his writing before committing himself on paper.

Nevertheless, Niebuhr had a profound effect on his students, the public, and, most notably, clergymen in the field, dedicated men who found in Niebuhr someone who understood well the social and religious current with which they had to deal on a day-to-day basis in their parishes.

Although Niebuhr was the best-known theologian of his day, he regarded himself primarily as a teacher of social ethics. He was one of the great social thinkers of his century and has been so acknowledged. He was not a scholar's scholar but, rather, communicated forcefully and persuasively to a broad range of laymen and parish clergymen. His theology probably had a greater impact on nonbelievers than that of any religious man of the period. Many significant thinkers of the period took Niebuhr more seriously than they did any other theologian.

Fox presents valuable portions of Niebuhr's correspondence with his younger brother, H. Richard Niebuhr, a professor of theology at Yale—in his own right, a much-respected theologian. Richard Niebuhr's influence upon his brother's thinking was great, as their correspondence attests, yet Richard always lived in his brother's shadow and felt inferior to him. Richard and Reinhold Niebuhr differed from each other philosophically, as Richard tended to trust exclusively in God's ability to direct the course of human events while Reinhold was an activist who believed that man must participate directly in human affairs and through that participation help control the course of events.

Niebuhr continued undaunted in his social and political activism throughout his life. He was once the Socialist candidate for Congress from his district in New York. He was one of the founders of Americans for Democratic Action. He was instrumental in the founding in 1941 of the journal *Christianity and Crisis*, resulting from his belief that the highly influential journal *Christian Century* was too liberal for the times and furthermore that its pacifist stand in the face of Adolf Hitler's aggression was unwarranted. Niebuhr's name remained on the masthead of *Christianity and Crisis* until 1972, a year after his death, when his family insisted that it be removed because the journal had become critical of Israel, a stand antithetical to

Niebuhr's Christian Zionism.

Shortly after Niebuhr rose to the position of full professor at Union Theological Seminary in 1930, he was offered a full professorship at Yale, but
Union had become the center of his life, the unifying thread that he seemed
to need for his own stability. He resisted the offer from Yale, just as he
resisted offers from other prestigious schools, including Harvard University,
where President James B. Conant wanted Niebuhr to become a professor
with no specific departmental affiliation and without affiliation with the
divinity school. Robert G. Sproul, president of the University of California
at Berkeley, also considered Niebuhr for a similar position at that institution, but Niebuhr was not inclined to leave Union.

Fox presents Niebuhr not only as a man of conscience but also as a man
who could shift his positions and who sometimes did. One of Niebuhr's less
glorious stands came in 1951, when he supported the execution of Julius and
Ethel Rosenberg, who had been convicted of passing secret documents to
the Russians. His early decision was based on his anti-Communism, which
at times seemed almost rabid. After further consideration, Niebuhr opposed
the Rosenberg's execution, but on grounds of expediency rather than on
moral grounds—he thought that their execution would subject the United
States to adverse opinion from other nations. Only after the Rosenbergs had
been executed did Niebuhr come to oppose the execution on moral
grounds.

Although such shifting of opinion is not overly common in Niebuhr's
thinking, he was capable at times of turning one hundred eighty degrees,
and when he did, he usually was quick to admit it and to apologize to those
hurt by his earlier stand.

More gradual changes also took place in Niebuhr's thinking. He moved
from a quite full commitment to socialism in the 1920's and early 1930's to
the acceptance of a capitalism that provided, through welfare and other such
institutions, security for the working class. Franklin D. Roosevelt's New
Deal was largely acceptable to him, even though it was carried out within
the framework of the capitalist system.

Although he had supported the involvement of the United States in both
world wars, Niebuhr stood in staunch opposition to the country's involvement in Vietnam, and was a strident advocate of withdrawal from that war.
Niebuhr tried to persuade his old liberal compatriot Hubert H. Humphrey
to repudiate the Vietnam engagement, but Humphrey continued to express
his support of United States involvement in the conflict. When supporters of
Humphrey approached Niebuhr seeking his support of Humphrey's bid for
the presidency in 1968, Niebuhr refused because of Humphrey's stand on
the war. In the 1968 election, however, Niebuhr voted for Humphrey rather
than for Richard Nixon.

Despite his widespread activities throughout the country, which made

great demands on his time, Niebuhr was devoted to teaching and to his students He is said to have canceled classes only on rare occasions to meet his
numerous outside commitments, often carrying a packed suitcase to his last
Friday lecture so that he could leave campus immediately to travel to weekend speaking engagements.

This first full biography of Reinhold Niebuhr is a model of excellent
research and lucid writing. Fox handles a great diversity of materials with
deftness and weaves them into an intriguing narrative about one of the
twentieth century's most fascinating thinkers. Fox has taken no shortcuts in
his research, and his complete mastery of the material shows. He exercises
admirable restraint, remaining objective and nonjudgmental, presenting his
materials fairly and leaving readers to make their own interpretations and
judgments.

R. Baird Shuman

Sources for Further Study

The Atlantic. CCLVII, January, 1968, p. 93.
Christian Century. CIII, January 1, 1986. p. 15.
Christianity and Crisis. XLVI, February 3, 1986. p. 5.
The New York Review of Books. XXXII, February 13, 1986, p. 7.
The New York Times Book Review. CXI, January 5, 1986, p. 1.
Publishers Weekly. CCXXVIII, November 29, 1985, p. 41.
Time. CXXVII, January 20, 1986, p. 71.
The Wall Street Journal. LXVI, February 21, 1986, p. 21.

RETURN TO REGIÓN

Author: Juan Benet (1927-   )
Translated from the Spanish by Gregory Rabassa
Publisher: Columbia University Press (New York). 288 pp. $18.95
Type of work: Novel
Time: 1925-1964
Locale: Región, a fictional place in Spain

A re-creation, from the reconstruction of events through memory, of the experiences of a man and a woman during the Spanish civil war

> *Principal characters:*
> DANIEL SEBASTIÁN, a doctor living in seclusion in Región
> MARRÉ GAMALLO, the daughter of a Falangist general killed during the Spanish civil war
> NUMA, a mysterious, mythical being that inhabits the reality of Región

In the preface to the 1974 edition in Spanish of *Return to Región* (published originally as *Volverás a Región*, 1967), Juan Benet explains that in 1951 he began a novel about a mythical guardian of a forbidden forest, which he rewrote in the years from 1962 to 1964 as an elaboration of three separate narratives—the myth of the guardian, a fictional history of the development and consequences of the Spanish civil war in a remote community, and the story of a frustrated marriage in the mountains of Northern Spain. When Benet received a rejection notice from a publisher indicating that the novel lacked the material most attractive to contemporary readers—sufficient dialogue—he intransigently set about revising his text by eliminating much of the dialogue from the manuscript. In 1967, two years after Benet's fifth rewriting of the material, the novel was finally published by Ediciones Destino.

Return to Región is a complex, difficult novel, rendered into English by Gregory Rabassa, a translator of consummate skill who has produced excellent translations of many Spanish and Latin American novels, including Benet's *Una meditación* (1978; *A Meditation*, 1982). Benet had to sacrifice many "insolences" and "impertinences" to make *Return to Región* acceptable to the publishers. After his success, he was able to preserve the integrity of his manuscripts, as is evident in the novels that follow *Return to Región*. *A Meditation* is considerably more complex than the first novel, as are *Un viaje de invierno* (1972; a winter journey) and *La otra casa de Mazón* (1973; the other house of Mazón). These later novels are genuinely "insolent" and "impertinent" in the context of the neorealism of Spanish fiction in the 1950's and 1960's. Benet wrote *A Meditation* on a long, continuous roll of paper, without paragraphs, chapters, or periods. Sentences go on for pages, filled with parentheses within parentheses and quotations within quotations. The punctuation is so chaotic that the text is decipherable only with considerable patience and determination.

Return to Región is somewhat more traditional in its narrative techniques, probably because of the strictures placed on the unknown novelist by the publishers. Even so, it is an extremely difficult novel that marked a significant change in the direction of Spanish fiction in the 1960's. In spite of the more conservative linguistic structures of the text, the narrative constructs a kind of reality similar to that found in Benet's later novels—a mythographic configuration of a world that operates according to its own rules. Benet's fictional reality is an uncertain one, posited through the process of memory. The characters of *Return to Región* recall the past, analyze the remembered facts, evaluate the reconstructed events, and leave the reader with a potential, partial truth that is not entirely accessible or understandable.

Benet divides his novelistic text into four sections. The first is a description and history of Región, an isolated village in the mountains of Northern Spain, in a dense forest guarded by the mysterious, mythical figure of Numa, the unseen presence that preserves the peace of the area. The second, third, and fourth sections of the novel narrate the visit of Marré the Gamallo to the house where Dr. Daniel Sebastián lives in isolation, caring for a retarded man who was abandoned by his mother during the civil war. The last three sections of the novel are devoted almost entirely to the spoken words of Marré Gamallo and Sebastián. It soon becomes evident, however, that these two characters are not engaged in a dialogue; rather, each is delivering a monologue not necessarily directed at the other. The purpose of the monologues—which at times become interiorized—is not communication but the re-creation of past experience through the act of recalling the events that established a relationship between the two characters, a relationship unknown to either of them until their meeting in Sebastián's house.

The two primary voices in the novel—those of Marré Gamallo and Daniel Sebastián—together with the voice of the unnamed narrator and the comments of an unnamed editor of the text form the narrative of *Return to Región*. At many points, it is not clear who is speaking or to whom the pronominal forms refer. Both these characters are obsessed with the wartime experience. Marré Gamallo has come back to Región in search of her lover, Luis Timonel, who disappeared into the forest at the end of the war. She forces Daniel Sebastián to remember his experience, although his monologues dwell on the theme of the destruction wrought by time rather than on the events of the war.

Through the testimonies of Marré and Daniel, the narrator's fragmentary history of Región presented in the first section is gradually clarified. Marré, the daughter of Colonel Gamallo of the invading Falangist forces, was held hostage by the Republican defenders of Región. After her first love affair, with a German soldier who was killed in the defense of the town, Marré had an affair with Luis Timoner, whose mother, María, was supposedly the lover of Colonel Gamallo. María rejected the advances of Daniel Sebastián, who harbors for her an unrequited passion years after her death. Daniel married another woman, with whom he lived in celibacy for twenty years, forever refusing to consummate the marriage. Since her death, he has lived alone in the house, caring for a violent retarded man abandoned by his mother during the war.

The novelistic text does not serve primarily to narrate this history of complex relationships. Rather, it is devoted to the obsession that each character has for the experience of the war in the remote Región. The details of the "plot"—the plot that hardly exists in the novel—are scattered throughout the monologues. Other related details are concentrated in a chaotic manner in the first section, which presents the obsessive remembrance of the other primary voice, that of the narrator.

The novel, then, is a revelation of the interior conflict of Marré and Daniel, and also of the abandoned child. The conflict of each has its origin in primal sexuality, aggravated by the prohibitions of civilized society. Marré, after an adolescence of repressed sexuality and the death of her first lover, became promiscuous and even spent a period in the inn of ill repute that figures significantly in the next novel Benet wrote, *A Meditation*. Her return to Región is a search for the happiness and sexual fulfillment of the period with her second lover, Luis Timoner. Daniel, rejected by the woman whom he loved, has spent his life first in a pseudomarriage, denying all sexual involvement, and then in isolation, nurturing a man whose infantile incestuous relationship with his mother was frustrated by her disappearance. The abandoned man-child lives out his life awaiting the return of his mother and even thinks that Marré is her and that Daniel is denying him access to her.

The wartime experience of Región, then, is merely a pretext for a more turbulent, interiorized experience. The war disturbs the isolation of the community and opens it up to the more cosmopolitan outside world. It aggravates the tension of the conflict between primal sexuality and civilized society, which in Benet's novel becomes a metaphor for the struggle between the liberal and conservative forces of the civil war. That the novel's central event—the encounter of Marré and Daniel—takes place in the mid-1960's, at the height of Francisco Franco's repressive reign, is significant. In the midst of a well-ordered, stagnant society, Marré and Daniel struggle to release the tension of their inner conflict through remembrance of the pervasive, frustrated sexuality of the wartime experience.

Throughout the narrative of the war in the first section of the novel, and also underlying the monologues of Marré and Daniel, is the image of the mythical Numa, who stalks the forest with carbine in hand, always ready to preserve the order of things and punish transgressors with rapid death. At the end of the novel, after Marré and Daniel have re-created the intense sexual transgressions of the past and the abandoned child has murdered

Daniel, a single shot rings out in the quiet forest. Marré and all that her reappearance in Región represents are eliminated by Numa, the complex of repressive prohibitions is reaffirmed, and the social order is restored.

In *A Meditation*, Benet continues his exploration of the experience of Región with a narrative of the events from the end of the civil war up to a point some years before the time of Marré's return. Once again, that experience is primarily sexual. Within Benet's Freudian concept of frustrated sexuality, the history of Región is a continual process of society's repressive prohibitions and the individual's frequent transgressions, or the eternal conflict between reason and instinct. In *Return to Región*, the emphasis falls much more on the obsession with the conflict than on specific examples of it. It is as if this novel should have followed, rather than preceded, *A Meditation*, for this is the theoretical formulation of the struggle between instinctual impulses and rational constraints that is worked out in the later novel.

The encounter between Marré and Daniel in *Return to Región* seems to occur outside of time, because of the emphasis on the obsession itself. Daniel's monologues concentrate to a great extent on the essential timelessness of experience. The impossibility of reconstructing a past or imagining a future inevitably renders the immediate present as the only reality. Región is a timeless, eternally stagnant representation of the repressive socialization of primal instincts. This pessimistic vision of society is reinforced by the eternal presence of Numa, to whom Marré sacrifices herself when she realizes the hopelessness of her attempt at fulfillment through restoration of the past.

Benet's distinctive narrative style contributes significantly to his representation of the fictional reality as one that exists beyond the confines of chronological time. The fragmentary record of events and the chaotic arrangement of episodes parallel the natural process of memory, but also compromise the authenticity and reliability that characterize more traditional novelistic texts. Yet, whether the testimonies of the characters of *Return to Región*—Marré, Daniel, and the narrator—are authentic and reliable is of no consequence, for the significance of their experience lies not in what it *was* but in what it *is* in its remembered state.

Gilbert Smith

Sources for Further Study

Choice. XXIII, November, 1985, p. 455.
Library Journal. CX, June 1, 1985, p. 141.
Los Angeles Times. September 20, 1985, V, p. 28.
The New York Times Book Review. XC, September 15, 1985, p. 24.
Publishers Weekly. CCXXVII, April 26, 1985, p. 72.

THE ROUNDHOUSE VOICES
Selected and New Poems

Author: Dave Smith (1942-   )
Publisher: Harper & Row, Publishers (New York). 182 pp. $9.95
Type of work: Poetry

An analysis of the past's hold on the present

The main subject of Dave Smith's *The Roundhouse Voices: Selected and New Poems* is the past, especially as he experienced it. He also focuses on women and ruminates about the nature of poetry.

Smith localizes in the past what he knows about decay. In "Near the Docks," he remembers a shed that burned down. He used to go there to smoke, and it is as if light itself in the form of fire causes and illuminates destruction for him, and the sea which gives life is also life's graveyard. Smith returns to the Southern town and train station he knew as a boy and finds them and their rural setting fallen apart, and this both repels and lures him ("How to Get to Green Springs," "Cumberland Station"). In "Goshawk, Antelope," an event full of power and death in the present reminds him of the past, which makes him realize that the past is dead and therefore different in his memory than when it was the present. Indeed, life moves forward and as such betrays what went into it ("Remembering Harpers Ferry"). The news of his father's death was full of meaning for him when it came but seems meaningless (dead in meaning) long afterward ("No Return Address"). Death itself is bad enough, but the past in which it happened makes it worse, for that past is itself dead. Thus the past offers little by way of understanding what happened in it ("De Soto") and repeatedly presents emblems of the failure appropriate to it, such as the lonely judge in "In the House of the Judge," whose job made him see the horrors of human life, and the boy in "Ear Ache," for whose illness no one could find a cure.

Sinister as the past may be for Smith, he also sees lessons of hope and endurance in it because love makes him stubborn. In "Sailing the Back River," he may see decomposition in his past, but that past—which he loves—makes him feel saved. At the same time that the past holds him in its grip and seems useless, it feeds him; in "Smithfield Ham," it causes a thirst which Smith equates with hope. "Kitchen Windows," with its annually renewed celebration from the past (Thanksgiving), moves him to accept the bad times which the past embodies and to see hope, not only death, as an essential part of life's meaning. What his dead father told him in the past when he wanted to run away he finds he can apply now that he is grown up. The event which brought about the advice is painful—a boy going out to test himself against the world—but the advice is still good: Keep in touch, be careful, and take time with decisions ("Runaway"). If the past, in short, is the history of hardship and decay, it also shows the way to live life and makes it possible, as in "Chopping Wood," to see that dead things (wood) nourish life (fire).

To understand how Smith relates women to his past, it helps to see what features about them he emphasizes in the present. "The Shark in the Rafters" shows violence and death associated with women. Perhaps to take revenge on the shark for eating humans, the women in the poem tear it apart after it is caught. The pregnant woman in "Black Widow" kills the spider but feels in tune with its savagery, neurotically imagining that she is full of its unborn offspring. Even the little girl in "Cleaning a Fish" quickly overcomes her shock at the butchery she is about and accepts it. Moreover, the impression of female passion from which he is cut off is so strong on the narrator of "Field Music" that he becomes a wild beast in his own eyes.

A quality of women that attracts Smith is the hope of which they are capable. The used girl in "The Soft Belly of the World" waits for her seducer to return, hoping thereby to free herself of the memory of what happened to her. Hope is what makes the widow in "Portrait of a Lady" try to withstand age and death by tending her flowers, despite all the weeds she has to pull. Hope raised to the level of enduring attraction in the woman in "James River Storm" is what keeps the narrator committed to his memories and his vision of their importance to him in the present.

Sex and the past often go together in Smith's poetry, mostly in an unhappy way. The women in "The Pornography Box" are pictures. They are the source of lust in the narrator's boyhood, and though he found such abstract women wonderful, they also encased him in a feeling of rot. "A Gold of Birds" associates a death-dealing hawk in the present with the first experience of sex. The mud in "Pond" reminds Smith of the sexual love of ancestors, while "Nekkid: Homage to Edgar Allan Poe" takes him back to the time when he was fourteen and his desire for women was full of terror. When he was seventeen, he was humiliated by the laughter of the man who caught him having sex with a girl, and it is this shame linked with sex that he remembers in "The Colors of Our Age: Pink and Black." In the same vein, a girl causes him to fall when he is ice-skating in his youth; he bleeds, and avers as an adult that everyone has a bloody story to tell about youthful sex ("Skating"). Remembering when he was drafted, the narrator of "Men Drafted" places women at the core of young men's sense of helplessness, for they wish for what they cannot reach in their condition, as though women have always expected an impossible strength from them. If "Wedding Song" insists that it is the impulsive feeling behind his early marriage that keeps that marriage alive now for the poet, the poem also emphasizes the pain of such a marriage.

Smith goes to the past not only to find out what death and love mean but also to define what poetry means to him. In general, pain is the source and goad of art, as "Ducking: After Maupassant" and "Snow Owl" reveal. The pain of parting from a known place, consigning it thus to the past, makes words the habitation of that place in "Leaving Town." The pain of paradox occupies "The Roundhouse Voices," in which the poet recalls his maverick boyhood, with its rules and lessons, and wonders how poetry and rebelliousness can accommodate each other. Smith says, furthermore, that poetry cannot fully capture the wildness of nature or the pain of composition but adds that it is akin to useful, earthy arts such as boat building and that it can reveal something of the elemental in life ("Rooster Smith's Last Log Canoe"). For Smith, poetry is like an old boat maintained against the specious glamour of the present ("Boats"), and though poetry may repeat the bad news of the past in the present, it is still a message that needs to be delivered, perhaps as a warning meant to preserve life ("Messenger"). Smith continues the boat metaphor in "Elegy in an Abandoned Boatyard," equating a verse-line to a keel-line and seeing poetry as effective an embodiment of the past as are old boats. Photography is another metaphor that Smith uses for poetry, especially photography's limits. "The Perspective & Limits of Snapshots" suggests that the subject of poetry is the past, and therefore failure. "The Traveling Photographer: Circa 1880," again locating art in the past, shows the artist confounded by his subjects in that he is forced to see life as it is, not as he might like it to be. The artist is compelled by this painful restriction not only to pursue his art but also to record the truth of its content.

Two things account for the popularity of Dave Smith's work in the current mainstream of American poetry: his addiction to his own past (particularly his family experiences in it) and his fascination with rural settings. He is forceful in his treatment and use of both, though not unique. His work broods with a kind of elegant subtlety on its subjects, but this is not enough to set it apart from the homogeneous verse of his contemporaries, which features a by now forced nostalgia for nature. In addition, what real passion there is in Smith's poetry tends to be weakened by overstatement. Many of his poems start with an unnecessary description of setting and go on simply to repeat his intention and conclusions. Such a strategy tends to drug rather than excite or renew the reader's attention.

Mark McCloskey

Sources for Further Study

Library Journal. CX, November 1, 1985, p. 100.
The Nation. CCXLI. October 5, 1985, p. 320.
The New York Times Book Review. XCI, January 12, 1986, p. 17.
Publishers Weekly. CCXXVIII, August 9, 1985, p. 72.

RUDE ASSIGNMENT
An Intellectual Autobiography

Author: Wyndham Lewis (1882-1957)
Edited, with an afterword, by Toby Foshay
With six letters by Ezra Pound edited and annotated by Bryant Knox
Publisher: Black Sparrow Press (Santa Barbara, California). Illustrated. 311 pp.
  $20.00; paperback $12.50
Type of work: Autobiography
Time: The first half of the twentieth century
Locale: London, Paris, and New York

An intellectual autobiography in which Wyndham Lewis, artist, writer, and critic, answers the various charges made against him and his works during his career and sets forth the difficulties facing the artist in the modern age

> *Principal personages:*
> WYNDHAM LEWIS, the author; a writer, artist, and critic
> EZRA POUND, an American poet and expatriate
> JAMES JOYCE, an Irish writer, the author of *Ulysses*
> FORD MADOX FORD, an English author and critic
> GEORGE ORWELL (ERIC BLAIR), an English author and political
> analyst

"It was, after all, a new civilisation that I—and a few other people—was making the blueprints for. . . . I, like all the other people in Europe so engaged, felt it to be an important task. It was more than just picture-making: one was manufacturing fresh eyes for people, and fresh souls to go with the eyes."

So Wyndham Lewis, years later, recalled the early years of the twentieth century, when indeed it seemed as if Lewis and his companions were fashioning new eyes and new souls. All the arts were in vibrant motion, and the names of the creators still capture some of the excitement of that time: Igor Stravinsky, Henri Gaudier-Brzeska, Ezra Pound, T. S. Eliot, James Joyce, and Wyndham Lewis.

Among a crew of gifted artists, Wyndham Lewis seemed, at the beginning of this century, to be one of the most widely gifted of them all. He was a novelist, a critic, an essayist, a painter, and a philosopher. He created the Vorticist movement, which began as a theory of pictorial art and moved— via Ezra Pound—into literature as well. For a time it must have seemed that Lewis himself would be the vortex, the driving, creative center of modern art.

Such was not the case, and *Rude Assignment: An Intellectual Autobiography*, first published in England in 1950 and only now available in an American edition, is Lewis' attempt both to explore and explain his career as a writer, thinker, and artist. The book has "one engrossing subject: namely to meet and to destroy unjust, prejudiced, and tendentious criticism—past, present, and future. It is my object to dispel misconceptions (about myself, or about my work) whether they derive from ill-natured and tendentious criticism, or some other cause."

Rude Assignment is, then, an "intellectual autobiography." Lewis addresses his personal history only as it affects his career and his work; this is not the story of Lewis the man, but of Lewis the artist. More than that, it is the story of Lewis as an example of the artistic-intellectual "type" and how that type fares in the contemporary world. As he states, "A secondary aim is to elicit a pattern of thinking: to show how any one of my books is connected with every other: that they are a litter of books, not really discrete: how the critical books carry forward what is, in fact, a type of thinking, belonging to a certain type of mind."

The type, to be sure, is the artist, particularly the writer; Lewis' contention is that the modern world is strikingly unsuited for real art—that is, art that is unbiased, unsentimental, and above all, unafraid of reality. Taken singly, any one of these qualities is a severe handicap to public acceptance; taken together, as Lewis notes in gloomy but undefeated remembrance, they lead to personal attacks on the artist and conspiracies against his work.

In reviewing his career, Lewis points to three fatalities that worked against him. The first was that, as an uncompromising intellectual—"Mr. Ivory Tower," as one woman called him—he was at odds with the majority of the public, since they were allergic to the masterpiece, averse to any exposure to serious literature. The minority public, the intelligentsia, the truly literate—where Lewis' books should have been met with some respect and understanding—was riddled with coteries and cliques, animated not by artistic concerns but by political quarrels.

The second fatality was Lewis' bent for satire. This made many enemies; it also provided his critics with an opportunity to dismiss his writings as either unimportant or as simply malicious. In fact, however, characteristic of Lewis' satiric works, as his most notable, *The Apes of God* (1930), is his primary interest in the type, not the individual. Satire, "the reflection of moral nausea," as intellectual historian Crane Brinton has termed it, at its best transcends the contemporary to attack universal human failings; Lewis may have reacted to a set of particularly irritating conditions—the between-war period and W. H. Auden's "low, dishonest decade"—but his work cannot justly be dismissed as either transitory or merely malicious. His true errors, he insists, were not artistic, but political—this was the third and most damaging fatality that haunted his career.

For Lewis, politics was more than the conventional ins and outs of party and faction—it was a serious view of the world that required both moral and intellectual integrity. He felt himself surrounded by partisans who rejected this standard of honesty, opponents who attached supreme importance to the labels and no value to the contents.

"Politics is for the Twentieth Century what Religion was for the Sixteenth and Seventeenth. In a time so exclusively political, to stand outside politics is to invite difficulties: or not to identify yourself, in passionate involvement, with one or other of the contending parties." In a sense, Lewis managed to commit both of these sins. He was outside politics in the usual sense, preferring to consider it as an objective observer, becoming a participant only in certain limited and specific struggles. Even then, he resolutely refused to hold to a false consistency and so was called everything from a crypto-Nazi to a Stalinist; no faction claimed him and all united against him.

According to *Rude Assignment*, "politics" in this sense cost Lewis dearly: in lost work, suppressed publications, and damaged reputation. His novel *The Roaring Queen* (1936) was printed and bound—and then kept from the public because of possible legal problems. It was not published until 1973. His series of antiwar pamphlets during the late 1930's, such as *Left Wings over Europe* (1936) and *Count Your Dead, They Are Alive* (1937), were discounted as pro-Nazi propaganda. Well might Lewis lament toward the end of *Rude Assignment*: "Today I should not write such books at all. People ought to be allowed to drop to pieces in any way they choose. I even disapprove of propping them up. Let nations, like men, die in peace."

It seems clear that politics did harm Lewis' literary career; he was too often and too much on the wrong—or at least the unacceptable—side. The tone of his polemics was guaranteed to irritate even the uncommitted, and it certainly infuriated his opponents, such as George Orwell. Nevertheless, one must question Lewis' self-assessment, for ultimately politics—even in the disputatious sense that Lewis practiced it—was not the major obstacle to his career or the main obstacle to full recognition of his achievements. Later generations are likely to be either forgiving or benignly neglectful of an artist's politics: Auden's flirtation with the Left, Pound's more serious dealings with the Fascists have not significantly disturbed their literary reputations; surely Lewis' antiwar writings and mild—and every qualified— praise of Adolf Hitler in the early 1930's cannot be held against him. The truth is, they are not.

What caused the most objections to Lewis during his career, and what still impedes his full acceptance as a major writer, was his thoroughgoing and vociferous rejection of the prevailing aesthetics of the literary revolution of the early part of the twentieth century. While Lewis was—and generally remained—on fairly friendly terms with authors such as Joyce, Pound, and Eliot, he was definitely opposed to what he perceived as their philosophical and theoretical foundations. His prime attack on these foundations came in *Time and Western Man* (1927), which remains his premier critical work, a study of considerable subtlety and complexity but one that rejects what many accept as the essential works of the modern period.

In *Rude Assignment*, Lewis restates his earlier purpose: "As to *Time and Western Man*, it will be sufficient to say that in my view, at the period at which I wrote it, the philosophy in the ascendant was destructive, and that it should be combated. In its pages—and it is a book of considerable length—I provide a very detailed answer to that disintegrating metaphysic."

Lewis viewed his work as a defense of Western culture, an attack on the "time-philosophers" he saw as picking apart the fabric of that culture. He rejected relativism, impressionism, and "time-philosophy" in general, and he rejected most of the individual works that sprang from them; in particular he undertook a lengthy, detailed, and highly critical analysis of Joyce's *Ulysses* (1922). Even Lewis admits that he might have been too sweeping in his attack: "I was perhaps too forcible. At that time I was about the only writer in English-speaking countries who gave utterance to such opinions, and I had to insist in order to be heard."

Lewis was heard, and in *Rude Assignment* he assesses the turmoil and damage that resulted; he does not back away from his criticism, and he insists that it remains valid. The idea of "Western man" may have become almost absurd after two bloody world wars and the increasing brutalization of, by, and for the omnipotent State—but Lewis maintains that the idea and the ideal were once worth defending—until events proved that Western man was determined to commit moral and intellectual suicide.

In a sense, *Rude Assignment* is Wyndham Lewis' account of his part in that struggle to preserve the essence of Western man. Once again, as so often in this work, he is concerned with the type, a type that once predominated. Isolated as he was, Lewis still felt kinship to that vanishing type: "I had all the confidence of a herd—that was not there. In England there had been numbers of us at one time. I knew that from the books I read. Many of their authors thought the way I did."

By the time he wrote *Rude Assignment*, Lewis had become convinced that this type had all but vanished and that the time of Western man was past. His pessimistic conclusions are belied by the vigor of his style, the toughness of his outlook, and the besieged yet enduring nature of his reputation. Even those who believe that he is mostly wrong about Joyce or mistaken concerning Pound know that Lewis still has something to say about these artists—something that inspires more than dismissal.

This edition of *Rude Assignment*, edited by Toby Foshay, with six letters from Ezra Pound edited and annotated by Bryant Knox, reveals Wyndham Lewis in the full power of his polemical, critical, and stylistic abilities. The illustrations—all, significantly enough, self-portraits—reinforce the essential point that Lewis was an artist in all senses of the word.

In the early years of the twentieth century, Wyndham Lewis considered himself to be one of those fortunate few chosen to draw up the blueprints for a new civilization. Yet by the time he wrote *Rude Assignment* at mid-century, he had come to realize that a variety of circumstances had made him not a primary architect but a critic of the vast design then abuilding. He might have preferred to be the prime draftsman (he certainly regretted the particular structure rising), but he realized that to be a critic was to play an important role, one which called for vision, clarity, and, above all else, unflinching intellectual honesty.

Michael Witkoski

Source for Further Study

The New York Times Book Review. XC, February 10, 1985, p. 29.

THE SAGA OF DAZAI OSAMU
A Critical Study with Translations

Author: Phyllis I. Lyons (1942-   )
Publisher: Stanford University Press (Stanford, California). Illustrated. 410 pp. $38.50
Type of work: Literary biography; short stories and a travel memoir
Time: 1909-1948
Locale: Japan

The first full account in English of the life and works of an important modern Japanese writer; this critical biography is supplemented by translations of five stories and a travel memoir

In her study of Dazai Osamu, Phyllis Lyons observes the Japanese practice with regard to names, the surname preceding the given name. For consistency's sake, that style will be followed here.

Dazai Osamu is best known in the West as the author of two novels, *Shayō* (1947; *The Setting Sun*, 1956) and *Ningen shikkaku* (1948; *No Longer Human*, 1958), and the short story "Viyon no tsuma" ("Villon's Wife"), which was included in Donald Keene's pioneering and widely read anthology *Modern Japanese literature* (1956). In contrast to such near contemporaries as Tanizaki Jun'ichirō, Kawabata Yasunari, and Mishima Yukio, however, Dazai is not a familiar figure to Western readers.

In Japan, the situation is quite different. "To the Japanese," Lyons writes, "Dazai Osamu is not just one of the most famous of all modern writers; he is a star," the subject of intense scholarly study and, at the same time, the kind of lurid journalistic speculation that still attends the life and death of an Elvis Presley or a James Dean:

> Annually on the anniversary of his death, television crews go out to film the memorial services at his graveside as a human-interest feature for the evening news; they are still well attended, though it is over thirty years since he killed himself.

More important, several editions of Dazai's complete works have been published since his death in 1948, and his books are still widely read in Japan.

There has been one previous book-length study of Dazai in English: James O'Brien's *Dazai Osamu* (1975), a volume in the Twayne series; among other sources, notable are the chapters on Dazai in Masao Miyoshi's *Accomplices of Silence: The Modern Japanese Novel* (1974), Makoto Ueda's *Modern Japanese Writers and the Nature of Literature* (1976), and Donald Keene's *Dawn to the West: Japanese Literature in the Modern Era* (1984). Lyons' study, however, provides by far the fullest account of Dazai's life and literary career available in English.

The Saga of Dazai Osamu is divided into three sections. The long first section, "Dazai's Life and the Osamu Saga," is a critical biography. The remainder of the book offers a sampling of Dazai's works: The second section, "Osamu Stories," comprises five short stories, while the third section, *Tsugaru*, presents in its entirety a book-length account of a journey which Dazai made to his home region after a long absence.

Although Lyons' professional field is Japanese language and literature, the emphasis in her study is primarily psychological and, to a lesser extent, sociological rather than literary. Explaining that "this is not a conventional 'life and works,'" she acknowledges that she "goes into Dazai's philosophy of literature (such as it is) largely as that has bearing on the progressive telling of the tale of [his] life." She adds, however, that since she hopes "to draw readers into a more intimate relationship with Dazai, they will find themselves guided through a number of the major stories." At the same time, Lyons is much concerned with what she regards as the distinctively Japanese quality of Dazai's writings; it is her intention to present his fiction in its cultural as well as its psychological context, showing "how Dazai, while a man like all other men of whatever society or culture, is at the same time specifically and revealingly Japanese."

To a certain extent, Lyons' approach was dictated by her subject, for Dazai's life and writings were intertwined to a degree rare even in the twentieth century. Much of Dazai's work is in the genre known in Japan as the *shishōsetsu*, or "I-novel." In this genre, which has affinities with the so-called confessional poetry of Robert Lowell, John Berryman, and Sylvia Plath, the "I" of the story or novel is indistinguishable (or nearly so) from the author. A number of critics regard Dazai as having taken the I-novel to its limits; in their view (largely shared by Lyons), Dazai's suicide was the logical—indeed, inevitable—culmination of his career: Having written exhaustively about his own life, he finally used up his material and had nothing left to do but die.

While such interpretations are open to debate (as Lyons herself demonstrates, in her finest pages of analysis, the relationship between truth and fiction, author and narrator in Dazai's works is much more complex than might first appear to be the case), the basic facts of Dazai's life have been well-documented, and Lyons has sifted through the memoirs and biographical studies that have appeared in remarkable profusion since his death, in addition conducting her own independent biographical research. Dazai was born Tsushima Shiji on June 19, 1909. (It was not until 1933 that he adopted the pen name by which he is known.) He was the tenth of eleven children in an affluent landowning family; frequently in his writings he describes the sense of guilt he felt, even as a boy, at his family's wealth. The region where he was born, Tsugaru, lies on the northeastern tip of Honshu, the main island of Japan. In Dazai's time—and, according to Lyons, even today—Tsugaru was regarded as extremely provincial, culturally backward; Lyons draws a parallel with Appalachia in the United States, noting that there was a social stigma attached to the highly distinctive Tsugaru dialect. As Lyons suggests, it is important to remember that Dazai the self-styled (guilty) aristocrat, the "Tokyo litterateur and would-be decadent," came from such a region.

In 1923, when Dazai was thirteen, his father died. A month later, Dazai entered high school (or the Japanese equivalent) in the nearby town of Aomori; this was the first time he had been away from his family. He wrote his first stories while in high school and, with two of his brothers, helped to start several short-lived literary magazines.

From Aomori, he went, in 1927, to Hirosaki College, and from there, in 1930, to Tokyo Imperial University. While at Hirosaki, he met a young geisha, Oyama Hatsuyo, and, like many Japanese students of the period, became involved in leftist political activities. In 1929, before he had entered the university, he attempted suicide for the first time, taking an overdose of sleeping pills.

Various explanations for this first suicide attempt have been proposed. Lyons suggests that fear of disgrace prompted by imminent academic failure—Dazai had been ignoring his studies at Hirosaki, as he was to do later at the university—was the most significant local cause, but ultimately she traces it to childhood insecurities.

Whatever the cause, this youthful suicide attempt set the pattern for Dazai's life. In 1930, he and a woman attempted suicide together, taking sleeping pills and then (according to some accounts, concerning which Lyons is skeptical) throwing themselves in the sea; the woman died, but Dazai survived. Shortly afterward, he married Hatsuyo. In 1935, he attempted suicide by hanging but survived. During a period of ill health, when he required prescriptions for painkillers, he became addicted to narcotics; he was also drinking heavily. He was cured of his addiction in a harrowing month spent in a mental hospital. A few months later, in 1937, he and Hatsuyo attempted suicide together; both survived, and they separated.

Some years passed before Dazai's fifth and final suicide attempt. Those years, which spanned the war, marked his most prolific and successful period as a writer. In 1939, he had married again; he and his second wife had two daughters and a son. After the war, which had seemed to demand of him a measure of stability, Dazai began to drink very heavily, and his life became increasingly disordered; he was also seriously ill with tuberculosis. In June, 1948, he and a woman named Yamazaki Tomie, who had become his mistress and had declared her determination to die with him, disappeared, leaving suicide notes; their bodies, tied together by a cord, were found in a canal several days later, on the morning of what would have been Dazai's thirty-ninth birthday.

What is one to make of this life, and what light does it shed on the writing that Dazai did between 1933 and 1948, enough writing to fill the dozen volumes of his collected works? There is much that is unsatisfactory in Lyons' answers to these questions. Masao Miyoshi observes that

> no one is more sensitive than Dazai to the possibility that any mode of speech may turn absurd. Whenever his writing turns a bit too ponderous, or affected, or cumbersome, or rigid, or just too formal, he shifts into reverse and writes with humor, or a meticulously measured colloquialism, or vulgarisms, or babyish onomatopoeia, or a sprinkling of learned diction and foreign words, here and there a grotesque word, an archaism or two, or he omits a pronoun or preposition, or he staccatos a passage with overpunctuation.

Unfortunately, Lyons lacks this awareness of potential absurdity. She shows no signs of realizing, for example, that the bare narrative of Dazai's life, the bungled suicides and all, however tragic, may strike the reader as something like a Woody Allen routine. Heedless to such vital matters of tone, she will instead discuss an anthropologist's schema of "three motivations for (or functions of) suicide in Japan."

More seriously—and this is a shortcoming which affects her translations as well as her critical study—Lyons lacks the sensitivity to language and literary values which distinguishes Miyoshi's observation quoted above and which also informs Makoto Ueda's and Donald Keene's discussions of Dazai. This lack is particularly glaring when Lyons, seeking to explain Dazai's enduring appeal, has recourse to the mushy jargon of pop psychology: "In reading Dazai one is able, as it were, to write one's own experience in his mind-space."

This is not a compelling argument for reading Dazai, nor is the suggestion that Westerners should read Dazai because he is "more Japanese" than other, better-known writers. The charm of Dazai's voice, conveyed in Miyoshi's account of his style, is a sufficient reason to read him—that charm is felt even in translation. Yet there is more to Dazai. Most of what he wrote is saturated with a painful awareness of human weakness (especially his own), of suffering, inequality, and loss. This mixture of acute sympathy and self-abasement can become wearying, exasperating—as one of Dazai's characters says, "when human beings get that way, they're no good for anything"—but it challenges the reader's indifference. Given this challenge, one must ask if the elaborate psychological and sociological framework constructed by Lyons is necessary or adequate to account for Dazai's heightened perception of the human condition. Do not such constructs block the reader's vision, making it difficult for him to see himself and his world in Dazai's fiction?

Nevertheless, while *The Saga of Dazai Osamu* is not without flaws, it is unquestionably a valuable resource, of interest to any reader of modern Japanese fiction and indispensable to students of Dazai. Supplementing the main text is a detailed chronology of Dazai's life and works, a list of the stories and novels by Dazai that are available in English, an extensive bibliography (most of the entries are in Japanese, but English-language sources are also included), and a superb index. The book is beautifully designed; the dust jacket (featuring a striking photograph of Dazai), the decorated title page, the typography—all combine to make this an exceptionally attractive volume.

John Wilson

Sources for Further Study

Choice. XXIII, September, 1985, p. 125.
World Literature Today. LIX, Autumn, 1985, p. 658.

SAINTS AND STRANGERS

Author: Andrew Hudgins (1951-   )
Publisher: Houghton Mifflin Company (Boston). 82 pp. $13.95; paperback $6.95
Type of work: Poetry

In this latest volume in the Houghton Mifflin New Poetry Series, Andrew Hudgins makes his impressive debut

Of the best books of poems published in 1985, an unusual number are first collections. It is difficult to recall a year when so many young poets made such impressive beginnings. In *Saints and Strangers*, Andrew Hudgins demonstrates some fruitful ways of emerging distinctively from the metrical confusion of the past decade or so, and he presents a wide array of memorable characters and situations.

In several respects, Hudgins is reminiscent of the early James Wright. His lines are most often decasyllabic; his diction is usually that of casual speech; his subjects are often more appalling than the speaker seems to think they are. The important differences between Hudgins and the early Wright are that Hudgins uses rhyme much more sparingly than Wright did, and that Hudgins avoids the predictable phrasing that sometimes weakened Wright's poems of the late 1950's and early 1960's. Nevertheless, the vocal similarities are sometimes striking, as in the opening lines of "Claims":

> It's boys who find the bodies in the woods
> and mostly boys who put them there.
> At cowboys and Indians—a murder game—
> they found two naked, dead, and rotting girls
> covered with leaves and brush—not even dirt.

As Wright acknowledged, this is an older voice than his; he said he was trying in those early books to write "in the mode of Robinson and Frost," and the same might be said, with reservations, of Hudgins. He works in sentences and in lines, and draws often on the power of narrative to carry the reader forward. Yet he is also willing to launch into something like surrealism, when speakers turn some alienated perspective on everyday occurrences. Throughout the collection, Hudgins' mature voice falters very rarely; upon reading the title section of the book, which is placed at the end, the reader knows that he is in the presence of something genuine and scarce.

The collection is divided into four sections; the divisions between them, in terms of the differences among poems, are unusually sharp for a collection whose unifying voice and style are as strong as Hudgins'. The first section consists of fifteen poems, most of them personal, in the sense that the reader does not much consider whether the speaker and the poet are separate; the second section includes among its ten poems at least seven which are spoken by characters easily distinguished from the poet; the third section blurs the distinction; and the final section consists of eight poems, all spoken by a woman remembering how it was to grow up as the daughter of a revivalist preacher, to marry twice, to come at last to being her father's guardian. In conviction, scope of time, immediacy, and power, this sequence rivals many novels. As John Frederick Nims says in his introduction to the collection, "Here, even more than in the other poems, readers are likely to find something as close to nobility as we can hope to know amid the paradoxical strangeness of our lives."

The tension in the first section of the book seems to arise from the conflict between the solidity and assurance of the poems, and the precarious life they seem to reveal. The speaker is often being surprised by some odd or threatening intrusion, as when he wakes up one night to hear the sound of someone sawing. "Not wood. It's too soft for wood." What he sees through his bedroom window is a pair of poachers butchering a doe which they have hung from the speaker's swing set. He mentions his ignorance of how to stop them or turn them in, but it seems strange, nevertheless. In "The Choice the Driver Makes," the speaker walks along a highway at night, aware that rain makes him nearly invisible, and that "the drunks are out." Then:

> Two lights veer off the road and aim at me.
> For a long moment I stand judging them
> almost convinced they'll swerve away, then leap
> full-length into wet grass, wholeheartedly,
> and cannot tell what choice the driver makes.

Three other poems—"In the Night Garden," "Sentimental Dangers," and "On Sentimentality"—make direct or glancing reference to a fragile domestic situation. "In the Night Garden" seems at first to be concerned primarily with the speaker's relationship with his garden, as he watches the evening settle over it, and declares that he works the garden for what it produces. In three references to his wife, however, it is easy to see that something must be rising between them. Picking a green tomato, he thinks of slicing it the next day, frying it in batter, and sharing it with his wife; then he remembers: "But tomorrow/ is not one of the days/ she spends with me." Clearly, though, she is in the house—"Soon, I'll walk to the house// and sleep beside my sleeping/ wife"—but he will rise early the next morning, and go to the garden:

> I'll be here when
> she leaves for work. Her bare
>
> legs will flash like scissors
> in the sun. Or maybe
> I will stay in bed until
>
> she's gone. I love to sleep

> and I refuse to be the hero
> or the villain of my life.

"Sentimental Dangers" recalls a time when the speaker and his wife were poor, he was out of a job, and his wife brought a stray dog home from near the office where she typed. The speaker, before he realizes he must take the dog to the pound, comes to have a deeply sympathetic relationship with him:

> I'd sit outside all afternoon and talk
> to him, to the hard knowledge in his face
> that she'd leave me when I was well enough
> to be left.

Finally, "On Sentimentality" recounts a departure. It begins with a discussion of the film *Limelight*; a scene in which a woman screams when she sees that she has been left arouses in the speaker a feeling that this is "too much, sentimental." Yet after he has been left, and does not scream, he sees the film again:

> I felt his absence sinking into her
> and thought, *Because she isn't real*
> *she'll do everything I did and do it better.*
> She finally understands he's gone. She screams.
> We're real, we cannot do it for ourselves.

Though these are personal poems, it has to be stressed that there is no way of knowing whether they are autobiographical, nor is there any need to know that. The world portrayed in the first section of this book is real enough, and Hudgins is so skillful with variations on the dramatic monologue and the soliloquy that the reader could easily believe all these poems to be fictional. In the second and third sections of *Saints and Strangers*, there are poems spoken by Holofernes, John James Audubon, Sidney Lanier, and Jonathan Edwards, as well as by fictional characters, such as one of Solomon's concubines, based on historical or biblical situations; there are also third-person narratives of episodes in the lives of such figures as Sigmund Freud and Carl Jung and Saint Francis of Assisi, or the eunuch attendant of Daniel in Babylon.

Sometimes such poems may be rather slight, having the charm mostly of an oddity discovered and shared. "Audubon Examines a Bittern" is a prime example of this kind of poem; it recounts, in straightforward language, Audubon's experiment with a bittern delivered to his studio alive. After standing still for ninety minutes while the artist sketches it, the bird walks, at Audubon's urging, between two books on the table; Audubon gradually moves the books closer and closer together, and the bird continues to pass between them, even when the books are only an inch apart. Afterward, Audubon reports that upon killing and dissecting the bird, he found the breast to be two and one-quarter inches wide. "Bedamned if I know what to make of that," he says, and the poem ends.

Such resonance as poems like these may have is small, perhaps, but this whole collection reminds the reader that the world is full of welcome (and unwelcome) oddities. A more usual effect of the dramatic monologue is to give distance to emotional conclusions the poet may have reached; it is a way of treating one's own experience without writing confessional poetry. Hudgins's explorations of the power of love and physical attraction are extraordinarily convincing; his compassion for his characters and the assurance of his language are remarkably steady.

In "Saints and Strangers," the sequence of eight poems which concludes the collection, compassion and assurance are incredibly secure. In a few of the poems which appear earlier in the book, one might occasionally feel jarred by an unexpectedly short line, or by a strained rhyme; such moments are rare, and they seem not to occur at all in this final section. It is spoken by a woman named Elizabeth Marie, the daughter of an itinerant revivalist preacher; in the first poem, she recalls an episode that occurred when she was barely twelve; as she was playing the piano, two drunks interrupted the service and beat up her father. The last several lines of this poem demonstrate the astonishing ease with which Hudgins can let his speaker vacillate between emotions; in this case, extended quotation is necessary:

> Can you imagine what it means to be
> just barely twelve, a Christian and a girl,
> and see your father beaten to a pulp?
> Neither can I, God knows, and I was there
> in the hot tent, beneath the mildewed cloth,
> breathing the August, Alabama air,
> and I don't know what happened there, to me.
> I told this to my second husband, Jim.
> We were just dating then. I cried a lot.
> He said, *Hush, dear, at least your father got*
> *a chance to turn all four of his cheeks.*
> I laughed. I knew, right then, I was in love.
> But still I see that image of my father,
> his weight humped on his shoulders as he tried
> to stand, and I kept plunging through the song
> so I could watch my hands and not his face,
> which was rouged crimson with red clay and blood.

The sequence captures a few more episodes from early youth: the father's touchingly right corrective when he finds Elizabeth Marie and her friends skinny-dipping in a baptismal font; her first menstrual period; her theft of change from the offering plate to tip waitresses in truck stops. As she grows up, she marries twice, first to a handsome young man who could sing

"Amazing Grace" like Donald Duck, and then to the man referred to above. The final two poems, "Glossolalia" and "Saints and Strangers," bring the reader to the present; the father suffers a stroke and must live with his daughter's family. These poems, and thus the sequence as a whole, balance love, resignation to duty, and gentle humor with astonishing delicacy; the final few lines of "Saints and Strangers," in which Elizabeth Marie explains how she must sometimes bring her father's table graces to an end, is both heartbreaking and uplifting. It is hard to believe that so much happens in the relatively short space of three hundred lines; this sequence is one of the richest poetic narratives to have appeared in several years. Andrew Hudgins is a gifted poet, and his first book is a superb achievement.

Henry Taylor

Source for Further Study

Publishers Weekly. CCXXVIII, October 11, 1985, p. 62.

SELECTED LETTERS OF E. M. FORSTER
Volume II: 1921-1970

Author: E(dward) M(organ) Forster (1880-1970)
Edited by Mary Lago and P. N. Furbank
Publisher: The Belknap Press of Harvard University Press (Cambridge, Massachusetts). Illustrated. 365 pp. $20.00
Type of work: Letters
Time: 1921-1970
Locale: Primarily England

Volume II of Forster's correspondence provides a sampling from the last fifty years of his life and shows his wide range of interests

In 1955, E. M. Forster wrote to American literary critic Lionel Trilling to thank him for a book that contained references to the poet John Keats. "I have been reading in his letters ever since," Forster says. "He is almost the only great man I have ever wanted to be with." Half a century earlier, Forster had read the Keats letters and observed that the poet must have been nearly the best person in the world.

Such, apparently, is the power of letters. At least, such is the power they can command over sensitive men such as Forster, whose own letters are now available in part, edited by an American and an Englishman, the first a college professor, the other an author and lifelong friend of Forster himself.

This selection may not make one feel about Forster as he did about Keats. On the surface, this correspondence does not seem to emanate from an exciting man; much of it is the everyday exchange of a devoted son, a loyal friend, and a concerned liberal worried about government encroachment on individual liberty. There is, however, more to the collection than that.

Forster has always been something of an enigma for students of modern British literature, especially for those who know him only as a novelist. One familiar only with Forster's fiction may indeed wonder why anyone would want to publish a volume of his letters that focuses primarily on the period after 1924, the year in which *A Passage to India* was published. Though he lived for almost five decades more, Forster published no long fiction during the remainder of his lifetime; the final addition to his canon, *Maurice* (1971), was published posthumously.

Skepticism over the value of this effort must be tempered, however, by the corresponding natural inquisitiveness that students of literature have shown over the question of Forster's long silence. Why did he publish nothing else? No one reason may be forthcoming, but a perusal of these letters offers several intriguing possibilities and offers valuable insight into the life of a man who believed that one who devoted himself to a career of letters could in fact make a contribution to society as a whole.

Reading this selection of Forster's letters can help readers interested in the novelist understand why Forster stopped publishing fiction after the publication of *A Passage to India*. The first reason is offered by Forster himself. Writing in 1966 to American professor Wilfred Stone, who had recently completed a book-length study of his works, Forster says that it seems that "the fictional part of me dried up." As far as he could recall, Forster "did not think of writing either a novel or short stories" after 1924. Instead, he turned his talents to other forms of communication: pamphlets, essays, radio broadcasts, even an operatic adaptation of Herman Melville's *Billy Budd*.

Beneath the surface answer lies another one, however, and careful readers can discover a more plausible explanation for Forster's silence. Scattered references to short stories which Forster had written and was circulating among friends and repeated comments about the manuscript of the unpublished novel *Maurice* suggest that Forster had not abandoned interest in his own fiction. His problem was that the subject of his writings was not one which he wanted associated with his name in public: homosexuality. Long before he brought out *A Passage to India*, Forster had turned his considerable talents to a fictional exploration of the topic; in fact, *Maurice* was drafted before *A Passage to India*, as were several short stories that were never published and which are now lost. Homosexuality was a subject from which Forster could not divorce himself, because it was one that was a part of his own real life.

Forster was a homosexual from the time he was a young man, but he kept that fact from all but a few close friends. It is interesting to note that even in personal letters to those who may have known about his homosexuality Forster scarcely ever made overt reference to it. There are some cryptic allusions, but only rarely (in this collection, at least) does Forster write to or about another man in language that betrays his true feelings. "The happiest hours of my life will always be the short hours we can spend together in the flat," he writes to Bob Buckingham in 1933, and in 1939 he complains to him, "If you call living a full life seeing me once a fortnight, I don't." Nevertheless, only from the notes provided by the editors does one learn the extent of the relationship between them, a relationship that lasted half a century. To protect his family and his lovers from embarrassment, Forster made certain that he did nothing to reveal his secret, keeping that part of his life shielded from public view.

On the other hand, he was not reticent about his political preferences. A confirmed believer in liberal humanism, Forster waged a lifelong campaign to promote the liberal cause. Scores of letters show his concern for the plight of various minority groups: Indians, workers, Communists, and especially writers. One must recall that in the 1930's, writers with leftist political leanings were quickly branded Communists, and many openly professed affinity with Communism. While not a Communist himself, Forster sympathized with the movement insofar as it promoted the rights of individuals over the state. Many of the most spirited letters in this volume are ones in which Forster launches strident attacks on various government agencies, especially the British Broadcasting Company, for attempts to censor writers in some way.

To suggest that this collection be read simply to ferret out details of Forster's sex life or his political leanings, however, would be to do the volume serious injustice. *Selected Letters of E. M. Forster* presents its subject from many angles, each interesting in its own right. Until his mother's death in 1945, Forster corresponded regularly with her, writing from as far away as India and from as close as the London flat that he rented to escape from her (though he would never have admitted openly that he was doing so). He was a dutiful correspondent with other family members as well. Then there is the large collection of letters to close friends, many of whom are in their own right important figures in the realm of British letters: J. P. Ackerley, novelist and literary editor of *The Listener*; Leonard and Virginia Woolf; W. J. H. Sprott, professor of philosophy and lifelong friend; and Charles Mauron, translator of Forster's works into French. There are letters to other literary luminaries as well: A. E. Housman, Robert Graves, T. E. Lawrence, T. S. Eliot, Siegfried Sassoon, Christopher Isherwood, Arthur Koestler, and Constantin Cavafy.

Forster's letters to these people are not mere exchanges of pleasantry. Most reveal that Forster had a working relationship with them and was not simply kowtowing to them or trying to raise his own stock by trading with these well-known figures. On the contrary, Forster more often than not appears to be the figure whose attention is sought when the correspondence is anything more than a simple exchange between real friends. From these letters alone, readers can gain some sense of the intellectual camaraderie (or lack of it) that existed among writers, especially British writers, during the middle decades of the twentieth century.

Much is also revealed about Forster as a workman laboring at his professed trade, the furtherance of letters. Correspondence to and about Cavafy shows Forster's influence in introducing the Greek poet's works to the English-speaking world. Exchanges with T. E. Lawrence display the strong kinship of feeling the two men shared and explain why Forster was asked to write a life of Lawrence and to edit the latter's papers after his death (though Forster eventually turned down both projects).

In these exchanges, and in other correspondence, both with close friends and virtual strangers, Forster gives glimpses of the principles upon which his own creative and critical works are based. Scattered comments may help both scholars and general readers expand their understanding of Forster's aesthetic. Some examples are worth noting: Referring to modern authors' extreme attempts to achieve consistency in point of view, he complained to his old professor Goldsworthy Lowes Dickinson in 1922, "The studied ignorance of novelists grows wearisome." To philosopher Sprott he observed that "Art is a better guide" to life "than Science." Though a critic himself, he noted to one unidentified correspondent that "when one is actually writing novels," it is important to "trust one's own inclinations, instincts, and tastes" rather than to turn to others for advice or models. Disgruntled students of Russian literature will find in Forster a partial ally, who thought Leo Tolstoy's *Anna Karenina* (1875-1877) not very good and its characters "not really masterpieces." As a reader, Forster wanted his books to provide either "accurate information" or "artistic achievement," by which he meant "good character drawing, exciting narrative... and a witty or poetical outlook." This sanguine, commonsense approach allowed Forster to appreciate a wide variety of writings, and his letters are filled with studied praise for many works that have only recently begun to receive critical attention. In the same vein, he was quick to debunk works that he thought were shams, even if they were in public favor; not surprisingly, most of these have fallen from grace, so to speak—evidence of Forster's ability to spot literature of lasting worth.

The impression one gets from a collection of letters is often dependent on the expertise of the editors in selecting and annotating materials for the volume. Perhaps the professional scholar will find fault with this offering. The letters are arranged chronologically, and there are "gaps"—in some cases, almost a year is skipped. The general reader will probably not be bothered by details such as this; instead, he will find the second volume of *Selected Letters of E. M. Forster* a book that illuminates the life of the novelist in many ways. The range of correspondents and of subjects is refreshing and entertaining: Forster appears as a "rounded" individual, not simply as a stuffy intellectual or a radical reformer, but both, and as a concerned son, devoted lover, and constant and loyal friend as well. Throughout the volume, one sees a steady balance between the public and private lives. Additionally, editors Mary Lago and P. N. Furbank have provided extensive annotations and notes. Correspondents and people mentioned in the letters are identified fully. Even the most cryptic allusions are traced and explained. On rare occasions readers may find an unidentified reference, but on the whole the notes provide as much information as is needed to fill out the background of every letter included in the book.

A volume of letters is not a biography, but for many readers some narrative about the subject is required to help establish a context for the individual letters. Furbank and Lago have solved the problem by dividing this collection into large chronological sections and including several short summaries of the major events in Forster's life. What is not present is extensive analysis of the individual entries: No attempt is made to move from what Forster says to what he means or to tell readers how they should judge the man from what he says in his letters. That seems to be appropriate. After all, one reads these letters to learn at first-hand something of the intriguing, complex figure who wrote them. The experience one gains from reading *Selected Letters of E. M. Forster* fulfills that expectation.

Laurence W. Mazzeno

Sources for Further Study

American Libraries. XVI, May, 1985, p. 282.
The Atlantic. CCLV, January, 1985, p. 94.
Choice. XXIII, November, 1985, p. 446.
Kirkus Reviews. LII, November 1, 1984, p. 1033.
The London Review of Books. VII, June 20, 1985, p. 9.
The New York Review of Books. XXXII, August 15, 1985, p. 19.
The New York Times Book Review. XC, May 5, 1985, p. 12.
Publishers Weekly. CCXXVI, December 14, 1984, p. 46.
Times Literary Supplement. May 24, 1985, p. 569.
Washington Post Book World. XV, May 26, 1985, p. 5.

SELECTED POEMS

Author: John Ashbery (1927-   )
Publisher: The Viking Press (New York). 349 pp. $22.95
Type of work: Poetry

A representation of thirty years' published work by a poet whose poems have proven difficult but rewarding to the attentive reader

For thirty years, John Ashbery has been hailed as a poet of substance whose each new book has been heralded with enthusiasm and awards. *Selected Poems* (the author is the selector) gathers representative poems from books ranging from *Some Trees* (1956), a Yale Series of Younger Poets choice, through the acclaimed *The Tennis Court Oath* (1962) and the Pulitzer Prize-winning *Self-Portrait in a Convex Mirror* (1975) to his last previous volume, *A Wave* (1984).

Many readers who delve bravely into the intricacies of modern poetry consider Ashbery among the most difficult of post-World War II poets, and anyone plumbing this volume will quickly sense how intimidating Ashbery can be. Although he does not associate himself with the school of poets that despises—or affects to despise—communication, he has been accused, even by admirers, of refusing to write English. His grammar is unconventional in a way that challenges the perspicacity of linguistically oriented critics.

Not surprisingly, his work has become the subject of book-length studies, including one by David Shapiro with the promising title *John Ashbery: An Introduction to His Poetry* (1979), but students are likely to find much of Shapiro's criticism as intimidating as the poetry. Shapiro often says or implies that one should not expect an answer to a question such as what does it mean? In the reader who demands "sense," Ashbery is likely to provoke disappointment, even exasperation. Nor can he be taken in at a gallop: "Modern poetry is a series of insults to the speeding reader," Shapiro observes wryly. This critic finds Ashbery's poetry to be autonomous and antireferential. One is as likely to encounter deliberate incoherence as coherence. Shapiro proceeds to analyze the poetry with great subtlety and with a determination to see the poetry in its own terms, for he too is a poet, but his very resolve to do justice to Ashbery can be bewildering. The reader must be prepared for such utterances as this concluding sentence in the chapter on Ashbery's early work: "Never again is limpidity employed so continuously concerning the themes of discontinuity and opacity."

Perhaps the best introduction to Ashbery's poetry, after all, is this new selection of 138 poems (some of them extracts from long poems and some of them prose meditations) from ten earlier books. Though each of Ashbery's books is brilliant in itself, *Selected Poems* is more than the sum of its parts, as it in fact constitutes the record of an inquiring mind's lifelong quest for the unknowable, Wallace Stevens' "poem of the act of the mind," in a world even less intelligible than that of a half century ago. One need not be a philosopher to appreciate the epistemological problems of modern philosophy or the importance that a poet such as Ashbery attaches to the pursuit of truth when truth itself seems fragmented, elusive, perhaps even illusory.

Samuel Beckett has said that "words are all we have," and, like Beckett's, Ashbery's language is brilliant and rich enough to carry the reader over the difficulties of the meaning. Ashbery is overwhelmed by the desire to know and to share his self-discovery, so both the desire and the discovery (or the void created where the desire preponderates) are the essence of a grammar that exists for itself.

An early poem, "The Grapevine," embodies the question of knowing. The basis of knowledge. "Of who we and all they are/ You all now know," is small compared to the question:

> But you know
> After they began to find us out we grew
> Before they died thinking us the causes
>
> Of their acts.

Then there is the crucial discovery. "But things get darker as we move/ To ask them:" So what began as a recognition of truth ends in a complex question: "Whom must we get to know/ To die, so you live and we know?"

A discovery does not put an end to the question, as there is always the further question and the further discovery. The early volume *Some Trees* already illustrates Ashbery's attempt to define reality—and also the early influences, one of the strongest being Wallace Stevens. Thus in "Le Livre est sur la table":

> We can only imagine a world in which a woman
> Walks and wears her hair and knows
> All that she does not know. Yet we know
>
> What her breasts are. And we give fullness
> To the dream

But when the woman leaves and goes into the house,

> Are there
> Collisions, communications on the shore
>
> Or did all secrets vanish when
> The woman left?

Here is the question of Stevens' "Martial Cadenza": "What had this star to do with the world it lit?" Does the poet concern himself with the thing itself or with that which it symbolizes?

Walt Whitman pervades another early poem, "As You Know."

> Goodbye, old teacher, we must travel on, not to a better land, perhaps,
> But to the England of the sonnets, Paris, Colombia, and Switzerland
> And all the places with names, that we wish to visit—
> Strasbourg, Albania,
> The coast of Holland, Madrid, Singapore, Naples, Salonika, Liberia,
>   and Turkey.

In its flexible blend of long and short lines, its fondness for catalogs of names, its folksy intimacy, its restless ambition to be on the move, the poem is in the tradition of Whitman. Ashbery does not, however, aspire to Whitman's earth and people but rather "to the nearest star," leaving to the earthbound "the endless, muggy night."

It is not Whitman's ambulatory movement but T. S. Eliot's episodic motion that is most useful to the point-by-point analysis characteristic of Ashbery's work from the beginning. There will be an affirmation or a denial, followed by another, and another, building progressively to a unified whole. Each image or situation is an episode representing an underlying reality. The relation between situation and definition is what is crucial in his poems. Where that relationship becomes very difficult to ascertain, Ashbery has been called a surrealist poet. His place, however, is probably between Eliot, with his episodic structure, and the Surrealists, with their language floating free of underlying reality. The key is the extent to which language substitutes for episode. Ashbery's language strikes the ear and eye with an independence of its own, but his episodes are not lost on the alert reader. Even when the total poem eludes precise understanding, it is possible to appreciate the episodes that make up the whole.

"The Skaters," a long poem from Ashbery's 1966 book *Rivers and Mountains* exemplifies well his penchant for telling episodes, even though some are only a line or two. Only an extract appears in *Selected Poems*, but it is sufficient to display the Eliot technique—though in a personal mode that is far from Eliot's way of extinguishing personality. From sandbars to apples to constellations, the poet skates along, observing, though scarcely pausing over, what comes into view, for like a skater, this poet maintains his balance by advancing. No other modern poet can have realized better than Ashbery on this poetic journey "the pleasurable activity of mind excited by the attractions of the journey itself," as Samuel Taylor Coleridge expressed it.

Ashbery's search for meaning on his journeys is a search for order that has a long history. He employs the vocabulary of today; the questions that he asks are perennial. Steven P. Schultz has suggested in his essay on Ashbery in *Critical Survey of Poetry: English Language Series* (1982) that a reader can begin anywhere in his poetry simply because it is constantly moving and not particularly concerned with arriving. Perhaps his long prose poem "The System," originally part of *Three Poems* (1972), is as good a place as any. Standing close to the middle of the current volume, this thirty-eight-page meditation is couched in language as beautiful and suggestive as that of his poetry—interestingly, another trait Ashbery shares with Whitman. It also sets forth many of the ideas that are reiterated both before and after it.

Ashbery avers that he is searching for an order that will make his days part of a unified life. At the beginning of a new year, he is beginning again also, and through a series of up-and-down discoveries he achieves—almost—an equilibrium. The desired end is nearly in sight and always just around the corner. There is a flame of light followed by a shadow: a building to a crescendo and a slow denouement, a vacillation that intermittently brings comfort to his tired soul. He discovers two kinds of happiness, one being the idealized version of the other. He is at one stage positive toward life: "it is certain now that these two ways [of happiness] are the same, that we *have* them both, the risk and the security, merely through being human creatures subject to the vicissitudes of time, our earthly lot." Three pages later, the reader is plunged "into a numbing despair and blankness. The whole world seems dyed the same melancholy hue. Nothing in it can arouse your feelings. Even the sun seems dead." Yet the mood becomes upbeat as the soul is again reassured. There follows a fine disquisition on the importance of history for the full realization of the present. The meditation ends on the prospect of a "pragmatic and kinetic future."

Ashbery need not be read in any particular sequence. Though his poetry has changed through the years, his poetic personality has remained remarkably constant, and his later books have not obscured his earlier ones. Several poems in *Some Trees*, the first book represented in the volume under consideration, remain popular with his readers. *Three Poems*, in which he mapped so much of his favorite territory, is in many respects central. *Self-Portrait in a Convex Mirror* has doubtless received the most acclaim. *A Wave* has already won adherents; in its long title poem (the final one in *Selected Poems*), he writes:

> One idea is enough to organize a life and project it
> Into unusual but viable forms, but many ideas merely
> Lead one thither into a morass of their own good intentions.

No, Ashbery is not advocating monomania here, for a "morass" is not necessarily an evil thing—if there is no necessity of tarrying too long. As he adds a few lines later, "It's fun to scratch around/ And maybe come up with something."

This enthusiasm for "scratching around" remains strong in Ashbery, who, like Samuel Beckett, pursues the unexplainable with unfailing good humor and confronts the possibility—the likelihood—of meaninglessness with undiminished élan. In this respect he is a writer not simply of, but for, today's world, though his reputation for difficulty has probably diverted too many readers from giving him more than a rapid glance. Like most twentieth century poets, Ashbery needs to be read at length, his vision of the world explored with some thoroughness, before he can be properly appreciated. More than most of his contemporaries, he will repay the time and effort spent in the endeavor.

Robert P. Ellis

Sources for Further Study

The New York Times Book Review. XC, December 29, 1985, p. 10.
Publishers Weekly. CCXXVIII, November 15, 1985, p. 50.
World Literature Today. CCXXVIII, November 15, 1985, p. 50.

SELECTED SHORT STORIES OF PADRAIC COLUM

Author: Padraic Colum (1881-1972)
Edited, with an introduction, by Sanford Sternlicht
Publisher: Syracuse University Press (Syracuse, New York). 130 pp. $19.95
Type of work: Short stories
Time: The late nineteenth and early twentieth centuries
Locale: Primarily rural Southern Ireland

Most of these thirteen stories by a minor short-story writer of the Irish Literary Revival focus on Irish peasant life

Padraic Colum is best known as a dramatist who was influential in the founding of the Irish National Theatre Society and the Abbey Theatre in the early twentieth century, the author of such realistic plays as *The Land* (1905) and *Thomas Muskerry* (1910), both dealing with the world of the peasant the small farmer. He is also recognized as a poet of the period known as the Irish Literary Renaissance and, after coming to the United States, as a writer of children's literature, having authored more than twenty-five children's books primarily about folklore and mythology. He is not, however, well-known as a short-story writer. Nor does Colum necessarily deserve such recognition, for he wrote only about thirty adult short fictions, of uneven quality; the thirteen reprinted here represent his best work in that genre, which his friend James Joyce pioneered as a distinctly modern form in the epoch-making collection *Dubliners* (1914).

Frank O'Connor, also a contemporary of Colum, and, like his countrymen Joyce, George Moore, and Seán O'Faoláin, a master of the short-story form, recounts an anecdote in *A Short History of Irish Literature* (1967), which perhaps explains why Colum failed in the form in which certain of his colleagues succeeded. O'Connor states that one night he was complaining to Æ (George William Russell), one of the leading founders of the Irish Literary Revival, of his indigestion. Æ roared with laughter and said, "Every serious Irish writer has a pain in his belly. Yeats has a pain in his belly; Joyce has a terrible pain in his belly; now you have a pain in your belly. Padraic Colum is the only Irish writer who never had a pain at all."

Indeed, there is little pain in these thirteen slight stories; there is much whimsy, nostalgia, and affection for what Colum sees as the dignity of Irish peasant life—but not the sense of displacement, grotesqueness, and hypocrisy that dominates the stories of Joyce. Nor do Colum's stories have what O'Connor has called, in his classic study of the short story, *The Lonely Voice* 1963), that sense of loneliness typified by Blaise Pascal's statement, "The eternal silence of those infinite spaces terrifies me," which characterizes the short-story form at its most intense and artistic. The short story is an art form, according to O'Connor, which is as elaborate, pure, and patterned as the sonnet.

Only a few of Colum's stories have the delicate restraint associated with the short stories of Joyce; one such piece is "Eilis: A Woman's Story," which is, as is typical of Colum, a story within a story told by an eighty-year-old woman, Eilis, who is of the "old culture" and who tells of contemporary events as if they were folktales. There is no real plot here, merely the poignant experience from Eilis' own past when she forsook the chance to marry Shaun Gorman, whom she loved, for Michael Conroy, the man whom her father arranged for her to marry. When she goes in secret to meet Gorman and comes to a ditch that separates his fields from her father's, her knees fail her and she cannot pass; thus, out of loyalty, or perhaps simply passivity, Eilis accepts Conroy, a good man, a man, whom she says, "wouldn't let me break a sod of turf across my knee, he took such care of me." As is typical of the Chekhovian notion of the modern short story, the piece is less a dramatic tale than it is the sensitive evocation of "a woman's story," similar to the stories about quiet and enclosed women in *Dubliners*.

More typical of the storytelling convention of which Colum makes use are such fairy-tale forms as "The Peacocks of Baron's Hall" and "The Slopes of Tara." "The Peacocks of Baron's Hall" is told in the true folklore tradition by an old huntsman as a tale within a tale; the motivation for its telling is to explain, in the manner of folklore, why anyone who lives in Baron's Hall must keep the peacocks that are hatched there on the estate. The central and almost mythical figures of the tale are the Little Baron and his sister Lady Sabrina, both no taller than a child of twelve. The villains of the piece are the uncles of the two, who are greedy for the estate and gradually drive them out to live in a small lodge nearby. The fairy-tale beauty of the estate becomes destroyed by the heirs of the greedy uncles, and the Little Baron and his sister die, but the peacocks remain as the sole reminder of a magical world of Irish folklore that no longer exists—the world of fairy itself.

"The Slopes of Tara" is a curious combination of the realistic and the fairy tale; Colum attempts to portray the young protagonist Shaun, "a survival from a vanished population," as caught in a kind of enchantment. Shaun dreams the folklore legend of a nobleman who built a turret for a beautiful young woman. In this highly stylized story, Shaun, displaced and drifting, living a life of lonely dreams, goes to the house of a female friend, who is then visited by a beautiful young woman he has seen earlier—a visionary girl from whom he recovers a sense of reality only when he turns away from her. Fancying her to be the beautiful lady of his dreams for whom the nobleman built the turret, Shaun is haunted by the experience. This is an elliptical story in the fairy-tale tradition—more a lyric meditation than a story, for it evokes life lived in the lost world of dream and imagination. It is perhaps stories such as these that suggest why Irish writers of the turn of the century found the short story such a natural form, for it has always remained close to the folktale from which it originated, and, indeed, the Irish imagination, regardless of the sophistication of Joyce's stories, somehow still remains close to the legendary world of fairy tales.

Much simpler are the comic stories, such as "The Little Pension," which takes place on the day that John Greggins goes to pick up his army pension check at the town post office. In gratitude to the government, he hires a professional letter writer to compose a formal letter of appreciation for him. On the way home, full of the high-sounding tone of the letter, he addresses some idlers about the bridge that he is crossing: "think of them that in the old, ancient days raised it in majesty and in glory to be a pattern and a credit to their posterity." Mocking him by tossing a coin at his feet, the idlers are each rapped on the head for their disrespect, and as a result John Greggins is put in jail for starting a fight. The next day, chastened, he goes home, and the "silence was upon him like unto the silence beyond the trees and hedges."

"Marcus of Clooney" is a bit of Irish nonsense and blather, truly much ado about nothing, in which a young man goes to elaborate lengths to be introduced to a young girl, only to have his plans foiled by his own timidity and by Marcus O'Driscoll's inconsequential chatter about whether the young man should carry a walking stick. When his chance to meet the young woman has been missed, he storms off, charging that fellows such as Marcus O'Driscoll have made "the country the way it is."

"Catherine Mulamphy and the Man from the North" combines folktale conventions with turn-of-the-century Irish peasant values to create another bit of comic nonsense. The chief characters are Martin Mulamphy, his wife, Catherine, and Neil, a Northerner who strikes a bargain with Martin to purchase Catherine. The story is filled with several small comic bits, such as the way Martin deals with the lamentable fact that he has no watch: He ties the lid of a small canister to his watch chain and puts it in his pocket, for appearance is everything to Martin. Neil gives Martin money for his wife as a result of an agreement that he will pick her up in one year and a day. When the time comes, however, Martin changes his mind and returns the money, but not until besting the Northerner in a fight. The story ends with Catherine angry at her husband, not for trying to sell her but because she has discovered that her ring, which Martin said was gold, is really only brass.

Colum's stories are widely uneven in quality and thematic significance. They range from such satisfying, illustrative tales as "The Flute Player's Story," which delicately recounts an experience that satirizes the mysterious "passion of women," to such vaguely unsatisfying episodes as "Marriage," which deals with a young woman's efforts to raise an adequate dowry for her husband-to-be. Moreover, whereas a story such as "Pilgrimage Home" is an ambitious attempt to focus on the gradual loss of the old, simple life and the realization of modern disorder, a piece such as "Land Hunger" is a quite simple tale of a father's desire to gain more land for his son's inheritance.

In addition to the eleven peasant stories, the collection also contains two "Dublin stories," which, although they are probably included because they seem to share the satiric worldview of Joyce's more famous collection, are not as effective as the simple and often-lyric meditations and tales of the folk. "A Dublin Day" focuses on a minor poet, Mortimer O'Looney, who sets out to sell an unused burial plot that he owns. He becomes so wrapped up in a poem that he is composing, however, that he forgets that he had earlier received a letter from the United Cemeteries Office informing him that the association has been dissolved and that no further claims on the plot can be liquidated. This story and the other Dublin story, "Three Men," might be satires of Dublin literary aspiration and the pseudointellectual life there, but they come nowhere near to equaling the biting criticism of that sterile and provincial city found in the stories of Joyce.

Sanford Sternlicht, in his long introduction to this slim volume, makes a valiant effort to justify Colum's short stories, claiming that Colum belongs in the tradition of George Moore's *The Untilled Field* (1903), which encouraged young Irish writers to write about Irish life in clear and direct language. The introduction reads like a traditional critical analysis of the stories, pointing out the various symbolic motifs that Colum uses and emphasizing his central theme of the nobility of the Irish peasant and their love of their land, their history, and their cultural tradition. Sternlicht claims that Colum's stories have received almost no critical attention, and the present book represents the first effort to bring his short fiction to the attention of the general reader.

Yet, except for those people who are particularly interested in turn-of-the-century Irish life or those who are academically interested in Irish literary culture (the book is one in a series of Irish Studies published by Syracuse University Press), it is doubtful that these stories will arouse great interest. The modern short story received an important impetus from such Irish writers as George Moore and James Joyce—an impetus that has been sustained by such others as Frank O'Connor, Séan O'Faoláin, and Liam O'Flaherty. Padraic Colum seems destined to remain a minor light among these Irish greats, if for no other reason, than, as Æ once observed, he has no real pain in his belly.

Charles E. May

Sources for Further Study

Choice. XXII, May, 1985, p. 1330.
The New York Times Book Review. XC, February 24, 1985, p. 26.
The New Yorker. LXI, April 1, 1985, p. 112.
Publishers Weekly. CCXXVI, November 30, 1984, p. 82.
Times Literary Supplement. September 6, 1985, p. 980.

THE SEVEN DAY CIRCLE
The History and Meaning of the Week

Author: Eviatar Zerubavel
Publisher: The Free Press (New York). Illustrated. 206 pp. $16.95
Type of work: Sociology of time

Zerubavel traces the history of the seven-day week from its beginnings in the ancient Middle East and examines some of the effects which this artificial scheme has had on modern man

One of the most pervasive features of late twentieth century American life is the emphasis on greater and greater control of smaller and smaller units of time. Elaborate daily planners are no longer the exclusive province of high-level executives. Best-selling books feature titles such as *The One-Minute Manager*, and advertising agencies are perfecting the fifteen-second television commercial.

This pervasive time-consciousness is one of the subjects of a new field of study, the sociology of time—the specialty of Eviatar Zerubavel, who excels at making the insights of his scholarship accessible to the general reader. While Zerubavel's first book, *Patterns of Time in Hospital Life* (1979), was narrow in focus, his second book, *Hidden Rhythms: Schedules and Calendars in Social Life* (1981), treated such topics as the nature of temporal regularity, private time and public time, and the origin of the schedule, which can be traced to medieval Benedictine monasteries. *Hidden Rhythms* is a fascinating book, rich in implications, and with his third book, *The Seven Day Circle: The History and Meaning of the Week*, Zerubavel has produced a worthy sequel.

The Seven Day Circle began, Zerubavel says, in answer to a question posed by his three-and-a-half-year-old daughter: "Daddy, what's Thursday?" In answering this question, Zerubavel explores the origins of the seven-day week and its sociological and psychological implications.

The very concept of the week, apparently universal, represents a revolutionary view of time. The day is tied to the alternation of light and dark. The month and year reflect the lunar and solar cycles respectively. All these measurements of time are thus tied to the rhythms of nature. The week, on the other hand, is artificial, a man-made construct created to break away from those natural patterns. Zerubavel points out that for many social activities, the day is too short an interval and the month too long—for market days, to cite one example. The solution has been some form of the week, a recurring cycle of time varying in length from five to twenty days.

The seven-day week of the Western world arose from two sources. The first is the Old Testament version of Creation, in which God made the world in six days and rested on the seventh. The Jewish Sabbath commemorating the Creation thus recurred every seventh day, and the six days in between were numbered to show their distance from the previous Sabbath: First

Day, Second Day, and so on, a system still used by Jews and Quakers and analogous to the way African tribes measure the intervals between regularly recurring market days.

The second origin of the week supplied the standard names of the days. The ancients knew of seven planets—wandering bodies as opposed to the fixed stars: Saturn, Jupiter, Mars, the Sun, Venus, Mercury, the Moon. According to Babylonian astronomy, each hour of each day was governed by one of these planets, and the ruler of the first hour was called the regent of that day. If Saturn ruled the first hour and hence was regent of that day, the Sun would rule the twenty-fifth hour, or the first hour of the next day. The Moon would then be regent of the third day, Mars of the fourth, Mercury of the fifth, Jupiter the sixth, and Venus the seventh. The eighth day would belong to Saturn, and the cycle would begin again. In the cases of Sunday and Monday, the English-speaking world has retained the Babylonian symbols; for the other planets, it has substituted Nordic deities corresponding to the planets (for example, Thor for Jupiter—Thursday—and Fria for Venus—Friday). Although the Jewish and Babylonian systems arose independently, the conquests of Alexander and the Caesars and the spread of Christianity led to a fusion, as well as the diffusion of the two throughout the known world.

Once established, the seven-day week could serve as a target for groups seeking to distinguish themselves through what Zerubavel calls "calendrical contrast." Christians separated themselves from Jews by switching the Sabbath to Sunday; Moslems marked their break from the other two major Middle-Eastern religions by celebrating their Sabbath on Friday. These breaks nevertheless retained the seven-day week and, oddly, even its Jewish order, Sunday still beginning the week and Saturday ending it.

More dramatic were the efforts of the French and Russian revolutions to abolish the traditional system for a more "rational" one. In 1793, the French National Convention substituted a metrical calendar—ten-day weeks, with each day divided into ten hours of one hundred minutes composed of one hundred seconds. The new calendar of *décades* would abolish Sundays, substituting decadal holidays celebrating the state for the previous hebdomadal religious rituals. The experiment lasted, ironically, ten years.

Even shorter lived was the Soviet effort in 1929 to institute a five-day week. Again a prime target of the reform was the Church, since Sunday would cease to be a national day of rest. According to the Soviet scheme, every worker would have a vacation every fifth day, but on any given day 80 percent of the work force would be at their benches or desks, while 20 percent would have the day off. Another goal of the reform—aside from once more signaling a break with the past—was weakening family ties, since one spouse was likely to be at work and the children in school while the other spouse had the day off. Family gatherings would thus be virtually impossible. This *nepreryvka* lasted two years.

Even the *décade* and the *nepreryvka* testify to the need for regular, recurring cycles longer than the day but shorter than the month. No society, however primitive, has failed to adopt some form of the week, and no society, however revolutionary, has attempted to randomize or completely abolish it. In Western cultures, the seven-day week persists despite seeming inconveniences. Workers who are paid every Friday will receive four paychecks some months, five in others. Holidays pegged to a fixed day such as Monday—as more and more are—have no fixed date, so that one no longer remembers when George Washington's birthday will be celebrated from year to year, and only a mathematical genius can calculate when Easter, tied to Sunday, will fall. Hospitals do not distinguish between Monday and Friday for staffing; both are treated as workdays, even through Monday is the busiest of the week, Friday among the slowest.

That Monday is the busiest day for hospital emergency rooms and has the highest suicide rate is the consequence of the psychological values attached to the various days of the week. Weekends are for socializing, so one feels worse about spending a Saturday night alone than a Thursday night. Even with added pay, less traffic to fight, less work to do, and less supervision, people are reluctant to go into the office on a Saturday or Sunday. Working on Friday, though, seems almost fun; at least Friday has the lowest absentee rate. What quality (and quantity) of work gets done that day is a different question.

Alexander Pope observed that the good writer makes the familiar seem new and the new seem familiar. Nothing can be more familiar than the week—even children recognize Sunday or Monday before they understand the more "natural" months. Yet Zerubavel makes it new, giving insights into the subtle ways the seven-day cycle affects our lives.

Despite the wealth of information in the book and the extensive research suggested by the eighteen pages of bibliography and thirty of notes, Zerubavel leaves certain questions unanswered. The seven-day cycle is largely irrelevant to agricultural and hunter-gatherer societies: Cows must be milked twice a day, Sabbath or weekday; horses must be fed no matter which planet is regent. Why, then, did ancient societies universally adopt this system? Why did it become so popular? Why does it retain its hold on a secular, postindustrial world? With the growth of service industries operating seven days a week, does it show signs of evolution or collapse? *The Seven Day Circle* fulfills its promise of telling how the week began and what it means culturally and psychologically. Can Zerubavel or another writer build upon that knowledge to answer these still unresolved questions? Zerubavel has laid an elegant and provocative foundation for such further investigations.

Joseph Rosenblum

Sources for Further Study

Library Journal. CX, June 15, 1985, p. 69.
Los Angeles Times Book Review. September 15, 1985, p. 1.
The New York Times Book Review. XC, June 23, 1985, p. 12.
Psychology Today. XIX, September, 1985, p. 78.
The Village Voice. September 12, 1985, p. 78.
Vogue. CLXXV, June, 1985, p. 156.
The Wall Street Journal. CCVI, July 30, 1985, p. 28.

SHAH OF SHAHS

Author: Ryszard Kapuściński
Translated from the Polish by William R. Brand and Katarzyna Mroczkowska-Brand
Publisher: Harcourt Brace Jovanovich (San Diego, California). 152 pp. $12.95
Type of work: Political commentary
Time: 1970-1980
Locale: Iran

   A firsthand account of the revolutionary movement that purged the Shah from power

> *Principal personages:*
> SHAH MOHAMMED REZA PAHLAVI, the last Shah of Iran
> AYATOLLAH KHOMEINI, a Shiite holy man and leader of the opposition against the Shah

In *Shah of Shahs* (published in Poland in 1982 as *Szachinszach*), Ryszard Kapuściński unfolds a rich story which merges factual reporting with his keen impressions and reflections. The book is both engrossing and revelatory and offers a highly personal portrait of the psychological condition of a country in the throes of revolution. The captivating volume is more an impressionistic commentary than a history of the causes and consequences of the Shah's overthrow and the Ayatollah Khomeini's ascendancy to power. The author appeals to his readers' imagination rather than to their intellect and makes his points with images rather than with tightly structured ranks of facts and analysis. In some respects, reading the book is like watching a potpourri of news broadcasts. The narrative jumps from place to place and from episode to episode with no seeming respect for standard historical or even literary conventions. Nevertheless, the text is as absorbing as it is acrobatic—a work of sublime creativity which provides a brilliant firsthand account of the Islamic upheaval that toppled the Shah.

   The book illustrates at many points how the extreme oil-derived wealth of Iran corrupted the Shah's social vision. Oil kindles extraordinary emotions of strength, wealth, and power among Mideastern leaders. To possess and control the fortune wrought by this resource seems to evoke an almost mystical conviction that a divine power has elevated a nation above others, electing it as its favorite. For the Shah and his minions, oil created the illusion of a paradisiacal life without work or effort. The great oil resources of Iran corrupted its leadership into believing that social progress and economic stability could be achieved through the vagaries of fortune rather than through sweat, anguish, and hard work.

   For Iran's rulers, one of oil's most alluring qualities was that it strengthened their authority; from their point of view, oil caused few social problems because it engendered neither a numerous proletariat nor a sizable bourgeoisie to challenge the status quo. The government, freed from pressures to split the profits with anyone, could spend the wealth according to its own ideas and desires. The Shah as well as governmental ministers became lords of energy, publicly and privately exhibiting their hubris and power. It seemed as though Iran were an elect nation, an attitude reenforced by the fact that Islam was enjoying a period of expansion as new crowds of faithful embraced the religion.

Inevitably, the Shah's grandiose but short-sighted ambition to build the "Great Civilization" in Iran was doomed to failure. From his isolated palace, the leader issued hundreds of decisions in the early 1970's that convulsed his homeland and set the stage for his overthrow a decade later. He doubled domestic investment, began importing modern technology, and created the third most advanced army in the world. He built atomic power plants, electronics factories, steel mills, and great industrial complexes. Iran became a sales mecca, and the presidents of multinational corporations, directors of great conglomerates, and lesser corporate sales representatives flocked to this flood tide of spending. For a time, it seemed that Iran was moving along a smooth current of development, but shoals and eddies began to appear. Billions of dollars were spent making purchases, and ships full of merchandise began steaming toward Iran from all the continents. When they reached the Persian Gulf, however, the country's small, obsolete ports proved unable to handle the mass of cargo. Several hundred ships backed up at sea and remained unloaded for up to six months. These delays forced Iran to pay nearly $1 billion annually to shipping companies.

Somehow the fleet gradually unloaded, but there were no warehouses to store the mass of goods. Millions of tons of cargo had to be stockpiled in the open and subjected to unrelenting tropical heat. Half of it, consisting of perishable foodstuffs and chemicals, was thrown away. The remainder needed to be transported to the country's interior, but, alas, there were few trucks, trailers, and other forms of transport. Two thousand tractor-trailers were accordingly ordered from Europe, but as there were not enough drivers, hundreds of people had to be flown in from Korea. When the goods finally began to move, the Koreans learned that Iranian drivers were earning higher salaries than they, and so they quit. Scores of trucks, unused to this day, still sit along the Bander Abbas-Teheran highway.

With time and the assistance of foreign freight companies, the machines purchased abroad finally arrived at their appointed destinations. No engineers or technicians, however, were available to build, operate, and maintain factories. From a logical point of view, the designer of a Great Civilization should have laid a foundation by training cadres of experts to form a native intelligentsia; unfortunately, the Shah and his advisers feared creating a freethinking university population that would challenge the status quo. Hence, the monarch kept the majority of his students far from home. By the late 1970's, more than a hundred thousand young Iranians were studying in Europe and America. The policy, which cost much more than it would have to create national universities, bled the nation of its best and brightest, for the majority of these young people never returned. More Iranian doctors currently practice in San Francisco and Hamburg than in Tabriz or Mashhad. They would not come home, even for the generous salaries the Shah offered. They feared the Savak (the Shah's security-and-intelligence organization) and did not want to live under the oppressive dictatorship that limited basic human freedoms. An Iranian at home could not read the books of his country's best writers (because they were only published abroad), could not view the films of its best directors (because they were not allowed to be shown in Iran), and could not ponder the ideas of its intellectuals (because they were condemned to silence). By destroying the nation's intelligentsia and culture, the Shah left a vacuous wasteland that was eventually filled by fanatic Muslims.

One of Kapuściński's best insights is his analysis of the impact of the Shah's Great Civilization upon the nation's psyche. In order to fulfill his vision, the Shah needed at least seven hundred thousand experts in various fields; and the only immediate option was to import them. Security considerations were an important part of this decision, because foreigners—concerned about doing their jobs, making money, and getting home—would refrain from organizing plots and rebellions or contending against the Savak. Tens of thousands of experts began to arrive from all over the world and to erode the nation's self-confidence. This army of Americans, Europeans, and Asians, by the very strength of its technical expertise, began to dominate the country and evoke an inferiority complex among the Iranians. There is an element of the Iranian national character which retards an individual's ability to admit that he cannot do something; such an admission constitutes personal shame and a loss of face. Large segments of the population grew restive, depressed, and finally began to hate the Shah, as it became clear that foreigners were the key elements of his social vision. Thus, the Great Civilization was seen by many as a great national humiliation.

Kapuściński is perhaps at his best when illustrating how the Shah's emphasis on militarization helped sow the seeds of his downfall. Although preoccupied with modernizing the nation, his true hobby and real passion was the army. It constituted the main prop of the throne, and, as years passed, it increasingly became its sole support. For much of the Shah's reign, the army was primarily an instrument of domestic terror, a kind of police that lived in barracks. For this reason, the nation looked upon further military buildup with fear, realizing that the Shah was swinging an ever thicker and more painful whip that fell heavily across the backs of the people. The Shah loved his uniforms and occupied his time reading arms magazines. The glut of oil money enabled him to indulge his fantasies, and huge orders of military hardware began flowing in to Tehran. Eventually, Iran had more tanks and artillery pieces than either the British army or the German armed forces (the Bundeswehr). Iran was quickly transformed into a great showplace for all types of weapons and military equipment. Showplace is the right word, for the country lacked the warehouses, magazines, and hangars needed to protect and secure military stores; hundreds of helicopters sat idle in the desert.

Kapuściński tends to view the toppling of the Shah and the assumption of power by the Shiites as simply the most recent expression of historical leitmotifs. For hundreds of years, Iranians have exhibited a particular talent for preserving their independence under conditions of subjugation. For centuries they have been victims of conquest, aggression, and partition. They have been ruled repeatedly by foreigners or local regimes dependent on foreign powers, and yet they have preserved their culture, language, and spiritual fortitude and exhibited an ability to arise reborn from the ashes of defeat and despair. During the twenty-five centuries of their history, the Iranians have sooner or later managed to outwit anyone with the temerity to try ruling them. At times they have resorted to the weapons of uprising and revolution and obtained their goal with a tragic levy of blood. On other occasions they have employed the tactic of passive resistance in a particularly consistent and radical way. The most common Iranian technique, however, has been absorption—active assimilation of the foreign sword, turning it into their own weapon.

This historical groundwork helps explain why Shiism is so compelling to Iranians: It expresses the nation's spirit, culture, and independence. Kapuściński convincingly argues that this variant of the Muslim religion is a faith for the wronged and conquered, an instrument of contestation and resistance, the ideology of an unhumbled people prepared to suffer in defense of their distinctness and dignity. Shiism became not only the Iranian national religion but also their refuge and shelter, a means of national survival, and, at the right moments, a tool for struggle and liberation.

Perhaps this strong impulse in Iranian history made the nation a sterile habitat for Western political forms. Within the revolutionary camp there were initially many philosophies and grand designs. All opponents of the Shah wanted to depose him, but different parties to the revolt envisioned the future differently. Some thought that Iran would become the sort of democracy they had experienced while studying in France, Switzerland, and the United States. The intelligentsia, however, though wise and enlightened, was also weak. Members of this group found themselves in a paradoxical situation: A democracy cannot be imposed by force, the majority must favor it, yet the majority wanted what Khomeini wanted—an Islamic republic.

The only major weakness of *Shah of Shahs* is the author's failure to explain why the Shah remained so out of touch with the feelings of his people. In fact, the Shah, despite the title of the book, remains an enigmatic figure. Kapuściński does a splendid job of showing how people reacted to the Shah's efforts to build the Great Civilization, but many fundamental questions remain unanswered. Why did the Shah fail to create a loyal middle class dependent on his policies and patronage? How could he fail to understand the resentment provoked by the large influx of foreign technology and professionals? Why did the monarch make no effort to accommodate or defuse the radical Shiites? Why did his plans for modernization ignore Iran's rural poor? To what extent did the general turmoil and tension in the Middle East serve to destabilize the Shah's government?

Despite this flaw, *Shah of Shahs* brilliantly reveals the pathology of an oppressive regime that was incapable of satisfying its people. It appears that the Shah tried to deceive his backward nation with grand but empty promises. Perhaps the greatest victim of these great delusions was himself.

Michael C. Robinson

Sources for Further Study

Booklist. LXXXI, March 1, 1985, p. 922.
Library Journal. CX, March 15, 1985, p. 52.
The London Review of Books. VII, July 4, 1985, p. 22.
Los Angeles Times Book Review. March 17, 1985, p. 1.
The Nation. CCXL, June 22, 1985, p. 772.
The New York Times Book Review. XC, April 7, 1985, p. 7.
Newsweek. CV, March 4, 1985, p. 66.
Publishers Weekly. CCXXVII, January 25, 1985, p. 83.
Virginia Quarterly Review. LXI, Summer, 1985, p. 94.
The Wall Street Journal. CCV, April 4, 1985, p. 28.

SIGISMUND
From the Memories of a Baroque Polish Prince

Author: Lars Gustafsson (1936-   )
Translated from the Swedish by John Weinstock
Publisher: New Directions (New York). 191 pp. $16.50; paperback $7.95
Type of work: Novel
Time: Primarily 1973
Locale: Primarily Berlin

A playful, episodic novel of ideas

> *Principal characters:*
> LARS GUSTAFSSON, the author and narrator
> LAURA G., a painter, his friend
> SIGISMUND III, King of Poland, 1587-1632

Lars Gustafsson's novel *Sigismund: From the Memories of a Baroque Polish Prince*, first published in Sweden in 1976, is bracingly eccentric in form yet eminently readable. Were it the work of a writer from Eastern Europe or Latin America, it would be much discussed. Coming from Scandinavia, it has hardly been reviewed.

Sigismund has an autobiographical base and a deftly established setting—Berlin, 1973—from which it freely departs. Here, as in his other novels, Gustafsson violates the conventional distinction between author and narrator: His narrator is Lars Gustafsson, a visiting professor—as was, presumably, the "real" Lars Gustafsson in 1973. From the beginning, however, it is clear that this is no naïvely autobiographical fiction, for, having suggested that the boundary between life and art has been erased, Gustafsson proceeds to indulge in brazen fancies which celebrate the writer's freedom to lie, to invent, to make up what he pleases.

Much of the pleasure of the novel derives from the unusual interplay between the "autobiographical" Lars Gustafsson, who seems to be addressing the reader with refreshing directness, and the shameless liar, the writer-as-counterfeiter. Here is the voice of the former:

> If there isn't a paradise it remains to be invented. Dry clear air, some trees that sway in a steady wind . . .
> Paradise is a place where it is dry, where sun and sharp shadows prevail.
> In any case that doesn't at all accord with the time and place for this story. BERLIN 1973. A drizzling, endless rain moves through the parks, highways, gasometers, among the cars parked on endless destroyed lots, a heavy coal smell in the air. Puffs of wind from the dead who move past in the twilight. And just like those Shakespearean kings who awaken in the middle of the night when a cold gust goes through the room, a gust of reproaches, of remorse, of remembrance, I often awaken.

Within the first few pages, this reflective, engaging voice describes the experience that sets the novel's sketchy, parodistic plot in motion. It is an experience that many readers will find familiar: a sudden awareness that one has been living "without noticing it," that a "stand-in" has been carrying on in one's absence, going through all the motions of everyday life. Where, then, has the "I" been, and how can its return be managed?

Here is a familiar human dilemma in a realistic setting, but the manner in which Gustafsson develops it is anything but familiar, or realistic. Having described the sensation of "waking" to his life after months of living without awareness, Gustafsson shows himself in the process of finding a metaphor for his condition. This is what the Russian Formalists called "baring the device": The writer shows the reader how the trick is done (and the trick *is* done, for all that). The metaphor which Gustafsson seizes on is deliberately outlandish, in the manner of Richard Brautigan (as the charming insouciance of Gustafsson's title, its inconsequential relation to the substance of the novel, recalls the appeal of Brautigan's *A Confederate General from Big Sur*, 1979): According to this metaphor, his slumbering self, his "I," is the Swedish-born King Sigismund III of Poland, who died in 1632 and who since that time has been entombed in a sarcophagus in the cathedral of Cracow.

It is a ridiculous conceit (a baroque conceit), and Gustafsson soon expresses his regret at having introduced it, but in fact it is this very quality that makes it suitable for his purposes. He wants to show that a fundamental question—"I really wonder who has charge of my soul?"—cannot be answered by a proper literary metaphor: The bizarre convolutions of human selfhood deserve a strange analogue. He wants to celebrate the anarchic freedom of the writer, and the human capacity for making meaning, for the metaphor of Sigismund, however farfetched, organizes diverse experiences, yields insights, as any story will do.

Insofar as *Sigismund* has a plot, then, a central action, it is an inner drama, worked out in terms of the governing metaphor. The novel is divided into two parts: "Memories from Purgatory," the long first section, and "Sigismund Walks Again," which takes up less than twenty pages. The resolution comes in the final pages, when Sigismund, liberated from his tomb and "clad in an elegant suit of the best English tweed," arrives at Gustafsson's house and reproaches him: "Young man, it's about time to pull yourself together!" The last words of the novel conclude this comic drama of the reintegration of the self: " 'Your Majesty,' I answered, 'your Majesty, in your absence I have done my best.' "

Such a description of the novel, however, is quite misleading, for this plot is but the loosest of structures. As befits a novel with an epigraph from *Don Quixote de La Mancha*, Sigismund is episodic, digressive to an extreme degree, but always entertaining. There are, for example, several interspersed chapters of science-fiction parody; while they drag a bit at times, presumably having lost in translation their verbal exactness, they are frequently very funny: The names alone ("the old dying sun Ham-Ofad"; "Chief Researcher Kiirk-Fa") are a delight. There is also the story of

Gustafsson's Uncle Stig, a genial Communist inventor, and the ill-fated 1949 test run of his revolutionary bicycle, which is pedaled from a prone position.

Several of the episodes are connected by a theme that runs throughout Gustafsson's fiction—a theme stated concisely early in *Sigismund*:

> When I ask a question it is *my* question, even if it sounds exactly like *your* question. Someone who doesn't understand this will never understand what it means to live.

For the writer, this means that all the archetypal stories await rediscovery. He has the right to make them his, just as each generation of lovers rediscovers love. Gustafsson tells the story of his Aunt Clara, petite and refined, whom he admired as a boy and who shocked her family by going off with a blind vagabond, Gottwald. For the first time in his life, Gustafsson recalls, he saw "how enormous man's freedom can be." Aunt Clara's health was not up to life on the road, and she contracted pneumonia ("I think she died completely happy"); Gottwald outlived her by several decades. After his death, two manuscripts are discovered among his possessions, and they end up in an archival collection of folklore, where Gustafsson reads them. As he summarizes them in a couple of sentences and praises their artistry, many readers will be moved to protest the implausibility of the tale. After all, a blind man.... If they reconsider, however, they might note that these thumbnail sketches of the two manuscripts of Gottwald the Blindman could serve equally well as descriptions of the *Iliad* and the *Odyssey*.

Of all the stories in *Sigismund*, the most fully developed is the story of the painter Laura G. and her Faustian bargain, related in several interspersed chapters. Laura G. (like Zwatt, to whom the book is dedicated, and Lars Gustafsson himself) is, one gathers, a real person as well as a character in *Sigismund*; Gustafsson describes her as "the only artist I've met in my entire life who is completely serious, and in the firm conviction that it is not at all unattainable for her, she strives for perfection."

In the story he spins around her, G. is visited by a "friendship delegation" from Hell. In her bargain with the three "foreigners" (who remind her of visiting professors), G. insists on a stipulation which they find very unusual: For one day, she wants to be another person. Ultimately, she agrees to visit the underworld for a week, and finds it very boring. (This Hell seems to be a parody of Paradise as envisioned in the Socialist states.) Even though she decides not to stay, one of her hosts, intrigued by the notion, grants her request: When she returns to the surface of the Earth, she does so in the form of a man; for one day, as she desired, she will see the world from a different perspective.

The chapter recounting G.'s return is entitled "Mirror Worlds." Suddenly it occurs to the reader that the extraordinary experience granted to G. is precisely the experience that *Sigismund* grants to its readers—which any novel, potentially, has to offer. Fiction is a kind of magic.

Though it stands on its own as an independent work, *Sigismund* is the fourth in a series of five loosely connected novels that concludes with *En biodlares død* (1978; *The Death of a Beekeeper*, 1981). To date, the first three novels in the sequence have not appeared in English; another Gustafsson novel which has been translated, *Tennisspelarna* (1977; *The Tennis Players*, 1983), although not part of the series, is cut from the same cloth. Readers of *Sigismund* who are interested in the genesis of the entire sequence will find this and other matters discussed in cotranslator Janet K. Swaffar's afterword to *The Death of a Beekeeper*, drawing on two interviews with Gustafsson conducted in 1979.

John Wilson

Sources for Further Study

Best Sellers. XLV, May, 1985, p. 48.
Kirkus Reviews. LII, November 15, 1984, p. 1061.
Library Journal. CX, February 1, 1985, p. 112.
Publishers Weekly. CCXXVI, December 14, 1984, p. 38.
World Literature Today. LI, Spring, 1977, p. 292.

THE SIMPLE LIFE
Plain Living and High Thinking in American Culture

Author: David E. Shi
Publisher: Oxford University Press (New York). 332 pp. $19.95
Type of work: Intellectual history
Time: 1630 to the 1980's
Locale: The United States

A history of the idea that the simple life is a virtuous life

> *Principal personages:*
> JOHN ADAMS, a revolutionary leader and the second President of the United States, 1797-1801
> SAMUEL ADAMS, a revolutionary leader
> EDWARD BOK, the longtime editor of *Ladies Home Journal*
> RALPH BORSODI, a social critic and homesteader
> JOHN BURROUGHS, a social critic
> RALPH WALDO EMERSON, an author and lecturer
> JOHN MUIR, a naturalist and the founder of the Sierra Club
> HENRY DAVID THOREAU, an author and social reformer
> JOHN WINTHROP, a leader and governor of the Massachusetts Bay Colony
> JOHN WOOLMAN, an early Quaker saint and reformer

The Simple Life: Plain Living and High Thinking in American Culture is a work of intellectual history written for the serious (though not necessarily academic) reader. In this book, David Shi traces the idea, from Colonial times to the Ronald Reagan presidency, "that the making of money and the accumulation of things should not be allowed to smother the purity of the soul, the life of the mind, the cohesion of the family, or the good of the commonwealth." Shi's treatment of the idea is sympathetic and chronological. The treatment in this essay will be sympathetic and analytic.

The first problem in writing or thinking about the simple life is the multiplicity of ideas, sentiments, and activities that have come under this title. As Shi writes, "a hostility toward luxury and a suspicion of riches, a reverence for nature and a preference for rural over urban ways of life and work, a desire for personal self-reliance through frugality and diligence, a nostalgia for the past and a scepticism toward the claims of modernity, conscientious rather than conspicuous consumption, and an aesthetic taste for the plain and functional" have all been advocated as the essence of simplicity.

Yet the reasons and motives which have kept the idea alive in America for almost four centuries have been relatively few. First, the simple life has been said to promote social justice; second, it has been said to promote an organic and cohesive society, instead of one based on crass economic individualism and self-interest; third, it has been said to prevent the deadening of the soul and the numbing of the mind; and finally, the simple life has been said to free time for worship, family, and community service.

While not denying the motivating power of reasons and arguments, Shi, like any good historian, uncovers the deeper factors that move men and societies. During the Colonial period these factors were primarily religious. It made little difference whether the call to the simple life came from governors or preachers: The ground of their appeal was the same—Holy Scripture.

The arguments extracted from Scripture included all those mentioned above. John Woolman, a Quaker saint and reformer, made it clear that in his opinion the "least degree of luxury hath some connection with evil." His argument was straightforward: Because luxuries are unnecessary for true happiness, those who demanded such goods caused "men and animals to do unnecessary labor," and thus they "were acting contrary to the design of the Creator."

On the way to the New World, in his famous speech aboard the *Arbella*, John Winthrop, an early leader and longtime governor of the Massachusetts Bay Colony, made it clear that this was not to be a money-making expedition. He warned the colonists that the material abundance of the New World might tempt them "to embrace the present world and prosecute our carnal intentions, seeking great things for our selves and our posterity." Therefore, vigilance was necessary to ensure that the "good of the public oversway all private interests." Lacking optimism about the power of words to control men's depravity, Winthrop convinced settlers to institute sumptuary laws and controls on wages, prices, and markets to make sure "the life of business be placed within a structure whose proportions had been drawn by the hand of God."

The spiritual state of settlers' souls was also an important concern to the early leaders of Pennsylvania and the New England colonies. While diligence at one's vocation was part of the Christian's duty, the material abundance that such diligence often produced was not considered an unmixed blessing. The Massachusetts colonists were not getting a new or original teaching when they heard their influential pastor, John Cotton, caution that "we are never more apt to forget God than when he prospers us." Time proved Cotton to be correct. Within two generations, preachers were lamenting that religion "had brought forth prosperity, and the daughter destroyed the mother."

Some of the clergy tried to threaten their congregations into obedience. Cotton Mather warned Boston merchants that God would find "an eternity to damn the man who cannot find time to pray." Others took the positive approach. Woolman spent most of his adult life speaking and demonstrating the freedom and opportunities that accrued to those who practiced simple living. Though the path to material abundance lay open, Woolman chose to sell his flourishing business so that he might have the "opportunity for retirement and inward recollection." Thereafter he vowed to spend no more time at his new job—tailoring—than was necessary to provide the necessities of life for himself and his family. As an added benefit, his renunciation of business enabled him to spend much time traveling around the colonies and England, proselytizing for a "humbler, plain, temperate Way of Living: a life where no unnecessary cares nor expenses may encumber our minds, nor lessen our ability to do good."

By the time the Puritan's "errand in the wilderness" and the Quaker's "holy experiment" produced grandchildren in the New World, the religious zeal of the original colonists had dissipated. A Quaker spokesman explained it thus: "Their fathers came into the country, and bought large tracts of land for a trifle; their sons found large estates come into their possession, and a profession of religion which was partly national, which descended like a patrimony from their fathers, and cost as little."

Yet no sooner was one impetus spent than another took its place. This time it was the republicanism of the founding fathers. Their texts were the classics of the Greeks and Romans. Sam Adams, John Adams, James Madison, Thomas Jefferson, and other leaders of the Revolution were all convinced from their reading of history that a republican nation depended on developing and sustaining a virtuous citizenry. The importance of a virtuous citizenry in the minds of the founding fathers is already well-known, but Shi adds to this historical understanding the comprehension of how large a place frugality and simplicity had in their conception of the virtuous man.

Sam Adams, for example, provoked a long exchange of letters in the Boston newspapers for suggesting that some young nabobs were acting contrary to the principles of the Revolution when they founded the Tea Assembly, an exclusive social club devoted to dancing and card playing. Such activities, Adams wrote, were "exchanging prudence, virtue and economy for those glaring spectres luxury, prodigality and profligacy." Benjamin Rush, a confidant to Jefferson, argued that unless both government and individuals developed the virtues of frugality and economic self-control the new republic would eventually see its citizens "devouring each other like beasts of prey." John Dickinson, a leader of the American Revolution, wrote that "luxury and corruption" must be curbed by "a general reformation of manners, which everyone sees is absolutely necessary for the welfare of this kingdom."

But again, the political zeal with which the nation began was unable to sustain the simple life that so many thought necessary for a just and cohesive society. Soon John Adams was forced to adopt his own style of jeremiad. "There is so much Rascality, so much Venality and Corruption, so much Avarice and Ambition, such a Rage for Profit and Commerce among all Ranks and Degrees of Men even in America, that I sometimes doubt whether there is public Virtue enough to Support a Republic." The general effect was similar to that of the Puritan divines' attempt to browbeat their auditors into returning to the simpler ways of their fathers: Soon the fashionable were ridiculing such sentiments as the ramblings of "rigid republicans" and of "men of contracted minds."

Though religious and political zeal would not sustain lasting and widespread support for the simple life, simplicity itself did not disappear from the list of American values. About the time of Andrew Jackson, Transcendentalists began preaching their own gospel of plain living. Unlike the Colonial and revolutionary leaders, Ralph Waldo Emerson, Henry David Thoreau, and other nineteenth century romantics seldom invoked social justice or communal cohesion as reasons to forgo the material goods that the economy was producing in such abundance. Simplicity, as they saw it, ought to be the result of a personal choice, not a socially imposed norm. The Transcendentalists were more interested in perfecting individuals than institutions. Their goal was the purity and elevation of souls; their inspiration was Nature and the simple blessings she provided.

Thoreau is famous for his twenty-six-month retreat to Walden Pond, and while he proved to himself that life could be carried on quite happily, perhaps even more happily, without the trappings of a modern, industrial society, he also discovered that plain living was not as closely connected with high thinking as Emerson had suggested. During his stay in the woods, Thoreau learned that the Indians of Maine were not the noble savages of Jean-Jacques Rousseau. The fact is, according to Thoreau, they were "sinister and slouching fellows" who made only a "coarse and imperfect use . . . of Nature." When Thoreau once had to take cover during a sudden storm in a ramshackle hut rented by John Field, he was forced to admit that the backwoodsman's unembellished life had not ennobled his thoughts. Though Thoreau began talking with Field "as if he were a philosopher, or desired to be one," he soon discovered that Field's poverty had blinded him to the higher things of life.

Later, Thoreau's spirits were buoyed when he met Alek Therien, another woodsman, who said that if "it were not for books [he] would not know what to do [on] rainy days." Thoreau's spirits sank, however, when he learned that the books consisted solely of an "almanac and an arithmetic." Furthermore, Therien knew and cared little about social issues, philosophical questions, or spiritual truths. Thereafter, Thoreau realized that plain living and high thinking would be combined only in the lives of an elite few.

Toward the end of the nineteenth century, Darwinian naturalism sapped nature's remaining romance. Thus, by the beginning of the twentieth century, the gospel of the simple life had looked to three different sources for inspiration—Scripture, the classics, and nature—and all had proved, in the end, to be unable to stand against the temptations of modernity. Shi's story, however, does not end at this point. As the concluding chapters of his book make clear, the virtues of the simple life have been touted throughout the present century. Without a unifying foundation, however, the proponents of the simple life take on the appearance of gadflies, not prophets. How many have heard of John Burroughs, Edward Bok, Ralph Borsodi, Arthur E. Morgan, or Scott Nearing? Nevertheless, as Shi's history reveals, they all played important roles in the struggle for plain living and high thinking in the twentieth century.

Shi's history concludes with the Reagan presidency and with the proponents of economic self-restraint in full retreat. Have they finally been defeated? They have not, according to Shi. "Like the family," he writes, "simplicity is always said to be declining but never disappears. No sooner do advocates in one era declare it dead than members of the next proclaim its revival." *The Simple Life* is a cornucopia of evidence for such a claim, and there is no reason to think that the ad-man's millennium is about to begin.

The Simple Life is also the work of one who is described on the dust jacket as "an avid organic gardener who aspires to lead a simple life." Though Shi does not preach, there are lessons in his work for those who share the author's aspirations.

In 1974, the English historian Arnold Toynbee remarked that "a society that is declining materially may be ascending spiritually." There may be something to Toynbee's quip. More than all other factors, outside forces which have served to limit prosperity—for example, the nonimportation agreements of the colonists, most of our several wars, and the Arab oil crisis—have rallied the nation around those who have tried to convince us that less may really be more. It is easier to persuade people to live and work in a tempting environment without coming to love it when the material world is not quite so lovable. Though many of simplicity's advocates have welcomed wars and other national crises when they have come for the sacrifices which they engender, there would be something incongruous in praying or working for such crises in hopes of catching the nation's attention. Besides, such historical forces are largely uncontrollable.

It is, however, within the control of simplicity's advocates to regulate their own style of living. Cotton Mather, William Penn, John Hancock, Thomas Jefferson, Ralph Waldo Emerson, William James, Theodore Roosevelt, and many others have all been brilliant advocates of the simple life in print and speech. Yet, as Shi reminds the reader, and as their contemporaries surely noticed, these men were hardly paradigms of plain living. Their lives all suggest that the simple life was only for men of lesser economic means. Some tried to justify their own luxurious standard of living by arguing that it was necessary to sustain the power and prestige of their office or position, yet one suspects Woolman spoke for more than just himself when he said, "Conduct is more convincing than language."

This is not to say that those whose lives do not conform to standards as strict as Woolman's are necessarily hypocrites. Once on a ship bound for England, Woolman noticed that the cabins were decorated with "carved work and imagery" and "some superfluity of workmanship." Since such luxuries "entangled many in the spirit of oppression," and since he could "not find peace in joining in anything which he saw was against the wisdom which is pure," he decided to spend the next six weeks in steerage, where he shared the hardship of the sailors, "their exposure, their soaking clothes, their miserable accommodations, their wet garments often trodden underfoot." It would be easy to argue that Woolman's standards were too strict and that they verged on asceticism. The problem lies in having the wisdom to know how and when to draw the line and the grace or will to be able to conform life to one's decision. Many advocates of the simple life will sympathize with the cry of William Dean Howells: "Words, words, words! How to make them deeds. . . . With me they only breed more words."

Ric S Machuga

Sources for Further Study

Choice. XXII, April, 1985, p. 1219.
Christian Century. CII, April 10, 1985, p. 364.
Commonweal. CXII, August 9, 1985, p. 442.
Kirkus Reviews. LII, December 15, 1984, p. 1195.
Library Journal. CX, February 1, 1985, p. 96.
Los Angeles Times Book Review. February 24, 1985, p. 1.
The Nation. CCXL, March 9, 1985, p. 277.
New England Quarterly. LVIII, June, 1985, p. 318.
The New York Times Book Review. XC, January 20, 1985, p. 14.
Psychology Today. XIX, March, 1985, p. 71.
Sierra. LXX, January, 1985, p. 136.

A SIMPLE STORY

Author: S. Y. Agnon (1888-1970)
Translated from the Hebrew, and with an afterword, by Hillel Halkin
Publisher: Schocken Books (New York). 246 pp. $14.95
Type of work: Novella
Time: The late nineteenth to the early twentieth century
Locale: Szybusz, Poland; Galicia

A tale of bittersweet romance set in a small town in southern Poland around the turn of the century, rich both in Jewish folk wisdom and universal truths about human nature

Principal characters:
> HIRSHL HURVITZ, a young storekeeper's son, too timid to declare his passion for Blume Nacht
> BLUME NACHT, the daughter of Mirl and Hayyim Nacht
> MINA ZIEMLICH, the daughter of a wealthy merchant from Malikrowik, later Hirshl's wife
> BARUCH MEIR HURVITZ, Hirshl's father
> TSIRL HURVITZ, Hirshl's mother
> GEDALIA ZIEMLICH, Mina's father
> BERTHA ZIEMLICH, Mina's mother
> DR. LANGSAM, a neurologist
> YONA TOYBER, a matchmaker from Szybusz

S(hmuel) Y(osef) Agnon's classic *A Simple Story*, first published in Hebrew in 1935 as *Sipur pashut*, is now available for a wider audience in Hillel Halkin's lucid English translation. For this Schocken edition, Halkin also contributes an insightful afterword, partly to provide for the general reader useful background information to the novella, partly to analyze Agnon's complex treatment of theme and structure. However simple the story appears to be, the work rewards close and careful attention. Like other fiction by the 1966 Nobel Prize-winner, this novella also re-creates the lost world of early twentieth century Jewish life. In general, Agnon's work is—at least superficially—nostalgic, conservatively religious, often moralistic. On a deeper level, his fiction treats a quest for values in a once-static society slowly disintegrating or changing because of modern pressures. As such, *A Simple Story*, like *Days of Awe* (1938), *A Guest for the Night* (1939, 1950), or *The Bridal Canopy* (1931), should be read not merely as an old-fashioned narrative depicting a bygone age but also as an ambiguous moral parable that concerns the human soul in turmoil.

From the point of view of an obtrusive narrator, a native of Galicia wise and tolerant concerning the foibles of men and women in love, Agnon tells a simple tale that grows ever more complex and meaningful. He begins with the fortunes of Blume Nacht, an attractive, clever, and industrious young woman who, as a penniless orphan, arrives at her cousin's home in Szybusz, a Jewish *shtetl* in southern Poland. Baruch Meir Hurvitz and his shrewd wife, Tsirl, look the girl over, decide that she might well serve as a maid in the household to earn her modest keep, but their only son, Hirshl, looks at the girl with deeper appreciation. In time he falls in love with her, but—too inexperienced in the ways of the world to approach Blume—he allows fate to take control of his romance. Hence the *shtetl* matchmaker, Yona Toyber, works out for the young man a much more promising match—with Mina Ziemlich, from the nearby village of Malikrowik.

Passively, Hirshl allows his parents to prepare for his marriage; passively he courts the equally inexperienced Mina; and passively he weds her. Always he had thought—or perhaps he had hoped—that Blume might intercede for him and that they might run off together. Such things, however, do not generally occur in the village of Szybusz; people follow Jewish traditions, and Hirshl is, if anything, obedient.

Only after his marriage does he show signs of agitation, which swell into revolt against the conventions of married life and finally turn to depression and near madness. Desperate with his unrequited love for Blume, Hirshl strays from his home, suffers an emotional breakdown in the forest, and— through the assistance of his worried family—is placed in the care of the wise Dr. Langsam and committed to a sanatorium. There, allowed time for sleep and the renovation of his frayed nerves, he regains his sanity. Indeed, he recovers more than his wits: He returns home to his wife and to his vocation as a shopkeeper with a new vigor. His rebellion is over. Restored to his wife and children, content with his lot as an ordinary townsman in an imperfect world, he resumes a life of complacency. As far as Blume is concerned, the narrator chooses not to discuss her fate; hers is another "simple story."

How simple, indeed, is Agnon's novella? His narrative pattern, seemingly straightforward, is full of strange twists. The reader at first supposes that Hirshl's love for Blume will, after overcoming the impediments of his parents' opposition, eventually triumph in wedlock. Instead, he marries Mina, a less spirited but otherwise suitable mate. At this point, Blume's role in the story as romantic focus diminishes, although it never entirely fades; she persists in Hirshl's imagination as the unattainable fair one. The reader now expects that Hirshl will persist in his quest for Blume and that, somehow (perhaps with tragic consequences), his desperate ardor will win her heart. Again, Agnon surprises: Hirshl, to be sure, is driven nearly mad with vexation over his unrequited passion, but Blume remains chaste and is indifferent to his clumsy advances. What therefore will become of the pining lover deprived of his amorous goal? The reader expects Hirshl to decline as a result of his erotic madness into a deeper pit of depression. Instead, he recovers and, against expectations, returns home as a solid, respectable Szybusz merchant—more mature a husband and a father, more responsible a businessman, more conventional a Jew.

What, then, is the moral of this parable? That the old ways, the ways of traditional obligations and traditional constraints upon freedom, are the best, so Hirshl finally comes to his senses by abandoning his foolish dreams of pursuing his romantic ego? Or does Agnon mean to say that Hirshl, a decent enough fellow but not a truly extraordinary soul, does not deserve the finely tempered Blume? Does Agnon side with the winds of change in complaisant Szybusz or with the solid verities of the past? More to the point: How is the reader to interpret this bittersweet story which lacks villains but also lacks heroes? The most nearly heroic figure is Dr. Langsam, who represents the emerging educated Jewish professional class but still maintains tenuous links to his orthodox religious heritage; a victim of existential doubt, he is torn between the two worlds, able to heal the neuroses of others but not his own psychological wounds.

What becomes of Blume? Agnon's treatment of this sharply defined character is curious indeed. The story begins with an account of her struggles to survive and concludes, enigmatically, with these sentences: "Hirshl and Mina's story is over, but Blume's is not. Everything that happened to Blume Nacht would fill another book." The reader is left to imagine the incidents of such a book, and indeed, in spite of Agnon's reticence to disclose information about Blume's future (she has rejected another lover), her image is powerfully suggestive. Will she emigrate from Szybusz to seek a more spacious, freer life abroad? Will she ever find a lover worthy of her? From what is already known about her, readers can imagine not only a different fate for her but also a better one than that of the historically doomed Galician Jews. As the dark (or nocturnal) flower that her name symbolically suggests, Blume's mystery remains fragrantly external to the central parable of the novella.

In effect, Agnon's parable lacks a distinct moral focus because his vision is comic. From the vantage of retrospection, he examines his characters with amused toleration for their follies, with compassion for their suffering. His tale ends, as most great comedies do, with an impulse toward reconciliation; with the ceremony of marriage for many of the minor characters; with the promise of integration and unity for the whole community. And, like most great comedies, Agnon's miniature world is touched by the sadness of life. No one who reads the account of Hirshl's early discontent in a loveless marriage can dismiss the book merely as a folk romance. More in the pattern of Ivan Olbracht's neglected masterpiece *The Bitter and the Sweet* (1937) than Shalom Aleichem's popular stories, Agnon's comic vision rarely sentimentalizes or trivializes the past. As both a realist and a man of deep religious faith, Agnon treats his characters no better than they deserve—but also no worse.

Leslie B. Mittleman

Sources for Further Study

Kirkus Reviews. LIII, October 15, 1985, p. 1094.
Library Journal. CX, November 15, 1985, p. 108.
The New York Times Book Review. XC, December 22, 1985, p. 8.
Publishers Weekly. CCXXVIII, October 11, 1985, p. 58.

SLOW HOMECOMING

Author: Peter Handke (1942-   )
Translated from the German by Ralph Manheim
Publisher: Farrar, Straus and Giroux (New York). 278 pp. $16.95
Type of work: Three interrelated prose narratives
Time: The 1970's
Locale: America, France, Germany, and Austria

In three increasingly autobiographical contexts, the author recounts his painstaking efforts to reclaim from the transience and formlessness of modern life shapes of enduring beauty and truth

> *Principal characters:*
> VALENTIN SORGER, an Austrian geologist trying to find his way back into society after having rekindled his passion for the forms of nature during fieldwork near the Arctic Circle
> A FIRST-PERSON NARRATOR, one who is in search of Paul Cézanne's vision, exploring the landscape of the painter's Southern France
> A FIRST-PERSON NARRATOR, one who is determined to bring up his daughter in a world hostile to the wisdom of her innocence

The noisy entrance with which in 1966 the twenty-three-year-old Peter Handke from Austria spoiled the party of some of Germany's most influential writers gathered at Princeton has by now become an almost legendary event in the history of German postwar literature. At first, his diatribe against the older generation's socially committed realism and his own attempt to sever all customary relations between words and things struck many as little more than the promotional antics of a self-styled enfant terrible. Yet despite the early Handke's insistence that literature is concerned with language, not with the representation of reality—an attitude which had all the trappings of an unpromising formalism—he did not exhaust himself or his theme in the sterile exercise of mere wordplay. After twenty years and eleven novels, ten plays, four volumes of poetry, three diaries, and numerous essays, the young man's deconstructionist approach to language must not only be acknowledged to have existed well within the context of a peculiarly Austrian preoccupation with language—a tradition which includes such men as Fritz Mauthner, Hugo von Hofmannsthal, Karl Kraus, Ludwig Wittgenstein, and even Sigmund Freud—but also must be recognized in retrospect as only the first radical step toward a new and demanding poetic realism. For Handke, to strip the incrustations of conventional language from the face of reality turns out to have been simply an unavoidable preparation for a successful reconstruction of the world's primordial beauty.

A few years after his provocative beginnings, Handke advanced beyond the austerity of his early works in such novels as *Die Stunde der wahren Empfindung* (1975; *A Moment of True Feeling,* 1977) and *Die linkshändige Frau* (1976; *The Left-Handed Woman,* 1978) by writing about men and women who managed to escape the deadening automatisms of their linguistic conditioning in moments of immediate and, therefore, as yet inarticulate experience. Still, the suggested mysticism can never be the last word for an artist who must love form even more than any true feeling. This love for form strives for intersubjectivity, for communication, for permanence in a valid linguistic system; it strives, as Handke is not at all embarrassed to state, for modern myths, stories that link the forms arising from the contemplation of reality into a new gospel of harmony between man and world. This latest and most ambitious turn in Handke's romantic quest can now be followed in *Slow Homecoming*, which in its solemn, at times ceremonious pursuit of what is real often reads like the story of a new Adam renaming his universe. The book, admirably translated by Ralph Manheim, contains one fictional narration, "The Long Way Around," and two clearly autobiographical accounts, "The Lesson of Mont Sainte-Victoire" and "Child Story." Though published in Germany as three independent books between 1979 and 1981, these texts have here justifiably and wisely been combined and should be read as a fictional project followed by two efforts toward its realization by the author.

"The Long Way Around," which takes up about half of the volume, represents the most programmatic and complete story because it allows its hero to proceed where Handke himself, as the two autobiographical reports will show, has not yet been able to follow. Valentin Sorger, an Austrian geologist, pursues fieldwork in Alaska to regain his sense for the essence of reality. Through patient observation, he gradually succeeds in reclaiming from the apparently numb presence of vast uniformity interlocking elements of form which begin to reveal to him the law of harmonious existence. To test this new vision and to systematize its wisdom, he finally decides to return to his university in California. Yet an unmotivated assault by a drunken Indian on the day of Sorger's departure from Alaska and nagging reminders upon his arrival of his citizenship in a nation of former mass murderers challenge his newfound faith in the goodness of things, confronting him with his troublesome social and historical identity. All efforts to shelter himself in the peace and permanence of spatial configurations fail, and in the end it takes only a minor instance of confusion in the streets to shatter Sorger's precarious sense of order and purpose. That in his ensuing panic a neighboring family appears in the role of a most welcome guardian angel abruptly converts the now diffident man to a grateful acceptance of social life's benign dispensations. Acknowledging the misguided pride of his lonely search for personal meaning from impersonal form, Sorger is suddenly willing and eager to lay claim to his native country and culture, to go back home. During a layover in New York, his confidence in the order of human history is buoyed by a vision in a crowded Manhattan coffee shop, which reveals to him its ordinary routines as nothing less than the fruit of centuries of peaceful creativity. There exists a possibility for human fulfillment after all because "history is not a mere sequence of evils, which someone like me can do nothing but despise—but has also, from time immemorial, been a peace-fostering *form* that can be perpetuated by anyone (including me)." So he flies home and is last seen still above the clouds but ready to descend.

More explicitly than the other two texts, "The Lesson of Mont Sainte-Victoire" is an extended essay on Handke's development as an artist, told with "the gentle emphasis and appeasing flow of a narrative." The author sets out to remember how moments of recognition in nature (in Austria, Yugoslavia, and France) and in front of paintings (by Edward Hopper and Gustave Courbet, among others) clarified his once-disturbed relationship toward colors into perceptions of form. His unguided desire to contribute to the realm of ordered life finally finds its longed-for teacher in Paul Cézanne, whose pictorial power the author experiences at an exhibition in the spring of 1978. Cézanne's *Man with the Folded Arms* inspires the narrator to conceive of Valentin Sorger. The master's many paintings of Mont Sainte-Victoire begin to fascinate Handke only several months later, and he finally decides on a pilgrimage to this most famous motif of Cézanne's latest period. The account of how the disciple stalks the mountain near Aix-en-Provence in the pursuit of the painter's artistic secret produces superb examples of what since Gerard Manley Hopkins can most adequately be called the "inscaping" of landscape. When the evil presence of human history tries to profane this sacred realm, Handke, not unlike the unregenerated Sorger, prefers to forget rather than face the dark force of formlessness. For the moment, his eagerness to communicate the experienced harmony dominates the remainder of the text, which now tells of its own genesis. Turning to the mountain for advice in his artistic uncertainties, Handke is taught by a fault line how to combine the differing materials of his report into one literary form. Still, like Sorger's Alaska, Handke's Mont Sainte-Victoire must ultimately be tested in landscapes, which were not fortunate enough to be the subject of sane creativity but instead were forced to provide the backdrop for the insanities of history. Even the Mont des Fusillés, a place of executions near Paris, and the Havelberg, from which one sees both sides of the divided Berlin, can now be viewed with the eyes of Cézanne as beloved space, though not yet with the eyes of Sorger in the context of beloved time. The mythic progression stops short of completion. History proves a recalcitrant subject to Handke's quest for harmony. His loving description of a forest near Salzburg, which concludes this narration, shows him reconciled to the landscape of home but not to its society.

"Child Story" recounts Handke's life with his daughter, Amina, from her birth to age ten, the years between 1969 and 1979. It constitutes the author's most direct attempt to achieve fulfillment through a communion with others. As such, it is probably the most moving of the three texts, though this quality results in no small measure from the fact that Handke's ardent wish proves so sadly divided against itself. Told with the solemnity that one expects from myths and placed in an atmosphere associated with legends rather than autobiography, the story intends to tell no piece of mere family history but what Handke perceives to be an archetypal process of immense significance: a father's reentry into a child's innocence. In spite of his unshakable confidence that this child will teach him what is real, Handke's touching devotion shows itself exclusive rather than inclusive of life and world. After a while, the mother seems curiously superfluous and leaves to pursue her own career while Handke's intense metaphysical yearnings create a bond with the child so strong as to provide a convenient "pretext for turning his back on history." Not until the daughter's need for social communion becomes inevitable—a diabolical inevitability for the narrator—does he accede to the demand and then is even prepared to experience her longing vicariously. Yet when his efforts to provide the Gentile child with a Jewish identity are rebuffed, Handke abjures again and curses "those non-beings who need history for their lives," a curse which Sorger for one would not easily have escaped. Children, however, cannot and do not want to remain in the "transtemporal Middle Ages" which their well-intentioned fathers might construct for their protection. After only one year of separation from his daughter, a time during which "The Long Way Around" seems to have been written, Handke is forced to ask with undisguised consternation: "Are you still a child or have you become a German?" At the end of the book, Handke and his daughter are painting over the swastikas that someone had daubed on birdhouses in a nearby forest. Could it be that the child's developing historical identity will finally bring the father to the point where he is ready to follow Sorger's lead and agree to intervene in the turmoils of time?

In the mid-1960's, Handke's destructive formalism was deplored as nihilistic. His present ambition to reconstruct the world through patient observation of worldly forms is frequently dismissed as the eccentric absolutism of a writer who has remained loyal to himself only in the megalomania of his artistic self-perception. Strident self-righteousness, intolerant snobbishness, condescension, and an unforgiving lack of humor are only the most common sins to which critics have objected in Handke's messianic message. The author leaves himself open to all these charges and, worst of all for the critic, seems not to care if he does because all such complaints are for him nothing but additional evidence against an obdurate age. For Handke, the truth about reality demands an act of faith, and so does this book, which has been written to evoke it. That the three narrations can arouse such a willing suspension of disbelief results ultimately from the fact that Handke actually succeeds in showing at least the trailing hem of an unexpected glory. His landscapes, the subjects of his most intense wooing, do become transfigured in a "thing-image-script-brushstroke-dance" which justifies the author's ambition and validates its truth. Where the same magical realism is applied to the world of daily life in community, however, it often does not elevate events to absolute significance but weighs them down with deadly pomposity. Does a room offered as a play area to neighboring children gain in stature by being described as "the material foundation of the idea, on the strength of which a proposal to others became possible"? Handke's inability to extend the myth of archetypal forms to the realm of history becomes here not simply a flaw in his creed but an artistic handicap. The artist who yearns so much for the redemption of the world through the discovery of its inherent harmony remains in the end unsure how much he can and wants to redeem. Should myth not have told him that in its sphere there reigns the law of all or nothing? Has Sorger really come home as long as his author continues to measure today's world by the wisdom of Alaska rather than that of Manhattan?

Joachim J. Scholz

Sources for Further Study

Booklist. LXXXI, June 1, 1985, p. 1370.
Choice. XXXIII, September, 1985, p. 122.
Kirkus Reviews. LIII, March 15, 1985, p. 237.
Library Journal. CX, June 15, 1985, p. 72.
Los Angeles Times. May 22, 1985, V, p. 18.
The New Republic. CXCII, June 17, 1985, p. 31.
New Statesman. CX, August 2, 1985, p. 28.
The New York Times Book Review. XC, August 4, 1985, p. 11.
Publishers Weekly. CCXXVII, April 19, 1985, p. 69.
Washington Post Book World. XV, July 28, 1985, p. 6.

SMALL WORLD
An Academic Romance

Author: David Lodge (1935-   )
Publisher: Macmillan Publishing Company (New York). 339 pp. $15.95; paperback,
   Warner Books, $4.95
Type of work: Novel
Time: 1979
Locale: Numerous sites of academic activity around the globe, beginning in the
   English Midlands and ending in New York City

*A comic novel in which numerous literary characters pursue their individual "holy
grails," chiefly romantic love and academic fame*

> *Principal characters:*
> PERSSE MCGARRIGLE, a young Irish poet-teacher who pursues his
>   beloved through a whirl of international literary conferences
> MORRIS ZAPP, a high-powered American critic who befriends
>   Persse
> PHILIP SWALLOW, a British professor, a traditional humanist who
>   seeks rejuvenation outside his marriage
> ANGELICA PABST, a beautiful young graduate student, the object of
>   Persse's affections
> SYBIL MAIDEN, an aged spinster folklorist who encourages Persse
>   in his quest
> ARTHUR KINGFISHER, the acknowledged king of literary theory,
>   who nevertheless suffers from intellectual and sexual impotence
> CHERYL SUMMERBEE, a London airport check-in clerk who falls in
>   love with Persse

Small World: An Academic Romance is the third entertaining volume in
David Lodge's single-handed revival of a genre that seemed to have become
virtually extinct: the academic novel. Few specimens of the breed have
appeared since its heyday in the 1950's, when comic exposés of faculty life
flourished in such novels as Mary McCarthy's *The Groves of Academe*
(1952), Kingsley Amis' *Lucky Jim* (1954), and Randall Jarrell's *Pictures
from an Institution* (1954). In later decades, the subject of academic life
became more the province of the drama, in such plays as Edward Albee's
Who's Afraid of Virginia Woolf? (1962), Simon Gray's *Butley* (1971), and
Willy Russell's *Educating Rita* (1982)—all of which were also made into
impressive films. Meanwhile, however, David Lodge was rising through the
ranks of the British university system (eventually becoming a professor of
English at the University of Birmingham) and producing not only six books
of highly regarded literary criticism but also six novels. Three of these novels—*The British Museum Is Falling Down* (1965), *Changing Places* (1975),
and *Small World*—bring his expert knowledge of literary history and
novelistic form into play on the subject of academic life.

Small World synthesizes and expands the lively talents for literary parody
and parallel plotting that Lodge demonstrated in his earlier two academic

novels. In *The British Museum Is Falling Down*, Lodge playfully modulated his narrative voice into the styles of numerous modern novelists; in *Small World*, he not only spices the narrative with numerous literary allusions but also parodies the current varieties of literary theory so skillfully that one critic remarked that the book could be used as a primer on the subject. Lodge's second fictional excursion into academia, *Changing Places*, traces the hilarious parallel experiences of two professors who exchange positions for a semester: the traditional British humanist Philip Swallow and the high-powered American critic Morris Zapp. In *Small World*, Lodge not only reprises these two characters, along with their wives and their colleagues, but also interweaves the experiences of some fourteen other academics, writers, publishers, and translators into an ambitious and uproarious satire of contemporary literary life.

Small World does have a central character, however, in the person of Persse McGarrigle, a young Irish poet-teacher (and an academic and sexual innocent) who travels to an academic conference in the English Midlands with the old-fashioned notion that he will participate in the exchange of ideas. Instead, he gains instruction from Morris Zapp in the bewildering new realities of the literary profession. "Scholars these days are like the errant knights of old, wandering the ways of the world in search of adventure and glory," says Zapp, in explaining why professors now spend so much time globe-trotting from conference to conference rather than in the traditional pursuits of teaching and research.

From Sybil Maiden, a kindly spinster folklorist, Persse gains another perspective that in fact also provides the novel with its underlying theme and structure. Miss Maiden sites Jessie Weston's book *From Ritual to Romance* (a genuinely pioneering work of literary criticism, first published in 1920, which provided T. S. Eliot with much of the imagery and allusion for his 1922 poetic masterpiece, *The Waste Land*) in arguing that the explanation for the academic spectacle which Persse is witnessing should be traced back even further than the quest of King Arthur's knights for the Holy Grail. For Miss Maiden, "it all comes down to sex, in the end," and medieval and academic quests alike are all versions of pagan fertility rituals, phallic thrusts in search of the feminine womb, "the life force endlessly renewing itself."

The novel goes on to fulfill its subtitle, *An Academic Romance*, in Miss Maiden's terms: by following the individual quests of its various characters while also self-consciously relating those quests to the quality of their sex lives. Persse McGarrigle (whose first name the book relates to the word "pierce" and to the archetypal quest hero Percival, and whose last name means "Son of Super-valour") remains the noblest, the most innocent, but also seemingly the most naïve of the questers as he pursues the elusive Angelica Pabst, a beautiful and sophisticated graduate student, from conference to conference around the world.

Meanwhile, Morris Zapp and several other established critics compete for their ultimate grail: a $100,000-a-year UNESCO honorary chair that requires no teaching or scholarly work whatsoever. Famous as these critics are in their respective literary fields, however, their love lives are all ridiculed for being repressed, shallow, sterile, or nonexistent. Zapp, who sublimates his libido into energy for his writing and traveling, has invested his critical efforts in the most modish and nihilistic of the literary movements: deconstruction. Seeing it as "the last intellectual thrill left," Zapp compares deconstruction to "sawing through the branch you're sitting on." He delivers the same paper at every conference: "Textuality as Striptease," an argument that literature endlessly teases the reader without ever enabling him to penetrate to the "womb" of authentic meaning. In contrast to Zapp, Fulvia Morgana, an Italian Marxist, is more confident that her ideological truths have a basis in economic fact and that her voracious erotic appetite can be satisfied through wildly unconventional sex. Her wealth and extravagant lifestyle make her seem a highly hypocritical Marxist, however, and her pursuit of kinky sex is made to appear ultimately shallow. The other contenders for the UNESCO chair similarly fall short of the ideal of faithful heterosexual love that the genre of the romance requires. Michel Tardieu, a French structuralist, is gay. The sinister Siegfried von Turpitz, a former Nazi tank commander who espouses reader-reception theory, keeps himself aloof from all human contact and seems to thrive only on power. Similarly, Rudyard Parkinson, an arrogant Oxford belletrist, is a celibate who derives his sole pleasure from his writing.

On a lower echelon of literary activity, many of the novel's characters that are not in contention for the UNESCO chair also suffer from some form of impotence or sterility. Howard Ringbaum, an American cursed with an abrasively competitive personality which deprives him of any chance for the academic success that he craves, drives his wife, Thelma, away from him. Rodney Wainwright, who yearns to find a better position than his teaching post in coastal Australia, struggles endlessly to get past the first sentence of a theoretical essay. Similarly immobilized in a provincial institution is Robin Dempsey, a British specialist in stylistics whose career frustrations lead him deeper and deeper into computer mania. Ronald Frobisher is a British novelist who contracts a crippling writer's block when Dempsey shows him a statistical analysis of his writing style, and Désirée Byrd is also a blocked novelist, bereft of material after a first novel based on her former husband Morris Zapp's supposed mistreatment of her. Philip Swallow seems to be the one character to break through these afflictions of personal isolation and professional frustration, for he is rejuvenated by an adulterous love affair and finds his literary reputation skyrocketing when Rudyard Parkinson (seizing on an opportunity to denigrate Morris Zapp's modish deconstructionism) praises Swallow's old-fashioned book on William Hazlitt. Yet even

Swallow eventually suffers for his excessive high spirits, for he is doubly stricken—by conscience at the unexpected appearance of his son, and by the symptoms of the dreaded Legionnaire's Disease—and he eventually declares that he "failed in the role of romantic hero."

The epitome of this prevailing sexual and literary impotence is the figure of Arthur Kingfisher, the recognized monarch of literary theory, who for years has not been "able to achieve an erection or an original thought," despite the loving ministrations of his beautiful mistress, Song-mi Lee. In the climactic scene of the book, however, at a Modern Language Association symposium where the recipient of the UNESCO chair will be decided, Persse McGarrigle puts a challenging question to the contestants which delivers Kingfisher from his creative stagnation. Persse thus fulfills the archetypal role of the virginal young knight who rejuvenates both the ailing Fisher King and vitality of his realm, and the novel concludes with other elements characteristic of the genre of the romance: the disclosure of secret or mistaken identities, the reunion of long-separated family members, and the matrimonial couplings of many previously despairing characters. Persse himself is liberated from his obsessive infatuation with Angelica and realizes that his heart belongs to the woman who has loved him all along: Cheryl Summerbee, a London airport check-in clerk and an ardent reader of romances.

No matter how seriously one delves into the thematic underpinnings of *Small World*, however, the book never flags in its appeal as a hilarious entertainment. Through Lodge's lighthearted mastery of parallel plotting, comic characterization, and witty dialogue, the novel abundantly provides the kind of exhilaration that Cheryl Summerbee describes when she explains her own pleasure in reading a classic romance: "It's full of adventure and coincidence and surprises and marvels, and has lots of characters who are lost or enchanted or wandering about looking for each other, or for the Grail. . . .Of course, they're often in love too."

Terry L. Andrews

Sources for Further Study

The Atlantic. CCLV, April, 1985, p. 140.
Commonweal. CXII, May 31, 1985, p. 344.
Library Journal. CX, March 15, 1985, p. 73.
The New Republic. CXCII, April 15, 1985, p. 30.
The New York Review of Books. XXXII, August 15, 1985, p. 26.
The New York Times Book Review. XC, March 17, 1985, p. 7.
The New Yorker. LXI, June 3, 1985, p. 124.

Publishers Weekly. CCXXVII, January 18, 1985, p. 61.
Saturday Review. XI, July, 1985, p. 71.
Time. CXXV, April 15, 1985, p. 100.
Virginia Quarterly Review. LXI, Summer, 1985, p. 92.

THE SOLACE OF OPEN SPACES

Author. Gretel Ehrlich (1946-   )
Publisher: The Viking Press (New York). 131 pp. $14.95
Type of work: Essays

In this collection of loosely connected essays, mostly autobiographical, the author records with a poet's sensibility her impressions of northern Wyoming—its people, weatherscapes, and landscapes

Few people would search for solace in the open spaces of northern Wyoming, the wind-blasted ranges or rolling hill country that sustains only grazing sheep, sheepherders, and some scattered tenacious ranchers. Fewer still, like Gretel Ehrlich, would abandon the sophisticated New York literary scene she well knew in order to discover this lonely solace. In 1976 she went to Wyoming to make a film, and stayed there. At that time her former world was already collapsing. She had recently mourned the death of a lover and now, disoriented, she "had the experience of waking up not knowing where I was, whether I was a man or woman, or which toothbrush was mine." The solitude of Wyoming, the bleak and vast horizons, seemed to fill her needs. Not at first did she experience a measure of healing from the open country, solace from pain, and the eventual reconstruction of a shattered life. In time, though, she did become whole, and her story, revealed in loosely connected essays, autobiographical impressions, and brief narratives, is one of spiritual adventure leading to sanity and renewed strength—even to ecstasy.

What sort of book is *The Solace of Open Spaces*? Although part of the genre of twentieth century travel literature, with its emphasis upon the writer's exploration of "spirit of place," Ehrlich's book contrasts with representative genre works in two particulars: She does not aggressively search out this "spirit" in order to define her special nature, one that is revealed through her connection with the landscape, and she requires from the landscape only its healing powers, not its impulse toward power or grandeur. D. H. Lawrence's travel books, in contrast—typical of travel literature as varied as books by C. M. Doughty, Lawrence Durrell, or Carlos Castañeda—explore both the place and the author's state of mind: Place teaches the author how to assert himself; it magnifies his soul. Ehrlich's work belongs to the subgenre of the literature of retreat, in which the author remains passive in the face of elemental nature; the author does not learn powers of assertion but of spiritual regeneration. Ehrlich's literary tradition has the paradigm of Henry David Thoreau's *Walden* (1854) and of such early twentieth century models as George Gissing's *The Private Papers of Henry Ryecroft* (1903) and Havelock Ellis' *Impressions and Comments* (1914-1924, 1926). Like these writers, Ehrlich retreats from a complex and stressful society to discover simple principles of working (or resting) in consonance with nature. As such, *The Solace of Open Spaces* is that rare book: a secular meditative essay that teaches the art of living.

Above all, Ehrlich teaches the reader how to work and survive in the harsh Wyoming valleys and uplands. She became a working shepherd, later a sheep rancher; hers is not the account of a visiting journalist soaking up local color but of an immigrant who has determined to stay on the land. That land she knows well. Her first chapter describes in sharp images the landscape, its people and its animals; the scenes of wildness and harsh beauty; the seasons, with their vast changes; the scents, sounds, and impressions of rugged hills, mountain ranges, declivities, and open country. She quotes a ranch hand to describe Wyoming's openness: "It's all a bunch of nothing—wind and rattlesnakes—and so much of it you can't tell where you're going or where you've been and it don't make much difference."

To a poetic sensibility such as Ehrlich's, however, everything makes a great difference. The special quality of her prose is her power of evocation. She sees into the heart of things. Whether she describes matters great (the upheavals of her life, from the period of mourning her lover to a time of mind-numbing toil, then to happier moments of courtship leading to marriage) or small (the obituaries of insignificant, quirky ranchers or ranch hands, who succumbed through disease, accident, or old age), she treats her themes with freshness and a sharp edge.

Ehrlich writes in the preface, "The truest art I would strive for in any work would be to give the page the same qualities as earth: weather would land on it harshly; light would elucidate the most difficult truths; wind would sweep away obtuse padding." Indeed, she describes scenes not so much with a brush as a palette knife, cutting and scraping so that the lines are sharp as bone on the plains, so that nothing superfluous is left. Whether she treats cowboys of the American West (true Wyoming cowboys, who are stripped of any Hollywood images), testy ranchers, or watering holes, she approaches her subjects with openness of spirit, honesty, and curiosity. Nothing escapes her attention: Indians at the Sun Dance, field corn "jackknifed and bleached blond by the freeze," rattlesnakes, blizzards, funerals. She captures her subjects not as a photographer—to record static images, beautiful, arresting, or ugly—but as a painter, to see into the significance of things.

What special significance does Ehrlich find in the open spaces of Wyoming? To a moralist, eager to seize upon portable wisdom and steal it from the printed page, the twelve essays in this book disclose little in the way of packaged philosophy. To be sure, Ehrlich has a philosophical bent and is keen to discover the mysteries of existence in the daily rounds of work and in the pleasures and struggles of ordinary people; even so, her meditations are not set pieces that can be lifted from the context of observation. At the same time, she is a naturalist in spirit, although she lacks scientific credentials to shore up her authority. She pretends, however, to be neither a naturalist nor a philosopher. She wishes to conserve the land, not for the sake of its austere beauty but for the sake of animals and men and women who need the land—who make the wilderness their home.

During her honeymoon, when Ehrlich departs the sheepherder's range to watch an Oklahoma City rodeo, her vision is as pure as Ernest Hemingway's at the Pamploma bull ring, though with a difference: Hemingway observed not as a Spaniard who belonged on the scene but as an outsider who wished to belong. Ehrlich, on the other hand, belongs with the cowhands and ranchers; she views the action with an eye practiced to understand the beasts and their riders. After all, she has witnessed the birthing of cattle, has seen also cattle skulls on the range, has been familiar with taciturn cowboys and even less communicative shepherds, knows the fears and the courage necessary for survival on the land.

It is appropriate, therefore, that Ehrlich alludes to Hemingway—also to Joseph Conrad—writers who knew poignantly the terrors of loneliness and the need to master these terrors. In a memorable essay, "On Water," she reveals how important water is to the sheepherder and rancher; in this context she mentions Hemingway's attitudes toward water in "Big Two Hearted River" and Conrad's in *Heart of Darkness* (1902). These allusions do not seem out of place in her work. Ehrlich brings to the writer's task skills that are formidable—particularly the skill to make the reader *see*, an objective that Conrad once described as his chief claim as an artist. In language that recalls Conrad's, she epitomizes the objective of her book: "Finally, the lessons in impermanence taught me this: loss constitutes an odd kind of fullness; despair empties out into an unquenchable appetite for life."

Leslie B. Mittleman

Sources for Further Study

Glamour. LXXXIII, December, 1985, p. 192.
Kirkus Reviews. LIII, September 1, 1985, p. 928.
Library Journal. CX, November 1, 1985, p. 105.
The New York Times Book Review. XC, December 1, 1985, p. 41.
Publishers Weekly. CCXXVIII, October 25, 1985, p. 56.
Texas Monthly. XC, December 1, 1985, p. 41.
Time. CXXVII, January 6, 1986, p. 92.

SOLZHENITSYN IN EXILE
Critical Essays and Documentary Materials

Editors: John B. Dunlop, Richard S. Haugh (1942-), and Michael Nicholson
Publisher: Hoover Institution Press (Stanford, California). 414 pp. $19.95
Type of work: Criticism and interpretation

Essays and materials concerning exiled Soviet author Aleksandr Solzhenitsyn

This volume is a welcome addition to the earlier *Aleksandr Solzhenitsyn: Critical Essays and Documentary Materials* (1973), which covered the period until Aleksandr Solzhenitsyn's enforced exile from the Soviet Union in 1974. Two of the three editors of the present volume also edited the earlier work; together, the two books present a thorough picture of Solzhenitsyn's literary works, political opinions, and controversial polemics, which have made him a center of attention throughout the world.

The book is divided into four parts: a series of informative essays which depict Solzhenitsyn's reception in various countries, including the United States; critical essays on the author's postexile writings and sociopolitical beliefs; documentary materials (letters, an interview concerning his views on literature, and Lidiia Chukovskaia's reminiscences of Solzhenitsyn); and finally, a lengthy and extremely useful bibliography of Solzhenitsyn's works and works about the author. Unlike the first volume, which was a compilation of essays and lectures printed or delivered under various auspices, this volume, according to the preface, contains articles specially commissioned for inclusion in *Solzhenitsyn in Exile*. At least one article, however, has appeared elsewhere; "Yugoslav Reactions to Solzhenitsyn" was recently published in an American journal for teachers of Russian.

All the essays are written with sympathy for Solzhenitsyn, castigating his opponents and praising his friends. For example, Edward J. Brown takes Soviet literary critic Vladimir Lakshin and others to task for criticizing Solzhenitsyn's less than flattering treatment of Soviet poet and editor Aleksandr Tvardovsky in *Bodalsya telyenok s dubom* (1975; *The Oak and the Calf*, 1980). Even some staunch supporters of Solzhenitsyn in his myriad battles with the Soviet establishment were critical of the author's picture of an alcoholic and sometimes less-than-bold Tvardovsky, the editor of the liberal literary journal *Novy mir*, which published *Odin den Ivana Denisovicha* (1962; *One Day in the Life of Ivan Denisovich*, 1963). Tvardovsky had also supported Solzhenitsyn before Party leaders and the bureaucrats of the Union of Soviet Writers. Brown defends Solzhenitsyn's portrait of Tvardovsky and counters that Solzhenitsyn does not owe the late editor the loyalty which Tvardovsky's friends and relatives believe that he does. This controversy has caused embitterment and considerable dissension among many Soviet liberals and dissidents.

The main point of the essays in this book, however, is not to portray the divisions among friends and allies of Tvardovsky but, rather, to ask one simple question: Why has the perception of Solzhenitsyn in the West changed so drastically in the ten years since his involuntary departure from the Soviet Union? His portrait of Tvardovsky may have caused some people to view Solzhenitsyn as an ingrate, but much more serious questions have arisen concerning his social and political views. Indeed, there is no doubt that his stock in the United States has gone down; many who viewed Solzhenitsyn as a suffering dissident speaking out for freedom in the Soviet Union now see him as a reactionary cold warrior who does not seem to believe in the fundamental freedoms of democracy. The essays dealing with his reception in various countries portray the confusion that commenced as Solzhenitsyn began to criticize what he perceived as the weaknesses of the Western democracies, which, in his opinion, have lost the religious foundations of Western civilization and are given over to unrestrained and licentious behavior.

Were there two Solzhenitsyns—a democratic liberal in the Soviet Union replaced by a conservative religious fanatic in the West? Perhaps Solzhenitsyn was traumatized as he was forcibly catapulted to the West, or perhaps he conceived of the West as Utopia and has understandably been disappointed and become bitter. David Halperin's essay "Continuities in Solzhenitsyn's Ethical Thought" pursues this question and points out that Western commentators often missed the points which Solzhenitsyn was attempting to make while he was in the Soviet Union. In fact, because of Soviet restrictions and Solzhenitsyn's legendary secretiveness, little was known of the author's beliefs except a strongly felt anti-Stalinism. Contrary to speculation, Solzhenitsyn was not a sincere Marxist-Leninist trying to undo the legacy of Stalinism, such as Soviet dissident Roy Medvedev, nor was he a constitutional democrat who believes in a secularized society, such as Nobel Peace Prize recipient Andrey Sakharov. He was, and still is, a member of the Russian Orthodox Church who firmly believes that the foundations of government and society should be Christian principles. Furthermore, Solzhenitsyn considers the fundamental tragedy of the twentieth century to be the turning away from God by those who are the heirs of Western culture and civilization. This process had already been noted in the nineteenth century by Fyodor Dostoevski, who predicted that the movement would lead to disaster. It is no accident that Solzhenitsyn, in his polemical writings, looks back to the nineteenth century as the beginning of this evolution in Russia, when the intelligentsia grew restive under the authoritarianism of the czars and also rejected religious belief in favor of science and utopian social theories. Solzhenitsyn believes, as Dostoevski loosely predicted, that these mistaken beliefs led directly to Marxism—a "scientific socialism"—and then to Stalinism, which Solzhenitsyn considers not to be an aberration from Marxism-Leninism but, rather, a logical conclusion to a theory fundamentally flawed by its rejection of God.

Donald Treadgold's essay "Solzhenitsyn's Intellectual Antecedents" points out that the author is in many ways similar to Nikolai Berdyaev, Sergei Bulgakov, and other Russian intellectuals of the early twentieth century who abjured Marxism and returned to Christianity. This group, in a book of essays entitled *Landmarks* (1909), called upon the intelligentsia to repent of its atheism and to reject dreams of a materialistic Utopia. Solzhenitsyn has done much the same thing in his collection of essays *Iz-pod glyb* (1974; *From Under the Rubble*, 1975), which calls upon Soviet intellectuals to reject Marxism, as he did, and return to Christian ideals, especially the pursuit of truth.

Perhaps the question should be placed in a broader context for readers who are not familiar with the vagaries of Russian intellectual history. Prerevolutionary Russia, untouched directly by the Reformation or the Renaissance and only superficially influenced by the Enlightenment, entered the twentieth century with a traditional theory of the connection between religion and culture, a theory which was generally rejected by the Protestant West in the nineteenth century and largely ignored by Catholicism in the twentieth century. In brief, this concept holds that religious belief and ideals form the basis of culture; the etymological connection between cult and culture is more than mere coincidence. The health of any civilization, therefore, is dependent upon the depth of its religious commitment; the chaos of the twentieth century, with its world wars and revolutions, antisocial behavior, and rebellion against tradition, is a mirror of the loss of faith. Religious belief served as a cohesive force in society; because of the loss of faith, that cohesion is disintegrating and society is on the verge of collapse.

Opposing this pessimistic point of view is the dominant belief of the twentieth century, which places more emphasis on secularized ideals, such as education and democracy, than on religious ideals. This theory tends to see disruptions of order as temporary aberrations from a basically progressive development of history rather than as manifestations of a general breakdown of civilization. As this contemporary belief became more important, it was accompanied by a gradual loss of faith and rejection of religion, at least among the educated classes in the United States and among almost all classes in Europe, and a corresponding growth in individualism as opposed to the communitarianism inspired by ideals held by the great majority.

With this background in mind, the reader can understand Solzhenitsyn's position when he left the Soviet Union in 1974. The author achieved great fame as a solitary opponent of a repressive regime, a man of courage against the behemoth of the Soviet state. With that reputation ensured, Solzhenitsyn came to the West and explained his beliefs, which turned out to be beliefs already jettisoned by the West. Instead of being a living reproach to the Soviet Union, he now became a reproach to the West and its loss of religious faith. Shocked at this turn of events and perhaps irritated that their hero had turned upon them, Western liberals began to criticize the exiled author and then to ridicule him for his strongly felt and sometimes strongly expressed beliefs. Mistakes of fact and hasty generalizations on Solzhenitsyn's part were eagerly seized upon as examples of the author's intellectual and political backwardness.

This book of essays and documentary materials records the many aspects of this continuing controversy, including the awkward handling of Solzhenitsyn by President Gerald R. Ford in 1975. Critics of Solzhenitsyn are cited, despite the bias of the contributors in favor of the author; the reader receives an accurate picture of the controversies surrounding Solzhenitsyn, although the critics themselves deserve a reading before a final judgment is rendered.

Solzhenitsyn has entered the second half of the twentieth century as a contemporary prophet in the biblical sense; like some of his Hebrew predecessors, he is experiencing the disapproval of those who are being called upon to repent. He is also criticized by those who believe that his residence of only twelve years in the West, most of it in isolation in rural Vermont, has led him to either mistaken conclusions or an exaggeratedly pessimistic diagnosis of the ills facing society. Whatever the outcome of these controversies, Solzhenitsyn has cast a long and broad shadow. This book will be extremely useful for the reader who wishes to understand what makes the exiled Soviet author persevere in his life's work.

Philip Maloney

Sources for Further Study

Best Sellers. XLV, December, 1985, p. 353.
Book Forum. VII, no. 2, 1985, p. 27
Kirkus Reviews. LIII, September 1, 1985, p. 926.
Library Journal. CX, September 15, 1985, p. 82.
Publishers Weekly. CCXXVIII, August 9, 1985, p. 68.

SOMETHING SAID

Author: Gilbert Sorrentino (1929-   )
Publisher: North Point Press (San Francisco, California). 266 pp. $15.50
Type of work: Critical essays

Critical essays from the past twenty-five years by a distinguished American novelist and poet

Gilbert Sorrentino is best known as a novelist whose darkly comic writing draws its inspiration from the extravagant Irish genius of James Joyce and Flann O'Brien. Among his many novels are *Mulligan Stew* (1979), *Aberration of Starlight* (1980), *Imaginative Qualities of Actual Things* (1971), *Crystal Vision* (1981), and *Blue Pastoral* (1983). In addition, he has published several books of poetry. As a poet he works consciously in the tradition of William Carlos Williams, Ezra Pound, Charles Olson, and the so-called Black Mountain School that Olson inaugurated in recent American verse. Olson's pupils have included Robert Creeley, Robert Duncan, Jonathan Williams, and Ed Dorn, all accorded honorific treatment by Sorrentino. Currently, Sorrentino is a professor of English at Stanford University.

This collection demonstrates Sorrentino's talents as a critic and literary essayist. Whenever "real writers" turn their attention to criticism, one is interested in learning more of their preferences and in following the profession of their aesthetic creed, but critical essays rarely do more than gloss aspects of a writer's "real" works—that is, his novels, stories, poems, and plays. Or perhaps one might consult such a writer's critical essays for suggestions on other writers to read (or not to read). Sorrentino, because of the range and diversity of his literary preoccupations, manages to transcend these horizons to comment forcefully on the arbitrariness of the academic literary canon that selects a few writers as masters while consigning so many deserving writers to oblivion. Sorrentino even avoids, at least most of the time, the annoying tendency in books such as his to indulge in narcissistic self-congratulation and knowing gossip about "those of us who are writers."

The arrangement of the book itself is unusual. It appears at first glance that the essays follow a sequence like the traditional one of the Koran, in descending order of chapter length. What Sorrentino has in fact done is to string together, in chronological order, all the pieces that he has produced over the years concerning a given writer or theme. To call attention to some of his deepest commitments, for example, to Williams, Olson, Louis Zukofsky, Jack Spicer, and Paul Blackburn, he has placed several longer essays among the first of the forty-seven "chapters" of *Something Said*. The reader gradually becomes accustomed to the steady accretions, working somewhat like time-lapse photographs, which make up these essays. The effect, indeed their effectiveness, is cumulative, Three brief selections near the end of the volume deal with the visual arts. They seem oddly out of place, dwarfed as they are by the amount of space devoted to literary considerations, but they breed curiosity about Sorrentino's potential as an art critic.

The source of the book's title can be found in the writing of Maurice Blanchot, whose texts are noteworthy for blurring the distinction between "criticism" and "writing." The *quelque chose dit* of Blanchot is what one writes in order to resist finality, and Sorrentino must be understood as struggling against academic shibboleths and received opinions concerning writers and texts. In effect, he turns this maneuver on himself by contrasting later and earlier pieces, showing graphically how something more always remains "to be said."

In the case of a writer he admires as passionately as he does William Carlos Williams, that something more takes the form of a deepening appreciation and an ever more anguished cry of protest that literary academe has at best embraced only grudgingly this great poet. This theme echoes throughout the essays on Olson, Zukofsky, Spicer, Kenneth Rexroth, and Lorine Niedecker. Sorrentino not only complains about these exclusions but also questions the prominent position given such moderns as Robert Frost, suggesting that Frost is much overestimated. Though the poetic canon is his chief preoccupation, he also expresses considerable dismay over the novelists typically selected for front-page reviews in *The New York Times Book Review*. One of the most thoroughly lionized novelists of the 1970's, the late John Gardner, is one of Sorrentino's least favorite writers. He resents Gardner's posturings—his willingness to designate himself in an interview as "one of the best" living writers—and perhaps even more Sorrentino dislikes Gardner's naturalist aesthetic, Gardner being conventionally regarded as one whose books encourage readers to "recognize" themselves and their society in all its oppressive contemporaneity. Although Sorrentino does not mention it, Gardner's ill-humored "plague on all their houses" tract, *On Moral Fiction* (1978), must also be a source of irritation.

Against Gardner, Sorrentino would oppose an enigmatic writer such as Italo Calvino, who eschewed the omniscient "I" of traditional narrative and created enough doubt concerning the "you" of the supposed addressee to suggest the complicity of the reader in the text's (re-)creation. This calls to mind the "writerly text" so highly prized by Roland Barthes, but Gilbert Sorrentino is no trendy poststructuralist when it comes to his literary enthusiasms. Two of the critics he quotes at key junctures in *Something Said* will give some indication of his position. He begins his first essay in the collection with a quote from Walter Benjamin: "No poem is intended for the reader, no picture for the beholder, no symphony for the listener." Much later, in his essay on Calvino, Sorrentino quotes the Russian formalist critic Victor Shklovsky: "The ideas in a literary work do not constitute its content but rather its material, and in their combinations and interrelations with other aspects of the work they create its form."

In a sense, then, writing is "for" writers themselves, but it would probably be more correct to point out that Sorrentino, somewhat like such an icono-clastic contemporary critic as Edward Said, attempts to walk a line between equally outmoded formalist and purely biographical approaches. The writer is seen as someone who transforms his or her (usually, for Sorrentino, "his," a problem which will be discussed below) historical situation into writing, although that writing is never understood as a mere reflection of spatio-temporality. In his essay on Spicer, Sorrentino writes, "The poet is nowhere to be found in his poem; he has disappeared behind the words." Out of context, this could appear to be an endorsement of New Criticism, but it is pre-cisely New Criticism which has led to the select pantheon of "great modern poets" that Sorrentino questions so forcefully.

Often, Sorrentino urges the reader toward critical appreciation in much the manner of Ezra Pound's *The ABC of Reading* (1934): "Use your ear, this is great writing!" he seems to say, proffering samples of overlooked po-etry and prose. The index of greatness in the writers Sorrentino champions is a stubbornly "American" quality, but not "American" in the agreeably affirmative sense of a Walt Whitman or a Carl Sandburg. Again, because of the political conservatism of the New Critics, the American poetic canon abounds either in writers who, like T. S. Eliot, pose in Continental garb or in "folksy" all-Americans such as Frost. To Sorrentino, William Carlos Wil-liams is a "great American writer" because he shows the darker side of the American experience: the heartbreak, the alienation, the shabby sentimen-tality, and the sleazy commercialism. Like Pound, Williams does this in both prose and poetry:

> Williams' vision is essentially bleak and tragic—not anything so fashionable as pessimis-tic. Here is America, the artist says. Let us investigate it and see what it is. It is dead. What has it done to its people? They are ruined.

Sorrentino's analysis confirms the suspicion that the academic guardians of the literary canon must exclude writers such as Williams on blatantly political grounds, whatever their purely "aesthetic" protestations to the con-trary. Williams, the "kindly small-town doctor," picked impertinently at the hideous scab of modern American experience. Or, in keeping with the above passage, perhaps autopsy would be a more appropriate metaphor. For Sorrentino, it is precisely such a grim postmortem that truly "American" writing must conduct. In an essay deploring the critical neglect of the writings of Edward Dahlberg, Sorrentino states that "American literature is wondrous because of the way in which it confronts the limping and shabby thing that is American experience."

Although not reflecting an obvious theme of his book, observations such as these open a window onto Sorrentino's trenchant brand of social criti-cism. It is reluctantly given, for it is his conviction that Americans are all under the spell of a post-Romantic "humanism," too strongly compelled to see the artist as "a kind of dazed egomaniac to whom we look for inter-pretations of the world that may be taken as revelatory of the world's reality." Nevertheless, Sorrentino's occasional complaints about the spiritual impoverishment at the heart of American culture are painfully wounding in their timely accuracy. At least once, this becomes prophetic: in a 1967 essay on Nathanael West, in which Sorrentino relates the personality of then California governor Ronald Reagan to the frighteningly one-dimensional characters of West's fiction. Sorrentino remarks bitterly that "Mr. Reagan, or someone very like him, will be our president, and *we* deserve him." This looms ahead for Sorrentino as "the final victory of a debased democracy to propose candidates who were conceived in celluloid and who speak with the voice of the sound track."

There is a relationship between these aspects of American culture and the highly arbitrary process by which a few novels appear on the front page of *The New York Times Book Review* and by which a select few novelists and poets acquire canonical status in American universities, and Sorrentino explores it well. Yet he displays an embarrassing lack of interest in the most glaring exclusion of all: women writers. Particularly in his earlier essays, one is struck by Sorrentino's use of the word "men" to refer to the handful of neglected writers he cherishes. Even though he pleas for overdue attention to Lorine Niedecker and Denise Levertov, he devotes precious few pages to them, compared to his lengthy considerations of Williams or Spicer. The chief reason for admiring Levertov appears to be her affinities with Sorrentino's much-cherished Black Mountain school of poets.

Much more space is allotted to demolishing the literary reputation of Marianne Moore. This is largely because of her willingness to pose, like Frost, as the prototype of the "eccentric, much beloved great American poet." Sorrentino also sharply criticizes the "retreat from life" apparent in her work. This appears to derive from his sense that the best American poetry springs from sleeves-rolled-up immersion in the dirt and grit of daily life, following Dr. Williams' dictum of "no ideas but in things themselves." Is Sorrentino suggesting that avoidance of the raw immediacy of life is a feminine trait? It would almost seem so, even if he avoids Harold Bloom's scenario of poetry as a manly vocation revolving around fierce grappling with one's fatherly predecessors. In a book whose urgency grows in the accumulation of justifiable complaints about the appalling neglect accorded so many fine contemporary American writers, especially poets, why is there no mention of Anne Sexton or Adrienne Rich, or of such talented young poets as Carolyn Forché or Sharon Olds? Like so many other significant books of criticism by men, this one, too, is incomplete—decentered by what it cannot, or would rather not, talk about.

Not that one should demand closure from a book whose very title denotes, via Blanchot, the poststructuralist critique of that concept; it is more to the point to say that feminism is not "just another" excluded topic. A revised canon will have to be more than, as with Sorrentino, the substitution of a few neglected men for the traditional figures. Serious consideration of writing by women, still at best a marginal concern for departments of English everywhere, will lead to radically revised estimations of works that will increasingly appear to have been overvalued more as a result of sexism (which works most effectively when it works unconsciously) than of most other imperatives.

In other words, there is much more that could be said in *Something Said*. Yet, to an extent, that is a criticism canceled in advance by the book's very intent. It is the kind of book that must never be taken as a "summing up," for it will have succeeded precisely to the extent that it invites and encourages other books to supplement and even supersede it. Despite its flaws, its continued importance may be that, as with this reviewer, it will send readers in search of the poems, stories, and novels of the neglected artists it rescues from oblivion.

James A. Winders

Sources for Further Study

Booklist. LXXXI, January 15, 1985, p. 680.
Kirkus Reviews. LII, October 15, 1984, p. 1001.
Library Journal. CIX, December, 1984, p. 2280.
Los Angeles Times Book Review. March 3, 1985, p. 7.
The New York Times Book Review. XC, March 3, 1985, p. 19.
Publishers Weekly. CCXXVI, October 12, 1984, p. 48.
Washington Post Book World. XV, February 10, 1985, p. 3.

THE SOONG DYNASTY

Author: Sterling Seagrave (1937-   )
Publisher: Harper & Row, Publishers (New York). 532 pp. $22.50
Type of work: Biography
Time: The twentieth century
Locale: Primarily China

An examination of the impact of the Soong family on modern Chinese history

Principal personages:
CHARLIE SOONG, a revolutionary and the patriarch of Soong family
AI-LING SOONG, his daughter, a speculator and the wife of H. H. Kung
CHING-LING SOONG, his daughter, a revolutionary and the wife of Sun Yat-sen
MAY-LING SOONG, his daughter, the wife of Chiang Kai-shek
T. V. SOONG, his son, the prime minister and financier of Kuomintang party
SUN YAT-SEN, a revolutionary
TU YUEH-SHENG, the Green Gang boss and a financial supporter of Chiang Kai-shek and the Soongs

Journalist Sterling Seagrave recasts Nationalist Chinese history of the twentieth century from the Christian, social democratic images projected by the China Lobby, a United States lobby group, to the utterly corrupt, authoritarian reality of the Soong dynasty. No longer does the reader look to those "pinkos" of the United States Department of State as those "who lost China" but to the members of the Soong family, who were responsible for maintaining Chiang Kai-shek at the head of the Nationalist Chinese government.

The Soong dynasty included three generations of Soong family members, family members by marriage, and close associates of this coterie. Charlie Soong (1866-1918), who initiated the dynasty, made valuable connections through American Christian missionary training and was active in Sun Yat-sen's revolutionary movement. Three of Charlie's daughters—Ai-ling, Ching-ling, and May-ling—and a son, T. V. Soong, were deeply involved in the Chinese revolution and the Nationalist government. Through marriage, Chiang Kai-shek and H. H. Kung joined the Soongs. Tu Yueh-sheng, the boss of a Shanghai criminal society, was financially and politically involved with the Soongs for many decades.

Seagrave's work comments on several themes running through Chinese history during the first half of the twentieth century. First in importance is the revolutionary tradition rooted in the Taiping Rebellion (1850-1864), the nine attempted rebellions of Sun Yat-sen, and the conservative revolution of Chiang Kai-shek. A second thesis involves the relations of the United States and Nationalist China, and how arrogant and naïve the former became. Finally, Seagrave's main focus centers on how the Soong family propped up the Nationalist government for so many years. Seagrave's interpretations of these main courses of Chinese history substantially revise previous outlooks and should find a receptive audience in this era of normalized relations between the People's Republic of China and the United States.

As presented by Seagrave, the Soong family was inextricably involved in the flow of Chinese history. Charlie Soong, the family's patriarch, established the major characteristics of the principal members of the Soong dynasty. He initiated the family practice of acquiring an American education at prestigious institutions, including Harvard University and Oberlin College. Fluent in English, ostensibly Christian in practice, and American in style, the Soongs were influential in both Eastern and Western business and political circles. At the same time, contrary to their carefully groomed public image, the Soongs maintained their close association with Tu Yueh-sheng, the leader of the Green Gang, a powerful criminal society which made vast fortunes in Shanghai from dealings in drugs, prostitution, protection, and numerous other rackets. Finally, in Seagrave's account, Chiang Kai-shek and H. H. Kung, who was for a time Chiang Kai-shek's finance minister, appear as virtual puppets of their respective wives, May-ling and Ai-ling Soong.

The anomaly of the Soong family emerged in the person of Ching-ling, Charlie's second daughter. Following her education at Wesleyan College in Georgia, she returned to China to serve Sun Yat-sen, first as his secretary and then as his wife. With his death in 1925, Ching-ling remained committed to Sun Yat-sen's liberal Socialist revolution, which isolated her from the mainstream of conservative Soong political interests as focused in Chiang's Kuomintang Party (KMT). True to her social beliefs, she remained on the mainland following the Communist takeover and lived in comfort and respect in Peking as the widow of Sun Yat-sen until her death in 1981.

Seagrave suggests that American conceptions (and misconceptions) of China for much of the twentieth century were significantly influenced by May-ling and T. V. Soong, who skillfully exploited American missionary endeavors and business interests in China. Their credentials of language, education, and style opened many financial and political doors in New York and Washington, D.C. As a result, the Soongs greatly benefitted from the support of Henry Luce, the owner of Time-Life, and Lend-Lease Act, and other foreign aid from the Roosevelt Administration. Indeed, American public opinion favored Nationalist China for decades until official American diplomatic ties were established with the People's Republic.

Throughout Seagrave's examination of the Soong family, Chiang Kai-shek, and the KMT, the theme of graft and corruption predominates. Seagrave disposes of the myth that KMT siphoning off of lend-lease and foreign aid came only at the end, prior to the Chinese Communist takeover. Rather, he demonstrates that from the start Charlie Soong accepted considerable financial aid from questionable sources, supplied by Tu Yueh-sheng in support of Sun Yat-sen's abortive revolutions. In similar fashion, Chiang Kai-shek relied on money from the Green Gang to support his revolution. T. V. Soong, in collaboration with Tu Yueh-sheng, became one of the world's wealthiest men through currency manipulation, bank embezzlement, and questionable real estate dealings in the United States, among other schemes. H. H. Kung, the husband of Ai-ling Soong, similarly fed well at the public trough. Not until after World War II ended did the Harry S Truman Administration begin to limit foreign aid to China as recognition of widespread corruption emerged.

Although Seagrave should not be called a knee-jerk liberal, individuals of the political Left are cast in a rosier light in his account than are the members of the Soong dynasty. Ching-ling emerges triumphant as the heroic widow of Sun Yat-sen. Seagrave favorably comments on those martyred heroes of the United States Foreign Service, Jack Service, O. Edmund Clubb, John Paton Davies, and John Carter Vincent, whose careers were terminated or who were persecuted in the McCarthy era. Their field reports, generally accurate but naïvely written, were highly critical of Chiang Kai-shek and the KMT and, by implication, supportive of the Communist Chinese by the understanding of those times.

A similar tilt to the political Left is evident in Seagrave's positive depiction of the Chinese Communist Party (CCP) and its dominant leaders, Mao Tse-tung and Zhou Enlai. When comparing KMT and CCP programs and their implementation, Seagrave usually interprets the latter's more favorably. Certainly the Communists had legitimate grievances, but they were capable of ruthless brutality, a point that Seagrave tends to muffle.

Every civilization sets a distinctive tone, whether it be one of material riches, war, art, or cruelty. Here, Seagrave catches fully the tone of the Soong dynasty in its corruption, moral decay, and intellectual rot. From this perspective, the emergence of Mao Tse-tung and the Chinese Communist Party could be seen as an inevitable historical result; the delay in reaching it can in part be seen as a measure of the extent to which American fear and gullibility were so ably played upon by May-ling. In the end, the Soong dynasty ended as do all dynasties, this one crumbling away in its own corrosion.

John F. Riddick

Sources for Further Study

Booklist. LXXXI, March 1, 1985, p. 922.
Kirkus Reviews. LII, December 15, 1984, p. 1195.

Library Journal. CX, March 1, 1984, p. 84
Los Angeles Times Book Review. May 19, 1984, p. 7.
Macleans. XCVIII, April 15, 1985, p. 56.
The New York Times Book Review. XC, March 17, 1985, p. 1.
Publishers Weekly. CCXXVII, January 25, 1985, p. 79.
Time. CXXV, April 29, 1985, p. 82.
The Wall Street Journal. CCV, April 19, 1985, p. 26.
Washington Post Book World. XV, March 24, 1985, p. 1.

STAINED GLASS ELEGIES

Author: Shusaku Endo (1923-   )
Translated from the Japanese, with an introduction, by Van C. Gessel
Publisher: Dodd, Mead & Company (New York). 165 pp. $13.95
Type of work: Short stories

The first collection of stories translated into English by one of Japan's foremost novelists

When asked about his fiction, Shusaku Endo has said that the subtleties of contact between Oriental and Western experience are at the center of his art. This is not surprising. He himself has experienced at firsthand the passion of Roman Catholic commitment in twentieth century Japan. The martyrdom of early Japanese Catholics in the sixteenth and seventeenth centuries was mirrored for Endo in the persecutions that he experienced as a young man. During World War II, Christian affiliation was considered a less than patriotic connection. Japan's life-and-death struggle with the Allies did not encourage tolerance of Western institutions. Even if, like Catholicism, such institutions were already well enough established to withstand the first attacks of the government, it eventually became necessary to punish "Europeanism" with isolating measures. Endo was subjected to a form of house arrest at a Christian college dormitory throughout the war years for his pacifism.

The stories in this collection add new stature to an international reputation already secured by several novels. Irving Howe was moved to the following praise after reading Endo's most recent novel, *The Samurai* (1980): ". . . surely one of the most accomplished writers now living in Japan or anywhere else." Endo's many literary prizes won in Japan testify to his reputation among his own countrymen despite the marginality of his principal theme: Christian identity in a non-Christian society. *Silence* (1969), his best-known work, sold more than eight hundred thousand copies in Japan alone. John Updike called it "a remarkable work, a . . . startlingly emphatic study of a young Portuguese missionary during the relentless persecutions of Japanese Christians in the early seventeenth century."

Stained Glass Elegies largely supports Endo's contention that he is primarily a writer about religious feeling at odds with cultural or personal reality. "Fuda-no-Tsuji" is a story in which a site associated with early Japanese Christian martyrs becomes the locus of a painful memory for the narrator. He cannot forget a vigil at the site shared with a pathetic but brave and selfless European-Jewish monk named "Mouse"—the butt of everyone's ridicule in the narrator's student days at the Christian college—who is later murdered by the Japanese authorities.

An even deeper and more haunting guilt is probed in "My Belongings." Here a man, long past youth, finds himself neither truly identified with his Christian faith nor lovingly attached to his wife. Nevertheless, his commitment is stronger than his desire; the man cannot abandon what he had chosen at a time in his life when choosing was a vital act. The residual power of his waning faith and love sustain his disillusioned character. The light of faith still shines mysteriously through the "stained windows" of experience. Whereas Western skepticism might call the husband's faith a victory of habit, Endo's realism and understatement lend a strange sanctity to the moment. In "Mothers," another story about guilt, the narrator conflates the guilt of the Kakure, who betrayed their Christian faith to avoid torture and death, with his own guilt for betraying his domineeringly pious mother.

In "Mothers," there is another dimension central to Endo's fiction—a dimension as important as Christian suffering. It is the world of the hospital room; the trauma of convalescence constitutes Endo's most trying experience in later life. His lengthy hospitalization for massive lung surgery becomes a pendant to the religious persecution of his youth. Both experiences test his faith and his capacities for perception and honesty. In "Mothers," the narrator dreams about his mother while he is hospitalized. In "A Forty-Year-Old-Man," which chronicles the daily trials of a seriously ill patient, a mynah bird gradually transforms from a natural creature into a Christ symbol and rewards the narrator-sufferer with something richer than the companionship of a pet—Christ's pity.

Endo's collection of stories has the intensity of a miracle play, and as with all such religious drama, there is a comic interlude. Halfway through the volume, the reader encounters a scatological tale so impish and irreverent that it almost seems blasphemous in the context of the tales as a whole. A naïve young doctor in "Incredible Voyage," a science-fiction fantasy (actually a parody of the 1966 American film *Fantastic Voyage*), is miniaturized and enters his sweetheart's bloodstream to operate on a tumor. He ends up blocked in her large intestine. Flatulence is the agent of deliverance in this story.

The stories are often breathless, choppy, and sometimes repetetive. Yet there is a rightness and deftness of feeling that sees many of them through to visionary statement. Most touching is "Old Friends," the closing story, an epilogue to the collection. An old European priest, tortured during the war by the Japanese on suspicion of espionage, casually announces that spring always returns. Suffering does not kill hope. Dishonesty, repression, and cowardice are more successful. Yet suffering and hope have a strongly paradoxical interdependence. It is finally deep wisdom such as this that pushes Endo's stories toward greatness.

Peter A. Brier

Sources for Further Study

Booklist. LXXXI, May 1, 1985, p. 1236.
Kirkus Reviews. LIII, February 1, 1985, p. 99.
Library Journal. CX, May 1, 1985, p. 76.
Listener. CXIII, January 10, 1985, p. 24.
New Statesman. CVIII, September 21, 1984, p. 29.
The New York Times Book Review. XC, July 21, 1985, p. 21.
The Observer. December 2, 1984, p. 19.
Publishers Weekly. CCXXVII, February 1, 1985, p. 350.
Times Literary Supplement. October 26, 1984, p. 1223.
Washington Post Book World. XV, June 23, 1985, p. 10.

STANLEY AND THE WOMEN

Author: Kingsley Amis (1922-   )
Publisher: Summit Books (New York). 256 pp. $14.95
Type of work: Novel
Time: The 1980's
Locale: London

A satirical novel that directs its animus against women and psychiatry

> *Principal characters:*
> STANLEY DUKE, the advertising manager of a daily newspaper
> SUSAN, Stanley's current wife, an assistant literary editor
> STEVE, Stanley's son, an acute schizophrenic
> NOWELL, Steve's mother and Stanley's former wife, an actress
> CLIFF WAINWRIGHT, Stanley's friend, a medical doctor
> ALFRED NASH, a psychiatrist
> TRISH COLLINGS, a psychiatrist in charge of Steve's case

Kingsley Amis' seventeenth novel, *Stanley and the Women*, has already become a *cause célèbre*. Its wicked satirical thrust and misogynistic sentiments allegedly provoked feminist editors of various publishing houses to try unsuccessfully to stop its publication in the United States. Whatever the truth of these allegations, the emergence of the novel was delayed, and the American edition appeared a year later than its British counterpart. There is substance to this furor, for the antifeminine slant of *Stanley and the Women* will continue to generate controversy, grievously offending those readers who harbor strong ideological convictions—feminist, leftist, or liberal. Like most satirical works which incline toward corrosive and subversive irony, *Stanley and the Women* is often unfair, uncharitable, and intolerant; it is also outrageously funny.

Stanley and the Women begins where *Jake's Thing* (1978) ends. In Amis' earlier novel, Jake Richardson, whose sexual drive has diminished almost to the point of nonexistence, submits religiously to the manifold "cures" of psychotherapists and sexologists. At the end of his travail, and after nearly three hundred pages of unrelenting exposure of the incompetence and stupidity of professional therapists and the institutions that sustain them, Jake discovers that the cause of his impotency may have been physical and reflects upon the desirability of reviving his malfunctioning "thing" and thereby regaining his libido:

> Jake did a quick run-through of women in his mind . . . their concern with the surface of things . . . with seeming to be better and to be right while getting everything wrong, their automatic assumption of the role of injured party in any clash of wills, their certainty that a view is the more credible and useful for the fact that they hold it, their use of misunderstanding and misrepresentation as weapons of debate, their selective sensitivity to tones of voice, their unawareness of the difference in themselves between sincerity and insincerity . . . their fondness for general conversation and directionless

discussion, their pre-emption of the major share of feeling, their exaggerated estimate of their own plausibility, their never listening. . . .

His decision as to whether he should undergo more tests is quite easy. "No thanks," he says, and on that note the novel ends.

These antifeminine sentiments, which through extremity Jake is driven to at the end of the story, pervade *Stanley and the Women* from the very beginning. The temptation is to equate the attitudes, ideas, and values of the first-person narrator with those of the implied author. Because one is privy to the innermost thoughts and feelings of Stanley Duke and is given an inside view only of him, one is imprisoned within his consciousness. Therefore it is difficult to determine the implied tone of the text, the author's own attitude or evaluative stance toward the material of his novel, and the amount of ironic distance between the norms of the narrator and those of the author. The problem is compounded when the novel in question is satirical and demands on the part of the reader skills in ironic discounting and interpretive reconstruction.

If only on a superficial level, Kingsley Amis is not Stanley Duke. Stanley has no interest in literature or culture, works in advertising, is mildly anti-Semitic, and drinks cheap Scotch. In fact, he is *l'homme moyen sensuel* with a vengeance, an upwardly mobile Everyman figure who married a class or two above his own. His sexism is a defense mechanism: in the beginning, a momentary stay against the chaotic confusion of an irrational world; in the end, an explanatory principle of reality, a coherent worldview that gives significance to his experience. Equipped with only his comic resistance to "offences against common sense, good manners, fair play, truth," Stanley is a sane antihero struggling to cope with an insane world.

At the beginning of the novel, Stanley Duke, the middle-aged advertising manager of a London daily newspaper, is faring well. His second wife, Susan, seems to be an ideal companion, despite her tendency to show off her genius and draw attention to herself. She is eminently preferable to his first wife, Nowell, who abandoned him for a director. As for Nowell, "all that scared her," Stanley muses, "was the prospect of everybody not looking at her for five seconds. . . . She makes up the past as she goes along. You know, like communists." Although he is still bothered by her desertion, he happily has no contact with her at present. In fact, Stanley seems the quintessence of the liberated husband, playing a subservient role to his wife at her literary parties and deferring politely to her social and cultural superiority.

The equilibrium of Stanley's comfortable existence is disrupted by the arrival of his son, Steve, the only issue of his marriage to Nowell. Suffering from what is eventually diagnosed as acute schizophrenia, Steve rips up one of Susan's novels and later, at his mother's place, hurls an ashtray into the television set. According to him, the Chosen, a group of Jewish conspirators who aim to conquer the world, are trying to seize control of the communications media. Nowell calls in Stanley, Stanley calls in his doctor friend Cliff Wainwright, Cliff calls in his psychiatrist friend Alfred Nash, and Stanley's problems multiply.

The central premise of the novel is stated incisively by Dr. Nash, the only psychiatrist on whom the author bestows respect and authority. "Ordinary people," he maintains, "are usually good judges of [madness], or they were until some lunatic went round telling them it was really the sane ones who were mad.... One of the troubles with psychiatrists in England is that because of the system here they don't often see a madman for months on end.... And there's no teacher like simple quantity of experience." The implication is unmistakable: Real madness is self-evident and incurable; antipsychotic drugs can control it, but nothing can eliminate it. Because neurosis is fashionable, psychiatrists are burdened with hordes of reasonably sane patients and are so inured to the "psychobabble" they mechanically utter that they seduce themselves into believing that it has curative value and render themselves incapable of recognizing real madness when it confronts them. Amis' satire is directed as much against the insanity of psychiatry as it is against the insanity of women. Stanley is willing to admit that Nowell may be "a bit mad" in her division of the world into people who are "sweet" to her and people who are "foul" to her, but he does not at first assent to Nash's proposition that all women are mad. At this point, he believes that there are some exceptions—Susan, for instance—though he will discover soon enough that he is sadly mistaken.

Stanley's miseries begin in earnest when Trish Collings, the hospital psychiatrist assigned to Steve's case, suggests that Stanley is the cause of Steve's psychosis. According to her, Stanley, like many "young primogenitors of high activity," had "a negative attitude towards parenthood and resented the difficulties it occasioned." Trish goes on to offer an explanation of Steve's problems, and the barrage of clichés, jargon, and buzzwords is staggering. Steve, she concludes, has a "problem in living," occasioned by his parents and by his having to cope with "unemployment . . . the nuclear holocaust, racial tension, urban pollution, alienation." Hence he feels "vulnerable" and "powerless" in "a big dangerous world" and therefore creates "a defence," making "a place to hide, a place we call madness, or mental illness, or delusions, or hallucinations." Her job is to "persuade him to lower his defences," to "help him to get in touch with his own feelings, including especially his anger," and to allow him "to find out who he really is."

This is Amis at his savage best. The notion that the puerile pap of pop psychology is of any relevance to a person suffering from acute schizophrenia is exquisitely absurd. As Stanley reflects, "Collings's general style and level of thinking would have done perfectly well for a psychiatrist in an American TV movie." According to Dr. Nash, the author's spokesman, the only valid thing one can say about schizophrenia is that it is an illness in which the brain becomes disordered. As Dr. Nash puts it:

All schizophrenia patients are mad, and none are sane. Their behaviour is incomprehensible. It . . . gives no insight into the human condition and has no lesson for sane people except how sane they are. . . . When [schizophrenics] laugh at things the rest of us don't think are funny, like the death of a parent, they're not being penetrating. . . . They're laughing because they're mad, too mad to be able to tell what's funny any more. The rewards for being sane may not be very many but knowing what's funny is one of them.

Trish's failure to grasp the true nature of Steve's schizophrenic condition impels her to send him home and to discontinue his drug treatment. Her incompetence has dire consequences, for Steve ends up incarcerated in an Arab embassy after the Arabs discover that his information about the Israeli conspiracy has its basis in psychotic distortion rather than political intelligence. After Stanley and the police negotiate his release, he climbs a tree, and once back on the ground, he allegedly attacks Susan with a switchblade. The evidence is a wound on her arm requiring stitches, though Steve vehemently denies responsibility. Without any apparent motivation, Susan accuses Stanley of thinking that her wound is self-inflicted and of believing his deranged and deluded son rather than her. She leaves him, calling him a "lower-class turd" with "no breeding" and "no respect for women." It turns out that the wound was in all probability self-inflicted, and a brief foray into Susan's history reveals that her assumed reasonableness was a charade. Stanley finds out that hers is "the dossier of any other deranged bleeding completely wrapped up in herself female." She is no exception to the rule that all women are mad.

Following the revelation of Susan's duplicity and egomania, the misogynistic frenzy of the narrative achieves its climax. Commiserating with Stanley, Cliff Wainwright drunkenly observes:

According to some bloke on the telly the other night . . . twenty-five per cent of violent crime in England and Wales is husbands assaulting wives. Amazing figure that, don't you think? You'd expect it to be more like eighty per cent. Just goes to show what an easygoing lot English husbands are, only one in four of them bashing his wife. No, it doesn't mean that, does it? But it's funny about wife-battering. Nobody ever asks what the wife had been doing or saying. She's never anything but an ordinary God-fearing woman who happens to have a battering husband. . . .

Stanley puts matters a little less elegantly—indeed, unprintably. Nevertheless, the novel ends with Susan on the phone to Stanley, asking him to forgive her for all the terrible things she said and did.

Given the superflux of outrageous hyperbole in *Stanley and the Women*, it is hard to imagine how any reader could take this novel at face value. In the fictional world of Kingsley Amis, nothing is sacred; irony and satire persist and pervade. As he himself puts it:

All comedy . . . all humor is unfair. . . . There is a beady-eyed view of women in the book, certainly, and as its author I had to spend some time thinking along those lines. But a novel is not a report or a biographical statement or a confession. If it is a good novel, it dramatizes thoughts that some people, somewhere, have had. Haven't most men, at moments of high exasperation, thought, "They're all mad"?

The ironic disparity between the norms of the author and those of the narrator can be ignored only if one is ideologically blinkered or comedically underprivileged. The rewards for being sane may not be very many, but knowing that *Stanley and the Women* is funny is one of them.

Greig E. Henderson

Sources for Further Study

The Atlantic. CCLVI, November, 1985, p. 143.
Booklist. LXXXI, July, 1985, p. 1474.
Los Angeles Times. September 25, 1985, V, p. 8.
The New York Times Book Review. XC, September 22, 1985, p. 9.
The New Yorker. LXI, October 21, 1985, p. 149.
Newsweek. CV, February 4, 1985, p. 80.
Publishers Weekly. CCXXVIII, July 26, 1985, p. 155.
Time. CXXVI, September 30, 1985, p. 74.
The Wall Street Journal. CCVI, September 23, 1985, p. 28.
Washington Post Book World. XV, September 1, 1985, p. 3.

THE STORIES OF MURIEL SPARK

Author: Muriel Spark (1918-   )
Publisher: E. P. Dutton (New York). 314 pp. $18.95
Type of work: Short stories
Time: From World War I to the 1980's
Locale: England and Africa

Twenty-seven intriguing stories, including six not previously published in a collection, by one of England's liveliest contemporary novelists

Muriel Spark is better known and more highly regarded as a novelist than as a short-story writer, for it is in her longer works, such as *Memento Mori* (1959) and *The Prime of Miss Jean Brodie* (1961), that her powers of character delineation and social satire are best displayed. In the short stories, virtually all of which are gathered in this new collection, she shows herself less interested in lampooning people and institutions than in jabbing the reader into an expanded awareness of life's dimensions and possibilities. This seems to have been her purpose form the beginning, for her first published story, "The Seraph and the Zambesi," takes the reader to a remote African outpost where preparations for a Christmas pageant are under way. When an angel visits this tacky celebration of God's presence among men, it is chased away as an intruder rather than welcomed as a manifestation of the divine. Because of Spark's interest in the supernatural, many commentators emphasize the importance of her conversion to Roman Catholicism, but few readers would sense any sectarian bias in these stories. "The Black Madonna," the most overtly Catholic of her stories, deals with a smug young couple's political and social liberalism and the blow that it receives when their child, conceived after repeated prayers to a Madonna carved of bog oak, is born black. Even here, however, the author's religious concerns are secondary to her interest in the couple's shallow convictions and elitist attitudes. A story that touches religious feelings more directly and profoundly—and also more ecumenically—is the semiautobiographical "The Gentile Jewesses," in which three generations of women are shown responding profoundly to religious impulses, but with less regard to the outward form of worship than to a deep sense of the divine in everyday life. Here Spark's view of the importance of religion is most forcefully and aptly expressed.

In the majority of her stories, however, Spark deals in the impact of the unforeseen and unpredictable. The best story in this vein is "The Portobello Road," the narrator of which was nicknamed Needle when she actually found a needle in a haystack. Years later, she is found murdered in a haystack, and she narrates her tale as a ghost, looking back with some regret on a life lived too mechanically by herself and her three best friends, one of whom strangled her when she threatened to tell his fiancée that he was already married to an African woman. Needle's manifestations to George on three successive Saturdays drive the man insane and render his belated confession of murder unintelligible. The narrator's cool objectivity contrasts sharply with the violence and supernaturalism of the tale, emphasizing the idea that life cannot be taken for granted nor its spiritual dimension ignored. These are characteristic themes for Spark, as is the story's unexpected violence. "The Curtain Blown by the Breeze," "Bang-bang You're Dead," and "The Go-Away Bird" include sudden—one is tempted to say, gratuitous—murders, except that these killings are calculated to show, along with the manifestations of the supernatural, the unpredictability and fragility of life.

These two themes are explored in another of Spark's finest stories, "The House of the Famous Poet," in which the narrator buys from a Neanderthal-looking soldier "the abstract idea of a funeral." Moments afterward, a poet's home is destroyed by a V-1 rocket, killing the poet and his housekeeper, both of whom had also bought abstract funerals. Exactly what Spark means by "the abstract idea of a funeral" is left tantalizingly vague, one of the few instances of the open-ended conclusion that reverberates and resonates back through the story and beyond it in the memory. This violent ending is especially unexpected because the story seemed to be exploring the subjective nature of reality—throughout, the narrator comments on how the appearances of people and things change, sometimes instantly. Overall, the story strikes down the complacent view of life and reality as fixed and knowable, and beyond this emphasizes that death, in the abstract and in the particular, throws existence into a new and more meaningful light. In this powerful story, the young narrator encounters the fluidity and brittleness of her existence.

Another fine story, "The Twins," abandons the supernatural to deal naturalistically with the forces outside people's lives that manipulate and control them. The metaphor for this truth is a pair of innocent-looking twins, a well-behaved and apparently normal boy and girl who, by a series of lies and sly innuendos, manipulate their parents and even determine their relations with each other.

Apart from their thematic interest, Spark's stories offer the enticement of carefully crafted, busy plots. Much happens in a Muriel Spark story, condensed into a short narrative frame by her spare and well-pruned prose. She is particularly good at describing with great economy and fidelity the ordinary objects of everyday life, and her dialogue at once sparkles and rings true to life. Her prose quickens the senses and enlivens the imagination. Nevertheless, this emphasis on plot and surface details makes the stories somewhat weak in character development and atmosphere. In all the stories mentioned above, except "The Gentile Jewesses," ideas and events predominate, with the result that in the end one feels little affinity with or affection for the characters about whom one has been reading. Objectivity becomes distance. The narrator and chief character of "The House of the Famous Poet," for example, lacks human warmth; she seems more a vehicle for recording impressions and events than a breathing human being. Even when the narrator focuses attention on character, as in "The Ormolu Clock" and "'A Sad Tale's Best for Winter,'" the reader remains outside the story, looking in with interest but not drawn empathetically into the action or the characters. These are the limitations of an author more interested in ideas than in people.

Among the six new stories, the best is "The Gentile Jewesses," which exudes a warmth and compassion seldom evident in Spark's short fiction. A contrasting story in her humorously satiric vein is "The First Year of My Life." Based on the proposition that children are born omniscient and lose their powers as they grow, this story is narrated by an adult who somehow recalls her first year, lived during 1918 as World War I was drawing to a close. The baby's family is preoccupied with getting the child to smile; for her part, the infant is alternately bored and appalled by the adults around her and those she can tune into through her telepathic powers. Her first smile occurs, not as her family thinks, because of the candle on her birthday cake, but from overhearing a fatuous remark made by Herbert Asquith about the glory of war. The child's naïve perspective is cleverly used here for trenchant, wickedly acute satire. Since this child and the author were born in the same year, it is inviting to equate them and to see in the baby's sarcastic laugh the origin of Spark's own satiric outlook.

The other four new stories fall well below Spark's highest standard. "The Executor" harkens back to "The Portobello Road" in dealing with the relations between the interfering ghost of a famous writer and his niece, whom he appointed his literary executor. When the niece holds back the manuscript of an unpublished and unfinished novel instead of including it with the other papers that she sells to a museum, the moralistic ghost haunts the woman until she does the honest thing. Unfortunately, the story is merely clever, and one is no more interested in the niece's petty crime than one is in the uncle's ghostly high jinks. "The Fortune-Teller" has a set of promising characters and a female narrator with an original and uncanny method of telling fortunes, but in spite of its potential, the story ends with a predictable irony. Similarly, "Another Pair of Hands" trades on the supernatural assistance which a dead housekeeper renders her inept successor, but even the dullest reader can see the ending pages in advance, and in any event the story has nothing new to say about life's spiritual dimension. "The Dragon" features a workaholic fashion designer who hires a "dragon" of a secretary to protect her privacy and then nearly throws away her prosperous business to join a truck driver on a jaunt through Europe. The seamstress-turned-haute-couture-designer is convincingly neurotic and recognizably eccentric yet greedy—the kind of character V. S. Pritchett brings to life—but Spark's attempt at unmasking shallow materialism, while skillful, fails to elicit the necessary sympathy.

Most short-story writers claim a social or psychological territory and spend most of their time exploring within it. Muriel Spark's territory is the frontier between the ordinary and the miraculous, and her tales are most often narrated by women who stand aside form the action that they describe. They are also a curiously sexless lot, only faintly interested in men and never driven by passion. Men in Spark's stories may commit murder in moments of anger but are seldom moved by the erotic or by any strong emotion. This is another reason why Spark's stories exist primarily at the level of idea. They work best when plot and character are well but not too obviously suited to theme. The best stories lay bare an aspect of society or life that is recognizable as real and true; when the tales become predictable or merely clever, they fail. Spark's glittering style and sure technical ability are obvious in everything that she writes, even in whimsical pieces such as "Miss Pinkerton's Apocalypse," and when all the elements come together, she is superb.

Of the twenty-seven stories collected here, roughly a dozen stand beside any written in England in the second half of the twentieth century. A handful of others warrant reading, while the remainder are clever trifles. Few writers can claim so high an average of success. Nevertheless, readers and libraries that already own *Collected Stories I* (1967) will have to decide whether the six new stories of this volume are worth the purchase price.

Dean Baldwin

Sources for Further Study

Kirkus Reviews. LIII, August 1, 1985, p. 750.
Library Journal. CX, October 1, 1985, p. 115.
The New Republic. CXCIII, October 14, 1985, p. 40.
The New York Times Book Review. XC, October 20, 1985, p. 1.
Newsweek. CVI, September 16, 1985, p. 70.
Publishers Weekly. CCXXVIII, August 16, 1985, p. 60.
Washington Post Book World. XV, September 29, 1985, p. 5.

"SURELY YOU'RE JOKING, MR. FEYNMAN!"
Adventures of a Curious Character

Author: Richard P. Feynman (1918-   ), as told to Ralph Leighton
Edited by Edward Hutchings
Introduction by Albert Hibbs
Publisher: W. W. Norton and Company (New York). 346 pp. $16.95
Type of work: Memoirs
Time: The 1930's to the 1970's
Locale: Primarily the United States; Rio de Janeiro

A Nobel laureate in physics recounts his adventures and encounters with the bureaucratic and the stolid as well as with some of his more noted contemporaries

Principal personage:
RICHARD P. FEYNMAN, Nobel laureate in physics

Nobel laureates in physics seem to be expected to write a book which explains their work and its relationship to people's lives. Sometimes, this is followed up with a memoir or chronicle of the development of the laureate's intellectual and scientific self. In all the history of laureate literature, there has been no equivalent of *"Surely You're Joking, Mr. Feynman!" Adventures of a Curious Character*; it can be argued that Dr. Feynman himself is unique if not peerless. What most sets it apart from other memoirs of famed physicists is its lack of introspection and self-analysis. The book is a collection of anecdotes, not diary entries expanded to chapter length. Yet in its way, *"Surely You're Joking, Mr. Feynman!"* epitomizes the man. The title itself is indicative of the intent and the effect of the book; he is both telling jokes and challenging the reader's preconceptions of what a physicist is and what kinds of books he or she should write.

As if the content were not shocking enough, the book was essentially, if not legally, ghostwritten—note the "as told to Ralph Leighton" at the bottom of the title page. Yet this is no ordinary ghostwriter seeking to make a popular hero's ramblings into something palatable or literate; Dr. Leighton teaches physics alongside Feynman at the California Institute of Technology and was instrumental in converting Feynman's lectures into a justifiably acclaimed physics text. Perhaps a Boswell to Feynman's Johnson, but a peer, not merely a foil.

The most important aspect of this book is that it consists of anecdotes collected and compiled by Leighton over a period of years in a highly informal setting (while playing the drums no less, according to the preface). They are arranged in chronological order and thus chronicle Feynman's increasing surprise at the respect accorded him; the more respect, the more surprise. He asks the question that drives publishers to sign up each new laureate: "What makes him (me) tick?" Or, in another formulation, "What makes him (me) special?" In almost every situation, Feynman casts himself as the naïf, often pointing out that the emperor is unclothed. He does not understand what prevents people from thinking clearly, or in some cases, thinking at all. Yet he rarely voices this opinion; he is more content to marvel at the contrast and at the pettiness that dominates so much of other people's lives.

The pattern is set from the outset of both the book and Dr. Feynman's life. He is asked to fix a radio by virtue of his reputation as a boy interested in electronics. As much as he tries to convince the reader/listener that he is unprepared for the repair job, his argument is undercut by his explanation of his thought processes. He just "realizes" the solution. To him, it is simply part of the puzzle-solving he enjoys. This chapter sets the tone for the book—the nonchalance of his solutions, the importance of impressing or astounding the audience, and his predilection for the unconventional. He closes with a brief mention of the various techniques he developed to tackle problems, emphasizing again the way he reshapes the world both to make it his and to make his further explorations easier. It is no wonder that part of his Nobel-winning contributions were called Feynman Diagrams.

Another major theme is introduced in the following chapter, which concerns a labor-saving method that fails. He is almost prouder of his efforts here than of those in the previous chapter, if one measures pride by counting details. The model for Feynman is not so much Albert Einstein or Wolfgang Pauli but Thomas Edison, or maybe even Nikola Tesla, someone with a tattered track record. He suggests that his success is more whimsical than anything else, and that furthermore, his forte is more novelty than philosophy, although the truth is more along the lines of subtlety. To Feynman, the physical world is a Gordian knot, to be unraveled as much as sawn through.

As the book progresses, so does the life of Richard Feynman. He gets to Princeton, where he encounters philosophers and other non-physics types. It is in this chapter that the reader first encounters Feynman the impatient. We see a man frustrated with the endless wrangling over terms that (to him) so characterizes philosophy, or the fascination with terminology that is so prevalent in biology or geology. Physics is reductionist and deductive, reasoning from abstractions, simplifications, and a minimum of special jargon. Throughout the book, one is struck by Feynman's antipathy to "knowledge by naming" and the barriers that the memorization of names erects to the untutored, such as himself.

There is a similar note of querulousness when it comes to the social graces. At every opportunity, Feynman poses the question "Why?" Why must we behave like this? Why don't we say what we mean? Why have protocol? When dealing with people that exude pomposity, the violation of protocol is cute, even funny, a reprise of Groucho Marx versus Margaret Dumont. When dealing with the military authorities, it seems daring and delightful; consider $M^*A^*S^*H^*$. At other times, the question seems adolescent; after all, didn't Holden Caulfield complain about these things, too?

Feynman is not complaining, however; he is only pointing out absurdity. Although in his art, he is representational even when he is abstract, in his dealings with other people, he is a Dadaist.

One of the most interesting sections of the book covers the wartime years at Los Alamos. It was a time of intense work, done in isolation and in secret; for Feynman, it was more than that. He was coming of age. It was also a time of personal tragedy, being stationed at Los Alamos and working feverishly on a secret project with the elite of high-energy physics while his wife was confined to a hospital, dying of tuberculosis. Yet this is not a book about a person's attempts to deal with death or a loved one's mortality. Nor is it a book about coming of age or intellectual rites of passage. Feynman's (first) wife, Arlene, is first mentioned on page 104, in the context of what he would do during his (infrequent) time off from his work at Los Alamos. He would visit Arlene, who was in a hospital in Albuquerque: There is a short anecdote about how well people can discern smells or recognize ones for which they have been keyed. The next mention of her, a few pages later, comes by way of introducing Robert Oppenheimer, who is described as solicitous: "He worried about my wife." All this is done to set up the classic Feynman story of following Oppenheimer's orders to disguise the mass exodus from Princeton to Los Alamos by being the only one to disobey. Arlene's name is brought up several more times in the ensuing pages, to set up other accounts of Feynman's triumphs over the bureaucratic mind. Indeed, it is only her name that is raised, leaving the reader not only at a loss to imagine her or their relationship (When did they court? What did they talk about? How did she feel about his inspired outrageousness?) but also angry at him. It seems callous, and that is not what one expects from heroes. As ever, he "pulls a Feynman" and astonishes the reader with his candor: He admits that her death was something he had much difficulty handling. He tried to suppress it. He still does. There is no question that the poignancy of his recounting is far more affecting than any mere traditional mourning.

The Los Alamos chapter is one of the longest and most substantial in the book, perhaps because it was taken from another anthology. Among other characters, it introduces Feynman's peers, both in physics and in quick insight. In one of the anecdotes, Feynman tells of being outflanked by Edward Teller, who figured out a prank as fast as Feynman could unveil it. As he says in the book, "The trouble with playing a trick on a highly intelligent man like Mr. Teller is that the time it takes to figure out from the moment that he sees there is something wrong till he understands exactly what happened is too damn small to give you any pleasure!"

It is instructive to compare Feynman's account of the days at Los Alamos with another's. Although not a Nobel laureate (probably only because there is no prize for mathematics), Stanislaus Ulam issued a very similar memoir, entitled *Adventures of a Mathematician* (1976). Ulam was educated in Europe, and his more formal and classical training shows throughout the book, especially when he comments on the antiphilosophical spirit among the junior American physicists. Ulam seems to include Feynman in this group of dedicated pragmatists, but quickly separates him from his contemporaries. "The younger scientists did not have much of an aura, they were bright young men, not geniuses. Perhaps only Feynman among the younger ones had a certain aura. Six or seven years younger than I, he was brilliant, witty, eccentric, original." Ulam repeats the safecracking stories, giving Feynman more credit than Feynman deserves, by his own admission. The point of Feynman's story was that he never really cracked a safe; he always let the owner give the combination away. Ulam thought it was a matter of listening to tumblers drop into place.

It is not obvious that a mischievous misfit would make a great teacher. On the other hand, there can be no denying Feynman's ability to teach or his commitment to teach. One of the finest sections in the book deals with his attitudes toward teaching. He starts off the section that deals with his pre-celebrity academic career with the forthright "I don't believe I can do without teaching." A man as vibrant and curious as he is cannot be removed from the lectern.

It is instructive to listen to Feynman the raconteur become Feynman the lecturer. In the midst of a fascinating section about a sabbatical in Brazil, Feynman launches into a discussion of how one teaches and the shortcomings of Brazil's educational system. The passion leaps from the pages, displaying the infectious enthusiasm of a good teacher. In the same way that Feynman decries the substitution of rote memorization for learning, the intensity of his discourse shows that it is not enough for a teacher to provide understanding; he or she must inspire students to proceed on their own. Throughout the book, one encounters such glimpses into the man, a man who is angry at those who want easy definitions, easy answers, and all those other safe but constricting constructs. This is especially true in the sections that deal with those who would define art, or pornography, Hasidic law, proper textbooks, or any of a dozen other items. The quality of this book seems as much the result of the stories themselves as their placement.

Perhaps the image that Feynman relishes most is that of the "wild child," the prankster with a flair for insight, based as much on genius as on naïveté. This first comes to the fore when he gets to the Massachusetts Institute of Technology. Humor plays a large part in this book, perhaps because it is a compilation of anecdotes and not a series of biographical sketches. Another likely reason is that humor is very often a concomitant of both insight and a skewed perspective. This latter interpretation is from Arthur Koestler's concept of bi-association and undoubtedly fits Feynman. An alternative explanation of humor derives from the ever-humorless profession of psychoanalysis, which takes humor all too seriously. Some analysts tend to associate humor with the fringes of mental instability. It is the definition of instability that makes this second definition appropriate here, because instability implies being poorly integrated or nonconforming, and that is just the kind of image that Feynman cultivates. Whether it is at a tea party in Princeton (the source of the title) at age twenty-three, at a high-security lab in New Mexico at twenty-eight, at Cornell at thirty, or at Caltech at fifty, he acts more like a man from Mars than a man of the world. This posture gives him enormous license and liberty and creates a dissonance in the reader's perceptions, a cognitive dissonance that makes the reader reexamine expectations about those who have achieved greatness on the basis of their minds alone.

Richard A. Strelitz

Sources for Further Study

Choice. XXII, April, 1985, p. 1184.
Library Journal. CX, March 15, 1985, p. 56.
Los Angeles Times Book Review. February 24, 1985, p. 1.
Nature. CCCXIV, April 25, 1985, p. 685.
The New York Times Book Review. XC, January 27, 1985, p. 13.
The New Yorker. LXI, February 25, 1985, p. 104.
Newsweek. CV, March 11, 1985, p. 75.
Publishers Weekly. CCXXVI, December 14, 1984, p. 44.
Time. CXXV, January 7, 1985, p. 91.
The Wall Street Journal. CCV, May 3, 1985, p. 21.

TABLE OF CONTENTS

Author: John McPhee (1931-   )
Publisher: Farrar, Straus and Giroux (New York). 293 pp. $15.95
Type of work: Essays
Time: 1981-1984
Locale: Rural Alaska, Maine, New Jersey, and New York

A collection of eight essays about dynamic and innovative Americans who apply their talents to such fields as conservation, family medicine, and hydroelectric generation.

At first sight, the title of this collection of essays may seem to be the product of an editor's fancy—a catchy phrase to adorn the dust jacket and nothing more. Yet *Table of Contents* becomes an entirely appropriate choice when the reader recognizes that, for John McPhee, the world is indeed a book to be read and subdivided into recognizable chapters, each one treating a particular place or occupation. What holds *Table of Contents* together is McPhee's unique vision of the world, his particular values and dreams, and the sharply defined men and women who exemplify these values in the day-to-day activities of their personal and professional lives.

It would be an oversimplification to say that McPhee is a diehard environmentalist who is generally opposed to technology and big business, although he clearly admires wild animals (especially bears), wilderness areas (especially northern Maine), and rugged individualists (especially small entrepreneurs). What inspires McPhee to write chapter after chapter in *Table of Contents* is fresh evidence of recycling and restoration. McPhee celebrates a certain kind of American hero who is intent on repairing, restoring, healing, or recycling some precious American resource that would otherwise be lost—whether that resource happens to be black bears in rural New Jersey, abandoned waterwheels in Upstate New York, or, more important, abandoned patients in the backwaters of Maine. The New Man and New Woman whom McPhee praises unabashedly rely on inexhaustible supplies of energy and enthusiasm. Their goal, stated in the simplest terms, seems to be the restoration of the present in order to guarantee the existence of a future. Such people are not above compromising and making accommodations; they use tools and technology in innovative and unexpected ways to produce results that always aim at the betterment of human life.

Patricia McConnell, a diminutive, forty-year-old biologist who works for the New Jersey Fish and Game Department, lures huge bears into traps baited with crullers and jelly-filled doughnuts which she buys from Dunkin' Donuts and further enhances with drops of anise. This creative approach to bear trapping yields consistent results, and McConnell immobilizes her prey with the help of the tranquilizing drug Ketaset. Her job is to arrive at an accurate census of the bear population in New Jersey, a state not generally associated with a resident population of bears. McPhee reports, however, that bears have been sighted on interstates, in supermarket parking lots, even in backyards. McConnell hopes that her efforts will result in a permanent habitat for the bears, possibly in the Pine Barrens area. "Man has a responsibility to other life forms," she states firmly.

McPhee is obviously awed by this small woman as she approaches these dangerous animals, armed with her tattoo box, jab stick, tape measure, weighing cuffs, and spring scales. Each bear is tagged and identified; some receive radio transmitters as well. McPhee appreciates every detail of her professionalism at the same time that he records the personal drama in the life of this brave biologist. For while Pat McConnell is driving her pickup truck over the mountain roads in search of bears, her eleven-year-old daughter is scheduled to appear in a gymnastics show. McConnell and McPhee arrive at the show just in time to see her daughter perform. McConnell, bear trapper and proud mother, arrives on the scene with mud up to the hips of her jeans. For McPhee, she is the exemplary New Woman, tireless, overworked, neglectful of her husband's shirts and other household duties, but completely responsible in every way that counts.

In his treatment of Patricia McConnell—and of her peers in the remainder of *Table of Contents*—McPhee is always sensitive to this double drama of private versus public lives, and that kind of attention to his subjects gives McPhee impressive credibility and depth. The essay on McConnell (entitled "A Textbook Place for Bears") is typical in other ways, too. McPhee admires dynamic and original personalities in all of his books. He likes pioneers, and he also likes bears, facts that are already apparent to readers of McPhee's justly famous book on Alaska, *Coming into the Country* (1977).

"A Textbook Place for Bears" also serves as a good example of McPhee's style throughout *Table of Contents*. It is not merely Patricia McConnell who falls under the sensitive gaze of his journalist's eye but the bears themselves and their lovely, secluded habitats. McPhee is an unusually sensitive and detailed writer. He catalogs every detail about the bears, such as their food (corn, string beans, hazelnuts, wasps' nests, and honeycombs), the trees of their habitats (black birch, sugar maple, and pink laurel), and the strange, sometimes beautiful place-names associated with their capture (Minisink Island and Silverthread Falls). Even though "A Textbook Place for Bears" is neither the longest nor the most important essay in the book, McPhee seems happiest in its realm. If he dwells on the bears, it is his indirect way of celebrating all wild creatures and their unique, irreplaceable qualities, including their noises. Thus, McPhee reports that bears whine, wail, hiss, and woof. He rarely waxes philosophical, and this lack may be considered a weakness in the work. Yet McPhee is constantly pressing his point through subtler devices: It is the poetry of his presentation that ultimately convinces.

McPhee's most ambitious essay, "Heirs of General Practice," accounts for more than a third of the book, but the complexity of his approach raises questions about the success of *Table of Contents* as a whole. Unlike the tightly focused piece on Patricia McConnell, "Heirs of General Practice" amounts to a dozen portraits of admirable young physicians who have rejected the lucrative fields of dermatology and radiology for the less glamorous and less remunerative branch of medicine known as family practice. These twelve doctors—young, hardworking, and visionary men and women who for the most part were not encouraged by their medical-school professors to go into family practice—wound up in rural Maine, in places such as Washburn and Mars Hill, where McPhee follows them through typical days. Patients "present" themselves with enough ailments to fill up a medical textbook, including those suffering from perforated eardrums, hypertension, genital warts, amnesia, herpes, asthma, and angina. The doctors treat all these ailments—and more—with a humane and extraordinarily sympathetic attitude—an attitude that is summed up rather neatly by Dr. Sandy Burstein, who says, "The purpose is to help people in a deep and personal way."

McPhee presents the family practitioners as informally dressed, casual men and women who bear up under their stressful days with remarkable equanimity. They are trapped in the paradox of trying to provide personal service to a larger and larger clientele. There simply are not enough hours— or doctors—to go around. Some sleep less; others contemplate the unpleasant alternatives of rushing patients through the visit or refusing to accept any new patients. Even success and goodwill cannot redress the imbalances of a system that rewards the urban specialists and penalizes the rural practitioners. McPhee again serves as a documentarian, noting patients' names, ages, and ailments. At one point he even begins to talk about "an elevation in levels of serum glutamic-oxaloacetic transaminase." The sheer weight of these details becomes overpowering in itself: Even the most dedicated and sympathetic reader may become lost in the welter of patients' names, ailments, doctors, place-names, and names of hospitals. Originally written for *The New Yorker*, "Heirs of General Practice" may have been more suitable in a magazine format; some reshaping would have made it more digestible for *Table of Contents* (perhaps fewer case histories and fewer doctors, with longer narratives on each one). "Heirs of General Practice" is a beautifully written example of literary overkill; the individual parts are superb, but the aggregate is unwieldy and unnecessarily complicated. The best moments, as always, are in the descriptions. Again and again, McPhee has an unerring ear, as in this description of the sounds made by a fetus: "The child sounds like a locomotive, like a swimmer doing laps, like water gurgling in a drain."

"Open Man," an affectionate portrait of Senator Bill Bradley of New Jersey, suffers from the same organizational weakness as "Heirs of General Practice," even though it is one of the briefest and liveliest essays in the book. McPhee chronicles one day in the life of Senator Bradley, suggesting the Herculean work of the politician by jotting down bits and pieces of conversations, especially questions and comments of voters as the senator moves through several cities of New Jersey. The effect is to re-create the chaos and confusion of Bradley's heavy schedule, but somehow the reader misses an overview, a conceptual slant, a summary judgment or assessment that pins down the meaning of that day. Like "Heirs of General Practice," "Open Man" was more appropriate in *The New Yorker* in its present form; to the reader of *Table of Contents*, the piece may seem rather rough and unfinished.

Perhaps McPhee was sensitive to these rough edges, because "Minihydro," which superficially resembles "Heirs of General Practice" in its use of many examples of practitioners, actually has a dramatic sense of unity. Perhaps the subject of waterwheels and the restoration of abandoned mill sites is simpler than the manifold miseries of the human body. In any event, "Minihydro" shows McPhee at his best, praising a wide assortment of engineers and entrepreneurs who saw the potential profit in refurbishing rustedout turbines and clearing the debris from dammed-up mill ponds. They were aided by the National Energy Act of 1978, which required large utilities to purchase electricity from the small generators and pay for it at the going rate. McPhee is clearly fascinated by this chance marriage of technology and conservation. By using the most advanced turbines of the sort designed by F. W. Stapenhorst and by applying ingenuity and hard work, small entrepreneurs can produce electrical energy cheaply and efficiently while renovating the eyesores that dominate many mill towns in New York and Massachusetts. McPhee appreciates the special skills, amounting to a kind of artistry, required to start up one of these old waterwheels in locations that are beautiful, inaccessible, and sometime dangerous. He notes that "each small hydro site is unique, like a thumbprint." McPhee even goes so far as to lament the apparently obstructionist tactics of environmentalists, who sometimes fail to appreciate the ultimate value of the small generating facilities. The key to his thinking lies in the criterion of intelligent application: Bears deserve a place in the universe, but so do small-scale generators that save hundreds of barrels of oil every day.

For the same reason, McPhee sings the praises of Richard Hutchinson in "Riding the Boom Extension," because Hutchinson single-handedly installed telephones and electric lines in the tiny hamlet of Circle City in the Yukon of Alaska. Similarly, physicist Theodore B. Taylor (in "Ice Pond") is heroic for having invented a "cryodesic dome," an ice pond that can be used to cool an entire office building. McPhee's vision is interesting and original; he cannot be pigeonholed. His thinking is every bit as bold and innovative as the actions of the people he admires. That originality of mind informs the whole of *Table of Contents*: No one can read it without sharing in the excitement of making a new world out of the old.

Daniel L. Guillory

Sources for Further Study

Cosmopolitan. CXCIX, October, 1985, p. 34.
Kirkus Reviews. LIII, August 1, 1985, p. 779.
Library Journal. CX, October 1, 1985, p. 98.
The New York Times Book Review. XC, October 13, 1985, p. 26.
Publishers Weekly. CCXXVIII, August 16, 1985, p. 57.
Smithsonian. XVI, November, 1985, p. 232.
The Wall Street Journal. CCVI, October 8, 1985, p. 28.
Washington Post Book World. XV, October 13, 1985, p. 10.

TEXAS

Author: James A. Michener (1907-   )
Publisher: Random House (New York). 1,096 pp. $21.95
Type of work: Historical novel
Time: 1535-1985
Locale: Texas

Texas history as seen through the lives of five fictional families

Principal characters:
> TRAVIS BARLOW, the narrator and chair of the governor's task force
> THE GARZAS, descendents of the first mestizo explorers of Texas
> THE QUIMPERS, among the first American settlers to arrive in Texas
> THE MACNABS, Scotch-Irish immigrants who number Texas Rangers and football players among their descendents
> THE COBBS, Southern aristocrats who came to Texas with the cotton trade
> THE RUSKS, cattle ranchers and oil barons
> MAGGIE MORRISON, a real-estate entrepreneur and modern-day immigrant to the Sun Belt

Texas holds a special place in the minds and hearts of Americans. The westward-seeking pioneers of the 1700's and 1800's, insatiable for land, infiltrated and began to settle the vast holdings of Spain and Mexico. Dreamers and visionaries as well as dirt farmers and hustlers were attracted to the promise of the immense territory. The scale of the land, coupled with the larger-than-life, almost mythic nature of its heroes, has led to the fascination that Americans have with the state and its inhabitants. Reinforced by the intense pride of Texans and spread around the world by Hollywood, there is a vision of Texas as symbolic of the best of the pioneering spirit of America: independent, proud of its past, looking toward the future, bursting with life and energy.

In *Texas*, his latest monumental novel, James A. Michener takes a wide-ranging look at the events and people that shaped the land and developed its legendary status among the states. As with several of his earlier novels, such as *Hawaii* (1959), *Centennial* (1974), and *Chesapeake* (1978), Michener uses the lives of fictional characters, intertwined with real personages and historical facts, to illustrate the history of a place. In this case, there are five families—the Garzas, the Quimpers, the Macnabs, the Cobbs, and the Rusks—each of which is representative of one of the different cultures that tamed and settled a vast and generally harsh region. Their stories are both tied together and moved forward by another group, a contemporary Texas governor's task force. Composed of five members, the task force is charged with researching what Texas children should be taught about their history and how it should be taught, in preparation for the sesquicentennial celebration of statehood. Four of the members are direct descendants of the principal families: Efraín Garza, a university professor; Lorenzo Quimper, a brash Texas tycoon involved in several business interests, politics, and football; Lorena Cobb, the daughter and granddaughter of two Texas senators; and Ransom Rusk, an oil and real-estate billionaire. The fifth member, Travis Barlow, serves as narrator when necessary. Michener's alter ego, Barlow is an "outside" scholar, returning to Texas from a position in Colorado.

After a brief introduction and explanation of the task force, Michener begins his story with the story of the first Garza. Fittingly enough, he is a mestizo, born of an Indian mother and a Spanish father. More important, however, he is bright, curious, and courageous. He accompanies the conquistadores as they explore the new land and search for gold, finally settling in the territory then known as Tejas. Among his descendants will be numbered artists, outlaws, and scholars.

As the focus shifts to the influx of settlers from Kentucky and Tennessee, the reader is introduced to the Quimper family. Down on their luck, they are lured by the promise of land in Tejas. The mother, Mattie, is representative of the indomitable women who helped to open the frontier and hold the family together. Her son, Yancey, is a lazy braggart who somehow manages to turn potential disasters into personal triumphs.

The Macnabs, father and son, exemplify the European immigrants who came to Texas, specifically the Scotch-Irish. They arrive just in time to participate in the great events of Texas independence: the Alamo, Goliad, and San Jacinto. Otto Macnab, the son, is one of the most fully developed characters in the book, figuring prominently as one of the original Texas Rangers.

The Cobbs emigrate to Texas from the Old South, bringing with them the cotton trade and the loyalties that divide the country in the Civil War. They maintain their gentility and remain the aristocrats of the state, with two generations serving Texas as senators.

Of all the families, the Rusks begin most deeply in tragedy and, perhaps, rise the highest. Again, a strong woman is the source of strength in the family. The victim of appalling Comanche cruelty, she overcomes her misfortunes to found a cattle empire based on the famed Texas longhorns. These riches multiply when her land is found to contain one of the richest oil fields in the United States.

Although the same families appear for generations, few characters are seen over a long period of time. Most appear in relatively short episodes or vignettes, which in themselves are memorable but do not necessarily contribute to a sense of continuous narrative flow. Rather there is a sense of the continual sweep of history as one character or family moves aside for another. While Michener uses characters to animate his descriptions of historical facts and events, he also seems to say that no one individual is important for long in the context of history. More important than individual personalities are the attitudes and dreams that individuals contribute to the bubbling mixture of cultures which gives Texas its special character.

Two exceptions to this somewhat anecdotal treatment are Yancey Quimper and Otto Macnab. They both are on the scene during the battle for Texas independence and reappear periodically even beyond the Civil War. In personality and character, they are almost diametrically opposed, and as such they become representative of the best and worst of Texans. Quimper is a blustering opportunist who will lie and cheat to gain an advantage. Outgoing and sociable, he attracts cronies who may help him in his shady dealings. He is a con man and hustler and represents the typical Texas wheeler-dealer. Macnab, on the other hand, is fiercely independent and aloof. Even as a Texas Ranger, he is not part of a group but operates alone. Self-reliant and honest, he is willing to fight for right as he sees it.

In attempting to set down and personalize more than four centuries of the turbulent history of a geographically, climatically, and culturally diverse land, Michener has given himself an unenviable task. Choices of who and what to include and how to approach the subjects must be made. It is these choices which determine the focus and the ultimate success of the work. Few authors approach Michener's success with his proven formula of individualizing history and overwhelming the reader with masses of detailed information. Although he does not begin *Texas* with the formation of the land and the emergence of flora and fauna as he has in other novels (*Hawaii* and *Centennial*, for example), he is still faced with an extraordinarily large subject, and one about which many people have very definite feelings. Therefore, it is easy to quibble about Michener's choice of characters. Native Americans and blacks are treated rather cursorily, yet comparatively broad coverage is given to the armadillo. A localized liquor war is given more attention than is the tragedy of the Great Depression and the Dust Bowl. In the light of such apparent discrepancies in balance and given Michener's propensity for meticulously presented research, it is important to keep in mind that this is a work of fiction and not a textbook, and it must be judged as such.

Underlying the detail and the action of *Texas* is the dominant theme of the land and its bounty. Humans pass in review, acting out their history, but the land endures. The first Spanish explorers came looking for gold and in doing so ventured into much of what is now the Southwest. They were disappointed in their search for the fabled Seven Cities of Gold, but they were successful in opening a land of promise. To the land-hungry settlers who followed, Tejas, or Texas, offered the promise of a new start and the possibility of unexpected wealth. Men who had little chance of success at home were able to acquire land with relatively little expense or effort, and with land they acquired status and a certain wealth. The settlers saw the potential of the land, but to gather its riches, they had to pay a price. Michener is at his best when he reveals his own love of the land through his characters and shows the reader what price was, and continues to be, paid. Through the centuries Texans have had to cope with a wide variety of natural disasters, ranging from droughts and freezes to hurricanes and tornados. They have been wiped out but fought back to regain wealth. They also have had to defend their land from outsiders and even from fellow Texans. This love of the land becomes a motivating factor for Michener's characters and one that underpins their existence. In a broad sense, Texas itself becomes one of the novel's principal characters.

Structurally, *Texas* switches from past to present with each chapter. One chapter of the book roughly equals a chapter of Texas history, or at least a significant time period, in Michener's view. As each chapter ends, the governor's task force is reintroduced to set the stage for the next chapter. Michener has the task force meet in different locations around the state, both to get a feel of the diversity of Texas and to meet with experts on different aspects of Texas history. In this manner, he can allow the narrative to leapfrog rather than flow. Relevant facts and events are summarized for the reader by the experts and by task force members as Michener moves on to a new period. Initially, the pace is slow, as befits the sense of time and space in the sixteenth century. The first descriptions of Texas paint a picture of an empty, desolate wasteland, hostile to man. Gradually the pace of the narrative picks up as events seem to fly by. In the twentieth century, especially since the 1960's, the reader sees the transformation in the competition for land. People no longer vie for seemingly limitless tracts of land but instead make or lose fortunes in the competitive urban real-estate business. In spite of the trappings of modern life, however, much remains unchanged. Like the early settlers, the Morrisons are attracted to Texas by the promise of a fresh start. Maggie Morrison proves to be another of Michener's strong women, worthy of being a Texan. Her husband tries to match the real Texas land hustlers but fails, with tragic results. Maggie, however, is willing to work honestly and to gamble in order to win. When she narrowly avoids disaster in the wake of Hurricane Alicia, she is ready to gamble even more in another venture.

It is obvious throughout the novel that Michener has great respect for Texas and its citizens. Even as disreputable a character as Yancey Quimper is treated rather sympathetically. Michener was invited to Texas by its governor, William P. Clements, in order to produce just such a novel as he has. Like his narrator, Travis Barlow, Michener was provided with research assistants and flown around the state to gather information. Also like Barlow, Michener decided to move to Austin when his work was done. With this knowledge, it would be easy for the reader to dismiss *Texas* as suspect in source and content. In reading the book, however, it is impossible not to feel that Michener's thoughts and emotions are truly engaged by his subject. His genuine love of the land and his admiration for the Texas character which can snap back from seemingly any defeat comes through on every page.

Barbara E. Kemp

Sources for Further Study

American West. XXII, January-February, 1986, p. 81.
Booklist. LXXXII, September 15, 1985, p. 91.
Library Journal. CX, October 15, 1985, p. 102.
The New York Times Book Review. XC, October 13, 1985, p. 9.
Newsweek. CVI, September 23, 1985, p. 73.
Publishers Weekly. CCXXVIII, September 6, 1985, p. 56.
Texas Monthly. XIII, November, 1985, p. 222.
Time. CXXVI, October 28, 1985, p. 96.
The Wall Street Journal. CCVI, November 12, 1985, p. 26.
Washington Post Book World. XV, September 29, 1985, p. 1.

TIME AND TIME AGAIN
Autobiographies

Author: Dan Jacobson (1929-   )
Publisher: The Atlantic Monthly Press (Boston). 213 pp. $15.95
Type of work: Memoirs
Time: The 1930's to the 1980's
Locale: South Africa and England

In these thirteen individual autobiographical pieces, Jacobson is faithful to the mysterious processes of memory, by the agency of which seemingly trivial events remain fresh in the mind while others seem hardly to have left a trace

Time and Time Again: Autobiographies is Dan Jacobson's fourteenth book. Jacobson, born and reared in South Africa but an emigrant to England in his mid-twenties, is best known for his novels and stories; he has also published essays, an earlier memoir, and—*Time and Time Again*'s immediate predecessor—*The Story of the Stories: The Chosen People and Its God* (1982), a critical account of the Bible (in both Jewish and Christian traditions) as fiction, in Jacobson's view clearly and fatefully untrue yet awesomely testifying to the power of stories "to help men shape their experience into patterns comprehensible to them, and thus to help sustain them, as individuals and in communities, in the face of the adversities which time never fails to bring."

This sense of the power of stories to give shape to the flux of experience also informs *Time and Time Again*, as Jacobson notes in a brief foreword which satisfies the reader's curiosity concerning the unusual subtitle (why "autobiographies" plural?) and in other ways illuminates what follows. Jacobson begins by avowing his fidelity, as autobiographer, to the truth; at the same time, he acknowledges that he has sought "to produce *tales*, real stories." Clearly, he observes, "there is a certain tension or even a contradiction between these two sets of aims," yet it can be a fruitful tension:

> What I was trying to do was to turn to advantage, as a story-teller, the surprise we all feel at discovering how difficult it is to remember some aspects of our past, and how difficult it is *not* to remember others, and how little either of these kinds of difficulty has to do with our wills or wishes or even with our sense of what has been important in our lives.

In short, while the recollections that make up this volume impose a degree of "narrative shapeliness" on the events of Jacobson's life, they also, by their episodic nature, "preserve or even dramatise something of the erratic or fitful nature of memory, and hence something of its intensity, too." Thus the subtitle "Autobiographies," plural and discontinuous, not autobiography, singular and seamless.

As a method for autobiography, Jacobson's approach has both strengths and weaknesses. On the one hand, his submission to the caprices of memory, coupled with his scrupulous resolve to tell the unvarnished truth, has produced a book that is almost pugnaciously undramatic—at times, simply boring. On the other hand, many readers will be attracted by the integrity of Jacobson's unemphatic recollecting voice, which gains in authority as one begins to appreciate the subtlety that complements his immediately evident decency and freedom from cant.

Time and Time Again is divided into two parts: The six chapters, or "autobiographies," that make up part 1 are set in South Africa, while the seven pieces that compose part 2 are set in England. The brief opening narrative, "Kimberley," sketches the landscape, the people, and the culture of that South African city, to which Jacobson's family moved when he was four years old. Kimberley had grown haphazardly, snaking around abandoned quarries, and Jacobson vividly evokes the essential strangeness of the place (and its charm for a young boy). The city's physical strangeness was matched by its human aspect. Kimberley at that time was dominated by the English-speaking segment of the populace, later (as Jacobson notes, ranging ahead in time) to be superseded by the Afrikaners. Both these groups simply took for granted the servitude and degradation of the native Africans and the so-called Cape Coloureds, people of mixed blood. In addition, there were in Kimberley smaller contingents of Indians and Chinese, Greeks and Jews; Jacobson's Latvian-born father and Lithuanian-born mother had come to South Africa separately many years before, in what he describes as a "freakish movement among Lithuanian Jewry, around the turn of the century: when more Jews from that corner of the Russian empire chose to go to South Africa than to any country other than the United States."

Thus, in the book's first piece, Jacobson unobtrusively but tellingly introduces one of his principal themes: the sheer contingency of all human arrangements. All these stories from memory are animated to some degree by a kind of wonder at the strange twists of fate. The theme is most mordantly developed in "Fair Seedtime," which recounts an episode from Jacobson's adolescence. One year at school, quite literally "for no reason" (not even the "reason" of anti-Semitism), Jacobson was singled out for ill treatment by his classmates, who pretended not to notice his existence for the last six or eight weeks of the term. A few ringleaders set the tune, with the tacit approval of their young schoolmaster; the others followed, some readily, some sheepishly. There was no violence, and when the next school year began, all was back to normal, but the experience left permanent scars:

A recollection of the blank, anti-climatic arbitrariness of it was to return to me when I set foot on the continent of Europe for the first time, at the age of twenty, knowing that had I been in that very place five years previously I would have been a hunted man, someone condemned to death. Now I was not. The ban had been lifted. That was all there was to it.

The same theme, given a different twist, can yield delight, as in "Fate, Art, Love, and George," in which he reflects on the unpredictable chain of circumstances whereby a chance conversation led to his meeting his wife-to-be.

It would be misleading, however, to suggest that this collection is limited to variations on a theme. There is great variety here, in keeping with Jacobson's attendance upon the mysterious processes of memory. "The Calling" begins with a one-word paragraph: "Chemise." The reader is taken by surprise: What is the drift of this fragmentary opening? An answer is immediately forthcoming:

> It was that one word, the pronunciation of which differed so mysteriously, to my ears, from its written appearance, that made me fully conscious of just how much I wanted to be a writer. More: it made me feel as if I had already become a writer. It had happened. The decision had been made. Now all I had to do was the writing.
> She-mēz.

The narrative that follows, fleshing out this arresting beginning, is one of the finest in the book. Also worth rereading is "Time of Arrival," easily the longest of the thirteen pieces; this account of Jacobson's first months in England, in the early 1950's, is a revised and expanded version of the title piece of a collection of essays published in 1962.

Finally, mention should be made of Jacobson's memoir of F. R. Leavis (and the formidable Mrs. Leavis). Valuable as a portrait of a great critic who was also an eccentric in the English manner, this piece is equally revealing of Jacobson himself. In a memorable passage, he identifies the primary appeal and lasting virtue of Leavis' work: "What Leavis offered in his criticism was a model or ideal community which anyone, any reader, could bring into existence without stirring from his room." As Jacobson goes on to evoke this community of writers and readers, this living tradition, one suddenly sees its particular relevance for a writer who cannot properly be labeled either South African (having left his native land for good as soon as he completed his formal education) or British (for although he has lived in England for decades and is no alien there, he remains in one sense an outsider).

One can describe Jacobson with accuracy only as an "English-language writer"; the awkwardness of the formula points to a much-needed critical reorientation. There has been, in the 1970's and 1980's, an increasing awareness of the rich diversity of English-language writing: Literature in English is being written in Africa and the West Indies, in India and Canada, in Ireland and Australia—drawing on an enormous range of linguistic and cultural traditions. While some writers find their inspiration in local differences, emphasizing that which distinguishes their English from others', Jacobson is representative of an opposing trend: His English is a kind of international reader's-and-writer's English, admittedly with a British accent but with none of the idiomatic quality of an Anthony Powell or a Kingsley Amis. By such various means, writers in English have been redefining the "living tradition" in ways that the Insular Leavis failed to appreciate.

John Wilson

Sources for Further Study

Kirkus Reviews. LIII, August 1, 1985, p. 776.
Listener. CXIV, September 12, 1985, p. 26.
The London Review of Books. VII, October 3, 1985, p. 8.
The New York Times Book Review. XC, September 15, 1985, p. 15.
The Observer. September 15, 1985, p. 22.
Publishers Weekly. CCXXVIII, August 16, 1985, p. 55.
Times Literary Supplement. September 13, 1985, p. 995.

TO THE HALLS OF THE MONTEZUMAS
The Mexican War in the American Imagination

Author: Robert W. Johannsen (1925-   )
Publisher: Oxford University Press (New York). Illustrated. 363 pp. $25.00
Type of work: Cultural history
Time: 1845-1848
Locale: The United States and Mexico

An examination of contemporary American perception of and reaction to the Mexican War in the press, popular culture, literature, and the arts

> *Principal personages:*
> JAMES FENIMORE COOPER, an American author
> RALPH WALDO EMERSON, an American essayist
> JAMES KNOX POLK, eleventh President of the United States, 1845-1849
> WILLIAM HICKLING PRESCOTT, an American historian
> WINFIELD SCOTT, major general in the United States Army
> ZACHARY TAYLOR, major general in the United States Army

Wars, by their nature, tend to engulf both participants and spectators in a fast-moving chain of events while generating much interest and comment. The war with Mexico (1846-1848) proved to be no exception. American public attention was already focused on Mexico in the wake of Texas' recent war for independence and the controversy surrounding Texas' annexation by the United States in 1845. The country was, it seemed, looking for an excuse to teach the Mexicans a lesson, and when events both real and imagined led to a declaration of war, the country responded with volunteers and a wide-ranging outpouring of expressions of approval.

Rather than a military history of the Mexican War, Robert W. Johannsen's *To the Halls of the Montezumas: The Mexican War in the American Imagination* is an examination of the ways in which the country perceived and interpreted the war—in the press, popular culture, literature, and the arts. The patriotism which the war inspired resulted in an outpouring of writing and artistic works that reflected many of the values and assumptions of nineteenth century American culture—attitudes toward romanticism, republicanism, nationalism, racism, and other aspects of nineteenth century life.

The war was a celebration of patriotism and nationalism, and it fostered a period of national unity even as its successful prosecution was laying the ground for disunity. Sectionalism was brushed aside, even though some said that this was a war to aid the slaveholders and to provide new territory for the expansion of slavery. Much of the popular sentiment, however, was expressed by a Southerner: "When fighting a common enemy, in one great common cause . . . we are all united." The war and its early victories offered a reassurance by lending "new meaning to patriotism, providing a new arena for heroism, and reasserting anew the popular assumptions of America's romantic era." The war was important for a number of reasons, both real and perceived. The territorial acquisitions, some two-thirds of Mexican territory north of the Rio Grande and west to the Pacific, provided the impetus for new settlement and the addition of new states to the union. As perceived by contemporaries, the war "held an even broader importance, for it strengthened republicanism, demonstrating to a doubting world that republics held the capacity to wage successful foreign wars, and legitimized long-held convictions of mission and destiny."

The successful prosecution of the war was made possible by the adoption of new technology. The steamship made possible the successful invasion of Veracruz and provided a means of supplying matériel to the invading forces and vital news dispatches to the home front. The advancing telegraph was pressed into use, along with dispatch riders, to provide rapid communication between forces in Mexico and President Polk, who actively directed conduct of the war.

The new technology which aided in the prosecution of the war also provided the means to supply the public with news of events in a matter of days rather than weeks. The demand for information led to innovations in news gathering and dissemination. Newspapers placed correspondents on the scene with the invading forces and printed their dispatches as well as those from the military. To speed the information along to New Orleans, newspapers outfitted a river packet with a complete typesetting operation and met each ship inbound from Mexico and set the latest news in type—thus ready for the press by the time the boat docked in New Orleans. Dispatches and news arriving in New Orleans were carried to New York via another innovation. Several New York newspapers had joined together to support a combination telegraph-courier operation to improve receipt of war news. This operation proved its value, and the cooperation continued as the Associated Press.

The early success of the army stimulated the war spirit and resulted in an overflow of volunteers for the fighting. Most of the volunteers ignored the dangers of combat and entered the war with "a spirit of enterprise and curiosity... with light hearts and bounding pulses we left our homes... in quest of wild adventures." Everyone was eager to do his part and prove that the nation had not lost its revolutionary spirit in pursuit of a just cause. As one volunteer expressed his feelings, "I am very anxious to have a chance to try my spunk.... I think I have the grit of '76." Many of the volunteers and regulars saw the war as an opportunity to travel to a foreign land and have something of an exotic vacation—"if those cursed Mexicans did not shoot at one so hard, Mexico would be a delightful country to be in." Many took an active interest in the land they traveled through, treating their experience as something of a grand tour and using William H. Prescott's *History of the Conquest of Mexico*, published in 1843, as a guidebook.

The exploits in Mexico gave rise to a new crop of heroes which the press was quick to recognize and exploit. While Winfield Scott gained new recognition for his command of the Veracruz invasion and the march to Mexico City, Zachary Taylor derived the most benefit. A relatively obscure colonel assigned to the Texas border, Taylor had the good fortune to be the right man in the right place at the right time and secured the first victory in the war. This propelled him to national attention, elevated him to general, and provided a strong base for his consideration as a serious presidential contender after the successful conclusion of the war. While the commanding generals naturally received much attention in the press, the popularity of the war and the intense interest in its progress, coupled with the increased coverage by correspondents, resulted in the adulation of many others who engaged in the conflict. The new heroes were pictured as exhibiting romantic and chivalrous qualities such as those of the medieval French Chevalier de Bayard. One example was Henry Clay, Jr. Clay became one of the "instant" heroes because of his courage when attacked and outnumbered by Mexicans. Surrounded, he defended himself with his sword while being attacked and wounded by rifles. There was something romantic about attempting to defend oneself against rifles with only a sword. Clay was one of many who claimed public attention as a result of the press coverage. Indeed, almost anyone could be a hero in some form or another by simply having taken part in some action or been with the invading armies. Yet for every hero paraded before the public, there were others who represented a truer picture of the war. They spent much time in camp and in trying conditions, ill supplied and suffering from disease; they found a different war filled with "sickness, fatigue, privations, and suffering." They quickly became disillusioned with the experience, and their description of their experiences and the harsh reality of the war was expressed as having "seen the elephant."

The rendering of events in Mexico quickly provided the raw material for an outpouring of expressions of patriotism and popular support. Songs associated with past accomplishments gained new popularity, especially "Yankee Doodle," and the army gave new life to both the stars and stripes and "The Star Spangled Banner." Others were momentary successes, such as the "Rough and Ready Polka" and "General Taylor's Quick Step," while still others received a lasting popularity, especially "The Girl I Left Behind."

The heroes, the average soldier, American values, exotic Mexico, all were inspiration for expression in popular literature, and this took many forms. Plays were written and performed about the battles and the war, including *The Battle of Mexico: Or, The Capture of the Halls of the Montezumas*, written and produced by Thomas Barry in 1848, and *The Siege of Monterey: Or, The Triumph of Rough and Ready*, written by Joseph C. Foster and produced in 1847. Much poetry was written by both amateurs and professionals celebrating the activities of the Americans. Perhaps the most memorable poetic expression of sentiment was "The Dying Soldier to His Mother."

New developments in technology were pressed into service to meet the almost insatiable demand for information about the war and about Mexico itself. The new art of lithography provided illustrations used in newspapers and magazine coverage of the war. Moving panoramas were created, exhibiting the course of the war, and these traveled throughout the country. Illustrated histories of the war were prepared and circulated. All this publication of news and information provided material for a new form of entertainment, the paperback novel. These were usually historical romances about Mexico at the time of the Spanish conquest under Hernán Cortés or were about the American experience in Mexico centering on "the stark contrast between the 'superior,' good, and patriotic American volunteer and the dark, skulking, 'inferior' Mexican ranchero."

In the midst of this seeming unity of support for the war, there were those who opposed it on various grounds. Most opposition was decidedly antislavery, but there were those who opposed the war from a pacifist standpoint as well. Many leading literary figures opposed the war, including John Greenleaf Whittier, James Russell Lowell, and Ralph Waldo Emerson. Yet "peace advocates, Whigs, antislavery reformers, all tempered their stands . . . by seeking some ultimate good in the conflict." This usually amounted to the benefits that American victory would bring Mexico—relieving the country from the oppressive, antiquated system of government, imparting republican ideals, and bringing Mexico into the nineteenth century. Thus, while they might decry the war, they would not deny its benefits to the nation. In the words of Emerson, "Most great results of history are brought about by discreditable means." On the whole, proponents and opponents alike accepted the success of the war and the victory as proof of "God's benign guidance of republican America" and the example it held forth for the world.

In addition to the stimulation of interest, new developments in literary expression, and adoption of new technology, the war also helped the nation to assimilate the newly acquired territory and fostered the entry of some new words into the language as well. "Adobe," "ranchero," "chaparral," "sombrero," "lasso," "corral," "hacienda," "peon," "calaboose," "fandango," "patio," and "cigarillo" entered into common usage as a result of the war.

Johannsen succeeds in providing a fascinating picture of the response to the Mexican War given by all segments of American society. One can understand why and how contemporaries viewed the war as more than territorial aggrandizement and proslavery and saw it as an affirmation of the nation's manifest destiny to occupy the rest of the continent. Johannsen concludes his portrait of the American nation at the conclusion of the Mexican War with a caveat. Whatever the war might have done for contemporaries in reaffirming their belief in and view of America's destiny, it also altered that destiny. The unity of spirit engendered by the war was quickly dissipated in the following decade, and the fruits of that victory—the new territories—sowed the seeds of discord which contributed to an event that overshadowed the victory and toppled it from the place in history its supporters sought to make for it—the Civil War.

Johannsen's *To the Halls of the Montezumas* is an excellent portrait of a nation at war and the response to that war. It provides a complement to other volumes on the Mexican War, notably K. Jack Bauer's *The Mexican War, 1846-1848* (1974).

Steven A. McCarver

Sources for Further Study

Booklist. LXXXI, March 1, 1985, p. 922.
Choice. XXII, July, 1985, p. 1691.
History: Reviews of New Books. XIII, May, 1985, p. 124.
Kirkus Reviews. LII, December 15, 1984, p. 1187.
Library Journal. CX, February 15, 1985, p. 167.
The New York Times Book Review. XC, April 14, 1985, p. 37.
The New Yorker. LXI, September 16, 1985, p. 123.

TOWARD A MORE NATURAL SCIENCE
Biology and Human Affairs

Author: Leon R. Kass (1939-   )
Publisher: The Free Press (New York). 370 pp. $23.50
Type of work: Popular science

Philosophical and moral reflections on the biomedical sciences and the conduct of physicians

As the technology available to the biomedical community has increased in power, new ethical challenges have arisen for society in general and for the medical community in particular. Scientists can, or will soon be able to, ensure the production of genetically perfect children, significantly expand natural life spans, produce new forms of life, and overcome infertility. At first glance, these all seem to be positive advances. They have the potential, however, of altering the fundamental structure of human life. More particularly, and perhaps more immediately, the new powers available to the medical community may force a reexamination of the self-conception and definition of the physician.

Leon Kass is a physician and biochemist by training and a philosopher and educator by vocation. He is an extremely articulate spokesperson for those who fear the consequences for the human race if current trends in biomedical science and technology are not reversed. In thirteen essays written over a dozen years (only two have not been published before), he examines three specific themes: the ethical questions raised by the new power of biomedical technology in the area of human reproduction and genetics, the proper goals of medical practice, and the true nature of nature. He seeks a more natural biology, one "true to life as found and lived" and not divorced from ordinary human experience.

Research on human reproduction has led to the development of several controversial techniques and results. Test-tube babies, cloning, genetic screening, and genetic engineering raise serious ethical questions. Cloning and other potential developments will generate additional problems. Kass analyzes and answers some of these questions. He argues persuasively, although many might not grant his first premises or agree with his conclusions. Underlying Kass's ethical discussions is a fundamental and controversial scientific belief—human life begins at fertilization. As a corollary, he holds that fetuses, whether normal or abnormal, as living things have a right to life. Abnormality is not a sufficient reason, at least ethically, to condone abortion.

If the reader accepts these cornerstones of Kass's philosophy, then his arguments concerning infertility, genetic screening, and abortion will be compelling. He does not believe that having a baby is an absolute right or that infertility is a disease to be cured at all costs. Society must accept some infertility. Although this will mean personal unhappiness for individuals, infertility is preferable to the experimentation on and death of human embryos which is a necessary by-product of efforts to solve infertility. Moreover, as Kass warns, although particular biomedical technologies were invented as a response to infertility, there is no reason to believe that the use of that technology will be limited to solving such problems. There are various possible eugenic applications. Again, the result would be the death of embryos and fetuses for questionable purposes.

Kass is not ignorant of the fact that in American society debates over some of these ethical issues are not limited to the philosophy class or the laboratory but have spilled into the streets, Congress, and the Supreme Court. One of his explicit objectives is to raise these ethical questions in the context of a "liberal democracy." He warns that advances in biomedical science and technology will not respect the boundaries on nature placed by judges.

His precepts for and criticism of the medical profession are equally thought-provoking and controversial. The proper objectives of the physician are, in his opinion, the preservation of health and the prevention of premature death. Health includes concepts such as "wholeness" and "working well," but it does not necessarily comprise happiness or being well adjusted to society. The physician-patient relationship is an asymmetric, participatory partnership assisting the natural processes of healing. Unfortunately, the medical profession is in danger of deteriorating into a trade responding to the wants and demands of its clients, irrespective of whether the clients' demands are in harmony with the values of the profession. It is becoming a set of means without clear ends. Cosmetic plastic surgery, abortions, altering or controlling human behavior, and keeping patients alive through mechanical means are not among the proper tasks of the physician, although they are commonplace medical activities because of client demand.

In denying that the physician should always worry about fending off death, Kass makes a very strong distinction between being alive and being healthy, and between premature and natural death. Life without health is possible, but it may not be desirable or natural. Keeping a patient alive through technology when hope for recovery—the restoration of wholeness and the proper functioning of the body, granting that these are relative and not absolute conditions—is gone should not be routine medical treatment. Death will and should come. It is the natural end.

There are many pitfalls to be avoided in confronting this issue. Kass admits that he has offered little in the way of practical solutions to the everyday ethical dilemmas facing physicians. He is confident, however, that the ultimate answers will not come about from committees constructing procedures, guidelines, and rules, but from the self-examination and self-understanding of the proper role of the physician.

Kass concludes his examination of the ethics of the medical profession with a gloss of the Hippocratic Oath. Claiming that the American Medical Association Principles of Medical Ethics defines the relationship of the physician only to modern, liberal, legalistic, and litigious society, Kass attempts to demonstrate that although the language of the Oath is time- and culture-bound, the values and standards of behavior incorporated in it are not. The Oath, properly understood, embraces the universal core of medicine—treatment, decorum, relations to teachers and students, and the role of nature in healing.

In the final section of the book, Kass offers his thoughts on some characteristics of nature which his fellow scientists usually overlook or deny. Again, he is attacking orthodoxy, this time in biology and in the philosophy of science. He claims that nature is teleological, hierarchical, and value-laden. Utilizing Charles Darwin's *On the Origin of Species* (1859) as a springboard, Kass constructs a complex argument which climaxes with the introduction of the concept of soul (defined as "the integrated vital powers of a naturally organic body") and the conclusion that evolution is the development of higher grades of soul. Nature tends toward ever greater freedom, awareness, and self-awareness. In short, Kass declares his allegiance to an antimaterialistic philosophy.

Having established his belief in the soul, he then attacks reductionist materialism by focusing on the attitudes of humans on their bodies. He argues strenuously for the need to view the human body as a whole, not the sum of the physical parts, as well as for the necessity of acknowledging that a human is more than his or her body.

Kass then turns to the question of aging and death. Assuming that biomedical technology will eventually be able to retard aging, should it be allowed to interfere with that natural process? He suggests some of the moral implications of keeping people healthy and active until the age of one hundred and beyond. The falling death rate would mean population growth, fewer opportunities and increasing frustrations for the younger generations, and reallocation of resources. Yet society might be willing to undertake the massive adjustments necessary to cope with an extension of the productive years of man. In that case, the next step would be making those productive years indefinite or infinite. Is not immortality an unqualified good? Kass concludes exactly the opposite. Mortality, not immortality, is a positive value. The knowledge that one must eventually die combats boredom, gives life a sense of seriousness, preciousness, moral value, and character. The existence of death makes life worth living.

An essay on looking and behaving well concludes the volume. Kass believes that nature does have values—there are activities that are more natural and more proper. To be in harmony with nature, one must look and be good. For evidence, he points to the phenomenon of blushing and the concept of shame.

One must come away from this book with a sense of unease. The issues raised are extremely disturbing. Even if the reader rejects some or all of Kass's philosophical musings, there is no way to escape the conclusion that technology, not the human spirit, is in control. One does not have to accept his image of the physician as a tradesman welcoming a customer to be upset by trends in physician-patient relationships. Sometimes Kass does not fully develop his arguments; sometimes his language appears to have been chosen less for its ability to convey information than for shock value; sometimes, especially in the final section of the book, his grasp far exceeds his reach, and the reader is left dissatisfied. Never, however, does he fail to engage one's attention and make one think.

Marc Rothenberg

Sources for Further Study

Choice. XXIII, October, 1985, p. 315.
Commentary. LXXX, August, 1985, p. 62.
Library Journal. CX, July 1985, p. 81.
Los Angeles Times Book Review. August 11, 1985, p. 2.
The New York Times Book Review. XC, April 21, 1985, p. 35.
Psychology Today. XIX, November, 1985, p. 82.
The Wall Street Journal. CCVI, December 4, 1985, p. 28.

THE TREE OF LIFE

Author: Hugh Nissenson (1933-   )
Publisher: Harper & Row Publishers (New York). Illustrated. 159 pp. $15.95
Type of work: Novel
Time: 1811-1812
Locale: Ohio

The imagined diary of Thomas Keene, a nineteenth century Ohio frontiersman, farmer, artist, and poet, whose daybook records that time's presence with uncanny verisimilitude

> *Principal characters:*
> THOMAS KEENE, a onetime pastor, now pioneer, and the diary's author
> JOHN CHAPMAN (JOHNNY APPLESEED), a Swedenborgian itinerant and friend of Thomas Keene
> FANNY COOPER, Thomas Keene's fiancée
> THE REVEREND COOPER, a Methodist minister
> TOMMY LYONS, a Delaware Indian brave, and shaman, the leader of raids on the white settlers

What was it like to live in the Ohio wilderness in 1812—hunting, farming, distilling whiskey, swallowing folk remedies, courting a woman, seeing tomahawks impact with skulls, having erotic fantasies, dodging black jaws (a biting insect), connecting socially with other pioneers, and being an artist and poet encountering nature the way one supposes Lascaux draftsmen knew it, with savage apprehension and skill? This question preoccupied Hugh Nissenson during the seven years it took him to write *The Tree of Life*, the diary of Nissenson's fictional character Thomas Keene, purportedly written between 1811 and 1812, in a calfskin ledger. It is a tour de force of verisimilitude, provoking in the reader the shock and surprise which he might be expected to feel were he to stumble upon such a volume, dusty and brittle, in a Cincinnati antique shop. Nissenson's quest, however, is not so much to awe the reader with illusions of a period as to wrest a fabulously factual image of a fictional man, Keene, from a period encrusted with decades of film and television banalization. Such intention required substantial factual knowledge of everything in Ohio at the time, from what people were wearing to the varieties of corn being planted. As well, it required the talent to compose in an original form, which in Nissenson's hands becomes, in places, as persuasively natural as the sound of birds singing and crickets chirping.

Anything *made* these days glints like a diamond in sludge; the craftsmanship of this book recommends it to the reader who has learned increasingly to adopt a distrust toward fiction. Nissenson has produced a book ostensibly written more than a hundred years ago: Such is his naïve assumption, upon which he builds Thomas Keene's cabin, consciousness, and paintings, prints of which appear throughout the book. So strikingly made up, *The Tree of*

Life proposes a sincerity about life which, in the twentieth century, is often only sensible in the form of the antique object.

Before writing *The Tree of Life*, Nissenson was lesser known as the author of short stories and novels and as a journalist—he covered Adolf Eichmann's trial for *Commentary*. This latest work, however, not only received critical acclaim (and a nomination for an American Book Award) but also was included by both *Time* and *People Magazine* in their lists of best fiction of 1985. Connoisseurs may regard the latter as a dubious honor, but certainly it attests the book's appeal as something original flowering in the bombed-out districts of deconstructionism.

Thomas Keene, Nissenson's diarist, is a voice and sensibility speaking and feeling with his time's condition bearing on every syllable. He has arrived in Ohio a few months previous to the diary's initial entry. The loquacity of a Robinson Crusoe is not present, nor is Crusoe's anxiously successful importing of all the prejudices of perception with which he landed. The transitional nature of life in 1811 America Nissenson brings out through Keene's minimalist frontier-shocked record. That part of the Middle West which Nissenson's readers cross on freeways was once all forest, stinging insects, fevers, strange animals only the Indians had named, and a hodgepodge of metaphysical orientations—animistic natives, Old Testament Methodists, Swedenborgian mystics, and shrugging unbelievers. This mishmash of culture and religion, and the corresponding agonies it engenders, is probably the book's central image. The epigraph, a quotation from William Blake's "The Human Abstract," attests:

> The Gods of the earth and sea
> Sought through nature to find this Tree;
> But their search was all in vain:
> There grows one in the Human brain.

"The Tree of Life" which the gods seek in Blake's poem is something they would eradicate if discovered, since it is the solid growing thing any particular brain becomes when its own abstractions, particularly religious abstractions about "the right way to do and see things," forbid adjustment to and accommodation of all the overwhelming splendors and terror served up by the universe.

Keen is Nissenson's liberated man, someone whose tree of abstractions has no fruit and few leaves. Seven years before arriving in Ohio, he was pastor of a church in Maine. He lost his faith when his wife's death agony led him to conclude that the Savior was not answering prayers. Now, as an infidel, though still entangled in the roots of guilt his Protestant theology established, he gives forth benignly disillusioned and respectfully reticent observations of the various and often warring convictions of white neighbors and the Delaware Indian tribe led by Chief Armstrong. Also, as a painter and poet, Keene develops his own new and, Nissenson would have the reader believe, better mythology, an outlook more explicitly sympathetic with the Indian's way of apprehending than with the white man's.

Keene's diary records the prosaic immediacy of his commercial ventures, social life, sexual fixations, and artistic concerns. Dated entries of business transactions, the state of his bowels after a several day-long drinking binge, snippets of dialogue between Keene and a neighbor (quoted directly), and educated but brief asides (Keene attended Harvard Divinity School) make up the random feeling of a life being lived. The book opens with Keene's inventory of his business possessions. He owns a cow named Juno worth thirty dollars, the components of a whiskey still, 160 prime acres in Richland County, miscellaneous weapons, writing pens, india ink for drawings, and a ledger "bought of Levi Jones at his store in Mansfield." Passing from entry to entry, the reader learns of Keene's neighbors. John Chapman (the legendary Johnny Appleseed) slips without fanfare onto the stage in a recorded transaction—his apples for Keene's cheese. The reader also learns the cost of things, as the diary is an account book as well as a journal; most of the characters do business with Keene, either through barter or by purchase. Tensions in the community are rapidly introduced. Trouble grows between the white settlers and the Delaware tribe after Phil Seymour and his father, holding a grudge for their mother and wife's death at the hands of some drunken Delaware braves, profane the Indian's sacred red cedar by burying a white man at its foot. Keene's internal tensions as well are carefully documented, including translations he makes from Juvenal for erotic stimulation in a diction Ezra Pound would approve: "Some girls love eunuchs./ Smooth cheeks & no worry about abortions." Only intermittently successful with the Juvenal, Keene soon receives more tangible fulfillment from Lettiece Shipman, a former slave. The details of her abuse at the hands of her previous owner excite Keene, as does Lettiece's fantastic willingness to perform Keene's fantasies behind his barn. Continued sex with Lettiece becomes problematic as Keene and Fanny Cooper, wife of Henry Cooper, who lies buried at the foot of the cedar, make plans to marry. Fanny's father-in-law, the Reverend Cooper, a Methodist minister, and Fanny, too, are dubious about marriage with an unbeliever, but the conditions of the frontier, which simply dictate finding a way to survive, favor the union of Keene and Fanny. Even though they disagree on religion, they fall genuinely in love.

Such are the complexities in the life of Thomas Keene, starkly and poetically rendered by Nissenson. Nissenson strives to make each entry poetic, both in its internal architecture and in the way it relates to the entries that precede and follow it. This diary is a form only the modern eye, attracted as it has become to fragments of texts and the potential eloquence of suspended bits and pieces (mobiles, cubism), could devise. With the goal of total verisimilitude in mind, Nissenson suggests that the record of a human voice creates the sense of a real person living in the early nineteenth century—not, as in so many historical novels, a twentieth century character garbed in the trappings of another age. Keene's records of conversations have that authentic feeling of a real voice put down as it speaks. Like most real voices, it speaks succinctly, as Robert Frost often related it, in part because of the awesome wilderness it finds itself inhabiting as a vulnerable speck. Accepting its vulnerability after successive shocks, this voice has also learned to speak frankly. Keene's neighbor Mrs. Lambright is concerned about Keene's relationship with Fanny: "Do you hanker after Fanny? . . . Then get your arse over there, for Christ's sake. . . . Marry the girl!" Mr. Lambright, equally practical, ponders other possibilities: "When you fight in the bush, you want to be able to axe a body, as well as shoot him." He advises the immediate purchase of a tomahawk. The entry begins "Do you hanker" and ends with "Get yourself a hawk." The Lambrights have lost four young daughters to disease. As a poem, the entry containing their words promotes life, urgent with the direction offered to one specific life, Keene's.

Other entries aspire to such a seemingly artless directness. Everything to which a novel ordinarily resorts—characterization by lengthy descriptions and dialogue, arduously imagined settings—the diary ignores for the sake of directness. What results is an image of beauty, love, terror, and incongruity in the lives of Keene and his neighbors. John Chapman encourages the chickenhearted Tommy Lyons to accept the role of shaman after his father, the current medicine man, dies. Swedenborgian Chapman, sympathetic with all manifestations of the spirit, tells Keene: "Tommy Lyons has had a vision. God worked a miracle thro' me." Keene's next sentence, referring to Chapman, reads: "He wears four pairs of pants." That Keene is dubious, tolerant, and kindly inclined is implicitly conveyed in this aside. The flatness serves to produce the picture of Keene's mind working, caught in its interest about the things Chapman describes and the questionable authority of someone so consistently unique. Chapman's main belief is that the universe is alive and speaks directly to its children. Never married, Chapman has a celestial fiancée, Beth, who tells him what to do. Keene is sympathetic, although leery of the excesses to which such a position might lead. His personal statements of belief or philosophy come through the paintings and short poems which he includes in the diary. The beauty of the paintings and poems is like that of the diary itself—nonornate and "hand-made."

Keene is slow to label Chapman, or anyone else, whether they be a familiar Protestant type or a strange painted savage. All identities are in flux, and a theology closely protected one day can be abandoned the next when the context for living is so physical in its threats and necessities. If Nissenson is guilty of riding any hobbyhorse it is this theme of the white man's Prot-

estant beliefs vaporizing in the reality of Indian America. The Reverend
Cooper observes that the difficulty in converting Indians to Methodism lies
in the paucity of their vocabulary, which lacks the terminology to translate
adequately the Lord's Prayer. (Keene, or Nissenson, suspects that the more
articulated a conviction, the more subject it is to decay.) By contrast, Indian
spirituality relies less on internal maintenance of doctrines and more on
identification with nature. If Chapman's mysticism is open to doubt, it still
relates better than does traditional Protestantism to the Indian's outlook,
which fears the ghost speaking through hooting owls and spirits living in
trees.

Keene finds his own behavior mysterious. He wonders why the repulsive
and grotesque sexual suggestiveness of Lettiece should hold him enthralled.
He yearns to share a bed with Lettiece and Fanny at the same time. While
he is watching a Delaware ceremony, the huge phallus of a Delaware medicine man impersonating The Horned Being rivets his attention. He stops
short of commitment to any creed, but his orientation becomes increasingly
a reverence for an inarticulate nature that kills without mercy and then
grows fresh life from the rotting corpse. A tree blasted by summer lightning
makes compost for next spring's violets, blue phlox, and wild hyacinth. Baby
owls nestle in half-eaten rabbits killed by the mother owl. No small marvel
that such a tooth-and-claw world gives birth to the ultimate pacifist, John
Chapman, who fears that lighting a fire in the forest will kill bugs, at the
same time that it creates the embittered Phil Seymour, who drinks a victory
potion from the scalp he takes from a young Delaware. Keene relishes these
incongruities and paradoxes, and he devises paintings to illustrate his awakening to a mythology of a tooth mother in a Quaker bonnet and the grim
reaper in a waistcoat.

Nissenson clearly desires to restore "the physical" for readers in concrete
jungles and subways. His oblique target is the inflated sense of shelter
which the modern world offers as the nature of things or the natural way to
live. Keene lives without medical insurance, social security, unemployment
compensation, and psychological counseling, as do his neighbors. The Delaware have constructed their "child-care programs" through the harshest in-
tuitions of human exposure. Vulnerability is central. Keene notes that a
Delaware father slashed the shins of his twelve-year-old son; the child was
then escorted from the village by his mother, who screamed and renounced
her love for the boy while whipping him into the bush. The true condition
of life now held the child: aloneness. If protection were to come, it would
be in the form of a vision, with which the boy could return in triumph,
transformed in the village's eyes. Without a vision, the boy is empty, "ah-
lux-so," and destined to follow his leader.

Keene's experience, recorded daily, is a comparable initiation. School
teaches little, and life teaches everything. Physical and mental exposure pre-

cede spiritual awakening. Other settlers, avowed Christians, undergo similar awakenings. The Reverend Cooper, advocate of peace, feels a wave of overpowering happiness during a Delaware attack as the passion to kill an attacker, "he's mine," overwhelms him. He dies a few moments later and requests that his wife not pray for his deliverance, as the experience of wanting to kill an enemy was too exhilarating to miss. Cooper's daughter, Fanny, kidnaped later by the same Indians, abandons Jesus when she is forced to observe the torture of Jethro Stone, who, buried to the neck, stares into the fire Tommy Lyons has built around his head until his brains boil and his eyes gush out. "Help me live without Jesus, Tom," Fanny says to Keene. John Chapman, who is responsible for negotiating Fanny's release from Tommy Lyons and who also observes the torture remains firm in his beliefs: "There is no death. . . . Jethro Stone is now an Angel in Heaven." Keene respects this stubborn idealism. Chapman is the only person who can walk through the coals of such evidence without burning his feet. His goodness is a combination of unshakable faith and selfless giving, and he becomes an emblem, a human ideal for Keene, which Keene represents in the diary's final picture, a woodcut, showing the bearded Chapman's head, eyes lifted like a saint's and surmounted by an arc outline. Within the arc is an apple tree that bears one large apple and one leaf on its two branches, characteristic of the single vision of serving nature by which Chapman has lived.

Chapman's fidelity influences Keene. He abandons the idea of sleeping with two women and marries Fanny. His wedding poem to Fanny celebrates the release from confusion:

> Thou art water
> Fit to drink,
> Fresh bread,
> The North
> That stopped the arrow
> Spinning in my head.

On the book's last page is a letter from Keene to his son Ezra, dated 1845, the year of Chapman's death and thirty-three years after the diary's final entry. He sends Ezra "Vol 1 of my Journal (1 July 1811-11 Oct 1812) how your Ma and I came to wed." "How we came to wed" is more poetry as understatement, Keene's testimony to the way life springs from death and horror. Eminently practical, as ever, the seventy-five-year-old Keene's last sentence in his letter to Ezra is, "How's your business?"

Bruce Wiebe

Sources for Further Study

Booklist. LXXXII, October 1, 1985, p. 192.
Kirkus Reviews. LIII, September 1, 1985, p. 899.
Library Journal. CX, October 15, 1985, p. 102.
Los Angeles Times Book Review. November 3, 1985, p. 14.
The New York Times Book Review. XC, October 27, 1985, p. 14.
The New Yorker. LXI, December 23, 1985, p. 89.
Present Tense. XIII, Autumn, 1985, p. 57.
Publishers Weekly. CCXXVIII, August 16, 1985, p. 63.
Time. CXXVI, October 21, 1985, p. 87.
The Wall Street Journal. CCVII, January 23, 1986, p. 30.

THE TRICK OF THE GA BOLGA

Author: Patrick McGinley (1937-   )
Publisher: St. Martin's Press (New York). 288 pp. $14.95
Type of work: Novel
Time: 1942-1943
Locale: County Donegal, Ireland

A crime novel in which an unmysterious murder provides a perspective on the insoluble riddles of love and death

> *Principal characters:*
> RUFUS GEORGE COOTE, the protagonist; an engineer and expatriate
> HUGH "THE PROKER" DONNELLY, a farmer, a neighbor of Coote
> MANUS "SALMO" BYRNE, a farmer, fisherman, and neighbor of Coote
> IMELDA McMACKIN, a neighbor, a mistress of Coote
> CONSOLATA O'GARA, a neighbor, a mistress of Coote

Patrick McGinley, an Irishman residing in England, published his first novel, *Bogmail*, in 1978; the American edition was issued in 1981. More novels followed in quick succession: *The Trick of the Ga Bolga* is his fifth (although it was the fourth in sequence to be published in the United States—thus the misleading information provided by the American edition). McGinley's novels have generally been classified as mysteries or crime novels—designations that are at once accurate and misleading, for he uses genre conventions in a subversive way.

In this latest work, murder provides a context for the protagonist's existential disposition. It strengthens his unenviable perception that everything in the world is itself and, more than likely, another thing. Murder occurs as a banality. As such, it seems a contradiction in terms, or at least a serious reversal of reader expectation. Yet by virtue of such contradictoriness, it provides a means for McGinley's larger and more problematic concerns—with nature, love, the psychology of perception, and death—to play their part in the rich and slightly unnerving matrix of his fiction.

At first sight, the protagonist of *The Trick of the Ga Bolga*, Rufus George Coote, seems himself a contradiction in terms, or at least a misfit. He is an engineer attempting to farm. He is a man of metropolitan tastes and background living in a rural community. He is an Englishman waiting out World War II in the remote northwest of Ireland—and not as a matter of conscience but rather of expediency. The twofold nature of his status and circumstances is not entirely hidden from Coote, but he lacks the means, and to a large degree the desire, to articulate a sense of them. Overshadowing the glimpses of doubleness which he receives are the demands and pleasures of mundane existence. To judge by appearances, he fits in very well with his neighbors in Garaross. At least his neighbors think so. From the moment of his arrival, he is treated as one of them, and he undergoes no trying period of adjustment. Surrounded by mountains and the sea, Coote believes that he is being offered the possibility of "peace, placidity and the sanity of the ordinary." Or, as a neighbor puts it: "You can get away with murder here."

Coote states that his ambition is to "live off nine acres of rocky land like everyone else." Nevertheless, he is an active participant in the community, sharing its work rhythms and economic rituals. He even becomes joint supervisor, with the local priest, in an abortive effort to build a bridge, an episode which may or may not have symbolic relevance to a general understanding of Coote's experiences. His participation allows the author to indulge one of his favorite artistic habits—namely, to provide lore. In this case, since he is writing about his native region, the lore of farming, fishing, and folkways is prominent. The second of these three is featured with particular vividness and obvious relish. In addition, local idioms in both English and Irish lend color and distinctiveness to the proceedings, giving the novel texture and averting attractively the danger of a merely schematic, intellectual piece of work.

Perhaps Coote fits in too well. When obliged to defend himself against The Proker, one of his neighbors, who makes unexpectedly unseemly advances toward him, the result is The Proker's death. It takes a long time, however, for Coote to make an appropriate moral response to the murder. (Morally speaking, The Proker's death is murder. Legally, a lesser charge might be entertained, on the grounds of self-defense.) He sees another neighbor, Salmo (The Proker's sworn enemy), arrested for the crime and jailed pending probable conviction and execution. He solicitously visits Salmo in prison. Only gradually, and because of the innocent and humane concerns of Consolata, one of his girlfriends, is Coote prompted to help Salmo. Even then, his objective is to free the prisoner, not incriminate himself. He fails, however. During the course of his imprisonment, Salmo has developed a fatalistic acceptance of his misfortune which is, ironically, made of much sterner stuff than Coote's amorality. As if to compound the irony, when Coote eventually goes to confess the crime to the plodding local constable, he is told that he is much too decent a person to have done such a deed.

The other, more invigorating aspect of Coote's sojourn—one that blinds him to his part in Salmo's plight—is his love life. He maintains simultaneous relationships with two local women, the immense Imelda and the benign Consolata. The intensity of his encounters with Imelda leads Coote to believe that she has taught him the trick of the Ga Bolga. (The novel ends with Coote being rudely disabused of this surmise by Imelda's husband, Denis, an Irish Nationalist ironically returned from fighting for the Allies in North Africa. Denis points out that the Ga Bolga is the infernal javelin forged by the legendary Irish hero Cuchulain for the fight to the death with his best friend, Ferdia. Death is the weapon's trick.) It is Consolata's modest ordinariness, however, which eventually wins Coote's serious attention.

Their affair is shockingly destroyed by Imelda, infecting Coote with a more violent strain of what is termed "the poison of self analysis" than any he has yet had to withstand. One of the results of his decline is the attempted confession of The Proker's murder.

Significant as these developments are for the novel's plot, Coote's two-timing has an even greater relevance to the novel's perhaps overelaborate structure of motifs. The simultaneous affairs are the most prominent enactment of the author's sense of doubleness and contradiction. Coote is in the position of being given Imelda, whom he does not need, and by virtue of that relationship's impersonality, he is deprived of Consolata. His position in his love relationships is a more intense repetition of the one that he occupies between Salmo and The Proker. Imelda's callousness is a more malevolent and egregious expression of Coote's implicit attitude to the imprisoned Salmo. Thus Coote, whose hope initially in this organic, or at least largely self-supporting, community was for "unity of experience," ends up as the merest of mortals, defined narrowly between the poles of love and death— poles that here, at one level, are obviously antithetical yet at another seem to share an uncanny mutuality.

One small example of the author's deployment of doubleness is that the affair with Imelda takes place indoors in darkness, whereas Coote's time with Consolata is spent outdoors in daylight. The sense of doubleness pervades the novel. Coote is presented with alternatives to himself in the form of a dead sailor, washed ashore from the war. Coote uses the dead man's name a time or two. Consolata's father reminisces fondly about an earlier English visitor, a travel writer named Spragg. Coote wonders if he is not Spragg's reincarnation. Coote even allows his neighbors to invent a history for him, to the effect that he is a veteran of the Battle of Britain.

In addition, the novel is suffused with hauntings of various kinds. Coote thinks that he sees ghosts. The author cleverly underlines this effect by tacitly invoking William Butler Yeats's poem "The Fisherman." (Perhaps this reference is also intended to be taken satirically. The eponymous figure of that poem goes native to the extent of wearing homespun. Coote's equivalent is a shroudlike nightshirt, woven from local materials.) Coote is prone to thinking of his surroundings as "a world elsewhere." He experiences "a sense of awayness." Sometimes he feels transports of pleasure from the landscape. At other times, "he sensed his life was being pushed out of shape by the pincer-grip of the landscape itself." He admits to Consolata, "I often think Garaross is not a place in Glen but a place in my mind."

Coote is the only character who experiences the world in those terms. He is the only character with a mind or, perhaps one should say, a psyche. What he subjectively suspects is as important as what the world objectively contains. Hence he has immense difficulty in determining how significance may be attached to, or derived from, his experiences. He views The Proker's death as "an event on a different plane"—and indeed it is. Yet that plane coexists with the plane of the diurnal, where Coote wants to lose himself. The author is careful not to judge his protagonist. Nor does he deride Coote's fears and presentiments. McGinley can hardly condemn Coote for falling victim to a playfulness of mind which the author himself has disciplined without distorting. As the novel's final sentence wittily and delicately puts it, Coote is not necessarily wrong when he thinks that he sees things, but he may be ignorant of what precisely it is that he sees.

The core of the novel, then, as distinct from the core of the plot, is deeply (though by no means heavy-handedly) preoccupied with the psychic chess of individual perception. In that sense, *The Trick of the Ga Bolga* seems to owe as much to the so-called magical realism of novelists such as Gabriel García Márquez as it does to the crime novel—although in McGinley's case, the magic is black. An author to whom McGinley seems clearly indebted is the Irish satirist Flann O'Brien, whose *The Third Policeman* (1967) has evidently acted as a foster parent to McGinley's fictional interests.

Overelaborate construction and slightly excessive length should not detract from this novel's undoubted pleasures. There are numerous diverting characters, much sly humor, and the intermingling of the uncanny and the mundane is handled effectively, producing a decided, if unconventional, sense of mystery and unease. Yet if, as a crime novel, *The Trick of the Ga Bolga* satirizes cavalierly the concept of evidence, it compensates for doing so by imaginatively enlarging the murder story so that it becomes the death story, a rather less cozy and, intellectually speaking, more worthwhile entity. *The Trick of the Ga Bolga* is also notable for some excellent descriptive passages, revealing the author's superb powers of observation and his closeness to nature. Very quietly, the novel is a tribute to the mountains, lakes, headlands, and seascapes of the author's formative years.

It may be that the novel's various ingredients—murder plot, recondite lore, and psychological interests—do not succeed in making up a satisfying whole. On the other hand, its color and prevailing sense of the uncanny and the uncertain, its quirky development and whimsical asides, distinguish it as the work of an author noteworthy and worthwhile by virtue of his idiosyncrasies as well as his unsettling themes.

George O'Brien

Sources for Further Study

Booklist. LXXXI, March 1, 1985, p. 928.
Kirkus Reviews. LIII, February 1, 1985, p. 105.
Library Journal. CX, April 15, 1985, p. 86.

New Statesman. CX, August 30, 1985, p. 26.
The New York Times Book Review. XC, July 21, 1985, p. 20.
The Observer. September 1, 1985, p. 18.
Publishers Weekly. CCXXVII, February 1, 1985, p. 350.
Times Literary Supplement. September 13, 1985, p. 1000.
Washington Post Book World. XV, May 5, 1985, p. 10.

THE TRIUMPH OF ACHILLES

Author: Louise Glück (1943-   )
Publisher: The Ecco Press (New York). 60 pp. $13.50
Type of work: Poetry

The fourth collection by a poet in mid-career juxtaposes myth and reality in austere lyrics of transformation and resignation

Much contemporary poetry, especially in international terms, leans automatically toward parsimony. The spendthrift school of improvident discourse seems out of joint, even immoral, in a culture already awash in its own verbosity. The reigning aesthetic in the poetry of this century has therefore been a countermove toward understatement, in which words, frugally doled out from the poet's silence, strive by their very scarcity to recapture the fullness of nuance and resonance that was once theirs. A poet who adopts this aesthetic will find that it offers three advantages. First, the truth-value of any situation stands in wary relation to overstatement, whose fussiness tends to pervert and obscure. It prefers the lean to the fat, the cool to the hot. Second, it apprises the poet of a constant obligation: He is, by default, the custodian of the language. Third, because he constantly directs his attention to the full measure of words, he is put in touch with their mythic beginnings—and with myth itself. Resonant structures lie at his disposal. Time becomes synchronic and history transparent. He brings, consciously, the whole history of denotations, connotations, usage, and inflection to bear on his subject matter. Preeminently among the poets of her generation (those born in the 1940's), Louise Glück has sought, with supreme indifference to fad, to hone a verbal instrument—laconic, severe, completely devoid of inconsequence—equal to the life-altering illusions, fictions, and longings she takes as the subjects of her poems.

The Triumph of Achilles, Glück's fourth collection, continues her demystifications of the most central and the talismanic facts of human existence—namely, love, aggression, mortality, and knowledge. Once a time-haunted poet, she seems now to have packed away her nostalgias—as beautiful as these were—and directed her attention to what it means to live in the present tense. What once was predominantly retrospective in her poems is now by turns introspective and prospective. Instead of the personal past, she invokes myth, where the typical gains ascendancy over the individual and where, therefore, the patterns of human behavior unfold. It is as if experience, to which we bring our vaunted individuality, generates a friction that forces us to act against the grain of our singular intentions and renders us, at last, typical. The recognition of this fact, and our accommodation to it, constitute the topos of this book. The projection of our acts into myth provides the method.

In the title poem, the gods forsake Achilles, himself "nearly a god," because he no longer aspires to their majesty and omnipotence. Instead, he grieves "with his whole being" for Patroclus, and the gods withdraw their patronage, since "he was a man already dead, a victim of the part that loved, the part that was mortal." For all the godlike features within his nature, Achilles turns to and embraces his mortality—that which most basically typifies humanity—through his love. His mortality, then, is his triumph, and the gods know this to be so. Because of his love, they see him as "Already dead." This implicit causal relationship between death and love permeates the collection.

Yet it is not only a case of "Because death, therefore love." The poet intimates that the reverse relationship is sometimes true as well. In "Hawk's Shadow," the poet and her lover watch a hawk "hovered with its kill," making one shadow, "Like the one we made,/ you holding me." The opening poem, "Mock Orange," refers skeptically to the love cry as expressive of the "low, humiliating premise of union." The premise never blossoms into its desired conclusion. Rather, it is stunted by the romantic fiction "love," which is not an auspice for true feeling but a license for manipulation. "Always in these friendships/ one serves the other, one is less than the other." In "Mythic Fragment," Apollo, the "stern god," approaches the female speaker, the unidentified Daphne, who begs her deity-father "in the sea" to save her. Transformed into a tree, she resists the god's advances but must forever accommodate her father's—another god's—silence. These transformations declare, in irrefutable terms, the death of previous states of being and the necessity both for recognition and acceptance. Considered as images, many of these poems bring to mind William Blake's last engravings, in which human figures tunnel through realms of being that remain after they have passed. In Glück's poems, the realms no longer remain, except insofar as they are the dead atmospheres of memory, and "no voice/ carries to that kingdom."

Glück's new book puts heavy emphasis on acceptance, accommodation, or, at the very least, resignation. A family poem, "Legend," speaks of her grandparents' generation, the generation of immigrants who had to erect "principles, abstractions/ worthy of the challenge of bondage." To justify their election of estrangement and servitude, they promulgate strict articles of proper outlook and behavior, which serve as means to block nostalgia. The soul of her grandfather is likened to a diamond: "In the whole world there is nothing hard enough to change it." It is taught to speak the truth since that has been "the salvation of our people," bestowing on them "the illusion of freedom." In "Liberation," the poet relinquishes the primal, instinctual desire to hunt, "because it is impossible/ to kill and question at the same time." She identifies with the victim and consoles herself that "only victims have a destiny." The hunter, who believes that "whatever struggles/ begs to be torn apart," becomes a part of the soul that is now "paralyzed."

The wounded, the victimized, the threatened—all become beautiful in

Glück's eyes and derive their power to command attention from the sense that their experiences have brought them to life's borders, journeys that authenticate their humanity. In "Day Without Night," an angel pushes the hand of the child Moses away from the rubies and toward the burning coals. To be maimed is to be blessed and vice versa. To be favored is to be denied the Promised Land. Repeatedly in these poems, what is truly human distinguishes itself from the godlike, the overaspiring and the power-driven, by its losses and disavowals: "the conscious being chooses not to enter paradise." Boundaries, self-limitings, discretions come to haunt Glück's world to the point that they serve as its chief values. In "A Parable," King David stands on his palace roof and feels nothing for Bathsheba: "She is like a flower in a tub of water." He feels nothing for "the shining city of Jerusalem." He suddenly realizes that "he has attained/ all he is capable of dreaming." In "Hyacinth," the poet finds the gods themselves sunk "to human shape with longing." She flatly asserts, "Beauty dies: that is the source/ of creation." In "Winter Morning," a series of tableaux about the incarnation of Christ, flocks of birds circle indifferently around the Crucifixion, "since men were all alike,/ defeated by the air."

Glück, who is perhaps best known for the cool intimacy of her portraits, here steps further back from the canvas. The poems are cooler, more remote and objective. Yet one senses a fullness here that was missing from her previous collections. Perhaps the fact that the book contains several sequences adds to this impression, but a deeper reason involves the poet's juxtaposing the mythic and the present worlds. The back-and-forth manner in which she has ordered the poems conveys, cumulatively, the impression that one has covered a great mental distance, even though the book is a mere sixty pages—a mite slim for most poets, but ample for Glück.

Understatement, properly understood both as a limiting device and a conciliatory gesture to the reader's imagination, is one of the great tools of rhetoric. Glück's poems derive much of their dark enchantment from radical understatement combined with a splendid, unnerving sense of diction, of the riveting single word that snaps a line into place. In "Metamorphosis," a sequence on the death of her father, she describes the brief surfacing of his consciousness as he lies on his deathbed: "Then his flushed face/ turned away from the contract." One realizes that the paternal attention and the filial response *are* a kind of contract, here reaching its expiration. Elsewhere, an old woman shopping for lettuce in a marketplace prefers heads that still retain a residue of earth to "the other, more/ estranged heads." Glück has also increased her use of the definitive, a penchant observable in her earlier work. Besides such already-mentioned assertions as "only victims have a destiny" and "Beauty dies: that is the source/ of creation," one also finds "The calm of darkness/ is the horror of heaven," "The context of truth is darkness," "The image of truth is fire," "There is no god who will save one man." These have the effect of immediately occupying a certain territory of abstraction, around which cluster relevant particulars. They also expose human experience as archetypal, and thus typical, each possible story but a variation on a theme, against which one's struggles only increase the theme's inclusiveness and significance.

Stringency and limitation, hallmarks of the classical, pervade these lyrics. Glück is obviously uncomfortable with notions of transcendence and only refers to such in order to get at their fictive bases. In "Winter Morning," she writes, "Today when I woke up, I asked myself/ why did Christ die? Who knows/ the meaning of such questions?" In "The End of the World," a man's imminent death reduces the sky to an "uncanny brilliance/ substituting for the humanizing sun." The human instinct for longing, torn away from its biological basis and floated among other characteristic abstractions—moral, emotional, ethical, or aesthetic—can cause whole lives to feel dreamed, not lived. "How short it seemed, that lifetime of waiting"—an old man's indirect thought—is as close as she gets to the truly cautionary subtext of her poems.

Glück's severe vision is Mediterranean in its clean contours, its sense of time, and its modal emphasis on light as a precondition of existence. From her compulsion to make experience transparent, she has fashioned an exciting vehicle that goes to the very roots of human life. Her epigraph from Bruno Bettelheim provides an apt motto: "Joey was beginning to know good from evil. And whoever does that is committed to live a human existence on earth." A human existence, then, begins in knowledge, where what is tragic lies within the field of vision. Only in this way do value, beauty, and dignity have meaning—and the poet a justification for his art. "Finally, this is what we craved,/ this lying in the bright light without distinction—/ we who would leave behind/ exact records." This is writing aware of its own strength: Even poetry itself is shaken of its foliage, revealing "The writhing, stationary tree," which "will take no forms but twisted forms."

In a sly boast from a previous book, Glück, facing the loss of youth, saw the ensuing age as one when "I shall begin/ the great poems of my middle period." What was a joke and a prompt now appears prophetic: There *are* "great" poems here, if that term still has any power to convey distinction. *The Triumph of Achilles*, winner of the National Book Critics Circle Award in the category of poetry, is her triumph, a book of high character that makes one understand, in problematical days when poetry is constantly forced to justify itself, the reason for the high claims and ancient prestige of the art.

David Rigsbee

Sources for Further Study

Library Journal. CX, September 15, 1985, p. 84.
The Nation. CCXLII, January 18, 1986, p. 53.
The New York Times Book Review. XC, December 22, 1985, p. 22.
Publishers Weekly. CCXXVIII, July 26, 1985, p. 161.

THE TRUE CONFESSIONS OF AN ALBINO TERRORIST

Author: Breyten Breytenbach (1939-   )
Publisher: Farrar, Straus and Giroux (New York). 396 pp. $18.95
Type of work: Autobiography and social history
Time: 1975-1983
Locale: South Africa

In poetically charged prose, Breyten Breytenbach describes the seven years he spent as a convicted "terrorist" in a South African jail

A leading Afrikaner poet, as well as a painter, Breyten Breytenbach emigrated to Europe in the late 1960's. There he established his literary reputation, married a Vietnamese woman—thus providing a further reason for his exile in the eyes of South African law—and became active in the antiapartheid movement. In 1975 he returned to South Africa, disguised as a Frenchman, in order to help organize a network of white resistance to the government. Arrested at the Johannesburg airport as he tried to leave, he was convicted of terrorism and sentenced to nine years in prison. After serving seven of those years, including two in solitary confinement, he was released and returned to Europe. This book, dictated into a tape recorder during his first months of freedom, is an account of his time in prison.

Although the issues at the base of the book are African race relations and the history of the struggle against apartheid, there is little about South African political groups or about race itself. This is not surprising, however, when one considers that the material for this book arose in large part from Breytenbach's experiences in solitary confinement—in a country in which even the prisons are segregated. In prison, other races were largely invisible to Breytenbach. With a few exceptions, he was aware of blacks only when he heard them singing—in defiance of prison regulations—on the nights before one of their number was to be executed. Though Breytenbach is a hero of the struggle, it is not with the struggle that he is most concerned; it is with prison life itself: the terrible fight, day by day, week by week, month by month, to stay sane under insane conditions.

Necessarily, perhaps, the book resembles other examples of the genre that has been called, with casual cruelty, "prison literature." Its detail is the detail of prison routine: eating, cleaning up, exercise, tricks to make time pass. Its surprises, like the decorating of artificial teeth with filed-down bits of colored glass or hearsay about ritual murders committed by prison gangs, are almost predictable. Its main events are the (too few) departures from routine: visits, letters, anything smuggled in or out, conversations with the guards, an injured wood-pigeon that flies over the wall and is tamed by Breytenbach, and then—while Breytenbach is enjoying a visit from his wife—is eaten by the jailers' cat. (Under the circumstances, it is difficult to avoid perceiving allegory in even the most ordinary events.) The book's characters are the prison staff and inmates. In the light of Breytenbach's

extraordinary poetic sensibility, the cast flashes into vivid life, but only intermittently. It is the cruel fact of prison literature, as of prison life, that there
can be no "rounded" or "developed" characters when so little contact
between people is permitted.

The narrative of Breytenbach's mission, capture, interrogation, and imprisonment should perhaps be the most gripping part of the book, but it is
not. Okhela, the white left-wing splinter group that Breytenbach helped
found and on whose behalf he made the ill-fated trip to South Africa, has
one real political accomplishment to its credit: It stole documents proving
West German cooperation in South Africa's attempt to develop the capacity
to produce nuclear weapons. Yet Breytenbach's mission was harebrained
from the start, and its execution was inept; ultimately it succeeded only in
getting the people he contacted into trouble. As a political thriller, this section of the book comes uncomfortably close to absurdist comedy. Nor does
the political line become more coherent thereafter. According to Breytenbach, the authorities agreed to lighten his sentence in return for his agreement not to "politicize" the trial. The trial was not politicized, but his sentence was not reduced.

In a sense, Breytenbach's time in prison is hardly more politicized than
his trial. Because South Africa is a totalitarian state, the regimentation and
surveillance of life in prison might be seen as a microcosm of its "ordinary"
life, but this is not Breytenbach's purpose in describing it. The real political
strength of the book lies in its attention to the state of mind of the *boere*—
the derogatory prison term for policemen and warders and, by extension,
for whites. It is because Breytenbach himself belongs to this extended category, though with an unease marked by the word "albino" in his title, that
he has so much insight. (Had he been black, he might well have been murdered rather than jailed.) From the beginning of his mission, he has wondered whether his own exclusive clandestinity does not mirror that of the
police. He himself is not tortured; as a famous Afrikaner poet and the
brother of a military hero, he is treated with a strange mixture of harshness
and indulgence. Yet the people with whom he deals are torturers.
Breytenbach conveys this without showing them simply as monsters. At
some risk to his own moral and political position, and even to his sanity, he
forces himself to understand how torturers think. The reader sees their anti-
Semitism combined with their admiration for Israel, their flaunting of power
that is most deadly at moments when compassion, even love, surface yet are
frustrated by the prisoners' "obstinacy." Breytenbach's portrait refuses to
deny the humanity of the enemy; it neither surrenders its indignation nor
falls into the slothful categories of "them" and "us."

Yet it is not his political convictions that uphold Breytenbach in his isolation. Prison does not confer on him a new political identity by teaching him
to see his time as a form of resistance: "Resistance," he writes, "if that is

what you want to call survival, is made up of a million little compromises and humiliations, so subtle that the human eye cannot perceive them." Belief in the justice and eventual success of the struggle plays a far smaller role in sustaining him than does Buddhism, which undermines the very notion of a firm, politically coherent self. You must learn, Breytenbach says, that you are nothing. Give up the sum of attributes by which you think of yourself, he counsels, and participate in the putting down of the I.

Along with the effort to extinguish his self, what sustains him most is his writing. Breytenbach is at his best when he is writing about writing—a natural subject when the physical act of inscribing, preserving, and distributing one's words is so difficult, and when it is nearly all he is allowed to do. Nevertheless, the very fact that he is allowed to write, although prison regulations ban any professional or lucrative activity, is a sign of the ambiguity of writing and of his identity as a writer. In prison, as he says, every word he writes will be read by his enemies over his shoulder. Yet even out of prison, he does not escape this contradiction: Writing in Afrikaans means addressing a community which is revolted by every opinion he expresses. Thus, the act of writing itself is tainted with antagonism toward the reader. In *The True Confessions of an Albino Terrorist*, an unfocused, unanalyzed hostility burns through the mode of address. Page by page, Breytenbach reminds both the reader and himself that his words are being read by one "Mr. Investigator." Sometimes this mysterious figure seems to represent a version of himself; one of the pseudonyms of Mr. Investigator is "I." At another point, Mr. Investigator is "my dark mirror-brother," a representative of black revolutionaries, from whom the Okhela group split off, and Breytenbach's hostility toward his hearer becomes an image of his fears for South Africa's future. "We must launch a dialogue. I must warn you that the system by which we're trying to replace the present one will grind us down, *me and you*, as inexorably. I must tell you that I cannot hold my criticism, my disaffection, in abeyance; that I cannot condone your (our) agreements and compromises—not even tactically. I love you too bitterly for that. I hear you chuckling, you who are Black. . . ." If this book is revenge for what he has suffered, it is also a repetition of that suffering, a continuing of the interrogations to which he was subjected by the police, and an extension of those interrogations to fellow opponents of apartheid.

This is another way of communicating that the book is self-consciously self-destructive. He writes, Breytenbach says, not so as to preserve his experiences but so as to erase them. This need to purge himself stems from disgust at his compromises with his enemies. In order to get a volume of his poems published, he had to agree to dedicate it to Colonel Huntingdon, the chief investigator. (He also had to permit it to be censored. One complete poem was deleted; its title was "Help," and the full text consisted of the single word "Help!") More important, the old theme of unwilling complicity between torturer and tortured, jailer and prisoner, is compounded by the special circumstances of the Afrikaans author. Despite his political stand, Breytenbach remained the darling of the Afrikaans literary world. On a brief trip home in 1973, two years before his arrest, he was lionized; for the Afrikaners, who associate their threatened language with their threatened ownership of the land, the fact that Breytenbach had raised their language to such literary prominence made him a hero despite himself, and even a de facto defender of their right to South African soil.

What he was to his Afrikaner readers was decidedly different from what he was to himself. Thus Breytenbach had every reason to problematize the theme of identity, one of the richest motifs in the book. In an extraordinary section called "Detainee and Interrogator," he writes:

> The self-disgust of the prisoner comes from the alienation he has been brought to. That in which he participated (because the mortification lies in that he is forced to participate in his own undoing) will play havoc with his conception of himself and it will forever modulate his contact with other people. He will have the leftover knowledge that he has been used as a tool, that he was coldly and expertly manipulated, that he was confronted with his own weakness. Worse, far worse, that he ended up looking upon his tormentor as a confessor, as a friend even. This development is so profoundly unnatural that it makes him sick of himself.

Examining himself with great courage, Breytenbach declares that the self-divisive damage he has suffered is permanent. In an interview just before his release, he tells the authorities that after five years in prison any man is no longer a man. When people ask him how he survived, he answers that he did not survive. In the modernist authors from whom Breytenbach has learned the most, this paradox is familiar: As one reads, the "I" whose actions and sufferings are described in the past is superseded by the "I" who *must* have survived in order to be describing them in the present. Yet here, for once, it is hard not to take these words at face value. Breytenbach did not survive. A fine poet and dedicated activist was incarcerated; the man who was released seven years later was still a fine poet, but his attention had been driven inward, on himself. He is no turncoat, but his voice is not that of someone who remains politically active.

There is a heroic myth which reflects that suffering in a just cause is ennobling. Willfully and also perhaps unconsciously, Breytenbach demystifies this consoling notion. Repeatedly he insists that he did not survive. He reminds his reader that he made no political statements and that he agreed with the authorities when he thought he could win points by doing so. Being in prison, he says, is never worth it. Unfortunately, the reader is obliged to believe him. The self who writes can take credit for these words; the self who acts and suffers demonstrates their sad truth. The book has a powerful but dispiriting moral: To go to prison for a cause can remove one from that cause. One must act without believing that action is worthwhile.

Little by little, Breytenbach's attractive modesty about his own political unimportance shades off into thoughts which are apolitical, nihilistic, merely individual. There are many political sentiments expressed here which will make Breytenbach's allies wince, and even perhaps a few that will bring a smile to the faces of his enemies. The activists of the European antiapartheid movement are portrayed quite unpleasantly. Those, on the other hand, who are bred within the system cannot be expected to change it significantly, he declares; only violence from without can shake it. Yet violence will inevitably be blind—and in conclusion he assures his readers that no cause can sanction the destruction of human life. This logic does not leave much hope for changing the lives of the people of Soweto. Accusing the African National Congress of antidemocratic and authoritarian practices, Breytenbach prophesies darkly that its victory would merely replace a racist totalitarianism with a nonracist totalitarianism. Such statements may explain why the South African government has decided to permit *The True Confessions of an Albino Terrorist* to be published in South Africa.

During the last five years of his imprisonment, Breytenbach was kept at Pollsmoor Prison in suburban Cape Town, the most recent home of Nelson Mandela. The two men crossed paths in the same jail, but they lived in different worlds. To mention Mandela's name is to be reminded that it is possible to "survive" in prison, and that regardless of whether one does, the cause for which one was imprisoned goes on. Still, the bitter honesty with which Breytenbach records his failure to survive has its own value. Even if it finally proves to be only a passing moment in his career, Breytenbach has done well to define and preserve it.

Bruce Robbins

Sources for Further Study

Commentary. LXXX, October, 1985, p. 71.
Foreign Affairs. LXIII, Summer, 1985, p. 1133.
Kirkus Reviews. LII, December 15, 1984, p. 1177.
Library Journal. CX, March 1, 1985, p. 83.
The New Republic. CXCII, March 11, 1985, p. 29.
The New York Review of Books. XXXII, July 18, 1985, p. 3.
The New York Times Book Review. XC, February 10, 1985, p. 1.
Publishers Weekly. CCXXVI, December 21, 1984, p. 79.
Washington Post Book World. XV, May 5, 1985, p. 5.
World Literature Today. LIX, Spring, 1985, p. 311.

UNDER THE BANYAN TREE
And Other Stories

Author: R. K. Narayan (1906-   )
Introduction by the author
Publisher: The Viking Press (New York). 193 pp. $16.95
Type of work: Short stories
Time: From World War II to the mid-1980's
Locale: Southern India, including assorted villages and Malgudi, a fictional city

A collection of twenty-eight stories, in which Narayan ranges over a wide swath of South Indian life with humor, compassion, and insight

R. K. Narayan, who is eighty years old, has long been admired as a native observer of Southern India and a craftsman of fiction in English. In more than two hundred short stories and twelve novels, Narayan has populated the fictional city of Malgudi and the surrounding region with an immense variety of characters. Most reviewers of *Under the Banyan Tree: And Other Stories* comment on the range of social classes about which Narayan writes, from beggars to rich merchants, and he convincingly portrays all ages, from small boys to old men (his only limitation, perhaps self-imposed, seems to be the expression of female points of view). In a brief but revealing introduction to this collection, Narayan states, "At one time I found material for my stories in the open air, market-place, and streets of Mysore." He did not roam the streets "deliberately or consciously to pick up a subject but for the sheer pleasure of watching people." The result in *Under the Banyan Tree*, a selection of recent stories and stories from earlier collections, is a panorama of South Indian life from a close and compassionate observer, an expert at putting himself into the skins of other people—and even of animals.

Besides portraying an impressive variety of characters, Narayan commands a variety of form. His short stories here recapitulate the history of the form from O. Henry to Donald Barthelme. A few stories rely on a formula or premise, such as "Like the Sun," about a man who resolves to tell the blunt truth for one whole day (and thereby alienates his wife and his boss), and "All Avoidable Talk," about a man warned by his astrologer to avoid making irritating remarks for one whole day. A few other stories contain ironic coincidence, such as "Half a Rupee Worth," about a greedy merchant suffocated by his hoard of rice, and "Another Community," wherein a peaceful man who shuns involvement in the Hindu-Muslim confrontation is the cause of its violent outbreak. Most of the stories develop more freely out of character and situation; one or two even have unresolved endings. Most are brief, tightly constructed, and occur within a short period of time, but a few are long, rambling, or cover years: "Uncle's Letters" consists of snippets of advice from an uncle to a nephew over the course of their lives. Three of the stories are related by an involved narrator, the Talkative Man, who is reminiscent of Joseph Conrad's Marlow. Two of the longer stories take on the appearance of memoirs, with Narayan himself playing prominent roles in them. Several others have an unnamed narrator who occasionally reflects on his authorial decisions.

Narayan's variety of form is controlled somewhat by the realistic tradition within which he works, and another controlling factor is his style. It must quickly be added that Narayan's realism, though faithful to South Indian life, is not the documentary, nitty-gritty type that dwells upon squalor and other physical detail; by contemporary standards, his work will seem cleaned up and sanitized, even if it does include stories about animals, prostitutes, beggars, and other poor folk. One reason for this is Narayan's style, which is restrained, discreet, and urbane. Sometimes called deceptively simple, Narayan's style is capable of much subtlety and of expressing a wry, compassionate personality. It seems well suited to *The New Yorker*, in whose pages Narayan's stories have frequently appeared.

Narayan writes in English so easily and naturally that he is in some danger of being considered a Westerner, which is perhaps why an occasional reviewer has judged his work amusing but otherwise puzzling, pointless, or without substance. While Narayan is too polite to hit his Western readers with the Caves of Malabar, the Hindu cultural context nevertheless supplies the essence of his work. The Hindu background is more obvious in his novels (and in his translations of Indian myths and legends) than in his short stories. Yet, even covered up by his Western manner, Narayan's Hindu roots are in some ways as apparent as the ear-splitting om resounding through the Caves of Malabar.

A simple demonstration occurs in the introduction to *Under the Banyan Tree*. Here Narayan alleges his inability to arrange the stories by "mood or theme" or even chronologically by order of publication. Instead, he arranged the stories "at random," thus giving the collection "a strange but convincing pattern of affinities and contrasts." He further alleges that "all theories of writing are bogus" and that he "cannot explain how a story comes to be written." All of his fussy disclaimers are a concession to the mysterious operation of divinity in the universe, in particular the forces of creativity but also disorder and destruction represented by the god Siva. In Narayan's stories, these forces are always contending with those of order and control—and usually winning.

A special case of these forces at work is women. In "House Opposite," a religious ascetic tries to carry on his meditations across the street from a prostitute, but her brisk trade and "seductive outline" prove to be too distracting. He finally moves out of his little hut and leaves the street to her, but, significantly, he gives her his blessing when she asks for it. Not so forgiving is an estranged wife in "The Shelter," who accidentally meets her husband when they take shelter from the rain under the same banyan tree. He uses the opportunity to seek a reconciliation, but she withers his advances with verbal fire and finally takes off into the rain. He might, in fact, be lucky, particularly if the spouses of the men in other stories are any indication. In "A Horse and Two Goats" and "Four Rupees," the wives shower their men with verbal abuse, send them off without food to find money, and, when they return with money, accuse them of stealing it.

Yet it is not only women in whom the elemental forces of Siva are at work. Children can also be treacherous, as in "Nitya" and "Crime and Punishment," and so can employers, as in "All Avoidable Talk" and "The Evening Gift," and so indeed can employees, as in "A Career." Not even animals can be depended on to be loyal: In "The Mute Companions," a deaf-mute beggar's only companion, a little performing monkey, abandons him after three years for richer pickings. Nothing can be depended on in Narayan's world, and nothing lasts: The universe is in flux, caught up in the unpredictable dance of Siva. Almost all of Narayan's stories develop this same general theme, either sadly or humorously, but following are some of the more notable examples in *Under the Banyan Tree*.

"A Breath of Lucifer" is based, Narayan says in a prologue, on a personal experience, an eye operation which required his eyes to be bandaged for a week, and he tells the story as a memoir, though it is apparently embroidered by a vivid imagination. The prologue is an occasion for existential musing, and the story itself is a metaphor for existence, Hindu style. During his hospital stay, Narayan says in the prologue, that he involuntarily practiced the ancient yogis' technique of visually screening out the world: He withdrew from the "unreal world" of flux and chaos into an inner space of sweetness and light where he was "blissfully free alike from elation as from fury or despair"—which sounds suspiciously like Nirvana. In the story itself, however, Narayan's temporary blindness takes on the opposite meaning, suggesting the way that most people live in the world of flux and chaos. He is dependent on a male nurse, Sam, to guide him even to the bathroom. About the time that Narayan begins to trust Sam, a model of courteous efficiency, Sam turns out to be more than he seems. Sam once excelled at playing Lucifer in a morality play, and, on the night before Narayan's bandages are due to be removed, Sam throws a celebration party, gets drunk, leads Narayan out of the hospital, offers to share his mistress, and finally abandons the befuddled author next to a bush. The patient suffers a relapse from "shock and exposure."

Also presented as a memoir is the long story "Annamalai," which traces Narayan's association with his illiterate gardener-caretaker. It is a beneficial association for both, freeing the writer from many distracting mundane concerns and providing a stable retirement for Annamalai. Annamalai has led an adventurous life, running off from his backward South Indian village, working on plantations in Ceylon and Malaysia, escaping from the Japanese during World War II, and, most recently, fleeing a tyrannical employer who had left him in a tiger-infested jungle to gather elephant dung. Originally, Narayan hired Annamalai to help him move to a quieter neighborhood, but Annamalai has stayed on as Narayan's gardener-caretaker for fifteen years. Though aging, Annamalai is a strong worker and fierce watchman, intimidating would-be thieves; Narayan can return from his travels and find his house intact and in good order. Above all, Annamalai is a sturdy representative of the villager mentality—proud, independent, stubborn, contentious, suspicious, but honest—which has enabled him to endure despite the handicap of his illiteracy. Yet the world catches up even with Annamalai. From afar, he has continued to receive mail detailing the chronic troubles of his family in the village—a microcosm of the world in flux. He originally had fled such entanglements, only to run into different ones elsewhere. In the end, he goes home to his village to sort out the family troubles and to die.

The villager mentality is also on exhibit in "A Horse and Two Goats," a story proving that Siva does not always stir up bad luck. The villager portrayed is old Muni, a herdsman whose flock has shrunk from forty to two goats and whose wife sends him off in the morning without feeding him. As he sits on the pedestal of an old clay statue—a warrior standing next to a prancing horse—and grazes his goats, a car drives by on the highway and skids to a stop, and out jumps an American tourist. The tourist wants to buy the clay horse from Muni, but Muni, who understands no English, fears that the tourist is an officer accusing him of some crime, perhaps a recent murder, and prays to Siva for protection. When the tourist gives him a cigarette and continues gabbing, Muni's suspicions are calmed; Muni in turn opens up and becomes voluble in Tamil. For pages, in a hilarious parody of intercultural exchange (and man's general confusion in the universe), the two carry on a mutually incomprehensible conversation. Yet much satisfied by their exchange, each man getting an opportunity to vent his own particular concerns, they conclude a deal for one hundred rupees (though Muni thinks that he has sold the goats)—thereby showing that man can live and thrive amid the chaos.

The final story in the collection, the title story, continues the theme of living amid the chaos, but much more somberly. "Under the Banyan Tree" deals with storytelling itself, a human activity designed to give order to the chaos and make it acceptable, though it is only fiction. In "Under the Banyan Tree," old Nambi, the beloved village storyteller who takes a month to "make up" a story and then, sitting under the banyan tree next to the goddess Shakti's temple, takes as many as ten evenings to narrate the story to his eager listeners, suddenly reaches the end of his string. One night he cannot tell his story, nor the next, nor the next. Finally he announces that the stories have come from the goddess Shakti, and then he takes a vow of silence: "The rest of his life (he lived for a few more years) was one great consummate silence." The old storyteller's lapse into silence sounds similar to Narayan's disclaimers in his introduction. Is "Under the Banyan Tree" Narayan's final statement on the nature of the universe and his art? Is this Narayan's farewell to the "unreal world"?

Harold Branam

Sources for Further Study

Booklist. LXXXI, June 15, 1985, p. 1436.
Kirkus Reviews. LIII, May 15, 1985, p. 442.
Library Journal. CX, July, 1985, p. 94.
Los Angeles Times. August 27, 1985, V, p. 8.
The New York Times Book Review. XC, July 21, 1985, p. 1.
Newsweek. CVI, August 26, 1985, p. 66.
Publishers Weekly. CCXXVII, May 17, 1985, p. 98.
Time. CXXVI, August 12, 1985, p. 58.
Washington Post Book World. XV, July 28, 1985, p. 7.

THE UNWANTED
European Refugees in the Twentieth Century

Author: Michael R. Marrus (1941-   )
Publisher: Oxford University Press (New York). 414 pp. $25.95
Type of work: Modern history
Time: 1919-1950
Locale: Europe

A survey of the plight of European refugees in the twentieth century

It has been drummed into our heads by poets, artists, and pundits that the modern world is haunted by the ghost of alienation; that despite the efforts of education, revived religion, government programs, and an endless cycle of psychological therapies, mankind continues to suffer from a sense of separateness. We are cut off from community. Even closer ties, formed in family and marriage, have lost their sustaining power. The strong can sometimes find within themselves the inspiration and strength to fashion accommodating worlds. Many people, however, lack the confidence (or arrogance) to go it alone and instead settle for a curious malaise. Many feel unwanted, and they embrace the ghost of alienation, considering marginality the true human condition. Many do not feel a sense of belonging and live out their lives straddling a metaphysical fence.

After reading Michael Marrus' account of forced wandering in the twentieth century, some readers may find themselves wondering if perhaps in his epic story of monumental social suffering there lies an important clue to the riddle of modern alienation. Since World War I, almost a hundred million people have been driven into homelessness, often under barbaric conditions. In the late nineteenth century, czarist persecutions drove millions of Jews westward. After World War I, the dissolution of the Habsburg Empire drove more Jews, as well as Slavs, Croats, and Italians, from their ancestral provinces. Almost half a million Czechs, Romanians, and Yugoslavs crowded into Hungary in 1921. In 1924, more than 300,000 Armenians fled Turkish persecution. They, too, came west. During World War II, first as a result of Nazi persecution and invasion and finally, in 1945, as a result of the Russian advance, the astonishing figure of more than sixty million describes Europe's homeless. The equivalent of the populations of both Great Britain and France constituted a nation in themselves—an unwanted nation. Is it unreasonable to suggest, with such a titanic example of social dislocation, that humanity was driven to internalize what had become a social reality? That unwantedness was transformed from a political tragedy into a cultural trauma?

These are but a few of the questions raised by Marrus' wide-ranging study, *The Unwanted: European Refugees in the Twentieth Century*. Marrus begins by distinguishing the experience of modern refugees from that of earlier generations; one of the purposes of his book, he notes, is "to trace the emerging consciousness of a refugee phenomenon since the 1880s." With a few exceptions (for example, "Jews banging on the gates of Palestine in the 1930s and 1940s or Polish refugees from Hitler who left the Soviet Union for destinations in the Middle East or Africa"), Marrus does not follow refugees after their departure from Europe; his focus is on refugees "moving within, out of, and into the European continent."

Marrus' previous book, *Vichy France and the Jews* (1981), cowritten with Robert O. Paxton, won a National Jewish Book Award, and while *The Unwanted* is by no means restricted to Jewish refugees, their fate is central to the book and is the source of the almost eerie dramatic irony that pervades it. Even before Adolf Hitler invaded Eastern Europe and began his murderous persecution of Jews, the governments of Poland, Romania, and Hungary expressed virulently anti-Semitic sentiments and urged mass emigration of what they believed were their excessively large Jewish populations. The Depression era's principal victim in Europe was the Jew. Jewish capitalists were blamed by Fascists and rightists everywhere for starting the Depression, and the impoverished Jews of Eastern Europe were considered a burden to the strained economies of the day. When Hitler finally made his move, the rest of Europe either acquiesced or ignored his solution to "the Jewish problem": slavery and extermination. Toward the end of the war and immediately after it, however, more than two million refugees of German stock fled before the Russian armies and crowded into what was to become the Federal Republic of Germany. Whereas Hitler had moved east to push back the Slavs and reclaim ancient German lands, the war ended with Germanic peoples, who had lived in Poland and the Ukraine for centuries, fleeing west. Hitler had sought greater territory to thin out German populations. What he "achieved" was a greater concentration of population in smaller territories.

Marrus insists that his study does not engage a close discussion of what he calls the "refugee experience"—the psychological and social problems of upheaval and assimilation. He is more concerned with "the impact of refugee movements on the international community in Europe," and he devotes extensive coverage to agencies such as the Red Cross, the League of Nations, and the United Nations, all of which became involved in political and humanitarian activities. When the famous Norwegian polar explorer Fridtjof Nansen was appointed to head the newly established High Commission for Refugees under the auspices of the League of Nations in the early 1920's, Europe took its first step to address refugee problems on an international level. In 1923, the Lausanne Convention, under Nansen's guidance, arranged a compulsory exchange of Turkish and Greek nationals involving one and a half million people from both nations. In 1925, the League avoided a Greco-Bulgarian clash by mediating a refugee problem. After a favorable start, the High Commission gradually lost prestige; it never gained inclusion in the League Covenant and was insufficiently funded. Leaning increasingly on charity assistance, primarily the Red Cross, the fettered politically, Nansen's High Commission dwindled in effect. This proved a disastrous precedent—an international organization of limited power—when the overpowering difficulties of refugee policy challenged Western nations after the advent of Fascism.

Germany had left the League of Nations in 1933. Nevertheless, diplomatic pressure from the League could have played a decisive role. Despite liberal anger at the persecutions in Germany in 1933, the League could not bring itself to act forcefully. A new High Commission for Refugees was established, and an American scholar of high reputation and proven humanitarian principles was elected to head it. James G. McDonald had high hopes. He worked vigorously to stop Hitlerian persecution of Jews, but after two years McDonald left his post in frustration. He simply could not get the League to back him in strong protests against Hitler. McDonald's successor, a retired British general, Sir Neill Malcom, managed to make major contributions toward improving the legal and social position of refugees already out of Germany, but he was not able to institute policies in aid of refugees about to arrive. Everyone knew that Hitler was determined to expel not only Germany's Jews but also those in occupied Austria after the *Anschluss* in 1938. Europe refused to formalize its capacities as a sanctuary. It had no intention of providing asylum on the large scale that Hitler's persecutions demanded.

France, for example, which had been a traditional refuge for "émigrés" in the nineteenth century, curtailed the entry of "refugees" to a trickle after a short six-month period of unrestricted asylum in 1933. France did allow Spanish loyalists fleeing Francisco Franco to find asylum in 1939, but after France's terrible defeat in June, 1940, her own roads were filled with an exodus south that rivaled any refugee wave in modern history.

Once the war had started, Jewish refugees were the most vulnerable of all. They constituted the overwhelming majority of the 350,000 refugees who had managed to escape Hitler before war broke out in 1939. Many had been able to leave Europe, but about 110,000 of these prewar Jewish refugees were still in Europe—many behind German lines. The Jews who had been fortunate enough to get to Great Britain were often interned as enemy aliens. From the beginning of the war until the end of 1941, a total of seventy thousand Jews managed to escape from Germany and Austria. Some got to Palestine. The United States liberalized its German-Austrian quotas briefly in 1940 and 1941, which enabled some sixty thousand Jews to reach the United States between 1939 and 1941. In June, 1941, however, Congress passed the Russell Bill, which severely curtailed further immigration.

Marrus ends his study by noting that after so many years of refugee experience, Europe now seems entirely free of it. Refugees are now largely a

Third World phenomenon. The wars in Biafra, Ethiopia, and Sudan have produced the new unwanted—along with Bangladesh, Vietnam, and Cambodia. In 1983, the *World Refugee Survey* reported a total of almost eight million "refugees in need" throughout the world; only 30,700 were in Europe, largely people passing through Austria on their way to permanent resettlement. These, by the way, were largely Jews allowed to emigrate by the Soviets.

Peter A. Brier

Sources for Further Study

Booklist. LXXXI, July, 1985, p. 1511.
Kirkus Reviews. LIII, July 1, 1985, p. 633.
Library Journal. CX, September 1, 1985, p. 196.
The New York Review of Books. XXXIII, February 27, 1986, p. 5.
The New York Times Book Review. XCI, February 2, 1986, p. 17.
Publishers Weekly. CCXXVIII, August 2, 1985, p. 56.
Times Literary Supplement. October 11, 1985, p. 1134.
Washington Post Book World. XV, September 8, 1985, p. 5.

VIRGINIA WOOLF
A Writer's Life

Author: Lyndall Gordon (1941-   )
Publisher: W. W. Norton and Company (New York). 341 pp. $17.95
Type of work: Literary biography
Time: 1882-1941
Locale: England

*A literary biography which draws on unpublished correspondence and manuscripts and on three of Virginia Woolf's novels—*The Voyage Out, To the Lighthouse, *and* The Waves—*to illuminate her life*

> *Principal personages:*
> VIRGINIA WOOLF, a novelist
> JULIA STEPHEN, her mother
> LESLIE STEPHEN, her father
> LEONARD WOOLF, her husband

At the age of forty-four, when she was writing *To the Lighthouse*, Virginia Woolf was photographed wearing a Victorian dress that had belonged to her mother. Her beautifully hooded eyes downcast, Woolf was gazing with a mixture of diffidence and amusement toward an exaggerated leg o'mutton sleeve. The dress did not quite suit her—its bulk almost overwhelms Woolf's slender frame—but the photograph, which appears on the dust jacket of *Virginia Woolf: A Writer's Life*, perfectly captures the spirit and emphasis of Lyndall Gordon's splendid biography. At first glance there might appear to be no need for yet another book, even a splendid one, about this much-written-of novelist. In the years since 1972, when Quentin Bell published the definitive biography of his famous aunt, Woolf's life and work have become subjects of intense literary and popular interest. Six volumes of letters, four volumes of diaries, and numerous reminiscences and scholarly treatises have fed an apparently insatiable appetite for information, interpretation, and gossip concerning one of the century's most important writers. Nevertheless, despite the amount of material about Woolf already in print, Gordon manages to see her subject in a new way. Her Virginia Woolf is neither an insistent modernist nor a committed feminist nor a madwoman with a collection of eccentric friends; rather, she is a writer who was motivated by the impulse to preserve her Victorian past, and whose richest sources were her own earliest memories.

One of the most striking attributes of Gordon's biography is the congeniality between Woolf's methods and Gordon's own. Woolf's innovativeness as a fiction writer arose in part from her belief that what is usually considered significant in a novel—births, deaths, marriages—is not nearly as important as "the way people look and laugh, and run up the steps of omnibuses." Gordon tries to follow Woolf's practice, on her long walks in the country and in London, of keeping to byways rather than main thoroughfares, of ignoring obvious markers and boundaries and finding natural paths. Drawing heavily on early drafts of *The Voyage Out* (1915), *To the Lighthouse* (1927), and *The Waves* (1931) and on unpublished memoirs and fictional fragments, Gordon does what Quentin Bell stopped short of doing: She examines Woolf's life in the light of the fiction and the fiction in the light of the life. This examination has three parts. The first, "Victorian Models," is a discussion of Woolf's childhood. The second, "Apprenticeship," deals with the twenty-year period between 1895, when Julia Stephen died, and 1915, when Woolf published her first novel. The long third part, which is called "The Life Composed" and which occupies half of Gordon's book, deals with Woolf's maturity.

Woolf's earliest and most enduring memories, according to Gordon, were of her parents and of the sound of the waves at Talland House, the family's summer home in Cornwall. Both these memories helped to shape *To the Lighthouse*, with its compelling portraits of Mr. and Mrs. Ramsay, drawn from the characters of Julia and Leslie Stephen. Gordon's discussion of Julia and Leslie is particularly illuminating in its treatment of young Virginia's relationship to her father. Far from being a domestic tyrant like Mr. Ramsay, Leslie consistently expressed loving fondness for his children, and especially for his youngest daughter. He read aloud to his children every night, and, as Virginia grew older, he gave her the run of his vast library and guided her in becoming a voracious and perceptive reader. Gordon convincingly demonstrates that through his tastes and interests, Leslie Stephen was his daughter's most important intellectual model; even her drafts, Gordon says, resemble his. Gordon uses correspondence to show that Leslie's encouragement of serious work on the part of the females in his family began even before his marriage to Julia, who insisted during their courtship that she intended to continue working as a nurse among the poor. She pursued her vocation until she died in 1895, when Virginia was thirteen. This event began a "decade of deaths": Virginia's stepsister, Stella, died in 1897, her father in 1904, and her brother Thoby in 1906. These early losses helped to shape an adulthood haunted by Victorian ghosts whose presence Woolf invoked in her fiction, most powerfully in *To the Lighthouse* and *The Waves*.

In the "Apprenticeship" section, Gordon delicately explores the connections between these deaths and the onset of Woolf's mental illness in early adolescence. Departing from the usual view that it was Julia's death that precipitated Virginia's first suicide attempt, Gordon suggests that Stella's death, not Julia's, triggered the illness, as well as a lifelong need for love from strong women. Gordon handles with equal delicacy the matter of Woolf's sexual abuse by her stepbrother George Duckworth. Without underestimating either the deaths or the abuse as factors in Woolf's illness, Gordon avoids lurid speculation where no certainty is possible. Neither does she exclude the more positive aspects of Woolf's apprenticeship: her inheritance of the "sensibility" associated with the nineteenth century Clapham Sect, her study of Greek in a bedroom "half... literary; half washing and dressing," and the flirtatious support of her brother-in-law, Clive Bell, during the writing of *The Voyage Out*.

Gordon is at her most discerning in the first two parts of the book, where she deftly weaves together biographical and fictional materials written at various times in Woolf's career to produce a coherent and fresh account of the writer's early life. In the long third section, chronology begins to dominate the presentation, and deftness is less in evidence, but Gordon's interpretations continue to offer insight. For example, she traces the origin of *The Waves* to a passage in William Wordsworth's "Ode: Intimations of Immortality" (1807). She distinguishes pre-1910 Bloomsbury from other literary circles by pointing out that its real basis was domestic affection, in particular the bond between Woolf and her sister Vanessa, rather than adherence to aesthetic principles. One of the most revealing sections of the book is Gordon's discussion, in a chapter called "The Trial of Love," of the relationship between Virginia and Leonard Woolf. On the basis of their correspondence—Leonard's is unpublished, and Virginia's letters to him are scattered throughout six volumes—Gordon argues convincingly that theirs was "a passionate and strange union" the basis of which was "Leonard's imaginative willingness to share a playful, private vocabulary." Readers who have been discomfited by the animal language in Virginia Woolf's intimate correspondence should find Gordon's analysis quite helpful. She insists that Woolf's habit in her letters of creating personas both for herself and for her correspondent was an extension to private life of the same imaginative energy she invested in her work. She also insists that Woolf's representation of herself as a "sexual failure," like her assertion that she was not well educated, may have been ironic, rather than literal. The Woolfs had their difficulties, to be sure, and Gordon does not gloss over them; instead, she stresses the couple's very Victorian devotion to each other—they were miserable apart—and their firm commitment to their marriage. In the light of Virginia's feelings for Leonard, Gordon is able to dismiss the relationships with Katherine Mansfield, Ethel Smyth, and even Vita Sackville-West as relatively insignificant.

In all three sections of *Virginia Woolf: A Writer's Life*, Gordon clearly delineates the themes of Woolf's fiction and demonstrates their connection to her experience. Central among these preoccupations was a concern for the middle-class Victorian woman's history and traditions: her confinement in domesticity, her training to silence, her need to deal positively with the past. Woolf herself escaped confinement when she and her sister moved from the family home in Hyde Park Gate to an establishment of their own in Bloomsbury, where each of the women had her own studio and where there were no restrictions on behavior or conversation. The opportunity to converse freely proved exhilarating to them. "In the Victorian age," Gordon explains, "women felt the pressure to relinquish language, and 'nice' women were quiet." In Woolf's fiction, silence is important both thematically and structurally; as Gordon puts it, Woolf "injects silence into the narrative, letting her own medium of expression—words—fail. . . . She turned Silence to effect in her novels but, initially, it was a weakness, the temptation not to speak at all."

The inefficacy of language is certainly a major issue in both *The Waves* and *To the Lighthouse*, whose central character, Mrs. Ramsay, will not even tell her husband that she loves him. In her silence and in every other way, Mrs. Ramsay is the quintessential Victorian woman, the woman both admired and resisted by the young painter Lily Briscoe, who represents Woolf herself. Lily comes to terms with Mrs. Ramsay by painting her, much as Woolf came to terms with her mother by writing the novel that many consider her masterpiece. *To the Lighthouse* is so powerful, Gordon believes, "because it is a triumphant book about the liberation of a woman from the past . . . all the more triumphant for not, in the process, abrogating the past but, in a controlled and selective way, using it."

Another of the preoccupations of Woolf's maturity was with the inadequacy of traditional methods of drawing character. Gordon points out that both of Woolf's parents were biographers: Leslie Stephen founded the *Dictionary of National Biography*, and Julia Stephen was well-known for her gift of summing up character from observation. Like her parents, Woolf was fascinated by the problem of portraying the essence of personality. She concluded that the best way to draw character was not to concentrate on the achievements or actions that the world might deem significant, but rather to rely on the suggestive power of apparently insignificant details. Her ideas about characterization, set forth in the essay called "Mr. Bennett and Mrs. Brown," are stunningly implemented in *To the Lighthouse* and *The Waves*. In both these novels, Woolf employed an elegiac blend of imagination, biography, and autobiography to draw portraits of her characters that extracted their essence. Her view of biography paralleled her view of history. For Woolf, history consisted not of public events but of "the acts of the obscure between the acts of kings and warriors." While some commentators have equated "obscure" with "trivial" and have faulted Woolf for her failure to deal explicitly with such momentous subjects as war, Gordon sees in Woolf's refusal to write about war "an outrage so complete that, taking a line more extreme than anti-war poets, she refused to treat war at all." Without diminishing the innovativeness of Woolf's fictional methods, Gordon says that her "true originality. . . lies in the heroic perversity of her sense of history."

At the end of her career, Woolf's preoccupation with the "lives of the obscure" led her to direct her fiction, as she had long directed her literary criticism, to the common reader. In this effort she achieved at least some measure of success. Her novel *The Years* (1937), in which Gordon says Woolf spoke for the women of her generation, was a best-seller. *Three Guineas* (1938) was both damned and praised for its feminist, pacifist polemicism. In *Between the Acts*, a novel published posthumously in 1941, Woolf dealt explicitly with the difficulty of reaching an audience of ordinary English villagers; the unpublished "Anon." was to have explored similar issues. Gordon suggests that in these last works, Woolf attempted to conquer her "obsession with the dead" in order to develop a more public voice. This view differs significantly from the usual judgment that the work of the 1930's represents a decline in Woolf's imaginative power after the brilliance of *To the Lighthouse* and *The Waves*.

Gordon's reinterpretation of the end of Woolf's career typifies the fresh approach she takes throughout *Virginia Woolf: A Writer's Life*. Although she deals fully with only three novels, her selectivity enhances her portrayal rather than detracts from it. From its careful documentation to its insightful handling of complex sources to its detailed bibliography and index, Lyndall Gordon's economical, energetic book is an admirable achievement, as valuable to the reader approaching Woolf for the first time as to the aficionado. Even the aptly chosen photograph on the dust jacket helps the reader see this most "modern" of novelists in the light of her powerful Victorian past.

Carolyn Wilkerson Bell

Sources for Further Study

Choice. XXII, May, 1985, p. 1332.
The Chronicle of Higher Education. XXX, April 10, 1985, p. 10.
Kirkus Reviews. LII, December 15, 1984, p. 1185.
Library Journal. CX, February 15, 1985, p. 169.
Los Angeles Times Book Review. March 3, 1985, p. 3.
New Leader. LXVIII, January 14, 1985, p. 12.
The New York Times Book Review. XC, February 10, 1985, p. 12.
The New Yorker. LXI, April 15, 1985, p. 131.
Publishers Weekly. CCXXVII, January 4, 1985, p. 64.
Times Literary Supplement. December 21, 1984, p. 1480.

THE WAR DIARIES OF JEAN-PAUL SARTRE
November 1939–March 1940

Author: Jean-Paul Sartre (1905-1980)
Translated from the French by Quintin Hoare
Publisher: Pantheon Books (New York). 366 pp. $17.95
Type of work: Diary
Time: November 1939-March 1940
Locale: Alsace, on the German-French border

A collection of the notebooks kept by the man who was to become France's most influential philosopher during the "Phony War" of September, 1939, to March, 1940

> *Principal personages:*
> JEAN-PAUL SARTRE, a philosopher, psychologist, essayist, dramatist, and fiction writer
> SIMONE DE BEAUVOIR, a philosopher, novelist, and essayist, Sartre's best friend
> ARLETTE ELKAÏM-SARTRE, his adopted daughter
> OLGA KOSAKIEWICZ, his mistress in 1935-1937
> WANDA KOSAKIEWICZ, Olga's sister and Sartre's mistress in 1939-1940
> PAUL NIZAN, a philosopher, Sartre's long-term friend
> PIETERKOVSKY (PIETER),
> PAUL, and
> KELLER, Sartre's military comrades

Jean-Paul Sartre's death in 1980 ended the career of a prodigiously creative one-man band of modern thought and literature who did important work in philosophy, psychology, fiction, drama, biography, literary criticism, journalism, political pamphleteering, and film writing. It also began the end of a brilliant era in French contributions to philosophy, linguistics, and anthropology, as Sartre's demise was followed within five years by the deaths of Roland Barthes, Jacques Lacan, and Michel Foucault, and the retirement from publication by Louis Althusser and Claude Lévi-Strauss.

Not content with producing four dozen volumes during his lifetime, Sartre left a rich mine of writings from which three books have so far been quarried: the two-volume *Lettres au Castor* (1983), a collection of his correspondence with Simone de Beauvoir; *Cahiers pour une morale* (1983), his notebooks for an unfinished treatise on moral philosophy; and the war diaries, originally published in 1983 as *Les Carnets de la drôle de querre* (notebooks during the phony war), portions of a diary he kept while a soldier during the months from his conscription in September, 1939, to his capture by German forces in late June, 1940.

When Sartre received his call-up notice, he was a thirty-four-year-old philosophy professor at the Lycée Pasteur in Neuilly, near Paris. He had begun to make his mark in both philosophic and literary circles but was far from reaching the worldwide fame which the postwar period would bring him. After graduating first in his class of 1929 from the formidable École

Normale Supérieure, he taught during the 1930's at various provincial *lycées* and spent the 1933-1934 academic year studying German philosophy at the Institut Français in Berlin. While at the École Normale, Sartre met Simone de Beauvoir, a philosophy student at the Sorbonne, and they soon formed a lifelong union more noted for intellectual than sexual intimacy. Two of her autobiographical texts, *La Force de l'âge* (1960; *The Prime of Life*, 1962) and *La Force des choses* (1963; *Force of Circumstances*, 1964), furnish a wealth of information about their lives together, particularly during the 1930's, when they undertook strenuous holidays, tramping through much of Europe and England with packs on their backs.

Sartre's first philosophical essays were influenced by the German phenomenologist Edmund Husserl, whose ideas he encountered in Berlin and partly agreed with, partly contested, in *L'Imagination* (1936; *Imagination: A Psychological Critique*, 1962) and *La Transcendance de l'égo* (1936; *The Transcendence of the Ego*, 1957). Sartre's literary career began with the 1938 publication of *La Nausée* (*Nausea*, 1949), commonly regarded as his best novel. *Nausea* is his most philosophically compact work of long fiction, dramatizing his views on such topics as freedom, anguish, authenticity, contingency, and absurdity. Since the novel's rootless protagonist, Antoine Roquentin, resembles Sartre in significant ways, it is worth noting that the work is cast in first-person diary form. One year later, in July, 1939, Sartre published a volume of five short stories under the title of what soon became his best-known tale, *Le Mur* (1939; *The Wall and Other Stories*, 1948). Again, each story seeks to illustrate a particular philosophical point, with "The Wall," for example, attempting to refute the German existentialist philosopher Martin Heidegger's contention that man can live meaningfully toward his own death.

By the early fall of 1939, then, Sartre had made a name for himself as a brilliant thinker and writer capable of both abstruse exposition and memorable dramatization of a far-ranging constellation of concepts. He had done his mandatory military service in 1929 in the meteorological corps, and was therefore assigned a decade later to a meteorological section attached to an artillery headquarters just behind the French-German front in Alsace. This station was moved only a few kilometers during the ten months Sartre served, with Strasbourg a close-by metropolis. His less-than-demanding duties are best noted in his sardonic summary:

> . . . my work here consists of sending up balloons and then watching them through a pair of field glasses: this is called "making a meteorological observation." Afterwards I phone the battery artillery officers and tell them the wind direction: what they do with this information is their affair. The young ones make some use of the intelligence reports; the old school just shove them straight in the wastepaper basket. Since there isn't any shooting, either course is equally effective.

When the Germans ended the Phony War by invading Belgium and

Northern France in late May, 1940, Sartre had transmitted fourteen of his completed war diaries to Simone de Beauvoir and other Parisian friends. Three or four of them, however, were lost by Jacques Bost, a colleague to whom de Beauvoir lent them. Through other circumstances, impossible to trace, a half dozen other notebooks have also been lost, so that the volume under review, though a substantial 366 pages, consists of only five of the fourteen completed notebooks. The numbers and dates of the surviving diaries are III (November 12–December 7, 1939); V (December 17–December 23, 1939); XI (January 31–February 19, 1940); XII (February 20–February 29, 1940); and XIV (March 3–March 28, 1940).

Why did Sartre write them? In a December 1, 1939, entry, he calls his journal "the notebook of a witness . . . the testimony of a 1939 bourgeois draftee on the war he's being made to fight." He emphasizes the commonplace nature of his situation: Unlike such diarists as André Gide or Jean Giraudoux, he is not a distinguished writer; unlike personnel in the intelligence or censorship divisions, he is "not in a privileged position." Yet his journal will be representative of millions of other soldiers. "It is a *mediocre*, and for that very reason *general*, testimony." He regards himself as a spokesman for a generation confronted by an apocalyptic historical crisis; therefore, he unabashedly states, "everything I write is interesting . . . in consequence this journal has no humility . . . no intimacy. It is a proud, pagan journal."

As an extremely complex person, Sartre surely kept his diary for a number of additional purposes: to explore his own mentality and character; to free himself from childhood trauma by describing them; to establish a solitary sanctuary amid the enforced claustrophobia of military life; to conduct freewheeling forays into intellectual and literary analysis; to prepare himself for future writing projects. The book's graceful translator, Quintin Hoare, states in his introduction that these notebooks "prefigure and map out the virtual entirety of the writer's subsequent oeuvre," as well as justifying themselves in their own right as a memorable exercise in a great thinker's self-examination. They "represent the essential transition from . . . apprenticeship to the full flowering of Sartre's talents."

In a November 19 entry, Sartre notes:

I went more than fifteen years without looking at myself living. I didn't interest myself at all. I was curious about ideas and the world and other people's hearts. Introspective psychology seemed to me to have yielded its optimum with Proust; I'd tried my hand at it rapturously between the ages of 17 and 20, but it had seemed to me that one could very quickly become a dab hand at that exercise, and in any case the results were pretty tedious. Furthermore, pride deflected me from it: it seemed to me that by prying into trifling acts of meanness, one inflated and reinforced them. It has taken the war, and also the assistance of several new disciplines (phenomenology, psychoanalysis, sociology) . . . to prompt me to draw up a full-length portrait of myself.

liant writing, ranking with *Les Mots* (1964, *The Words*, 1964) as a painfully honest self-portrait, often self-mocking and mordant, sometimes witty, other times pompous and portentous, occasionally elegantly aphoristic ("One is totally responsible for one's life"; "all happiness has to be paid for, and there's no affair that doesn't end badly"; "a book read is a corpse"). In *The Words*, Sartre persistently denounces himself as a play-actor guilty of a series of impostures vis-à-vis other people, of hypocrisy, insincerity, self-deception; the book reeks with self-recrimination.

   The War Diaries of Jean-Paul Sartre is an equally unsparing self-critique. Sartre accuses himself of moral buffoonery and pedantry, of lecturing his unlearned comrades and thereby discharging his bile. Again and again, he lashes himself for lacking what was soon to become his most significant existentialist touchstone: authenticity. He accuses himself of being remote and detached from other people's emotions. Like Roquentin in *Nausea* and Orestes in his later play *Les Mouches* (1943; *The Flies*, 1946), he feels himself incapable of sharing others' feelings: "I look like a sensitive person but I'm barren. . . . I haven't felt Nausea, I'm not authentic." Still, like Orestes in the closing speech of *The Flies*, "I point the way. . . and others can go there. I'm a guide, that's my role."

   In a probing essay on the nature of love, Sartre discovers its roots in sadism: The desire to be loved amounts to a "hit at the Other in the Other's absolute freedom." Therefore the commonest and strongest type of love, "the love that craves slave-freedom; the love that wants freedom in others only so that it can violate it—that form of love is utterly inauthentic." The wish to be loved, Sartre summarizes in a byzantinely tortuous definition, amounts to *"effecting the unification of the for-itself and the world in accordance with the type of unity of the for-itself and the for-the-Other, while existing in safety in the midst of a freedom which subjugates itself in order to desire you as world."* In his next sentence, he grants that "it will be said that I'm expressing quite simple things in a complicated way." Yes.

   Sartre recalls himself as a contriving little monster when he was a child, winning other children's affection by giving puppet performances. Later in his life, he tried to become "a scholarly Don Juan, slaying women through the power of his golden tongue." Since the age of seventeen, he says, he has "always lived as part of a couple"—not a loving pair, but qualities warring with one another. Like Paul Valéry's self-absorbed character Monsieur Teste, "I was living dissociated from myself." As he does later in *The Words*, Sartre charges himself with the sins of overabstraction and emotional aridity: "I'm not cut out for friendship. I've disappointed all my friends— not by betrayal, neglect or lack of consideration, but by a profound lack of warmth." He takes this declaration to its logical conclusion: "I have no *need* of friends because, basically, I don't need anybody: . . . I prefer to derive everything from myself."

Surely such a self-indictment is too severe. Sartre is an emotional puritan, who distills and then denounces those threads of imposture and insincerity with which virtually all lives are stitched. Surely the uninterrupted devotion between him and the extraordinary Simone de Beauvoir bears a more affirmative witness than these harsh self-harrowings. At the École Normale he is known to have become the firm friend of such talented people as Raymond Aron and Paul Nizan. A number of his mistresses remained on friendly postlibidinal terms with him.

Speaking of women: Despite his self-proclaimed ugliness, Sartre had many affairs besides and during his companionship with Simone de Beauvoir. Hoare says that during the period covered by the war diaries, Sartre was also writing, on virtually a daily basis, not only to de Beauvoir (nicknamed "the Beaver," hence *Castor*) and his mother also, but to his then-current mistress, Wanda Kosakiewicz, with whom he had an intense relationship after having previously loved her sister Olga, and to whom he was to dedicate *L'Âge de raison* (1945; *The Age of Reason*, 1947), having dedicated "The Wall" to Olga. In the diaries Sartre expresses his distinct preference for female over male association: " . . . it's very rare for the company of women not to entertain me. . . . I *get on* with women. I like their way of talking, and of saying or seeing things; I like their way of thinking; I like the subjects they think about."

Nevertheless, Sartre's intellectualism clearly overshadows his interest in both people and current events. He worries, for example, about having added several kilos of extra weight and not having had a letter for several days from Wanda. His main interest, however, centers on Arthur Koestler's book *Spanish Testament* (1937; abridged in the Danube edition as *Dialogue with Death* in 1942), which recounts Koestler's imprisonment by Falangist forces in Spain. Sartre admires Koestler's authentic confrontation of the fear of dying and quotes his testimony that overcoming the fear of death constitutes "the most complete experience of freedom that can be granted a man." As for letters, they prompt Sartre to a meditation on time, being "scraps of present surrounded by future; but it's a past-present surrounded by a dead future."

Philosophically, the main interest of the war diaries lies in their rehearsal of many ideas that would soon suffuse his masterwork, *L'Être et le néant* (1943; *Being and Nothingness*, 1956). The stagnant situation of the Phony War enables Sartre to devote as many as thirteen hours a day to concentrated reading and writing, as he elevates himself from his mundane, boring military surroundings into stratospheres of rarefied metaphysical speculation to which untrained readers will have difficulty following him. One makes the acquaintance here of such significant concepts as the state of *pour-soi*, being-for-itself, as opposed to *en-soi*, being-in-itself, and *pour-autrui*, being-for-others. Man, Sartre insists, brings with him into the world the essential but elusive concept of *néant*, Nothingness, which causes him to feel the anguish, *angoisse*, which is the normal condition of his liberty in a world lacking universal values.

Repeatedly, Sartre seeks the almost unattainable goal of authenticity, whereby man fully understands his condition in the world. "To be authentic," he states in one notebook, "is to realize fully one's being-in-situation, whatever this situation may happen to be: with a profound awareness that, through the authentic realization of the being-in-situation, one brings to plenary existence the situation on the one hand and human reality on the other." Since Sartre regards man as an absurd creature, existing without justification or purpose, he feels unwanted and frustrated except for art: "Only the work of art could give man that justification, for the work of art is a metaphysical absolute. So, lo and behold!, the absolute is restored—but *outside* man. Man is worth nothing."

As for morality, Sartre has no difficulty positing it in his atheistic universe: "Dostoevsky used to write: 'If God does not exist, all is permitted.' That's the great error of transcendence. Whether God exists or does not exist, morality is an affair 'between men' and God has no right to poke his nose in."

Sartre is fascinated by the concept of Nothingness, to which he returns repeatedly, seeking to illuminate it. Since "freedom is the apparition of Nothingness in the world . . . [then] anguish at Nothingness is simply anguish at freedom, or, if you prefer, freedom's anguish at itself." The argument soon turns highly technical, as in these statements: ". . . in the urgency of the possible, there's a certain nothingness-ness [*néantité*]. It can also be seen that the possible couldn't be anterior to being. Quite the contrary, the original possibles are my own possibles and flow from my 'facticity-as-being-which-is-its-own-nothingness.'"

As just shown, Sartre often yields to the temptation to envelop his subject in a thick cloud of abstraction, demonstrating his nature as an extreme example of the Continental intellectual who takes to language and speculation at an early age and remains inside these domains as his breathing element. One gets the strong impression that he prefers the organized flow of words and charged current of methodized thought to the variable dynamics of human relationships. A metaphysical axiom is far more welcome than the unpredictable tug-of-war exerted by feelings. An addiction to the Word—millions and millions of words—is the one constant obsession in Sartre's life. *The War Diaries of Jean-Paul Sartre* furnishes, for both better and worse, a representative opportunity for his exercise of this commitment.

Gerhard Brand

Sources for Further Study

Booklist. LXXXI, March 15, 1985, p. 1024
Foreign Affairs. LXIII, Summer, 1985, p. 1123.
Kirkus Reviews. LIII, January 15, 1985, p. 87.
Library Journal. CX, April 15, 1985, p. 69.
The London Review of Books. VII, February 7, 1985, p. 19.
The Nation. CCXL, April 20, 1985, p. 470.
The New Republic. CXCII, April 15, 1985, p. 32.
The New York Times Book Review. XC, March 31, 1985, p. 12.
Publishers Weekly. CCXXVII, February 8, 1985, p. 65.
Times Literary Supplement. January 4, 1985, p. 16.

WHAT'S BRED IN THE BONE

Author: Robertson Davies (1913-   )
Publisher: The Viking Press/Elisabeth Sifton Books (New York). 436 pp. $17.95
Type of work: Novel
Time: 1855-1981
Locale: The Ottawa Valley, Toronto, Oxford, Bavaria, and London

Francis Cornish is an individual of great resources and great potential, but like the country he reflects, he can never find his creative selfhood—his cultural and aesthetic signature

> *Principal characters:*
> FRANCIS CORNISH, a spy, art restorer, and world-famous art collector
> MARY-JACOBINE "Mary-Jim" McRORY CORNISH, his beautiful but distant socialite mother
> MAJOR FRANCIS CHEGWIDDEN CORNISH, his ambitious, politically astute father, an intelligence operative
> SENATOR JAMES "HAMISH" McRORY, his grandfather, a self-made lumber baron and financier
> ISMAY CORNISH, his attractive, promiscuous, and selfish wife
> RUTH NESBIT, a governess-spy with whom Francis has an affair
> TANCRED SARACENI, his mentor in the art of restoring paintings

How many fictional characters—or historical ones, for that matter—are fortunate enough to have their lives rehearsed by a recording angel? Perhaps only Francis Cornish, the hero of *What's Bred in the Bone*, has had such luck. Robertson Davies' novel is filled with formal surprises such as this one, which will bring smiles from his growing legions of avid readers. As the Lesser Zadkiel reruns the tape of Cornish's life, he is joined by the Daimon Maimon, Cornish's private daimon, who is always ready to take bows for prompting Francis toward his mixed fate. Between them, these eternal beings exercise a playful, Olympian control over the unraveling of the hero's life and its meaning. The novel's title is straightforward enough: Davies' work explores the mysteries of human personality as shaped by heredity, environment, accident, and nudges from the spiritual realm. The display of Cornish's unfolding destiny—which is his character—is masterful and joyous art. This challenging, ambitious novel is one of Davies' most entertaining, and it shows his abundant skills in grand form.

What is bred into Francis Cornish? One strand is the isolation of living in the Canadian frontier town of Blairlogie as a young boy and the double isolation of being teased by other children. As a member of the privileged class, Francis finds himself in a complex exile, especially as his parents leave him to his own devices and to the ministrations of peculiar relatives and household employees. Davies gives lavish attention to this place and to his hero's forebears.

From Francis' maternal grandfather, James Ignatious "Hamish" McRory, the hero inherits a surprising toughness and some of his aesthetic gifts.

McRory, who was brought to an untamed Canada as a boy in the middle of the nineteenth century, rises to become a lumber baron, a banker, and a member of the Canadian Senate. Francis knows him best as an amateur photographer who introduced his grandson to the magic of light. Married to Marie-Louise Thibodeau, Senator McRory works to build a liberal base of power. Although a Scot, he is Catholic, and he intends to maintain that Catholic inheritance even in the Ottawa Valley where the Presbyterian Scotch have held sway over the larger population of French Catholics and the laborer-servant stratum of Poles.

The senator's first daughter, Mary-Jacobine, is his darling. For her he makes great plans that culminate in an appearance before Edward VII. At this pinnacle of success, Mary-Jim (as she is called), flushed with excitement, champagne, and the power of her own spectacular beauty, allows herself to be compromised by a temporary hotel employee. Her mother, in spite of her rigorous Catholicism, explores various exercises to end the unwanted pregnancy, but all the jumping and horse-riding result only in a deformed, severely retarded son.

Major Francis Chegwidden Cornish, who attends the McRorys during their London adventure, is a man with polish and practical clear-sightedness. He has a name; he needs a marriage into money to secure his future. At first, the McRorys resist his overtures, but a deal is made when they become alarmed over Mary-Jim's condition. This marriage of convenience works well because each partner respects the other's selfishness and leaves room for it. Each also supports the other's drive for social prominence, and neither finds time for their children.

Mary-Jim's unwanted child is named Francis. Some five years later, when Mary-Jim becomes pregnant by her husband, this earlier child—an ordeal and an embarrassment to the ambitious couple—is allowed publicly to die. In fact, he is alive, sequestered in an upstairs, off-limits room in the senator's house. Mary-Jim herself has been led to believe that her son is dead, already having outlived the predictions of the family doctor.

To the major's biological son, this first Francis becomes an emblem of feared possibilities. For the hero, this misshapen, demented namesake—even more isolated, more removed from parental care, less able to control his animal impulses—serves as a grotesque double (one of many instances of doubling in the novel). It is only when the first Francis finally dies that the second begins to blossom fully, though the image of the "Looner" haunts him thereafter—a warning of how much of what man becomes is subject to forces over which he has no control. The case of the first Francis seriously complicates the question of "what's bred in the bone."

Reared apart from his parents, Francis Cornish finds a spiritual mother in his great-aunt, Mary-Benedetta McRory, who serves as an upper servant in the senator's house. Mary-Ben feeds Francis a tantalizing, partially inhibiting, but imaginatively stimulating brand of Catholicism—this in spite of the fact that Major Cornish has insisted on a Protestant upbringing as part of the deal with the McRorys. Mary-Ben's collection of religious pictures intrigues Francis; their images and manner sink into his sensibilities. Victoria Cameron, the family cook and a stern Calvinist, is a kind of alter-ego double for Mary-Ben and the other mother figure for the hero, while Victoria's friend, a strange fellow named Zadok Hoyle, serves as Francis' father figure.

Zadok—groom to the McRory stable, carriage and hearse driver for a local businessman, and veteran of the Boer War—befriends Francis and encourages his art. Zadok's own arts include those of embalming (ironic, given Francis' later career doing somewhat fraudulent restoration work on old portraits), and through watching Zadok practice his profession, Francis finds subjects for his self-taught (with the aid of a how-to book) figure drawing. To complicate the hero's sense of himself, it is Victoria and Zadok who are charged with the care of the first Francis. So, by these coincidences, both the hero and his double have the same nurturers. (Only the heavenly narrators know that this same Zakok is the biological father of the first Francis.)

Francis is left to find his own path, though Daimon Maimon claims that he made all the proper moves that any responsible daimon could make. The aspiring artist seizes what opportunities come his way. The major, whose prominent monocle suggests his ability to look into things deeply but narrowly, imparts some of this trait to his son. Moreover, he maneuvers Francis into the world of secret intelligence gathering—the major's own specialty. Otherwise, the father keeps his distance. Francis attends the University of Toronto and then Oxford University, where his young adulthood becomes severely complicated. In presenting these complications, Davies shows an artist's mastery over all that Sigmund Freud, Carl Jung, and their followers have taught the world about human personality.

The bulk of the novel elaborates Francis' growth as an artist, his entanglements as a spy, and his relationships with two women. Every episode is rich with wit, with exciting settings and situations, and with intriguing aesthetic and ethical concerns. Repeatedly, the reader is assured that the working out of Francis' fate stems from what was "bred in the bone." The intricate webs of cause and effect are always convincing, highly imaginative, and rarely predictable. Davies' genius resides simultaneously in his probing of humanist and religious values, his mastery over the smallest details of craft, and his blazing inventiveness.

At Oxford, Francis is used by his promiscuous and beautiful cousin, Ismay, who leads him to believe that she is pregnant by him. She is a coarse version of the Arthurian lady fair he imagines her to be. After their marriage, she reveals who the true father is and soon leaves Francis to join her lover. Ismay is a double for Francis' own mother; his attraction to her and his consequent sense of betrayal stem from this mirroring. At the same time, Ismay is treated as part of Francis' quest to complete himself by finding and blending with his female side, a quest begun in his youth when he would posture before the mirror in women's garments. Clearly enough, one thing bred into Francis is a need planted by Mary-Jim's indifference toward her maternal responsibilities.

Later, Francis meets a woman, Ruth Nesbit, who shares his interests and is worthy of his affection, but she is taken from him by the wartime bombing of London. In one way or another, all of Francis' attachments to women seem doomed.

Doomed as well is his career as an artist. Though his skills blossom, he is aesthetically at home only with the Renaissance art of religious passion and shared cultural symbols. His own inclinations and his arduous apprenticeship under the master restorer Tancred Saraceni prepare him to produce masterpieces in the Renaissance manner, but he finds no way of developing a contemporary style of his own. After his involvement in deliciously devious anti-Nazi intrigues, he finds himself a minor celebrity in the art world, then a respected art consultant and collector, and finally a reclusive eccentric. These latter periods of Francis' life are summarized briefly. Indeed, a possible flaw in this novel is the imbalance of attention paid to the last forty years of his life after the meticulous treatment of the first thirty. Nevertheless, the overall impression is that the patterns are so well-fixed that further elaboration would risk repetition. Whatever the ebbs and flows of Francis' worldly success, Davies insists on the magnitude of the inner Francis as he struggles to know himself and to accept his fate.

Davies' vision of Francis has many levels, one of which is an allegory of Canada. Like his country, Francis is an uneasy mix of Catholic and Protestant, as well as English, Scotch, and French. The turmoil and tension of this dislocated spiritual and ethnic diversity parallels the uncertain identity of the Canadian nation. Francis is an individual of great resources and great potential, but, like the country he reflects, he can never find his creative selfhood—his aesthetic and cultural signature. The forces which play upon him and within him are too large and contradictory to synthesize into a new and dynamic entity. Though much greater in potential than many of his contemporaries, Francis Cornish is left to play a relatively obscure role in the affairs of art. Such also, suggests Davies, is the role of Canada in world affairs.

As Davies builds Francis' education in art, he simultaneously educates readers. Running through *What's Bred in the Bone* is a lesson in art history and in the philosophy of art—a lesson that glows with love. Davies' descriptive prose handles any subject with clarity and vigor, but his descriptions of paintings, of the process of painting, and of the ways in which art communicates, enriches, and ennobles human experience are truly stunning. Ironically, his plot requires that he set this kind of material against other aspects of the artist's world: art as national treasure, art as business, art as political instrument. Indeed, much of the novel is concerned with the paradoxical relationship of art and money.

Francis Cornish has something of the McRory banker's blood in him. He wants full value for his money. He wants to be a creative spender. Such a summary sounds crude, but Davies makes this strand work in his complex characterization. The Francis Cornish who leaves behind a significant collection has done something to shape art history and the future of art. He has had an impact on what is valued and on the value itself. Francis Cornish, a rather mysterious figure who is nevertheless easy enough to overlook, would make an excellent subject for a biography.

To other personages invented by Robertson Davies, Cornish is certainly real, and after he dies, those left to administer the Cornish Foundation for Promotion of Arts and Humane Scholarship (three characters central to Davies' *The Rebel Angels*, 1982) appoint one of their number to tell his story— a story about which they know surprisingly little. The Reverend Simon Darcourt has done some research but has found only more questions. Arthur Cornish (Francis' nephew) and Arthur's wife, Maria, debate with Darcourt the wisdom of looking into the past of a man whose dealings are reputed to be somewhat shady. Might they not turn up something to discredit the great Canadian financial empire—the Cornish Trust? The novel opens with these deliberations. Then the recording angel and the daimon take over, revealing matters that even the skilled Reverend Darcourt could never unravel. As the novel ends, Darcourt is given the green light to write Francis Cornish's life, and the reader is left to wonder—knowing all that there is to be discovered—what kind of success Darcourt will have.

In *What's Bred in the Bone*, Robertson Davies' success is complete. The novel is a formal triumph, a deep well of human compassion and understanding, and a treasure of learning and wit.

Philip K. Jason

Sources for Further Study

Booklist. LXXXII, October 1, 1985, p. 190.
Commonweal. CXII, December 20, 1985, p. 705.
Library Journal. CX, November 15, 1985, p. 109.
The New Republic. CXCIII, December 30, 1985, p. 47.
The New York Review of Books. XXXIII, February 27, 1986, p. 16.
The New York Times Book Review. XC, December 15, 1985, p. 6.

Newsweek. CVI, December 2, 1985, p. 95.
Publishers Weekly. CCXXVIII, September 20, 1985, p. 104.
Time. CXXVI, December 2, 1985, p. 94.
The Wall Street Journal. CCVI, November 19, 1985, p. 28.

WHITE NOISE

Author: Don DeLillo (1936-   )
Publisher: The Viking Press (New York). 326 pp. $16.95
Type of work: Novel
Time: The 1980's
Locale: Blacksmith, a small college town near Glassboro, New Jersey

Jack Gladney is a history professor whose life suddenly becomes complicated by two events: a dangerous toxic-waste leak that forces a mass evacuation, and his discovery that his wife is taking a mysterious drug to ward off her insistent death panics

Principal characters:
> JACK GLADNEY, a history professor and chairman of the department of Hitler studies at College-on-the-Hill
> BABETTE, his wife, whose drug experiments disturb Jack
> MURRAY JAY SISKIND, the Gladneys' friend, a former sportswriter now turned lecturer on popular culture
> OREST MERCATOR, a chum of the Gladneys' teenage children

Jack Gladney is chairman of the department of Hitler studies at College-on-the-Hill, but he feels insecure because he can neither speak nor read German. He lives harmoniously with his wife, Babette, and with his kids, her kids, and their kids. They are a likable, bright family, and the children are especially vulnerable and appealing. Uneasy about a conference on Hitler studies soon to be hosted by his department, Jack studies German with an eccentric autodidact who has studied meteorology by correspondence and "got a degree to teach the subject in buildings with a legal occupancy of less than one hundred."

Howard Dunlop, the self-taught meteorologist, makes up a comic trio along with Murray Jay Siskind, Jack's friend who rummages around in the debris of popular culture, and the imaginative teenager Orest Mercator, obsessed with spending a record time in a cageful of black mambas. Readers of earlier novels by Don DeLillo, especially *End Zone* (1972) and *Ratner's Star* (1976), will quickly recognize in these three characters a special kind of amiable looniness that DeLillo is adept at creating. Such characters in his fiction are always charming, guileless, and original. Dunlop, the German teacher, for example, besides German, teaches Greek, Latin, and ocean sailing, as well as the weather classes in small buildings. When Jack gets to know Dunlop better, he learns that Dunlop became obsessed with weather patterns and data as a relief from the shock he suffered at his mother's death. This insight helps Jack to understand Dunlop, and it fits him into the main theme of the novel: the insidious, debilitating, omnipresent sense of one's eventual death.

Murray Jay Siskind's life has another kind of pathos. He has come to the College-on-the-Hill to escape the city's heat and the sexual entanglements that he claims torment him there. He lives in a crumbling house near an insane asylum, sharing his address with seven other boarders whose spiritual malaise appears in a variety of dark guises. He craves winning the minds of women, especially those whose sensibilities are complex, neurotic, and difficult. Murray reads the ads in *Ufologist Today*, takes Jack to see the most photographed barn in America, and hires a prostitute on whom he wants to perform the Heimlich maneuver. Despite Murray's inventive ways of coping with life, his loneliness is apparent. His efforts to develop a "vulnerability that women will find attractive" produce only a "half sneaky look, sheepish and wheedling."

Jack's son Heinrich introduces him to Orest Mercator, whom Jack tries to dissuade from his mad hope to spend sixty-seven days in a cage with poisonous reptiles. Orest appears only briefly in *White Noise*, but his bravado about death is touching, and it captures well the courage and the aspiration for self-realization that characterize the children in the novel.

Jack's own struggles with the German language are comic, and his well-meant but futile earnestness is at once sad, funny, and very human. Preparing for the Hitler conference, he compiles long lists of words that are the same in both German and English. The result is a conference speech that is bewilderingly narrow in the range of its diction but spotted with allusions to Adolf Hitler's dog, whose name, Wolf, is the same in both German and English. After this "disjointed and odd" speech, as Jack calls it, he spends much time trying to hide from the Germans at the conference. His summation of his misery when forced into hearty social intercourse catches exactly the discomfiture of many people in the presence of fluent bilingual speakers: "All I could do was mutter a random monosyllable, rock with empty laughter. I spent a lot of time in my office, hiding."

One somber theme of the novel is prefigured in its title, *White Noise*. Sounds from various sources fill up the background everywhere, with a steady hiss that dominates all frequencies like white noise. Part 1, "Waves and Radiation," abounds in noise and discussions of noise. When Jack goes to the supermarket in Blacksmith, the little town where he lives, he realizes that the cavernous interior is "awash in sound. . . . And over it all, or under it all, a dull and unlocatable roar, as of some form of swarming life just outside the range of human apprehension." The remark fills out the earlier observation by his son Heinrich that sensory perceptions are often deceiving and that there are sounds "out there" that go unheard.

For Murray, who spends hours taking notes on his television watching, television is a matter of waves and radiation, a "primal force in the American home," a source of "coded messages and endless repetitions, like chants, like mantras." Just as television comes alive as a primal force, technology emerges as a "species of beast" in the form of the local hardware store. It is a "vast space" filled with a "great echoing din" and people speaking a spectrum of languages: "English, Hindi, Vietnamese, related tongues."

Yet by far the most impressive sound in *White Noise* is the seven-hour outburst of crying that overwhelms the Gladneys' young son Wilder. His unexplainable grief is terrible and exhausting to them all. The conclusion to his outpouring is cathartic to the whole family:

> It was as though he'd just returned from a period of wandering in some remote and holy place, in sand barrens or snowy ranges—a place where things are said, sights are seen, distances reached which we in our ordinary toil can only regard with the mingled reverence and wonder we hold in reserve for feats of the most sublime and difficult dimensions.

The ubiquitous noise in the background of the Gladneys' lives represents perhaps the insistent whispering in the depths of consciousness that death conquers all. Fear of death is never far from Jack's mind, or from Babette's, either. Jack wakes up one morning at 3:51 "in the grip of a death sweat," and when he reads the obituaries he notes the age of the deceased. He observes, "The power of numbers is never more evident than when we use them to speculate on the time of our dying." In one passage, Babette considers the possibility that death is only sound which goes on and on. Jack's description of this death sound as "uniform, white" is chilling and definitive.

All of Jack's anxieties are intensified in part 2, "The Airborne Toxic Event," when a poisonous cloud of Nyodene Derivative is accidentally released into the air. Everyone is evacuated from Blacksmith for nine days, an episode of tensions in people's lives that DeLillo develops with convincing psychological realism. The event forces everyone's apprehensions about death out into the open, spurring Murray on to a lyric lecture about the nature of modern death and a theory that people are now experiencing incidents of which they have long ago had precognitions that have been repressed. Now that "death is in the air" it is "liberating suppressed material," Murray explains. The toxic event becomes an inescapable *memento mori* that wears down everyone's spirits.

The third part, "Dylarama," is the story of Babette's obsession with a new drug, Dylar, supposedly capable of alleviating death fears. When Jack and Denise, Babette's daughter, both find evidence of her drug use, they snoop around until Jack finds a capsule, which he then has analyzed by a neurochemist. Dylar turns out to be a potent experimental drug manufactured illegally with human volunteers as guinea pigs. Its manufacturer claims that it works on the part of the brain in which the fear of death originates, and Babette is so desperate in her misery that she allows the distributor to sleep with her in payment for two bottles of the capsules.

The toxic-waste cloud has also changed Jack's life while Babette has been experimenting with Dylar, for computer studies of his medical history indicate that he is doomed. Although he shows no symptoms yet, he is convinced that the poisons have done their work on his body and that he can do nothing but wait helplessly for their effects to bloom. Faced with this challenge to his self-control, he is especially loving and understanding with Babette when he finally forces her to tell him the story of her Dylar experiments and adulteries under duress. When he confesses to her his own computer-predicted fate, they console each other in their human misery. Thus, the two incidents—the toxic-gas leak and the Dylar experiment—converge in *White Noise* in the mutual love of the emotionally exhausted Gladneys.

A long philosophical discussion of death with Murray gives Jack a new perspective on his plight. Murray argues that all humans must repress their fear of death if they are to cope with it. He explains to Jack that there are two kinds of people in the world—killers and diers—and that the killers try to accumulate strength from their victims. Murray admits that is he speaking theoretically, but he argues for the existence of "a fund, a pool, a reservoir of potential violence in the male psyche." Their discussion leads, in effect, to Murray's advising Jack to become a killer rather than a dier, and, with this advice to guide him, Jack undertakes to say good-bye to himself by ransacking the house for possessions to throw away.

Jack's resolve to act violently coincides with the visit of his father-in-law, an aging roustabout who leaves him a small pistol, thus providing him with a convenient agent of death. Furthermore, he is briefed on Dylar by his neurochemist friend, learning in the discussion the name—Willie Mink—of his wife's lover and the motel in which he can be found. He has also had a recent and comprehensive physical examination which hints at a "nebulous mass" that he interprets as the result of Nyodene Derivative poisoning. Jack, then, is intellectually and psychologically prepared for an act of violence that will, he hopes, not only assuage his death fears but also offer him a satisfying blood revenge on the man who has cuckolded him.

Jack executes his plan in a surrealistic fashion, beginning with the theft of his neighbor's car and a reckless drive to the motel, where he finds Mink. He does not reveal himself to Mink as Babette's husband but instead represents himself as someone who wants Dylar for himself. In the mad motel-room denouement, Jack manages to shoot Mink twice, but when he puts the gun in Mink's hand to make the affair look like a suicide, Mink straightens up and shoots Jack in the wrist. The bizarre conclusion finds Jack driving them both to the emergency room of a nearby hospital and surreptitiously returning the neighbor's blood-stained car.

White Noise has the characteristically bright surface of DeLillo's novels, with language that is always inventive and often poetic. The wry comic dialogues of Orest Mercator and Murray Jay Siskind are also standard DeLillo features, coming from individuals whose yearnings seem very real and whom DeLillo never savages or patronizes. The Gladneys are all exceptionally likable people who retain the reader's sympathy throughout, and their harrowing tale achieves a deep archetypal attraction that makes *White Noise* an exceptionally satisfying novel.

Frank Day

Sources for Further Study

America. CLIII, July 6, 1985, p. 16.
The Atlantic. CCLV, February, 1985, p. 100.
Commonweal. CXII, April 5, 1985, p. 219.
Library Journal. CX, February 1, 1985, p. 112.
Los Angeles Times Book Review. January 13, 1985, p. 1.
The New York Review of Books. XXXII, March 14, 1985, p. 6.
The New York Times Book Review. XC, January 13, 1985, p. 1.
Newsweek. CV, January 21, 1985, p. 69.
Publishers Weekly. CCXXVI, November 9, 1984, p. 58.
Saturday Review. XI, March, 1985, p. 65.
Time. CXXV, January 21, 1985, p. 71.

WITH ALL DISRESPECT
More Uncivil Liberties

Author: Calvin Trillin (1935-   )
Publisher: Ticknor & Fields (New York). 230 pp. $14.95
Type of work: Essays
Time: 1981-1984

Humorous reflections on myriad topics, from the Publishers Clearing House Sweepstakes to the Reagan Administration

Theorists who believe that humor should be composed of two parts of hostility, mixed vigorously with one part of aggression, and deftly spiced with small, but essential, amounts of humiliation and degradation, will certainly be disappointed with Calvin Trillin's *With All Disrespect: More Uncivil Liberties*. Trillin, if asked whether this disagreeable recipe were, in fact, essential to that hearty brew called humor, would no doubt reply both gently and characteristically: "It's too soon to tell." This is the same reply that he gives to his daughter when she asks for the formula for finding the area of an isosceles triangle. It is, in fact, the answer that he gives to a great many of life's interesting little questions.

Readers who believe that an essayist for *The Nation* must be interested only in the big, leftist issues such as imminent nuclear holocaust, the plight of the street people, or corruption in high places will almost certainly be disdainful when they discover that in the forty-six essays presented in *With All Disrespect*, covering the politically and satirically fertile years from 1981 to 1984, Trillin has taken notice of the Reagan Administration a mere eight times. Part of Trillin's charm is that he is clearly as amused when exposing the silliness of his far-to-the-Left straw horse, Harold the Committed, as he is when gently chiding the political Right. Asked why he writes for a magazine which he himself describes as "Pinko," he answers quite sensibly that it is, after all, the closest magazine to his house. When asked further if he would write for a conservative, supply-side journal if one were to open shop within walking distance to his house, he answers with another of his incisive rejoiners: "I'd just as soon not say."

Readers who require their wit in rapid, shotgun bursts may find Trillin somewhat discursive for their tastes. He is not a natural descendant of Ambrose Bierce or Philip Wylie, both of whom believed with Louis Kronenberger that "humor is criticism." He lacks the brittle cynicism of Dorothy Parker and the paradoxical wit of Oscar Wilde. He follows, rather, the lead of the early American humorist Washington Irving, who is often credited with having popularized the short, semiautobiographical sketch, filled with gentle observations of men and manners. Trillin clearly admires the American monologist, Marshall Dodge, to whom he dedicated, in memoriam, *With All Disrespect*. As a humorist, Trillin probably has more in common with Robert Benchley than with Sidney Joseph Perelman. At his best, he is reminiscent of E. B. White.

He is, at all times, a most congenial comedian. He serves Thalia, the muse of comedy, with a whimsy devoid of malice, with an inspired nonsense unencumbered by apology, and with a clear sense that trivial things benefit most from careful observation. His persona in *With All Disrespect* is a simple man, with simple tastes and simple ideas. He takes things at face value. The smallest detail will send him off on an orgy of rumination, much to the impatience of his wife, Alice, who always has something more practical to do than to fall in with his seemingly aimless musings. He has a notable affinity with underdogs, such as Philip Caldwell, chairman of the Ford Motor Company, whose base pay increased from $400,000 to $440,000 but who got no incentive bonus at all in 1980 or 1981. Trillin's persona is also a man who is catholic in his interests: He gives the reader a complete account of the amortization of his tuxedo; he considers founding an organization dedicated to attacking the stereotypes that are so disturbing to gout sufferers, and he takes notice of Brooke Shields's advertising campaign against teenage smoking. Nothing slips by this simple, thinking man.

Eschewing sarcasm and bitter satire, Trillin's aim is to tickle, not to eviscerate. For example, in "The Mailbag," his handling of the spurious letter to the editor, which becomes such a grotesque and sometimes pornographic weapon in the hands of magazines such as *National Lampoon*, is an almost M. C. Escher-like series of self-referential jests. The essay begins with a letter asking Trillin if he can be trusted, in the light of recent disclosures about Ann Landers' and Abigail Van Buren's recycling of previously used letters. He answers, "As to concocting letters, I can assure you that yours is the first," which generates a series of letters, all intricately tied together and all calling into question their veracity.

Trillin is also a master of litotes, that special brand of understatement that tends to heighten the importance of what is being discussed. For example, in "Getting Serious," Harold the Committed rebukes Trillin for his lack of concern regarding the serious issues of the time. Trillin, however, appears to have thought deeply about the major issues, and his positions on them are impeccable: He is a passionate supporter of liberalizing the immigration laws; he definitely wants more Russian chefs, especially the ones who can make those distinctively light dumplings; he wants more *crabes farcis* cooks from Martinique; and he wants more culinary artists from Hong Kong. As to the fate of the baby seals, his record is again flawless—he does not go to the local fish market and demand filet of baby seal. Finally, regarding the environment, Trillin demands that barbecue restaurants cook on real hickory wood, thereby conserving the world's supply of natural gas. Trillin's interest in food is no passing fancy. His earlier books *Third Helpings* (1983), *American Fried: Adventures of a Happy Eater* (1974), and *Alice, Let's Eat* (1978), sometimes called by him "the tummy trilogy," are all paeans to his hearty appetite, delicate palate, and real commitment to gourmet pursuits.

Good-natured parody is another of Trillin's special gifts, as is clear from "Invitations," the only essay in *With All Disrespect* that is reprinted not from *The Nation* but from *Vanity Fair*. It is a wonderful burlesque of those ubiquitous letters of flattery and invitation that stuff America's supposedly elite mailboxes. Trillin's interest is inescapably aroused when he is not solicited to subscribe to *Vanity Fair*. The essay develops, in a roundabout way, into a consideration of letters of invitation from *Women's Wear Daily*, the *Newsletter of the Tarrytown Group*, and a company that markets beautiful and exclusive heraldic coats of arms. The article climaxes when all the various signatories of these invitations sit down to discuss Trillin's qualifications for membership. Inevitably, he is passed over by *Vanity Fair*, which, not unlike the marines, is only looking for a few good men.

To say that Trillin's humor is more like a soufflé than a dumpling is not to suggest that he cannot handle, with considerable felicity, the technique of hyperbole. One of the most successful pieces in *With All Disrespect* is the essay "Voodoo Economics: An Eyewitness Account," which takes the frequently difficult and perplexing elements of Reaganomics to their logical, or illogical, extreme. In "Voodoo Economics," Edgar and Emily, naïve tourists in an uncertain land, follow a guide, who talks like an African native but looks suspiciously like an oil-company lobbyist. They are promised that they will see many wonders, for example, "machine tools [that] depreciate lightning fast" and "poor folk [who] bounce on safety nets" while "rich folk bounce on poor folk." When the voodoo sorceress finally appears, she is wearing an Adolfo gown. Trillin does not miss a chance to exaggerate the bewilderment of the American citizen in the face of an increasingly complicated economic world, the contradictions in the stated fiscal position of the Reagan Administration, and the possibilities for conflict of interest built into the American way of doing business. What is unusual in Trillin's use of exaggeration is his bemused tone and his total lack of stridency and rancor.

Even when Harold the Committed's favorite topic, imminent nuclear holocaust, is at issue, Trillin manages to deal with it in an inordinately casual way—a way that would certainly make the proponents of comedy-as-hostility gnash their collective teeth; a way that would delight equally the followers of Arthur Koestler and Stephen Leacock, who theorized that the mainspring of humor is not animosity but incongruity. People laugh, they say, when things do not fit—when a human acts in a mechanical way, when ideas are ill-suited to one another, and when situations are seen in an unusual light. It is unlikely that anyone sees the possibility of nuclear holocaust in a more unusual light than does Trillin in his essay "Nuclear War: My Position." Trillin sees the nuclear holocaust as highly improbable, given the shoddiness of Russian television and the poor quality of cars coming out of Detroit. Trillin thinks, in fact, that the world is quite safe and will remain so until either the United States or the Soviet Union can get the Japanese to make reliable missiles for them. This viewpoint is graced with incongruity but not deformed by futile outrage. If there is one consistent characteristic of Trillin's work, it is this light touch.

On August 16, 1776, Horace Walpole, minister of Parliament and gothic novelist, wrote in a trenchant letter to the Countess of Upper Ossory that "the world is a comedy to those that think; a tragedy to those that feel." This time-tested dichotomy can only lead a reader to conclude that Calvin Trillin, so adroitly amusing, so roguish and droll, is a thinker, after all—and indeed a very engaging one.

Cynthia Lee Katona

Sources for Further Study

America. CLIII, August 31, 1985, p. 1.
Booklist. LXXXI, March 1, 1985, p. 892.
Kirkus Reviews. LIII, March 1, 1985, p. 225.
Library Journal. CX, May 1, 1985, p. 61.
Los Angeles Times Book Review. August 4, 1985, p. 4.
National Review. XXXVII, July 26, 1985, p. 53.
The New York Times Book Review. XC, April 14, 1985, p. 10.
The New Yorker. LXI, July 15, 1985, p. 86.
Publishers Weekly. CCXXVII, February 22, 1985, p. 148.
The Washington Monthly. XVII, May, 1985, p. 58.

WITH FRIENDS POSSESSED
A Life of Edward FitzGerald

Author: Robert Bernard Martin (1918-   )
Publisher: Atheneum Publishers (New York). Illustrated. 313 pp. $17.95
Type of work: Literary biography
Time: 1809-1883
Locale: England

A sympathetic biography of the author of The Rubáiyát of Omar Khayyám, *attacking the common view of him as an amiable eccentric and emphasizing his complex personality*

> *Principal personages:*
> EDWARD FITZGERALD, a minor English poet and noted letter writer
> LUCY BARTON, his wife of less than a year
> WILLIAM MAKEPEACE THACKERAY, a major Victorian novelist; a friend and correspondent of FitzGerald
> ALFRED, LORD TENNYSON, a major Victorian poet; a friend and correspondent of FitzGerald
> WILLIAM KENWORTHY BROWNE, a young friend patronized by FitzGerald
> JOSEPH "POSH" FLETCHER, a young sailor friend patronized by FitzGerald

It is the purpose of this biography to demonstrate the complex nature of the poet Edward FitzGerald and to attack or at least to qualify the legendary image of "Old Fitz" as "only a delightful, learned, and eccentric recluse in funny clothes who lived in untroubled ease in rustic surroundings from which he issued a constant flow of cultivated letters to the famous literary men who were his friends." It must be said at the outset that, with the exception of the phrase "untroubled ease," the description remains essentially true. It is that "untroubled ease," however, which the biographer principally settles upon, demonstrating to the reader that in addition to being an amiable eccentric FitzGerald was frequently lonely, often melancholic, occasionally despairing, and generally suffering from a stunted emotional life. FitzGerald certainly lived in what most people would consider ease, and the troubles which beset him were almost entirely of his own making, from within his own nature; the vicissitudes of the outside world little disturbed the even tenor of his way.

The biography is based principally upon the recent four-volume edition of FitzGerald's letters, *The Letters of Edward FitzGerald* (1980). Robert Bernard Martin, a former professor of English at Princeton University and the author of numerous award-winning studies of Victorian figures, states explicitly his own love for FitzGerald (it would be entirely appropriate to call this book a "labor of love") and posits that, though FitzGerald is already loved, the reader's love of him should be based on a true knowledge of him and not on a sentimental image. Thus the book quotes extensively from the letters, and Martin makes shrewd guesses about FitzGerald's thoughts and feelings from what is not said as well as from what is expressly said.

FitzGerald is one of those poets unfortunately (or perhaps fortunately) known for a single poem. The most obvious parallel is with Thomas Gray, and Martin explicitly draws that parallel several times in the book. FitzGerald did write and publish other things, but they are of scant value or interest. Martin mentions them and briefly discusses them, but even his love for FitzGerald cannot lead him to claim for them more than they deserve. The reputation of FitzGerald and his one poem has been over the years greatly enhanced by the romantic story of the poem's reception: Published in 1859, *The Rubáiyát of Omar Khayyám* sold almost no copies until later "discovered" by the young Pre-Raphaelites, whence a word-of-mouth campaign caused it to become a best-seller, creating a demand for more and more editions. In the chapter "The Discovery of the *Rubáiyát*," Martin issues many qualifications of this story and removes a fair amount of the romance surrounding it.

Martin does not deal at great length with *The Rubáiyát of Omar Khayyám* specifically or with any other of FitzGerald's works. He makes some insightful comments about the themes and about the origins of the work, but he does not become involved in the traditional scholarly squabbles over exactly how much FitzGerald "translated," how much he "adapted," or how much he "invented." Nor, concerned mainly to relate the content and mood of the work to FitzGerald's own personality and beliefs, does Martin deal with the vexing question of which of the four editions published in FitzGerald's lifetime is the best, or "truest."

The man himself, then, is the focus of this work. All in all, FitzGerald led a quiet life, certainly by choice. Money was never a problem, he was intelligent if indolent, and he and his family had friends of substance and standing who could easily have helped him in a chosen career had he so wished. Yet there is a tentativeness of nature in FitzGerald, which emerges clearly in the biography, that led him away from commitment and from direct engagement. He seems to have cared deeply about few things (and those mostly close and personal); he had no urge to change the world or even to make his voice heard in wider public spheres. His religious views he pretty much kept to himself and a few close friends, though FitzGerald eventually acquired something of a reputation as a genteel and hedonistic skeptic, evincing what Martin felicitously describes as a "lightly disbelieving tolerance of Christianity."

Simply from the incidents presented by Martin of FitzGerald's life, the contemporary reader would almost immediately conclude that FitzGerald was a prime candidate for psychoanalysis. Martin, however, deliberately eschews all but the most obvious conclusions about the state of FitzGerald's psyche—a refreshing approach which allows the reader to form his own conclusions about some of the deep-seated motives for FitzGerald's way of life. Martin does frequently return to the influence of FitzGerald's family, especially his mother, upon him. Until 1818, the family name was Purcell, his father having married a FitzGerald. In that year, when Edward was nine, Mrs. Purcell's father died, leaving great sums of money to his daughter; though apparently not required to do so, Edward's father took the Fitz-Gerald name, perhaps partly because he himself had come from a branch of the same FitzGerald family. Edward loved his father, who was, however, an ineffectual man, not on the best of terms with his wife and thus frequently living apart from her. Apparently trouble existed in the family because the wife was much more wealthy than the husband, though until he went bankrupt in 1848 he was by no means dependent on his wife's largess.

FitzGerald's mother, who was reputed to be the richest commoner in England, was a large, domineering woman, who apparently liked to have the young Edward by her side to adorn her attempts at fashionable entertainment in London and Paris. From Martin's description, she would have been a walking example of all the unpleasant things implied by the term nouveau riche. It is almost certainly in opposition to his mother's ostentatious display and social striving that FitzGerald acquired his almost pathological disgust at any form of opulence. His mother could be overpowering in other ways; until her death in 1855, whenever she called for him to attend her, he came. Without excessive psychologizing, one could reasonably attribute FitzGerald's later difficulties with women, except perhaps with his elder married sister Eleanor, to the inexpungible presence of his mother.

With the exception of Eleanor, with whom he spent many holidays, the remainder of the eight FitzGerald children were not close to Edward. The eldest son, John, was decidedly strange, and another son, Peter, was apparently something of a natural. FitzGerald had a lifelong fear of madness and at times thought that he was insane or could easily become so. His own parents had been first cousins, and there were similar matings in his family tree. FitzGerald was well aware that there had been too much intermarriage and mingling of Geraldian blood. It is little to be wondered that in later years FitzGerald had as little as possible to do with most members of his family. Thus, when called to London to dance attendance upon his mother after his graduation from Cambridge, he came—but he refused to live in her London mansion, setting himself in a cheap rented room several blocks away.

Yet the theme of the life and the title of the book center on friendship. In FitzGerald's early years at Bury St. Edmunds' King Edward VI Grammar School (1818-1826), he began to make those friendships that would be the feature of the remainder of his life. At the grammar school, he came to know William Donne, James Spedding, and John Kemble, all of whom were to become further acquainted at Cambridge and all of whom became gentlemen amateurs on the fringes of Victorian literary circles. John Kemble also provided FitzGerald with one of his more famous correspondents in later years, his sister Fanny Kemble, the actress. At school, not only did FitzGerald begin some of his lifelong friendships, but he also demonstrated an aspect of those friendships that was to continue—their intensity, which was often embarrassing to the recipients.

As a student at Cambridge (1826-1830), FitzGerald made even more important friends: John Allen, Richard Monckton Milnes, later Lord Houghton, and William Makepeace Thackeray. He had seen Alfred, Lord Tennyson during those years, but they did not formally meet until a year after FitzGerald was graduated. Tennyson was to benefit from FitzGerald's generosity for a number of years following, though he could be a prickly friend, no doubt occasionally resenting having to accept money from the much less talented FitzGerald. These friends, especially Thackeray, were to be the recipients of FitzGerald's long, entertaining, and vivid letters for years to come. It must be admitted that as the years passed for these correspondents, and for others, the friendships tended to become less intense on the part of FitzGerald's friends. They never entirely gave him up, but they do not seem to have attached the importance that FitzGerald did to trying to keep up the spirit of all-boys-together established at Cambridge. There remained to the end something of the youth in FitzGerald, while many of his friends matured and grew into other interests.

FitzGerald's talent for friendship, however, had its more embarrassing side. It was noted even when he was in grammar school that he had an eye for physically attractive young lads. In the course of his years after Cambridge, he became attached to (and openly cherished and supported) at least three young men. The first was William Kenworthy Browne, in whom FitzGerald professed to find a pattern of gentlemanly poise and conduct, though others were unable to see anything noteworthy about the young man. The others were Edward Cowell, who introduced him to Persian and ultimately to *The Rubáiyát of Omar Khayyám*, and Joseph "Posh" Fletcher, whom he found after several years of trolling for companionship among the sailors of Felixstowe. All these young men were handsome, if only conventionally so, and in all of them FitzGerald professed to find qualities hidden from others. FitzGerald's conduct and some of the more effusive letters strongly suggest a definite homosexual bent, but Martin's ultimate judgment, which is almost certainly correct, is that there is no proof of physical relations with either man or woman (including his wife.) Nevertheless, FitzGerald's intense affection could make some of his closest friends uneasy—and many letters that might have been illuminating were destroyed by various correspondents. Though FitzGerald gives all the appearances of *le vice Anglais*, it is probable that, as in many of his other relationships, at the last moments he would step back, fearful of involvement.

Perhaps the most devastating moment in FitzGerald's life came with his marriage to Lucy Barton, daughter of Bernard Barton, the Quaker poet. At the time of his marriage, FitzGerald was forty-seven and the bride about forty-eight, and even FitzGerald's friends were appalled. The marriage was an absolute disaster, and FitzGerald's letters and conduct at this time can be seen only as nasty. FitzGerald and Barton separated permanently, after some months of living apart, in August of 1857. FitzGerald seems to have entered into the whole thing as a sort of aberration. The author suggests that because of certain possible promises made to Bernard Barton on his deathbed, FitzGerald was maneuvered into having Lucy accept a proposal he never made. The whole incident would be laughable if it had not clearly been so painful for all concerned. Martin makes clear that at least one of the forces at work here was FitzGerald's antipathy to women in general. He regarded them as lowly creatures and, for example, had almost nothing good to say of any woman writer.

This biography, then, is sympathetic without indulging in whitewashing. FitzGerald's warts are all on view, and the author has succeeded in his intention of demonstrating the complexity and personal terrors of a man usually viewed as a bit of a genial old buffer. It is problematic whether one ends up loving FitzGerald more, as Martin would have one do, but it cannot be denied that one sees him, and to some extent his famous poem, more clearly and truly.

Gordon N. Bergquist

Sources for Further Study

Booklist. LXXXI, August, 1985, p. 1623.
Contemporary Review. CCXLVI, May, 1985, p. 276.
Economist. CCXCV, June 15, 1985, p. 108.
Kirkus Reviews. LIII, January 1, 1985, p. 34.
Library Journal. CX, May 1, 1985, p. 56.
The London Review of Books. VII, April 4, 1985, p. 6.
The New York Review of Books. XXXII, April 25, 1985, p. 3.
The New York Times Book Review. XC, April 21, 1985, p. 11.
Publishers Weekly. CCXXVII, January 25, 1985, p. 83.
Spectator. CCLIV, March 23, 1985, p. 32.
Times Literary Supplement. March 15, 1985, p. 275.
Washington Post Book World. XV, May 12, 1985, p. 6.

WITNESSES AT THE CREATION
Hamilton, Madison, Jay, and the Constitution

Author: Richard B. Morris (1904-   )
Publisher: Holt, Rinehart and Winston (New York). Illustrated. 279 pp. $16.95
Type of work: Biography and historical narrative
Time: The 1780's
Locale: The United States

Short biographical sketches of Alexander Hamilton, James Madison, and John Jay, along with a narrative description of the writing of the Constitution of the United States

> *Principal personages:*
> ALEXANDER HAMILTON, an American statesman
> JAMES MADISON, fourth President of the United States, 1809-1817
> JOHN JAY, the first chief justice of the United States Supreme Court

Every Fourth of July, across the nation, Americans celebrate the signing of the Declaration of Independence. Every September seventeenth, not one American in a hundred is even conscious of the fact that on this day, in 1787, thirty-five of the nation's brightest political thinkers put their signatures on the document which would soon become the supreme law of the land. Why the difference? Though the opening paragraphs of Thomas Jefferson's most famous work lay down in immortal words a political philosophy to which most Americans still subscribe, the majority of his declaration is an indictment of an English king for crimes that only a historian remembers. The Constitution of the United States, on the other hand, except in those places where it has been amended, continues directly to affect the lives of all Americans.

Writing on the assumption that that which touches all the people ought to be understood by all the people, Richard B. Morris has produced a history of the Constitution and its framers that can be read and enjoyed by the general public. While the product of outstanding scholarship and erudition, *Witnesses at the Creation* does not attempt to adjudicate scholarly disputes concerning interpretations of the Constitution or the motives of its authors. Morris is neither a venerator nor a denigrator of the Constitution or of his three witnesses to its creation, Alexander Hamilton, James Madison, and John Jay. Instead, his goal is didactic. As cochairman of "Project '87," an organization jointly sponsored by the American Historical Association and the American Political Science Association, Morris' announced purpose is "to stimulate nationwide interest in the origins of the Constitution," a document whose bicentennial will be celebrated in 1986 and 1987.

John Adams once described Hamilton as "the bastard brat of a Scotch pedlar." Understood as a simple description, the first and third parts of Adam's quip are accurate. (That Hamilton was a brat is open to question.)

Yet, it is easy to understand why Hamilton might take offense at such a remark. What is surprising, at least to contemporary Americans, is the extent to which the purely factual nature of his entrance into the world drove Hamilton to excel from a very early age. Modern society and Hamilton's differ, however, on questions of "honor." In the eighteenth century, "honor" was as much the product of one's birth as was the color of one's hair.

Born without honor, Hamilton spent all of his life in a quest for fame. "The love of fame," he wrote, is "the ruling passion of the noblest minds." The only question was, How does a schoolboy on the island of St. Croix achieve fame? By the time he was twelve or fourteen (depending on which record one prefers in dating his birth), Hamilton had formulated a clear answer: Writing to a friend at King's College (now Columbia University), he said, "Ned, my ambition is prevalent that I contemn the groveling and condition of a Clerk or the like, to which my Fortune, etc. condemns me . . . but I mean to prepare the way for futurity. . . . I shall conclude saying, I wish there was a war."

While a student at King's College, Hamilton began writing revolutionary tracts to bring about the war that he so desired. To ensure that he would be part of the war with England, he recruited his own company of soldiers. He even used his personal credit to clothe and equip them. His persistence paid off. Standing high on the west bank of the Raritan River, Hamilton masterfully covered George Washington's retreat from Charles Cornwallis' pursuit. His "cocked hat pulled down over his eyes, apparently lost in thought, with his hand resting on a cannon, and every now and then patting it, as if it were a favorite horse or a pet plaything," not to mention his brilliant aim, caught Washington's eye. Soon thereafter he was appointed Washington's aide-de-camp. Hamilton's star was on the rise.

Yet even Washington's favor and the sheer ability that he exhibited in his post were insufficient to expunge Hamilton's ignoble beginnings. Once again, Hamilton was clear about how he would achieve his goal. He needed a wife. Furthermore, she must be young, beautiful, shapely, "sensible (a little learning will do), well bred, chaste, and tender." Such paragons are hard to find, and whether his wife-to-be, Elizabeth Schuyler, met all these specifications is unclear. She did, however, meet the crucial one—being wellbred. By marrying the daughter of General Philip Schuyler, "a commanding figure among the Albany Dutch gentry," Hamilton achieved "honor by association."

Achieving honor and maintaining honor are, however, two different things. While serving as secretary of the Treasury, Hamilton was accused of secretly purchasing Revolutionary War bonds at huge discounts in hopes that the new government of the United States would one day honor the bonds at their face value. Such groveling for money was unacceptable for a man of honor. Hamilton was forced publicly to set the record straight: "My real crime is an amorous connection with his [James Reynolds's] wife." His defense, in other words, was that he was being blackmailed for sleeping with another speculator's wife.

Hamilton's last defense of his honor was a fatal duel with Aaron Burr. While it would have done great harm to his honor if he had refused Burr's challenge, the cold-blooded killing of another man was equally distasteful to Hamilton. One final time, Hamilton's analytic mind found the solution. There was nothing in the duello that made one's honor contingent upon winning the duel. Merely fighting the duel was sufficient to maintain one's honor. A duel in which both parties fired and missed was the optimal outcome from Hamilton's perspective. Thus, the night before he met Burr, Hamilton wrote to his wife: "The scruples of a Christian have determined me to expose my life to any extent rather than subject myself to the guilt of taking the life of another. This must increase my hazards, and undoubtedly my pangs for you." The next day Hamilton would fire into the air; Burr would not. Hamilton died several days later with his honor and Christian scruples intact.

Hamilton spent all of his life working for what money could not buy. Madison spent none of his life working for what money could buy—he did not have to. Born to James Madison, Sr., on the family estate of Montpelier, the young Madison never worked for a living and never pursued a paying profession. Even when he tried to manage the family plantation, he did not make much money. His talents lay elsewhere.

Physically small and frail, shy or aloof depending on one's perception, born with a feeble voice in an age in which great orators would spellbind audiences without electronic wizardry, Madison found solace in books. His range of reading was encyclopedic, though he was particularly interested in international law and political theory. He was a principal architect of the Constitution, and all Americans have benefited from his scholarship.

Fortunately, he lived in a period when political influence was not dependent upon winning the favor of the masses. "How a man with so frail a constitution, so introspective, sedate, and prim," writes Morris, "could have withstood the rigors of campaigns on the hustings which were to be widely initiated within a few years of his death, or the one-on-one wooing of voters considered a necessity today, would be truly incomprehensible." Even in his own day, Madison had trouble winning elections. Having won election to the Virginia Convention in 1776, he promptly lost his seat the following year when he refused to provide free whiskey or to buy votes, which, as Morris notes, were "both common practices of that day."

John Jay was neither the energetic and able man in search of honor nor the frail young scholar. Rather, he was a principled aristocrat. Jay was born into a socially prominent, politically influential, and economically well-established New York family, and there was never any question about his class standing.

Nevertheless, Jay had to learn the principles of aristocracy. While he was a student at King's College, some of his classmates got rowdy and broke a dinner table one night. After Jay denied his involvement in the incident to the president of the college, the interrogation continued:

> "Do you know who did break the table?"
> Jay's answer: "Yes, sir."
> "Who is it?"
> "I do not choose to tell you, sir."

Summoned before the faculty and threatened with dismissal, Jay came prepared with a set of the college statutes. He argued that there was nothing in them that obliged one student to inform on another. "Feeling no sympathy with lawyerlike undergraduates," writes Morris, "the faculty promptly suspended him."

To stand on principles when one's own well-being is at stake is difficult; to stand on principle when the well-being of a longtime friend is at stake is even more difficult. Yet Jay learned to do precisely that. While head of a committee investigating those who would not swear loyalty to the patriot cause, Jay was forced to pass judgment on Peter Van Schaack. In what Morris calls "Jay's bitterest decision," Van Schaack was banished from his home and forced to set himself up as an exile in London. Writing to him there, Jay explained his decision: "Your judgment, and consequently, your Conscience differed from mine on a very important Question. But though as an independent American, I considered all who were not for us, and You among the Rest, as against us, yet be assured that John Jay did not cease to be a friend to Peter Van Schaack." After the war, Jay arranged for Van Schaack's return to America and was the first to greet him when he returned to New York.

Jay's principles and his willingness to follow the evidence wherever it led would even provoke him to stand publicly against his country when it was in the wrong. In the Treaty of Paris, Great Britain was undeniably generous to her rebellious, but now independent, subjects. Yet she did expect something in return. For example, Great Britain expected the courts in the United States to erect no obstacles to the collection of bona-fide prewar debts. When the Americans protested that English forts on the Western frontier had not been dismantled per treaty stipulations, the British responded that Americans, acting under the protection of state courts, had not been forthcoming in paying their English creditors. As secretary for foreign affairs, Jay investigated the charges and concluded that the British were correct: Testifying before Congress, he announced that the legislatures of the individual states had in fact been violating the treaty and had been doing so before the British violations had begun. Principles would not allow even the patriotic fudging of the evidence.

In the second half of his book, Morris calls these three honorable men to testify to the creation of a single nation out of a group of thirteen petty states that shared only "unity in misery." In this regard, Morris has clearly distanced himself from earlier historians of this century. In *An Economic Interpretation of the Constitution* (1913), Charles Beard characterized the framers of the Constitution as counterrevolutionaries anxious to conserve their own wealth against the leveling tendencies of the Revolution. Historians sympathetic to Beard have thus sought to downplay the inadequacies of the Articles of Confederation. The reason is clear: If the period between the Revolution and the writing of the Constitution were not all that bad for Americans, then the *de facto* proclamation of the framers that the previous constitution was null and void begins to look suspect. Morris' position is equally clear: If there were nothing but a unity in misery prior to the Constitutional Convention, then, whatever the legality of the framers' action, their moral and political wisdom is evident.

Morris' catalog of ills is certainly impressive. Shackled by its inability to collect taxes, Congress had no funds to pay an army on the brink of mutiny. Its navy was decimated and powerless to enforce even the minimal rights of its citizens abroad. Its credit was exhausted by a flood of red ink. Its superintendent of finance, Robert Morris, after trying to convince the individual states of the urgency of the matter, likened talking to the states with preaching to the dead. Its citizens were engaged in conspiratorial plots everywhere. A privately funded militia was necessary to put down one such rebellion in Massachusetts. John Hancock, however, running on a platform of amnesty for the rebels, overwhelmingly defeated the incumbent governor who had been principally responsible for restoring order. Individual states, such as Rhode Island, were printing so much money and making it legal tender for all debts that creditors were fleeing across state lines to avoid being paid with the worthless script. There was even talk of bringing over European royalty and making the United States a limited monarchy. Perhaps there was something to Washington's quip immediately prior to the convention: "No morn ever dawned more favourably than ours did, and no day was ever more clouded than the present."

The convention itself was characterized by "a cautious optimism that prevailed over a widely shared and deep-seated pessimism about human nature." The pessimism centered on the ability of the people to govern themselves. Only a lifetime president and senators, Hamilton argued, would "have firmness enough to answer the purpose. When a great object of government is pursued which seizes the popular passions, they spread like wildfire and become irresistible." Though Hamilton stood on the extreme right of the political spectrum, even the political middle at the convention was far to the right of its current location. John Dickinson argued that the Senate should be patterned after the British House of Lords. Thus, the states, not the people, would select senators; this would make it more likely that the Senate would attract "the most distinguished for their rank in life and their weight of property." Dickinson's proposal was adopted, and it was not until the passage of the Seventeenth Amendment in 1912 that senators were elected directly by the people. Concerning the presidency, George Mason argued that having the people choose the chief executive was as unnatural as asking a blind man to pick out colors. Thus, the elaborate electoral college system was proposed and adopted.

The reason that any national political officers were to be elected by the people was more a matter of expediency than of democratic principle. James Wilson argued that the lessons of the confederacy were clear: One must have a strong national government. Yet, to raise "the federal pyramid to a considerable altitude," he said, makes it "necessary to give it as broad a base as possible." Provision was therefore made for the direct election of the members of the lower house. There was even enough "cautious optimism" at the convention to entrust the House of Representatives with considerable powers, including control over the nation's purse strings.

The product of that convention held in 1787 has served America well. Yet, it had its flaws. In what Morris refers to as "one of the most stirring speeches of the Convention," George Mason, a Virginian who had firsthand knowledge of his subject, warned his audience:

Every master of slaves is born a petty tyrant. They bring the judgment of heaven on a country. As nations cannot be rewarded or punished in the next world they must be in this. By an inevitable chain of causes and effects providence punished national sins by national calamities.

Why did Mason's warning go unheeded? The crucial eight-to-four vote at the convention was not a straight sectional issue—the North was divided, and Virginia voted with the minority—nor was it a purely economic issue: Cotton had not yet become the king that ruled over all. Morris chooses to describe it as a matter of deferring to "Southern sensibilities." If this is all it took to blind men to sin's inevitable consequences, perhaps Americans should take more seriously their Founding Fathers' "deep-seated pessimism about human nature."

Ric S Machuga

Sources for Further Study

Best Sellers. XLV, November, 1985, p. 313.
Choice. XXIII, February, 1986, p. 920.

Kirkus Reviews. LIII, July 15, 1985, p. 704.
Library Journal. CX, September 1, 1985, p. 197.
Los Angeles Times Book Review. September 1, 1985, p. 1.
The New York Times Book Review. XC, November 17, 1985, p. 31.
Publishers Weekly. CCXXVIII, July 12, 1985, p. 43.

WORDS THAT MUST SOMEHOW BE SAID
Selected Essays of Kay Boyle, 1927-1984

Author: Kay Boyle (1903-   )
Edited, with an introduction, by Elizabeth S. Bell
Publisher: North Point Press (San Francisco, California). 288 pp. $16.50
Type of work: Essays

Essays selected to reiterate the author's moral concerns

Words That Must Somehow Be Said consists of selections from Kay Boyle's writing from as far back as 1927. Representative of the author's unique experiences in Europe and the United States, the essays in this collection vary in tone from satiric and self-mocking to intensely serious. The author's arrangement of the essays, reviews, and one short story in the collection suggests that she intends a message for all who will hear, but especially for writers.

The first of the four sections, an autobiographical piece entitled "The Family" and the only section previously unpublished, shows how the author's values were formed. Recalling her unusual childhood, Boyle credits her mother for early years free of boredom, unusually free of dogma, and even relatively free of formal education. Boyle's remarkable mother, although not formally educated herself, made her daughter aware of important musicians, authors, and artists, and even took the child to such significant cultural events as the Armory Art Show in 1913. Other family members, such as Boyle's Grandmother Evans, who told her of crossing the plains in a covered wagon, also influenced her; yet by reading to her children, by showing kindnesses to down-and-out individuals, and by championing women's suffrage, it was Boyle's mother who achieved the most significant influence upon her daughter. As a child, Kay Boyle had difficulty learning to read because of her hit-and-miss education, but she grew up to become a political activist, a teacher, and a noted author.

In assessing her roots in the relatively brief opening section, Boyle explains her distrust of the autobiographical "I." She finds neither the child nor the adult voice entirely authentic; therefore she chooses to say those words which she believes must be said through selections from her own earlier writing. The title phrase comes from "A Man in the Wilderness," a 1967 review of two collections by Edward Dahlberg. In it, she applauds Dahlberg's "philosophy of rebellion, but of dignity and discipline as well." The rebels of the 1960's, Boyle goes on to say, were not sure that their leaders were saying "fearlessly and honestly enough the words that must somehow be said." Still fearful of loss of freedom, Boyle chose the essays in this volume to make a statement in freedom's defense.

Boyle prefaces the second section, "On Writers and Writing," with the phrase "Interpreters of This Deep Concern," a line from "A Declaration for 1955." This section demands that artists and writers be authentic. In her review of *In the American Grain* (1925), she finds William Carlos Williams to be authentic, but in another early review, "Mr. Crane and His Grandmother," she finds Hart Crane's poetry false and patronizing, even of his grandmother. Boyle finds Katherine Mansfield's writing inadequate and narrow and judges Elizabeth Bowen's fiction disconnected from reality for the most part. Despite some faults with his characterizations, in a 1938 review she finds William Faulkner, like Edgar Allan Poe, obsessed with "the unutterable depths of mankind's vice and even more with his divinity."

Not only must writers express truth in their art, according to Boyle, but also they must have a social conscience. Acknowledging the heresy of her position, she asks that writers take responsibility for the "transforming of the contemporary scene": "The artist's deeper concern has always been not with what is taking place, but with the dimension of what might, within the imagination and the infinite capacity of man, take place." She shows that an artist has the capability of using words to draw out the best in humans when a Spaniard deflects a near confrontation with a waiter in her "Farewell to New York." When she was a professor at San Francisco State University in the 1960's, she had an opportunity to put into practice her belief that the writer's obligation is to speak out. In "Excerpt from 'The Long Walk at San Francisco State,'" Boyle judges her own poetry less "relevant to life and death" than that of the students of black poet Sonia Sanchez. Boyle ends this second section with "The Teaching of Writing," an essay addressed to teachers. The quotation that she selects from James Baldwin expresses the essence of her charge to writers: "The interior life is a real life, and the intangible dreams of people have a tangible effect upon the world."

The third section, "On the Body Politic," opens with Boyle's "Farewell to Europe," originally published in *The Nation* in 1953. As she leaves Europe after several decades of life there, her clearest memory of life in the United States is the individual freedom enjoyed by its citizens. She recalls with pride her thrice-great-grandfather, who fought in the American Revolution and who in her eyes was an early model of the tradition of freedom. She recalls others in her family's history who were pioneers, such as her great-grandfather, who settled on the Kansas plains at a time when Indian camp fires were still visible. His granddaughter, Nina E. Allender, pioneered in another sense as a cartoonist and suffragette. These ideals and traditions were very much a part of Boyle's consciousness during her European years, but the American political climate in 1953 was menaced by McCarthyism. Ironically, European friends warned her that the censorship taking place in the United States was comparable to that in Nazi Germany and that civil liberties were endangered in her native land. As if nudged by her forebears, Boyle resolved to return and to speak out, a sentiment in keeping with the phrase that prefaces this section—"Shout Aloud Our Disputed Tongue."

The next selection, "No Time to Listen," suggests that Boyle did not become an activist immediately, for in this piece of self-mockery, the author chides herself for not listening to what Mr. Dodson, a black man, had to say while she was writing a novel. A school principal, Dodson tried to tell the author about segregated schools near where she lived, but she wrote about a problem with the educational system in another country. Other selections, however, show that Dodson's words were not long lost on the author, for she did become a leader of the social activism of the 1960's. "A Day on Alcatraz with the Indians" recounts the Christmas that she spent there during the Indian occupation of the old prison facility and describes the place as a "symbol of the Indian's imprisonment on his own soil." In "The Crime of Attica," a review of Tom Wicker's *A Time to Die* (1975), Boyle emphasizes his conclusion that prisons have failed as places of rehabilitation but succeeded as schools for crime. In "Report from Lock-up," Boyle re-creates her own experience in the jail where she was sentenced to serve thirty-one days for demonstrating at the Induction Center at Oakland, California. Her account of the dehumanizing experience ends tellingly with a deputy's statement that she does not need a name, only a number.

"A Quite Humble Pageant" is the phrase that prefaces the final section, "On the Human Condition." This section opens with the mock-heroic "Battle of the Sequins," in which women fight over sequined blouses in a department store. This satiric piece and those that follow must indeed be a commentary on their author's view of the precarious human condition. "The Jew Is a Myth" is a 1945 review of a book on the German occupation of France; the book demonstrates how Jews became scapegoats for Germany's problems. A short story, "Frankfurt in Our Blood," presents two women on a train traveling to Frankfurt; the older woman, the widow of a professor, speaks of the cultivated, liberal city that Frankfurt had been before the rise of the Nazis and how "the free men of Frankfurt had seen freedom die." Boyle's review of Nancy Cardozo's book on the life of Maud Gonne, *Lucky Eyes and High Heart* (1978), contains a crucial observation by the subject: "Men are destroying themselves, and we are looking on."

Boyle's tone is devastatingly sarcastic in the next two selections. "Sisters of the Princess" deals with *The New York Times* article about the 1975 International Women's Year World Conference held in Mexico City, by Princess Ashraf Pahlavi, the sister of the Shah of Iran. Boyle charges that the princess should have concerned herself with "the specifics in her own country rather than in high-sounding generalities." Boyle then points out specific examples of atrocities against women in Iran. "Seeing the Sights in San Francisco" takes the tone of a travel guide, but the sights Boyle describes include the Golden Gate Cemetery, where American soldiers who fought in the Vietnam War are buried, a background visit to the mortuary where the bodies were delivered by truck several times daily, and a naval station from which weapons were sent to Vietnam.

In "The Triumph of Principles," Boyle reiterates her message that writers bear a moral responsibility and takes hope from those authors who have participated in demonstrations. She recalls Thomas Mann's assertion that with the right words, writers might have deflected Adolf Hitler's seizure of power, and she agrees with Chester Bowles that in contemporary America the "Bill of Rights might not be voted because too few of us understand the need to protect the freedoms of those with whom we disagree." This quotation is preparation for the last and most lengthy selection in the book, in that the reader is implicitly warned that events such as those described in "Preface from *The Smoking Mountain*" could be repeated if Americans are not vigilant about human rights.

People were the fuel for the smoking mountain; the mountain is a metaphor for the German military-industrial complex. The preface from Boyle's collection of short stories about post-World War II Germany tells of the trial of Heinrich Baab, a mid-level member of the Frankfurt Gestapo. The temper prevailing in Germany before the war had allowed this narrow-minded man with a violent disposition but unquestioning respect for authority to become the agent of destruction for many lives. Boyle makes clear that a puzzling duality of the German people allowed atrocities to happen because those who were people of goodwill did not speak out against evil. Persecution evolved from derogatory signs to burned synagogues to people being tortured and loaded onto cattle cars headed to death camps. Euphemistic explanations such as "protective custody" persuaded citizens to accept genocide.

Like a woman in the wilderness, Boyle follows her own admonition to writers in this volume. Read selectively, some of the essays could seem dated, but read consecutively, Boyle's words are still relevant in the mid-1980's.

Roberta Sharp

Sources for Further Study

Booklist. LXXXI, May 15, 1985, p. 1289.
Christian Science Monitor. LXXVII, June 19, 1985, p. 21.
Kirkus Reviews. LIII, May 15, 1985, p. 453.
Library Journal. CX, June 15, 1985, p. 62.
Los Angeles Times Book Review. September 29, 1985, p. 10.
Ms. XIV, August, 1985, p. 74.
The New York Times Book Review. XC, August 25, 1985, p. 20.
Publishers Weekly. CCXXVII, May 3, 1985, p. 59.
Saturday Review. XI, November, 1985, p. 72.
Washington Post Book World. XV, July 14, 1985, p. 10.

WORLD'S FAIR

Author: E. L. Doctorow (1931-   )
Publisher: Random House (New York). 288 pp. $17.95
Type of work: Novel
Time: The Depression era
Locale: Bronx, New York

A fictional memoir of a young boy growing up during the Depression

> *Principal characters:*
> EDGAR ALTSCHULER, a young boy
> DAVID and
> ROSE ALTSCHULER, his parents
> DONALD, his older brother
> MEG, Edgar's childhood sweetheart

"Essentially," E. L. Doctorow told one interviewer, "I believe you have to reinvent fiction with each and every book; you've got to take the conventions and break them down, reconstitute them." The strongest impulse in twentieth century literature, Doctorow told another, has been "to assault fiction, assault the forms, destroy it so it can rise again. You let go of the tropes one by one. You get rid of the lights, you get rid of the music, you forego the drum roll, and finally you do the high-wire act without the wire."

In practice, what the attitudes expressed in these statements mean is that Doctorow's work has combined an aversion to repeating himself with a persistent intention. The aversion has made versatility and daring distinguishing marks of his fiction; the intention has made his individual books take on the status of pieces of a single oeuvre.

Each Doctorow book seems a new departure. With each, he creates a different narrative voice, focuses on a different time and place, experiments with a different style, and explores a different aspect of American experience. In *Welcome to Hard Times* (1960), the time is the nineteenth century, the setting is the Old West, and the narrator is a cowardly mayor plagued by existential angst. In *The Book of Daniel* (1971), the time is the Cold War 1950's and the explosive 1960's, the focus is the Old Left's legacy to the New, the narrator is an angry, self-mocking graduate student whose life story incorporates the radicalism of both eras. In *Ragtime* (1975), the time is the turn of the century, the style mixes real and imagined figures, and the narrative voice is a verbal equivalent of ragtime music. In *Loon Lake* (1980), the time is the Depression, the form is a 1970's blend of Horatio Alger and proletarian novel, and the narrators include the main character, a failed poet, and a computer. In *Lives of the Poets* (1984), the time is the 1980's, the form is a series of related stories, and the narrative voice is pastiche of the sounds of contemporary American fiction. In *World's Fair*, the time is, again, the Depression, the setting is the Bronx, the form blends fiction and memoir into a *Bildungsroman*, and the narration is divided between a young boy, his older self, his mother, and his brother.

Beneath its variety and versatility, however, each of Doctorow's books represents another contribution to a continuing project. That project has focused on testing the limits of genre, blurring (and so, challenging) the accepted boundaries between the real and the imagined, the historical and the fictional. (Thus, to accuse Doctorow, as some reviewers have, of failing to be "fully novelistic" in *Ragtime* and *World's Fair* is to miss his artistic point completely.) In *Ragtime*, the metaphor for this artistic challenge to conventional notions of reality and fiction is Harry Houdini, forced to think of increasingly more dangerous escapes so that his illusions can compete with "the real-world act." In *World's Fair*, Doctorow's project is embodied in a circus clown who climbs the high wire after "the experts" are done.

> Slipping and sliding about . . . holding on to the wire for dear life, he was actually doing stunts far more difficult than any that had gone on before. This was confirmed, invariably, as he doffed his clown garments one by one and emerged . . . the star who headlined the high-wire act. . . . I took profound instruction from this hoary circus routine. . . . There was art in the thing, the power of illusion, the mightier power of the reality behind it. What was first true was then false, a man was born from himself.

Doctorow's versatility and his effort to bring about the rebirth of fiction by the high-wire act of redefining it have combined with his special strengths as a novelist to gain for him both critical and popular praise. He has a special knack for seizing on the telling detail in an archetypal experience; for mentioning exactly the right brand name and cultural artifact to capture an era; for juxtaposing images from different times in a way that surprises and compels attention; for creating and re-creating American myths through his use of the familiar images of our shared past; for describing the events of personal lives from a perspective that calls attention to social forces, and so for turning explorations of individual psyches into journeys through the storehouse of his readers' common memories.

All of Doctorow's concerns and virtues are abundantly displayed in *World's Fair*, a novel in the guise of a memoir. By labeling his book a novel and then presenting it as a memoir in which his and his family's names are assigned to his characters, he focuses his reader's attention on the ways that both personal and collective histories are, at best, selective reconstructions built of fragmentary memories.

The book ends with its nine-year-old hero burying a personal time capsule, in imitation of the one he has seen on display at the 1939 World's Fair in Flushing Meadow. The capsule at the fair "had been devised to show people in the year 6939 what we had accomplished and what about our lives we thought meaningful." The fictional Edgar buries his Tom Mix decoder badge "with the spinner shaped like a pistol," his four-page handwritten biography of Franklin Delano Roosevelt, his M. Hohner Marine Band harmonica, two Tootsy Toy lead rocket ships, one of his mother's torn silk stockings, and a pair of prescription glasses with a cracked frame that belongs to a friend. (He withdraws his copy of *Ventriloquism Self-Taught* from the capsule at the last minute and walks off in the book's last paragraph, practicing.)

World's Fair is another time capsule, by another Edgar, which combines mementos of the public and private experiences of a Bronx boyhood during the Depression. For this Edgar, ventriloquism—projecting one's thoughts, feelings, and words through imagined characters—is not a hobby but a calling. Like the boy's capsule, Doctorow's book is made up of pop cultural objects and personal, highly charged images; like the capsule, the book is meant to provide a foundation for understanding the meaning of an era through the cherished, carefully selected memories of a representative individual. By mixing the small boy's limited, child's-eye view of experience with those of Edgar as an adult and the oral testimonies of his mother and older brother, Doctorow renders those memories multilayered and appropriately complex.

Much of the pleasure of *World's Fair* lies in its lovingly recorded images of the era's sights and sounds. Edgar's world includes treats from the Sweet Potato Man; visits to Irving's Fish Store and Rosoff's Drugstore; excursions to Times Square for the frenzied rites of the "Flinging of the Textiles" and the "Try-On"; summer evenings by the radio, listening to shows such as "Easy Aces," the "Chase and Sanborn Hour," "The Royal Gelatin Hour," "Green Hornet," "Jack Benny," "Traces of Lost Persons," "Information Please," and "The Shadow," and commentators such as Fulton Lewis, Jr., Boake Carter, H. V. Kaltenborn, Father Coughlin, Gabriel Heatter, and Walter Winchell; Giants' games at the Polo Grounds; film serials such as the *Lone Ranger*, *Dick Tracy*, *Flash Gordon*, and *Zorro*; Little Blue Books; Ringling Brothers and the Barnum and Bailey's Circus at Madison Square Garden; and, of course, the World's Fair.

Against this background, Edgar's private family history unfolds as a saga of two adored parents increasingly alienated from each other by conflicting temperaments and disappointed expectations. His father is a lively, charming character full of schemes that never succeed. His mother, embittered by her husband's irresponsibility and failure, grows old in the struggle to have the life that she imagined when they first met. Edgar, adoring them both, at first vaguely and then clearly aware of the gulf dividing them, takes on the role of mediator.

At the same time, Doctorow records the growth of Edgar's consciousness of the world beyond his family. He tags along behind his older brother and begins to learn about friendship, sports, and sex. He enters school and begins to discover a route to success and acceptance through writing. He meets a girl and, through her and her mother, is introduced to romance and adventure. He begins to explore other neighborhoods.

His public and private lives converge at the fair. Doctorow's World's Fair is not the fair of vanity and façade of James Joyce's "Araby." It is, instead, a place where past, present, and future coexist for a while in a harmony that is extraordinary. Edgar enters a writing contest sponsored by the fair, and when his essay on "The Typical American Boy" is awarded honorable mention, he gets free tickets for his family. Together they enter the wider world of the fair and share a glimpse of the wonders it contains, setting aside for a day the tensions that divide them.

For the young Edgar, it is a lesson about the power of words and of art to change lives—if only for a while—a lesson about the power of imagination to shape reality. The lesson is one another Edgar—Edgar Laurence Doctorow—has never forgotten.

Bernard Rodgers

Sources for Further Study

The Atlantic. CCLVI, December, 1985, p. 119.
Booklist. LXXXII, September 15, 1985, p. 90.
Cosmopolitan. CXCIX, November, 1985, p. 66.
Esquire. CIV, November, 1985, p. 25.
Glamour. LXXXIII, December, 1985, p. 192.
Nation. CCXLI, November 30, 1985, p. 594.
The New York Review of Books. XXXII, December 19, 1985, p. 23.
The New York Times Book Review. XC, November 10, 1985, p. 3.
Newsweek. CVI, November 4, 1985, p. 69.
Publishers Weekly. CCXXVIII, September 13, 1985, p. 124.
Time. CXXVI, November 18, 1985, p. 100.
Vogue. CLXXV, November, 1985, p. 286.

YEAGER
An Autobiography

Author: Chuck Yeager (1923-) and Leo Janos
Publisher: Bantam Books (New York). 342 pp. $17.95
Type of work: Autobiography
Time: From the 1920's to the 1980's
Locale: Primarily the United States

Chuck Yeager, perhaps the greatest American test pilot, tells his life story with fascinating reminiscences from his wife and those colleagues who have known him well

> *Principal personages:*
> CHUCK YEAGER, the first man to fly faster than the speed of sound
> GLENNIS YEAGER (NÉE DICKHOUSE), a California beauty and his wife for more than forty years
> CHARLES E. "BUD" ANDERSON, Yeager's fellow World War II ace who became a lifelong friend
> JACQUELINE "JACKIE" COCHRAN, a World War II WASP colonel and internationally acclaimed aviatrix who triumphed over an impoverished childhood
> PANCHO BARNES, the female owner of a notorious Mojave Desert bar and ranch house who befriended the Yeagers
> COLONEL ALBERT BOYD, Yeager's commanding officer at Muroc Air Force Base who recommended Yeager for the sound barrier assignment

On October 14, 1947, Chuck Yeager, American test pilot, broke the sound barrier. While flying a Bell X-1 rocket airplane beyond Mach 1, this country boy from the hollows of West Virginia proved that there was no invisible brick wall in the sky to keep mankind from supersonic flight. This achievement was not Yeager's first claim to fame but only another milestone in his Air Force career.

Though *Yeager*—an autobiography coauthored by Chuck Yeager and Leo Janos, a former correspondent for *Time* magazine—reads like a heroic saga, it is based on documented fact. Yeager tells his own story throughout much of the book, but he occasionally stops to let others comment as well; Yeager's wife, Glennis, his friend Bud Anderson, former commanders, and previous rivals relate their own stories about him. The result is a fresh, lively narrative filled with anecdotes in which Yeager's legendary feats are episodically recollected.

"Starting from Scratch" is the only one of thirty-two chapters focusing on Yeager's early life. Born into poverty in Myra, West Virginia, near the Mud River, Yeager learned as a child to hunt, fish, and trap. He fondly recollects shooting and cleaning rabbits and squirrels before school and, at the age of six, being a crack shot. His father, an expert mechanic, taught the boy how to disassemble and reconstruct engines, and on hunting trips, he taught the young Yeager survival skills. Equipped with 20/10 vision and a determination to excel at whatever interested him, Yeager performed superbly in combat and test aircraft and later won both the Harmon and Collier trophies.

As narrated in his autobiography, Yeager the combat pilot was a terror. Although he was the most junior officer in the 363rd squadron stationed in England during World War II, Yeager frequently led missions; fellow officers recall him as the best and most reliable leader among them. Not all officers who outranked Yeager, however, wanted to follow his orders: Yeager recalls one incident when he had to force a flyer into formation by opening fire on the officer's plane. Yeager's was a brutal warrior's world: An officer had to be tough, he insists, to save the lives of his men as well as his own life.

This self-made hero was never short on courage or resourcefulness. He excitedly recounts those World War II missions when he shot down German Messerschmitts over occupied Europe. Tracking Axis aircraft and dogfighting Messerschmitts was a challenge requiring both courage and clear thinking. Aborted missions always left him disappointed because he enjoyed combat. Known as a risk taker, he insists that those he took were calculated, and fellow combatants agree that this was so.

At the age of twenty-two, with the war ending in Europe, Chuck Yeager returned home a national hero and a reluctant former combat pilot. Dogfighting was his life, and it became a sport he would never outgrow. Yeager repeatedly credits the United States Air Force for his success as a pilot. Referring to himself as an undereducated hillbilly whose potential was recognized and developed by astute commanding officers, he has always been grateful for the opportunities that have advanced his career. Yeager may be a supermacho figure when under fire or when facing the animosities of fellow pilots, but he is always humble about personal accomplishments. He is referred to in the book as a good team player, and his praise of other people certainly corroborates this assessment.

Yeager joined the air force at the age of eighteen shortly after being graduated from high school. A recruiter visiting Hamlin, West Virginia, where Yeager had lived since he was four years old, promoted the air force as an enjoyable career and a way to see the world. Yeager enlisted as an airplane mechanic and applied to the flying sergeant program because it offered an escape from gofer work. His first plane ride made him sick, but he soon enjoyed flying and discovered that he had a natural aptitude for it. Learning to become a pilot was hard work, he admits, but if one wanted to stay alive, he worked hard at it. Yeager has no sympathy for the pilots who died during flight training or for those who made foolish mistakes in combat. To be a pilot, he states frankly, one has to put a lid on grief and use anger as a defense mechanism—a ruthless, defiant attitude that probably saved his life many times. This is only one side of Yeager, however, the side that had to survive the deaths and maimings of many friends.

Yeager, too, was shot down. On his eighth mission, he parachuted from his exploding Mustang into a heavily forested section of Southern France. Wounded with shrapnel, Yeager hid under his parachute while German patrols looked for him. Saved through his own resourcefulness and with the help of the French underground, Yeager eventually escaped over the Pyrenees into Spain, but before then, he hid in shacks and haylofts for a time and lived with the Maquis (the French Resistance fighters) in secret woodland camps. He aided the Maquis as an explosives technician until he and some other downed flyers were spirited away to a trail at the base of the Pyrenees. This mountain trek was arduous, and Yeager's companion, a pilot named Pat, was shot and wounded by a German patrol. Yeager describes how he had to amputate Pat's leg with a penknife and then carry the flyer on his shoulders over the mountains.

Yeager's successful escape made him an evadee, and according to military code, an evadee was sent home immediately. To return to combat was unthinkable, because the Gestapo kept dossiers on missing Allied flyers, and if he had been captured by the Germans, an evadee could be forced to reveal everything he had learned about the Resistance. Because he wanted to resume combat duty, however, Yeager petitioned senior officers up the chain of command to the Chief of Allied Operations in Europe, General Dwight D. Eisenhower, who accomplished a military first by reinstating Yeager (and another petitioner) to active combat. Eventually, Yeager logged seventeen kills and vindicated Eisenhower's decision. Without this reinstatement, Yeager's air force career would have screeched to a halt after the war.

Yeager also describes various other events which jeopardized his daredevil career, a career that was not without blemish: As a corporal, he was court-martialed for shooting a horse with a machine gun; he lost a Cold War command in Europe after his pilots destroyed a bar and Yeager damaged a staff car; as a fledgling pilot, he was frequently reprimanded for low-level flying over farms and towns, stunts which ripped shingles off houses and incited cattle stampedes.

Yet, this aggressive pilot was also a caring man. Friendships with Bud Anderson, Jack Ridley (a fellow pilot and engineer who tutored Yeager), Pancho Barnes (the female owner of a Mojave Desert bar and motel), Jacqueline Cochran (an American aviatrix), Eisenhower, and numerous others of varied backgrounds and occupations commanded his loyalty. Yeager speaks proudly of his children and of his wife, Glennis, who overcame cancer. He respects his West Virginia heritage and praises certain commanding officers. General Albert Boyd, his superior at Muroc, the desert training center for experimental planes that later became known as Edwards Air Force Base, figures throughout as a guardian as well as a respected, exacting boss. After Yeager broke the sound barrier, some influential officers tried to prevent him from obtaining his test pilot's certification; only Boyd's intervention saved Yeager's career.

Yeager piloted may experimental planes besides the Bell-X1 and suffered some serious injuries. Nevertheless, he always resumed test piloting. He even tested a captured Russian MIG-15 for American pilots fighting in the Korean War and evaluated jets for the French. In the 1950's, Yeager tested everything from supersonic interceptors to prototype bombers, challenging what the pilots called the "Ughknown." His career spanned a golden period of postwar aviation, when jets replaced propeller planes and when the era of space travel was dawning. Yeager was the first pilot to glimpse the blackness of space, when in another Bell rocket-powered craft he exceeded the speed of Mach 2.

Yeager's account of what led to the first piloted space flight is fascinating history. In the late 1950's, he was appointed commandant of the newly created Aerospace Research Pilots School at Edwards Air Force Base. Before the school was closed by President Lyndon B. Johnson in the 1960's, Yeager's faculty and staff trained the first generation of military aerospace test pilots and developed the first space simulator. Astronauts Frank Borman, Thomas Stafford, and James McDivitt were faculty members later recruited by the National Aeronautics and Space Administration (NASA) for space missions. Before the school closed, NASA recruited thirty-eight graduates. The promise of the Space Age excited Yeager, particularly when he envisioned orbiting space laboratories and transportable shuttles. He accepted the fact that although he could be instrumental in laying the foundation for the nation's new commitment to space exploration, his lack of a college education prevented his becoming an astronaut. In characteristic matter-of-factness, he states that he did not see where the risks involved were as great as some research flying done at Edwards over the years. Yeager always understood and respected the nature of his job as well as the limitations of his career because of his lack of education.

He was for many years the air force's showpiece, and from the time he first broke the sound barrier he was flooded with speaking invitations. Because he considered his West Virginia accent and poor grammar to be liabilities, he tried to decline all requests. Forced under orders to make those speeches, he eventually overcame his difficulties, and as a retired one-star general he has continued to accept speaking engagements.

Glennis alludes to Yeager's rough edges, which she claims Jackie Cochran, the famous American flyer and a longtime friend of Yeager's, helped to refine. Cochran figures prominently in Yeager's life as one of two women (the other being Pancho Barnes) who lived vicariously through Yeager's accomplishments. Their friendship lasted more than twenty-five years until Jackie's death. During that time Yeager trained Cochran to break high altitude speed records, and she in turn introduced him to important people. Yeager attended international aviation conferences with

Cochran, and in 1959, while accompanying her to a conference in the Soviet Union, he managed also to spy on Soviet airfields. The Yeagers were an adopted family to Cochran and her husband, wealthy industrialist Floyd Odlum, who knew air force brass on a first-name basis. The chapter on Cochran gives a detailed example of the effect Yeager had on other people and how he was regarded by influential contemporaries. Cochran so admired Yeager that she lobbied politicians until he was awarded the Congressional Medal of Honor.

Glennis recalls that Pancho Barnes was, frankly, no lady, but was, nevertheless, her husband's good friend. As he did with Cochran, Yeager traveled with Barnes and he and his family were recipients of her generosity. Her bar/motel in the Mojave Desert was an oasis of notorious entertainment, with frequent brawls among fighter pilots. A second home to Yeager, it was eventually closed down by the air force (because of its additional business operation as a brothel). As crude as Barnes was (and Yeager's description is frank), she repeatedly proved herself to be Yeager's friend, and he bemoans her lonely death. Yeager accepted Barnes and others at face value, and he either fully liked or disliked the people he came to know. He admits that he had no patience for nuance, a characteristic that probably accounts for his ability to make quick decisions. Considering the Yeager's primitive, makeshift lodgings during their married life in the desert, it is easy to understand why they frequented Barnes's bar as an oasis of fun. In Yeager's narrative, the Barnes stories provide bawdy comedy and a look back in time to a vanishing American frontier.

The final chapters of *Yeager* cover his last assignments: commands in Vietnam, in Pakistan, and a second command in West Germany. Once, as wing commander in Vietnam, where his son, Don, was serving as a paratrooper, Yeager flew back to an air base in a helicopter with Don as gunner; Yeager also proudly recalls how his son used survival skills Yeager had taught him. While Yeager speaks of his son's heroics, Glennis remembers Don's disillusionment with the war in Vietnam. In contrast, Yeager, the professional soldier, accepted orders with little, if any, rumination and continued to act as the World War II intrepid hero.

This truly is an autobiography which presents a life's career in all its richness, a life experience in full dimension. Coauthor Janos manages to stay behind his subject so that Yeager speaks for Yeager in a fascinating self-portrait. The inspiration for the film *The Right Stuff* (1983), about America's space program, Yeager is also an inspiration to the reader of this book, where the myth of Chuck Yeager becomes the reader's pleasurable experience.

Anne C. Raymer

Sources for Further Study

Best Sellers. XLV, September, 1985, p. 220.
Booklist. LXXXI, May 1, 1985, p. 1219.
Business Week. XV, June 30, 1985, p. 1.
Christian Science Monitor. LXXVII, August 6, 1985, p. 28.
Kirkus Reviews. LIII, May 15, 1985, p. 480.
Library Journal. CX, September 15, 1985, p. 77.
Los Angeles Times Book Review. August 4, 1985, p. 2.
National Review. XXXVII, July 26, 1985, p. 46.
The New York Times Book Review. XC, July 7, 1985, p. 3.
Publishers Weekly. CCXXVII, May 31, 1985, p. 51.
Time. CXXVI, July 29, 1985, p. 69.
The Wall Street Journal. CCVI, July 3, 1985, p. 12.
Washington Post Book World. XV, June 30, 1985, p. 1.

THE YEARS OF MACARTHUR
Volume III: Triumph and Disaster, 1945-64

Author: D. Clayton James (1931-)
Publisher: Houghton Mifflin Company (Boston). Illustrated. 848 pp. $29.95
Type of work: Political biography
Time: 1945-1964
Locale: Japan, Korea, and the United States

The final volume of a major three-part biography of one of America's most brilliant and controversial military commanders

> *Principal personages:*
> DOUGLAS MACARTHUR, Supreme Commander for the Allied Powers (SCAP)
> HARRY S TRUMAN. thirty-third President of the United States, 1945-1953
> HIROHITO, Emperor of Japan
> DEAN G. ACHESON, Secretary of State during the Korean War
> SYNGMAN RHEE, President of South Korea
> MATTHEW B. RIDGWAY, Commander of the Eighth Army in Korea
> SHIGERU YOSHIDA, Prime Minister of Japan

What better subject for biography than Douglas MacArthur, whose career embraced momentous events and whose elusive personality inspired awe and apprehension. Rather than embellish the life and times of this almost legendary general, D. Clayton James sets out to separate fact from myth. This final volume in a monumentally researched trilogy is balanced, judicious, and understated in tone. "My nearly two decades of tracking him," the author admits modestly, "have led me only to a few fascinating shells along the edges of a long beach." In fact, after interviewing hundreds of contemporaries, James concludes that MacArthur was a man of paradox: to some, decisive, sincere, chivalrous; to others, haughty, insecure, theatrical. Fiercely loyal to his staff and one who demanded the total support of those under him, he could be disdainful of and insubordinate with superiors.

MacArthur's postwar career went from a triumphant stint as Supreme Commander (SCAP) in Japan to a disastrous break with President Harry S Truman over Korean war strategy; the indispensable man suddenly became expendable. James praises MacArthur's reconstruction policies while noting that most did not originate with him. Similarly, while the author concurs with Truman's dismissal decision, he demonstrates that vacillation in Washington and confusion at the battlefront created a treacherous, no-win situation for the vain general. Throughout the book, historical conclusions are unobtrusive and consistent with the evidence.

Arriving in Japan with a minimum of security but a maximum of pomp and fanfare, MacArthur cultivated the image of an omnipotent shogun, fair but firm, flexible but unflappable. Even so, James stresses the constraints under which he had to operate. Largely ignorant of Japanese history, ethnocentric but not a racist, he set out, according to James, to introduce "large portions of the American heritage that he thought were transferrable, especially political democracy." In his office were portraits of his chief "advisers," George Washington and Abraham Lincoln. MacArthur worked virtually every day at his Dai Ichi headquarters and hardly ever traveled anywhere. He envisioned a Christianized, nonmilitarized, progressive new Japanese society. Once, after a woman prostrated herself at his feet, MacArthur gently picked her up and said, "Now, now—we don't do that sort of thing any more." He was at his best during formal troop reviews or entertaining visiting dignitaries, pacing back and forth with corncob pipe in hand and telling spellbinding stories.

MacArthur got along well with most Japanese leaders; as Prime Minister Shigeru Yoshida later concluded, his tasteful handling of Emperor Hirohito was the most important factor in the occupation's success. Hirohito gave up his claims to divinity and sovereignty, but MacArthur found his ceremonial role useful as a symbol of acceptance. Japanese officials tried to suppress photographs of their initial meeting because the general seemed to tower over the emperor (although MacArthur stood less than six feet tall). SCAP insisted that the pictures be printed in the newspapers.

Aside from needlessly destroying three cyclotrons, hastily convening war-crime trials, and bowing to Catholic pressure on the matter of disseminating birth-control information, James gives MacArthur high leadership marks in the occupation's early, idealistic phase. He ordered a purge of ultranationalists, pushed for decentralization of the police, the bureaucracy, and business cartels (the Zaibatsu), and eagerly embraced women's rights and land reform. His general staff handled the repatriation problem efficiently and made outstanding inroads against communicable diseases. On his own, MacArthur ordered the army to feed the hungry, and his influence was probably decisive in the Japanese constitution's no-war clause.

Conservative Japanese politicians tried to minimize the effect of the most sweeping of the occupation's antitrust measures. In time, the Truman Administration switched its emphasis from reform to recovery. Sensitive to press criticism, MacArthur defended his liberal record while going along with the "reverse course." In fact, he was probably more comfortable purging Communists than Zaibatsu leaders. James disagrees with revisionist historians who stress economic motivations for the policy shift and instead stresses strategic considerations connected with the containment of Communism in Asia.

Indeed, MacArthur was a political animal, even though he denied it. In 1948, he allowed political operatives to float his candidacy for the Republican presidential nomination, but his high standing in popularity polls did not translate into delegates. In fact, MacArthur's poor showing in the

Wisconsin primary not only doomed his candidacy, but it also hurt his image of nonpartisanship in Japan.

Nevertheless, in James's opinion, MacArthur's image helped create a consensus of support for occupation policies, among Republicans and Southern Democrats as well as the Japanese. During the Korean War, Japan became a forward staging base for American troops as well as a vital supplier of goods and services. The relationship served both countries well, stimulating the Japanese economy and freeing American troops from many noncombat duties. MacArthur even secretly authorized Japanese agents to infiltrate Sakhalin and the Kuriles, then recently acquired by the Soviet Union at the Yalta Conference.

America's postwar Korean policy, according to James, was ill conceived. In charge at the outset was a general who remarked tactlessly that "these Koreans are the same breed of cat as the Japanese." The Truman Administration's lack of clarity about whether South Korea lay within America's defense perimeter may have precipitated the North Korean invasion, although James emphasizes the declining popularity of South Korean president Syngman Rhee's regime. MacArthur, first optimistic about blunting the attack, grew almost despondent until his troops established a defense perimeter at the Naktong line.

MacArthur was an unfortunate choice to assume command in Korea, given his myriad responsibilities, his advanced age, and his personality. Without approval from the Joint Chiefs of Staff, he ordered North Korean airfields bombed. Contrary to myth, he did receive permission to visit Chiang Kai-shek in Formosa, even though it unsettled the State Department. Except for flying the Stars and Stripes rather than the United Nations flag at ceremonies in Seoul, MacArthur's handling of the Inchon operation was beyond reproach, but success emboldened him to make rash statements. A message to the Veterans of Foreign Wars provoked Washington's wrath, as did his authorization of American troops to proceed into northern border areas despite a contrary directive from the Joint Chiefs of Staff.

The shift in war strategy from containment to liberation did not originate with MacArthur but had the support of Truman and his national security advisers as well as United Nations sanction. The Wake conference, in James's opinion, was more a political stunt than a serious policy review. MacArthur did not snub Truman, as legend has it, and discussions were cordial, if rambling. MacArthur speculated that Red China would not enter the conflict but admitted that political intelligence was not really his domain.

Another unfortunate remark was MacArthur's expressed hope, as the United Nations offensive commenced, that "the boys" would be "home by Christmas." Slow to pick up the Chinese counteroffensive, American forces pressed ahead, then belatedly retreated as MacArthur ordered massive raids on bridges across the Yalu River. The Joint Chiefs of Staff subsequently canceled the bombing missions, but after a bitter protest from MacArthur, Truman himself reauthorized them.

As United Nations forces withdrew into defensible positions, MacArthur chafed at constraints which in his opinion would lead either to annihilation or evacuation unless he received reinforcements. Eight times in the next three months, MacArthur flew on exhausting, risky inspection trips near the front, taking credit for operations which General Matthew Ridgway had devised and with which he had little to do. He developed a bizarre ten-day victory plan (never submitted to the Joint Chiefs of Staff) involving the placement of radioactive waste along an impenetrable zone between Manchuria and Korea. When Truman opened delicate peace negotiations, MacArthur made several hostile public comments, despite orders to get prior clearance for all such statements. For Truman, it was the last straw. MacArthur took leave of his post with considerable grace, although he later blamed the entire flap on Truman's uncontrollable temper.

More popular than Truman at the time of his dismissal, MacArthur received a hero's welcome—which, according to James, reflected support for his military accomplishments more than for his hawkish policy proposals. During senate hearings he was less than candid in claiming that he and the Joint Chiefs of Staff were in virtual agreement and that he had not been given a clear summary of Truman's foreign policies. By the end of the hearings, public interest had waned, and MacArthur found himself on the periphery of power.

Living in the Waldorf Tower near his old friend, former president Herbert Hoover, MacArthur continued to draw a general's salary and don his uniform, even while lashing out at Truman on a speaking tour sponsored by wealthy Texas oilmen. Joining a "stop Ike" movement a the 1952 Republican convention, he delivered a disappointing keynote speech. Marred by annoying mannerisms and vapid rhetoric, it was his final political misadventure. In later years, MacArthur groused that President Eisenhower avoided him. With John Kennedy, relations were more cordial. Elected board chairman of Remington Rand, he kept active and eventually got around to his memoirs, which glossed over his defeats and admitted to no mistakes in judgment.

James does not conclude with any sweeping generalizations. The layman will probably be disappointed in the paucity of colorful anecdotes, while the scholar will look elsewhere for a full treatment of the economic history of postwar Japan or the military history of the Korean War. Even so, despite a tendency to use too many long documentary quotations, the author has succeeded admirably in his stated objective of producing a "fair, full account of this man, who has been the subject of too much adulation and condemnation."

James B. Lane

Sources for Further Study

American History Illustrated. XX, November, 1985, p. 8.
Booklist. LXXXI, April 15, 1985, p. 1155.
Library Journal. CX, April 1, 1985, p. 137.
The New Republic. CXCIII, August 26, 1985, p. 37.
The New York Times Book Review. XC, August 25, 1985, p. 8.
Publishers Weekly. CCXXVII, March 15, 1985, p. 105.
The Wall Street Journal. CCV, June 3, 1985, p. 20.

THE ZONE
A Prison Camp Guard's Story

Author: Sergei Dovlatov (1941-   )
Translated from the Russian by Anne Frydman
Publisher: Alfred A. Knopf (New York). 178 pp. $14.95
Type of work: Linked stories
Time: The 1960's to the 1980's
Locale: The Komi Autonomous Republic of the Soviet Union; the United States, primarily New York

In this deftly constructed, unconventional, and highly entertaining work, letters to the author's émigré Russian-language publisher alternate with tales from a Soviet prison camp for regular criminals

Sergei Dovlatov, who emigrated from the Soviet Union to the United States in 1978, differs in several respects from his most celebrated fellow émigrés. He is neither ethnic Russian nor Jewish; he is largely apolitical; he was unknown as a writer when he left his native land, achieving publication—and a measure of recognition—only in the United States. Two of his books have appeared in English translation following their issue in Russian by émigré publishers: *Kompromiss* (1981; *The Compromise*, 1983) and *Zona* 1982; *The Zone: A Prison Camp Guard's Story*). Excerpts from both these books appeared in *The New Yorker*, to which Dovlatov has become a regular contributor.

The freshness of Dovlatov's voice is immediately apparent in *The Zone*. The title and subtitle suggest a rather grim, straightforward narrative; instead, the text begins with the surprising heading "Letter to the Publisher," followed by a letter, datelined New York, from Dovlatov to Igor Markovich Yefimov, head of an émigré Russian-language publishing house, Hermitage Press. Dovlatov is sending to Yefimov a fragment of his "prison camp book," *The Zone*—which, he admits, has already been rejected by several publishers, all of whom said that the "prison camp theme is exhausted. The reader is tired of endless prison memoirs. After Solzhenitsyn, the subject ought to be closed." The objection is unfair, Dovlatov notes—to begin with, he is writing about camps for regular criminals, not political prisoners.

Having made a case for his "right to exist" as a writer, Dovlatov then explains to Yefimov the fragmentary condition of his work. Before leaving the Soviet Union, he microfilmed the manuscript of *The Zone*; later, "a few courageous French women" smuggled it in bits through customs:

> Over the last few years, I have been receiving tiny packages from France. I've tried to compose a unified whole out of the separate pieces.
> The film was damaged in places. A few fragments were entirely lost.
> The reconstruction of a manuscript from microfilm is a laborious job. Even in America, for all its technological greatness, it is not easy. And, by the way, not inexpensive. I've restored about thirty percent of it to date.

Here is a marvelous modern variation on a favorite device of Romantic storytellers, the fragmentary manuscript—a device which Dovlatov lightheartedly exploits throughout the book.

Following this opening letter is a brief and ironic narrative of camp life. This establishes the pattern: Letters to Yefimov (who did in fact publish the Russian-language edition of *The Zone*) alternate with prison camp episodes. Thus, there are two distinct narrative lines. Dovlatov's letters—there are about fifteen of them, the first dated February 4, 1982, the last dated June 21 of the same year—trace the process by which he was transformed from a Young Pioneer to a prison camp guard to a writer who associated with dissidents; there are also reactions to letters from and conversations with Yefimov (to which the reader is not privy) and wry reflections on Dovlatov's acclimation to life in the United States. The second narrative line consists of a series of loosely linked but self-contained stories set in the Ust Vym camp complex in the Komi Autonomous Republic of the Soviet Union. Finally, the book works on a third level: the interaction between the two narrative lines. Sometimes this interaction is explicit, for Dovlatov frequently refers to the stories when writing to Yefimov; sometimes it is implicit, when the reader supplies connections between a given letter and the story that follows it.

All of this sounds rather schematic, and perhaps rather self-conscious as well. In fact much of the pleasure of *The Zone* derives from Dovlatov's lightness of touch, his insouciance, his humor. Style is inevitably flattened and distorted in translation, and a slangy, informal style is particularly difficult to render. In this respect, *The Zone* is exceptionally successful among recent translations from Russian. Dovlatov is fortunate indeed in his translator, Anne Frydman; in turn, Frydman acknowledges the help of her husband, Stephen Dixon, a prolific short-story writer and a novelist, who may have contributed to the translation's idiomatic rhythms.

The prison camp narratives which make up the bulk of the book vary in length and form, ranging from anecdotes or sketches of two or three pages to fully shaped stories with a conventional dramatic structure (conflict and resolution), though even the latter tend toward the anecdotal. The stories are loosely unified by two themes, both of which are outlined by Dovlatov himself in his letters to Yefimov: first, the emblematic significance of prison life; second, the making of a writer, the growth of a writer's consciousness.

There is a long tradition of Russian prison literature, Dovlatov observes, in which "the inmate appears as the suffering, tragic figure, deserving of admiration and pity. The guard, correspondingly, is a monster and villain, the incarnation of cruelty and violence." On the other hand, he notes, there is a tradition of "police" literature ("from Chesterton to Agatha Christie"), in which "the inmate appears as the monster, the fiend, while . . . the policeman is a hero, a moralist, a vivid artistic personality. His own experiences as a guard, Dovlatov says, taught him that these opposing viewpoints are both wrong. Instead of a sharp moral distinction, he detected a "striking similarity between the camp and the outside, between the prisoners and the guards":

> We were very similar to each other, and even interchangeable. Almost any prisoner would have been suited to the role of a guard. Almost any guard deserved a prison term.
> I repeat—this is the main aspect of prison life. Everything else is peripheral.
> All of my stories are written about this.

Dovlatov does not seem to realize that this perceived identity between camp and outside, prisoner and guard, far from being a radical alternative is in fact a cliché of contemporary literature—a cliché, fortunately, that is being treated with increasing skepticism. Dovlatov's infatuation with the appealing but morally blurred viewpoint is the book's only notable weakness, but it is not as serious a weakness as one might conclude from the passage quoted above, for the stories themselves are not quite so thesis-ridden as Dovlatov's declaration suggests. The stories indeed show prisoners and guards alike as fallible, often ridiculous human beings, but they do not for the most part insist on the naïve and pernicious theory of moral equivalence that Dovlatov advances in his letters.

The second unifying theme, Dovlatov's birth as a writer, is more interesting. In one of the early letters to Yefimov, dated February 23, he explains how the horrors of camp life, instead of overwhelming him, transformed him:

> I felt better than could have been expected. I began to have a divided personality. Life was transformed into literary material. . . .
> Even when I suffered physically, I felt fine. Hunger, pain, anguish—everything became material for my tireless consciousness.

Indeed, he adds, in his mind he was "already writing. . . . What was left was to transfer all this to paper. I tried to find the words." Thus concludes the letter to Yefimov, and immediately there follows a story in which Dovlatov's alter ego, prison guard Boris Alikhanov, experiences the transformation that Dovlatov has described in the letter.

Dovlatov's account of his "calling" is animated by a tension which allows him to avoid both cynicism and sentimentalism. On the one hand, he describes the growth of a writer's consciousness in religious terms: "Flesh and spirit existed apart. The more dispirited the flesh, the more insolently the spirit romped." Similarly, in the story that follows, Alikhanov the newborn writer experiences a quasi-religious epiphany:

> "The world had become alive and safe as in a painting. It looked back at him closely

without anger or reproach.
And it seemed, the world expected something from him.

On the other hand, Dovlatov acknowledges, "there is a large measure of immorality in all this"—that is, in the detachment whereby life becomes "material" for literature: "When a camp thief was strangled before my eyes outside of Ropcha, my consciousness did not fail to record every detail." Throughout the book, Dovlatov is sensitive to this conflict without belaboring it.

Ultimately, then, the story of *The Zone* is the story of the making of a writer, telling of the strange and wonderful capacity of the human mind to float detached from the organism in which it is nested. Appropriately, the last words of the book, in the last letter to Yefimov, offer a backhanded, self-referential tribute to the writer's calling:

> It was not I who chose this effete, raucous, torturous, burdensome profession. It chose me itself, and now there is no way to get away from it.
> You are reading the last page, I am opening a new notebook . . .

John Wilson

Sources for Further Study

Booklist. LXXXII, October 15, 1985, p. 312.
Kirkus Reviews. LIII, August 15, 1985, p. 805.
Library Journal. CX, October 15, 1985, p. 101.
The New York Times Book Review. XC, October 27, 1985, p. 45.
The New Yorker. LXI, December 23, 1985, p. 90.
Publishers Weekly. CCXXVIII, August 16, 1985, p. 61.

MAGILL'S
LITERARY ANNUAL
1986

BIOGRAPHICAL WORKS BY SUBJECT
1977-1986

I

III

BIOGRAPHICAL WORKS BY SUBJECT

V

BIOGRAPHICAL WORKS BY SUBJECT

BIOGRAPHICAL WORKS BY SUBJECT

BIOGRAPHICAL WORKS BY SUBJECT

BIOGRAPHICAL WORKS BY SUBJECT

CUMULATIVE AUTHOR INDEX
1977–1986

Note: Titles from *Magill's History Annual*, 1983, and *Magill's Literary Annual, History and Biography*, 1984 and 1985, have been merged into the Cumulative Author Index, 1977-1986. These titles are indicated parenthetically by an "H" followed by the year of the Annual in which the review appeared.

CUMULATIVE AUTHOR INDEX

CUMULATIVE AUTHOR INDEX

CUMULATIVE AUTHOR INDEX

CUMULATIVE AUTHOR INDEX

XXXIII

XLI